T0305576

Vietnam

Harvard East Asian Monographs 462

Vietnam

Navigating a Rapidly Changing Economy,
Society, and Political Order

Edited by
Börje Ljunggren and Dwight H. Perkins

Published by the Harvard University Asia Center
Distributed by Harvard University Press
Cambridge (Massachusetts) and London 2023

The Harvard University Asia Center publishes several monograph series and, in coordination with the Fairbank Center for Chinese Studies, the Korea Institute, the Reischauer Institute of Japanese Studies, and other faculties and institutes, administers research projects designed to further scholarly understanding of China, Japan, Vietnam, Korea, and other Asian countries. The Center also sponsors projects addressing multidisciplinary and regional issues in Asia.

Cataloging-in-Publication Data is on file at the Library of Congress.

ISBN 9780674291331 (cloth) | 9780674291348 (paper)

Index by Julie Shawvan

♾ Printed on acid-free paper

Last figure below indicates year of this printing
32 31 30 29 28 27 26 25 24 23

Contents

Tables and Figures

Tables

Figures

Preface

Emerging from decades of war and an aborted attempt at a traditional centrally planned economy transition, Vietnam has quietly risen to become an important economy, transforming the standard of living of its people and gradually developing a comprehensive partnership with the United States. China's phenomenal economic rise has been reported and analyzed in countless publications, overshadowing another important Asian transformation—the Vietnam story. Vietnam remains a Leninist party-state, maintaining political control in the face of rapid economic development, deepened global interdependence, and mounting social change. Increased demands for openness brought about by the internet revolution and an emerging civil society, however, is a growing challenge. How the country will navigate these challenges, beyond repression, is a core focus of this volume.

This volume provides a contemporary and comprehensive view of Vietnam's political, socioeconomic, and diplomatic emergence; how it arrived to where it stands today; and where it appears to be heading. Central issues analyzed include the nature and limits of the economic reform process, the nature of the party-state, social dimensions of change, and security implications for Asia in the next decade. This collaborative effort is the product of a project launched in 2018, resting on several pillars: Harvard University, with the Ash Center of the Harvard Kennedy School led by Tony Saich and the Harvard Asia Center led by James Robson, has been the locus of the project. The Cambridge-based China Medical Board led by Dr. Lincoln Chen provided important research and financial support. The Stockholm University Forum for Asian Studies and its coordinator Dr. Eva Hansson have been a key pillar, and Fulbright University Vietnam (FUV) in Ho Chi Minh City yet another. We are deeply indebted for the generous funding of the project provided by the Asia Center and the Ash Center at Harvard, the China Medical Board, Riksbankens Jubileumsfond, the research foundation established by the Swedish Central Bank, and the Stockholm University Forum for Asian Studies. In addition, FUV hosted a workshop in early 2020.

The project has been developed in collaboration between Dr. Börje Ljunggren, former Swedish ambassador to Vietnam and China, and Professor Dwight Perkins, Department of Economics and former director of the Asia Center at Harvard University, as coeditors of the volume. Dr. Eva Hansson, at the Forum for Asian Studies at Stockholm University and a Vietnam scholar, is a third member of the project core team. The collaboration between Dwight Perkins and Börje Ljunggren dates back to the early 1990s, resulting in 1993 in an edited volume, *The Challenge of Reform in Indochina*, published by Harvard University Press. The volume was based on a seminar series held at the Harvard Institute for International Development (HIID), then headed by Dwight Perkins. Börje Ljunggren, visiting fellow at HIID at the time, was the editor.

Dwight, while known by most as a specialist on China, began working in Southeast Asia in the 1960s. His involvement with Vietnam began when, in January 1989, he led an HIID delegation to explore whether the Institute could be of help in Vietnam's economic transition. That in turn led over the next twenty-plus years to regular visits to the country for lecturing and advising/consulting with the Vietnamese government. He also taught for two semesters in Vietnam's Fulbright Economics Teaching Program (FETP), established by HIID, and had a formal oversight role of the program during its first fifteen years. The Fulbright Economic Teaching Program in Ho Chi Minh City subsequently became the first building block of what in 2016 became a full-fledged university, Fulbright University of Vietnam.

Börje has devoted almost his entire career to Asia. In 1970 he joined the Swedish International Development Agency (SIDA) as regional economist for Asia and was from the outset involved in the planning of the Swedish reconstruction program for Vietnam, for many years serving as head of SIDA's Asia Department and also as the Agency's deputy director general. In the late 1970s he served as Swedish chargé d'affaires to Laos, coordinating the Swedish reconstruction program. In 1994 he joined the Swedish Foreign Ministry as ambassador to Vietnam, followed by an assignment to develop a Swedish Asia strategy as head of the Asia Department in the Ministry and in 2002 as ambassador to China. In recent years he has devoted most of his time to China, but has remained a close observer of Vietnam. He is an associate of Harvard University Asia Center.

The current project has been an interactive process, with two major workshops and a series of webinars. The first workshop took place at Stockholm University in May 2019 where draft papers were presented. As a result of the successful outcome of the Stockholm conference, the dean of the Fulbright School of Public Policy and Management, Dr. Vu Thanh Tu Anh, announced that FUV would host a midterm workshop in HCMC, taking place in early February 2020. A final conference was scheduled to take place at Harvard in June 2020, but no workshop could be held due to COVID-19. The final versions of the seventeen chapters in the volume were instead discussed in a series of webinars held in 2020–22, with a concluding webinar in November 2022. The volume was, hence, completed in the shadow of the pandemic. Vietnam's way of handling the challenge posed further questions about the nature and capacity of the nation and its system of governance that are addressed by a number of the contributors to this volume.

We wish to thank the following people who played an essential role in the preparation of the manuscript. Gretchen O'Connor edited and formatted both the version that went out to the outside readers and the final version sent to the press. Mark Seah of the Ash Center ably arranged the many Zoom meetings that substituted for a conference in Cambridge. Angela Piliouras oversaw the final copy editing for the press. The publication process from the beginning of the manuscript approval process through to the final production of the book was ably managed by Bob Graham, head of the Harvard Asia Center Publication Office.

Short Biographies of the Authors

(Authors are listed in order of the chapter each has written or co-written.)

1. Börje Ljunggren, a leading Swedish Asia expert, is a former Swedish ambassador to Vietnam (1994–97) and China (2002–6), and has served as Deputy Director General of the Swedish International Development Cooperation Agency (SIDA) and head of the Asia Department in the Swedish Ministry of Foreign Affairs. He holds a Ph.D. in political science from Southern Illinois University. Currently, he is an Associate of Harvard University's Asia Center and the Swedish Institute of International Affairs. His publications include *The Challenge of Reform in Indochina* (HIID/Harvard, 1993) and *Den kinesiska drömmen—Xi, makten och utmaningarna* (The Chinese dream—Xi, power, and challenges, 2017).

2. Alexander Woodside taught modern Chinese and Southeast Asian history at Harvard University and the University of British Columbia between 1963 and 2003. He is the author of *Vietnam and the Chinese Model* (1971, 1988), *Community and Revolution in Modern Vietnam* (1976), *Lost Modernities: China, Vietnam, Korea and the Hazards of World History* (2006), and coauthor of *The Emergence of Modern Southeast Asia: A New History* (2005). He is a Fellow of the Royal Society of Canada. In 2017 the Phan Chau Trinh Foundation in Vietnam awarded Woodside its prize for Contributing to Global Scholarship about Vietnam.

3. Pham Duy Nghia holds undergraduate and graduate degrees from Leipzig University, Germany. At Fulbright University Vietnam he teaches Law and Public Policy, Public Governance, and Research in Public Policy. He has published extensively on business law, good governance, and the transparency and accountability of government.

4. Eva Hansson is Senior Lecturer in Political Science and Coordinator of the Stockholm Center for Global Asia at Stockholm University. Hansson's research and teaching centers on democratization, state–society relations, democracy, and protest movements, with empirical focus on Southeast Asia, in particular Vietnam and Thailand. Among her publications are *Growth without Democracy: Challenges to Authoritarianism in Vietnam* (2011) and *Political Participation in Asia: Defining and Deploying Political Space* (2019). She is currently working on a book project based on many years of fieldwork on and with the Vietnamese and Thai democracy movements, and the forthcoming *Handbook on Civil and Uncivil Society in Southeast Asia*.

5. Le Dang Doanh was a member of the Committee for Development Policy of the United Nations from January 2016 to December 2018. He was a Board Member of the first (private, independent) Institute of Development Studies, Hanoi. He served as President of Central Institute of Economic Management (CIEM) from 1993 to 2001 and was Senior Economist to the General Secretary of the Communist Party Nguyen Van Linh from 1989 to 1990. Le Dang Doanh was also a member of the Research Commission of Prime Minister of Vietnam Vo Van Kiet and Phan Van Khai from 1993 until June 2006.

6. Dwight H. Perkins is currently the H. H. Burbank Professor of Political Economy, Emeritus at Harvard University. He is the author, coauthor, or editor of twenty-six books and 100-plus journal articles, many focused on East and Southeast Asian economic history and development. He was Director of the Harvard Institute for International Development, Chairman of the Economics Department, and Director of the Harvard Asia Center. His work with Vietnam began in 1989, consulting with the government of Vietnam on economic reform issues. He taught and had a long oversight role in the Fulbright Economic Teaching Program in Ho Chi Minh City (now part of Fulbright University of Vietnam).

6. Vu Thanh Tu Anh has been the Dean of the Fulbright School of Public Policy and Management (FSPPM) since 2017. He led the transformation of the Fulbright Economics Teaching Program (FETP) into FSPPM, the first public policy school in Southeast Asia accredited by NASPAA. His research interests include the political economy of development, public finance, industrial policy, and institutional economics. He was a Global Leaders Fellow at the Blavatnik School of Government (University of Oxford) and the Woodrow Wilson School (Princeton University), and also a member of the Economic Advisory Group of Prime Minister Nguyễn Xuân Phúc (2017–21). He holds a Ph.D. from Boston College.

7. Nguyen Xuan Thanh is Senior Lecturer in Public Policy at the Fulbright School of Public Policy and Management, Fulbright University Vietnam. His research interests lie in financial sector reforms and private sector development. In 2008, Thanh helped design and launch the first MPP program in Vietnam. Thanh is also a senior fellow at the Ash Center for Democratic Governance and Innovation, Harvard Kennedy School. At Harvard, Thanh works on comparative public policy issues and coordinates the Vietnam Executive Education Program. Since 2018, Thanh has been serving as a member of the Economic Advisory Council of the Prime Minister of Vietnam.

8. Ari Kokko is a Professor of International Business at Copenhagen Business School (CBS), where his teaching and research focus on international trade, foreign direct investment, and economic development, often in an East Asian context. Before joining CBS in 2009, he was Professor of International Business at Abo Akademi University in Finland, 1999–2001, and held various positions at the Stockholm School of Economics in Sweden, 2001–9. He is also affiliated with Tartu University, Estonia. In the past, Kokko has been a board member of SIDA in Sweden and a consultant to various corporations, international organizations, and governments.

8. Le Hai Van has a Ph.D. in Economics from Trinity College in Dublin, Ireland. She graduated from the National Economics University in Hanoi and is a former Deputy Director General of the

Vietnam Foreign Investment Agency at the Ministry of Planning and Investment in Hanoi. She is currently counselor at the economic section of the Embassy of Vietnam in Washington, D.C.

8. Curt Nestor is Senior Lecturer in Economic Geography at the School of Business, Economics and Law at the University of Gothenburg, Sweden. He conducted Vietnamese language studies at Institut national des langues et civilisation orientales (INALCO), Université Paris III— Sorbonne, and Hanoi University before engaging in Swedish official development assistance projects in Vietnam during the 1980s. His research interests focus on Vietnam's trade and foreign direct investment relations, and industrial and regional economic development.

9. Jay Rosengard, Adjunct Lecturer in Public Policy at the Harvard Kennedy School, specializes in public finance; public administration; banking and financial institutions development; financial inclusion; micro, small, and medium enterprise finance; and mobile banking. He is Director of the Mossavar-Rahmani Center for Business and Government's Financial Sector Program, and for fifteen years ran the Financial Institutions for Private Enterprise Development executive education program. Rosengard has taught at Fulbright University Vietnam and has served as Faculty Chair of the Vietnam Executive Leadership Program. Together with Nobel Laureate Joseph Stiglitz, he coauthored *Economics of the Public Sector*, 4th edition.

9. Huynh The Du is a Senior Lecturer at the Fulbright School of Public Policy and Management. His teaching and research interests include urban economics, local and regional development, infrastructure development, and finance and banking. He is particularly interested in theories of collective actions and public entrepreneurship. He has worked as an adviser to some provincial governments in Vietnam to help them define long-term development strategies. He worked at the Bank for Investment and Development of Vietnam from 1996 to 2005. He frequently participates in policy dialogues in Vietnam. His recent book is *Making Megacities in Asia: Comparing National Economic Development Trajectories*.

10. Malcolm F. McPherson is Senior Development Fellow, Ash Center for Democratic Governance and Innovation at the Harvard Kennedy School. He gained a Ph.D. in Economics from Harvard University in 1980. Following a stint at the Rockefeller Foundation, McPherson joined the Harvard Institute for International Development in 1982 and shifted to the Kennedy School in 2000. Over the last four-plus decades he has worked in Africa and Asia on structural adjustment, economic reform, and capacity building. His research in Vietnam, which began in 2009, has focused on land reform, resource management, water governance, and agricultural development.

10. Le Thi Quynh Tram was the Director of the Lower Mekong Public Policy Initiative (LMPPI), a USAID-funded socioeconomic and environmental policy research project for the Lower Mekong region. LMPPI was co-managed by the Ash Center of Harvard Kennedy School and Fulbright Economics Teaching Program—now the Fulbright School of Public Policy and Management at Fulbright University Vietnam. Tram is currently the Director of the admissions and financial aid office at Fulbright University Vietnam. She holds a master's degree in Public Administration from the Harvard University Kennedy School and a bachelor's degree in Electrical-Electronics Engineering from Ho Chi Minh City University of Technology.

11. David Dapice is an Emeritus Professor of Economics at Tufts University and the economist of the Vietnam Program at Harvard's Kennedy School, a position he has held since 1990. He first worked in Indonesia in 1971–73 for the Harvard Advisory Group and continued working on Southeast Asia and other regions during a year at the World Bank and Rockefeller Foundation. His work has ranged across development topics including agriculture, energy, health, poverty, and public finance. His most recent work has focused on Vietnam, Myanmar, and Indonesia.

12. Jonathan D. London is Associate Professor of Political Economy at Leiden University. His recent publications include three Vietnam-focused edited volumes: *The Routledge Handbook of Contemporary Vietnam* (2022), *Politics in Contemporary Vietnam* (Palgrave, 2014), and *Education in Vietnam* (ISEAS, 2011). Other publications include *Welfare and Inequality in Marketizing East Asia* (Palgrave, 2018) and numerous scholarly articles and book chapters addressing Vietnam-focused and Asia-focused themes. London's current research includes a major study of Vietnam's education system. Beyond his scholarship, London has served as a consultant for such international organizations as UNDP, UNICEF, and OXFAM. He holds a Ph.D. in Sociology from the University of Wisconsin–Madison.

13. Helle Rydstrom is a Professor in the Department of Gender Studies, Lund University, Sweden. She has a background in Social Anthropology and International Development Studies. Her research explores entanglements between gender, crises, precariousness, and harm in Vietnam compared with, for example, China, India, Pakistan, and the Philippines, thanks to collaborations in projects coordinated by Rydstrom. Publications include *Embodying Morality: Growing Up in Rural Northern Vietnam*; *Gender Practices in Contemporary Vietnam* (with Drummond); *Climate Hazards, Disasters, and Gender Ramifications* (with Kinnvall), and articles in such journals as *Ethnos*; *European Journal of Women's Studies*; *Gender, Place & Culture*; *Global Discourse*; *Men and Masculinities*; and *Signs*.

14. Le Nhan Phuong has been the Southeast Asia Regional Representative for the China Medical Board (CMB) since 2016. Prior to the CMB, Phuong was the Viet Nam Country Director for the Atlantic Philanthropies from 2003 to 2013, and oversaw grant-making in primary health care systems development, health human resources development, and supporting policies and advocacies for improving health equity. Phuong earned a B.S. degree in Aerospace Engineering at the Georgia Institute of Technology, an M.D. degree at the Medical College of Georgia, an M.P.H. from Johns Hopkins University, and a Master of Business Administration from the University of Hawaiʻi.

14. Lincoln Chen is President Emeritus of the China Medical Board, which he served as President from 2006 to 2014. Earlier, Dr. Chen was the Director of the Global Equity Initiative, the Taro Takemi Professor of International Health, Director of the university-wide Harvard Center for Population and Development Studies, and Chair of a department in the Harvard School of Public Health. In 1997, Dr. Chen served as Executive Vice President of the Rockefeller Foundation, and during 1973–87 he represented the Ford Foundation in India and Bangladesh. Dr. Chen graduated from Princeton University, Harvard Medical School, and Johns Hopkins School of Public Health. He was trained at Massachusetts General Hospital.

14. Sarah Bales is a Visiting Professor at the Hanoi University of Public Health. She is currently concentrating on health system efficiency and provider payment reforms in Vietnam, but has worked as an international consultant on a wide range of health systems and health financing projects since moving to Vietnam in 1992. Her research covers a wide range of topics, largely focused on Vietnam, including COVID-19 response, reproductive health, primary health care, diagnosis-related group and capitation payments, health equity including health care for the poor, health insurance, and tobacco control.

15. Alexander L. Vuving is a Professor at the Daniel K. Inouye Asia-Pacific Center for Security Studies. His research focuses on the ways of power, soft power, the evolution of great power competition, Chinese strategy, Vietnamese politics and foreign policy, and the South China Sea disputes. He has published in major journals and presented at leading universities and think tanks. Numerous news outlets, including the *New York Times*, the *Financial Times*, the Associated Press, *Bloomberg*, and *Foreign Policy*, have featured his views. He is an Editorial Board member of the journals *Asian Politics and Policy* and *Global Discourse*.

16. Bill Hayton is an Associate Fellow with the Asia-Pacific Programme at Chatham House in London. He is the author of *Vietnam: Rising Dragon* (2nd edition, 2020) and *A Brief History of Vietnam* (2022). He was the BBC's reporter in Vietnam during 2006–7. He is also the author of *The South China Sea: The Struggle for Power in Asia* (2014) and *The Invention of China* (2020).

17. Edward Miller is Associate Professor of History at Dartmouth College. He is a historian of modern Vietnam and the Vietnam War. His research explores the international history of the Indochina wars, especially the themes of nation building, sovereignty, violence, and civil warfare. His publications include *Misalliance: Ngo Dinh Diem, the United States, and the Fate of South Vietnam* (Harvard, 2013) and *The Vietnam War: A Documentary Reader* (Wiley, 2016). Miller previously served on the Board of Trustees of Fulbright University Vietnam. He is also a historical consultant for Independence Palace, a museum in Ho Chi Minh City.

Abbreviations

APEC	Asia Pacific Economic Cooperation
ASEAN	Association of Southeast Asian Nations
CAR	Capital Adequacy Ratio
CC	Central Committee
CHS	Commune Health Station
CPC	Communist Party of China
CPV	Communist Party of Vietnam
DRV	Democratic Republic of Vietnam
EEZ	Exclusive Economic Zone
EL	Enterprise Law
EPZ	Export Processing Zone
EU	European Union
FDI	Foreign Direct Investment
FIA	Foreign Investment Agency
FIE	Foreign Invested Enterprise
FIL	Foreign Investment Law
FTA	Free Trade Agreements
FUV	Fulbright University of Vietnam
GDP	Gross Domestic Produce
GVC	Global Value Chain
HCMC	Ho Chi Minh City
HRW	Human Rights Watch
IMR	Infant mortality rate
MDP	Multi Dimensional Poverty

MIA	Missing in Action
MOET	Ministry of Education and Training
MOF	Ministry of Finance
MOH	Ministry of Health
NA	National Assembly
NPL	Non Performing Loan
ODA	Overseas Development Assistance
OECD	Organization of Economic Cooperation and Development
OTC	Over the Counter [market]
PAPI	Public Administration Performance Index
PAVN	Peoples Army of Vietnam
PC	Peoples Committee
PPC	Provincial People's Council
PPP	Purchasing Power Parity
RVN	Republic of Vietnam
SBV	State Bank of Vietnam
SHI	Social Health Insurance
SME	Small and Medium Enterprises
SOCB	State Owned Commercial Bank
SOE	State Owned Enterprise
SPC	Supreme Peoples' Court
TFP	Total Factor Productivity
TI	Transparency International
TPP	Trans Pacific Partnership
TVET	Technical and Vocational Education Training
U5MR	Under-five mortality rate
VND	Vietnam Dong
VPA	Vietnam Peoples Army
VSS	Vietnam Social Security
VWP	Vietnam Workers Party
WHO	World Health Organization
WTO	World Trade Organization

INTRODUCTION

Vietnam has emerged from one of the twentieth century's most destructive wars to become one of the twenty-first century's more dynamic societies, in spite of its prevailing authoritarian order. Forty years ago, Vietnam was one of the poorest places in the world. Now, it is a "lower middle-income country." In the late 1980s, most of the world associated Vietnam with resistance and war, hardship, large flows of refugees (the "boat people"), and a mismanaged planned economy. During the 1990s, by contrast, major countries began to see Vietnam as both a potential economic partner and a strategically significant actor, particularly in the competition between the United States and an emerging China. In our current decade, foreign politicians and international investors alike see Vietnam as a land of opportunity.

This transformation did not happen overnight and, in most respects, Vietnam's role in the global economic and political system remains a work in progress. Change has been uneven: rapid in the economy, slower in other areas of life. Before *Đổi Mới*, the economic reforms formally launched in 1986, half of Vietnam's population lived below the poverty line. By 2020, just prior to the COVID pandemic, the official figure was just 5 percent. Life expectancy stood at seventy-five years, and literacy at 95 percent. Before 1986, central planning dominated the economy and foreign trade played a marginal role. Today, foreign trade, much of it from foreign direct investment firms, literally dominates the economy. In 2019, the value of Vietnam's exports became greater than the value of its nominal GDP.

Despite three decades of rapid GDP growth, however, Vietnam's economy remains relatively small. With close to 100 million inhabitants, the country is the fifteenth most populous in the world but only forty-fifth in terms of GDP (as of 2019) and even lower in terms of GDP per capita: roughly US$10,516 in 2021 (PPP in constant 2017 dollars).[1] That is about half the level of China. Even though the pace of growth in recent years has been quite fast, it will take decades for the country's GDP rank to match its population rank. One of the main purposes of this book is to investigate what Vietnam must do to close that gap.

Political change has been slow and uneven. Vietnam remains a Leninist party-state ruled by the Communist Party of Vietnam (CPV). The Party has managed to reconcile the supposedly irreconcilable: a one-party system and a market-based economy linked to global value chains. More than this, over the last few years, Vietnam's increasing economic openness has been combined with increasing political control and repression. Yet there are also areas of openness. Unlike in China, where sovereign control over the Internet prevails, Facebook (and its Instagram and WhatsApp subsidiaries) and Google (and its YouTube subsidiary) are part of everyday life in Vietnam. This active online world reflects both the vitality of Vietnamese society and also the increasing sophistication of the CPV's techniques of information and enhanced political control, increasingly high priority being attached to "cyber security."

On July 2, 1976, when the two halves of Vietnam were formally reunified, the Communist Party saw itself as a vanguard party in the developing world, supported by the Soviet Union and China, and with a worldview shaped by the Cold War. Years of great difficulty followed, aggravated by bloody border clashes, including Vietnam's invasion of Pol Pot's Kampuchea, and the subsequent Chinese invasion of Vietnam. It was not until the early 1990s that Vietnam moved away from Cold War relationships defined by the Sino-Soviet dispute, normalized relations with China, developed ties with a wider range of countries, and then, in 1995, established diplomatic relations with the United States. Vietnam joined ASEAN, negotiated closer ties with the European Union, and, in response to China's vigorous assertion of claims in the South China Sea, moved closer to the United States.

This book examines that journey and looks ahead to what might come next. It is a joint undertaking by scholars from Vietnam, North America, and Europe. It aims to deepen the understanding of Vietnam's development along these many fronts from the Đổi Mới period through 2021. The seventeen chapters that follow this introduction focus on the way Vietnam is governed and how that governance shapes the country's politics, its economy, its social development, and its relations with the outside world. There is also analysis of the further reforms required in the economic and social sphere if Vietnam is to become a sustainable modern high-income country in the coming decades. Ultimately, institutional political reforms will be of critical importance.

The Central Role of Politics

Politics is central to any understanding of Vietnam's path to a strong modern economy and society, and the Communist Party of Vietnam (CPV) is central to understanding Vietnamese politics. The CPV, like its counterparts in China and the former Soviet Union, is much more than a political party as that term is understood in Europe and North America. It is a system that constitutionally monopolizes control of the government, the economy, and all legal civil organizations. Organizations not formally controlled by the party-state are mostly prohibited or suppressed, but there is, nonetheless, a vibrant civil society. We take the view that Vietnam is best characterized as a repressive but responsive one-party state.

Members of the CPV are expected to share certain philosophical beliefs based loosely on Marxist-Leninist thought, and they must accept the "democratic centralist" decision-making process. Democratic centralism allows debate and information from below to rise to the top, but decisions flow in the opposite direction, primarily from the Party's Central Committee and Political Bureau (Politburo). Once those bodies make a final decision, Party members are obliged to support and implement it.

Party committees are found at all levels of all government organizations, forming, in effect, a powerful parallel line of information flow and control within the formal government structures. Party committees exist at levels below the lowest levels of formal government institutions. They are also present in most enterprises, schools, and other organizations. Challenges to this system are dealt with through an elaborate security apparatus backed ultimately by the Vietnamese security forces. In the Vietnamese constitution, the loyalty of the military is first to the CPV and then to the country.

In practice, no political structure is likely to last if it is as rigid as the above description implies. The Đổi Mới period began by turning a "blind eye" to many of the economic rules, taking allocation decisions away from government planners and leaving them to the market. User rights in agriculture were returned to farming families, and the party-state gradually accepted private ownership of some economic enterprises (see chapter 5). Debates over just what role the CPV should play in society were vivid and real, but they concluded with the Party's refusal to share political power. Nonetheless, the CPV's mode of coping in today's complex society can be just as deliberative now as it was then.

The first part of this book, therefore, is devoted to an in-depth understanding of how this political system works in practice, mainly during the Đổi Mới period. Chapter 1 by Börje Ljunggren is devoted to explaining how the CPV is structured and operates in the complex setting of a rapidly changing Vietnam. In his analysis, the Vietnamese party-state rests on six mutually supportive "pillars," with the Party at the core.

The CPV, like its Chinese counterpart, has "failed to fail." It not only survived with its power intact when the Soviet Union and the Communist Parties of Eastern Europe collapsed, but like China, it managed to combine the party-state with the market and keep developing at a rapid pace. Internally, the CPV has relied on assembling a ruling co-alition of four leaders (Party secretary, premier, president, National Assembly president) who usually represent different interest groups including, among other things, the country's regional differences. During his second term in office (2016–21), Party Secretary Nguyễn Phú Trọng did, for a time, also hold the position of president after the death of the incumbent. At the Thirteenth Party Congress in 2021, however, the Party returned to a four-person coalition. When no agreement could be reached on Trong's successor, he was elected to a third term, unprecedented in the Đổi Mới era. The new leadership upset the traditional regional balance since no southerner was included among the four. Just one woman was elected among the eighteen members of the Politburo, with no woman in the core "quartet."

While the basic structures of most Communist party-states are similar, as described above and in chapter 1, there are variations in the way different Communist party-states are governed and how particular leaders meet the challenges they face. In Vietnam, for example, there are sometimes vigorous debates within the system over both minor issues of bureaucratic reform and, occasionally, over more fundamental structural governance issues. In this and in other areas, explaining how Vietnam is different and even in some respects unique is best done by comparing how Vietnam is similar to or different from other Communist party-states.

The Communist party-state closest in its history and contemporary issues to that of Vietnam is China. Börje Ljunggren, drawing on his experience as an ambassador to both Vietnam and China, argues that there are important differences as well as similarities between the Communist Party of Vietnam (CPV) and the Communist Party of China (CPC). The differences are most apparent when the CPV is compared with the CPC of Xi Jinping. The CPV during the Đổi Mới period has been ruled by a significant element of consensus among the top leadership quartet, whereas power in today's China has become concentrated in a way that seems inconceivable in Vietnam. Vietnam has been open to, and influenced by, a wide range of ideas from outside, while Xi's China increasingly has turned inward, drawing on its own history and intellectual traditions and "Xi Jinping thought." China is, as Ljunggren notes, a deeper party-state. Vietnam's population, with its memory of resistance to rule by China, puts some constraints on the CPV's ability to cooperate with the CPC. These are reinforced by China's increasing assertiveness in areas such as the South China Sea and the headwaters of the Mekong River in ways that threaten Vietnam's interests.

For the first millennia of our current era, what is now northern Vietnam was ruled by various "Chinese" states. One result of that history, as chapter 2 by Alexander Woodside shows, is that Vietnam's approach to governance, from a twenty-year occupation by the Ming in the fifteenth century to the final loss of the country's independence to France in 1887, was governed in a fashion patterned on that of China. Like China, Vietnam had a ruler supported by a bureaucracy recruited in part through civil service examinations based on the Confucian classics. On occasions when this system was perceived as not fitting the needs of the country, the solution sought was technocratic reform of the bureaucracy (better training, meritocratic appointment, and promotion, etc.) rather than a more fundamental restructuring of governance. Core elements in traditional approaches to governance have carried over to the two countries' current Leninist states. While there are differences between Vietnamese and Chinese Leninism, the two have, as Woodside notes, addressed political crises in roughly the same way. Both countries' systems remain highly authoritarian, with structures deepening the administrative system that largely makes "bystanders" out of the people they rule. Organized efforts to replace the monopoly power of the CPV with a more democratic system are outright prohibited.

The CPV, during its early years of existence, was a secret organization opposed to French colonial rule. Then, for most of the two decades after 1954, the Party ruled a country at war. In that context, both the CPV and the government it controlled were largely governed through the internal and secretive rules of the CPV together with domestic versions of Soviet regulations for managing a centrally planned command economy. There was no real legal system. But with unification in 1976 followed by reform and opening of the economy after 1986, it became clear such a system was wholly inadequate for managing the government, business, and society at large.

As Pham Duy Nghia shows in chapter 3, the CPV and the government had to develop rules or laws that would make it possible to govern an increasingly complex economy and society. Initially, these laws were mostly driven by the CPV itself. Over time, however, pressures from the society outside the Party required the creation of additional laws and a judiciary to administer those laws. Vietnam's increasing opening to the global economy also required new laws to reassure foreign investors that their investments would be safe.

The development of a modern legal system in Vietnam is still a work in progress. The constitution that broadly sets the parameters for the laws has undergone many changes, as have the laws. Of greater importance, various components of the judicial system are also in the early stages of development. However, CPV rules take precedence over the formal legal system whenever the two are in conflict. Furthermore, the judicial system often lacks the power to enforce its decisions. Disputes between the party-state and private entities are generally decided in favor of the party-state. On the rare occasions when that is not the case, the party-state often simply ignores the judgment against them. Over time, formal law has become more predictable, pushing the party to be accountable to the public. An independent judiciary and the due process of law within this system, however, remain unattainable within the party-state.

Given that the formal legal system lacks the authority to deal with disputes between the public and the party-state, and sometimes between two organizations if one has more political influence, the public lacks a means for asserting its rights. The result is that many kinds of disputes over land, labor rules, and much else are not satisfactorily resolved in court and lead, instead, to public demonstrations and occasionally even violence against the authorities.

In these circumstances, the party-state does not rely solely on the loyalty of party members or on the judiciary to maintain control. An elaborate police apparatus is in place to deal with most threats from domestic opponents and critics. As chapter 4 by Eva Hansson shows, this party-state enforcement apparatus severely limits protests against party-state actions and prohibits outright most organized efforts to do so. Still, in recent years Vietnam has seen a marked rise in publicly expressed contention in the form of large-scale protests focused on issues such as land, labor rights, corruption, the environment, and relations with China. Politically oriented civil society organizations remain limited, however, forcing disputes between the public and the party-state at both local and national levels to become more frequent. Efforts by organized groups to promote alternatives to CPV monopoly control of politics are dealt with particularly harshly. The emerging educated and informed society clearly constitutes a growing challenge for the CPV, particularly when it responds to challenges with repression.

As pointed out earlier, once the leading decision makers in the CPV have made a firm decision on the path forward in any given area, the Party and the state are expected to carry out the decision without dissent. Prior to a final decision being made, however, debate within the party, the government, and even the public can be vigorous. The best illustration of this is the long debate over whether, and to what degree, private enterprises would be allowed in Vietnam. In chapter 5, Le Dang Doanh shows that once reunification was formally achieved in 1976, the Party leadership was determined to apply in the south the same Soviet-type centrally planned command economy that already existed in the north, with full state ownership of most enterprises and collectivized agriculture. Originally the CPV intended for a time to allow the private sector in the south, largely run by the Hoa (ethnic Chinese) community, to continue operating. However, the deteriorating political relationship with China led the leadership to reverse that policy. Collectivizing agriculture faced immediate resistance from farmers, most of whom owned the land they tilled, and was never implemented. State takeover of all urban private enterprises was implemented, however, and an effort was made to put a centrally planned command economy in place that included organizations that distributed food. That effort, however, led to stagnant or falling production, rampant inflation, and, in the north, severe malnutrition.

The death of CPV General Secretary Le Duan in 1986, along with awareness of China's successful reform and opening after 1978 and ongoing changes in the Soviet Union, led the new CPV leadership to institute what became known as *Đổi Mới*. The reforms abandoned the Soviet-type centrally planned economy in favor of a system based on the distribution of goods through the market. One feature carried over from the previous economic model, however, was that the state, and hence the CPV, retained ownership of most of the industrial and larger-scale service sector enterprises. Throughout most of the 1990s, domestic private enterprises outside agriculture and very small-scale shops and restaurants remained proscribed.

In an effort to attract foreign investment, Vietnam allowed foreign private ownership of enterprises from the outset of the reform period—mainly to encourage firms that would export their production. The debate over whether to allow domestic private ownership, in contrast, continued into the 1990s. Only at the turn to the new century, and after considerable debate and some resistance, were new laws passed that made private enterprise ownership possible. The number and size of such enterprises rose rapidly, although their share of output remained small.

The Economy and the Environment

The Đổi Mới economic reforms, as already noted, led to the rapid abandonment of the centrally planned command economy in favor of greater reliance on market forces. The immediate result of reform was an acceleration in the rate of growth of Vietnam's gross domestic product (GDP). Over the next three decades, Vietnam's average per capita income rose 4.7 times[2] and the most extreme poverty was eliminated. The structure of the economy changed from one where agriculture accounted for 40.5 percent of GDP (1991) and 72 percent of the labor force (1988)[3] to one where industry and services constituted 75 percent of GDP and agriculture less than 14 percent (2020).[4]

This economic transformation occurred without much change in the formal governance structure of the CPV. By the second decade of the twenty-first century, however, Vietnam was an increasingly urban society. It was also a much more complex economy requiring additional, and often fundamentally different, supporting institutions, and it was an economy that was increasingly integrated into the global economic system. In the economic chapters in this book, the focus is on how the country was able to sustain rapid economic growth despite the possible contradiction between a radically changed economic system and an unchanged political system. Did the contradiction create tensions that slowed the economic transformation or might slow it in the future? Our answers to this question will not be comprehensive. Instead, the chapters go in depth into key aspects of the transformation that illustrate the challenges of sustaining growth in an increasingly complex economy.

The economics section begins with an overview of Vietnam's economic performance. It examines how much of the country's economic performance was due to reforms that increased the productivity of the economy, and how much was the result of the mobilization of more capital and educated labor. At this macro level, continued close ties between the party-state and the economy did not undermine the dramatic impact that the Đổi Mới market reforms had on economic growth. As chapter 6 by Vu Thanh Tu Anh and Dwight H. Perkins makes clear, replacing the Soviet-style command system with a market system led to large jumps in "total factor productivity" in the 1990s. This is what made Vietnam one of the fastest growing economies in the world, topped only by a few Asian neighbors, notably China and the Republic of Korea. However, even after the dismantling of the command economy in the 1990s, Vietnam's investment rate continued to rise, and high GDP growth continued. State ownership of enterprises and the politicized allocation of state investment funds dragged the growth rate below its full potential, but it remained above that of most developing countries, including most other economies in Southeast Asia. COVID did slow growth as it did elsewhere in the world, but Vietnam's GDP growth fared better than most in 2020–22.

Some large-scale private enterprises or enterprise groups did develop and prosper, but as Nguyen Xuan Thanh's chapter 7 makes clear, the entrepreneurs or oligarchs who developed large-scale private enterprises and enterprise groups depended on close ties to the party-state, actively cultivating political support for "wealth defense." Banking and real estate were their preferred initial sectors. With periodic changes in political leadership, however, this approach became less effective. The oligarchs instead invited the participation of large-scale foreign investors and the protection of international legal systems. Most recently, oligarchs have been encouraged to invest in new industries with the government's official support. In a symbiotic relationship with the oligarchs, the party-state thus retains a degree of control over many of the more successful private enterprises. That level of party-state involvement goes well beyond the state regulatory environment that enterprises in most market-based countries experience. In fact, while the CPV gave high priority to foreign direct investments and allowed oligarchs to play an important role, its attitude toward domestic small and medium-sized enterprises remained more ambivalent, its potential still to be realized.

The single largest change in policy early in the Đổi Mới reform era was the economic turn outward, both by welcoming foreign direct investment and by expanding trade beyond the Soviet-led COMECON bloc. Chapter 8 by Ari Kokko, Curt Nestor, and Le Hai Van describes the truly rapid development of the role of foreign direct investment (FDI) in Vietnam and the equally rapid increase of Vietnam's partnership in regional and bilateral free trade agreements since its entry into the World Trade Organization in 2007. An inward-oriented economy gradually gave way to a more market-oriented and increasingly internationalized economy. Still, until now, value added has largely been limited to the input of labor, with limited technology diffusion and with few linkages between FDI and the local economy. Moving beyond these constraints will be critical if foreign direct investment and international trade are going to sustain high growth into the future. It will also involve much more than just trade policies. Creating an enabling environment for domestic private entrepreneurship and major upgrades in the education system, particularly at the tertiary level, will also be critical, for example. Major free trade agreements, like the one with the European Union, add an international dimension to domestic discussions around potential important issues such as labor rights.

The Đổi Mới move to a market-based system necessitated, in turn, major changes in the country's economic institutions. Vietnam's experience illustrates the challenges involved in creating a new set of institutions for a fundamentally changed economic system. Vietnam's command economy arrangements were completely inappropriate for a modern market economy. Chapter 9 by Jay Rosengard and Huyhn The Du describes how, within a relatively short time, Vietnam transformed this command economy financial system into a rudimentary modern market-oriented financial system. The central bank, through its control of the money supply, became responsible for maintaining price stability, and price controls were removed for almost all goods and services. The state-owned policy banks became quasi-commercial banks and were joined by many new joint stock private and state-owned banks. These were followed in subsequent years by foreign banks, by finance, leasing, and insurance companies, as well as by two stock exchanges. However, while this system may have had the appearance of a modern system, its core functions, particularly prudential regulation, remained weak. The financial system was gradually strengthened over time, but major flaws remained, leading to periodic financial crises.

Similar problems existed with other institutions created after the transition to the market economy. The party-state made major efforts to create large conglomerates (State General Corporations) that could become domestic and international leaders on the model of the Korean chaebol or the Japanese keiretsu. However, these Vietnamese conglomerates continued to behave much like the state-owned enterprises from which they were formed. They remained dependent on state subsidies and other special privileges. To date none have become internationally competitive.

A central feature of the Đổi Mới market reforms has been a strong focus on achieving a high rate of GDP growth. The CPV expected that growth, together with a continued large state role in the economy, would secure political stability and its own unchallenged rule. However, an increasingly serious shortcoming of the exclusive emphasis on

GDP growth was the neglect of other societal goals, notably the protection of the environment. This could threaten both growth and quality of life of the Vietnamese people.

Chapter 10 by Le Thi Quynh Tram and Malcolm McPherson illustrates this challenge by looking in depth at efforts to promote rapid growth in the Mekong Delta, Vietnam's largest and most productive agricultural region. The Mekong Delta agricultural sector grew rapidly during the Đổi Mới reform period. Improved plant varieties, irrigation expansion, and the deployment of chemical fertilizers and pesticides led to a rapid rise in yields and production. Vietnam went from a country unable to adequately feed its population to one where malnutrition was essentially eliminated. Farm incomes rose and the agricultural surplus led to dramatically expanded exports of rice, aquatic products, and coffee, among other products. This was achieved while the farming population stopped growing and then began to decline as increasing numbers of rural people moved to the cities for more lucrative work.

The process of achieving these gains, however, was destructive to the environment. Land degradation, coastal erosion, cropland salinization, and land subsidence, together with water pollution and excessive agrichemical use, are continuing to undermine the long-term prospects for agricultural development. Agriculture is not the sole source of this and other forms of environmental damage, but it is a major one. Current policy is not sustainable, and climate change is rapidly aggravating the situation.

Human Welfare: Poverty, Family, Health, and Education

Economic growth is necessary for the elimination of poverty and to generate the resources required for a modern education and health system, but it is not sufficient. The distribution of income, education, and health care significantly help determine the degree to which the entire population will enjoy the benefits of growth. Markets particularly fail when it comes to the equitable distribution of education and health. They also can fail in achieving an efficient balance between curative and public health–based approaches. For many other aspects of what constitutes human welfare—relations within families, for example—markets play little or no role. Vietnamese society and the party-state have been challenged in these areas throughout the past three decades.

One of the greatest achievements of the Đổi Mới reform era was that poverty, as measured by both an income line and on a more multidimensional basis, has fallen sharply. Less than 5 percent of the population is classified as poor when measured by income alone, and less than 10 percent if one also takes into account health, education, housing, and similar measures. As chapter 11 by David Dapice explains, this success was mainly achieved by a fourfold increase in national average income. While those gains were shared broadly, the quality of the estimates of income inequality is poor, and inequality may well have risen. Urban incomes were higher in absolute terms and grew more than rural incomes, but in relative terms rural incomes fared better. Important exceptions were the regions of the Central Highlands and the mountains north of Hanoi, which had lower incomes than the rest of the country and may even have experienced a relative decline.

Millions of people living in poorer areas took the opportunity to migrate to work in the cities. The growth of wage employment, as distinct from household employment, particularly in the export-oriented foreign investment enterprises, was a major source of wage growth. The expansion of education to all areas of the country and the increasing time children spent in school also facilitated easier migration to higher-paying employment. The expansion of universal education may have been the one area where the party-state's professed belief in greater equity was clearly translated into government action, with some impact on income inequality. Most of the gains in income and the reduction in poverty, however, came from the response of different components of the economy to market forces, amplified by Vietnam's increased integration in the global economy.

Was access to education equitably distributed, and is the quality of education improving rapidly enough to sustain a continued rise in incomes? As chapter 12 by Jonathan London, on education, indicates, Vietnam made a greater financial commitment to education, including the allocation of greater resources to the sector, than most other Southeast Asian countries. In financial terms this commitment came mainly from the government but also from individual households. Both devoted large sums to the sector, combining both socialist and Confucian values together.

The quantitative expansion of the education system is clear. Major efforts were made to reach all areas of the country, basic education became nearly universal, and the average number of years spent in school increased dramatically. Minority areas, however, did less well and higher-income and higher-ranking urban households obtained access to better schools than others—as is true in most of the world. Equitable access to education therefore has not been achieved, with widespread corruption having serious distorting effects on access.

A major problem in the Vietnamese education system is the quality of the upper-secondary and postsecondary levels. None of Vietnam's universities, for example, rank within the top five hundred universities worldwide in international rankings. This may not differentiate Vietnam much from its Southeast Asian neighbors, but it does separate it dramatically from its northern neighbors such as China and the Republic of Korea. Most Vietnamese academics teach long hours, leaving little or no time for research and improving their skills.

The weakness of tertiary education to date has not inhibited economic growth so far, mainly because that growth has been based on labor-intensive, low-skill industrialization. As the economy moves up into higher-technology products, however, it is likely to be a major obstacle. As London notes, how well Vietnam's education system performs in preparing its citizens for a future competing in local and global markets has huge implications for Vietnam's long-term trajectory.

Improved human welfare, of course, depends on much more than rising incomes and levels of education. As chapter 13 by Helle Rydstrom shows, most Vietnamese still live within families, but there is far more variety within these families than is recognized by the idealized official view of family composition and behavior of the party-state. The traditional Confucian view of the family positioned the husband as the head of household, with his wife and children subordinate to him. At the beginning of CPV rule, however, the law was changed to give men and women equal rights within the family. This legal change by the government did make a significant difference for many. But, as in most countries around the world, this official ideal in Vietnam comes up against a range of pressures and problems where the ideal does not fit the reality. The Confucian preference for a male heir, for example, has led to a seriously distorted sex ratio at birth, with more men than women.

The official view of the family is a heterosexual couple living together with their two children. Rydstrom discusses the evolving views of both government and society toward the presence of increasingly open same-sex relationships and also the continued existence of considerable physical and sexual violence within heterosexual marriages. The legal prohibitions against homosexuality have been removed, but same-sex marriage is still not permitted by law. As in most countries, efforts to eliminate violence within marriage in Vietnam fall far short of what is needed. Pressures for change have come mostly from the changes within the values and perceptions of the Vietnamese people themselves reacting in part to what they see happening elsewhere in the world. The Vietnamese government and the CPV have been more reactive than proactive, no doubt also because women play a limited role in the higher echelons of the party.

Good health is essential to a high quality of life, and health status has some correlation with income increases. As chapter 14 by Sarah Bales, Le Nhan Phuong, and Lincoln Chen points out, Vietnamese achieved relatively high levels of health for a low-income country when the Vietnamese party-state mainly followed a Soviet economic model. Like China, the period before market reforms included a vigorous low-cost public health program that brought mortality and morbidity rates down to levels typically associated with much richer countries. The shift to reliance on market forces led to the adoption of new health financing measures, including health insurance, user fees, increased foreign aid, and private commercial health care. At the same time however, there was a shift from low-cost but highly effective preventive measures to more expensive and hospital-based curative care. Unlike China, however, Vietnam did not totally dismantle its government-funded, commune-based health care system, which continued to provide basic primary care.

Overall, Vietnam's health programs and institutions have achieved reasonably equitable and effective health outcomes. There are, however, serious inefficiencies, distortions, and inequities in the private public system that followed the Đổi Mới reforms. Health inequality could, as the authors note, become an increasingly serious problem, especially if the voice and role of civil society do not advance adequately.

When COVID-19 first entered Vietnam from China, the party-state led a full mobilization. It immediately cut off travel from China, and it tested, traced, and rigorously quarantined infected populations. In 2020 it successfully contained the epidemic and endured relatively few infections or deaths; COVID cases, hospitalizations, and deaths rose rapidly in 2021. However, quick government action to mobilize imports of vaccines and administer them to a majority of the population allowed Vietnam to regain control over severe coronavirus disease and deaths later that year and into 2022. Overzealous control measures, in particular in Ho Chi Minh City, caused widespread concern. Due to high-level corruption affecting vaccine procurement, senior leaders, including the president, were forced to resign.

The Changing International Economic and Political Context

All countries must deal with pressures from other states and external interests. Vietnam, however, has faced larger external challenges than most, both during the Cold War and today. For thirty years after its declaration of independence in 1945, that pressure mainly took the extreme form of huge, sustained military interventions: first from France, trying to re-create its colonial past, and then from the United States, turning Vietnam into a major Cold War arena. Following the end of the Vietnam War, Vietnam hoped to inaugurate a new era of peace and prosperity, but soon found itself embroiled in a new conflict in Cambodia and clashes with its former ally, the People's Republic of China.

Vietnam eventually did find a route to more peaceful relations with its neighbors, following the CPV's adoption of the Đổi Mới reforms and "new thinking" in its approach to foreign relations. Since 1991, Vietnam has enjoyed considerable success in pursuing its policy of "becoming friends" with all nations, with the ongoing tensions in the South China Sea as the only major exception. External pressures and opportunities for Vietnam have instead mainly involved political issues (diplomatic relations, territorial claims, etc.) and economic issues (foreign trade, foreign investment, and aid). A central issue is whether Vietnam's responses to these various challenges can be best understood as ad hoc efforts to deal with one problem or one country, or as aspects of a more systematic approach. In the early years after reunification the CPV's foreign policy was largely driven by a more unified and ideologically driven conception of who its friends and enemies were, but today that is hardly the case.

Vietnam for a long time has had formal diplomatic ties with almost all the countries in the world. Its most important and complex relations, however, are embedded in its relationships with China and the United States. Chapter 15 by Alexander Vuving gives an overview of the evolution of Vietnamese foreign policy since Đổi Mới and the relationship of that evolution to changes in the domestic political situation. Chapter 16 by Bill Hayton and chapter 17 by Edward Miller analyze the evolution of Vietnam's relations with China and the United States, respectively. Book-length considerations regrettably preclude additional chapters on the country's relations with ASEAN, the EU, Russia, and several of its other Asian neighboring countries.

As Alexander Vuving explains, Vietnam's foreign policy was much like that of the Soviet Union both before and after reunification. That view saw the world divided into two opposing camps, a Communist or socialist camp and a capitalist camp. This conception was complicated by the split between the Soviet Union and China and later by the collapse of the Soviet Union and the end of Communist Party governments in Eastern Europe. The overall approach of Vietnam was to place countries in four levels rather than just the two of the Cold War era. Those countries that had retained Communist Party rule were placed at the top, and former Communist Party countries were next. At the bottom were many high-income capitalist countries including the United States, where relations were mostly adversarial.

As the country opened through the Đổi Mới reforms, there was increasing support within the CPV for an international view that would allow Vietnam to integrate broadly with the rest of the world, including the leading capitalist countries. There was much resistance to this in the 1990s, both domestically and internationally, but by the beginning of the twenty-first century the integrationists were clearly dominant. In concrete terms, this led to closer ties with many countries, including its decision in 1995 to join and work with ASEAN, as well as to normalize relations with the United States and enter into a cooperation agreement with the European Union. A new, more "accurate worldview" began to emerge. As Vuving notes, domestic currents within the CPV and to some degree also within the Vietnamese public, influence how the CPV determines its national interests and foreign policy. Vietnam's close relations with Russia became, as Vuving shows, a delicate issue when Russia invaded Ukraine in late February 2022, challenging the global order. While that invasion reminded Vietnam of the dangers involved in living next to a major power, its main influence was to strengthen what Vuving describes as Vietnam's "bamboo" approach, reinforcing its policy of four "no's" (no military alliances, no siding with one country against another, no foreign basing on Vietnamese soil, and no use of force).

Vietnam's relations with China, as Bill Hayton points out in chapter 16, are the most complex. This is primarily because of the two countries' proximity, but also because of the close but complex relations between the CPV and its Chinese counterpart, a relationship that goes back to before the CPV's forerunner was formally founded in 1930. After the Communist Party came to power in China in 1949, it continued to actively support the Vietnamese war against the French and in the 1960s against the South Vietnamese government and the Americans. During most of this time Vietnam welcomed support from both China and the Soviet Union, and the bitter split between the two major Communist powers enabled Vietnam to play one off against the other to increase aid.

By the late 1960s, however, Beijing's "big brother attitude" began to affect Vietnamese state policy, and the CPV began to shift its allegiance toward the Soviet Union and away from China. Concerns about Chinese policy in the 1970s, including China's increasingly close ties to the Khmer Rouge government in Cambodia, made both Beijing and Hanoi fear strategic encirclement. This led to mounting tensions with the Khmer Rouge regime, the Vietnamese invasion of Cambodia. and then to the Chinese invasion of the northern provinces of Vietnam in 1979. The two countries would not formally reconcile their differences and reestablish formal government and Party relations until a little more than a decade later after the collapse of the Soviet Union.

Differences, however, remained. With the collapse of Communist Parties in the Soviet Union and Eastern Europe, the CPV, and particularly conservative members within the CPV leadership, felt the need for CPC support against "peaceful evolution" pressures emanating from the West and the pluralism supported by some within the CPV itself.

At the same time, history, national interests, and a desire to avoid becoming subservient to China have inhibited close relations. As Chinese claims to the South China Sea became more assertive, Vietnamese national interests and popular feelings dictated an increasingly vigorous response. Part of that has involved getting closer to the United States. Vietnamese foreign policy toward China, therefore, continues to evolve as a balancing act between dealing with popular resentment toward China and resisting China's aggressive moves in disputed territory versus the "natural position" of the CPV leadership to keep close to China. This love/hate relationship that Hayton describes is one of the most serious challenges facing the CPV.

The case of Vietnam's relations with the United States since 1975 offers fascinating similarities and differences in comparison to the country's ties to China over the same period. As Edward Miller argues in chapter 17, this relationship can be viewed as a drawn-out and highly contentious peacemaking process. As early as 1973, both Washington and Hanoi had professed their desire for postwar reconciliation. During 1977–78, US and SRV officials briefly held high-level talks on the possibility of normalizing diplomatic relations, but this chance slipped away due to the crisis in Cambodia, Hanoi's tilt toward the Soviet Union, and the resurgence of Cold War strategic thinking in Washington.

As Miller demonstrates, leaders on both sides remained deeply invested in their respective narratives about the war and its implications for each state's legitimacy. Vietnam's embrace of the Đổi Mới reforms and its "new thinking" in foreign policy during the late 1980s helped pave the way for a normalization agreement, which was finally concluded in 1995. But normalization did not lead automatically or inevitably to reconciliation. SRV officials continued to worry about American plots to promote "peaceful evolution" toward liberal democracy in Vietnam, while their US counterparts refused even to discuss the idea of American moral culpability for the war or the damage inflicted on Vietnam.

Real progress toward US-Vietnam reconciliation came only in the twenty-first century. This shift was facilitated by a 2001 bilateral trade agreement, by Vietnam's 2007 accession to the World Trade Organization, and by Washington's willingness to display support for Vietnam's position in its emerging conflict with China in the South China Sea. But as Miller shows, the most dramatic changes took place in the realm of ideas and culture, and in the willingness of various actors on both sides to embrace new narratives about collaboration and shared responsibility.

Vietnamese Americans, a group that had once overwhelmingly opposed reconciliation with Hanoi, played increasingly prominent roles in Vietnamese business circles by the early 2000s. Meanwhile, polls showed that large majorities of ordinary Vietnamese had adopted strongly favorable views of American society and culture, and even US political leaders. Amid these developments, US and CPV leaders began launching new efforts to ameliorate the lingering impact of "war legacies" such as unexploded ordnance and Agent Orange. In the early 2020s, US-Vietnam reconciliation appears remarkably strong, even though a common understanding of the war and each side's responsibility for it remains elusive.

Looking toward the Future

In the early days of the third decade of the twenty-first century, Vietnam continues to be governed as a party-state led by the CPV, determined to retain its control of government and politics. Its democratic centralist approach to governance and its willingness to use repression to preserve stability has increased, but Vietnam combines this with a degree of openness not found in its Chinese neighbor. That degree of openness to information and ideas could continue at its current level for some time. There is also a chance that it could expand into a more open and pluralistic society, or, as recent developments have shown, it could move in the opposite direction, toward a "controlocracy" along lines similar to Xi Jinping's China. This book cannot answer that question, but suggests that neither of the latter two scenarios seems most likely. Demand for change is likely to grow, increasingly testing the ability of the Party to respond in ways that promote the interests of the country.

As pointed out in this introduction and in the chapters that follow, however, this book can, and does, describe the many forces that will influence Vietnam's direction. Many of these are only under the control of the CPV to a rather limited degree. That is most obvious in Vietnam's desire and ability to successfully maintain its independence in the face of an ever more powerful China, and a Vietnamese population that is increasingly favorably inclined toward America and more open to liberal societies in general.

These political pressures will also play out in the coming decades in an economic context that will be challenging. As this study shows, sustaining a high rate of economic growth over the next two decades will be difficult and may not even be possible given the policy direction that the country and the CPV are following today. The COVID-19 crisis will retreat into the past, and the economy, less damaged by the pandemic than many others, will recover. What is less clear, as this book shows, is whether the Vietnamese education system, particularly at the postsecondary level, will improve sufficiently to support a move up the technology ladder. Vietnam's success as a destination for foreign direct investment and integration into global value chains suggests opportunities for the country, provided it develops the human resources—and institutions—necessary for playing that role.

A crucial question is whether economic growth will move the country toward rising inequality and an economy controlled by politically connected oligarchs, as has occurred elsewhere. The unchecked official and private rent-seeking and corruption, already a chronic problem, that would likely accompany such a move would undermine critical public support. An alternative way forward, one featuring a renewed commitment to equity, would strengthen the foundations of Vietnamese society.

There is also the issue of whether the current policy direction will be sustainable given the increasingly serious damage currently being done to the environment. At the global level, policies implemented by the rest of the world will hardly be sufficient to avoid the impact of climate change upon Vietnam. A new sense of urgency is required.

Many of the chapters in this book outline what needs to be done in Vietnam to continue making progress in achieving transparent governance, a more effective education system, more sustainable development, less crisis-prone financial regulation, and more equitable and efficient health care. This book also outlines areas, particularly in the family and social sphere, where further changes in society are most likely to occur as social values evolve under pressure from forces largely beyond the control of government policy.

Despite the many challenges, some of which clearly are highly systemic, we remain optimistic about Vietnam's future. The chapters in this book describe those challenges openly and candidly, but also convey the evident vitality of a society determined to shape an ever better future.

Notes

1. This is the World Bank estimate of per capital PPP GDP in 2020 in current prices multiplied by the growth rate in per capita GDP in 2021. Vietnam did revise its GDP figures upward, leading the IMF to report a per capita PPP GDP in 2021 of $11,677. Because the chapters in this book require growth data over long periods and GDP figures for earlier years have not been adjusted upward, this book is mainly using the GDP estimates prior to the revision.

2. This is purchasing power parity GDP per capita in constant prices for 2020 over 1991 (World Bank, WDI online).

3. General Statistical Office, Economy and Finance of Vietnam 1991, 12; and General Statistical Office, *Nien Giam Thong Ke*, 1996, 16.

4. General Statistics Office, Vietnam Statistical Yearbook, online, 2020. The Vietnamese GDP data include a component "product taxes and subsidies" in addition to the standard three production sectors.

PART I

The Central Role of Politics

CHAPTER I

The Nature and Durability of Vietnam's Party-State

BÖRJE LJUNGGREN

Few countries have changed as much in the last decades as Vietnam. At a rapid pace it has developed a diversified economy with domestic and global markets playing crucial roles, dramatically reducing poverty and undergoing profound social transformations. Yet, when Đổi Mới (Renovation) was launched in 1986, at a time of grave economic difficulties and international challenges, a common narrative advocated by modernization theorists was that Vietnam was "in transition," not only from state command to market-driven economy but also toward democracy. This has not happened. Even though considerable institutional development has taken place and the Vietnamese society today is far from monolithic, the country remains a party-state.

In Vietnam, as in China and the other remaining party-states (Cuba, Laos, and North Korea), the Communist Party ultimately commands, controls, and integrates government, the legislature, the judiciary, the armed forces, and all political organizations and institutions. Society is diverse, organizations are formed, protests occur, and markets play a decisive role, but the hallmark of the Leninist party-state in contemporary Vietnam and the other four party-states is, as London notes, "the assertion and enforcement of the complete (by design) permanent political monopoly of the vanguard Party and its domination of social life and organizations across all fields, including the ideological domain."[1]

The concept of the party-state reflects the Leninist origin of the Democratic Republic of Vietnam (DRV). The constitution explicitly mandates the leading role of the Communist Party. With Marxism-Leninism as the ideological basis, ultimate sovereignty lies with the Party itself. But the country is far from "communist" in the original sense of collective ownership of the means of production, but rather a "market-Leninist system," which clearly has given it a new lease on life.

The essence is deeply rooted in Leninism and nationalism, shaped by Vietnam's resistance against French, Japanese, and American colonization and aggression. In this

I would like to express special thanks to Nayan Chanda, Joseph Fewsmith, Adam Fforde, Björn Jerdén, Ray Mallon, Jonathan London, Sam Sternin, and Stein Tönnesson for invaluable comments and suggestions.

process, the CPV emerged and established itself as the prevailing national political force. Like the Communist Party of China (CPC), it was not imposed by outside forces, but rather secured its dominant national role through its capacity to mobilize resistance against such forces. Hence, it is more resilient.

The concept of the Leninist party-state is in frequent use, yet lacks a clear definition. Even though five party-states have survived in the post-Soviet era, there has been little recent comparative analysis. In his recent book on how the Vietnamese system deals with public political criticism, Benedict Kerkvliet describes the system, using a summary label, as a "responsive-repressive party-state" where the CPV at all levels is "entwined with the state."[2] That characterization, based on Kerkvliet's decades of interaction with Vietnam, catches much of the essence of the system. My analysis below is based on the thesis that a party-state can be said to rest on six mutually supportive "pillars," with the Party at the core:

- Political power rests with the Party.
- The Party controls the army, armed police, and police through Party leadership and a high degree of Party membership.
- The Party controls the legislature and the administrative state.
- The Party controls the judicial system and the domestic security apparatus.
- The Party ensures that civil society is kept within the constraints of the party-state.
- The Party exercises ultimate control over media and the interpretation of history.

It is, hence, not just a single-party state, of which there are many in today's world, but a comprehensive system of a different nature, different from other political systems in its explicit ambition to ultimately maintain control of all political activity.[3]

Broadly speaking, the Communist Party of Vietnam meets all six criteria above. It has to cope with dynamic environments and cannot unilaterally exercise power, but power ultimately rests with the Party, sustained by its control of the other five dimensions of the construct and the success of market Leninism, with the country's tragic modern history and nationalism as critical glue.

Even though it is a party-state, Vietnam has succeeded in combining its authoritarian political system with the dynamics of global capitalism and, contrary to the predictions of leading scholars such as Acemoglu and Robinson, according to whom economic development in countries such as China and Vietnam, "like all examples of growth under extractive conditions . . . will not be sustained."[4] They have "failed to fail."[5] Global economic integration, with foreign direct investment as a driving force, has in fact emerged as a key source of growth, a development that has served the CPV well, while also deepening the dynamics of Vietnam's evolving challenges.

For the Communist Party of Vietnam, the Communist Party of China (CPC) is both a close ideological partner and a constant national challenge, deepening national identity. Party-states, including the Vietnamese one, are by nature not inclined to deconstruct themselves but rather prioritize "stability," while adapting within the system, attaching decisive importance to sheer system survival at the expense of systemic reform that might cause institutionalized uncertainty.

Understanding the nature and endurance of the Vietnamese party-state is the purpose of this chapter.[6] As a Swedish civil servant, diplomat, and scholar specializing in Asia, I have during my career served in three of today's party-states—Laos, Vietnam, and China—interacting with the system, while always trying to remain close to the academic world. Since retiring from government I have been writing and lecturing, primarily on China but also on Vietnam and key global challenges. Given these experiences, and China's importance, it has been natural for me to use the Chinese party-state as a *systemic comparison* in order to deepen the understanding of the Vietnamese system, focusing on significant similarities and differences.

The Setting at the Time of the Collapse of the Soviet Union—and Thirty Years Later

In December 1991, two years after the fall of the Berlin Wall, the Soviet Union ceased to exist. According to Marxist theory, history could only move forward and socialism only make further gains, but now the impossible had happened.[7] Suddenly the entire Soviet empire had collapsed, leaving just a handful of Communist countries in the world. The old worldview through which Vietnamese leaders made sense of the world was undermined. Hanoi clearly "felt the chill," as Nayan Chanda noted, especially as the 1980s had been a difficult decade internally as well as internationally.[8] The CPV was "rattled but unbowed."[9]

"The third wave of democratization," which began in the mid-1970s, had been growing steadily.[10] Now, a dozen Eastern European countries were added, making this wave appear as the only possible future. Market economy and democracy were seen as two inseparable dimensions of transition—according to Fukuyama, "the end of history as such."[11]

However, there was not just one but "two 1989s," the fall of the Berlin Wall but also, five months before the wall came down, the Tiananmen Square massacre.[12] History did not end. Three decades later, in 2022, five Leninist party-states remain, having survived the collapse of the Soviet empire. Furthermore, the democratic wave also turned out to be far from invincible. "2021 was the 16th consecutive year of global decline, with no end in sight."[13] Autocracy was on the rise.[14]

The CPV has shown considerable staying power—and capacity to adapt. As regards China, Ivan Krastev and Stephen Holmes conclude that: "They *borrowed* exuberantly but refused to *convert*," successfully borrowing the means but not the goals.[15] The Vietnamese story is less dramatic, but the image makes sense.

After the Tiananmen Square massacre, two schools of thought emerged as regards China, one saying that the system was bound to collapse, another that the Chinese party-state was considerably more resilient than conventional wisdom suggested. "Authoritarian resilience," a concept coined by Andrew Nathan, became a reality.[16] Deng Xiaoping's 1978 launch of "reform and opening" was evidence in favor of the resilience school.[17]

For Vietnam, the decade immediately after the Second Vietnam War was much more difficult than foreseen. Under the leadership of Party General Secretary Le Duan, long before Ho Chi Minh's death in 1969, the most powerful leader of the Party, the country's postwar reunification was based on the North Vietnamese state-dominated command economy model. Inevitable challenges were aggravated.[18] More than 2 million people left the country, many as boat refugees, and many belonging to the ethnic Chinese business community, distrusted by Hanoi. Vietnamese-Chinese relations were deteriorating, and in 1978, relations were further strained when Vietnam entered a friendship treaty with the Soviet Union.

Vietnam entered an era of further challenges when Vietnamese troops, in December 1978, after a period of serious border confrontations on the Vietnamese-Cambodian border, invaded Cambodia and removed the Pol Pot regime.[19] Burdened by the involvement, Vietnam became an increasingly isolated shortage economy, barely able to feed itself, and in the mid-1980s, in the absence of economic reforms, suffered from hyperinflation. The hardships resulted in the recognition of grassroots-level reform initiatives. In 1986 Đổi Mới was launched, laying the foundation for more comprehensive changes, in particular the crucial 1989 price reform. In any event, with the emergence of reformist Mikhail Gorbachev as Soviet leader, Hanoi could no longer count on Soviet support, and with the ultimate collapse of the Soviet Union, new realities prevailed. "The crisis and death of utopia" was a fact.[20]

Economic reforms gained further momentum. Foreign trade and foreign direct investments began to matter. Millions saw life improving. Diplomatically Vietnam, within a few months in 1995, enjoyed what the late Foreign Minister Nguyen Co Thach in a conversation with a visiting Swedish minister once described as a "bumper crop": diplomatic relations with the United States, ASEAN membership, and a cooperation agreement with the European Union. These developments helped restore confidence within the Party in its ability to cope with change, while also generating new challenges.

Global economic integration emerged as a driving force. In 2007 Vietnam joined the World Trade Organization, laying the foundation for increasing foreign direct investment–driven growth and integration into the global economy, in 2019 becoming what the *Financial Times* called a "super-exporter." Exports exceeded the size of nominal GDP, but Vietnam was still at the lower end of the global value chain. Oligarchs were, as Xuan Than shows in his chapter in this volume, seen as more "system friendly" than a truly dynamic small and medium-sized private sector.[21] In recent years, Vietnam has entered into a number of major free trade agreements. The EU-Vietnam agreement, finally approved in 2020 by the European Council, includes potentially important articles about labor rights.[22]

As regards China, a similar, though limited, development seems highly unlikely. EU-Chinese negotiations on a comprehensive investment agreement (CIA) have stalled due to growing resistance in the European Parliament, including tit-for-tat sanctions, with China increasingly being seen as a "systemic rival."[23] Globalization is supposed to serve as a vehicle for social and political liberalization and Western values. Yet, as noted above, both countries clearly "failed to fail," while the world witnessed an era of growing strategic competition, economically, technologically, militarily, and ideologically, with democracy in recession, China emerging as an ultimate techno-autocracy. Vietnam was destined to navigate in turbulent waters.

The Leninist Order—Mandate, Organization, and Leadership Culture

THE LENINIST MANDATE

All through Vietnam's modern history, ever since the French colonization, the "national question" has been at the core. For Ho Chi Minh, who in 1911 at the age of twenty-one left Vietnam for Europe, and for his compatriots in France, that was the question to which they wanted an answer. When approaching delegates at the 1919 Versailles Peace Conference, they wanted to know what Woodrow Wilson's Fourteen Points, which came to be interpreted by anti-colonial forces as supporting self-determination, meant for their country. They did not get an answer. The French socialists, not yet split into socialists and communists, were divided between those advocating a more civilized form of colonial rule and those joining the Third International, taking a clear anti-imperialist stand. For Ho Chi Minh, these experiences were decisive. As Brocheux notes in his Ho Chi Minh biography, "in his tireless pursuit of the anti-colonialist struggle, he moved progressively towards more radical positions, finally adhering to the communist revolutionary venture proposed by the Russian Bolsheviks."[24] In 1923 he became a Comintern agent, a Leninist nationalist. When in August 1944 he finally returned permanently to Vietnam, he did so as the leader of the Viet Minh and the Vietnamese anti-Japanese resistance movement.[25]

A leading historian of Vietnam, David Marr, in his book *Vietnam 1945*, argues that the nationwide rising against the French was led not by the Communist Party or Viet Minh in any coherent way, but by a broader popular manifestation.[26] Ultimately, the Communist Party, led by Ho Chi Minh, emerged as the leading force.

The August Revolution, launched by the Viet Minh against French and Japanese colonial rule on August 19, 1945, and the September 2, 1945, declaration of Vietnam's independence, was "a turning point in the process of transplanting Marxism-Leninism to the Vietnamese sociopolitical environment. The Communist Party had ceased to be an illegal organization, becoming the party in power," but not the sole power.[27]

In his speech in February 2020, at the ninetieth anniversary of the Party, Party general secretary and then President Nguyen Phu Trong described the emergence of the Party as "dictated by history."[28] Vietnam's modern history does, however, contain decisive moments, in particular 1946, when France launched its lost effort to regain control of its colony, and 1954 when the Americans, "determined to maintain its non-Communist bastion in southern Vietnam, helped deny the Viet Minh the full fruits of victory as they set about creating and building up the Republic of (South) Vietnam."[29] Facing these exceptional challenges, the CPV consolidated its dominant role.

In the Democratic Republic of Vietnam, as in China, the party-state is thoroughly institutionalized. The overriding role of the Party and the people's "democratic dictatorship" are centerpieces of recent Vietnam constitutions.[30] Early constitutions of Vietnam were, however, less explicit regarding the Party's leading role. The first constitution of the Democratic Republic of Vietnam (DRV), seen as a temporary constitution "not meant to last," had no mention of the CPV.[31] It was first mentioned in the fourth revision, in 1992, shortly after the fall of the Communist regimes in Eastern Europe and the collapse of the Soviet Union. Shocked by these events, the leading role of the Communist Party was for the first time explicitly affirmed. Đổi Mới was confirmed, but glasnost must be prevented. Economic openness and one-party rule were combined. Two small parties, which had been allowed to exist alongside the Communist Party, were dissolved in this party-state consolidation process. In China, eight such subservient parties have been allowed to remain, playing a purely decorative role.

The current Vietnamese constitution was adopted in 2013 and is, hence, the fifth one adopted since 1946. The leading role of the CPV is unequivocally stated in Article 4.1: "The Communist Party of Vietnam—the vanguard of the working class, concurrently the vanguard of the laboring people and Vietnamese nation, faithfully representing the interests of the working class, laboring people and entire nation, and acting upon the Marxist-Leninist doctrine and Ho Chi Minh Thought, is the force leading the State and society." No other parties are allowed to be formed, and only carefully screened independent candidates are allowed to run in national elections, reconfirming the systemically subordinated role of the National Assembly.

The 2013 revision did not, however, happen without a certain drama, marking the changing context of the party-state. When the Constitutional Amendment Committee released its draft new constitution to the public for debate, a group of seventy-two intellectuals, senior scholars of the country, many of them Party members, publicly submitted a highly controversial petition known as Petition 72 to the Drafting Committee.[32] Two of their recommendations were of substantial magnitude: the absence of any role for the Party in the draft constitution, and the removal of the dual role of the military in defending not only the country but also the Party. The draft was disseminated on the Internet and became the subject of extensive blog discussions, receiving thousands of supporting signatures.

Ultimately, some changes were made, including that the Party shall "operate within the framework of the Constitution and the law," reflecting growing pressures to present the party-state as operating through and subject to law.[33] But not unexpectedly, the Party chose to confirm the existing order, hence, the party-state.

But this was not a party-state operating in a placid and controlled context. "The party-state leaders found themselves," Bui Hai Thiem concludes, "struggling to manage the diverse and strident calls for change and to accommodate wider political participation from emerging players," "struggling to maintain hegemony . . . by ideational coercion and propaganda strategy."[34] Some petitioners suffered consequences, but no one was put on trial.

The outcome of the process was basically a defense of the status quo, but it was also a reflection of a dynamism that had to be reckoned with. The question of the future of the party-state was postponed rather than put to rest. For the CPC, especially under Xi, public debate on such a crucial matter seems alien.

PARTY STRUCTURE, CULTURE, AND PRESENCE

The CPV governs Vietnam from central to local levels through an all-encompassing party structure intertwined on each and every level with government structures, all modeled on principles developed in the Soviet Union. *Democratic centralism*, a decision-making practice and disciplinary policy adopted by the Communist Party of the Soviet Union and subsequently followed by Communist Parties in other countries, is a fundamental principle. Mass organizations form an integral part of the Party, and the Party is present all through the Vietnam People's Army, the police and the legal system, state enterprises and businesses of any size, media and cultural institutions, and NGOs of any significance. London notes that it does "not make sense to speak of any unit of the party-state independently of the Party."[35]

The *Politburo*, chaired by the Party secretary, is the Party's most powerful body, currently consisting of eighteen persons, seventeen men and one woman. In principle, the Party Congress, convened every five years, is at the top of the Party's hierarchy, followed by the 175-member Central Committee (CC) and its executive body, the Party Secretariat. While the Politburo is, hence, formally accountable to the CC and the Party Congress, in practice that body, and in particular the general secretary, dominates the entire Party. The "leading quartet" plays a critical role, and so does geographical distribution of key positions (see below).

The Politburo operates as a collective, balancing interest and power among police, army, state-owned enterprises, provinces, and the north, the center, and the south. Normally one of the top leadership positions is held by a southerner, but not during the current mandate period. The traditional practice of electing a southerner to one of the four top positions of national leadership, the quartet, was abandoned, with no woman included in the quartet. During the previous term, the chairperson of the National Assembly was a woman. According to Human Rights Watch, of the eighteen members, at least seven, including Vietnam's new prime minister, Pham Minh Chinh, have an affiliation with the Ministry of Public Security.[36] For the first time in twenty years, the Politburo includes two top generals. The number of military representatives in the Party's Central Committee also increased from twenty to twenty-three, cementing the status of the Vietnam People's Army (VPA) as the largest voting bloc in the CC, reflecting the central traditional role of the military in the Party as well as current South China Sea–focused security concerns.[37]

The Central Committee's Secretariat together with the Central Military Commission, the Central Party Commission for Public Security, and commissions on organization, discipline, and propaganda, play central roles in managing and controlling the

Party. Since 2001, the Politburo has no standing committee, a significant difference compared to the CPC. The CPV's more decentralized culture, with provinces playing an important role on the Central Committee, contributes to the stability-focused consensus-building tradition.

The Party's presence in society is therefore huge, albeit not as comprehensive as that of the CPC. While the CPC clearly is on the ideological and organizational offensive, the CPV's party-building efforts under the leadership of Party General Secretary Trong have been focused rather on ensuring the Party's leading role, coping as society becomes increasingly diverse and individualistic.

As a "vanguard party," based on Leninist principles, the CPV has strict rules of admission and discipline. Membership is not just up to the individual but remains based on a screening process, and membership requires loyalty under strict party discipline. In 2021, the total number of Party members was 5.2 million, 5 percent of the population, with the least concentration in the south, and more than 100,000 admitted annually.[38]

In both Vietnam and China there has been an evolution in the organization and composition of Party membership. In the case of the CPV, no changes as dramatic as the CPC's launch in the year 2000 of the so-called "three represents," but with Đổi Mới greater openness emerged. Loyal tycoons were welcome as members. A clear ambition is to recruit young, well-educated people.

Party reforms have for a long time been on the agenda of both the CPV and the CPC, and an element of electoral competition within the parties, the idea of "intraparty democracy," was introduced a few decades ago. Neither party has, however, pursued such reforms in any determined way, and they have not been sustained. In his book *Rethinking Chinese Politics*, Joseph Fewsmith, an insightful observer of the Chinese reform process and its limits, concludes that "in the end, Leninism proved stronger than institutionalization."[39]

Following Leninist practices, "mass organization," funded by the state, constitutes a fundamental part of the system. The official Trade Union of Vietnam, the Vietnam Peasants' Association, the Ho Chi Minh Communist Youth Union, the Vietnam Women's Union, and the Vietnam War Veterans' Association are all written into the current constitution. The Vietnam Fatherland Front, consisting of carefully screened members from the mass organizations, including the Buddhist community, is said to "constitute the political base of the people's administration," and it is supposed to "participate in the building of the Party and the State" (Article 9). By all accounts, it is entirely subordinated to the Party.

THE LEADERSHIP QUARTET

The CPV has a culturally rooted antipathy to excessive concentration of power, and Vietnam has never gone to China's extremes as regards the role of the Party with concentration of power in a single person.[40] The 1953–56 class struggle-driven land reform in the DRV was strongly influenced by China's Maoist agrarian transformation. Ho Chi Minh has remained the subject of a cult and been made a part of Vietnamese traditional worship of heroes, but there is no comparison to the cult of Mao or the current cult of Xi, described by Geremie Barmé, a leading Sinologist, as "all cult and no personality."[41] From an institutional perspective, the CPC has undergone a retrogression under Xi.

Ever since the death of Le Duan, less power has been concentrated in one person. For a long time, Vietnam has rather been ruled by a quartet of Politburo members consisting of the Party secretary, the prime minister, the president, and the chairperson of the National Assembly most of the time, with the Party secretary as the foremost among them. An important feature of this "four-pillar" order has been the relative separation of power between the Party secretary running the Party and the prime minister running the government. Also, in contrast to the situation within the CPC, the CPV has no standing committee of the Politburo in which power is concentrated, and the Central Committee, consisting of Party representatives from all provinces, plays an important cohesive role different from the one played by the Central Committee of the CPC, creating a certain measure of accountability.[42]

General Secretary Nguyen Phu Trong has been holding more political power than any party leader since Le Duan, who played a dominating role in the CPV from 1958 (officially 1960) until his death in 1986. Through his dual appointment as president in October 2018, following the death in office of President Tran Dai Quang, Trong also became chairman of the party's Central Military Commission. He is the first party chief to sit on both the Central Military Commission and the Central Party Commission for Public Security, the two Party bodies that lead the military, police, and security forces.

Trong is a party builder rather than a reformer, focused on strengthening Party legitimacy and the party-state. Central goals have been to clean up the Party by fighting the widespread corruption that characterized the era of his main contender at the 2016 Party Congress, the powerful but hugely corrupt Prime Minister Nguyễn Tấn Dũng (2006–16). Hence, one should purify Party membership by stressing moral duties and expulsions from the Party, recentralize power from the provinces back to Hanoi, and ensure that the Party maintains legitimacy among the public through economic growth and by upholding a stable status quo. In his speech in February 2020 on the ninetieth anniversary of the Party, Trong declared that "it is imperative for our Party to exert utmost efforts to bolster Party building and rectification, for the Party to be increasingly clean and strong, and to successfully fulfill its responsibility as the vanguard exercising leadership over the revolutionary cause in the new period."[43]

When Trong was named the country's new president in October 2018, this led to numerous news reports that claimed that Trong would be following the same path as China's "paramount leader," Xi Jinping. Such a scenario has always seemed remote, and Trong has rather been seen as a powerful gray party-state CEO. Vietnam's entire political culture made the very idea of "paramount leader" appear alien.

While the Twelfth Party Congress (2016) was characterized by an intense competition for the leadership position, the Thirteenth Congress, held in late January 2021, was expected to show the Party's capacity to manage balanced leadership change. No such agreement could, however, be reached. The newly elected eighteen-member Politburo reflects little generational change. The median age of its members is sixty-three, suggesting that many would reach the formal age limit for reelection during this term.

Trong failed to win support for his own party-building candidate as successor, but had the strength to stay on for a third term, in spite of thereby breaking the two-term rule. At seventy-six he was also far above the sixty-five-year age limit, and furthermore is in frail health after a stroke in 2019. A potential successor, reformist Prime Minister Nguyen Xuan Phuc, was designated to become president, a rather ceremonial position that Trong then relinquished. Phuc was in turn succeeded as prime minister by Pham Minh Chinh, a sixty-three-year-old general of the People's Public Security Forces, and former deputy minister of public security, with limited broad government experience, but a strong position within the Party. An economic policy expert with huge government experience, Vuong Dinh Hue, Phuc's principal deputy and natural successor, became chairman of the National Assembly. Deputy Prime Minister Vu Duc Dam (fifty-eight), nationally recognized for his leadership in fighting COVID-19, was not promoted to the Politburo. A rising star, Vo Van Thuong (born in 1970), the youngest member elected to the 2016 Politburo, was elected a standing member and executive secretary of the Central Committee's Secretariat.

The focus of the Congress was clearly on stability through party building: "the Party must enhance party building and rectification work to a strong and clean Party and political system."[44] The party-state and the leadership quartet, all of them top ranked, were reconfirmed, while the leadership question and necessary reforms were left pending.[45]

The Armed Forces—the Ultimate Guarantor?

The armed forces, together with the huge security apparatus, are pillars of the Vietnamese party-state, deeply rooted in the origin of the system. The armed forces must be directly under the control of the Party and be its ultimate guarantor. Serving the nation and the Party should be synonymous. According to Article 65 of the revised Vietnamese constitution (2013), "the People's Armed Forces shall show absolute loyalty to the Fatherland, the People, the Party and the State; protect the independence, sovereignty, unity and territorial integrity of the Fatherland, national security, and social order and safety; safeguard the People, the Party, the State and the socialist regime; and join the entire people in national construction and the performance of international duties." According to the same logic, "the State shall build a revolutionary People's Public Security" (Article 67), that is, not just state public security but a "revolutionary" one, loyal to the Party.

The Vietnam People's Army (VPA) was founded toward the end of the Second World War (December 1944), shortly before the 1945 declaration of independence of the DRV. Decades of war gave the military a central role, and maintaining close links with, and ultimate control over, the military has remained crucial. The CPV exercises absolute, direct, and all-around leadership over the VPA through a system of Party organizations and political organizations. The Central Military Commission (CMC)—the highest Party organization in the VPA—for example, is appointed by the Politburo. The CMC's members come from the Party Central Committee both within and outside the VPA. The

General Political Department (GPD), led by the CMC, is the top political organization in the VPA.

The professional character of the defense forces has become an issue of growing importance, with somewhat less emphasis on Party loyalty, but loyalty remains the CPV's overriding concern. Increased emphasis on professionalism was also evident in China during the Hu Jintao era, but since Xi came to power, absolute loyalty to the Party has clearly become a more central demand than in Vietnam.

The political role of the VPA was reconfirmed by the Thirteenth Party Congress. "Continuing building a politically strong Vietnam People's Army to meet the new task requirements" was a central theme of the resolution adopted by the Congress. The *National Defense Journal* conveyed the task of the VPA, expressed in language characterizing the ideology: "Being fully aware of the necessity of making the VPA politically strong," the Communist Party of Vietnam had always "concentrated their leadership and direction on turning the VPA into a political and combat force absolutely loyal to the Homeland, the Party, the State, and the people as well as on making it ideologically strong and 'immune' to the hostile forces' sabotage and social negative impacts. The Military had always successfully fulfilled the 'combat mission in peace time,' overcome nontraditional security challenges, and proactively fought against wrong, hostile viewpoints to defend the Party's ideological foundation."[46]

The comprehensive nature of the party-state is clearly illustrated. A crucial question is when and how the VPA might be used to curtail protests, the primary role being performed by the national security apparatus. It is difficult to imagine a situation being allowed to emerge where the CPV in a major way would risk its prevailing mandate by resorting to the use of the armed forces to defend itself against the people, as the CPC did when in 1989 it crushed the democracy movement. Still, given the nature of the system, scenarios involving considerable use of force to defend the party-state, fulfilling its "combat mission in peace time," cannot be excluded.

The Party, the Legislature, and the Administrative State

THE LEGISLATURE—A HIGHLY DEPENDENT VARIABLE

Running parallel to the Party structures, Vietnam has multitiered legislative structures to approve budgets, pass legislation, and so on. In the beginning of the country's reform and opening era, the role of these structures increased, but neither Vietnam nor China has experienced a sustained institutional evolution. They are by systemic definition loyal, disseminating bodies, rather than initiators. Examples of a certain independence of the Vietnamese National Assembly include cases where a proposed minister has not been approved.

The candidates per seat ratio in elections to the Vietnamese National Assembly has increased marginally over the years, and a small number of closely screened "independent" candidates were allowed. But the assemblies, especially at the national, regional, and township levels, remained instruments of the ruling Party rather than countervailing or supervising forces. In the 2021 national elections, the number of independent candidates was in fact lower than in previous elections. A total of 868 candidates contested 500 seats, of which 499 were ratified by the National Election Council for the 2021–26 tenure. Only four of the deputies were self-nominated. The voter turnout in the elections was reported to be 99.57 percent, or 68.7 million out of the total of 69 million voters, higher than the rates recorded in the previous elections, which were over 98 percent.[47]

One independent candidate, Le Trong Hung, was arrested two months before the election, charged with conducting propaganda against the state in violation of Article 117(1) of the Vietnamese Penal Code. On December 31, a court in Hanoi sentenced him to five years in prison and five years of probation after his release. According to reports, the court ruled that Hung's reporting had infringed on national security, defamed the government, caused instability, and affected "public confidence in the political institution and state."[48]

THE NOMENKLATURA

The development of Vietnam's administrative capacity is continuously assessed in the annual Public Administrative Performance Index (PAPI), a governance program initiated by the United Nations Development Programme in Vietnam in 2009. "PAPI measures and benchmarks citizens' experiences and perception on the performance and quality of policy implementation and services delivery of all 63 provincial governments in Vietnam to advocate for effective and responsive governance," including public trust in government. The index, based on data collected by the Fatherland Front, indicates a certain measure of progress over the years, especially as regards anti-corruption and public service delivery. Hardly any improvement has been recorded as regards transparency.[49]

The capacity and professional skills of the central government as well as lower-level bodies have developed through sustained efforts to professionalize the administrative state in order to meet new challenges emerging from the tasks of a modern government. The development of complex financial institutions is a salient example.

The relationship between the Party and the state has varied over time in both Vietnam and China, with periods of marked institutional development, but also of regression. In Vietnam the role of government changed as Đổi Mới evolved, but within the constraints of the party-state and with renewed emphasis under Nguyen Phu Trong on party building. Deng Xiaoping's China entered a period of an evolving state-party relationship, but since Xi came to power, the paramount role of the Party has been manifested more strongly than at any time since Mao.[50]

In both Vietnam and China, the cadre system and the right to appoint and remove top-ranking political and administrative personnel is an essential pillar of the party-state. Central cadres, the *nomenklatura*, are appointed, rotated, monitored, and disciplined by the Organization Department of the Central Committee, be it Party, government, administration, judiciary, state-owned enterprises, public service units, other organizations, or the military.[51] A fundamental, systemic fact is, as Adam Fforde has noted, that their legal systems are dual, preventing investigation of Party members by anti-corruption agencies without the formal approval of the Party.[52]

The "civil service" concept is used, though hardly adequate in a party-state system resting on Party-affiliated cadres rather than on Weberian principles of civil service. In the case of Vietnam, it may possibly suggest an ambiguity not seen in Xi Jinping's China, the Vietnamese system being less comprehensive and less definitive. Nonetheless, when in February 2020 Vietnam introduced more "specific quantified" criteria for top officials (Regulation 214), the regulations issued by Party Secretary Nguyen Phu Trong covered senior Party as well as government positions, heads of provincial Party committees, as well as ministers.[53] In January 2019, a Code for Civil Servants "to keep civil servants in line" was issued.[54]

ENDEMIC CORRUPTION

Corruption is an endemic and systemic dilemma for the party-state. No country is free from corruption, even if the legal system is highly developed and based on due process of law, and even if the press is free to play a truly scrutinizing role. In a party-state, lacking an independent legal system and a free press, corruption is an inevitable part of the system. Fighting corruption, a perennial goal, is a given priority, bound to remain unrealized within the prevailing institutional framework.

In Vietnam, corruption has been of a magnitude perceived as a threat to the legitimacy and survival of the Party. Widespread and personal corruption was a major reason why the then Prime Minister Nguyen Tan Dung, at the Twelfth Party Congress in 2016, failed in his bid to take over as Party secretary. Nguyen Phu Trong was reelected and began his second term by initiating an anti-corruption campaign against scores of high-profile officials. Trong still heads the Central Steering Commission for Anti-Corruption (CSCA), which he once described as a "blazing (or hot) furnace." For Xi Jinping, anti-corruption has been a trademark ever since he became Party secretary in 2012, and as he was set for an unprecedented third term in 2022, he launched an anti-corruption drive as part of his "common prosperity" strategy and as a political weapon.[55]

According to the annual rating of Transparency International (TI), corruption remains severe in Vietnam even though a certain improvement has been recorded. According to its 2021 ranking of corruption, Vietnam was ranked 87 out of 180 countries, nine positions better than in 2019, but with a total score of 39/100 it was just two points better. Over the last decade, the score had, however, improved by eight points. China, ranked 66, was considered a "significant improver," with a score of 45/100. In both countries, more than 60 percent of people thought that corruption was a "big problem."[56]

Furthermore, the encouraging shift in Vietnam reported by TI does not reflect the effects of grave corruption related to COVID. Vietnam saw the threat very early on and successfully mobilized the population to control the spread. The country's handling of the challenge became a source of national pride. However, during 2021, as new variants of the virus emerged, Vietnam faced growing challenges, met by uncompromising and dramatic lockdowns. Trust in the government was, as Pham Duy Nghia notes in his chapter in this volume, affected by serious cases of high-level corruption and lack of transparency. The sheer scale of it, and the fact that it involved high-ranking public officials, shocked the country, again revealing the systemic nature of the problem.

While certain improvements have been made, both Vietnam and China demonstrate the limitations of party-driven anti-corruption campaigns in lieu of sustained systemic reforms. The campaigns are managed by the Central Disciplinary Commissions of the parties, while the role of the legal system is to implement rather to initiate. Hence, a prosecutor would act on instructions from the Commission rather than on his or her own initiative when opening an investigation of suspected corruption.

Still, though Vietnam's legal system is dual, requiring formal Party approval before an investigation, a former Politburo member and several provincial Party secretaries have been prosecuted and sentenced, as have senior government officials and oligarchs. A serious dilemma is that a growing part of today's economic assets is the consequence of reinvestment of corrupt revenues.[57] Support from political elites is, as noted by Xuan Thanh in his chapter on the Vietnamese oligarchs, crucial for "wealth defense."

Rule by Law, Not of Law, and Denied Civil and Political Human Rights

THE LIMITS OF LAW

In his chapter on constitutional development in this volume, Pham Duy Nghia asks a fundamental question: "Is it possible for a country ruled by the supremacy of the Communist Party to be ruled at the same time by the supremacy of the law?" The chapter illustrates both possibilities and systemic difficulties. There are, as Nghia notes, "at least three forces that drive and facilitate the development toward the rule of law in Vietnam, namely the Party, the society, and global integration," making it necessary for the Party to adapt, while maintaining its "supremacy."

In his book *The Party: The Secret World of China's Communist Rulers*, Richard McGregor recounts a conversation with a retired Chinese judge who, when asked about interference of party officials in his court rulings, responded, "you call it interference, we call it leadership."[58] The conversation catches an essential dimension of the nature of the party-state and its inherent lack of legal security. *Rule by law* is an ambition, while *rule of law*—assuming a qualitatively different system with independent courts, due process of law, lawyers committed to the defense of their clients, and freedom of the press—is alien to the system.

After the launch of *Đổi Mới*, the Vietnamese legal systems underwent significant development, and today Vietnam has a comprehensive system expanded to serve the needs of its diversified economy, not least when it comes to commercial law. Still, the ambition of the Party is *not* to develop an independent legal system allowing for rule of law. As

Lubman has noted about China, the legal system is bound to develop without evolving into an independent legal system.[59]

The legal profession has also developed rapidly within the constraints of the party-state. Today, Vietnam has approximately 13,900 licensed lawyers with permits for litigation at courts, with the remaining large number of law graduates working as in-house lawyer/consultants in business.[60] Licensed lawyers are organized in the Vietnam Bar Federation. All leaders of bars and the federation must be Party members, and their appointments agreed to by Party leadership. An oath of loyalty to the Party is not required, but a lawyer acting contrary to the Party line will face difficulties, such as increased tax control and inspection. Defending a "dissident" involves particular risks.

While there are many similarities to China, the Vietnamese situation is, in this respect, more fluid and less far-reaching than the Chinese. After the Cultural Revolution, China had fewer than five hundred lawyers, and they were all poorly trained state lawyers, whose task was to convict rather than defend "the client." Today, China has more than a quarter of a million lawyers, required to swear an oath of loyalty to the Party.[61]

THE LIMITS OF HUMAN RIGHTS

The 2013 Vietnamese constitution states that "in the Socialist Republic of Vietnam, human rights and citizens' rights in the political, civic, economic, cultural and social fields are recognized, respected, protected and guaranteed in concordance with the Constitution and the law" (Article 14.1). The practice of rights "shall be provided by the law," as defined by the Party. Vietnam has both signed and ratified a large number of UN covenants on human rights, including the crucial Covenant on Civil and Political Rights. China has never ratified the covenant, and in recent years has shown a clear intention not to do so. China has, in fact, explicitly moved away from the fundamental notion of the universality of human rights. Social and economic rights have improved dramatically, while the opposite has been true for civil and political rights.

The detention and imprisonment of a growing number of democracy activists and human right defenders is a sign of mounting challenges for the CPV. In its 2020 *World Report*, Human Rights Watch's (HRW) overall assessment was that "Vietnam did little to improve its abysmal human rights record in 2019."[62] In its 2022 report, HRW noted that critics of the government or Party faced "police intimidation, harassment, restricted movement, arbitrary arrest and detention, and imprisonment after unfair trials." "Party-controlled courts" sentenced "bloggers and activists on bogus national security charges."[63]

The judicial system, while expanded and modernized, is ultimately determined by the nature of the party-state, and the human rights situation leaves a lot to be desired. Improvements can and have been made, but they are limited and not irreversible. The CPV has adopted a number of resolutions on legal reform, such as the Judicial Reform Strategy to 2020, but implementation has been slow. The contrast between the rapid development of society at large and the serious lack of protection for human rights is striking. Demands for change are likely to grow.

A qualitative difference compared to China is that, although Vietnam has pursued policies to encourage majority-*Kinh* citizens to settle in sensitive border areas home to ethnic minorities, there is no corollary to China's systematic efforts to suppress Tibetan or Uighur cultural, religious, linguistic, and ethnic identity through mass repression, surveillance, and detention.

CIVIL SOCIETY—IN A CAGE

The relationship to civil society is by nature complex and contradictory. A profound ambivalence in both Vietnam and China characterizes the attitude toward NGOs and, even more so, to the idea of a proactive and scrutinizing civil society. So-called "peaceful evolution" was and is seen as a Western-promoted threat to the socialist system, perceived as very real after the Ukrainian Orange Revolution (2004–5) and the Arab Spring (2011).

Following Leninist practices, there are a number of mass organizations, funded by the government, forming key elements of the overall formal political structure. By all accounts, they are entirely subordinated to the Party. "The right to association" is written into the Vietnamese constitution (Article 25). The exercise of those rights "shall be prescribed by law." In 2019 some 650 NGOs were registered by the state as active in the social sphere, environmental protection, and even in research. The Chamber of Commerce plays an advocacy role, and, for example, informal associations of farmers play a recognized role. NGOs can make a difference. However, though a draft law on NGOs was prepared as early as the mid-1990s, with a large number of drafts having been produced since then, until now no law has been adopted, a clear illustration of a profound systemic dilemma.

The attitude of the Party has become more controlling rather than more open. In December 2018, Vietnamese authorities, for example, broke up a civil society conference in Hanoi.[64] The control of NGOs is still clearly less stringent in Vietnam than in China, but organizations are closely monitored, requiring permission to organize conferences, and they may even be closed down at short notice. The prevailing model based on Party-affiliated mass organizations is bound to be challenged from inside Vietnam as well as through deepening external economic commitments, not least by workers trying to form their own associations.

In its 2019 Global Rights Index on labor rights, the International Trade Union Confederation (ITUC) puts Vietnam in the category of countries where no rights to formal organization of workers' organizations are respected.[65] Since then the Vietnamese legislature has adopted a potentially important new Labor Code, enacted in January 2021. For the first time, workers are allowed to form worker organizations not affiliated with the Vietnamese General Confederation of Labor (VGCL). But they are not unions and are only allowed to be formed at the individual enterprise level, unable to form sectoral or regional federations to represent the interests of workers from different companies. Actual implementation will be a test of the CPV's preparedness to recognize evolving realities. As Hansson shows in her chapter on state–civil society relations in this volume, the primary ambition of the CPV, hence the Vietnamese government, is to restrain the effects of the law. ITUC noted no improvements in its 2022 Global Rights Index.[66]

During the last few years Vietnam has also become more repressive, in the sense of imprisoning more democracy activists and protest leaders, while the number of protests, as Hansson shows in her chapter, has grown. The year 2018 was a year of protests. One issue that caused major protests was the Law of Cyber Security, discussed below.[67] The planned special economic zone caused large-scale anti-Chinese protests and detentions in a number of cities, leading to the postponement of the adoption of the law.[68] A number of protests and severe confrontations, such as the brutal and tragic one in Dong Tam village outside Hanoi in January 2020, are caused by land disputes.[69] These disputes appear increasingly to show growing public concern over the use of violence by the party-state. In February 2022 a serious incident widely circulated on Vietnamese social media occurred at a construction site in Thanh Hoa Province. The citizens who were assaulted during the conflict were members of a local family who had disputes over land ownership with an investment company carrying out a luxury resort project at the locality.[70] A more transparent and more predictable sustained mode of conflict resolution will be required if escalation is to be avoided.

Press, Social Media, Cyber Security, and the Narrative

THE SUBJUGATED ROLE OF MEDIA

In the "World Press Freedom Index 2022," Vietnam was found at the bottom of the index, and so is China, with Vietnam as number 174 and China as 175 out of 180 rated countries. Only five countries, Myanmar, Turkmenistan, Iran, Eritrea, and North Korea, were given a lower ranking.[71] While the full picture in both countries appears more complex than suggested by this ranking, the fact is that traditional media in both countries have become more rather than less controlled. Journalists are detained and imprisoned. In Vietnam, the Party has reinforced its control over the editors-in-chief of eight hundred journals and mass media outlets and further developed sophisticated censorship. However, the situation for traditional media is only a part of the picture. China has again gone much further than Vietnam, the assigned role increasingly being to amplify, not criticize.

Although Vietnam has constrained it, there is still considerable access to global cyberspace and social media such as Facebook, in contrast to China, where the party-state has created increasingly comprehensive control systems with the firm ambition of establishing "Internet sovereignty," controlling access behind the Great Firewall.[72] Still, as all over the world, the most dramatic development in Vietnam as well as China has happened on the Internet. This development has had dramatic effects on society, but it has not led to the open society that was envisaged following the development of the World Wide Web. In the beginning of 2022, Vietnam had approximately 72 million users, 90 percent of them using the Internet every day. Vietnam, in sharp contrast to China, allows (supervised) access to Facebook and Google. Though civil society is severely constrained, it is very active on social media.[73] China in 2021 had 940 million frequent users, but their access to information was tightly controlled by a state firewall.

In mid-2018 the Vietnamese government exposed its ambition to control social media with the introduction of a cyber law that led to widespread protests. In January 2019, a slightly modified version became law. According to a transcript of a question-and-answer session with lawmakers in October 2018, the law was aimed at staving off cyberattacks and weeding out "hostile and reactionary forces" using the Internet to stir up violence and dissent.

The new law requires Facebook to censor anti-government content among its 70 million Vietnamese users and allow authorities to access users' online data. It requires Internet companies to remove content that the government regards as "toxic" and compels them to hand over user data if asked to do so. Tech giants such as Facebook and Google also had to open representative offices in Vietnam if they wished to continue operating in the country. In a draft decree released in November 2018 on how the law should be implemented, the Ministry of Public Security gave companies offering Internet services in Vietnam up to twelve months to comply.[74] Facebook chose to remove items. A week after the law came into force, Vietnam's Association of Journalists announced a new code of conduct on the use of social media by its members, forbidding reporters to post news, pictures, and comments that "run counter to" the state.[75]

The purpose of the law was clearly to increase the control of the Internet, hence a further step away from freedom of expression. Critical bloggers constantly run the risk of being sentenced to long prison terms. In June 2019 an environmental activist urging people to take part in a peaceful protest, for example, was jailed for six years for "anti-state" Facebook posts, as part of the country's continuing crackdown on social media.[76] During the months prior to the Thirteenth Party Congress, a wave of arrests occurred. Journalists were charged with spreading anti-state propaganda under Article 117 of the penal code and sentenced to several years of imprisonment.[77] Still, Facebook is today part of the Vietnamese people's DNA, and it is hard to imagine the CPV trying to establish Internet sovereignty of the kind prevailing in today's China, or to build an AI-based surveillance system such as the one built by the CPC to control and correct behavior.

CONTROLLING THE NARRATIVE

Control of thoughts and knowledge production are important features of party-states. Both the CPV and CPC regard it as fundamental to maintain ultimate control of the narrative. The CPC in a massive way, as Ian Buruma has put it, determines history "by decree," Vietnam less so but without any clear sign of genuine preparedness to recognize the value of further openness.[78]

In Vietnam, a central task of the Party remains controlling the meaning of the wars between 1946 and 1975. When then–Party Secretary Nguyen Van Linh in the spirit of Đổi Mới urged intellectuals, civil servants, and journalists to speak their minds, it led to critical assessments of the war, such as Bao Ninh's novel *The Sorrows of War* (1987) and novels by Duong Thu Huong, since 2006 living in France, who in her writing presented a more severe critique of the war.[79] Such writings were more than the Party could easily tolerate.

In the last few years, the Party has escalated its efforts to set the limits more broadly, with a focus on Party members. Hence, in November 2017, the CPV Politburo issued Regulation 102 on disciplining Party members who violate Party rules. This rule states that expulsion from the Party would be applied to Party members who "deliberately spoke or wrote in order to distort history and truth, or denied the leading role and revolutionary achievement of the Party," "rejected or negated Marxism-Leninism, Ho Chi Minh's principle of centralized democracy," "demanded implementation of the separation of powers," "civil society," "political pluralism," "a multiparty system," or "founded and/or joined associations in contravention of law."[80]

One prominent case concerned Chu Hao, a former vice minister and well-known intellectual and publisher. He was disciplined by the Party after publishing translations of several classics of political philosophy: John Stuart Mill's *On Liberty*, John Locke's *Second Treatise of Government*, Alexis de Tocqueville's *Democracy in America*, and Friedrich A. Hayek's *The Road to Serfdom*. Hao had also signed petitions and open letters critical of the Party, including Petition 72, and been accused of being involved in founding and joining associations and other organizations that "spread views contrary to the views of the Party."[81] More than two hundred Party members and intellectuals signed an open letter asking the Party leadership to retract its decision to discipline him. Joining the open letter signers, a group of eighty-one international scholars, academics, and researchers sent a letter expressing their "profound disagreement and disappointment with accusations directed at Professor Chu Hao" to the Vietnamese leaders.

Shortly after Trong took the office of the presidency, the disciplining of Chu Hao was announced. In a meeting with his constituents in November 2018, Trong, as a member of the National Assembly, said Chu Hao was expelled from the Party not for corruption, but "self-evolution" and "self-transformation," personal qualities that the Party secretary considered unsuitable for a true Party member.[82] The Party line stands in stark contrast to the vitality of Vietnamese society.

Beyond the Party-State?

Few countries have, in a number of respects, changed as much in the last few decades as Vietnam. The country has shown a lot of social and economic vitality, yet has remained a party-state. As noted above with reference to Krastev and Holmes, Vietnam has also "*borrowed* exuberantly but refused to *convert*," pursuing market economic reforms and opening, while retaining the party-state. In a sense, it should not come as a surprise, given Vietnam's history and the fact that hardly any party-state by its own design has transformed itself into a pluralistic democracy, determined to maintain itself through adaptation and repression.

Is the CPV, then, "mimicking" the CPC? Under Xi, China has entered an era of authoritarian consolidation, using digital technologies to create a "controlocracy," with big data and artificial intelligence serving the interests of the party-state.[83] The prospects for a more "eclectic state" seem remote.[84] Also, Vietnam has in recent years developed further in an authoritarian direction, trying to counter changes in society perceived as threatening to the Party, and the Thirteenth Party Congress confirmed the overarching importance attached to "party building." Broadly speaking, the CPV meets all six criteria discussed above. It has to cope with dynamic environments and cannot unilaterally exercise power, but power ultimately rests with the Party, sustained by its control of the other five dimensions of the construct, with history and nationalism as a critical glue. But the CPV is still hardly just copying the CPC. China is, according to all six dimensions, a clearly deeper and more penetrating party-state than Vietnam, and as a geopolitical superpower is driven by visions very different from Vietnam's ambition to cope in a complex environment. Vietnam is more outward oriented, more deliberative, with a less authoritarian relationship between the Party and society, hardly about to become a full-fledged controlocracy, clearly autocratic but not totalitarian. Developments during 2021–2022 deepened the differences, though the CPV also became more rather than less unwilling to accept any challenges to its authority.

So far, the CPV has succeeded in managing the country's unorthodox path to a market economy, but it could soon face tougher choices. Using economic jargon, one could talk of a "supply side" perspective (the Party), and a "demand side," reflecting the population's growing rights consciousness and demands for greater openness.

Increased repression would meet growing popular resentment and not offer a viable alternative. In order to realize the country's huge potential, the Party will have to make more forward-looking choices. Many forces, not least economic, are at work, putting pressure on the CPV to develop its decentralized ability to adapt.

While the identities of both the Vietnamese and the Chinese systems have been shaped in response to Western global dominance and by Leninist party-state principles, and even though Sino-Vietnamese party contacts are frequent, the Vietnamese look upon China's rise with considerable concern and popular anger. Ideology brings them together, national interest and nationalism draw them apart, with Vietnam trying to counter China's growing power by deepening its global integration. China defines its relations with Vietnam not only as a "neighboring state" but also as a country of "comrades and brothers," anchored in ideological affinity and historical linkages. Vietnam's evident ambivalence toward China's huge Belt and Road Initiative (BRI) is a telling example, while growing tensions in the South China Sea signify distrust. As the geopolitical situation evolves, Vietnam will not, in spite of shared ideology, want to be a part of a Chinese order.

Vietnam's dramatic history matters. A profound dilemma is that the constraints of the party-state will make it increasingly difficult to develop a shared twenty-first-century vision for the country that resonates with the richly varied aspirations of society. "Vietnamese republicanism" emerged more than a century ago, as French rule exposed Vietnamese intellectuals to the ideas of the Enlightenment. It does, thus, date back further than communism, and will not cease to keep questions of political reforms alive.[85] The Party may, as Jonathan London concludes, remain the dominant force for decades to come, a multiparty system being unlikely to emerge in the foreseeable future. Still, internal and external pressure can be expected to increase, and commitment to a broader reform process, involving enlarged representation, steps toward a more independent judicial system, and laws protecting civil society could narrow the gap between supply and demand, making economic, social, and political reforms mutually supportive. Vietnam's growing dependence on the global economy makes labor rights a dynamic issue.

A truly significant forward-looking step would be to cut the constitutional cord between the Party and the army. Such a change, however, only appears possible in a perspective beyond the predictable. Tuong Vu notes that "men loyal to Marxism-Leninism are in control of the Party leadership."[86] They are at least loyal to the party-state and its justification of "stability."

David Marr notes, with reference to how closely the CPV is linked to the events of 1945, that the year might "lose its glow," "as prior generations disappear from the scene."[87] The late Prime Minister Vo Van Kiet once told his colleagues on the Politburo "not to be afraid of the future."[88] Ultimately, such boldness would take Vietnam beyond the party-state, releasing the vitality that defines Vietnam, and again "surprise us as they do."[89]

Only posterity can tell how Ho Chi Minh, as a revered founding father of the DRV, may be viewed in a Vietnam transitioned to democracy.[90] Would he be written off, or would his commitment to the "national question" remain a lasting legacy in complex future times?

Notes

1. London, "The Communist Party of Vietnam," 26.
2. Kerkvliet, *Speaking Out in Vietnam*, 6.
3. Arendt, *The Origins of Totalitarianism*.
4. Acemoglu and Robinson, *Why Nations Fail*, 441.
5. Acemoglu and Robinson, *Why Nations Fail*.
6. For a more comprehensive picture of the system and its history, see in particular London, "The Communist Party of Vietnam."
7. Before leaving Laos in July 1980 after two years as Swedish chargé d'affaires, I made a courtesy call on the then foreign minister and Politburo member Phoun Sipaseuth. During our conversion, I made a reference to recent developments in Poland, where Solidarity was emerging as a political force. The foreign minister kindly told me that I needed to understand that the development of socialism was irreversible.
8. Chanda, "Indochina beyond the Cold War," 19–38.
9. London, "Communist Party of Vietnam," 21.
10. Huntington, *The Third Wave*.
11. Fukuyama, "The End of History?"; Fukuyama, *The End of History and the Last Man*.
12. Rachman, "Beijing, Berlin and the Two 1989s."
13. Repucci and Slipowitz, *Freedom in the World 2022*.
14. V-Dem, *Democracy Report 2022*.
15. Krastev and Holmes, *The Light that Failed*, 195.
16. Nathan, "China's Changing of the Guard."
17. Heilman and Perry, *Mao's Invisible Hand*.
18. In his chapter in this volume, Le Dang Doanh notes that the original intention was to allow the private sector to continue operating in the south, and that perceived Chinese interference made the party leadership reverse the policy and decide to move the whole country to socialism.
19. Chanda, *Brother Enemy*.

20. Vu, *Vietnam's Communist Revolution*, 237–64.

21. Gainsborough, *Vietnam: Rethinking the State*.

22. On November 20, 2019, the National Assembly of Vietnam adopted Labor Code No. 45/2019/QH14 ("New Labor Code") after an amendment process lasting nearly four years. The new code took effect on January 1, 2021.

23. Ni, "EU Efforts to Ratify China Investment Deal."

24. Brocheux, *Ho Chi Minh*, 13.

25. Duiker, *Ho Chi Minh*, 275.

26. Marr, *Vietnam 1945*, 8.

27. Khanh, *Vietnamese Communism 1925–1945*, 338.

28. Trong, "Speech at the Ceremony."

29. Tönnesson, *Vietnam 1946*, 259; Logevall, *Embers of War*, 712.

30. For a thorough review and analysis of Vietnam's constitutional development, see Pham Duy Nghia's chapter in this volume.

31. Tönnesson, "Not Meant to Last."

32. Bui Ngoc Son, "Petition 72."

33. SRV, The Constitution.

34. Bui, "Pluralism Unleashed."

35. London, "Communist Party of Vietnam," 27.

36. Human Rights Watch, *World Report 2022*.

37. Le Hong Hiep, "Vietnamese Army's Rising Influence."

38. London, "The Communist Party of Vietnam," notes that the figure understates the Party's "ubiquity and influence. If we consider the total number of persons with direct family links to a CPV member," then the number "exceeds 20 million, approximately one fifth of the country's population."

39. Fewsmith, *Rethinking Chinese Politics*, 189.

40. Fforde, "Amongst Factors Conditioning Political Evolution."

41. Quoted in Schell, "Xi's Big Show."

42. Malesky, Abrami, and Yu, "Institutions and Inequality," 401–19.

43. Trong, "Speech at the Ceremony."

44. "13th National Party Congress Adopts Resolution," *Vietnamnews.vn*, February 2, 2021.

45. Nguyen, "Vietnam's Unresolved Leadership Question."

46. "Theory and Practice—Continuing Building a Politically Strong Vietnam People's Army to Meet the New Task Requirements under the Resolution of the 13th National Party Congress," *National Defense Journal*, April 5, 2021.

47. "National Election Council Ratifies 499 Elected Deputies for 15th National Assembly," *Hanoi Times*, June 10, 2021.

48. "Vietnam: Independent Political Candidate Faces Charges—Le Trong Hung Could Get Up to 12 Years in Prison for Election Campaign," *Human Rights Watch*, December 29, 2021; "Vietnam Sentences Journalist Le Trong Hung to 5 Years in Prison," *Committee to Protect Journalists*, January 5, 2022.

49. VUSTA/UNDP, "The Viet Nam Provincial Governance and Public Administration Performance Index (PAPI)."

50. Shirk, *The Political Logic of Economic Reform in China*; Fewsmith, *The Logic and Limits of Political Reform in China*.

51. Heilman, *China's Political System*.

52. Politburo Directive No. 15, dated July 7, 2007, referred to in Fforde, "Vietnamese Patterns of Corruption."

53. "Criteria for Top Officials," *Vnexpress International*, February 2020.

54. "Code of Conduct Written to Keep Civil Servants in Line," *Vietnamnews.vn*, January 13, 2019. Read more at http://vietnamnews.vn/society/483603/code-of-conduct-written-to-keep-civil-servants-in-line.html#XzEvY2tRSbA7GZco.

55. White and Mallet, "Xi's Anti-Corruption Crusade."

56. Transparency International, "Corruption Perceptions Index 2021."

57. Fforde, "Vietnamese Patterns of Corruption," 8.

58. McGregor, *The Party*, 23.

59. Lubman, *Bird in a Cage*.

60. The number was mentioned at a meeting on January 7, 2020, chaired by the minister of justice to review the MOJ Plan for 2020, including development of lawyers. https://moj.gov.vn/qt/tintuc/Pages/hoat -dong-cua-lanh-dao-bo.aspx?ItemID=4306.

61. Wee, "China Orders Lawyers to Pledge Allegiance to Communist Party."

62. Human Rights Watch, *World Report 2020*.

63. Human Rights Watch, *World Report 2022*.

64. "Vietnamese Authorities Break Up Civil Society Conference in Hanoi," *Radio Free Asia*, December 20, 2018.

65. ITUC Global Rights Index 2019, https://www.ituc-csi.org/rights-index-2019.

66. ITUC Global Rights Index 2022, https://www.globalrightsindex.org/en/2022/countries/vnm.

67. Hiebert, *Under Beijing's Shadow*.

68. Murray, "Vietnamese See Special Economic Zones as Assault from China"; "Vietnam Jails 10 More for Protests over Economic Zones," *Reuters*, July 23, 2018.

69. Hutt, "State vs People Conflict"; "Vietnam Sentences Brothers to Death After Three Policemen Killed in Dong Tam Land Rights Clashes," *South China Morning Post*, September 14, 2020.

70. "Local Citizens Assaulted over Land Rights Disputes," *The Vietnamese Magazine*, February 25, 2022.

71. Reporters without Borders, "World Press Freedom Index 2022."

72. "Digital 2021: China," https://datareportal.com/reports/digital-2021-china?rq=Digital%202021%20 China.

73. "Digital 2021: Vietnam," https://datareportal.com/search?q=Digital%20Vietnam%202021.

74. "To the Dismay of Free Speech Advocates, Vietnam Rolls Out Controversial Cyber Law," NPR, January 1, 2019.

75. "New Year, New Repression: Vietnam Imposes Draconian 'China-Like' Cybersecurity Law," *South China Morning Post*, January 1, 2019.

76. Ellis-Petersen, "Vietnam Blogger Jailed for Six Years."

77. Human Rights Watch, "Vietnam: Crackdown"; Humphrey, "Vietnam Arrests Prominent Journalist."

78. Buruma, "History by Decree."

79. Goscha, *The Penguin History of Modern Vietnam*, 495.

80. Politburo Regulation no. 102, "Handling Violations of Party Discipline," November 2017.

81. Vu, "Anti-Intellectualism in Vietnam."

82. Vu, "Anti-Intellectualism in Vietnam."

83. Ringen, *The Perfect Dictatorship*.

84. Shambaugh, *China's Communist Party*, 181. Shambaugh, *China's Future*, 115–24.

85. Goscha, *The Penguin History of Modern Vietnam*, 489.

86. Vu, *Vietnam's Communist Revolution*, 298.

87. Marr, *Vietnam 1945*, 552.

88. Memo from Vo Van Kiet to the Politburo, dated August 9, 1995, on a new worldview.

89. Goscha, *The Penguin History of Modern Vietnam*, 507.

90. Vu, *Vietnam's Communist Revolution*, 298.

References

Acemoglu, Daron, and James A. Robinson. *Why Nations Fail: The Origins of Power, Prosperity and Poverty*. New York: Crown, 2012.

Agence France-Presse. "New Year, New Repression: Vietnam Imposes Draconian 'China-Like' Cybersecurity Law." *South China Morning Post*, January 1, 2019.

Arendt, Hannah. *The Origins of Totalitarianism*. New York: Houghton Mifflin Harcourt, 1973. (Originally published 1951.)

Brocheux, Pierre. *Ho Chi Minh: A Biography*. Translated by Claire Duiker. Cambridge: Cambridge University Press, 2007.

Bui Ha Thiems. "Pluralism Unleashed: The Politics of Reforming the Vietnamese Constitution." *Journal of Vietnamese Studies* 9, no. 4 (2015): 1–32.

Bui Ngoc Son. "Petition 72: The Struggle for Constitutional Reforms in Vietnam." *I-CONnect*, March 28, 2013. http://www.iconnectblog.com.

Buruma, Ian, "History by Decree." *Project Syndicate*, January 7, 2022.

Chanda, Nayan. *Brother Enemy: The War after the War*. New York: Harcourt Brace Jovanovich, 1986.

———. "Indochina beyond the Cold War: The Chill from Eastern Europe." In *The Challenge of Reform in Indochina*, edited by Börje Ljunggren. Cambridge, MA: Harvard Kennedy School, 1993.

Duiker, William. *Ho Chi Minh: A Life*. New York: Hyperion, 2000.

Ellis-Petersen, Hannah. "Vietnam Blogger Jailed for Six Years for Facebook Posts Calling for Peaceful Protests." *The Guardian*, June 7, 2019. https://www.theguardian.com/world/2019/jun/07/vietnam-blogger-jailed-for-six-years-for-facebook-posts-calling-for-peaceful-protests.

European Council. "EU-Vietnam: Council Gives Final Green Light to Free Trade Agreement." March 30, 2020. consilium.europa.eu/en/press/press-releases/2020/03/30/eu-vietnam-council-gives-final-green-light-to-free-trade-agreement.

Fewsmith, Joseph. *The Logic and Limits of Political Reform in China*. Cambridge: Cambridge University Press, 2013.

———. *Rethinking Chinese Politics*. Cambridge: Cambridge University Press, 2021.

Fforde, Adam. "Amongst Factors Conditioning Political Evolution in Vietnam, What Are the Legacies of the CPSU-VCP Relationship?" Draft article, January 2020.

———. "Vietnamese Patterns of Corruption and Accumulation: Research Puzzles." *Journal of Contemporary Asia*, April 1, 2022.

Fukuyama, Francis. "The End of History?" *The National Interest* 16 (1989): 3–18.

———. *The End of History and the Last Man*. New York: Free Press, 1992.

———. "The Pandemic and Political Order—It Takes a State." *Foreign Affairs* 99, no. 4 (2020): 26–32.

Gainsborough, Martin. *Vietnam: Rethinking the State*. London: Zed Books, 2010.

Garner, Dwight. "'Wuhan Diary' Offers an Angry and Eerie View from Inside Quarantine." *New York Times*, May 15, 2020.

Goscha, Christopher. *The Penguin History of Modern Vietnam*. London: Allen Lane, 2016.

Heilman, Sebastian, ed. *China's Political System*. Lanham, MD: Rowman & Littlefield, 2017.

Heilman, Sebastian, and Elizabeth Perry, eds. *Mao's Invisible Hand: The Political Foundation of Adaptive Governance in China*. Cambridge, MA: Harvard University Asia Center, 2011.

Hiebert, Murray. *Under Beijing's Shadow: Southeast Asia's China Challenge*. Lanham, MD: Rowman & Littlefield, 2020.

Human Rights Watch. "Vietnam: Crackdown on Peaceful Dissent Intensifies." June 19, 2020. https://www.hrw.org/news/2020/06/19/vietnam-crackdown-peaceful-dissent-intensifies.

———. *World Report 2020*. https://www.hrw.org/world-report/2020.

———. *World Report 2021*. https://www.hrw.org/world-report/2021.

———. *World Report 2022*. https://www.hrw.org/world-report/2022.

Humphrey, Chris. "Vietnam Arrests Prominent Journalist as State Cracks Down on Free Speech Online," *The Guardian*, October 8, 2020. https://www.theguardian.com/global-development/2020/oct/08/vietnam-arrests-prominent-journalist-as-state-cracks-down-on-free-speech-online.

Huntington, Samuel. *The Third Wave: Democratization in the Late Twentieth Century*. Norman: University of Oklahoma Press, 1993.

Hutt, David. "State vs People Conflict Rocks and Roils Vietnam." *Asia Times*, January 18, 2020. https://asiatimes.com/2020/01/state-vs-people-conflict-rocks-and-roils-vietnam/.

Ikenberry, John. "The Rise of China and the Future of the West: Can the Liberal System Survive?" *Foreign Affairs* 87, no. 1 (2008): 23–37.

Kerkvliet, Benedict J. Tria. *Speaking Out in Vietnam: Public Political Criticism in a Communist Party-Rules Nation*. Ithaca, NY: Cornell University Press, 2019.

Khanh, Huynh Kim. *Vietnamese Communism 1925–1945*. Ithaca, NY: Cornell University Press, 1982.

Krastev, Ivan, and Stephen Holmes. *The Light that Failed: A Reckoning*. London: Allan Lane, 2019.

Le Hong Hiep. "How Vietnamese Army's Rising Influence in Politics Reflects South China Sea Security Concerns." *South China Morning Post*, May 2, 2021.

Lei, Yu-Wen. *The Contentious Public Sphere: Law, Media and Authoritarian Rule in China*. Princeton, NJ: Princeton University Press, 2018.

Ljunggren, Börje, ed. *The Challenge of Reform in Indochina*. Cambridge, MA: Harvard Institute for International Development, 1993.

Logevall, Fredrik. *Embers of War: The Fall of an Empire and the Making of America's Vietnam*. New York: Random House, 2012.

London, Jonathan. "The Communist Party of Vietnam: Consolidating Market Leninism." In *Routledge Handbook of Contemporary Vietnam*, edited by Jonathan D. London. Abington, UK: Routledge, 2022.

Lubman, Stanley. *Bird in a Cage: Legal Reform in China after Mao*. Stanford, CA: Stanford University Press, 1999.

Malesky, Edmund, Regina Abrami, and Yu Zheng, "Institutions and Inequality in Single-Party Regimes: A Comparative Analysis of Vietnam and China." *Comparative Politics* 43, no. 4 (July 2011): 401–19.

Marr, David. *Vietnam 1945: The Quest for Power*. Berkeley: University of California Press, 1995.

McGregor, Richard. *The Party: The Secret World of China's Communist Rulers*. New York: HarperCollins, 2010.

Murray, Bennett. "Vietnamese See Special Economic Zones as Assault from China." *This Week in Asia*, June 7, 2018. https://www.scmp.com/week-asia/politics/article/2149785/vietnamese-see-special-economic-zones-assault-china.

Nathan, Andrew. "China's Changing of the Guard: Authoritarian Resilience." *Journal of Democracy* 14, no. 1 (2003): 6–17.

Nguyen, Hung. "Vietnam's Unresolved Leadership Question." *East Asia Forum*, February 25, 2021. https://www.eastasiaforum.org/2021/02/25/vietnams-unresolved-leadership-question/.

Ni, Vincent. "EU Efforts to Ratify China Investment Deal 'Suspended' after Sanctions." *The Guardian*, May 4, 2021. https://www.theguardian.com/world/2021/may/04/eu-suspends-ratification-of-china-investment-deal-after-sanctions.

PhaPluat. "Đảng Cộng sản Việt Nam hiện có 5,2 triệu đảng viên." December 25, 2019. https://plo.vn/thoi-su/chinh-tri/dang-cong-san-viet-nam-hien-co-52-trieu-dang-vien-879702.html.

Rachman, Gideon. "Beijing, Berlin and the Two 1989s." *Financial Times*, June 4, 2019.

Reporters without Borders. "World Press Freedom Index 2022: A New Era of Polarisation." https://rsf.org/en/rsf-s-2022-world-press-freedom-index-new-era-polarisation#:~:text=The%202022%20edition%20of%20the,encourages%20fake%20news%20and%20propaganda.

Repucci, Sarah, and Amy Slipowitz. *Freedom in the World 2022: The Global Expansion of Authoritarian Rule*. Freedom House. https://freedomhouse.org/report/freedom-world/2021/democracy-under-siege.

Ringen, Stein. *The Perfect Dictatorship: China in the 21st Century*, Hong Kong: Hong Kong University Press, 2016.

Schell, Orville. "Xi's Big Show: What the Olympics Reveal about China." *Foreign Affairs*, February 6, 2022.

Shambaugh, David, *China's Communist Party: Atrophy and Adaptation*. Hong Kong: University of California Press, 2008

———. *China's Future*, Cambridge: Polity, 2016.

Shirk, Susan. *The Political Logic of Economic Reform in China*. Berkeley: University of California Press, 1993.

Socialist Republic of Vietnam. The Constitution. 2013. http://vietnamnews.vn/politics-laws/250222/the-constitution-of-the-socialist-republic-of-vienam.html#jlBHrmOmoX96LE4H.99.

Thayer, Carlyle A. "Background Brief: Vietnam: Measures against Corruption." *Thayer Consultancy*, July 5, 2020. https://www.scribd.com/document/468657750/Thayer-Vietnam-Measures-Against-Corruption.

Tönnesson, Stein. "Not Meant to Last: Vietnam's First Constitution." In *Constitutional Foundings in Southeast Asia*, edited by Kevin YL Tan and Bui Ngoc Son. London: Bloomsbury, 2019.

————. *Vietnam 1946: How the War Began.* Berkeley: University of California Press, 2010.

Transparency International. "Corruption Perceptions Index 2020." https://www.transparency.org/en/cpi/2020.

————. "Corruption Perception Index 2021." https://www.transparency.org/en/cpi/2021.

Trong, Nguyen Phu. "Speech at the Ceremony in Honor of the 90th Anniversary of the Founding of the Communist Party of Vietnam." *Vietnam Pictorial*, February 3, 2020. https://vietnam.vnanet.vn/english /speech-by-party-general-secretary-and-state-president-nguyen-phu-trong-at-the-ceremony-in-honor-of -the-90th-anniversary-of-the-founding-of-the-communist-party-of-vietnam/439572.html.

V-Dem Institute. *Democracy Report 2022: Autocratization Changing Nature?* Varieties of Democracy Institute, March 2022. https://v-dem.net/media/publications/dr_2022.pdf.

Vietnam News. "Resolution Issued on Building Army's Party Committee in 2019." January 8, 2019. https://en .nhandan.vn/politics/domestic/item/7034002-resolution-issued-on-building-army%E2%80%99s-party -committee-in-2019.html.

Vietnam Times. "The 13th National Party Congress: Maintaining Security and Social Order." May 6, 2020. https://vietnamtimes.org.vn/the-13th-national-party-congress-maintaining-security-and-social-order -20058.html.

Vu, Cu Huy Ha, "Anti-Intellectualism in Vietnam: The Case of Professor Chu Hao—Professor Chu Hao's Fate Is Revealing of the Communist Party's Priorities in Vietnam." *The Diplomat*, November 29, 2018.

Vu, Tuong. *Vietnam's Communist Revolution: The Power and Limits of Ideology.* Cambridge: Cambridge University Press, 2017.

VUSTA/UNDP. "The Viet Nam Provincial Governance and Public Administration Performance Index (PAPI) 2012." June 3, 2013. https://www.undp.org/vietnam/publications/viet-nam-provincial-governance -and-public-administration-performance-index-papi-2012.

Wee, Sui-Lee. "China Orders Lawyers to Pledge Allegiance to Communist Party." Reuters, March 21, 2012. https://www.reuters.com/article/us-china-lawyers/china-orders-lawyers-to-pledge-allegiance-to -communist-party-idUSBRE82K0G320120321.

White, Edward, and Victor Mallet. "Xi's Anti-Corruption Crusade," *Financial Times*, February 23, 2022.

CHAPTER 2

The Leninist State and Its Predecessors

Classic Political Questions

ALEXANDER WOODSIDE

By the standards of the two hundred or so member states of the United Nations, autonomous Vietnamese political systems in their various manifestations are among the oldest in the world, being traceable back to the tenth century. The Vietnam we know today, comprising both the northern Red River Delta and the southern Mekong River Delta, first came together under the rule of the Nguyen dynasty in 1802. By our contemporary standards, perhaps, the kingdom's integration was weak. Of the roughly 1 million adult male taxpayers listed in the dynasty's tax registers in 1847, almost half lived in central Vietnam, where the national court was located, suggesting the regional nature of the dynasty's practical power.

Even so, the political unification of Vietnam in 1802 was historically precocious. Many national states we take for granted now, including major European ones, did not yet exist. In 1802 there was still no "Germany" or "Italy" on any European map. Bavarians and Saxons, and the peoples of the Papal States or of the kingdom of Naples, would still not have anticipated membership in a future German or Italian state. The Leninist party-state that has ruled all of Vietnam since 1975 is the heir of Vietnam's preindustrial kingdoms, including the nineteenth-century one.

Moreover, the contemporary Leninist party-state shares a common characteristic with Vietnam's preindustrial kingdoms. That is its reliance upon transnational transfers of political and legal institutions and ideas that originated elsewhere. For centuries, Vietnam has exemplified the phenomenon known to some analysts as the "internationalized state." Such states have political systems whose national boundaries remain intact, but whose governing elites have formed close connections with sources or symbols of power outside those boundaries. From the 1400s, if not before, Vietnamese courts duplicated many of the political institutions of the Chinese empire. These included six specialized central government ministries and an agency with varying names in different eras that we usually call the Censorate in English: a bureaucratic organ whose task was to conduct an internal surveillance of the government's operations and monitor them for waste and corruption. Like China itself, and also Korea, Vietnam was a mandarinate. At least part of its governing elite was recruited through success in winning degrees in written examinations.

This upheld the principle of meritocracy (rule by merit) as against the principle of the hereditary power of an aristocracy.

As for most of the forms and structures of Vietnam's post-1975 Leninist state, they were first invented in Lenin and Stalin's Russia in the first three decades of the twentieth century. As Vietnam did not share a common civilization with Russia, as it did with China, this was a much more drastic form of state internationalization. In Leninist states, a single "theocratic" political party maintains cells in every state institution, as well as party administrations at all levels, paralleling and overshadowing those of the state. To some outside observers, it all seemed very Russian. As Bertrand Russell put it after a visit to the USSR in 1920, Leninism was "a close tyrannical bureaucracy," but perhaps it was the right government for Russia: "if you ask yourself how Dostoyevsky's characters should be governed, you will understand."[1]

Vietnam, however, has never had a proper abundance of Dostoyevskyan characters. And the imposition of a Leninist state with a command economy upon a peasant society that lacked the large numbers of engineers, statisticians, computer specialists, and lawyers who served the Soviet state by the 1950s meant that the Leninist party-state in Vietnam was more hollowly neo-traditional. Generalist cadres without specialized training were far more dominant than in the technocratic USSR. In the mid-1980s, one Vietnamese investigator found, the USSR had eighty-eight central state agencies, of which only a minority were concerned with general administration; Vietnam's more than seventy central state agencies of all kinds reversed this pattern.[2]

Moreover, the parallelism of party and state administrations, with overlapping jurisdictions, generated administrative confusion and an alienating sense of a lack of sufficient transparency. The legitimacy of Leninist states, enhanced by the Soviet victory in World War II and by Soviet scientific achievements (e.g., Sputnik) in the 1950s, began to erode by the 1970s. But in eastern Asia, criticism of the Leninist state's confusions began as early as the 1930s.

In that decade the government of Nationalist (Guomindang) China, while honoring the Western doctrine of separation of powers as reimagined by Sun Yat-sen, then contradicted it by also borrowing institutions from the Leninist-Stalinist party-state in the USSR. These included all-encompassing economic development commissions, such as a National Reconstruction Commission, which concentrated power severely rather than dividing it. In 1935 one Chinese critic, Luo Longji (1896–1965), denounced this top-heavy government for being "more complex than any other national political system in the world." Its complexity was such that the Chinese people did not feel qualified to be citizens with rights to participate. Their psychological attitude was that of "bystanders."[3]

The criticism that the complex structures Leninist states create make bystanders out of the people they rule has thus had a long life in East Asia. Five decades later, in 1988, a dissident member of the Vietnamese Party Politburo, Tran Xuan Bach (1924–2006), was to use roughly the same language in attacking his own Leninist party-state for denying the Vietnamese people adequate democratic freedom. The result, Bach complained, was that the people had the manners of bystanders, full of distrust and indifference. Bach proposed, as a solution, that Vietnam combine political pluralism with planning by scientific experts. Scientific expertise, in his view, was the necessary antidote to "subjective human elements" in the party leadership.[4] Significantly, Luo Longji, the Chinese critic of 1935, had wanted the same thing: a fusion of democracy with a "government by experts" skilled in public administration.

It has never been easy to be a public critic in Vietnam: Tran Xuan Bach was expelled from the Party Politburo in 1990. This is all the more reason to regret that Vietnamese traditions of political criticism have never received enough appreciation outside Vietnam. In what follows, we will try to overcome this shortcoming by citing only Vietnamese insider critics of the contemporary Leninist state, and leave aside Western liberals' criticisms. And for the precolonial kingdom, we will draw upon the views of two of the most formidable scholar officials of the 1700s and 1800s, Le Quy Don (1726–84) and Phan Huy Chu (1782–1840). In the early days of "renovation," critics from inside the system assailed the Leninist state's high costs and low administrative efficiency. In 1986, a Vietnamese legal specialist described this state as a triumph of form over substance. Its visible organization was impressive: a National Assembly, more than seventy central ministries or ministry-like bodies, a council of ministers directing the work of some 850 offices, specialized bureaus, and institutes; and similar agencies at lower levels in provinces, counties, and townships. But its cumbersome machinery distanced it from the people. And the actual relationship between the Party and the state, between Party committees and state organizations, remained confused and mysterious.[5]

Moreover, as an internationalized state, the internal dynamics of the Vietnamese government were subject to forces outside Vietnam. Jim Glassman has shown how the government of Cold War Thailand, dependent on Japanese and US investment, became the site of an ongoing struggle over the orientations and relative empowerment of the Thai government's various ministries. Some Thai ministries gained in importance, while others lost out, through their degree of internationalized involvement. East of the Mekong, the Vietnamese Leninist government exhibited the same patterns because of an equivalent dependence on Soviet-bloc aid.

In 1977, one official declared that Vietnam had to "hire" foreign countries to prepare the technical and economic arguments for its various development plans, and that the government's competing agencies then "hid" the plans that they hired foreigners to draw up for them from other parts of the Vietnamese government. This behavior blocked any capacity for internal circulation of information. In 1988 a member of the Ministry for External Economic Relations complained that the government was characterized by "walls" between each of its branches and each of its levels, making the coordination of decision making impossible. The government's stronger ministries might even "repress" the activities of less-favored government agencies for "making rebellion" against the stronger ministries' programs.[6]

Then there was the problem, common to all Leninist states, of the bloated numbers of officials. Leninist government structures became bloated because of their efforts, under centralized planning, to try to control every branch of economic life. Reference has already been made to the Hanoi government's seventy or so ministries in the mid-1980s. China, which suffered from the same problem of administrative inflation, actually had one hundred government ministries or ministry-like bodies in 1980; in contrast, the average number of central government organs in Western countries at that time was fifteen. Indeed, between 1951 and 1993 China conducted six large-scale shrinkages of its administration, only to see a revival of its unchecked expansion after each one.[7]

To control the swelling numbers of officials and their salaries, the Party adopted "cadre positions lists" (*bien che*), which allocated fixed numbers of personnel and their salaries to different government agencies. But this term was a covering formula for the Soviet nomenklatura system, invented in Russia in 1923 to allow Bolshevik leaders to oversee all appointments within the Party and the state. A form of centralized executive patronage for such leaders, it allowed them to control their cadre force. In some eyes it resembled a privileged feudal hierarchy. When combined with the principle, added by Stalin, of lifelong tenure for leadership cadres, it modernized Russia's historical tradition of hereditary privileges for its nobility. No such tradition existed in Vietnam or China.

Effective as a hierarchical patronage system, the Vietnamese nomenklatura nonetheless failed to reduce government bloat. In 1996 the number of officials on Vietnam's Ministry of Finance payroll was almost six times the number the cadre positions lists allowed. Indeed, in the 1980s, a period of rice shortages and widespread malnutrition in Vietnam, the swollen government administration was publicly blamed in part for the crisis; an issue was made of the excessive numbers of salaried personnel in the state administration who consumed rice without producing it. Finally, in 1992, some insider critics demanded an examination of what they called the "real face" of Vietnamese officialdom. One critic charged that a majority of Vietnamese officeholders owed their appointments to "nepotism," and could not serve the purposes of their job titles.[8]

There are many differences between China and Vietnam in the early twenty-first century: not just their obvious differences in size and wealth, but the fact that the Vietnamese state has never produced single leaders as powerful and as charismatic as Mao Zedong or Deng Xiaoping. This difference can be extended back into the past. No Vietnamese emperors had centralizing ambitions as grandiose as those of some of China's Ming and Qing emperors. And there is no equivalent in contemporary Vietnam of the profusion of "emperor" books—encyclopedias about Chinese emperors, multivolume biographies of Qing dynasty empresses, anthologies of Chinese emperors' poetry—that have been published in China since the late 1980s.[9] Yet the two Leninist party-states have addressed their political crises in roughly the same way. This makes it important to keep China in mind in our present discussion. The two states have reacted to their crises by substituting bureaucratic reform for political reform.

Following China, Vietnam "restored" its civil service system in 1991, in order to introduce "scientific management" to its government. A minority of Communist Party cadres were converted into salaried public officeholders, to be recruited through competitive examinations. They were to be given specialized training of the sort found in professional civil services elsewhere, ranging from Singapore to Canada, and controlled by laws regulating their promotions, retirements, and dismissals. In 1991 the Seventh Party Congress demanded that this new civil service be steeped in the "administrative sciences," which were seen as a remedy for the catastrophic under-conceptualization of the state (as contrasted with the Party) in Leninist thought.

This meant, in the words of a Chinese technocrat in 2003, assimilating the laws and administrative practices of such international bodies as the World Trade Organization, given that the Chinese and Vietnamese states were "late development exogenous types," a new and more specialized term for characterizing internationalized states in this particular reform mode.[10] Vietnamese Party leaders acknowledged what an uphill struggle it would be to convert their Party cadres, many of whom were military men, into civil servants. Nguyen Phu Trong complained in 1991 that even leadership cadres were more familiar with orchestrating mass movements than with "market mechanisms" and compliance with domestic and international legal norms.[11] Hence the need to make the rules of the WTO game seem transcendent, rather than the product of messy compromises among world leaders and the vested interests behind them.

At the same time as Vietnam rediscovered the ideal of a meritocratic civil service, in 1991 its leaders also legitimized the study of political science, previously disdained by Leninist revolutionaries in their heyday as a "false science" and a "capitalist class" subject. Vietnam's embrace of political science was belated by Soviet-bloc or Chinese standards. (Czechoslovakia legitimized the study of political science in 1965, China in 1980.) The political science that arrived in Hanoi as part of the "renovation" process had a technocratic flavor. As one of the architects of Vietnam's vernacularization of political science put it, in the West political science has the function of "defending" Western societies, through the training of managers and planners adept at systems analysis.[12] Vietnamese and Chinese reformers now claimed that all states, regardless of their ideologies, shared the common problem of administrative efficiency. Therefore the administrative sciences did not have a class nature or a political party nature.

This promotion of administrative reform over political reform is not entirely inspired either by Leninism or by authoritarian traditions in the Vietnamese (or Chinese) past. Quite to the contrary, Western political scientists themselves, however unintentionally, have also supplied the justification. Two of them in particular have proven to be useful to this task: Frank Goodnow (1859–1939) and Samuel Huntington (1927–2008). That Frank Goodnow's ideas circulate in contemporary China or Vietnam is ironic. This American professor of administrative law was a controversial adviser to the new Chinese Republic after 1912, and proceeded to draft a constitution for the new China that would have restored China's outdated emperorship. Goodnow's excuse was that the Chinese people were not politically mature enough for a democratic form of government. For this act Chinese liberals have reviled Goodnow ever since, even though the actual attempted restoration of the emperorship failed. But Goodnow argued (in books like *Politics and Administration*, published in 1900) that political activity and administrative authority should be separated, with the administrative realm serving as a sort of utopian counter-environment to the unstable passions and interests of the political world. Contemporary Chinese and Vietnamese disciples of Goodnow claim that such arguments uphold their belief that the most "rational" model of political progress for "developing countries" should be to improve administrative capacity first, as in Singapore.[13]

Perhaps Samuel Huntington's greatest admirer in Leninist East Asia is Wang Huning, a major Chinese ideologue and reform theoretician and (since 2017) one of the seven
members of the Chinese Politburo's Standing Committee. In a famous 1968 book about
political order in changing societies, translated into Chinese in 1988, Huntington con-
ferred hero status on administrative reformers. Huntington proposed that their "way was
hard," and that they needed a much higher level of "political skill" than did revolutionaries, as well as a greater talent for manipulating social forces. Wang Huning used Huntington as early as 1993 to demand the creation of a new power structure in China, through
administrative modernization and a revised kind of consultative authoritarianism. This
meant a strengthening of the People's Congress system. But it had to be combined with a
powerful elite civil service and better government management.[14]

The substitution of bureaucratic reform for political reform raises at least three major
issues. These issues bear the mark of the past. They were also classic problems in Vietnam's nineteenth-century mandarinate, albeit in different forms and circumstances. First
of all, in a political system that might be characterized as one of consultative authoritarianism, how broad should the consultation be, and with whom? At one extreme it might
mean simply that the ruler publicly seeks advice from elite specialists, as when the general
secretary of the Party visited Hanoi's new National Center for the Social Sciences and
Humanities in 1993 to ask what its scholars thought of the new Draft Political Report of
the Party's Central Committee. (The social scientists demanded that the report include a
reference to Vietnam's becoming a "law-governed state.") At the other extreme it might
mean recognition of the popular masses' "right to be insiders" (as contrasted with "bystanders") in appointing and supervising party cadres.[15] In the mandarinates, there were
debates about the legitimacy of the Censorate, the bureaucracy's surveillance organ; some
scholars felt that the censors, recruited from examination-taking scholars, had usurped a
better tradition of consultation that had encouraged ordinary people to criticize the government by writing their complaints on roadside notice boards.

Second, given that no political system could ever be wholly meritocratic, how far is
the meritocracy to be extended? In contemporary Vietnam, how compatible is a Party-
based civil service, recruited through competitive examinations, with a surviving nomenklatura system in which Party leaders at different levels still dispense appointments as
patronage on the basis of personal ties, perceived ideological virtue, and bargaining? Concerning the Chinese situation, Eric X. Li in 2013 hailed the remade Chinese Communist
Party as "one of the most meritocratic political institutions in the world"; in the same
journal in which he made this assertion, Yasheng Huang ridiculed his claim.[16] The Vietnamese situation is likely to be equally enigmatic.

Third, the precolonial mandarinates tended to convert what we would regard as political problems into administrative ones. That raised the question of how they could legitimize their authority independently of administrative and legal procedures, through
a normative order with its own general persuasiveness. The far more ambitious and far
stronger Leninist party-state of today nonetheless faces the same challenge. The elite cult
of scientific management is not enough to address the "bystander" problem.

Foreign scholars, at least, have yet to achieve a fully satisfactory understanding of the conceptual universe of Vietnamese politics between the eleventh and the nineteenth centuries, under multiple dynasties and (between 1528 and 1802) regional lords. But between 1075 and 1919 Vietnam was governed in varying degrees by an elite recruited in part through competitive written examinations. Together with the equivalent Korean and Chinese civil service examinations, these examinations rejected the principles of rule by a hereditary aristocracy, or of rule through the distribution of offices by a "division of the spoils." They are no doubt eastern Asia's single greatest contribution to modern politics. (Britain only acquired a civil service recruited through competitive examinations in 1854; the United States only acquired the nucleus of such a system in 1883.) As I have written elsewhere, such examinations were not modern in their content (poetry tests, and expositions of the ancient Confucian classics and of the thought of China's medieval neo-Confucian thinkers, as well as more modern "policy" questions). But they were modern in their transparency, their competitiveness, and the meticulousness of their precautions against cheating and other abuses.[17]

The examinations produced an administrative elite much of whose power was based on their command of written information. In the 1800s, for example, the new dynasty compiled land registers for 15,000 to 18,000 villages, some 10,000 of which survive to the present. Local officials had to send to the court monthly "rice price reports," which analyzed the strength of local harvests, sudden changes in prices, and the differences in rice prices between those in provincial capitals and those in outlying provincial borderlands. As early as the 1400s, bureaucrats had their performance in office evaluated every three years. As early as 1470, such evaluations even quantified peasant discontent, measuring local officials' administrative fitness, by counting the number of peasants who had fled their jurisdictions. In the 1840s, the mandarinate codified its own behavior by compiling a comprehensive inventory of all its bureaucratic procedures and case precedents; this giant guide to the dynasty's administrative evolution, in the form of its reprinted romanized translation of 1993, comes to fifteen volumes and 7,830 pages.

The result was in Western eyes a seemingly self-contradictory political system that defied Western political classifications (as Vietnam and China perhaps defy them now). A startled French observer in 1874, C. E. Bouillevaux, called Vietnam a challenging "mixture of tyrannies and of precious liberties," an "academic democracy" ruled by a "hereditary Caesar." Perhaps "consultative authoritarianism" is too static or banal a term to capture all the dynamics of such a polity.

Mandarins worked to create general rules that set written standards for government activities. There was a trend, best exemplified by Phan Huy Chu in the early 1800s, to use this creation of written rules to tame power by depersonalizing it. In the epic administrative history of Vietnam that he wrote between 1809 and 1819, Phan Huy Chu argued that there were responsible administrative principles for the collection of taxes and the management of property relations that no dynasty or emperor could evade.[18] In addition, their training in East Asia's classical culture supplied mandarins with a self-esteem that no less-educated "hereditary Caesar" could totally humble. Vietnamese poetry celebrated good scholar-officials by comparing them to immovable banyan trees or upright betel palms or rare wild orchids. The prodigiously learned mandarin Le Quy Don proposed that the most capable "gentlemen" the polity recruited through the examinations could, with their talent for poetry writing and statecraft, be imperial surrogates and speak on the monarch's behalf.[19] The lack of any sense of a strong juridical divisibility of power at various levels encouraged mandarins to occupy some of the monarchy's own space, as its colleagues.

Meritocracy by itself, however, could not legitimatize the political system sufficiently to guarantee its existence. Meritocracy can be divisive. Examinations may produce arrogant winners and angry losers; a hereditary aristocrat remains an aristocrat even if he is professionally unsuccessful, but a commoner who fails examinations becomes a nobody, or even worse, a rebel against the state, like the poet Cao Ba Quat in 1854. Hence, Le Quy Don pleaded in 1777 that the subject matter of the examinations be kept relatively simple, so that "the people below" could make success in the examinations their "ladder for advancing upward to be ministers."[20]

On the other hand, the fact that the ruler was the ultimate patron of the examinations certainly helped him to hold power. Vietnamese monarchs did not have the benefit of public coronations that involved religiously binding feudal oaths of allegiance from their subordinates, the way European monarchs did. The bureaucratic ratings system for officials in office did not even test the officials' loyalty, as contrasted with their administrative capacity. Whatever the weight of Confucian indoctrination in Vietnam and China, it could hardly compete with the religious conditioning of Europe's "confessional" states, or with that of the Ottoman Empire, in which Friday prayers in mosques from Belgrade to Cairo included the reverential invocation of the ruling sultan's name. Had Confucian indoctrination been more comparable to Europe's confessional forms of it, it would be hard to explain the Chinese reformer Kang Youwei's famous 1898 proposal to convert Confucianism into a state religion, with congregations and weekly temple services for everyone in order to compete with those of Western churches.

Apart from the examinations, rulers' legitimacy depended upon how well they practiced the political obligation of "teaching and nourishing" (*giao duong*) their people. "Teaching" meant moral education. But "nourishing," in its most ambitious form, meant top-down welfare policies ranging from tax remissions to land reforms designed to limit inequitable patterns of property ownership. By the 1800s, no emperor of China would have had the courage, or probably the capacity, to enact major land reforms. But in 1839 one of Vietnam's last emperors tried to do precisely that in selected localities. And Saigon newspapers in the 1960s, when I was there, demanded that South Vietnam's land reformers, and their American advisers, consult Minh-mang's 1839 reform plan as a valuable precedent.[21]

At first glance, trying to find explicit mandarin influences in contemporary Vietnamese administrations is a little like looking for seventeenth-century Puritan influences in contemporary New England. And yet modern reprinted versions of Phan Huy Chu's administrative history, and of the Nguyen dynasty's big codified inventory of its own administrative practices, do circulate today in the Leninist state, coexisting with the writings of Frank Goodnow and Samuel Huntington. One anthropologist has called this a kind of hybrid modernity occurring in conditions of "multitemporal heterogeneity."[22] Yet the precolonial mandarinate and the contemporary Leninist state do share three concerns. To recapitulate, they are the need to debate the scope of the consultative nature of an authoritarian polity, the need to negotiate the breadth of the new meritocracy, and the need to legitimize an administrative state whose thickening web of rules may seem increasingly oppressive.

What remains of Leninism in Vietnam, apart from the structure of the party-state and the commitment to planned economic growth, is Lenin's admiration for Western, especially American, management theory. Lenin openly praised the theories of Frederick Winslow Taylor (1856–1915), which identified the central problem of "scientific management" as the struggle to increase labor productivity. Stalin, lecturing to Bolshevik cadres in 1924, stated that "the combination of Russian revolutionary sweep and American efficiency is the essence of Leninism in party and state work."[23] East Asian revolutionaries for a long time did not agree. Chinese Maoists and their Vietnamese disciples denounced scientific management as capitalist class oppression of workers, and its promotion of economic efficiency as putting profit making, not politics, in command.

This changed after 1976. In 1996, one Chinese high official celebrated the (American) management sciences as the indispensable antidote to Chinese cronyism and China's rent-seeking, subsidies-demanding, state-owned enterprises.[24] Vietnamese officials seem to have followed suit. If Chinese reformers like Kang Youwei, little more than a century ago, admired Western churches, today their successors in both China and Vietnam exalt Western business schools.

Far from there being a "clash of civilizations" here, it is remarkable how compatible the Western behavioral sciences are with modern East Asian authoritarianism, once those sciences are detached from their Western context of parliamentary democracy and independent judiciaries. Some Vietnamese officials have gone as far as to claim that Confucius is the real founder of management studies, with people like F. W. Taylor continuing his work; they propose that Vietnam's "Oriental culture" anticipated some of the administrative sciences' theories of leadership, for example, in Le Quy Don's expositions about the importance of cultivating human talent.[25] Taylorism and its successor theories, as they spread to Asia, mutate and take on indigenous characteristics.

As for the Leninist party-state itself, administrative reform can be used to protect the ruling party's vested interests. Political reform, on the other hand, particularly political reform in the direction of what Tran Xuan Bach called "pluralism" in 1988, is another matter. Yet we should not dismiss the objective need, in global terms, for Vietnam (and China) to struggle to increase administrative efficiency and creativity.

Unlike the mandarinates, the contemporary Vietnamese state operates in a world with increasingly dense networks of international organizations and institutions. Expanding regimes of global juridification accompany the accelerated globalization of capital and technology, without being authorized by democratic means. The administrative powers of existing states must perform at a higher and higher level merely to hold their own in a situation in which the boundaries between the concerns of national governance, and those of international governance, have become blurred to an unprecedented degree. Hence the complaint of one Chinese critic in 2003 that Chinese administrative operations were too "unstandardized" to be able to engage with the World Trade Organization; what China needed were much more standardized "Weber type" administrative agencies.[26]

But it is just here, in this invocation of Max Weber, that we discover some of the differences between the party technocrats of today and the scholar-officials of the precolonial mandarinates. Max Weber's models of bureaucracy, and those of the apostles of the management sciences who have succeeded him, have little place in them for values, apart from the value of operational efficiency. The danger is that the modern administrative sciences will pay too much attention to the technical side of government, and will develop a trained incapacity to understand those features of politics (such as public opinion, mass psychology, cultural traditions) that evade rational standardization efforts.

Confucian learning always had multiple possibilities. So it is dangerous to generalize about it. But the Confucian rationality of the preindustrial mandarins was bound up with values, in particular the value of the development of individual moral self-awareness. The theme that moral rectitude was more important than profits restrained Confucian enthusiasm for any purely instrumental rationality of the type found in much contemporary management thought. The "gentleman," Vietnamese thinkers like Le Quy Don were inclined to argue, was entitled to take power as an official only if his virtue had been cultivated to the point that his reputation was good enough to ensure support for him in "court and countryside" alike. This at least was the ideal.

Mandarins also lived in a Buddhist society that believed that even officials could become "lost souls" after death, as one of Vietnam's most famous mandarins, Nguyen Du (1765–1820), warned them in a famous poem.[27] Conscious of the frailty of human achievement, mandarins were more sensitive than many contemporary managers are to the danger that bureaucracies could subvert themselves. Hence, to take just one example, Phan Huy Chu feared that if the cycles of evaluation of officials' performance in office did not occur at least once every three years, corruption would become pervasive.

Even if we concede with Ian Shapiro that modern democratic theory "has been oddly innocent of the research on power," especially the multiplying forms of internationalized power of the present age, it is unlikely that systems analysis can make politics, including the dream of democracy, disappear. A Chinese political scientist concluded recently that substituting bureaucratic reform for political reform has bought the Chinese Communist regime time, if nothing more than that.[28] The same is surely true of Vietnam. But both countries currently confirm the reality of the old joke that when Marxists gain power, many of them inevitably turn into Weberians.

Notes

1. Kotkin, *Magnetic Mountain*, 380.
2. Trinh Nguyen, *Luat hoc*, 40–49.
3. Luo Longji, *Duli pinglun*, 5–10.

4. See Tran Xuan Bach's address to a Soviet bloc congress of social scientists in *Nhan dan*, 1988, 1–4; also Bui Tin, *Following Ho Chi Minh*, 157–62.

5. Nguyen Nien, *Luat hoc*, 7–12.

6. Glassman, "State Power beyond the Territorial Trap," 669–96; Vu Thach Gian, *Nhan dan*, 1977, 4; Ngo Van Hai, *Nhan dan*, 3.

7. Zhang Zhijian, *Zhongguo*, 102–5.

8. Tran Van Ta, *Tap chi Cong san*, 35–38; the report of Vo Van Kiet on the food crisis in *Nhan dan*, 1; Hoang Chi Bao, *Co cau xa hoi-giai cap o nuoc ta*, 181–87.

9. For a meditation on the size difference, see Woodside, "Exalting the Latecomer State," 15–42.

10. Li Wenliang, *WTO yu Zhongguo zhengfu guanli*, 40.

11. Nguyen Phu Trong, *Tap chi Cong san*, 11–15.

12. Nguyen Duy Quy, "Mot so y kien ve khoa hoc chinh tri," 9–14.

13. For Goodnow in contemporary China, see among others Tian Suisheng, "Zhengzhi fazhan moshi xuanze," 27–31; for Goodnow in Vietnam, see Nguyen Duy Quy, "Mot so y kien ve khoa hoc chinh tri," 9–14.

14. Wang Huning, "Xin quanli jiegou," 3–7; for the parts of Huntington's theory Wang uses, see Huntington, *Political Order in Changing Societies*, 344–55.

15. *Nhan dan*, November 5, 1993, 1–3; Li Wenliang, *WTO yu Zhongguo zhengfu guanli*, 199.

16. Li, "The Life of the Party."

17. Woodside, *Lost Modernities*.

18. Phan Huy Chu, *Lich trieu hien chuong loai chi*, 47–53.

19. Le Quy Don, *Van dai loai ngu*, 237.

20. Le Quy Don, *Kien van tieu luc*, 93–98.

21. Viet Anh and Viet Son, *Chinh luan*, 2.

22. Escobar, *Encountering Development*, 218.

23. Sun Yaojun, *Xifang guanli sixiang shi*, 75–136, 822; Rogger, "Americanism and the Economic Development of Russia."

24. Zhu Rongji, *Xinhua yuebao*, 42–43.

25. Nguyen Thy Son, *Tap chi Cong san*.

26. Li Wenliang, *WTO yu Zhongguo zhengfu guanli*, 37–38.

27. Huynh Sanh Thong, *The Heritage of Vietnamese Poetry*, 25–30.

28. Yuen Yuen Ang, "Autocracy with Chinese Characteristics." See also Shapiro, *The State of Democratic Theory*, 5–7.

References

Bui Tin. *Following Ho Chi Minh*. Translated by Judy Stowe and Do Van. Honolulu: University of Hawai'i Press, 1995.

Clark, Ronald W. *The Life of Bertrand Russell*. London: Jonathan Cape, 1975.

Escobar, Arturo. *Encountering Development: The Making and Unmaking of the Third World*. Princeton, NJ: Princeton University Press, 1995.

Glassman, Jim. "State Power beyond the Territorial Trap: The Internationalization of the State." *Political Geography* 18, no. 6 (August 1999): 669–96.

Hoang Chi Bao. *Co cau xa hoi-giai cap o nuoc ta: Ly luan va thuc tien* (The structure of society and of class in our country: Theory and practice). Hanoi: Nxb Thong tin Ly luan, 1992.

Huntington, Samuel. *Political Order in Changing Societies*. New Haven, CT: Yale University Press, 1968.

Huynh Sanh Thong. *The Heritage of Vietnamese Poetry*. New Haven, CT: Yale University Press, 1979.

Kotkin, Stephen. *Magnetic Mountain: Stalinism as a Civilization*. Berkeley: University of California Press, 1995.

Le Quy Don. *Kien van tieu luc* (A small chronicle of things seen and heard). Hanoi: Nxb Van hoa, 1977.

———. *Van dai loai ngu* (Classified discourse from the library). Hanoi: Nxb Van hoa, 1961.

Li, Eric X. "The Life of the Party: The Post-Democratic Future Begins in China. *Foreign Affairs* 92, no. 1 (January–February 2013): 34–46.

Li Wenliang. *WTO yu Zhongguo zhengfu guanli* (The WTO and Chinese government management). Changchun: Jilin renmin chubanshe, 2003.

Luo Longji. *Duli pinglun* (The independent critic) 12, no. 171 (October 1935): 5–10.

Ngo Van Hai. *Nhan dan*, November 9, 1988, 3.

Nguyen Duy Quy. "Mot so y kien ve khoa hoc chinh tri" (A few opinions about political science).. *Nha nuoc va phap luat* (The state and law) 1 (1992): 9–14.

Nguyen Nien. *Luat hoc* (Journal of legal studies) 3 (1986): 7–12.

Nguyen Phu Trong. *Tap chi Cong san* 2 (1997): 11–15.

Nguyen Thy Son. *Tap chi Cong san* 6 (1998): 33–35, 43.

Phan Huy Chu. *Lich trieu hien chuong loai chi* (A classified survey of the institutions of successive courts). Hanoi: Nxb Su hoc, 1962.

Rogger, Hans. "Americanism and the Economic Development of Russia," *Comparative Studies in Society and History* 23, no. 3 (July 1981): 382–420.

Shapiro, Ian. *The State of Democratic Theory*. Princeton, NJ: Princeton University Press, 2003.

Sun Yaojun. *Xifang guanli sixiang shi* (A history of Western management thought). Taiyuan: Shanxi renmin chubanshe, 1987.

Tian Suisheng. "Zhengzhi fazhan moshi xuanze yu xingzheng gaige" (The choice of political development models and administrative reform). *Shehui kexue* (Social sciences) 4, (1993): 27–31.

Tran Van Ta. *Tap chi Cong san* (The communist journal) 2 (1997): 35–38

Trinh Nguyen. *Luat hoc* (Journal of legal studies) 4 (1985): 40–49.

Vo Van Kiet. *Nhan dan*, June 28, 1988, 1.

Vu Thach Gian. *Nhan dan*, April 4, 1977, 4.

Wang Huning. "Xin quanli jiegou" (A new power structure). *Shehui kexue* 2 (1993): 3–7.

Woodside, Alexander. "Exalting the Latecomer State." In *Transforming Asian Socialism: China and Vietnam Compared*, edited by Anita Chan. Lanham, MD: Rowman & Littlefield, 1999.

———. *Lost Modernities*. Cambridge, MA: Harvard University Press, 2006.

Yuen Yuen Ang. "Autocracy with Chinese Characteristics." *Foreign Affairs* 97, no. 3 (May–June 2018): 39–46.

Zhang Zhijian. *Zhongguo: Zhengfu guanli yu gaige wushinian* (China: Government management and fifty years of reforms). Beijing: Guojia xingzheng xueyuan chubanshe, 1999.

CHAPTER 3

The Emergence of Constitutional Government in Vietnam

Pham Duy Nghia

Early in 2021, as the Thirteenth National Congress of the Communist Party adopted the development strategy toward 2025 and beyond, Vietnam's future looked bright. Among developing countries, Vietnam is a success story. According to the World Bank, the lives of millions of Vietnamese have been improved, poverty significantly reduced, and more than half of the Vietnamese population is projected to join the ranks of the global middle class by 2035.[1] By the centenary of the republic in 2045, Vietnam should be a high-income developed country.[2]

Then the fourth wave of the COVID-19 pandemic suddenly hit the country hard, with a dramatic drop in GDP and far-reaching social implications. Overlapping authorities, absence of a clear reporting and accountability system, inconsistency of law and regulation, and particularly poor policy implementation weakened the government's capacity to contain the outbreak. Amid the outbreak, provinces arbitrarily interpreted and implemented guidance from Hanoi. Disobedience of the law and national policy complicated the return to a new normal and hindered economic recovery. This experience made it clear that public governance matters, with more resilience toward unforeseeable internal and external threats in the years ahead.

It was imperative to build up a well-functioning bureaucracy, disciplined by the rule of law. At the Thirteenth Congress, the Party reaffirmed the strategy of fostering a socialist state ruled by law. Subsequently, in August 2021 the Politburo decided to establish a steering committee to draft a strategy on building the socialist state ruled by law by 2045. Half of the Politburo are members of this steering committee, which is headed by President Nguyen Xuan Phuc.[3] This strategy was finally adopted by the Party Central Committee in October 2022.[4]

The notion of a socialist state ruled by law, like many other political and legal changes in Vietnam, remains somewhat unclear. Is it possible for a country ruled by the supremacy of the Communist Party to be ruled at the same time by the supremacy of the law? What is a socialist state ruled by law? How far has Vietnam progressed in its ambition to achieve comprehensive legal reform toward a socialist state ruled by law? How did legal reform work within the context of the Vietnamese party-state? What are the challenges facing legal and judiciary reform in Vietnam in the post-pandemic era?

This chapter argues that, as elsewhere, efforts to build the rule of law are always complex and may lead to mixed achievement. As the Vietnamese example will show, there is more than a single road toward the rule of law. Within the socialist party-state system, voice and accountability, government efficiency, regulatory quality, and to some extent the rule of law are all indicators of good governance that can be improved.

With that in mind, this chapter first focuses on legal and administrative reform. It attempts to explain how such reform works in the context of the Vietnamese party-state. Whether party-driven, society-driven, or global integration–driven, the demand for change in Vietnam is largely homegrown. The chapter explores the transition from socialist legality toward a socialist state ruled by law and attempts to clarify some distinctive characteristics of the rule of law in Vietnam. Finally, it briefly discusses aspects of judicial reform as one essential part of the socialist state ruled by law. The chapter concludes with an example of administrative justice to demonstrate how difficult it is to build the judicative power within the party-state.

The Driving Forces behind Institutional Reform in Vietnam

Generally, there are at least three forces that drive and facilitate the development toward the rule of law in Vietnam, namely the Party, the society, and global integration. As analyzed in other chapters of this volume, after the collapse of the Soviet Union, Vietnam remains a party-state ruled by the Communist Party of Vietnam (CPV). Borrowed from its Soviet origin, it is hard to separate the Party from the state. Under Party rule, lawmakers, the administration, and the judiciary are merely agencies assigned by the Party with different tasks that are not separate or independent from the Party. Legal, administrative, and judicial reform in Vietnam, therefore, needs to be explained in the context of institutional changes that are taking place within this unique socialist party-state.

From a secret organization with fewer than five thousand patriots at the time, the Party seized power in 1945, and has developed into a huge apparatus with more than 5 million members. The Party controls government policy and law, and decides all key personnel issues for the whole political system and state apparatus. The CPV's political cadres hold all leading positions and are frequently rotated within all government offices, mass organizations, and elsewhere in public agencies. Success or failure in improving public governance in Vietnam, therefore, has deep roots and is directly connected to the Party's struggle for legitimacy in its ruling of the country over the last eighty years.

The year 1986, when reform was initiated, was one of many critical junctures the party-state has faced during its existence. As elaborated in more detail by Le Dang Doanh and other authors of this volume, by the end of the 1980s the country faced overall stagnation. Sensing its near collapse, the party-state decided to loosen its control over economic life, granting agricultural land use back to the farmers and legalizing market transactions. This early move decisively saved the regime from collapse. Isolated from the world community following decades of war and regional conflicts, Vietnam fought its way to open the country to the market and to the world.

In exchange for economic liberalization, the Party kept political changes tightly under its control. On the one hand, political opposition within and beyond the Party, political pluralism, separation of power between the Party and government, free elections, free media, and civil society à la Western democracies are not tolerated. Criminalized as a hostile force against the socialist state, political pluralism is banned. On the other hand, driven by pragmatism, profound political and public governance reform is feasible in Vietnam when it helps to save, to strengthen, and to reinforce the CPV's rule. Vietnam recognizes a wide range of political rights and civil liberties in its existing 2013 constitution and continues to harmonize national law with international law and practice.[5]

Although Party internal politics remains opaque as elsewhere, the dynamic process of institutional reform emerges within the elite leadership of the Party apparatus, including the 180-member Central Committee (CC) and the eighteen-member Politburo. Ultimate Party programs are made by the National Party Congress, which meets every five years. These Party programs are the foundation of government policy, law, and regulation. Law is made and interpreted in compliance with the Party programs.

If the pivot point from Marx to market was made at the Sixth Party Congress in 1986, the need for reforming law and government to make them fit to facilitate the economic liberalization was recognized by the Party leadership some five years later, at the following Seventh Party Congress in the year 1991. Departing from the rigid dictatorship of the proletariat as provided by the 1980 constitution, the Party redefined the nature of the socialist state as a state of the people, by the people, and for the people under the leadership of the Party. That change then led to the first constitutional revision in 1992.

In the early stages, political and legal reforms are initiated by the Party and are Party-driven. The first pragmatic program to overhaul the entire government structure was adopted by the Party in January 1995.[6] Based on this 1995 pragmatic program, a further set of separate strategies for legislative, judicial, and public administration reform toward 2020 were adopted during the years 1995 to 1997.

Based on three strategies, the National Assembly, the government, and the Supreme Court worked on implementing master plans. The government, for example, adopted two successive administrative reform (PAR) master plans for the periods of 2001–10 and 2011–20. To monitor its performance, measurable annual targets in all sectors and regions were then determined. The PAR pillars include, inter alia, reform of the legal and regulatory framework; streamlining administrative organization and simplification of procedures; reform in recruitment, compensation, and assessment of public officials; and, more recently, the digital transformation in the public sector. All such profound public governance reforms toward modern institutions took shape gradually beginning from the year 1995.

That, in a nutshell, is a description of how Party-driven reform works in Vietnam. All Party organizations and members are obliged to obey the constitution and the law (Article 4.3 of the constitution), but the Party can initiate the process to amend or revise the constitution at any time it is considered necessary.

Planning mentality dies hard. The Vietnamese party-state still operates habitually within planning cycles. The party revises the constitution at intervals of roughly every ten years (1992, 2001, 2013). Important laws are revised almost every five years (for example, the Land Law was revised in the years 1987, 1993, 1998, 2003, 2008, and 2013). Government decrees and ministerial circulars are then revised at shorter intervals of every one or two years.

Reform in Vietnam, however, can also be society-driven. With the recovery and expansive growth of the domestic private economy, Vietnam's public became increasingly demanding, including in the political arena. The people became aware that doing business should not be a privilege granted arbitrarily at the will of the state authority. It should be a liberty, a citizen's right, a natural right of any individual. Economic liberalization transforms, then, into constitutional debates over fundamental rights and freedoms.

Both Party-driven and society-driven are homegrown demands for reform. In making the country attractive for domestic and foreign investment, the government must operate in a transparent, efficient, and reliable way. Closer connection to the world also creates additional momentum for domestic reform. Vietnam's size and its geopolitical position make the country receptive to international norms.[7]

The process of opening up and integrating into the global economy started with the normalization of diplomatic relations between Vietnam and the United States in 1995. Vietnam also joined ASEAN in 1995, joined the WTO in 2016, and has actively integrated since then into the global economy. Vietnam now is among the most open economies worldwide, given that its foreign trade volume is more than double its GDP.[8] The country is a signatory of at least seventeen new-generation free trade agreements (FTAs), including bilateral FTAs with Korea, Japan, and the EU, and multilateral agreements with the Trans-Pacific Partnership (CPTPP) and the Regional Comprehensive Economic Partnership.[9] The content of these new-generation FTAs involves far more than just trade. For example, in accordance with agreements with the CPTPP and the Vietnam-EU FTA, Vietnam commits to the rule of law, transparency, regulatory coherence, access to justice, and the like.

As a result, over the last thirty years Vietnam has created a comprehensive legal framework enabling the successful transition toward one of the most vibrant economies in the region. Major legal foundations have been created relating to property law, corporation, contracts, transaction, trade, banking, securities, dispute settlement, and bankruptcy. In public administration the country has implemented two successive PAR master plans, 2001–10 and 2011–20, designed to overhaul the whole state apparatus.

Foreign scholars and international agencies may view and measure the progress of public governance reform in Vietnam differently, subject to their paradigms and indicators. According to the World Bank's Worldwide Governance Indicators, Vietnam's public governance remains consistently low and has not improved for decades.[10] For Transparency International, the country remains seriously corrupt.[11] For Human Rights Watch, Vietnam's record is dire in all eras.[12] This list of critical assessments may continue. On the other hand, since the collapse of its Communist allies in the 1990s and its struggle for survival, Vietnam's party-state has proved extremely resilient and inventive in responding to all internal and external threats.[13]

The COVID-19 pandemic was a deadly test to verify governmental efficiency worldwide. Vietnam, as a low middle-income country not recognized for government efficiency by international donors and development agencies, was surprisingly among the few nations successful in containing the pandemic, at least during the first wave in 2020. The party-state proved able to formulate timely policy and to implement that policy efficiently to constrain the outbreak of COVID-19.[14] Competition among Party leaders to secure their position at the Thirteenth Party Congress, together with the trust of Vietnam's population in public authorities and sound policies in containing the pandemic, all contributed to Vietnam's early success in 2020 in combating the disease.

By contrast, in 2021 the Vietnamese government responded to the delta variant with unclear messaging, creating uncertainties among implementing agencies. Vietnam was also far behind the other ASEAN countries in purchasing and implementing the vaccination program. As the pandemic worsened in Ho Chi Minh City and the Mekong Delta beginning in May 2021, public health systems were poorly equipped to respond to this large-scale emergency. Social security could not be ensured for millions of low-income and other vulnerable groups, causing a factory worker exodus from the city.

The deadly COVID-19 pandemic made clear a threat to the Party's legitimacy if it could not deliver the leadership the country needed in a time of emergency. Overlapping authority and unclear reporting mechanisms within the party-state delayed decision making and worsened policy implementation from the central to the local level. A functioning bureaucracy ruled by law was badly needed to make the party-state more resilient to such threats and emergencies.

Legal and Administrative Reform within the Party-State Boundary

Theoreticians may debate endlessly the correct term—either socialist legality, rule of law, or rule by law—to describe the party-state ruled by a single Communist Party that has the authority to enforce law and to control the political system and society as a whole. This chapter will use the term constitutional government. Constitutional government is defined here as the existence of a constitution, law, and other rules that effectively control the exercise of political power, ensure a functioning bureaucracy, and discipline public servants, holding them accountable to the Party and to the public.

This broad definition works well for Vietnam. Authority can be exercised either by the Party, by the state apparatus, or in extreme cases by authorized mass organizations.

Within Party internal processes, with or without public participation, institutions can be formal and informal, with legal, political, and other social norms supplementing each other. Broadly, the most important stakeholders in the Vietnamese government consist of the Party apparatus, the state apparatus, the armed forces, the Fatherland Front as an umbrella organization supporting the Party to mobilize the masses, the media, and all other mechanisms that relate to the formulation and exercise of authority.

Within the umbrella of constitutional government, the state apparatus is a narrower concept. The state apparatus in Vietnam consists of the armed forces, the public administration, the representative bodies, the judiciary, the people's procuracy, and others. Notably, the army and police enjoy a special position and privilege within the party-state. The armed forces do not belong to and are not subordinate to the public administration. Given the overlapping and competing authorities within the party-state apparatus, there are many formal and informal circles of power. Instead of one ultimate power source, the power base in Vietnam is rather diffuse. For example, the prime minister heading the government does not have the final authority to nominate ministers and vice ministers. This power either belongs exclusively to the Politburo (for nomination of ministers) or to the Central Committee Secretariat (for nomination of senior public officials at the rank of deputy minister and government director upward). The CC subcommittees also oversee policy relating to organization and cadres, the economy, ideology, or Party discipline.

For readers familiar with the rule of law in multiparty democracies, concepts and institutions in the party-state may use the same vocabulary, but they often depart significantly in meaning. The government, army, police, mass organizations, state-owned business sector, and provinces are decisive power circles within the Vietnamese party-state. They are proportionally represented both in the Party Congress and in the National Assembly (NA). That representation makes the Party Congress or NA primarily forums for consolidation of power and building coalitions among diverse power circles.

In this context, the public administration system constitutes only one part of the authority and power of the Vietnamese party-state. Statistically, the number of public officials working in the public administration is only a small percentage of the personnel employed in the public sector.[15] Note that the public sector in Vietnam includes the public administration (with 247,344 public officials), public utilities (public health care, education, cultural entities, etc., with 1,783,174 employees), and local governments (with 1,031,151 employees). In addition, employment in the public sector also includes employees in the Party and mass organizations.

At the central level, Vietnam's government is only one among at least five ultimate power centers, including the Politburo, the Central Committee, the CC Secretariat, the government, and the National Assembly. These diffuse power bases repeat and extend to all levels. The People's Committee—the name for the local administration—is only one among several power circles under the local Party leadership. The army and police traditionally are accountable directly to the Party. Their hierarchy is vertically organized. The armed forces coordinate closely with the public administration at all levels, but politically and legally, they are not entirely subordinate to the national or local government.

This fragmented, diffuse power base complicates the system of reporting and accountability within the party-state. Leaders of any public agency must be responsible to multiple supervising authorities, vertically, horizontally, and professionally. The director of the public health agency at the provincial level, for example, is responsible to the local Party leadership, to the People's Committee, to the local elective people's council, and is subject to further vertical supervision by the Ministry of Public Health, the State Auditor, and the government inspectorate (in charge of administrative compliance).

That diffuse power explains why legal and government reform can only be successful if it is approached taking into account the complexity of public governance in the party-state. Indeed, the two successive PAR master plans encompassed a comprehensive and inclusive process of change across a broad range of areas. The six pillars of the PAR master plan for 2011–20 consist of: (1) the creation of a legal and regulatory framework; (2) the simplification of administrative procedures; (3) streamlining of administrative organization; (4) improving the quality of cadres, public officials in public authorities, and human resources in the public utilities sector; (5) reforming the public finance; and (6) modernizing public service delivery.[16]

Based on these master plans, five-year and annual measurable targets for all sectoral regulatory bodies at all government levels were determined. To implement and monitor PAR progress, steering boards were established at all levels. The prime minister chairs the PAR board at the national level, ministers chair the PAR board at the ministerial level, and mayors chair the local PAR boards. A periodic reporting system is set in place to monitor PAR performance of all agencies. Although initiated primarily in a top-down approach, PAR is not static. It is a dynamic, steadily evolving process, subject to manifold forces inside and outside the administration. Vibrant social networks, citizen perception toward market and privatization, events such as the COVID-19 pandemic and digital transformation—all these diverse factors contribute to evolving the scope and intensity of PAR. Understandably, PAR achievement can be quite different among the six pillars, with different short- or long-term impacts on the quality of public service delivery. The impact of legislative reform, for instance, is more difficult to measure than the simplification of administrative procedures or the streamlining of administrative organizations.

There are two decisive factors in explaining PAR success and failure in Vietnam. The first factor relates to the Party's priority to sustain and improve its legitimacy to rule. The second factor relates to the diffuse power structure within the Vietnamese party-state. As an example, the following analysis takes a closer look at implementation of the first PAR pillar, namely the creation of a legal and regulatory framework, and explains why the two mentioned factors are crucially important for the success or failure of PAR.

In the early 2000s the Party faced wide distrust and discontent among Vietnam's population, a result of the failure to contain rampant corruption, mismanagement of state-owned businesses, and the inefficiency of public investment. It was urgent for the Party to exercise discipline and enforce the law, primarily to limit the abuse of power by the government in allocating land, public finance, and other national resources. Subsequently, the Party took the lead to reinforce its rule over the government. The Politburo quickly ordered a stop to the government policy of experimenting with large state-owned conglomerates. It then re-created the CC Committee for Internal Affairs and reinforced the power of the CC Committee for Party Discipline, both powerful agencies in combating corruption among high party officials. Finally, the Party also initiated constitutional reform, which led to the adoption of the revised 2013 constitution.

The 2013 constitution inches toward a checks-and-balances system among executive, legislative, and judicial branches within the party-state.[17] The government still leads the legislative procedure; it can suggest and implement certain policy for piloting policies. For example, 95 percent of legislative initiatives come from government.[18] Operating under overlapping authority with the parallel party apparatus, the government seeks ways to gain legal certainty for its operation. By 2021 all fundamental legislation concerning the state apparatus had been issued or revised in accordance with the 2013 constitution.

In the legislative process, priority was given to legislation embracing market-conforming rules, such as improving the business environment, increasing certainty in property law, and further liberalizing trade. The private sector is encouraged to invest in public infrastructure. Public providers of health care services, education, and cultural life were separated from the public administration system and converted into self-financing public entities. In implementation of the two successive master plans between 2001 and 2020, comprehensive legislation has been adopted to facilitate these changes. PAR works well, primarily in areas where the legitimacy of the party-state could be strengthened.

By contrast, legislation stalls where it enters the political sphere, where it may expose some risk to the Party. The rights to associate or to demonstrate are such issues. The two draft laws, namely the Law on Association and the Law on Demonstration were postponed several times during the last six years.[19] Although these liberties are recognized by the 2013 constitution, their implementation is stalled because of the lack of administrative regulation and guidance. Hesitating to unleash such political liberties, the Party also devoted efforts to improving a sophisticated system of censorship to ensure that research, teaching, journalism, and cultural life comply with the Party line.[20] In contrast to Western liberal democracies, the army, police, and public servants in Vietnam are required expressly by law to be loyal to the Party.[21]

The party-state appears to be hesitant to simplify cumbersome procedures in politically sensitive eras. Procedures to register a nonprofit association or to operate a nonprofit fund remain as cumbersome as ever. Likewise, procedures to register strikes or mass demonstrations remain totally unclear because of the absence of relevant regulations. The second factor decisively affecting the course of PAR is the diffuse power structure within the party-state. Competition and infighting among diverse power circles within the party-state sometimes facilitate PAR, particularly by installing some sort of checks and balances. On the other hand, overlap in authority hinders clear responsibility and worsens governmental operations.

The legislative process in Vietnam has become more transparent, thanks to improvements in the checks and balances within the diffuse power structure. Under existing law, the government can only issue administrative regulations if explicitly allowed to do so by a particular law.[22] That is a meaningful restriction of the government's power and shifts the power in lawmaking toward the National Assembly.

The National Assembly assumes a more active role in keeping the government in check. Although often labeled as a rubber stamp of the Party, NA members may explore the space given by the Party to exercise parliamentary oversight over the government. Several draft laws and large public investment proposals have been rejected by the NA in the past, such as the draft Law on Road Traffic and the draft Law on Road Traffic Order and Security.[23] Public grievances, particularly land disputes and discontent with cumbersome administration, are often raised in controversial questioning sessions at the NA. Interestingly, the NA is also authorized to hold so-called votes of confidence for all cabinet members, primarily as a means of measuring their performance. These changes may impact the legislative process and thus contribute to achieving the first PAR pillar, namely creating a workable legal and regulatory framework for Vietnamese administration.

However, the overall result of implementing the first PAR pillar remains mixed. The authority of agencies in Party and state bodies still overlaps. Responsibility in formulating policy and lawmaking lies across several agencies within the Party and state. This conflicting competency sometimes has led to self-contradictory legislation. For example, Vietnam's criminal code and two other laws, although adopted, had to be postponed in 2016 because of their poor quality, technical errors, absence of internal logic, or the infeasibility of enforcement.[24]

Generally, this observation can be applied to all other remaining PAR pillars, including simplifying procedures, streamlining organization, improving public officials' quality, reforming public finance, and the modernizing of service delivery. PAR could succeed in areas where the party-state is forced to improve the legitimacy of its rule. Responding to ever-changing internal and external threats, PAR is dynamic, with priorities and intensity being adjusted over time. Continually on the road toward economic liberalization, PAR makes the Vietnamese party-state confident in managing political changes under its terms and hopefully will become more resilient in time of crisis.

From Socialist Legality toward a Socialist State Ruled by Law: The Interchange between Party Internal Rules and the Law

The essence of socialist legality is that Party rule, rather than the legal and judicial system, is supreme in governing the society. Law helps to implement Party policies by translating them into written normative legal documents, which are binding on the society as a whole. That tradition dies hard in Vietnam. The preamble to the 2013 constitution, for example, states that "in institutionalizing the Party program to build socialism, we Vietnamese people make, enforce, and protect this constitution." Rather than the sovereignty of the people, Party rule is precisely the soul and spirit of the Vietnam constitution.

The notion of socialist legality was included in Vietnam's constitution in 1960[25] and continued in the following 1980 and 1992 constitutions. According to socialist legality, law should be made and enforced efficiently as tools of the Party. The society as a whole must strictly obey the law. Through this obedience, the Party is capable of managing the society. Law and the legal system are understood primarily as the body of written normative legal documents, adopted by the hierarchy of the state apparatus. Although adopted early in the 1960s, little attention could be paid to the socialist legality during the Vietnam War. Having been dissolved since 1960, the Ministry of Justice was reestablished only later in 1981. Only a handful of laws were adopted by the National Assembly during the war. The society was largely governed directly by Party rules and by existing social norms. Efforts to intensify socialist legality occurred only briefly during the period from 1976 to 1986.

Imported from the former Soviet Union, socialist legality was originally a state doctrine, an ideology imposed by the elites within the party-state. The judiciary (people's court system), the public prosecutor (people's procuracy), the state inspectorate, and the legal professions (adjudicative bodies for economic dispute settlement—the so-called state economic arbitration, people's defenders in criminal procedures, state notary, justice enforcement authorities) were reorganized in the 1980s, modeled on institutional designs and knowledge learned from the former Soviet Union and Eastern Europe Communist bloc.

In contrast, the rule of law is a by-product of Vietnam's economic liberalization and integration with the world. Natural law, the supremacy of the law, and the constitutional concept of constraining the power of the party-state—all these liberal concepts are unintended side effects of the economic reform. The public discourse around the 1999 Law on Enterprise to prevent the abuse of power of local governments in granting business licenses, and to protect the natural right of people to do business, became subject to debate on the rule of law prior to the Ninth Party Congress in early 2001.[26] This debate gained momentum as Vietnam integrated more deeply with the world. Encouraged by international commitments within APEC (Asia-Pacific Economic Cooperation) and in preparing for WTO accession, the concept of the rule of law was then received by the Vietnamese public as a common, globally accepted value.

As a result, the constitution was then revised in 2001, replacing socialist legality and adding a new phrase into Article 2 that Vietnam is a socialist state ruled by law. Since then, within the Party and beyond, the debate on the rule of law has never stopped. It remains unclear how to settle peacefully the supremacy of the Party with the supremacy of the law. Occasionally, the discussion becomes explosive. One example was the rise of Petition 72 during the public discourse leading to the 2013 constitution.[27] The rule of law debate may flame once again at the time the Party implements the strategy on building a state ruled by law toward 2045 as adopted on October 9, 2022.

Out of this inconsistency and contradiction, what is a socialist state ruled by law in Vietnam? Obviously, people can understand this concept differently, as they understand the rule of law. According to the 2013 constitution, a socialist state ruled by law is defined as a state ruled by the Communist Party (Article 4). Rule by law means that the law must be a sufficient means in the hands of the Party to manage the society (Article 8). For this purpose, law must be predictable, consistent, transparent, accessible to the public, and generally applicable to all individuals and organizations. The forms of legal normative documents, and the procedure to draft and to issue, revise, and abolish such documents are strictly regulated by the law (Law on Issuance of Normative Legal Documents, 2015, revised 2020).

From a technical perspective, the legislative process in Vietnam has been significantly improved in terms of transparency and public participation. Over the years, the hierarchy of normative documents has become more transparent. They consist of laws and resolutions adopted by the National Assembly, governmental decrees, ministerial circulars, regulations issued by the Supreme Court, the Supreme Inspectorate resolutions, and decisions made by local authorities. Improvement has been made in terms of technical codification and systematization of the law. Vietnamese legal sources, from central regulation to local rules, are now largely available online, and they are accessible at an affordable cost.

The legislative process has also become increasingly inclusive. The agency initiating a draft law must conduct a regulatory impact assessment and publish this report and the draft law for public comment. The public is empowered to have its voice heard. Although a functioning judicial review over legal normative documents is still absent, a system of screening to detect noncompliance is managed by the Ministry of Justice. Normative legal documents that were improperly promulgated in violation of such procedures can be declared unlawful and void, theoretically by the higher supervisory authority or finally by the Standing Committee of the National Assembly.

Those and other changes in legislative process occurred under Party control. The Party decides the legislative program, supervises policy deliberation, and controls the process to translate the Party's intentions into legal documents. For this purpose, the Party operates through its own hierarchy, which exists parallel to all government and mass organizations at any level. Đảng đoàn Quốc hội is the Party organization overseeing the activities at the National Assembly. Ban cán sự Đảng Chính phủ is the Party organization overseeing the activities of the government. When initiating any draft law, the initiator must quote the specific Party program and clarify the Party's intention. Policy and law must provide solutions consistent with the Party's intention. The legislative process can end at any time the Party leadership senses that policy deliberation may go beyond the envisaged Party intention. That occurred several times during the drafting of the Law on Demonstration, the Law on Association, and the Law on Specific Economic Zones.

Emerging from a secret organization, the Communist Party's internal politics remain secret. The way the Party's internal rules were initiated, debated, and adopted remains somewhat mysterious, leaving much room for rumor and speculation. However, with public policy deliberation and transparency in the legislative process, the Party is under pressure to transform itself into an institution accountable to the public. In recent years, the Party has begun to systemize and codify its rules. Compatibly with the hierarchy of normative legal documents, the mountain of Party internal rules begins to take shape.

According to the Law on Issuance of Legal Normative Documents, 2015, as revised in 2020, the normative legal document is considered the source of Vietnam's written law. Party rules, in contrast, are not normative legal documents. By the letter of the law, Party rules may be binding only on its members; they are not laws generally applicable to the public. From the perspective of law in action, however, one can hardly ignore the Party rules in cases where they conflict with the normative legal documents.

In the Party documents, the Party uses political terms such as socialist-oriented market economy, ownership by the entire Vietnamese people, the leading role of state-owned enterprises (SOEs), equitization of SOEs, or socialization of public facilities. Obviously, these phrases are extremely ambiguous. They make the legal system less reliable. Land law is an example. Despite multiple revisions, the concept of so-called "ownership by the entire Vietnamese people" endures in the law. People cannot own their land plots as private property; only some land use rights were granted to them. Likewise, Vietnamese business law must deal with the political fiction that SOEs should assume the leading role in the economy. Risk occurs when the majority of shares in SOEs are transferred to private hands. Privatization of SOEs is taboo; only equitization is in conformity with the party lines.

Those kinds of examples may be found easily across the legal system. Because the law is not supreme and cannot bind the rule of the Party, Vietnamese law is somewhat of a hybrid. Party rules and public norms continue to coexist. They may substitute for and compete with each other. It is hard to forecast whether the supremacy of law or the supremacy of the Party may dominate in the ruling ideology of the Party leadership.

Judicial Reform: The Example of Administrative Court

Rule of law is meaningless without capable courts. Liberty can only be ensured if people can rely on a functioning justice system. The 2013 constitution will remain a nice book with a lengthy catalog of human and citizen rights if there is no mechanism to enforce them. That is particularly important when disputes emerge between public authorities and citizens. Those disputes are qualified in Vietnam as administrative disputes to be heard by administrative courts.

In what follows, this chapter demonstrates that administrative justice was borrowed by Vietnam under the influence of efforts to harmonize Vietnamese law with international commitments. It is a strange, foreign concept for the party-state that an individual may initiate a lawsuit against the state, and possibly will have the means to force the party-state to execute the judgment. The party-state is not prepared to accept this strange concept. Unsurprisingly, administrative justice cannot function with the current court system.

There are alternative ways and channels to prevent and to settle public grievances within the party-state. They include, for instance, the system of petitions and denunciations, the tradition of receiving citizen complaints, the system of the state inspectorate, the system of Party discipline oversight, the ways to measure and evaluate public concerns and opinions, and so forth. This wide range of alternative channels may possibly replace the role of the court in creating administrative justice. (The discussion of alternative justice in the party-state goes beyond the scope of this chapter and needs to be treated separately in further research.)

The first ordinance on the administrative court was adopted in 1996. A new division and new procedure, with very narrow jurisdiction to hear only a handful of certain categories of disputes as listed by the law, was carefully inserted into the ordinary court system. Land disputes, for example, were initially not included in the administrative courts' jurisdiction. They were added by the 1998 revision but soon removed again by the subsequent 2006 revision.[28] The 1996 ordinance was replaced by the Law on Administrative Procedure in 2010. But this law was also rather short-lived. It was soon replaced by the 2015 Law on Administrative Procedure. Subject to changes over the last twenty years, the administrative court does not have real power to hear disputes between citizens and public authorities. Its mandate is not to replace, but at best to supplement the existing political and social mechanism of grievance settlement within the party-state.

In implementing the 2013 constitution, the courts' organization was thoroughly revised. The Supreme People's Court (SPC) has seventeen judges, and its jurisdiction is narrowed to revision and to make so-called case law. The former three SPC branches in Hanoi, Da Nang, and Ho Chi Minh City were transformed into three new high courts. These high courts are courts of appeal, overseeing the sixty-three provincial courts. The provincial court is typically organized into six divisions: criminal, civil, economic, labor, administrative, and most recently the division for family and minors. The provincial court is the court of appeal for cases heard by lower district courts. There are 713 district courts throughout Vietnam.

At the district court, the lowest level within Vietnam's judiciary system, the separation into six divisions is not mandatory by law. District court leadership, however, usually practices some form of specialization among judges. Individual judges are selected and additionally trained to become specialized in administrative or economic cases.

The following short description demonstrates how the court operates. Among the provinces, Ho Chi Minh City (HCMC) People's Court has had the most extensive practice in dealing with administrative cases. The workload of a judge in HCMC is extremely heavy. Each judge must handle 298 cases annually, with an average of ten cases in a month. In other words, the judge has only two working days for the settlement of a case.[29] Judges are not properly honored. The average monthly salary of judges is less than US$400, much lower than salaries paid in the vibrant private sector.[30] Not surprisingly, the court cannot attract and keep talented legal professionals. In 2018, fifty-one judges in HCMC quit their jobs to enter the private sector. The shortage of personnel, inappropriate compensation, absence of societal recognition for judges, lack of independence, lack of integrity, and other organizational, legal, and procedural weaknesses may explain the limited role of the administrative court in Vietnam.[31]

Back in the 1990s, when drafting the first rule on administrative court procedure, Vietnamese lawmakers were already aware of the risk that within the party-state it is impossible for a judge to decide contrary to the will of the government.[32] A judge is appointed for an initial term of five years, and for ten years if reappointed. As a Party member he or she must obey Party discipline. Under these circumstances, decisions collectively made by the party-state authority cannot be challenged by a single judge.

The discussion of judicial independence gained additional momentum once again during the process of drafting the constitution in 2013. Article 2.3, section 102.1 of the constitution provides that judicial power is vested with the court. Theoretically, the court has the power to control the legislative and executive power. In addition, section 102.2 of the constitution provides that the mission of the judiciary is to protect justice, to protect the socialist regime, and then to protect the legitimate rights and interests of citizens. This priority setting and emphasis are remarkably new in Vietnam's political context. Previously, the protection of the socialist regime was always the very first priority of all state agencies.

According to the Party's strategy on judicial reform, by 2020 the court organization should be based on special jurisdiction, and not be dependent on geographic affiliation.[33] To create some independence for judges in administrative procedure, there were suggestions, for instance, to establish regional courts, independent from the existing ordinary court system. A regional court is then responsible for several districts. In this way, local party-state leadership could be prevented from exercising influence on the judges. But resistance from local authorities was strong. As a result, no change was possible; the court organization remained as it was, strictly embedded within the local political and administrative substructures of the party-state.[34] The 2015 Law on Administrative Procedure modifies the jurisdiction of administrative courts only slightly. According to sections 31.1 and 32.8 of the Law on Administrative Procedure, district courts are still responsible for hearing administrative cases challenging acts by district governments at the same level, except those adopted collectively by the District People's Committee (PC) and by the PC chairman, and except those considered important, which will be heard by the higher provincial court.

The influence of district governments on district judges is obvious. In accordance with Party internal rules, the chairman of the People's Committee is at the same level as the vice secretary of the Party organization. A judge can hardly escape the influence of his supervising Party organization. When being sued, the district government as defendant most often wins at the district court.[35] The plaintiff may have a slightly greater chance at the provincial court as the court of appeals.[36]

This outcome can be explained partly because judges at the provincial court level may be less sensitive to the influence of the lower district government. But different causes may also lead to this outcome. In certain cases against the local government for land taking on a large scale, judges tend to seek guidance from the court leadership. The latter again may seek guidance from the local Party committee for internal affairs.[37] The Party and the court are unwilling to disclose this informal practice. Only in some politically sensitive cases attracting large public attention does the Party sometimes disclose the composition of the Party steering committee in its handling of such cases.[38] It also indicates that there are different internal party channels to adjust local policy. The administrative court judgment in those cases appears merely as the formal decision that will be presented by the court to the public. The judgment often reflects the consensus reached among local elites, which has been already made prior to the court proceedings.

In summary, the organization of the administrative court is ill-designed to exercise judicial power over the government. As an extension of the current people's court system, the administrative court is subject to the influence of local substructures of the party-state.

Additionally, procedural rules are also inappropriate. Although the jurisdiction of administrative courts was to some extent widened over the last two decades, other constraints still endure.[39] Administrative courts have the jurisdiction to hear only disputes concerning individual decisions, and not generally legal normative documents. In land disputes, for example, land price is determined by resolution of the provincial people's council (PPC). According to Vietnamese law, a PPC resolution is a legal normative document and therefore not subject to judicial review. On the contrary, the compensation for an individual land plot is individual, decided by the PC chairman in the form of an administrative decision. Only this individual decision may be challenged in an administrative court.[40] Similarly, a business may challenge individual decisions made by a certain tax authority, but it cannot challenge normative ministerial circulars on tax policies in an administrative court procedure.

This boundary substantially narrows the scope of power of the administrative court. The court can correct certain administrative wrongdoings, but it is not designed to exercise judicial power over the entire administrative system. In the Vietnamese party-state, administrative acts must follow state policies, and the latter must follow Party guidelines. Limited to individual acts, administrative courts have no power to correct injustices incurred by unlawful policies and Party directions. In land-taking disputes, for example, administrative courts do not have the power to review unjust policies adopted by the local people's council to convert land use (from agricultural land to residential or commercial use) or to determine policies on land prices in cases of compulsory acquisition. In addition to the absence of a clear mechanism for constitutional review, the fact that the court does not have the power to exercise judicial review over normative acts seriously weakens the judiciary in Vietnam.[41]

In addition to narrowly defined jurisdiction, administrative procedure remains burdensome, time consuming, and a clear disadvantage to both the claimant and the trial panel of the court. The rules on representation of public authority as defendant remain somewhat inflexible and irrational. In a lawsuit against a local government, known as People's Committees (PC), only the PC chairman or vice chairman is authorized by law to represent the defendant before the court.[42] If these local politicians are absent, the trial panel must postpone the hearing, and this is the common practice at administrative courts in recent years.[43] Only if these local politicians still don't appear at the hearing when duly summoned for the second time may the trial panel conduct the hearing in their absence.[44] However, without active participation of the defendant, prior hearing reconciliation and adversary proceedings cannot be productive.[45] Given the complexity of facts and circumstances leading to an administrative act, the court appears to be very reluctant to proceed with the hearing in the defendant's absence.

Court procedure is also unpredictable because of the intervention of the procuracy. This unique role of the public prosecutor (in Vietnam, people's procuracy) is a relic from the Soviet legal heritage. Although Party strategies on judicial reform by 2020 envisaged that the people's procuracy should be transformed and limited within the public prosecutor's role, in fact the people's procuracy still enjoys the unique power to supervise the judiciary. The procuracy is authorized by law to attend any court procedure, including administrative. Thus, the procuracy is entitled to present legal opinions and to make suggestions during the hearing, consequently having immense influence on the court's decisions. Finally, the procuracy may file a protest against the first-instance verdict, thus initiating the appellate procedure by itself, independent of the plaintiff and defendant.[46] Currently there is no clear strategy in Vietnam on how to restructure this Soviet-style people's procuracy and transform it into a public prosecutor. The interference of the procuracy during administrative procedures is certainly a constraint not only on the parties' autonomy but also on the independence of the court. Without profound change in procedural rules to widen the court's jurisdiction, to ensure the parties' autonomy, and to limit intervention from third parties, administrative courts can only play a minor role in supplementing the existing mechanism to settle administrative disputes between individuals or organizations and the party-state in Vietnam.

A fundamental legal principle is that once a verdict is reached, the public agency (as so-called judgment debtor) must implement the judgment. In case it fails voluntarily to execute the judgment, a company or individual (a so-called judgment creditor) has the right to request, and the court may order, the compulsory execution of judgment. However, there is no capable executor to enforce such a judgment in Vietnam. The courts have no meaningful power to force the administration to obey the verdict, and public authorities frequently disregard the court judgment and refuse to implement it properly.[47]

Conclusion and the Way Forward

Vietnam's party-state is approaching its eightieth birthday in 2025. By 2045 the country will be among the group of high-income developed countries. A socialist state ruled by law will help to facilitate the development of the country, possibly with entrepreneurial spirits and innovative forces of the digital age. This grand strategy was adopted at the Thirteenth Party Congress in January 2021. The outbreak of the COVID-19 pandemic later in 2021, with a dramatic drop in GDP, suddenly made this ambitious goal seemingly unrealistic. Inherent old and new weaknesses in public governance of the country were exposed. Overlapping authorities and unclear accountability hinder the party-state in forming and implementing sound policies. Vietnam appears to be vulnerable to emergencies, threats, and uncertainties. To be resilient, the country needs a strong and efficient state, and a functioning bureaucracy disciplined by the rule of law.

Thirty years have passed, and Vietnam is well on the way to becoming a socialist state ruled by law. Two characteristics are important under this concept: (1) *socialist* state means that the Communist Party rules the country, and (2) *ruled by law* means that the law must be efficient, predictable, consistent, transparent, and generally applicable to all. To this end, the Party manages to keep the legal, administrative, and judicial reform under its control. Good law, and good implementation, will hopefully lead to good outcomes. Its legitimacy to rule is ensured so long as the Party continues to deliver its leadership performance.

Reform may occur under a mixture of different driving forces, events, and causes, accidentally or intentionally. The Party liberalized the economy and unleashed endless potential for millions of Vietnamese to pursue happiness and develop their dignity. At some point, law appears not to be merely a means in the hands of the ruling Party, but also the value, the power, the source that individuals may rely on to protect themselves against the abuse of power by public authorities, by the party-state. At this point, socialist legality starts to evolve from rule by law to rule of law. At this point, the law on the books turns into the law in action.

Vietnam is on the road toward the rule of law. It has left behind the non-law heritage of the dominance of customs, social norms, ethics, Confucian teachings, or directly applicable Party guidance. It has inched forward toward a society governed by the supremacy of the law: the existence of a constitution, law, legal institutions, and legal professions, all of which make the exercise of public power predictable. This stage, called constitutional government, describes the achievement the country has made and the uncertainties the country will face along the unknown road toward the rule of law.

Notes

1. World Bank, *Vietnam 2035*.
2. CPV, 13th Party Congress documents, https://en-daihoi13.dangcongsan.vn/congress-documents.
3. Vietnam+, "Strategy for Building Rule-of-Law."
4. "Party Central Committee Releases Announcement of Sixth Session."
5. Pham Duy Nghia, "From Marx to Market."
6. CPV, "Resolution 08/NQ-TW," https://tulieuvankien.dangcongsan.vn/van-kien-tu-lieu-ve-dang/book/sach-chinh-tri/ve-can-bo-va-cong-tac-can-bo-trong-thoi-ky-doi-moi-trich-van-kien-dang-378.
7. Fu Hualing and Bui, "Diverging Trends in the Socialist Constitutionalism."
8. The Global Economy, "Trade Openness."
9. WTO Center, http://wtocenter.vn/fta.
10. WGI, https://info.worldbank.org/governance/wgi/.
11. Transparency International, "Corruption Perceptions Index 2020."
12. Human Rights Watch, *World Report 2022*.
13. Nguyen Hai Hong, "Resilience of the Communist Party of Vietnam's Authoritarian Regime."
14. Hong Kong Nguyen, "Vietnam's Low-Cost COVID-19 Strategy."
15. Nguyen Trong Thua, "Assessment of Implementation of PAR Master Plan 2011–2020."
16. Government Resolution no. 30c/2011/NQ-CP, November 8, 2011.
17. See 2013 constitution, Article 2.
18. Ministry of Home Affairs, "Role of Government in Legislative Process."
19. Le Hiep, "6 năm thi hành Hiến pháp, Chính phủ vẫn 'nợ' luật về Hội, luật Biểu tình."
20. Libby, "The Art of Censorship in Vietnam," 209–28.
21. Article 6.2.a, Law on Professional Soldiers, Workers, and Servants in Armed Forces, November 26, 2015; Article 31.1, Law on People's Police, November 20, 2018; and Article 8.1, Law on Cadres and Public Servants, November 13, 2008, provide that army, police forces, and public servants must absolutely be loyal to the Party.
22. See Article 19, Para. 1, Law on Issuance of Normative Documents, June 22, 2015.
23. *Tuoi Tre*, November 17, 2020.
24. *Vietnam News*, July 1, 2016.
25. Hoang Quoc Viet, "Viec xay dung phap che xa hoi chu nghia va giao duc moi nguoi ton trong phap luat," 14.
26. Tran Ngoc Duong, "Continue Building the Socialist Rule-of-Law State."

27. Bui Ngoc Son, "Petition 72."
28. Dao Thi Xuan Lan, "Jurisdiction of Administrative Court over Land Disputes."
29. *Tạp chí Tòa án*, July 7, 2018.
30. Navigos Search Salary Report 2021, https://www.enworld.com.vn/blog/2019/03/jobseeker-salary-report-in-vietnam-in-2019.
31. *Tạp chí Tòa án*, September 5, 2019.
32. Nguyen Quang, "The Organization and Operation of Administrative Courts in Vietnam."
33. Resolution 49-NQ/TW, June 2, 2005.
34. *Vnexpress*, November 16, 2005; June 23, 2015.
35. *Vnexpress*, June 4, 2015.
36. *Vnexpress*, September 27, 2019.
37. *Báo Chính phủ*, November 15, 2018.
38. CPV Internal Affairs Committee, Decision 32/QD-TW, September 16, 2021, https://noichinh.vn/gioi-thieu/ban-chi-dao-tw-ve-phong-chong-tham-nhung/.
39. Tran Viet Dung, "New Administrative Procedural Rules."
40. Supreme People's Court Guideline No. 02/2018/QD-TANDTC, September 19, 2018, https://tapchitoaan.vn/bai-viet/phap-luat/giai-dap-15-vuong-mac-ve-to-tung-hanh-chinh.
41. Section 119.2 of the 2013 constitution.
42. Sections 60.2.d and 60.3 of the Law on Administrative Procedure, 2015.
43. Đoàn Thị Ngọc Hải. "Những vướng mắc, bất cập của Luật Tố tụng hành chính và hướng đề xuất hoàn thiện."
44. Section 157 of the Law on Administrative Procedure.
45. Sections 130–45 of the Law on Administrative Procedure.
46. Section 211 of the Law on Administrative Procedure.
47. *Vnexpress*, October 10, 2019.

References

Bui Ngoc Son. "Petition 72: The Struggle for Constitutional Reforms in Vietnam." *I-CONnect*, March 28, 2013. http://www.iconnectblog.com/2013/03/petition-72-the-struggle-for-constitutional-reforms-in-vietnam/.

Dao Thi Xuan Lan. "Jurisdiction of Administrative Court over Land Disputes." 2019. https://tapchitoaan.vn/bai-viet/nghien-cuu/ky-nang-giai-quyet-vu-an-hanh-chinh-trong-linh-vuc-quan-ly-nha-nuoc-ve-dat-dai.

Do Muoi. *Sua doi Hien phap xay dung Nha nuoc Phap Quyen Viet nam, Day manh su nghiep Doi moi* (Amending the constitution: Establishing a law-based-state and promoting Doi Moi achievements). Hanoi: Nha xuat ban Su that, 1992.

Đoàn Thị Ngọc Hải. "Những vướng mắc, bất cập của Luật Tố tụng hành chính và hướng đề xuất hoàn thiện." *Tạp chí Tòa án Nhân dân*, December 10, 2018. https://www.tapchitoaan.vn/bai-viet/phap-luat/nhung-vuong-mac-bat-cap-cua-luat-to-tung-hanh-chinh-va-huong-de-xuat-hoan-thien.

Fu Hualing and Jason Bui. "Diverging Trends in the Socialist Constitutionalism of the People's Republic of China and Socialist Republic of Vietnam." Paper delivered at the "What Is Socialist about Socialist Law? Exploring Epistemic and Institutional Change in Socialist Asia" Conference, University of Hong Kong, October 28–29, 2015. https://www.researchgate.net/publication/319585124_Diverging_Trends_in_the_Socialist_Constitutionalism_of_the_People's_Republic_of_China_and_Socialist_Republic_of_Vietnam.

Gillespie, John. "Understanding Legality in Vietnam." In *Vietnam's New Order: International Perspectives on the State and Reform in Vietnam*, edited by Stéphanie Balme and Mark Sidel. New York: Palgrave Macmillan, 2007.

The Global Economy. "Trade Openness—Country Rankings." 2021. https://www.theglobaleconomy.com/rankings/trade_openness/.

Hoang Quoc Viet. "Viec xay dung phap che xa hoi chu nghia va giao duc moi nguoi ton trong phap luat" (Building up socialist legality and educating people to respect laws). *Hoc Tap* (Study review) 16 (1962): 14.

Hong Kong Nguyen. "Vietnam's Low-Cost COVID-19 Strategy." *Project Syndicate*, April 8, 2020. https://www.project-syndicate.org/commentary/vietnam-low-cost-success-against-covid19-by-hong-kong-nguyen-2020-04?barrier=accesspaylog.

Human Rights Watch. *World Report 2022: Vietnam*. https://www.hrw.org/asia/vietnam.

Le Hiep, "6 năm thi hành Hiến pháp, Chính phủ vẫn 'nợ' luật về Hội, luật Biểu tình" (Six years of implementing the constitution, the government is still "debt" to the Law on Association and the Law on Demonstration). *Thanh Nien*, September 20, 2020. https://thanhnien.vn/thoi-su/6-nam-thi-hanh-hien-phap-chinh-phu-van-no-luat-ve-hoi-luat-bieu-tinh-1289149.html.

Libby, Samantha. "The Art of Censorship in Vietnam." *Journal of International Affairs* 65, no. 1 (Fall/Winter 2011): 209–18.

Ministry of Home Affairs. "Role of Government in Legislative Process." *MOHA Journal of State Management*, May 27, 2018. https://tcnn.vn/news/detail/40111/Vai_tro_trach_nhiem_cua_Chinh_phu_trong_viec_soan_thao_chinh_ly_hoan_thien_du_thao_luat_phapall.html.

Nguyen Hai Hong. "Resilience of the Communist Party of Vietnam's Authoritarian Regime since *Doi Moi*." *Journal of Current Southeast Asian Affairs* 35, no. 2 (2016): 31–55.

Nguyen Quang. "The Organization and Operation of Administrative Courts in Vietnam." In *Asia Examined: Proceedings of the 15th Biennial Conference of the ASAA, 2004, Canberra, Australia*, edited by Robert Cribb. https://webarchive.nla.gov.au/awa/20110214164008/http://pandora.nla.gov.au/pan/124461/20110211-1446/coombs.anu.edu.au/SpecialProj/ASAA/biennial-conference/2004/proceedings.html.

Nguyen Trong Thua. "Assessment of Implementation of PAR Master Plan 2011–2020." January 27, 2021. https://tcnn.vn/news/detail/49669/Ket-qua-10-nam-thuc-hien-Chuong-trinh-tong-the-cai-cach-hanh-chinh-nha-nuoc-giai-doan-2011-2020-va-dinh-huong-trong-thoi-gian-toi.html.

"Party Central Committee Releases Announcement of Sixth Session." *Nhan Dan*, October 10, 2022. https://en.nhandan.vn/party-central-committee-releases-announcement-of-sixth-session-post118702.html.

Pham Duy Nghia. "From Marx to Market: The Debates on the Economic System in Vietnam's Revised Constitution." *Asian Journal of Comparative Law* 11, no. 2 (December 2016): 263–85.

Than Quoc Hung. "Quality of Handling of Administrative Cases by the Court." 2018. https://hcma.vn/Uploads/2018/5/8/LA%20_%20Hung%20_cap%20HV_.pdf.

Tran Ngoc Duong. "Continue Building the Socialist Rule-of-Law State as the Focus of Renovation of the Political System in Light of the 13th CPV Party Congress." August 31, 2021. https://tcnn.vn/news/detail/51958/Tiep-tuc-xay-dung-Nha-nuoc-phap-quyen-xa-hoi-chu-nghia—nhiem-vu-trong-tam-cua-doi-moi-he-thong-chinh-tri-theo-tinh-than-Nghi-quyet-Dai-hoi-lan-thu-XIII-cua-Dang.html.

Tran Viet Dung. "New Administrative Procedural Rules: An Analysis from Judicial Reform Perspective." *Chonnam National University Law Review* 34, no. 1 (2014). https://papers.ssrn.com/sol3/papers.cfm?abstract_id=2435204.

Transparency International. "Corruption Perceptions Index 2020: Vietnam." 2021. https://www.transparency.org/en/cpi/2020/index/vnm.

United Nations. *E-Government Survey 2020: Digital Government in the Decade of Action for Sustainable Development*. New York: UN Department of Economic and Social Affairs, 2020. https://publicadministration.un.org/egovkb/Portals/egovkb/Documents/un/2020-Survey/2020%20UN%20E-Government%20Survey%20(Full%20Report).pdf.

Vietnam General Inspectorate. "Report of Vietnam General Inspectorate." November 14, 2018. http://baochinhphu.vn/Utilities/PrintView.aspx?distributionid=352065.

Vietnam Law and Legal Forum. "Building Rule-of-Law State to Better Serve People." July 4, 2021. https://vietnamlawmagazine.vn/building-rule-of-law-state-to-better-serve-people-president-37801.html.

Vietnam+. "Strategy for Building Rule-of-Law Socialist State Debated." August 26, 2021. https://en.vietnamplus.vn/strategy-for-building-ruleoflaw-socialist-state-debated/207035.vnp.

Wang, Maya. "China's Techno-Authoritarianism Has Gone Global." *Foreign Affairs*, April 8, 2021. https://www.foreignaffairs.com/articles/china/2021-04-08/chinas-techno-authoritarianism-has-gone-global.

World Bank. "Individuals Using the Internet (% of Population)—Vietnam." 2021. https://data.worldbank.org/indicator/IT.NET.USER.ZS?locations=VN.

World Bank and Ministry of Planning and Investment of Vietnam. *Vietnam 2035: Toward Prosperity, Creativity, Equity, and Democracy*. Washington, DC: World Bank, 2016. https://openknowledge.worldbank.org/handle/10986/23724.

CHAPTER 4

Coping with Contention

The Party-State and Political Opposition

Eva Hansson

In recent years, Vietnam has seen the rise of publicly expressed contention in the form of mass protest movements and the establishment of groups and organizations addressing a wide variety of political issues relating to human rights, democracy, corrupt officials, land grabbing, labor rights, women's rights, protection of the environment, social welfare, LGTBQ rights, the party-state's relations with China, and other issues. In the summer of 2018, massive nationwide demonstrations emerged against a proposed law on special economic zones (SEZ), which protesters claimed increased China's grip on Vietnam and allowed China to use Vietnam as its own backyard, and a cybersecurity law that increased party-state control over online content and social media users,[1] displaying the capacity and ability for nationwide mobilization and organization among ordinary citizens. In addition to their goal of targeting government policy, these protests had in common that their "issue-specific" claims were translated into broader debate and demands for accountability and transparency aspects of the party-state—in short, the legitimacy of the single-party regime. Vietnam's modernization has clearly produced new social forces that are increasingly claiming political space, and new ways of participating in politics. At the same time, the Party leadership under General Secretary Nguyễn Phú Trọng is on a crusade to save the Party and the political regime by attacking mass degeneration and corruption in the party-state apparatus. The recent corruption scandals have made it clear that the political regime for years has facilitated groups or individuals within the Party or their close affiliates to amass almost unimaginable fortunes, forming informal power centers within and around the political system. The many corruption scandals have provided the arguments for the general secretary to recentralize political power, emphasize programs of party-building, and strengthening Marxist-Leninisr and Ho Chi Minh ideology in all spheres of society (culture, media, education, civil service, judicial system, security police, army, etc.)—reminiscent of the power centralization, party-building, and ideology promotion program initiated by Xi Jinping in China from 2012. The major challenge in Vietnamese politics today is how the VCP will manage the rising claims for political representation and participation of ordinary citizens in today's profoundly pluralist society under its single-party regime. The solutions launched by the Party thus far include assigning the Fatherland Front and its organizations greater responsibilities for "social management," and absorbing criticism and points of view from citizens into the system through "invited spaces." But in a simultaneous move, the Party's aim is to cleanse itself of those with wrong views or ideologies, such as proponents of democratic reforms, civil society, or multipartyism, who could be suspected of having "self-transformed" or being victims of "self-evolution" and who may contribute to "peaceful evolution," leading to regime change.[2] While being a significant part of political life in the southern republic before 1975, large-scale public protests only reemerged in the 1990s among farmers protesting land grabbing and local corruption, and among workers against labor conditions in the new southern industrial zones following economic liberalization. Some of these protests were notably large in scale, gaining public attention through official media,[3] and causing concerns in sections of the Party, leading to the so-called "grassroots democracy decrees."[4]

These early farmers' and workers' protests displayed a significant lack of bridging between issue-specific groups and their particular grievances, and there was a lack of linkages between "elite dissidents" and ordinary protesters. Claims did not translate into more general demands for political change. This chapter argues that this reality has started to change. The repeated waves of labor strikes that led up to the massive "minimum wage strike" in 2005–6 have had the important consequence of normalizing public protests as a peaceful political expression. In addition, when some high-profile pro-democracy activists publicly expressed their support for striking workers, public links emerged between some pro-democracy activists and workers on the factory floors. A process of bridging between mainly well-educated middle-class civil society groups and ordinary people was reinforced through major consecutive waves of public protest movements in 2009, 2011, 2014, 2016, and 2018, resulting in emerging networks of activists across ideological boundaries and geographic space. Vietnam today is a profoundly pluralist society under a single-party regime, and a major challenge for the Party is how to manage rising claims for political representation of a pluralism of interests, ideologies, and ambitions among individuals and groups in society that have emerged with economic reforms. This chapter starts with a discussion of how labor protests propelled a process of bridging between some civil society groups, activists, and movements, and then proceeds to discuss the formal possibilities of political opposition.

Political Opposition and Political Unity

Vietnam has a long history of social movements and of individual and collective protest, often formed in response to unjust rule, rights, or in opposition to government policy. In a context where political unity is officially saluted over everything else, the term "political opposition" is considered wrong and unlawful by the Party. Indeed, much of the recent party-building policy of the VCP has targeted political opposition inside the Party. For observers of Vietnamese politics, however, it is clear that the party-state has long harbored multiple opinions on various policies and issues, indicating different ideologies embraced by various individuals and more or less organized groups of insiders. Sometimes prominent Party members have joined a "policy opposition," such as when national hero General Võ Nguyên Giáp joined the bauxite protests by writing several letters criticizing Party policy toward China.[5] These are in general individual acts of political opposition, although networks of "insiders" have emerged in recent years, and long-serving Party members have collectively published public petitions for political change, as will be discussed below. But political actors outside the party-state's institutional frameworks are also pushing their agendas and political interests. Studies of political opposition have mainly focused on the formal political sphere in established democracies, or in semi-democracies. The informal politics of opposition in authoritarian single-party regimes such as the Vietnamese is much less understood. Political space and oppositional politics in Vietnam include actors emerging both from civil society and from party-state institutions, operating across a formal-informal divide, a reason why a traditional liberal shorthand of state-civil society relations fits the Vietnamese political realities on the ground poorly.[6] During the last two decades, informal political actors, sometimes in conjunction with party-state insiders,[7] have pushed to define and expand their political space. This process began in important ways with the early labor protests.

Labor Strikes and the Opening of Political Space: Normalization of Public Protest and the Formation of a Democratic Opposition

The first labor protests after economic liberalization started took place in the FDI-oriented industries in the south. The number of strikes per year from the early reform years until the end of the 1990s was generally fairly low, which perhaps also indicated the slowness of the process of attracting foreign investments to the EPZs in the early reform years. When they occurred, strikes were often against low wages, long working hours, or other Dickensian labor conditions. In these first years, strikes tended to be small-scale and to last for a very limited period of time. According to official statistics, strikes occurred mainly in three southern provinces: Đồng Nai, Bình Dương, and the greater Ho Chi Minh City area, the sites of most foreign investment and with a long history of intense labor struggles among a pluralism of trade union organizations before unification. Although all the strikes emerging in the zones were technically illegal,[8] the state's response was generally benevolent, although patronizing in its attitude toward the protesters. Officials often stated that the workers did not understand the law and that strikes broke out because of cultural misunderstandings between foreign managers and Vietnamese workers, and not because of the diverging interests caused by the reintroduction of capitalism. At this stage the Party never saw such protests as a threat. On the contrary, the Party and the official trade union often referred in official media, including the newspapers run by the official trade union, to their role in protecting workers who were in the hands of abusive foreign managers. Nor did a clear ideological cleavage develop at the top Party level, as was the case in China, where a "new left" developed among Party elites who publicly supported the workers' and farmers' plight in the new economic conditions.

A change in the party-state's attitude toward protests followed the 2005–6 strike wave over minimum wages. The strikes were massive in scale, drawing hundreds of thousands of protesters.[9] In 2006 alone, an estimated 350,000 people were involved in labor protests. The Party increasingly saw them as threatening to social and political order. In contrast to previous protests, the strikes were now fairly well-organized, much larger in scale, and spread from the southern industrial hub to the north, and from the FDI sector to other economic sectors, including to state-owned enterprises (SOEs).[10] And, importantly, strikes were increasingly expressions of struggle over "interests," beyond what the law stipulated.[11] When the state's responses became more confrontational, the strikes also turned violent, with protesters destroying property and reportedly attacking trade union and Fatherland Front officials when they came to strike sites to try to negotiate with managers and workers to persuade them to get back to work.

Strikes were by then no longer exclusively a "southern problem." Nor could they be seen as a problem related purely to working conditions and foreign bosses with different cultural values, as Party and trade union officials had claimed in the early reform years. In the face of rising inequality and human rights atrocities in the factories in the southern provinces, citizens found few formal possibilities to influence their situation and policies through any existing political institutions. It is reasonable to argue that the southern labor protests were closely related to the failure of attempts to revitalize the political system and institutions of political representation, especially the role of the party-led trade union, VGCL, which still refused to take a lead in the strikes or to officially take sides with the striking workers against employers or politicians. The Party started to interpret strikes as a threat to national unity and, thus, increasingly as a problem of national security. The "people's security" responded with several different measures, for example, by placing "spies" in workers' dormitories, with the task of reporting on any suspicious activity on the part of workers, in an attempt to prevent conflicts from turning into strikes.[12] Another approach was captured in the phrase to "reconnect to the masses," through different policies supposedly addressing inequality and programs to "revitalize" representative institutions such as the National Assembly and the mass organizations of the Fatherland Front, but it proved to be difficult.

Some high-profile pro-democracy activists, such as the Buddhist activist Thích Quảng Độ, came out in public support of the workers and published a nine-point demand including demands for freedom of association and the right to form unions independent of the Party. Others started to set up organizations to assist workers in legal matters, or to advocate for labor rights. The strikes opened up political space for other forms of protest by normalizing public protests as a political expression, but they also opened up links between some pro-democracy groups, activists, and popular protesters.

In a parallel development with the strikes, Vietnam saw the development of a lively sphere of political blogs. Several pro-democracy groups openly publicized parties, and two independent trade unions formed with the stated aim to "protect and promote workers' rights, including the right to form and join unions without government interference

[and] for justice for people whose land had been confiscated by government officials, and for the end of dangerous working conditions."[13] After petitioning the Tenth Party Congress in February 2006, Nguyễn Tiến Trung, a young student at the time, initiated the Assembly of Vietnamese Youth for Democracy (Tập hợp Thanh niên Dân chủ) in May.[14] A central pro-democracy activist was lawyer Lê Công Định, who later came to defend several of the activists, who emerged during this period, in court. In October of the same year, the first independent labor union, the International Workers Union (IWUV; Công đoàn độc lập Việt Nam), was formed, and only ten days later the United Workers-Farmers Organization (UWFO; Hiệp Hội Đoàn Kết Công Nông) was established. Their stated aim was to "protect and promote workers' rights, including the right to join unions without government interference." The latter organization also called for justice for people whose land had been confiscated by government officials, and for an end to exploitative cheap labor and dangerous working conditions. The UWFO publicly announced they had been behind the organization of the 2006 labor protests. Between April and October 2006, a number of other pro-democracy petitions, organizations, and political parties were announced, among which the most well-known was Bloc 8406. In Hanoi, lawyer Nguyễn Văn Đài and his colleague Lê Thị Công Nhân formed the small group Committee for Human Rights in Vietnam, with the aim of spreading education about human rights and democracy to a wider audience, operating out of Văn Đài's law office in Hanoi. Bloc 8406, initiated by Roman Catholic priest Nguyễn Văn Lý, published a manifesto on the Internet, "Manifesto 2006 for Freedom and Democracy," followed by the establishment of a political party called Vietnam Progressive Party (Đảng Thăng Tiến Việt Nam), for which he was sentenced to eight years in prison a year later. Some dissidents supported the workers' strikes, both abroad and in Vietnam. Referring mainly to Bloc 8406, Carlyle Thayer has described the period as one in which "pro-democracy groups began to coalesce into an identifiable movement."[15] Also in hindsight, the observation by Thayer at the time appears plausible. It was, in fact, a turning point for public expressions of pro-democracy sentiments and public expression of opposition. However, it could not have turned into a "critical juncture" at the time, because the forces were just too fragile, organizations were too limited, and they gained little support from the official political sphere or from international actors.

In political blogs, all types of criticism were launched, including criticism of what was perceived as the Party's lenient position against an all the more powerful China that was seen as increasingly transgressing Vietnam's sovereignty. China was even accused in blogs of colluding with Vietnamese Party leaders in a plan to mine for bauxite in Vietnam's Central Highlands. The public uproar caused by these plans was reinforced by the actions of the ninety-seven-year-old revolutionary war hero, General Võ Nguyên Giáp, who spoke up against the potential harm to the environment by the Chinese bauxite mining in Vietnam.

But there were important factors that diminished the power of this nascent movement. Although not exclusively so, many of the organizations emerged in the south, and the importance of religion among southern political organizations and activists was one such factor. Despite the wide variation of actors and backgrounds of those who joined

Bloc 8406, the emerging democracy movement was fragmented. There was more bonding within each of the new organizations than bridging between them. In general, the Catholics had their "democracy heroes," and the Buddhists had theirs. For some of the political activists, their struggle for democracy had even started with demands for religious freedom and refusal to join the church organizations initiated and controlled by the Party. A further dividing characteristic was that the vocal democracy activists often belonged to a well-educated professional middle class who, together with other Vietnamese elites such as most members of the Communist Party, shared few experiences of the conditions of the majority of the population, including in the industrial zones right outside their city. Nevertheless, the massive protest among workers in the zones and among farmers who lost their land, taking to the streets to protest corruption among local party leaders and officials, affected the way activists perceived their opportunities. The developments in these fairly separated fields of activism coincided and expanded political space, and the networking around emerging protest activities was to start bridging differences between them, especially between the different religions.

There are several possible reasons why the 2005–6 movement was allowed to form and was not met by harder repression at an earlier stage of its development. First of all, it must be said that we know little about the internal discussions within the Party and how different important factions viewed the developments. It is not at all unlikely that some sections of Party members actually supported the demands, not only by the workers in the zones but also the wider political demands by democracy activists. Second, the party-state has proved to be sensitive to international criticism against the status of civil, political, and human rights, and in this period there were two important international events occurring in parallel with the above-described developments, which were seen as bringing Vietnam into the international spotlight. In November 2006, Vietnam was hosting an APEC meeting in Hanoi, and the government was also in the process of closing negotiations over Vietnam's WTO membership. Just before and during the APEC summit, some of the democracy activists were hindered from leaving their houses.[16] Signs were placed outside their homes reading "no foreigners" and displaying a crossed-over camera. After twelve years of negotiations, the WTO negotiations were expected to be finalized at a meeting on October 26. The negotiations had brought human rights issues to the table and, according to a document from the Ministry of Labor (MoLisa), there were pressures on Vietnam from international actors to legalize and permit trade unions and other independent labor organizations, as well as demands relating to freedom of association in general. According to the MoLisa document, Vietnam "strongly opposed these demands" and saw the demands for freedom of association and the right to form independent trade unions as tools for international actors to press for change in the political regime. Their position against allowing autonomous trade unions was very clear: "some countries require us to allow free labor unions that are independent of the Vietnam General Confederation of Labor. This is absolutely against the Labor Union Law of Vietnam."[17] It is perhaps too strong to say that security forces had their hands tied behind their backs, but at least these international developments certainly affected the way pro-democracy actors perceived their opportunities—many saw it as improbable that repression against peaceful democracy and human rights activists would occur in front of an open international scene.

At the national level, the Tenth Party Congress was organized in April the same year. The Congress marked twenty years of economic liberalization, and many reports were distributed through media and discussed in public that evaluated achievements of the Party. But the Congress was embarrassingly overshadowed by a huge corruption scandal centered in the Ministry of Transportation, where a management unit called PMU18, led by the deputy minister of transportation and Party Central Committee member, was accused of spending around US$7 million of the unit's budget—government funds and funds from international donors for construction and infrastructure projects—on gambling on European soccer matches. New details were published by news media almost on a daily basis.[18] Political bloggers delved into the details of the story and openly discussed the possibility that the PMU18 affair went all the way up to the office of the prime minister, or the possibility that the revelation was orchestrated by one faction of the Party in an attempt to tarnish the reputation of another. The Party Congress did not issue any statements that indicated a desire for dialogue with labour protesters and the organizers of political groups. The focus in national media was instead on the Party's decision to formalize the right of Party members to operate private businesses and to allow "capitalists" to join the Party. It was after the government's completion of the WTO negotiations and the APEC meeting in Hanoi that a concerted crackdown by public security forces came, and in a matter of months most leaders of the organizations that were established in 2005–6 had been detained and were later prosecuted in courts over different charges relating to national security.

Activists and leaders of Bloc 8406, the UWFO, the Committee for Human Rights in Vietnam, and others who were suspected of being in leading positions of the new organizations were arrested. In a period of just four days, between November 14 and 18, at least six persons directly involved in the leadership of the UWFO were arrested in the Ho Chi Minh City area and adjacent Đồng Nai Province. One of the arrested labor activists was accused of "joining reactionary organizations through the Internet" and that "under the disguise of helping members of the public to lodge petitions, he and his accomplices incited demonstrations and posted distorted articles on the Internet,"[19] and was sentenced to five years in prison plus two years of house arrest for the union activities.[20] Nguyễn Văn Lý, the founder of Bloc 8406, was arrested and later sentenced to eight years in prison for "carrying out propaganda against the Socialist Republic of Vietnam." Once the trials of protest leaders and dissidents commenced, others were targeted too, such as lawyers and journalists of large newspapers (or their editors) who reported on corruption scandals; they were reprimanded or lost their jobs. There soon followed an attempt to tighten the grip over media, social media and blogs, cinema, theater and cultural activities, and even social science research[21]—over most independent sources of opinion.

The repression of the still fragile and very limited rights and justice movement was temporarily successful. The events around 2005–7, however, combined into a turning point for political activism. There was a strengthening of civil society control through new laws and decrees and the party's repeated encouragements to increase political, cultural, and ideological security. This involved all party-state organizations, including the mass organizations, media, higher education, and the security forces, in the fight against every expression of "peaceful evolution" caused by "evil forces and reactionaries" who "abuse their democratic rights to oppose the Party and state." The Party's suggested policies to revitalize representative institutions proved unsuccessful. In the aftermath of the minimum wage strike, the then-chairman of the Central Committee of the Fatherland Front, Phạm Thế Duyệt, admitted that the Central Committee of the Party had issued a number of policies to reconnect the party to the masses, "yet it has been difficult to persuade people to join relevant organizations."[22] The new informal groups and organizations that had emerged were not supported by the mass organizations, but were rather seen as illegitimate competitors or as troublemakers. But public protest and demonstrations from then on became normalized as political activities, and, a few years later, new protest movements would expand and tie networks of activists and groups a bit closer together.

Layers upon Layers of Activism

With the arrest of leaders of the new organizations, oppositional politics were temporarily shut down, but protests and oppositional political activities were soon to reemerge. The years 2011 and 2012 were particularly intensive, with several land-grabbing conflicts leading to the use of violence both by the state and by protesters protecting their land. At a National Security Conference in December 2012, the then Prime Minister Nguyễn Tấn Dũng warned that under no circumstances should opposition groups be allowed to take root in Vietnam, and he encouraged the police to fight such attempts by all available means.

This strict message may have appeared confusing to some because, at the same time, the Party had opened up a process for feedback in which citizens were invited to comment and give suggestions in the process of revising the 1992 constitution. The chairman of the National Assembly claimed that during the three months' feedback period, more than 30,000 meetings had resulted in 20 million comments from citizens.[23] But the response to the invitation included a group of seventy-two senior intellectuals who submitted their comments in a petition delivered to the National Assembly by constitutional law scholar and former minister of justice Dr. Nguyễn Đình Lộc in front of state media.[24] In "Petition 72" (*Kiến nghị 72*) they called for fundamental reforms of the political regime, including multiparty democracy and abolition of Article 4 of the constitution, which stipulates the Party's leading role over state and society. They insisted further that the armed forces should protect the country and the people rather than a political party and its regime. Within a couple of weeks of being posted on the Internet, the petition had allegedly garnered thousands of signatories and triggered discussions in web forums and elsewhere. Although the suggestions by the group of petitioners were not heeded, the petition contributed to adding yet another layer of activism.

Other new and soon-to-be influential political civil society groups were formed in the coming months,[25] including the Brotherhood for Democracy (Hội anh em dân chủ), a loose association of activists and human rights defenders with the aim of bringing together a broad coalition of forces across the country for peaceful democratic change, founded by human rights lawyer and former political prisoner Nguyễn Văn Đài. Later the same year a number of civil society organizations announced the formation of the Civil Society Forum (Diễn đàn Xã hội Dân sự) with the stated purpose to "exchange and gather opinions aimed at contributing to the transformation of our country's political regime from totalitarian to peaceful democratization."[26] The Vietnam Women for Human Rights (Hội phụ nữ nhân quyền), the Network of Vietnamese Bloggers (Mạng Lưới Blogger Việt Nam), and in 2014 the Vietnam Association of Independent Journalists (Hội Nhà báo Độc lập Việt Nam) were formed with the intent to promote independent journalism and policy debate in the country.

Between 2012 and 2015, several of the key actors who had contributed to the opening of political space in the important years 2005 and 2006 were released from prison.[27] Most of these high-profile activists were under house arrest after their release, which is more or less a normal procedure for democracy and rights activists convicted in accordance with articles of the criminal code related to regime security issues. Upon their release from prison, a new generation of civil society organizations and groups had appeared. When new protests were to rock parts of the country in the coming years, old and new networks became increasingly interconnected.

The 2014 "anti-China demonstrations" were preceded by anti-China sentiments in 2006 after the government signed a contract with a Chinese SOE to extract and refine bauxite in the Central Highlands, a highly controversial project because of its risk of contaminating regional waterways that could have disastrous environmental effects, and because of the Chinese participation in the project. This step by the government prompted opposition voices to form into groups and networks, both online and offline (in what later has been regarded as a starting point of Vietnam's environmental movement). The immediate opposition came from a variety of sources, and for some of them the bauxite problem could not be seen in isolation from a wider political agenda, including the legitimacy of the single-party regime. As with several other burning political issues, the opposition to the bauxite plans served to knit more tightly a national network of activism.

The blog *Bauxite Vietnam* emerged from this movement, started as a forum to discuss and publish criticism against the party-state's bauxite mining policy, but it soon developed into a very influential site among intellectuals and the general public to discuss all types of political problems, including corruption among Party and state leaders, as well as different policy areas such as health care, education, foreign affairs, the environment, and democratization.[28]

Protests gained new steam in the summer of 2011 with low-key "Sunday marches," only to explode into massive protests in several cities across the country in 2014, after China had moved an oil rig into disputed waters in the South China Sea. Tens of thousands then took to the streets, primarily in the southern provinces of Bình Dương, Đồng Nai, and the greater Hồ Chí Minh City area. These protests have generally been interpreted as anti-Chinese, but they had their roots in several issue areas, and the reason they could evolve so quickly can be explained by the organizational networks between individuals, organizations, and groups that had evolved in the industrial zones in the area for years. Despite the view propagated through official Vietnamese media of protests as "spontaneous reactions," these protests did not emerge out of the blue. The "anti-China protests" had the typical wave-like development that they share with other protests, with a more or less decisive starting point after a certain decision or event, leading to formal complaints or petitions handed over to authorities at central or local levels, and taking off after the absence of reaction by authorities.

Protests also spread to other parts of the country. In Hà Tĩnh Province, where workers were aggravated by a contractor that had allegedly brought Chinese workers to build a new steel plant for Taiwan's Formosa Group, they turned particularly dramatic. Two years later, the same steel plant would form the context for a major environmental disaster caused by the Formosa factory. Under the slogan "I choose fish," demonstrators accused party-state officials of turning a blind eye to polluters and corruption, and of choosing economic growth at the expense of environmental destruction. In some protesters' view, the massive environmental disaster in which two hundred kilometers of the coast was flushed with millions of tons of dead fish[29] was caused by a corrupt and nontransparent political system without sufficient accountability mechanisms and institutional limits to political power, which allowed impunity and power abuse to flourish.

On March 26, 2015, protesters were back on the streets in the south. An estimated 90,000 workers took to the streets outside Hồ Chí Minh City to protest a new social security bill that would change the rules and procedures relating to payments of their earned pensions. The local People's Committee invited the deputy minister of labor to meet with media to "provide information related to the new article to help workers better understand it." The deputy minister said workers had "gone on strike as they have not fully grasped Article 60" and added that the changes to the social security bill were in fact "a positive move to ensure the interest of laborers."[30] The protesting workers disagreed and protests continued,[31] blocking the main road connecting Ho Chi Minh City industries to the rest of the country. Workers' protests quickly spread to nearby Bình Dương Province. To get protesters off the streets, Prime Minister Nguyễn Tấn Dũng had to withdraw the proposal and announce that the policy would be redrafted. Only after "competent agencies" had promised to meet protesters' claims did they move away from the streets. Some Vietnam scholars contended that the Party had underestimated the force behind protests.[32] The same month, the "Green Trees Movement" burst out in Hanoi after the city administration decided to cut down 6,708 old trees in 190 streets across the capital. A well-organized, broad-based movement utilized an "interplay of formal and informal channels, strategizing the online activism coupled with real-life demonstrations."[33] Several well-known pro-democracy activists participated in the protests,[34] such as author and journalist Phạm Đoan Trang, known for authoring books such as *Chính Trị Bình Dân* (Politics for the masses, 2017) and *Phản kháng phi bạo lực* (Nonviolent resistance, 2019), a handbook for political prisoners, cofounder of the Nhà xuất bản Tự do (Freedom Publishing House), and cofounder of the web journal *Luật Khoa Tạp Chí*, a journal dedicated to law, politics, and human rights. In December 2021 she was sentenced to nine years in prison for opposing the Party and state.[35]

These episodes of protest suggested that a new pattern of public protest was taking form, differing from that of the past when claims were mainly directed against factory managers who were not complying with laws, labor conditions, or wages. Unlike previous patterns, the social security protests and the Green Trees Movement directly targeted the government, the procedures of political decision making, and included the direct involvement of civil society groups and networks of activists engaged in several of the protests. This pattern continued in the summer of 2018, when massive nationwide demonstrations emerged against a proposed Law on Special Economic Zones (SEZ), which protesters claimed increased China's grip on Vietnam and allowed China to use Vietnam as its own backyard, and against a proposed cybersecurity law that would increase party-state control over online content and social media users.[36]

In addition to their goal of targeting government policy, the protests had in common that issue-specific claims were translated into broader political debate. The early labor protests had brought contention out in the open and were in that way a departure from the previous "everyday politics" through which citizens challenged policies, norms, and rules by more hidden and subtle acts.[37] The social security, Formosa, SEZ, cybersecurity, anti-China, and Green Trees demonstrations were, in contrast, directly targeting national party-state policy and politics. They were better organized through networks of individuals and civil society groups and organizations—and the protests themselves also brought networks and activists closer together.

Despite the rather successful Party strategy to limit political opposition, in particular of pro-democracy organizations, by strategies aiming to sow division among civil society groups on the one hand, and between the pro-democracy "loyal opposition" within the Party and in civil society on the other, political space and the democracy movement have continued to expand, slowly and step by step. Despite repressive actions against political opposition and pro-democracy groups that from time to time disable their public activities, it is clear that people's very experience of acting as citizens has changed the disposition of protesters themselves. There is today much less fear among key activists, despite long prison sentences handed down to activists by courts as well as harassment by security. Another change, in contrast to earlier, is the development of solidarity networks among activists and political prisoners, as evidenced by the gathering of activists and supporters outside courts hearings, the collection of money for families when an activist is imprisoned, and the large gatherings at dissidents' funerals. There is today also a network of lawyers who are prepared to defend activists in courts, despite the professional risks involved.

The scale of public demonstrations has changed from small-scale local protests to large mass protests involving a wide variety of actors. The old image of the lonely intellectual dissident speaking out against specific party policies, or for increased democracy and human rights, has been replaced by a new generation of political opposition, with the aim of organizing collectively to pursue their political goals. In contrast to the spontaneous protests emerging in the southern industrial zones in the early reform years, demonstrations are today well-organized, using on- and off-line mobilization. The previous bonding within a specific identity group has been complemented by bridging between organizations and networks. Despite these changes in oppositional and pro-democracy politics, the democracy movement still suffers from weaknesses and fragmentation caused in part by successful repression, the Party's denial of public dialogue with political opposition, and the lack of substantial support by international actors.

The solutions launched by the Party thus far to counter this trend include assigning the Fatherland Front and its sociopolitical mass organizations greater responsibilities for "social management," and absorbing criticism and points of views from citizens into the system. In a simultaneous move, the Party is aiming to purge itself of members with "wrong" political views and ideologies, who could be suspected of having "self-transformed" or of being victims of "self-evolution" and who could contribute to peaceful evolution or to the formation of a color revolution.[38] At least formally, this program amounts to a classical party rectification campaign and has already removed many high-profile intellectuals from the Party. So what are the formal possibilities for political participation and political opposition in today's Vietnam? The following section will address the party-state institutional framework.

Possibilities for Formal Political Participation, Representation, and Opposition

The state plays a major role in setting limits for political expression in civil society and the public sphere through institutions, laws, and regulations,[39] and through its form of policing of these arenas. These institutional structures and power relations in society encourage or discourage the formation of certain collective actors in society. An analysis of opposition politics therefore requires an analysis of the organization of the political regime, its coercive institutions, and the legal space for expressions of political opposition and organization in civil society.

In political science terminology, Vietnam would be defined as a consolidated, single-party regime led by the Vietnamese Communist Party (VCP), since the mid-1950s in the north and since reunification of the entire country in 1975–76. Inspired by Leninist organizational principles, Vietnam has parallel structures of state and Party at all levels of administration, from the central level down to the ward level, echoed in the organizations of the Vietnamese Fatherland Front and the state security forces.

The regime is said to be guided by principles of "democratic centralism," where lower levels of the system do not seek their authority and legitimacy primarily from citizens, but respond to the immediately higher level of organization. Democratic centralism has reemerged as an important theme in Party documents and propaganda in recent years, as evidenced, for example, by the frequent use of the term in legitimizing disciplinary action taken by the Party against high-level officials and leaders in the ongoing purge of Party cadres aiming at cleansing the Party of corruption, self-evolutionary tendencies, and other political problems.[40] In Party discourse, democratic centralism promotes democracy and unifies the will and action of the Party, while aiming to ensure the unitary power of the Party over the state and over society. Article 9 of the Party charter requires that all Party members and organizations at all levels must strictly adhere to the principle of democratic centralism. In theory, it means that within the Party, "individuals must submit to the organization, subordinates to superiors, localities to the Central Committee," and so on.[41]

Although the principle of democratic centralism and its implementation have been vividly discussed in Party media, policy, and research in recent years, it has rarely been addressed outside of the Party. Democracy activists and groups tend to see democratic centralism as irrelevant because it is a component of an accountability system that excludes the role of ordinary citizens, and instead tends to centralize political power and decisions in the hands of a few. While democratic centralism is not publicly questioned per se in Party circles, debate has arisen over problems related to its lack of "correct implementation." Lê Hồng Tiến of the Ho Chi Minh Political Academy, for instance, argues that it is shortcomings in implementation that have led some political leaders to take advantage of the principle. Through deceit and bribery, they have managed "to serve personal interest, create factionalism, that is affecting leadership capacity, fighting strength, the role and prestige of the Party, reducing people's confidence in the Party, threatening development and the survival of the Party." Indeed, Tiến warns that problems with an incorrect implementation of democratic centralism led to the dissolution of the Soviet Union and the Soviet Communist Party, which should serve as a lesson for the Party.

The party-state's institutional origin is traced back to Leninist ideas on the creation of a dictatorship of the proletariat and the establishment of a revolutionary "vanguard party." Even after thirty years of capitalist reforms, the Party officially embraces the idea of a required unity in political power, and thus a necessity to reject any separation of powers (in democracies, typically thought of as a separation between legislative, judicial, and executive powers). Any ideas or reforms that risk destroying the unity in political power under Party leadership, such as an independent judiciary, are strongly rejected. Recent policy programs are instead aiming to increase the efficiency of party leadership of the police, the army, the judiciary, media, and other organizations. Several recent decrees, regulations, and articles in Party and police press view demands and ideas of separation of powers as signs of self-evolution, self-transformation, even part of a process of peaceful transformation pushed by external or internal "hostile forces."

Along with claims for multiparty democracy, separation of powers, depoliticization of the police and army, and promoting civil society are now considered among "things that Party members cannot do."[42] Resolution 04-NQ/TW, October 30, 2016, in turn, specifies twenty-seven manifestations of ideological degeneration and expressions of internal self-evolution and self-transformation, divided into three groups of "degeneration of thoughts" in politics, morality/lifestyle, and expressions of self-transformation. Expressions of self-evolution and self-transformation would include opposing or denying of Marxism-Leninism and Hồ Chí Minh Thought and the Party's organizational principles, especially the principle of democratic centralism. In addition, the resolution includes demanding pluralism or a multiparty system; opposing and denying socialist democracy and the socialist rule of law state; demanding the implementation of separation of powers between the executive, judicial, and legislative powers; and the development of "civil society" (*xã hội dân sự*) among the views that may not be propagated or embraced by Party members.[43] This resolution was a response to the emergence of a substantial (loyal) political opposition within Party ranks, and as such it precludes possibilities for policy or political opposition related to decisions and policies of the party or the development of the political regime. In the preface to the resolution, it is emphasized that the wise leadership of the Party in the reform period had been no less than fantastic, "a miracle in the 20th century," winning victory after victory. According to the resolution, party building had created positive changes in the political system as the process of self-criticism and criticism had contributed to combating "wrong thoughts and behaviors" and had contributed to combating, preventing, and repelling the ideological regression to actively fight against the "peaceful evolution of hostile forces." Despite these gains, it is stated that there are continued problems with "the content of party activities," which in many places were "monotonous" and low in efficiency. The leadership and fighting power of many party organizations were low; even in some places the fighting power was lost. The resolution continues, concluding that the "deterioration of political ideology, morality, and lifestyle of a large part of cadres and Party members have not been pushed back," and that "internal conflicts and disunity are not only at the grassroots level, but also in a number of central agencies, economic groups, and corporations," and "many Party organizations and Party members still have limited awareness, neglect, or are not alert or are confused in identifying and fighting 'self-evolution' and 'self-transformation.'" For many in the pro-democracy movement in Vietnam and among Party members who see the urgent need to move away from "totalitarianism" (which is the term used among several pro-democracy actors today, especially among the senior generation of retired Party members who have entered the public sphere with voices for democratization of the political regime), Resolution 4 precludes opposition and also puts many of the Party's "loyal" opposition out in the cold.

There are several examples, but probably the case that caused the most public resentment was when public intellectual Professor Chu Hảo, former deputy minister of science and technology, then-editor-in-chief of the Knowledge Publishing House, was publicly expelled from the Party for self-transformation and self-evolution.[44] According to Party media, from 2005 to 2018 Professor Chu Hảo "let the Knowledge Publishing House publish 29 books with wrong content," among which were a "number of books with complicated and sensitive contents and contents contrary to the views, policies, and guidelines of the Party and state, violating the Law on Publications, and handled and collected by competent authorities for destruction." He had further, from 2011 to 2018, "participated in signing, and directly drafting seven proposals and open letters with content that was not correct, inappropriate, and contrary to the Party's and the state's lines and point of view, allowing bad elements to take advantage of and distort the truth and affect the prestige of the leadership of the Party and state."[45] According to the People's Army newspaper, there were also:

> articles and speeches contrary to the Party platform, the Party charter, resolutions, directives, and regulations [that] had affected public opinion in an adverse way by demanding the implementation of pluralism, a multiparty system, separation of powers, development of

civil society; speaking, writing contrary to the Party's views and lines, the state's policies and laws; downplaying and denying revolutionary achievements; exaggerating defects of the Party and state; denying the Party's leadership of the press, literature, and arts; promoting extremist democratic views and ideas exaggerating the downside of society; composing and promoting cultural and art works that are misleading, distorting history and degrading the Party's prestige.[46]

The website of the Party Central Inspection explained why it was necessary to expel Chu Hảo from the Party, despite the fact that he resigned from the Party before being formally excluded. The Central Inspection explains that his violation was of "such serious nature," and that he had violated Decree 102-QD/TW of November 15, 2017, of the Politburo on disciplinary punishment for Party members violating regulations (violation of political views and internal politics of the Party), and he had, according to the Inspection, been reviewed many times for these problems, which had further aggravated his situation. Through his political views and publication of books with wrong views, he had displayed "acts of opposition."[47] Two weeks before being disciplined, Professor Chu Hảo renounced the Communist Party in a letter and announced his continued commitment to "improving people's knowledge in the spirit of . . . Nationalism, Democracy, and Development through cultural and educational activities."[48] Cases like that of Chu Hảo push political opposition out of the Party and alienate the loyal opposition that does not primarily aim for profound change of the political regime, as was indicated by the spate of public resignations from the Party by several previously loyal members who chose to exit in protest against the treatment of Chu Hảo.

Institutions for Formal Political Representation: The Sociopolitical Organizations, the Fatherland Front, and the National Assembly

The mass organizations, or sociopolitical organizations, are formally assigned the role of serving as the link between the Party and the people. Organized under the Vietnamese Fatherland Front (VFF), they are constituent components of the party-state and are under the leadership of the Party. Officially, they monopolize the organization and political representation of important political interests in society, such as women, labor, youth, farmers, and war veterans, but are also expected to proactively participate in the fight against so-called "hostile forces" and their "schemes for peaceful evolution" that are "using the cover of 'democracy' and 'human rights' to change our country's political regime."[49] In total, Vietnam has seventeen mass organizations, the most important ones organized from the grassroots level up to the central level. The largest and politically most important organizations are the so-called sociopolitical organizations, which include many millions of members. According to official statistics, the Vietnam Women's Union, for instance, claimed a membership base of 51 percent of all women in Vietnam over eighteen years old, or 13 million members in 2013.[50] The Vietnam General Confederation of Labor (VGCL), the party-state trade union organization, had, according to its own reports, a membership of around 10 million in 2019. In each of the mass organizations, at various levels of the organization, there is a Party committee that decides on important organizational issues, leadership positions, and communication of Party lines and policies. In the ongoing party-building program, the role of the Party in the mass organizations is to be strengthened rather than giving the organizations a more independent role.

The most important and largest of the mass organizations, such as the VGCL and the Women's Union, have formal roles in the political system. In accordance with procedural rules, these organizations are responsible for popular representation, mass mobilization, implementation of policies, dissemination of Party lines and propaganda, as well as taking part in surveillance of possible threats to security and social order threatening the Party or the political regime.

According to analyses by the Party leadership, the mass organizations of the Front have lost much of their credibility. In opening the Eighth National Congress of the VFF in 2014, the general secretary of the VCP commended the work of the VFF and its member organizations for their proactive dissemination of and mobilization around the Party's guidelines, state policies, and laws. But their role in Vietnam post–Đổi Mới has been sidelined and they have, according to the general secretary, long suffered from a lack of legitimacy from below because of their inability to represent their own constituencies. These problems have, as far as this author is aware, been recognized by the Party at least since the mid-1990s. The general secretary clarified in his speech in 2014:

> [F]rankly speaking, there have been constraints and restrictions in the Front's work. Methods of mobilization and rally of force have not been on par with new requirements; the Front has not yet had coordinating mechanisms and not coordinated regularly with member organizations to understand and reflect people's thinking and aspirations; campaigns and emulation movements in some places have been nominal and not effective: the role as representative, protector of legitimate interests of the people, supervision, and social criticism has been limited.[51]

This does not mean that reformist forces do not exist within the sociopolitical organizations. At least from the end of the 1990s there were individuals in the central organization on the VGCL, for example, who expressed such views in interviews with the author. According to them, the organization needed a more independent role in relation to the Party and the state, and legal possibilities to play the role of representatives of their constituency in a more obvious way. While it is impossible to assess how common such a view was, or is, in the organization, one can conclude that the development has not moved in such a direction for the past twenty-five years.

Article 4 of the constitution is central to an understanding of political representation and the organization of the political regime. It stipulates the dominating role of the Vietnamese Communist Party (VCP) over all political and social institutions of the state and society. Although there have been attempts to separate the state organization from the parallel organization of the Party in function and role at least since the early 1990s, in reality they remain intertwined at all levels of administration, from the village level up to the central level, both informally but also in rules and regulations. The role of the Party in state organizations in the past few years has aimed at being strengthened rather than weakened. This is evident in recent laws and regulations that govern these relations. Possibly, these new policies of strengthening the role and leadership of the Party in organizations and institutions may signal a perceived weakness of Party organizations and problems of recruiting quality members who join the Party out of conviction, rather than for opportunistic reasons.

Next to the mass organizations of the Fatherland Front, there are also professional organizations organized under the Viet Nam Union of Science and Technology Associations (VUSTA), such as the Viet Nam Lawyers Association. Besides its purely professional oversight duties, such as revoking licenses of lawyers to practice law, the association also plays a role in the political system by providing comments on new legislation and contributions to the judicial reform agenda. Another organization, the Vietnam Chamber of Commerce, has since its establishment gained an important role in politics, representing entrepreneurs and the business sector. It has a shared interest with the Party elite and has thus acquired greater influence than other organizations in policymaking.[52] The business sector's political influence is further secured by its formal representation in the National Assembly, to which twenty-five senior business managers were elected already in 2002.[53]

The single-party parliament, the National Assembly (NA), for which elections are held every five years, is expected to mirror the composition of Vietnamese society, with the help of the VFF's vetting. The right balance among deputies from different segments of the population to stand for election is decided beforehand. The deputies are usually nominated in their capacity as representatives of different party-state agencies, including important mass organizations, ministries, religious organizations, the People's Army, and the police, as well as with regard to ethnicity, gender, age, and educational levels.[54] In the election to the Fourteenth National Assembly in May 2016, there were, according to the National Election Council, 162 candidates who had registered as independent candidates, and only eleven of them made it through the vetting process of the Fatherland Front.[55] Of these eleven, only two were finally elected.[56] The nonparty representatives in the assembly were at an all-time low, with only two elected independent candidates.[57] Among those who gathered the highest percentage of votes were Prime Minister Nguyễn Xuân Phúc, who reportedly won 99.48 percent, followed by the minister of national defense at 95.87 percent, and Party General Secretary Nguyễn Phú Trọng at 86.47 percent. All members of the Politburo were elected, as well as the seventeen cabinet ministers, as were all candidates nominated by Party agencies, presidential agencies, government agencies, the Supreme People's Court, Supreme People's Procuracy, Ministry of National Defense, and Ministry of Public Security.[58] The *Vietnam Law & Legal Forum* commented on the election result: "especially, the new legislature sees a record on the rate of Party members . . . and the number of Party Central Committee members winning the election with nearly 100 deputies (including full 19 members of the Political Bureau)." A further indication of the

Party's influence over the National Assembly was reflected in the fact that the Thirteenth Party Congress in January 2021 continued the practice of nominating both the highest offices of the state, the state president and the chairman of the National Assembly, *ahead* of the national elections. The nominees were then confirmed by the newly elected National Assembly in May 2021.

But political opposition in today's Vietnam also challenges the rules of the National Assembly. In the 2016 election, party officials complained in the media about a "movement of independent candidates" before the elections to the National Assembly. Several pro-democracy candidates had announced their candidacy and some even published election campaign posters on the Internet. Although they never thought they would get through the vetting process, their interest was probably more to expose the practice of exclusion of political opposition in the competition for votes to the National Assembly, the highest organ of people's political power.

Legal Space: Laws on Demonstration and Association

Similar to previous constitutions, the constitution of 2013 contains sections on the protection of freedom of speech, assembly, and demonstration. But even if the right to demonstrate has been secured in Vietnam's constitutions since 1946, seventy-five years later Vietnam still has no law to regulate demonstrations, nor a law covering the right of association, despite decades of debates and proposals that later have been withdrawn.[59]

Activists and the formal political and judicial sphere interpret the lack of such a law in different ways. Lawyers and some pro-democracy activists expressed in my interviews, for example, that while lacking both a law that codifies the freedom of association and the freedom of demonstration, it is clear that in the Vietnamese legal system, the constitution is the highest law, and because the constitution grants these rights, "one should not worry too much about the lack of further codification."[60] But despite these constitutional guarantees, without a law and subsequent decrees clarifying the implementation of the law, the legal status of peaceful protests is unclear. When the issue has been debated in the National Assembly, delegates have expressed a wide spectrum of views. For some delegates, the right to demonstrations is, along with other civil and political rights, enshrined in the amended constitution of 2013, and must therefore also be codified into law. The current legal situation produces a gap between legal possibilities and the necessity for genuine political participation. It leaves room for repression against people who are using their rights to express their political views in accordance with the constitution. Without proper legislation, "Party law" continues to trump "public law," with important repercussions.

The other side of the debate has argued that a law on demonstration would only serve to cause trouble and conflict in society. When a renewed debate on the law emerged in the National Assembly after the long episode of anti-China protests in 2011, a delegate to the Assembly expressed that a law on demonstrations was "unnecessary" and that "in many countries demonstrations are for people to protest their governments or to protest some government policy," and he continued: "Does Vietnam need anti-government demonstrations to protest government's policies? If not, why do we have to introduce the bill on demonstration?"[61]

In March 2019, however, Prime Minister Nguyễn Xuân Phúc announced that, "following the documents of the Politburo, the National Assembly, and the government," the Ministry of Public Security was "continuing to coordinate with relevant agencies and units to study theory, legal basis, and conduct field surveys at units and localities to study and develop a Law on Demonstration to ensure the rights of people, basic rights and obligations of citizens," while at the same time avoiding "hostile forces taking advantage of demonstrations to disrupt order and fight against our Party and state." A similar promise had been made in 2011 by then–Prime Minister Nguyễn Tấn Dũng, who had entrusted the Ministry of Public Security to draft the Law on Demonstration. So far, laws on demonstration and association have not been endorsed by the National Assembly.

Policing the Political Opposition

The political role of the state security forces as the protector of the Party and the political regime—the "sword and shield of the party"—has important consequences for how opportunity structures are perceived for contentious politics and peaceful political opposition. The People's Army is an important component of the Vietnamese political system, with representation in the highest political organ, the Politburo, as well as in the Central Committee of the Communist Party.[62] Several current ministers and high-level officials have a background in the police, and the Thirteenth Party Congress in 2021 resulted in increased participation in the Politburo by the People's Army and several members with police backgrounds.[63] There is no popular control over the police forces; even the annual budget is a protected state secret not known to citizens. The Ministry of Public Security is in charge of fighting against groups and individuals who are seen as challenges to national security, including threats to ideological, cultural, economic, Party, and regime security.

Scholars of social movements in Southeast Asia in general have paid little attention to the role of security forces and their central role in shaping contention. An exception is Vincent Boudreau,[64] who in his study of social movements in three Southeast Asian countries could show how the nature of repression also creates legacies in subsequent movements. State repression and policing of political space in Vietnam has gained even less scholarly attention. The exceptions are a few book chapters and articles by Carlyle Thayer[65] and a full-length book by Ben Kerkvliet,[66] and they arrive at partly different conclusions, perhaps reflecting their different approaches and research questions, relating to the repressive capacity of the party-state and its propensity for repression of alternative visions of society and politics. While Kerkvliet's analysis arrives at the conclusion that state responses toward citizens who are "speaking out" vary between responsiveness, toleration, and repression, depending on the issue, scale, and whether they attempt to organize collectively, Thayer's analysis provides an image of a finely knitted security apparatus.

The role of the army and the people's security forces came under public discussion in debates related to the promulgation of the new constitution in 2013. Several pro-democracy groups and other petitioners, including senior Party members, argued that the constitution must clearly state that the primary role of the security forces is to protect the nation and the people, rather than the Party and its political regime. The end result of that debate was that the Party strongly rejected the depoliticization of state security forces. In speeches and debates published in official Party, public security, and military journals, the role of the state security forces in safeguarding the Communist Party's rule should instead be strengthened, and a depoliticization of the people's security forces was strongly rejected in hundreds of articles in the official press, in comments and speeches by the Party secretary, and in regulations. Several articles were published in which high-level people's security officials expressed rejection of any move toward pluralism and depoliticization of state security forces. Even though the public debate indicated that there were differing views within the Party, the official line affirmed that one of the goals in the current situation was "to reach awareness that in whatever circumstance and conditions, the ultimate and direct leadership of the Communist Party of Viet Nam over the Vietnam People's Army in all areas should be maintained. . . . The Communist Party of Vietnam is the sole organization leading the Vietnam People's Army. The leadership over the army cannot be shared with any other individual or political force."[67] To accomplish their role in the "new complex situation," the army instead had to:

> step up to foil all schemes by hostile forces to instigate "peaceful evolution" in general and "military depoliticization" in particular. In fact, "military depoliticization" of the army is an extremely wicked scheme of the hostile forces against Vietnam's revolution, attempting to separate the army from the Party leadership and disempower the army as a sharp tool and a trustworthy political force of the Party and State.

At least in 2014, and again in December 2019, there were 4,000 police and military organized security forces drilling in central parts of Ho Chi Minh City and 5,000 in Hanoi, to prepare security forces to address illegal mass gatherings and demonstrations in which the scenario was that a "number of local reactionaries who had been backed and induced by hostile forces from other countries caused social disturbances in the city,"[68] indicating that the Party is preparing to deal with "hot spots" and popular demonstrations.

In the view of the police and other security agencies, including in the official views of the Party leadership and other component party-state organizations, individuals and organizations in civil society that challenge policies or the authority of the party-state are still today perceived as threatening to national security. In Party documents and regulations, peaceful opponents of policies and politics can be regarded as reactionary forces that are suspected of being supported by foreign forces and should therefore be eliminated.

The resolution of the Eleventh National Party Congress of January 2011 put "peaceful evolution" next to issues of territorial integrity and economic security as primary national security challenges for Vietnam.

Regime security, as further developed in more recent official documentation, is widely defined as, and more or less coincides with, national security, and includes, for example, "ideological security" and "cultural security." In the current situation, the political regime is understood as being challenged both from within the Party itself and from forces external to the party in a "double process" consisting of "degradation in political ideology, morality, and lifestyles" among party officials. These officials suffer from so-called "self-change" and "self-transformation" in their thinking, causing threats to ideological security, while on the other hand, the "[h]ostile forces [are continuing] to implement their peaceful evolution scheme, causing disturbances and using so-called 'democracy' and 'human rights' in order to change the political system in our country."[69] This threat analysis is, of course, not new, but has accompanied the Party and the party-state since its inception. With inspiration from the Russian revolutionaries and their security apparatus, the party realized early on that it needed to protect itself from real and suspected political enemies and potential counterrevolutionaries. In the early years, these enemies included not only those suspected of having a pro-French agenda, but also those who held other ideological views or sympathized with other political parties at the time.

The current people's public security forces trace their own history to the Red Guard that was formed in the 1930s with the goal of protecting the "masses and Party officials" against oppositional and counterrevolutionary elements. After the August Revolution, the People's Public Security of Vietnam was formed, with the task of "fighting counterrevolutionary and hostile organizations, maintaining social order and security, protecting the Party, the revolutionary government, and the people."[70] It was further institutionalized in 1953, when the Ministry of Public Security (Bộ Công An) was formally established, and today continues to organize the regular police as well as internal intelligence and security services. The formal Vietnamese public security institutions were initially modeled after the Soviet KGB (and its predecessors) and their Chinese counterparts (which were also modeled after Soviet state security).[71] According to historian Martin Grossheim,[72] the East German Stasi also assisted in developing and modernizing North Vietnam's security apparatus between 1965 and 1989.

Article 4 of the revised Police Law (2018) confirms that the People's Police is in all aspects under the absolute and direct leadership of the Vietnam Communist Party, the president, and under the management of the government and the Ministry of Public Security. The law reconfirms the role of the police in fighting "political crimes"; protecting political security and security in the fields of ideology, culture, and the economy; protecting the Party; and strictly abiding by party lines and strict loyalty with the Party. However, the role of the Party in leading the security sector is not clearly defined, nor is the budget of the national police public to citizens who fund the organization. Pro-democracy activists have expressed deep concerns about the People's Police and their involvement in policing ideology and peaceful political expression.

Concluding Remarks: The Challenge—Representation, Political Opposition and the "New" Pluralism

While the Vietnamese Communist Party has been successful in embracing new business interests and expanding the political and legal protection of the private sector, the influence on policy and politics of ordinary citizens is much more limited. Early in the process of economic liberalization, independent organizations representing business communities were allowed to influence policy processes and lobby for their political interests, while other sectors of civil society seeking self-representation and the ability to organize themselves independent of party-state influence were denied such rights. In the same vein, the announcement in May 2019 by Party General Secretary and President Nguyễn Phú Trọng that he would pass a bill to the National Assembly to ratify ILO Convention 98 (the right to organize and collective bargaining) came in response to demands by international actors in the free trade negotiations with the EU and CPTPP, not as a concession to Vietnamese political activists who were disputing political inequality and lack of political representation and participation. Only a year earlier, several of these activists received long prison sentences for voicing demands for these rights.

A political regime never exists in a vacuum, but is underpinned by societal forces. Decades of economic liberalization and high growth under an authoritarian political regime with few mechanisms for power control has, according to many political activists and organizations, resulted in a system in which economic power is easily converted to political power, and political power converted to economic power. Recent massive corruption scandals have made it clear that the political regime for years has enabled groups or individuals within the Party and their close affiliates and relatives to amass almost unimaginable fortunes. The Party has publicly debated how such groups are forming informal power centers within and around the political system. Contrary to the hopes of the pro-democracy opposition, the many corruption scandals have provided arguments for the general secretary to attempt to recentralize political power and emphasize programs of party building, strengthening "correct" ideology in all spheres (culture, media, education, the civil service, judicial system, security police, and army), and increasing the Party's control over these institutions. Weaknesses in the political system are in general interpreted as individual flaws rather than systemic problems. Instead of embracing the moderate democratic opposition among loyal party-state insiders, party-rectification programs are pushing out actors who support political liberalization. But political space is never just a reflection of state policies and the policing of that space. Despite increased efforts to limit the fragile informal pro–political rights and pro-democracy opposition, it continues to develop, to diversify, and to define space for itself, online and in the real world. Waves of protest movements with a variety of claims have added layers upon layers of activism during the last couple of decades, knitting a web of actors across the country closer together, while occasionally being disrupted by policing of that space. Protest action in itself affects the disposition of individuals and collectives who participate—

ordinary people start to think of themselves as actors rather than subjects. This is a process that is hard to reverse.

One of Vietnam's political challenges today is to think of ways to improve political participation and representation of the political and ideological pluralism that has emerged in society. Some measures to expand political participation have been taken through various initiatives, such as the "grassroots democracy decrees" in the late 1990s. But attempts made after 2000 to "reconnect to the masses" by reinvigorating the sociopolitical mass organizations have so far obviously not met the expectations by sections of "the masses," despite accompanying programs to open up invited space for participation, such as the right to file petitions and similar efforts.

An obvious problem lies in thinking of today's pluralist society as "the masses," as if a single unit could be envisioned with shared goals and interests. The Party has recently engaged in programs of party building in party-state institutions and in the private sector to strengthen Party leadership "everywhere," as well as programs aiming at "continuing to innovate and strengthen the Party's leadership" in civil society associations. For the moment, the Party seems to have concluded that the challenges emerging from a pluralist society can be managed within the current political regime, with improvement of intraparty democracy and intraparty accountability, improved Party discipline, better morale among officials, better adherence to the principle of democratic centralism, modernized and more efficient propaganda, and sustained economic growth, while using the Party's "sword and shield"—the public security forces—to resolutely fight against "peaceful evolutionaries" outside and inside the Party.

Notes

1. Drafted by the Ministry of Public Security, passed by the National Assembly on June 12, 2018, and went into effect January 1, 2019.
2. The struggle against "peaceful evolution" can be traced back to Mao's policy in 1959, basically referring to regime change without arms by Western goverments. "Self-evolution" and "self-transformation" emerged as themes in Vietnam after the analysis of the collapse of communism in the Soviet Union and Europe by the end of the 1980s and early 1990s. Even today, the concepts remain important components in explaining the collapse of the Soviet Union, with Gorbachev regarded as a main culprit who betrayed the revolution, beginning with his proposal to separate the Party from the security forces and finally by abolishing the Party's constitutional role as the leader of state and society. In this strand of thinking, the protest movements emerging across the Eastern Bloc were caused by external forces who manipulated people to protest and cause civil unrest. This same "plot" is identified by the Chinese and Vietnamese parties' thinking today identifying "external hostile forces." In a time when embassies from democratic countries, with a few exceptions, stay away from supporting pro-democracy actors, such fears seem unwarranted. Only in the documents of the Thirteenth Party Congress in 2021 did the VCP recognize that the largest threats to Party and regime survival are likely not posed by "external forces" but from degeneration inside the party-state itself, yet the theme is recurrent in the websites of pro-regime "opinion shapers" and news outlets by the Ministry of Public Security.
3. Ngọc Trần, "The Third Sleeve," 257–79.
4. These decrees were announced by the party in the late 1990s after prolonged and troublesome protests in Thái Bình Province southeast of Hanoi, in which angry protesters destroyed the homes of officials and attacked the People's Committee building and several police stations, over power abuse and corruption

among party officials that started in spring 1997 and continued into 1998. See, for example, Nguyễn Hồng Hải, *Political Dynamics of Grassroots Democracy*; Malarney, "Observations on the 1997 Thai Binh Uprising."

5. Morris-Jung, "The Vietnamese Bauxite Controversy."

6. Liberal perspectives postulating civil society as comprising associations that are characterized primarily by their presumed autonomy from the state fail to capture civil society in authoritarian contexts (Hansson and Weiss, *Handbook of Civil and Uncivil Society in Southeast Asia*; Hansson and Weiss, "Political Participation in Asia"). For an early conceptualization of state–civil society relations in the Vietnamese single-party regime, see Kerkvliet, "Grappling with Organizations and the State"; Hannah, "The Mutual Colonization of State and Civil Society"; Wishermann, "Civil Society and Governance in Vietnam," 3–40.

7. See Wells-Dang, *Civil Society Networks in China and Vietnam*.

8. They were considered illegal because they did not follow the cumbersome legally prescribed steps for organizing strikes. In 2022, Vietnam has not yet had one single legal strike.

9. Trần, "Alternatives to 'Race to the Bottom.'"

10. Hansson, "Growth without Democracy."

11. Clarke et al., "From Rights to Interests."

12. Trần, *Ties that Bind*, chap. 10.

13. Amnesty International, "Viet Nam: Lead a Union, Go to Prison."

14. London, *Politics in Contemporary Vietnam*.

15. Thayer, "Vietnam and the Challenge of Political Civil Society," 22.

16. One of the activists interviewed by the author in August 2015 said that two security officials were posted immediately outside the front door of their home over the entire APEC summit.

17. Ministry of Labour, Invalids, and Social Affairs, "Labour and Social Issues Emerging from Vietnam's Accession to the WTO."

18. Two investigative journalists working for the *Thanh Niên* and *Tuổi Trẻ* newspapers who had been reporting on the case were arrested, and one of them was sentenced to prison for "abuse of democratic freedom"(see "Ex-Reporters Tried for Abuse of Democratic Freedoms").

19. Amnesty International, "Viet Nam: Lead a Union, Go to Prison."

20. Human Rights Watch, "Not Yet a Workers' Paradise."

21. The Institute of Development Studies (IDS), Vietnam's first think tank composed of sixteen of the most prominent scholars, announced their decision to close the institute in 2009 in a protest against "Decision 97," which stipulated a list of approved topics for research and prohibited publication of results related to government policies without prior approval of relevant party-state authorities.

22. Phạm Thế Duyệt, "Bringing into Full Play the Glorious Tradition Enhancing the Strengthening of National Unity."

23. *Vietnam News*, March 29, 2013.

24. Bui Ngoc Son, "Petition 72."

25. It should be noted that several of the leading figures emphasized in interviews that they were *not* "civil society," but *political* organizations that should be seen as parts of the political sphere. Other groups, however, self-identified as civil society organizations, or civil society activists.

26. *BBC Vietnamese*, September 23, 2013.

27. Among these were lawyer Lê Công Định, who prior to his arrest on "national security" charges in 2009 had defended high-profile pro-democracy lawyers Nguyễn Văn Đài and Lê Thị Công Nhân in court (see Lê Công Định, "What Crime Have They Committed?").

28. See Bùi Hải Thiêm, "The New Meaning of Political Participation in Cyberspace," for the development of the political blogosphere in Vietnam.

29. "Vietnamese Blogger Jailed for Environmental Reports."

30. "New Social Insurance Rule Sparks Worker Strike in Ho Chi Minh City."

31. There were several reasons behind people's anger: they had not been allowed a say in a policy change of essential meaning for their livelihood, and they feared the new policy would limit their power to walk out on an employer if conditions were unbearable, wages were too low, or other problems.

32. Fforde, "Vietnam's Workers Use Local Strikes."

33. Ngoc Anh Vu, "Grassroots Environmental Activism," 1183.

34. Interviews with activists in Hanoi.

35. According to the People's Police online journal (*Công an nhân dân Online*, December 14, 2021), she was punished for opposing the Party and state, spreading propaganda against the Party and state, and giving interviews to foreign media in which she slandered the regime and the state of democracy and human rights in Vietnam. Her crimes were considered particularly serious (https://cand.com.vn/Phap-luat/tuyen -phat-pham-thi-doan-trang-9-nam-tu—i637998/).

36. Drafted by the Ministry of Public Security, passed by the National Assembly on June 12, 2018, and took effect in 2019. The law has similarities with China's Cybersecurity Law of 2017, and aims to give the party-state greater control over digital giants, and of users who are posting anti-government propaganda.

37. Kerkvliet, *The Power of Everyday Politics*.

38. "Peaceful evolution" refers to regime change without arms; it emerged as a theme after the Party's analysis of the collapse of communism in the Soviet Union and Europe by the end of the 1980s and early 1990s; "color revolution" (*cách mạng màu*) is, according to the VCP's official view, a phenomenon closely related to peaceful evolution, and refers to popular nonviolent movements against authoritarian rule, mainly in states of the former Soviet Union in the early twenty-first century and onward. In line with the view of the Chinese Communist Party, the official view of the VCP is that these movements are likely orchestrated by Western governments, in particular by the US (see, e.g., Võ Văn Thưởng [Politburo member and head of the Central Propaganda Department], *Nhân Dân* online, June 17, 2019), some of the protests that are described in this chapter are interpreted by Party conservatives as being components of a color revolution plotting to overthrow rule by the VCP and its political regime (see, e.g., *Quân đội nhân dân* [People's Army newspaper], "Từ 'cách mạng cây,' 'cách mạng cá' đến 'cách mạng màu'").

39. Cohen and Arato, *Civil Society and Political Theory*.

40. One of many cases in which the principle of democratic centralism has been evoked as the basis for disciplinary action was the Party Secretariat of the Central Committee's decision in May 2018 to dismiss the deputy secretary of the provincial Đồng Nai Party Committee from all of her Party positions and as head of the Đồng Nai National Assembly Deputy delegation (*Vietnam News*, May 5, 2018). In the Central Highlands province of Đắk Nông, the Party inspection found that more or less the entire cohort of Party delegates to the People's Committee for the 2016–21 period had violated the principle of democratic centralism, along with economic violations.

41. CPV, "Điều lệ Đảng (do Đại hội đại biểu toàn quốc lần thứ XI của Đảng thông qua)."

42. CPV, 47-QD/TW, "Quy định về những điều đảng viên không được làm."

43. The list of unacceptable views and what Party members may not do is comprehensive and includes further denying the socialist market economy or the system of people's ownership of land; speaking or writing contrary to the Party's viewpoints, decisions, and lines; denying revolutionary achievements; exaggerating the shortcomings of the Party and state; distorting history; slander of senior party leaders; inciting dissatisfaction, dissent, and internal opposition; taking advantage of using media and social networks to defame or degrade the Party's leadership; causing internal division and suspicion among cadres and Party members and the people; denying the absolute leadership of the Party in all aspects of the armed forces; demanding "depoliticized" army and police; linking and connecting with "hostile forces," reactionary forces, and opportunistic and dissatisfied elements to spread opposing ideas and views, mobilize, organize, and gather forces to oppose the Party and state; giving false information; distorting the foreign policy of the Party and state; giving one-sided information on the international situation that is detrimental to the relationship between Vietnam and other countries; denying the Party's leadership role toward the press, literature, and the arts; influencing, manipulating, and driving social opinion not to follow the Party's line; advocating for radical democratic ideology; emphasizing the difficulties in society; composing and promoting cultural and artistic work that is misleading, that distorts history, and that degrades the Party's prestige; having a narrow nationalist ideology or extreme religion; taking advantage of "democracy," human rights, the nation, and religion to cause internal divisions; and causing divisions between religions or between religion and the Party and state.

44. According to Politburo member, secretary of the Party Central Committee, and head of the Party Central Committee's Organizational Department, Trương Thị Mai, 25,104 Party members were disciplined between 2016 and 2020 for displaying signs of self-evolution or self-transformation (Le Hiep, "Hơn 25.000 đảng viên suy thoái bị kỷ luật từ 2016–2020").

45. "Giữ gìn phẩm giá, uy tín của người trí thức chân chính."

46. "Giữ gìn phẩm giá, uy tín của người trí thức chân chính."

47. "Kỷ luật khai trừ Đảng ông Chu Hảo—Nhìn vấn đề dưới góc độ công tác kiểm tra, kỷ luật đảng."

48. "ĐCSVN khai trừ GS Chu Hảo 'vì chống đối."

49. Dang Dung Tri, "Guarantee of Human Rights in Vietnam."

50. Waibel and Glück, "More than 13 Million," 344.

51. Nguyễn Phú Trọng, General Secretary of the CPV, "Tổng Bí thư Nguyễn Phú Trọng phát biểu tại Đại hội MTTQ Việt Nam lần thứ VIII."

52. Stromseth, "Business Associations and Policy-Making."

53. Salomon, "Power and Representation in the Vietnamese National Assembly."

54. Thayer, "Vietnam and the Challenge of Political Civil Society."

55. *Tuổi Trẻ*, June 21, 2019; "How Vietnam's Elections Run," *Tuổi Trẻ*, May 21, 2021.

56. "National Election Council Announces Election Results for 14th Legislature," *Vietnam Law & Legal Forum*, April 24, 2016.

57. *Vnexpress*, "Chỉ hai người tự ứng cử trúng đại biểu Quốc hội khóa 14."

58. *Vnexpress*, "Chỉ hai người tự ứng cử trúng đại biểu Quốc hội khóa 14."

59. See Sidel, *The Constitution of Vietnam*, on the lack of implantation and the "gap between rhetorical rights and real rights" and the process, at least since 1992, to enact a law on associations (chap. 7).

60. This did not mean they saw such codification as unnecessary; their argument was instead that the constitution should be treated as the highest law, and as the constitution guarantees these rights citizens should just take them for granted and not wait for them to be codified into laws.

61. *Thanh Nien*, November 18, 2011.

62. Thayer contends that the Vietnam People's Army's (VPA) involvement in political institutions and "elite politics" has been fluctuating, but overall "significant." Thayer, "Vietnam: How Large is the Security Establishment?," 71.

63. Abuza, "The Fallout from Vietnam's Communist Party Congress."

64. Boudreau, *Resisting Dictatorship*.

65. Thayer, "How Large Is the Security Establishment?"; Thayer, "The Apparatus of Authoritarian Rule."

66. Kerkvliet, *Speaking Out in Vietnam*; Kerkvliet, "Government Repression of Dissidents."

67. Nguyễn Phú Trọng, "'Không phân chia sự lãnh đạo quân đội cho lực lượng khác ngoài Đảng.'"

68. "4,000 People Join Anti-Terror Drill in HCMC," *Public Security News*, December 17, 2019.

69. *Nhân Dân*, January 20, 2011.

70. Ministry of Public Security, "History of the Public Security Forces of Vietnam."

71. Goscha, "Intelligence in a Time of Decolonization," 100–138.

72. Grossheim, *The East German "Stasi."*

References

Abuza, Zachary. "The Fallout from Vietnam's Communist Party Congress." *The Diplomat*, February 2, 2021. https://thediplomat.com/2021/02/the-fallout-from-vietnams-communist-party-congress/.

Amnesty International. "Viet Nam: Lead a Union, Go to Prison." AI Index ASA 41/011/2007, November 1, 2007.

Boudreau, Vincent. *Resisting Dictatorship: Repression and Protest in Southeast Asia*. Cambridge: Cambridge University Press, 2009.

Bùi Hải Thiêm. "The New Meaning of Political Participation in Cyberspace: Social Media and Collective Action in Vietnam's Authoritarianism." In *Political Participation in Asia: Defining and Deploying Political Space*, edited by Eva Hansson and Meredith L. Weiss. London: Routledge, 2018.

Bui Ngoc Son. "Petition 72: The Struggle for Constitutional Reforms in Vietnam." *I-CONnect*, March 28, 2013. http://www.iconnectblog.com.

Clarke, Simon, Chang-Hee Lee, and Do Quynh Chi. "From Rights to Interests: The Challenge of Industrial Relations in Vietnam." *Journal of Industrial Relations* 49, no. 4 (2007): 545–68.

Cohen, Jean, and Andrew Arato. *Civil Society and Political Theory*. Cambridge, MA: MIT Press, 1992.

CPV. "Điều lệ Đảng (do Đại hội đại biểu toàn quốc lần thứ XI của Đảng thông qua)" (Party Charter [approved by the Eleventh National Congress of the Party]). 2011. https://tulieuvankien.dangcongsan.vn/van-kien-tu-lieu-ve-dang/dieu-le-dang/dieu-le-dang-do-dai-hoi-dai-bieu-toan-quoc-lan-thu-xi-cua-dang-thong-qua-3431.

CPV, 47-QD/TW. "Quy định về những điều đảng viên không được làm" (Regulations on what Party members cannot do). November 2011. https://thuvienphapluat.vn/van-ban/Linh-vuc-khac/Quy-dinh-47-QD-TW-nhung-dieu-dang-vien-khong-duoc-lam-132578.aspx.

Dang Dung Tri. "Guarantee of Human Rights in Vietnam and Current Problems." *Tap Chi Cong San*, 2014. http://english.tapchicongsan.org.vn/Home/Culture-Society/2014/781/Guarantee-of-human-rights-in-Viet-Nam-and-current-problems.aspx.

"ĐCSVN khai trừ GS Chu Hảo 'vì chống đối'" (The VCP expelled Professor Chu Hao "for protesting"). *BBC Vietnamese*, November 15, 2018. https://www.bbc.com/vietnamese/vietnam-46223846.

"Ex-Reporters Tried for Abuse of Democratic Freedoms." *Vietnam Law Magazine*, October 24, 2008. https://vietnamlawmagazine.vn/ex-reporters-tried-for-abuse-of-democratic-freedoms-761.html.

Fforde, Adam. "Vietnam's Workers Use Local Strikes to Push Party to Push for Reforms." *World Politics Review*, April 17, 2015. http://www.worldpoliticsreview.com/articles/15556/vietnam-s-workers-use-local-strikes-to-push-party-for-reforms.

"4,000 People Join Anti-Terror Drill in HCMC." *Public Security News*, December 17, 2019. https://en.cand.com.vn/law-society/4-000-people-join-anti-terror-drill-in-HCMC-i547506/.

"Giữ gìn phẩm giá, uy tín của người trí thức chân chính" (Preserve the dignity of a true intellectual). *Báo điện tử Quân đội nhân dân* (People's Army newspaper), October 26, 2018. https://www.qdnd.vn/chinh-tri/cac-van-de/giu-gin-pham-gia-uy-tin-cua-nguoi-tri-thuc-chan-chinh-552971.

Goscha, Christopher G. "Intelligence in a Time of Decolonization: The Case of the Democratic Republic of Vietnam at War (1945–50)." *Intelligence and National Security* 22, no. 1 (2007): 100–138.

Grossheim, Martin. *The East German "Stasi" and the Modernization of the Vietnamese Security Apparatus, 1965–1989*. Washington, DC: Woodrow Wilson Center, 2014.

Hannah, Joseph. "The Mutual Colonization of State and Civil Society Organizations in Vietnam." In *Local Organizations and Urban Governance in East and Southeast Asia*, edited by Benjamin L. Read. London: Routledge, 2009.

Hansson, Eva. "Growth without Democracy: Challenges to Authoritarianism in Vietnam." Ph.D. dissertation, Stockholm University, 2011.

Hansson, Eva, and Meredith Weiss, eds. *Handbook of Civil and Uncivil Society in Southeast Asia*. London: Routledge, 2023.

———. *Political Participation in Asia: Defining and Deploying Political Space*. London: Routledge, 2018.

Human Rights Watch. "Not Yet a Workers' Paradise: Vietnam's Suppression of the Independent Workers' Movement." 2009. https://www.hrw.org/report/2009/05/04/not-yet-workers-paradise/vietnams-suppression-independent-workers-movement.

Kerkvliet, Benedict J. Tria. "Government Repression of Dissidents in Contemporary Vietnam." In *Politics in Contemporary Vietnam: Party, State and Authority Relations*, edited by Jonathan D. London. Basingstoke, UK: Palgrave Macmillan, 2014.

———. "Grappling with Organizations and the State in Contemporary Vietnam." In *Getting Organized in Vietnam: Moving in and around the Socialist State*, edited by Ben J. Tria Kerkvliet, Russell Hiang-Khng Heng, and David Wee Hock Koh. Singapore: Institute of Southeast Asian Studies, 2003.

———. *The Power of Everyday Politics: How Vietnamese Peasants Transformed National Policy*. Ithaca, NY: Cornell University Press, 2005.

———. *Speaking Out in Vietnam: Public Political Criticism in a Communist Party-Ruled Nation*. Ithaca, NY: Cornell University Press, 2019.

Kerkvliet, Benedict J. Tria, Russell H. K. Heng, and David W. H. Koh, eds. *Getting Organized in Vietnam: Moving in and around the Socialist State*. Singapore: Institute of Southeast Asian Studies, 2003.

"Kỷ luật khai trừ Đảng ông Chu Hảo—Nhìn vấn đề dưới góc độ công tác kiểm tra, kỷ luật đảng." Party Central Inspection Committee, November 16, 2018. http://kinhtedothi.vn/ky-luat-khai-tru-dang-ong -chu-hao-nhin-van-de-duoi-goc-do-cong-tac-kiem-tra-ky-luat-dang-330016.html.

Malarney, Shaun Kingsley. "Observations on the 1997 Thai Binh Uprising in Northern Vietnam." *International Christian University Bulletin III-A, Asian Culture Research Supplement*, no. 10 (2001): 137–48.

Lê Công Định. "What Crime Have They Committed?" *Journal of Vietnamese Studies* 5, no. 3 (2010): 208–18.

Le Hiep. "Hơn 25.000 đảng viên suy thoái bị kỷ luật từ 2016–2020" (More than 25,000 depressed party members were disciplined from 2016–2020). *Thanh Niên*, September 12, 2021. https://thanhnien.vn/hon -25-000-dang-vien-suy-thoai-bi-ky-luat-tu-2016-2020-post1409674.html.

London, Jonathan, ed. "Politics in Vietnam." In *Politics in Contemporary Vietnam: Party, State and Authority Relations*, edited by Jonathan London, 1–20. New York: Palgrave Macmillan, 2014.

Ministry of Labour, Invalids, and Social Affairs (MoLisa). "Labour and Social Issues Emerging from Vietnam's Accession to the WTO." Hanoi, 2006.

Ministry of Public Security. "History of the Public Security Forces of Vietnam." 2018. http://en.bocongan .gov.vn/about/history-of-peoples-public-security-forces-of-vietnam-t4446.html.

Morris-Jung, Jason. "The Vietnamese Bauxite Controversy: Towards a More Oppositional Politics." *Journal of Vietnamese Studies* 10, no. 1 (2015): 63–109.

"New Social Insurance Rule Sparks Worker Strike in Ho Chi Minh City." *Tuổi Trẻ*, March 31, 2015. https:// tuoitrenews.vn/news/society/20150331/new-social-insurance-rule-sparks-worker-strike-in-ho-chi-minh -city/29764.html.

Ngoc Anh Vu. "Grassroots Environmental Activism in an Authoritarian Context: The Trees Movement in Vietnam." *Voluntas: International Journal of Voluntary and Non-Profit Organizations* 28 (2017): 1180–1208.

Ngọc Trần, Angie. "The Third Sleeve: Emerging Labour Newspapers and the Response of the Labour Unions and the State to Workers' Resistance in Vietnam." *Labour Studies Journal* 32, no. 3 (2007): 257–79.

———. *Ties that Bind: Cultural Identity, Class, and Law in Vietnam's Labor Resistance*. Ithaca, NY: Southeast Asia Program Publications, 2013.

Nguyễn Hồng Hải. *Political Dynamics of Grassroots Democracy in Vietnam*. London: Palgrave Macmillan, 2016.

Nguyễn Phú Trọng. "'Không phân chia sự lãnh đạo quân đội cho lực lượng khác ngoài Đảng'" (Do not divide military leadership with other forces than the Party). *VietnamNet*, 2014. https://vietnamnet.vn /khong-phan-chia-su-lanh-dao-quan-doi-cho-luc-luong-khac-ngoai-dang-212612.html.

Nguyễn Phú Trọng, General Secretary of the CPV. "Tổng Bí thư Nguyễn Phú Trọng phát biểu tại Đại hội MTTQ Việt Nam lần thứ VIII" (General Secretary Nguyen Phu Trong speaks at the Eighth Vietnam Fatherland Front Congress). September 26, 2014. https://cand.com.vn/thoi-su/Tong-Bi-thu-Nguyen-Phu -Trong-phat-bieu-tai-Dai-hoi-MTTQ-Viet-Nam-lan-thu-VIII-i274680/.

Phạm Thế Duyệt. "Bringing into Full Play the Glorious Tradition Enhancing the Strengthening of National Unity." *The Communist Review*, 2006.

Quân đội nhân dân (People's Army newspaper). "Từ 'cách mạng cây,' 'cách mạng cá' đến 'cách mạng màu'" (From "tree revolution," "fish revolution" to "color revolution"). June 3, 2019. https://www.qdnd.vn /phong-chong-dien-bien-hoa-binh/tu-cach-mang-cay-cach-mang-ca-den-cach-mang-mau-575691.

Salomon, Matthieu. "Power and Representation in the Vietnamese National Assembly." In *Vietnam's New Order: International Perspectives on the State and Reform in Vietnam*, edited by Stephanie Balm and Mark Sidel, 198–216. New York: Palgrave Macmillan. https://link.springer.com/chapter/10.1057/9780230601970_12.

Sidel, Mark. *The Constitution of Vietnam: A Contextual Analysis*. Oxford: Hart Publishing, 2009.

Stromseth, Jonathan. "Business Associations and Policy-Making in Vietnam." In *Getting Organized in Vietnam: Moving in and around the Socialist State*, edited by Ben J. Tria Kerkvliet, Russell Hiang-Khng Heng, and David Wee Hock Koh. Singapore: Institute of Southeast Asian Studies, 2003.

Thayer, Carlyle A. "The Apparatus of Authoritarian Rule in Viet Nam." In *Politics in Contemporary Vietnam: Party, State and Authority Relations*, edited by Jonathan D. London. Basingstoke, UK: Palgrave Macmillan, 2014.

———. "Vietnam and the Challenge of Political Civil Society." *Contemporary Southeast Asia* 31, no. 1 (2009): 1–27.

———. "Vietnam: How Large Is the Security Establishment?" *Thayer Consultancy Background Brief,* April 2, 2017. http://viet-studies.net/kinhte/Thayer_VNSecuritySize.pdf.

Trần, Angie Ngọc. "Alternatives to the 'Race to the Bottom' in Vietnam: Minimum Wage Strikes and Their Aftermath." *Labour Studies Journal* 32, no. 4 (2007): 430–51.

"Vietnamese Blogger Jailed for Environmental Reports." *BBC,* November 28, 2017. https://www.bbc.com /news/world-asia-42153142.

Vnexpress. "Chỉ hai người tự ứng cử trúng đại biểu Quốc hội khóa 14" (Only two self-nominated candidates won the Fourteenth National Assembly). June 8, 2016. https://vnexpress.net/chi-hai-nguoi-tu-ung -cu-trung-dai-bieu-quoc-hoi-khoa-14-3416212.html.

Waibel, Gabi, and Sarah Glück. "More than 13 Million: Mass Mobilisation and Gender Politics in the Vietnam Women's Union." *Gender & Development* 21, no. 2 (2013); 343–61.

Wells-Dang, Andrew. *Civil Society Networks in China and Vietnam. Informal Pathbreakers in Health and Environment.* Houndmills, UK: Palgrave Macmillan, 2012.

Wishermann, Jörg. "Civil Society and Governance in Vietnam: Selected Findings from an Empirical Survey." *Journal of Current Southeast Asian Affairs* 29, no. 2 (2010): 3–40.

CHAPTER 5

The Evolution of Vietnam's Institutional Reforms

Progress and Challenges

LE DANG DOANH

This chapter discusses the evolution of Vietnam's institutional reforms during the past decades, with a focus on the business sector. A single-sentence summary could be that the transformation of the institutional environment has been truly impressive, but it is still a work in progress. The objectives of Vietnam's economic policies and institutions have shifted from ambitions to eradicate private capitalistic businesses, collectivize small producers, and force farmers into cooperatives in the late 1970s to the promotion of both domestic and foreign private investors, including powerful private conglomerates and multinational enterprises, in recent years. Despite impressive achievements in terms of economic growth, employment creation, and internationalization, the domestic private sector remains relatively small, and in particular, small and medium-sized enterprises (SMEs) operate in a difficult business environment. They face tough competition from state-owned enterprises (SOEs) and foreign-invested enterprises (FIEs) that are not only larger and technologically more advanced, but that also enjoy various kinds of privileges related to access to land and capital. Leveling the playing field and reducing the remaining obstacles to private-sector development are some of the remaining challenges for Vietnam's continuing reform process.

The Sixth National Congress of the Party in 1986 constituted a pivotal moment in Vietnam's economic transformation from plan to market. The Congress strongly criticized the failures of past policies and launched the Đổi Mới (Renovation) process. The loss of important material support from the Soviet Union and other Eastern European socialist countries in 1989–90 accelerated the reform process that had been started a couple of years earlier. It created, on the one hand, critical imbalances in the economy, but on the other hand allowed and pushed Vietnam to make bolder policy reforms. The political leadership was pressed to accept domestic grassroots experiments and to draw on the market economic legacy of South Vietnam, gradually reducing the scope of central planning.

Introducing the "contract plan system" for farmers, opening up the domestic private sector, encouraging inflows of foreign direct investment, and introducing market economic elements and gradual reforms of the state-owned enterprises were important parts of this reform process. Over time, Vietnam's domestic reforms have also become linked to international agreements. With more liberal and market-oriented policies, Vietnam has been welcomed into regional integration agreements (like ASEAN), multilateral trade agreements (like WTO), and bilateral treaties (like the bilateral trade agreement with the US and the free trade agreement with the EU). At the same time, these agreements have pushed Vietnam to further reforms that have benefited both domestic and foreign investors and entrepreneurs.

The first two sections of this chapter will provide a background by describing Vietnam's economic institutions before 1986 and the problems leading up to the start of the Đổi Mới process. The next two sections will focus on the reforms of company laws and enterprise laws, as well as other parts of the legal framework defining the status of the private sector. The discussion on the Enterprise Law promulgated in 1999 is particularly important, since this law constituted a crucial step in creating space for a more independent private sector. After highlighting some of the remaining obstacles for private-sector development, this chapter will briefly discuss the external pressures for change that have made it possible to carry out fundamental reforms despite opposition from important domestic interest groups, and will conclude with a summary of the current state of Vietnam's private sector by looking at some indicators of its international competitiveness.

Economic Institutions before 1986

Before the beginning of the formal reform process (*Đổi Mới*) in 1986, the private sector was insignificant and in principle illegal in the former North Vietnam. It primarily existed in the form of very small micro household enterprises in agriculture, handicrafts, and some services in the urban areas.

In 1957–58 the North Vietnamese government had carried out a heavy-handed campaign of "socialist reconstruction" directed against private ownership, confiscating "private capitalist enterprises" that were turned into state-owned enterprises, and collectivizing small farms, handicraft producers, traders, and even micro businesses, such as rickshaw drivers and small eateries serving traditional *pho* (noodle soup). The majority of the takeovers were expropriations, where the state paid a symbolic lump sum to the previous owner(s). These new firms often started as state–private joint ventures, but in 1964 most of them were transformed into SOEs. As a result, the share of direct state ownership of economic resources increased from about 18 percent in 1957 to 45 percent in 1965. The share of cooperatives grew from almost nothing in 1957 to 45 percent in 1965, while the share of the private sector declined from 72 percent to 10 percent over the same period. By 1975, the share of direct state ownership had increased to over one-half, mainly at the expense of the cooperative sector (see table 5.1).

However, the "socialist reconstruction" campaign in North Vietnam was not successful, although the weaknesses of the system were not clearly manifested until later. The losses related to the forced nationalization and collectivization of private assets and

Table 5.1
Ownership structure in North Vietnam, 1957–75 (%)

	Socialized sector			Private sector
	Total	State owned	Cooperatives	
1957	18.1	17.9	0.2	71.9
1960	66.4	37.8	28.6	33.6
1965	90.0	44.6	45.4	10.0
1970	91.4	40.3	51.1	8.6
1975	91.6	51.7	39.9	8.4

Source: Tran Van Tho et al., *Vietnam's Economy 1955–2000.*

the inefficiency of the command economy were dwarfed by the costs of the ongoing war—in terms of casualties and the destruction of infrastructure, farmland, and productive capital, as well as the priority given to the war effort in the allocation of economic resources—until the reunification of Vietnam in 1975.

Although the economy of South Vietnam was also badly affected by the war, it was largely based on private enterprise, and the high level of demand that was generated by US military procurement and large inflows of US aid made it appear much stronger and more dynamic than the command economy of North Vietnam. In particular, Saigon, the capital of South Vietnam, was seen as a center for private business and entrepreneurship. Before 1975, 80 percent of the production capacity of South Vietnam was concentrated in Saigon, where an estimated 38,000 businesses were operating in trade and industry (mainly light consumer goods), including 766 joint stock companies and 8,546 private industrial enterprises.

After the national reunification on April 30, 1975, the Communist Party of Vietnam (CPV) hoped that the entrepreneurial capabilities of South Vietnam could be used for the economic development of the nation, and the Twenty-Fourth Plenum (meeting of all members) of the Central Committee of the CPV decided to allow the private sector to continue operating in the south during a transition period. It was a hopeful move—a government with several well-known politicians in Saigon before 1975 like Dr. Nguyen Xuan Oanh, who served as adviser, and Dr. Duong Quynh Hoa, who served as minister of health in the newly formed government. A private press was tolerated (the private *Tin Sang* newspaper closed in 1981), and big private companies could continue to operate.

Unfortunately, these meaningful developments could not last very long due to complicated political developments. The business sector in South Vietnam was dominated by Vietnamese of Chinese origin (the *Hoa*), who controlled 80 percent of industrial production and 100 percent of wholesale trade. However, the activities of the Beijing administration among the *Hoa* community in the Chinatown Cho Lon in Ho Chi Minh City caused concern and worry among Vietnamese leaders. There were reports that the *Hoa* were loyal to Beijing rather than Vietnam, claiming Chinese citizenship, using the Chinese national flag, and pledging allegiance to the picture of Chairman Mao. Together with the quickly deteriorating political relationship with China, this development led the country's leadership to reverse the policy from the Twenty-Fourth Plenum, and the Fourth National Congress of the CPV in December 1976 decided to move the "whole country to socialism."

In line with this move, the Politburo of the CPV decided to conduct three campaigns of "socialist reconstruction" between 1976 and 1978, aiming to "liquidate private capitalist business, liquidate private capitalist ownership of production means, liquidate capitalist exploitation." This meant that private capitalist enterprises were labeled as "illegal and anti-socialist," and all private enterprises in the southern part of the country, employing about 250,000 workers in all, were socialized. In some cases, the nationalized enterprises were formally turned into state–private joint ventures. In addition, by 1979, 60,000 private household enterprises trading industrial inputs had been closed and 30,000 other household businesses had been nationalized. By that time, the authorities had also established 1,286 new cooperatives and 15,000 "production groups" in the agricultural sector, nominally covering about 50 percent of all farmers in southern Vietnam (although resistance to collectivization meant that most of these production units existed only in name).

The Five-Year Plan for 1976–80, passed at the Fourth National Congress of the CPV in December 1976, set very ambitious targets for the unified national economy. It was declared that GDP should increase by 13–14 percent per annum, agricultural production output should grow at an annual rate of 8–10 percent, and social productivity should increase by 7.5–8 percent per year. However, the heavy-handed socialization of the private business sector in South Vietnam was costly. It had been hoped that the use of the expropriated or confiscated machinery, real estate, and other assets of private entrepreneurs, together with the collectivization of land, would lead to greater efficiency and productivity. These hopes did not materialize. Many of the Chinese-Vietnamese businessmen who had made up Saigon's entrepreneurial class left Vietnam as "boat people" (and many educated professionals had fled South Vietnam in connection with the US withdrawal in 1973). The cadres replacing them in the nationalized enterprises lacked business experience, know-how, and management skills. Accountability and personal responsibility were limited, and many crucial decisions were made in the form of collective resolutions of various committees of the CPV. There were no effective material incentives for workers and farmers. The new investments channeled into SOEs did not produce the expected economic growth. Instead, production started to decline, and the efficiency of the cooperatives and SOEs was low. The lack of accountability and efficient control of power led to abuses of power, wastefulness, and corruption.

The government had established a large number of ministries and general departments to manage the economy. The State Committee for Planning was responsible for balancing and allocating the limited resources to the ministries and provinces, including the main SOEs. Line ministries were established according to narrowly defined industrial branches, such as silviculture, aquatic products, food products, mining and coal, mechanics and metallurgy, and so forth. Individual state enterprises were typically obliged to interact with several different ministries as part of their regular operations. For example, when the Saigon Beer Company was nationalized after 1975, responsibility for management and control was divided between the Ministry of Light Industry (for the water

Table 5.2
GDP growth 1977–81 (index 1975 = 100)

Year	Total GDP	Agriculture	Industry	Services
1977	105.3	100.7	113.2	104.9
1978	101.1	93.6	107.5	109.0
1979	98.2	103.3	95.4	92.4
1980	96.4	105.6	88.7	87.8
1981	102.3	104.3	99.9	100.7

Source: Dang Phong, *History of Vietnam's Economy*, vol. 2: *1954–1975*.

supply), Ministry of Food Industry (for the production of the beer bottles), and the General Department for Chemistry (for the production of carbon dioxide).

As shown in table 5.2, GDP stagnated after the initial "normalization" following re-unification. Total GDP in 1980 was well below its 1975 level—here, it should be recalled that the economy in 1975 was still heavily depressed by the war.

Vietnamese central planning was not as sophisticated as that in the Soviet Union, but the state was still directly involved in the operations of the cooperatives and SOEs. The central planning system included 105 socioeconomic indicators and 338 products and services; it allocated capital, raw materials, and financial resources to state-owned companies, and procured rice, pork, and other agricultural products at fixed prices from agricultural cooperatives. Due to slow output growth and increasing inflation, these prices were soon below the cooperatives' costs of production, and compulsory sales to the state simply led to cumulating losses. Unsurprisingly, those farmers who were able to do so reduced their production to a level that mainly covered their own demand. The public press frequently reported on "natural disasters" that made it impossible to reach the production targets, and Vietnam was forced to use its very scarce foreign reserves for importing crops to cover the minimum consumption needs of the people.

The shortage economy also made it necessary to introduce various forms of rationing. A system of coupons for purchases of rationed products was established, distinguishing between different classes of people. Public officials and public servants were highest on the list of priorities. Ministers and vice ministers were categorized in classes A and B, and were not only allocated larger rations than others, but were also given access to special shops where they could buy rice, meat, sugar, and other foods, as well as imported clothes, chocolates, powdered milk, and other products at low official prices. Officials of class C and below (general directors, directors, and public servants) had access to shops for meat and foods only, while their other consumer goods had to be purchased in regular public state-owned shops with limited supplies of goods and long queues. Table 5.3 illustrates the differences in rations for the five classes of public officials and public servants. The subsidized rations for ordinary citizens were smaller and subject to availability: in 1981, the monthly quota for each individual in Ho Chi Minh City was 2 kg of rice and 5 kg of subsidiary crops (e.g., sorghum, manioc, or sweet potatoes), while the monthly meat ration for a household of six persons or less was 500 grams.[1] Obviously, this was not suffi-

Table 5.3
Monthly food rations for officials and public servants

Classification	Type of coupon	Meat (kg)	Sugar (kg)
Special level	A1	More than 7	More than 3.5
Minister	A	6	3
Vice minister	B	5	2
General director	C1	3	1.5
Vice general director	C	2	1
Director of division	D	1	0.5
Public servant	E	0.3	0.5

Source: Đặng Phong, *History of Vietnam's Economy*, vol. 2: *1954–1975*.

cient for a healthy diet. Most people were forced to buy more food (at much higher prices) in the "free market" that was tolerated by necessity.

Similar distribution systems were in place for other commodities (clothing, other consumer goods) as well as for services like health care and education. For example, in the health care sector, citizens with classification A1 had access to special personal doctors and special pharmaceuticals. For classes A, B, and C there was a special hospital with different departments for each class of citizen. There were other public hospitals for categories D and E. Across the board, hospitals had different equipment and staff depending on what class of patients they were serving.

To manage their daily life, people had to develop extensive networks of "connections" to shops for rice, meat, other food products, and consumer goods as well as "free market" or "black market" vendors. Connections with hospitals, schools, kindergartens, and so forth were also necessary to get access to services when needed (often requiring extra payments in addition to the low official fees). The system not only created opportunities for extra earnings from corruption and trading on the black market, but the system also required these parallel market activities for its functioning. For many citizens, access to food and other goods outside the official quotas was essential for survival. The supply of goods in the free market came from several sources. Speculation, goods stolen from factories and state stores, and the resale of goods that had been purchased at subsidized prices from special shops provided some of the supply; the parallel market was profitable, with prices that were often several times higher than the subsidized prices in the state shops. In addition, the "socialist reconstruction" campaign in Vietnam had left some leeway for farmers to act outside the plan.

Members of agricultural cooperatives were allowed to use their household plots (typically 5 percent of the cooperative's total farmland) for some private farming activities. This was one of the major cash income sources for the farmers, since they could sell products from these household plots in the free market at free market prices—the income from the cooperative was mainly in the form of rice and other products. The productivity of the household plots was much higher than that of the remaining 95 percent of farmland that was cultivated by the cooperatives. This gap worried government economists and policymakers. In the cities, small traders were morally condemned and harassed by the administration, but not to the degree that they would have disappeared altogether—it was recognized that they were needed to satisfy some of the population's demands, which were neglected by central planning and the rationing system.

Gradually, these departures from traditional socialist ideology began to gain more ground. Already in the 1960s, Kim Ngoc, the head of the CPV Committee of Vinh Phuc Province, had initiated a "contract plan system" to provide stronger incentives for the farmers. Under this system, farmers agreed to produce and deliver a certain quota to the state, but were allowed to dispose of any production beyond the agreed quota as they wished. Kim Ngoc was punished and put under house arrest for this initiative. Similar low-level reforms were attempted in Do Son (Hai Phong) in the late 1970s, but without any immediate impact on the overall policy framework (although it was allowed to spread to the rest of the province during the following years). However, by the end of the decade, it had become clear that more extensive economic reforms of these types were needed to avoid continued stagnation. The top leadership was open-minded and pragmatic enough not to ignore or reject the early grassroots initiatives, which were carefully studied and eventually translated into partial adjustments of the planning system.

Hence, the Sixth Plenum of the Central Committee of the Fourth Legislation of the CPV promulgated Resolution no. 20 on September 20, 1979. It criticized the "centralized bureaucracy, which did not combine planning and the application of market economic relations," and requested microeconomic reforms.

Simultaneously, both farmers and SOEs were trying to find ways of escaping the rigidity of the command system. The experiments with the "contract system" had amounted to a de facto decentralization of responsibility and an allocation of arable land to the farming households. SOEs initiated a "fence-breaking" movement with a "three part plan," which enabled them to generate more financial resources, and allowed them to buy and sell their products at market prices. Resolutions 25/CP and 26/CP of the government in 1981 legalized the "three part plan," and Directive 100-CT of the Secretariat of the Central Committee of the CPV, issued the same year, allowed the contract system in agriculture. Meanwhile, in Long An Province, an experiment to abolish the dual price system and introduce market-based pricing brought positive results. Although these reforms seemed to raise economic efficiency and productivity, they were not uncontroversial, and a stormy debate ensued in the Party. There was strong criticism of the "bureaucratic central planning system" and continued isolated attempts to eliminate the private sector and collectivize agriculture, as well as conservative rebuttals. As late as 1983, when some private businesses had already been established throughout the country, the Hanoi Party Committee and the People's Committee launched a campaign with the title "administrative control and inspection," which confiscated the assets and real estate of more than fifty successful private enterprises, including the well-known fish restaurant Cha Ca La Vong and the producer of rickshaw tires, the so-called "king of tires." It was evidence of how difficult the reform process was. Later, after the launch of the Đổi Mới reform program, the confiscated assets were partially returned to their owners, but such campaigns created deep and bitter memories in the minds of private entrepreneurs.

The inefficiency of the system and the failures in economic policies of the late 1970s and early 1980s were severe, but not strong enough to lead to a broad systemic reform. Instead, the reforms that came in the early 1980s were partial adjustments within the command economy. One reason for the resilience of the system was the massive inflow of aid from the Soviet Union, which saw Vietnam as an important ally in the ideological battle against China. This changed gradually from the mid-1980s, when economic stagnation and *perestroika* in the Soviet Union led to a reduction in Soviet support. By this time, the weaknesses in Vietnam's collectivized production system, in both agriculture and industry, were aggravated by a combination of growing trade, government budget deficits, and galloping inflation. SOE production was stagnating because of the lack of imported inputs and raw materials, and the flow of agricultural commodities through the state's distribution system was diminishing because the prices paid to farmers fell short of increasing production costs. In 1985, inflation peaked at an annual rate of nearly 700 percent (see graphic below), and food shortages were reported from several parts of the country. Faced with a deep socioeconomic crisis, political leaders were forced to acknowledge that more fundamental reforms to mobilize internal resources and to give more space to the private sector were necessary to handle the critical situation.

ĐỔI MỚI

Some months after the death of the CPV General Secretary Le Duan on July 10, 1986, the reelected General Secretary Truong Chinh delivered the Party's political report at the Sixth National Congress of the CPV in December 1986.[2] It presented an unprecedentedly harsh self-criticism of the CPV, analyzing the failures of the central planning models, without naming any persons to blame. Terms like "voluntaristic," "subjective," "conservative," and "bureaucratic style of management" were used to characterize the recent past. In response, the Congress initiated the Đổi Mới process by introducing policies that would gradually help Vietnam's transition to "an economy based on product-money relations, economic accounting, and multi-economic sectorial structure" (including state sector, cooperative, domestic private sector, and foreign direct invested sector), as well as "developing international economic relations" and "restructuring the state administration agencies."[3] The reforms of "Price-Salary-Currency" in 1985 had led to hyperinflation (see figure 5.1).

The government of Vice Prime Minister To Huu took responsibility and resigned in 1986. At the time, the Sixth Party Congress of the CPV did not refer yet to the currently popular term "market economy with socialist orientation." These policies were to some extent based on the "fence-breaking" experiments undertaken in various parts of the country during the previous years, as well as insights and experiences from the implementation of Resolutions 25/CP and 26/CP and Directive 100-CT mentioned earlier. They were implemented under difficult conditions, with a deep socioeconomic crisis plaguing the nation, continued military activity in Cambodia, a broad international embargo, and without international consultations.

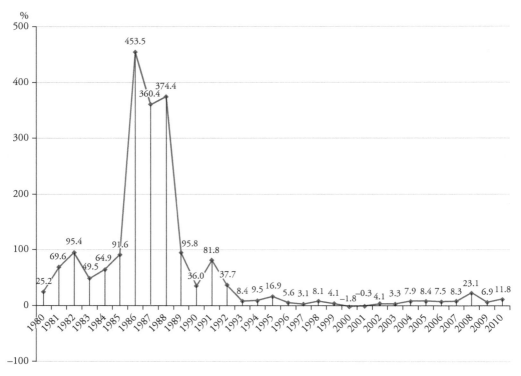

FIGURE 5.1 Inflation in Vietnam

The Sixth National Congress reaffirmed its commitment to the reform program and issued a statement in which the reform objectives were highlighted in five points:

- To carry out concerted efforts to increase the production of food, consumer goods, and exportable items;
- To continue the efforts to control small merchants and capitalists, while at the same time acknowledging the reality of supporting a mixed economy;
- To regenerate the planning bureaucracy while making the economic management system more efficient by decentralizing authority and making room for more independent decision making;
- To clarify the powers and jurisdiction of the Council of Ministers, and reorganize the state management apparatus to make it more efficient; and
- To improve the party's organizational capabilities, leadership, and cadre training.

The Đổi Mới reform program adopted at the Sixth Party Congress initiated a step-by-step liberalization of the private sector. The decision to carry out this controversial reform was primarily induced by the practical needs of daily life, rather than from theoretical rethinking of the nation's economic model.

The effects of the early reforms in agriculture were so impressive that other measures were introduced to allow more scope for the private sector in other fields. In 1987, the government promulgated two ordinances allowing private businesses to operate more freely. During the next two years, with mounting pressures on available resources, the government undertook bold, unprecedented, and extraordinary measures that allowed individuals to trade gold and jewels, and as a result, the price of gold was immediately normalized. Private housing construction was also allowed in 1989, which helped to ease the ongoing housing crisis. Private traders in retail trade, including rice retail, were also accepted. State control on prices was reduced drastically so that prices of goods and services would reflect demand and supply in the market, and price subsidies on rice, meat, and other consumer goods were canceled. Public reactions were surprisingly positive and revealed the negative impacts of the subsidies. As the free market could provide a sufficient supply of rice and other foods, the state-owned rice shops were suspended.

These measures produced such positive results that the government decided to prepare a company law to be presented to the National Assembly in December 1990 to legalize the private sector. This was an important formal step in the evolution of the relationship between the state and the economy in Vietnam: to regulate by law instead of by administrative order.

Vietnam promulgated the Law on Foreign Direct Investment on December 29, 1987, hoping to attract foreign capital and technology to make up for the disappearing assistance from the Soviet Union and Eastern European socialist countries. Thanks to a combination of low labor costs, an increasingly liberal trade environment, and a favorable policy environment (with various investment incentives such as tax exemptions and privileged access to land), inflows of FDI have gradually increased, as discussed in the chapter by Ari Kokko, Curt Nestor, and Le Hai Van in this volume.

A subtle indication of the deep changes that were in progress came in September 1989, when the Sixth Plenum of the Central Committee of the CPV for the first time replaced the "dictatorship of the proletariat" by the term "political system." The promulgations of the Company Law in 1990 and the Enterprise Law in 1999, both of which have been of great importance for the development of Vietnam's private sector, illustrate some of the challenges inherent in the complex and difficult process of institutional change in Vietnam. The following section will focus on these laws.

Company Law and Enterprise Law

The initial draft of the Company Law, prepared by the Central Institute of Economic Management (CIEM), tried to build on the relevant contents of the Company Law of South Vietnam from before 1975, which consisted of more than three hundred articles. However, several deputies of the National Assembly were unfamiliar with the market economy, as well as with the standards and practices of joint stock companies and companies with limited liability. They therefore rejected the draft on the grounds that it was too complicated and decided instead to promulgate a very simple law in 1990, with only thirty-four articles but without detailed regulations on internal company operations. They also required the authorization of state officials for the establishment of a company, and mandated specific amounts of chartered capital for different industries and services. The law was split into two separate laws: a Company Law for joint stock companies and companies with limited liability, and a Law on Private Enterprise with unlimited liability. Despite some weaknesses and limitations, the promulgation of the Company Law and the Private Enterprise Law at the very beginning of the reform process was a bold and important step toward a market economy and the development of a private sector. As a result, during the following nine years (1991–99), some 45,000 companies and private enterprises were established, signaling the emergence of a new private sector in Vietnam.

FIELD STUDIES AND SURVEYS

The decision to promulgate the highly simplified (and incomplete) versions of the Company Law and the Private Enterprise Law led to substantial challenges in the implementation of the laws. Surveys conducted by CIEM in 1998–99 highlighted some of the shortcomings and challenges.

Both laws required that companies be authorized by a high-ranking official, the chairman of the People's Committee of the province or municipality, before registration. This cautious and certainly not ill-intended step was in reality a seedbed for corruption, abuse of power, and harassment. Before the chairman of the People's Committee of the province signed the authorization, the chairmen of the ward and the district committee had to sign in order to provide political backup; the directors of relevant departments of the province also had to sign as a confirmation that they had checked and confirmed the submitted documents and materials. The surveys discovered that thirty-five signatures from officials at several administrative levels and agencies were required, together with thirty-two seals of various agencies before authorization could be granted. In many cases, applicants had to pay several extralegal "lubrication fees" to keep this process moving.

As the law did not identify specifically what documents and materials were required for authorization, the civil servants routinely requested an unlimited number of officially notarized copies of documents or materials to be included with the application. However, the number of required documents was not constant, but could be reduced if "special" fees were paid. Because the law did not stipulate explicitly how the status of a company should be defined, the applicants gradually learned that the best way to get the application approved was to pay for the services of the registrar to draft the necessary documents.

The registration fee of 0.2 percent of the chartered capital stipulated by the law was counterproductive. This fee unnecessarily added to the cost for the establishment of an enterprise. Applicants tried to avoid establishing large joint stock companies, because the registration fee increased with the size of the company. It was no surprise that with these cumbersome procedures it took from six months to a year to finalize all the formalities and to get the authorization to establish a private enterprise from the chairman of the provincial People's Committee. The costs in terms of money varied from 10 to 30 million VND, depending on the type and the size of the company. The costs in terms of time and money were exceptionally high in comparison with international standards, which was an obvious obstacle for the development of the private sector.

The politically sensitive nature of promoting private enterprise made the administrative process difficult for the provincial leaders as well. For example, the vice chairman of the People's Committee of Hanoi routinely called a meeting of all relevant general directors of city departments and chairmen of all districts every week to collectively approve the applications of private companies. This approach was chosen as an insurance measure for the vice chairman, because supporting the private sector was still politically risky at the time—with collective approvals, the individual decision makers were less exposed to criticism. On average, it was possible to authorize only two private companies in Hanoi each working week.

THE ENTERPRISE LAW OF 1999

The Drafting and Promulgation Process A resolution of the Fourth Plenum of the Central Committee of the CPV on December 28, 1997, decided that a new law on companies should be prepared. The findings from the CIEM surveys on the shortcomings of the Company Law of 1990 and the Private Enterprise Law of 1990 formed a basis for preparing a new Enterprise Law (EL) that would replace both the older laws.

The Politburo of the Central Committee of the CPV discussed the draft of the EL based on the presentation of the government and the comments of the National Assembly, and eventually accepted the draft. It also provided guidance on the main principles and conceptions of the law and sent it forward to the plenary session of the National Assembly for consideration and possible approval. During the stormy, critical, and open debate in the plenary session of the National Assembly, which took several days, one article after another was passed, but not without opposition. For example, the chairwoman of Bac Giang Province insisted she knew the people in the province very well, including who was "good" and who was "bad," and that she should therefore have the right to decide who could establish a company. However, she could not refer to any legal regulations that allowed her to classify citizens as good and bad or show what legal criteria she could apply to so classify citizens. The chairman of the coastal Khanh Hoa Province also declared that he had stopped the opening of new private hotels in his province, because he believed there were already too many hotels there. However, he was not able to show convincingly how he could determine what was the right number of hotels. It was not easy for the provincial leaders to give up their power over the authorization of private businesses.

The new Enterprise Law was passed by the National Assembly by majority vote (84.5 percent) on May 29, 1999. The main idea of the EL was to provide one unified legal framework for all types of enterprises and to grant the freedom to conduct business to the people. In actual fact, the EL became a law for the domestic private sector; at the time, there were already separate laws on state-owned enterprise, on cooperatives, and on foreign direct investment.

It is useful to look specifically at some of the articles of the EL. Article 2 regulates the relation between this law and other specialized laws: "where a difference exists on the same issue between this Law and a specialized law, the provisions of the specialized law shall apply." This article opens the way for other laws regulating business in specific areas, for example, to request chartered capital (for insurance companies) or licenses, standards, or permits that aim to protect public interests.

Article 4 provides state guarantees for enterprises and their owners: "the lawful assets and investment capital of enterprises and their owners shall not be nationalized or expropriated by administrative measures." Such guarantees were strongly requested as a legal protection for private business during the drafting process. Considering the experiences of the past, such demands were understandable.

For implementing the freedom to carry out business according to laws, Article 6 was important. It stated that "as prescribed by law, an enterprise may autonomously register and conduct lines of business other than those stipulated in Clauses 2, 3, and 4 of this Article." Clause 2 stipulated the prohibited lines of business. Clauses 3 and 4 stipulated that "where a law, an ordinance, or a decree prescribes conditions for conduct of line of business, an enterprise may only conduct such line of business if it satisfies all the prescribed conditions" and "where a law, an ordinance, or a decree requires an amount of legal capital, or a practicing certificate, for a line of business, an enterprise may only register such line of business if it has sufficient capital or a practicing certificate as required by law." This article effectively canceled all the numerous permits, licenses, and certificates required by ministers or chairmen of People's Committees under the earlier laws. But because nobody knew what licenses existed, the government had to explicitly review the license requirements and cancel them as described below.

Article 9 stipulated clearly the rights to establish and manage enterprises. It stated that "organizations and individuals have the right to establish and manage enterprises, except for the following cases." Article 6 used a "Negative list" to exclude state officials and others from establishing and managing enterprises. Article 10 regulated the right to contribute capital, allowing a larger circle of people, including foreign organizations and others, to contribute capital.

In the same direction, Article 12 stipulated: "The business registration body is not entitled to request the founder of an enterprise to submit additional documents other than those prescribed by this Law for each type of enterprise." For the first time, a law stipulated a clear restriction of the rights of a state agency. In that way, the *prior registration checking*, exercised under the previous Company Law of 1990, was replaced by *post-registration monitoring, internal control, and openness and transparency*. More importantly, the EL effectively upheld the freedom to do business according to laws and ended the requirement to get the authorization of the chairman of the People's Committee at the provincial level. In that way, red tape and abuse of power were significantly reduced.

Articles 20 and 21 stipulated the provision of information on business registration and publication of the business registration. It aimed to introduce transparency to the business registration and to provide interested people with access to this information. The law required the enterprises to "declare and periodically report fully and accurately the information regarding the enterprise and its financial situation."

On the one hand, the intention of the law was to implement the freedom to do business according to laws. On the other hand, the law emphasized the internal control of the shareholders, the creditors, mass media, and other interested people, and last but not least, the efficient governance of the state agencies. That aimed to ensure that freedom should not lead to chaos, as opponents of the EL had argued during the whole process of drafting and promulgating the Enterprise Law.

The Implementation of the Law Fully aware of the difficulties and challenges related to the implementation of the EL, the prime minister, for the first time, established a task force to assist in the process. The task force was responsible for elaborating the two ordinances issued for the implementation of the law, for exchanging views with related ministries on their guidance, and for helping to apply information technology in the registration process

One of the most important contributions of the task force was a number of revealing studies on required licenses and permits for doing business. As mentioned before, Article 6 of the Enterprise Law automatically canceled all licenses and permits issued by ministries and provinces. But since there was no overview of all licenses and permits that were required by different authorities, it was necessary to identify all permits that were considered to be redundant and then explicitly cancel each of them. Responding to a request by the task force on this issue, all ministries and state agencies ensured that they did not require any special permits or licenses. However, a survey on the licenses and permits showed that at least 402 permits and licenses existed and were required by authorities at different levels. After a process of long and difficult negotiations with the related ministries and agencies, the prime minister and the government abolished a total of 180 licenses and permits. This greatly reduced the administrative costs in terms of time and money for private enterprises. Unfortunately, it turned out that this reduction in the administrative burden of enterprises was temporary. Table 5.4 summarizes some of the changes in the regulatory environment following the implementation of the Enterprise Law of 1999.

Altogether, the Vietnamese government issued seventy-two documents guiding the implementation of the Enterprise Law, including twenty-two decrees, twelve decisions by the prime minister, and thirty-five circulars and decisions by relevant ministries and government authorities. The National Assembly and its Standing Committee issued two further laws and six ordinances related to the Enterprise Law. These legislative efforts made the EL one of the most comprehensive and rapidly implemented laws in the history of Vietnam.

Despite these efforts toward simpler and more transparent administrative processes, the regulatory landscape in Vietnam remains complex, and requirements for new licenses and permits have been introduced over time. In 2018, new surveys revealed that various state agencies had inflated the number of licenses to 6,191, with obvious costs in terms of cumbersome administrative procedures and expenditure of time and money. The government therefore decided in 2018 to abolish 3,345 of these licenses, but the business community continues to complain about harassment and requests for extralegal payments connected to many of the remaining licenses and permits.

Table 5.4
Comparison of regulatory practices: Company Law 1990 and Enterprise Law 1999

Company Law (1990)	Enterprise Law (1999)
Main concept: establishment of private enterprises controlled by authorities	Main concept: freedom to carry out business within framework of law
Authorization prior to registration required	No prior authorization needed
Complex business registration process: duration 6–12 months, cost VND 10–30 million, 35 signatures and 32 seals/stamps of different agencies required	Simpler business registration process: duration 15 days, cost VND 220,000, no prior authorization needed
More than 400 licenses and permissions required for business operations	180 of 400 licenses and permits canceled or transformed to business standards
In 9 years, 43,000 private enterprises were registered, mainly in big cities and urban areas	88,000 new private enterprises registered during 2000–2004 (before new unified law was promulgated in 2005)

THE UNIFIED ENTERPRISE LAW OF 2005

The Enterprise Law of 2005 extended the legislative reforms to facilitate the development of the private sector. Until 2005, Vietnam had separate laws for private enterprises, SOEs, and foreign-invested enterprises. In order to comply with WTO commitments, Vietnam promulgated a new unified Enterprise and Investment Law in 2005 that applies to all three ownership categories. SOEs can now take the form of sole owner, joint stock company (jointly or without private partners), or conglomerate (see further below). While the EL of 1999 was subject to extensive debate, the Enterprise Law of 2005 was passed with less controversy. One reason was probably that the 2005 law was mandated by an external commitment that had already been agreed upon—the accession to the WTO—whereas the EL of 1999 was a more fundamental internal decision related to important reforms in the Vietnamese economy and state administration.

CONTINUOUS GROWTH OF THE PRIVATE SECTOR SINCE 2000

If the success of the legal reforms supporting the private enterprise sector is measured by reduction in the relative shares of the state sector, the Enterprise Law has undoubtedly been a success. From January 1, 2000, to February 1, 2004, 88,000 new private enterprises were registered, which is nearly twice the number of companies established during the preceding nine years. As shown in table 5.5, the GDP share of the state sector has fallen continuously, from about 40 percent in the mid-1990 to an estimated 27 percent in 2019. Meanwhile, the share of formal private enterprises has increased throughout the period.[4] However, the rate of increase has been relatively slow because of remaining weaknesses in the business environment for domestic private firms, in particular SMEs. Instead, the reduction in the state's share of GDP has mainly been captured by foreign-invested enterprises, which saw their GDP shares more than triple between 1995 and 2019, from 6 percent to over 20 percent. Yet it should be noted that the private sector in Vietnam

Table 5.5
Ownership shares of GDP, 1995–2019

	1995[a]	2005[a]	2010	2015	2019 est.
State	40.2	37.6	29.3	28.7	27.0
Non-state	53.5	47.2	43.0	43.2	42.7
Collective	10.1	6.6	4.0	4.0	3.6
Private	7.4[b]	8.5	7.0	7.9	9.7
Household	36.0	32.1	32.0	31.3	29.4
FDI	6.3	15.2	15.2	18.1	20.4
Product taxes less subsidies on production	..[c]	..	12.6	10.0	9.9

Sources: Statistical Yearbook of Vietnam 1998 and General Statistics Office, Vietnam, https://www.gso.gov.vn /default_en.aspx?tabid=775.

Notes:
[a] Sectoral shares were not corrected for product taxes and production subsidies before 2010.
[b] Includes "mixed ownership."
[c] Data not available.

increased its capital investment one hundred times, increased its employment by a factor of seven, and contributed more to budget revenue than foreign-invested enterprises over the period 2000–2017, according to CIEM.[5]

Increasing Support for the Private Sector

The state in Vietnam has made a slow and difficult transition from central planning with discretionary decision-making processes toward a state that is officially governed by the constitution and formal law. The constitution outlines not only the fundamental principles that form the legal basis of the nation and how it is governed, but also the roles of the state and the private sector. The constitution of Vietnam from 2014 defines the Vietnamese state as follows:

> Article 2 1. The Socialist Republic of Vietnam is a socialist rule of law State of the People, by the People, and for the People.
>
> 2.2. The State powers are unified and delegated to state bodies, which shall coordinate with and control one another in the exercise of the legislative, executive, and judiciary powers.

This article clearly rejects the idea of the separation of power into autonomous legislative, executive, and judicial branches.

The central role of the Communist Party is explicitly spelled out, but Vietnam has not yet promulgated any law on the leadership and governance of the CPV, and it is not likely that such laws will be on the agenda for the foreseeable future. That is why there is de facto no clear distinction between the CPV and the state—the real power rests with the CPV.

On the economic system the constitution states:

> Article 51.1. The Vietnamese economy is a socialist-oriented market economy with multiple forms of ownership and multiple sectors of economic structure; the state economic sector plays the leading role.
>
> 51.2. All economic sectors are important constituents of the national economy. Participants in different economic sectors are equal, cooperate and compete in accordance with the law.

The term "state economic sector" (*kinh tế nhà nước*) was first used at the Seventh National Congress of the CPV (1996), replacing the previously used term "state-operated economy" (*kinh tế quốc doanh*). The state economic sector has been understood to mean state ownership of land and natural resources, state budget, and state foreign reserves. The "leading role of the state economy" has been elaborated as "the important material power and instrument of the state to fix the direction and keep the macroeconomic balance of the national economy."[6] When it comes to the state versus the non-state or private sector, Communist Party leaders on the one hand argue that "private enterprises shall be an engine of growth and development in Vietnam," but they also make it clear that "SOEs shall continue to play a leading role in the economy."[7] This tension characterizes much of the institutional development in Vietnam, and causes substantial confusion.

The Vietnamese government and the Communist Party have become increasingly aware of the importance of the private sector and have gradually introduced various reforms to strengthen its position. In addition to the company and enterprise laws discussed above, this has required reforms in the financial sector, where a private banking system, financial companies, credit cooperatives, and a stock market have been established to complement the state banking system.

Already in 2001, the government published a decree whereby it recognized that "Development of SMEs is an important task in the Socio-Economic Development Strategy, [and] accelerates the industrialization and modernization of the country." Further, the document stated that "the State shall encourage and facilitate SMEs to release their initiatives and creativity, improve their managerial capacities, and develop their science, technology, and human resources. The Government shall support the investment [of SMEs] through financial and credit measures." More recently, in 2017, the Fifth Plenum of the CPV's Central Committee adopted a resolution identifying "the private sector as a driving force for the market economy with socialist orientation in Vietnam." At the same time as these various steps have constituted important political moves to legitimize the private sector, they also illustrate the gradual process that Vietnam has gone through over the past thirty years.

Overall, the result of the reform process has been substantial growth in private-sector activities. In 2019, the private economic sector contributed 43 percent of GDP (legally registered companies accounted for 10 percent of GDP, while the household sector contributed the remaining 33 percent of GDP). Very importantly, 25 percent of private registered companies are led or headed by female leaders, much higher than the regional average in Southeast Asia, contributing significantly to gender equality in Vietnam. The private sector, excluding farming, accounts for 51 percent of total employment and creates 1.2 million new jobs per year.

Although most private enterprises belong to the SME category, some large private conglomerates have also emerged. For example, in the car manufacturing industry, where no Vietnamese SOEs are active, the private conglomerate Vingroup has established the first Vietnamese car, Vinfast, while the Truong Hai Group is successfully assembling cars for brands like Hyundai, Kia, and Mazda. The private Hoa Phat Group has grown to be the largest steel producer in the country, while the state-owned Thai Nguyen steel conglomerate is on the brink of bankruptcy, its leadership facing prosecution.[8]

At the same time, the transitional character of Vietnam's economy means that this development has not been without problems. Various state agencies are still prominent in many sectors, and one troubling issue concerns the habit of relying on "connections" (in Vietnamese, *quan he*) with state actors when doing business. This is relevant in Vietnam for "lubricating" the decision process in order to get access to land, timber, minerals, and other resources, or even to get tax reductions, tax holidays, and permission for imports and exports. While these practices are common and widely accepted in some circles, it is clear that this is nothing but bribery and corruption on the part of the related state officials.

Another problem is that domestic private firms sometimes operate in a less favorable legal environment than foreign investors, who may have access to favorable tax rules, subsidized land, and investment guarantees.[9] Furthermore, although the Đổi Mới process has introduced the market economy in Vietnam and reforms have strengthened the position of the private sector, elements of planning remain, and the ambition that SOEs should play a leading role in the economy sometimes distorts the competitive environment. In some industries, SOEs have a monopoly position; in many others, they enjoy various privileges, to the detriment of their privately owned competitors.

Obstacles to Private-Sector Development: Planning and SOEs

The measures to promote private enterprise have led to significant economic and social change in Vietnam. State agencies as well as state officials and public servants have had to learn to operate in a new legal framework. Planning agencies still exist, but their power to distribute resources to selected enterprises is limited. State agencies cannot readily intervene in the business operations of SOEs and private companies, but they still hold substantial power through their role in administering various licenses, permits, and plans. The continuing use of various licenses has been discussed above. In addition, in 2017, the Vietnamese government still had 11,667 master plans controlled by the ministries and local government agencies in force, significantly limiting market mechanisms in the specific sectors targeted by the plans (e.g., master plans on cement, catfish production, and so forth).[10] These master plans impose restrictions and conditions on enterprises and businesspeople. The newly promulgated Law on Master Plans, which entered into force at the beginning of 2019, reduces significantly the number of master plans and opens more room for market operations.[11] According to Decision No. 995 QD-TTg of the prime minister, dated August 2018, thirty-nine master plans should be elaborated for the period 2021–30, with a vision to 2050.[12]

Vietnam's "market system with socialist orientation" has allowed the private sector to emerge and grow to a certain size and level in many industries, but the SOE sector retains an important role in other parts of the economy. SOEs hold virtual monopolies in many strategically important sectors, such as petroleum products, electricity, coal, basic chemicals, telecommunications, and railroad transportation, as well as leading positions in many other industries, such as food products, cement, steel, paper, rubber, shipbuilding, air transportation, trade, and finance and insurance. Many of the state-owned conglomerates are highly diversified, with multiple activities outside their core business, meaning that private SMEs often find themselves competing with SOEs even when they operate in less strategic industries. Given their privileged access to resources such as land and financial capital, as well as close contacts with political decision makers, SOEs are often able to dominate the local and regional markets where they operate. Moreover, in the past, the management of SOEs has often not been based on transparent business considerations, largely because of weak accountability and, at times, soft budget constraints.

The government aims to implement the political concept "market economy with socialist orientation" according to the principle "collective leadership combined with personal responsibility" in the management of SOEs. However, the CPV decides on all political issues, and there is de facto often no clear "personal responsibility." A famous example of the consequences of this structure was the collapse of the huge state-owned shipbuilding conglomerate Vinashin, which led the National Assembly to request "personal responsibility" from Prime Minister Nguyen Tan Dung. However, his counterargument was that "all decisions have been approved by collective resolutions," and "my position has been endorsed by the Party," rejecting the call to take responsibility and resign from his position.[13]

More generally, the CPV exercises its leadership in all domains of the political system, and there is no division of power between the legislative, administrative, and judicial branches.[14] The personnel decisions regarding political positions and other leading representatives of the state are made by the CPV. The CPV controls the press, the mass media, and cyber activities. Hence, there is no counterbalance of power to the CPV, although the Commission of Control and Inspection of the CPV has some responsibilities in this direction, reporting to a CPV committee at the same hierarchical level, and it is not autonomous. This political structure remains largely unaffected by the transition to "market economy with socialist orientation" and Vietnam's integration with the world economy.

In this political landscape, it is not surprising that it has been difficult to reform the SOEs, many of which have proven to be grossly inefficient. The efficiency of state-owned enterprises (SOEs) is low. Their share of GDP is 28 percent (and their share of investment even higher), but they contribute only 22 percent of revenues of the state budget. The rate of return and other criteria of SOE performance are weaker than those of private enterprises.[15] The government had the strategy to develop the state-owned conglomerates to be the "iron fists of the national economy," but nearly all major state-owned conglomerates have been sanctioned in various ways because of corruption charges or wastefulness—the list of examples includes Vinashin (shipbuilding), Vinalines (maritime transportation), PetroVietnam, Vietnam Electricity, state-owned conglomerates in chemicals, coal mining and minerals, and others. The outstanding debts of the SOEs were reported to reach US$73 billion in 2016.[16] The Ministry of Industry and Trade (MOIT) alone has twelve inefficient mega-investment projects, and several leading officials of the SOEs under MOIT have recently faced criminal charges and prosecution.[17]

The plans to restructure SOEs have proceeded very slowly. Equitization and partial privatization have been at the core of the policy debate in Vietnam over the last decades, but the government's attitude has been ambivalent. On the one hand, equitization is emphasized in policy statements as a necessary step to create more efficient enterprises. On the other hand, the progress on equitization has been slow and relatively modest.

The government started a pilot equitization program in 1992 that was extended in 1996 with a formal decree on equitization. The decree targeted so-called nonstrategic SOEs that were allowed to become joint stock companies. The equitization process was very slow and at the beginning restricted to a limited number of unprofitable SOEs (by 1998 only eighteen SOEs were equitized). One reason was the resistance to equitization from many vested interests, above all SOE managers. New targets have been introduced over time, and the number of wholly state-owned enterprises has fallen dramatically, from over 12,000 in the early 1990s to 5,600 in 2000, 1,350 in 2010, and fewer than 1,000 by 2020. However, much of the privatization process underlying this trend—in particular for the larger SOEs—has focused on partial divestment. The state keeps significant—often controlling—ownership shares in about 3,000 enterprises, in addition to the wholly owned SOEs. From the perspective of purely private firms, it is often equally difficult to compete with partly state-owned firms as with wholly state-owned enterprises. Moreover, the aggregate capital stock of SOEs has grown continuously during the past two decades, despite the privatization and divestments that have taken place.

External Pressure for Change

As noted earlier, Vietnam's early economic reforms were driven primarily by urgency and need rather than theoretical rethinking of the nation's economic model. Over time, as Vietnam's reforms have contributed to increasing international integration, some reforms have gradually been locked in through international agreements. Further pressure for reform comes from various trade and investment agreements with other economies.

For example, Vietnam's accession to ASEAN and its free trade agreement AFTA in 1995 required several steps in the direction of economic liberalization and opening up.

The BTA with the US, which took effect in December 2002, added further reforms extending beyond trade, for example, in the areas of intellectual property rights, business facilitation, and transparency. In order to join the WTO, Vietnam had to amend several laws, for example, moving the Law on State-Owned Enterprises to one chapter of the Enterprise Law of 1999, and unifying the Law on Promotion of Domestic Investment and the Law on Foreign Direct Investment to one unified Law on Investment. More recently, Vietnam has also joined the CPTPP (Trans-Pacific Partnership), which has repercussions on domestic regulation and business policy.

In addition, Vietnam has signed free trade agreements (FTAs) with fifteen economies in the framework of six regional ASEAN agreements and an FTA with the EU (the EVFTA). The CPTPP and EVFTA, in particular, have translated into bold and unprecedented commitments from the Vietnamese side on a range of important issues—including labor rights, SOEs, government procurement, intellectual property rights, transparency, and openness—which are expected to result in substantial changes in the domestic legal framework on these sensitive issues. The commitments related to labor rights are particularly notable. Both agreements include specific requirements on work conditions, the freedom of association, and the right of collective bargaining. These requirements aim to contribute to sustainable development and enable workers and businesses to enjoy their fair share of economic gains, in line with the objectives of the International Labour Organisation (ILO). Once the two agreements come into effect, it is expected that workers will gradually be allowed to establish or join organizations of their own choosing, which, in turn, can decide whether they will be part of the Vietnam General Confederation of Labour (VGCL) or remain autonomous.

Although external factors like those discussed above have typically put pressure on Vietnam to reform its institutions, it is possible that there may also be external events that reduce the pressure for change. The COVID-19 pandemic that started in January 2020 and continues until today could be a case in point. The successful responses to the pandemic have strengthened the legitimacy and power of the Vietnamese government, and contributed to the view that Vietnam is an attractive alternative to China for FDI.

Is the Private Sector Competitive?

Despite these examples of progress, the public administration system in Vietnam remains relatively complex and untransparent, and accountability is not yet clearly defined. This has severe consequences for the efficiency of state investment.

Some of the challenges for the private sector are related to corruption: the complex and opaque restrictions coupled with unclear accountability open up many alternative interpretations of rules and discretionary decision-making processes. These problems are not unknown to Vietnam's top leaders: a major concern is that corrupt Party officials undermine the legitimacy of the CPV. There is a widespread belief that large companies and other interest groups are able to influence government policies and decisions in their own favor.

In addition to the areas discussed above, it should be noted that Vietnamese society— and therefore the Vietnamese state—is facing a number of formidable challenges related to environmental protection, rising inequality and criminality, and the weak state of higher education and vocational education in Vietnam. The policies to address these challenges and their efficiency will have significant effects on the business sector and its international competitiveness.

Conclusion

During the transition process from central planning to a "market economy with socialist orientation" that is integrated into the regional and global economy, Vietnam's institutions have undergone a significant transformation, where existing institutions have been renovated and new institutions, both domestic and international, have emerged. For example, associations of business communities and new NGOs have emerged, multiple newspapers have been established, the Internet has created access to information and changed people's ways of communicating, experiments with e-government have been initiated, and the role and visibility of the National Assembly have increased. There is, however, still no law on NGOs, and most existing ones are focused on professional activities like associations of SMEs.

Some elements of the institutional framework in Vietnam still create bottlenecks for economic and social progress. Higher education and vocational education have so far not been able to provide the skills and capabilities demanded by the private sector, and innovation in science and technology is insufficient. There is still excessive state intervention in many markets, legal regulations often change unexpectedly, and state agencies operate with limited oversight, transparency, and openness. One consequence is that the costs in time and money to engage in formal business in Vietnam are comparatively high. There are also challenges in public administration. Overstaffing, wastefulness, corruption, and vested interests reduce the efficiency of the public sector and contribute to chronic fiscal deficits and public debt. Vietnam's political structure, with a one-party state under the Communist Party of Vietnam, exacerbates some of these problems. Political objectives and resolutions are adopted by CPV committees at various levels and forwarded to the government, which is expected to prepare drafts of formal laws to be approved by the National Assembly. Accountability and personal responsibility are weak, both because of the lack of transparency and because the collective resolutions of the CPV serve to protect the individuals involved in the decision. New problems like climate change, environmental concerns, inequality, and the digital transformation will also need to be addressed in a timely and efficient manner. It is obvious that further systemic reforms are needed in countries like Vietnam to find solutions for these issues. Vietnam must also continue to reform its institutions to build the "state of the people, by the people, for the people" that it claims to be.

Anti-corruption and "control of power" has been a core theme of CPV General Secretary Nguyen Phu Trong's more than decade-long era as party leader. An unprecedented anti-corruption campaign ("burning furnace") was launched and in 2012, a Central Steering Committee for Anti-corruption chaired by Trong was established. Since the 2021 Thirteenth National Congress of the CPV, fifty high ranking officials have been punished, including eight members of the Central Committee and twenty generals from the Army and Public Security.[18]

The Thirteenth National Congress of the CPV, held at the end of January 2021, confirmed the reforms of market institutions, the state, and social organizations. Several important targets were highlighted by the Congress, including "continuing the fight against bureaucracy, corruption, wastefulness, vested interest groups," "reform of public administration," "reforming the legal framework of the market economy with socialist orientation," "improving transparency, openness, and accountability," "controlling power in operations of the state, of state officials and civil servants," and "encouraging innovation and creativeness." For the first time, the terms "transparency, openness, and accountability" were accepted in a political report of a National Congress of the CPV, marking some modest progress. This is particularly encouraging against the backdrop of the COVID-19 pandemic, which has been a serious challenge to Vietnam's political system and the national economy over the past two years—it gives hope that Vietnam's institutional reforms will continue despite unforeseen new challenges.

Notes

1. Nguyen Van Canh, *Vietnam under Communism*, 28.

2. http://dangcongsan.vn/tu-lieu-van-kien/van-kien-dang/van-kien-dai-hoi/khoa-vi/doc-39242015357 1056.html.

3. http://dangcongsan.vn/tu-lieu-van-kien/van-kien-dang/van-kien-dai-hoi/khoa-vi/doc-59242015402 2856.html.

4. The reduction in the share of private enterprises between 2005 and 2010 is due to a change in methodology: taxes and subsidies on production were not reported separately before 2010.

5. http://www.ciem.org.vn/Content/files/2018/vnep2018/C%C4%9018%20-Ph%C3%A1t%20tri%E1%BB%83n%20kinh%20t%E1%BA%BF%20t%C6%B0%20nh%C3%A2n%20v%C3%A0%20c%C6%A1%20c%E1%BA%A5u%20l%E1%BA%A1i%20n%E1%BB%81n%20kinh%20t%E1%BA%BF%20trong%20%C4%91i%E1%BB%81u%20ki%E1%BB%87n%20CMCN%204_0-converted.pdf.

6. http://www.hids.hochiminhcity.gov.vn/web/guest/cac-khu-vuc-kinh-te?p_p_id=EXT _ARTICLEVIEW&p_p_lifecycle=0&p_p_state=normal&p_p_col_id=center-top&p_p_col_count=1& _EXT_ARTICLEVIEW_struts_action=%2Fext%2Farticleview%2Fview&_EXT_ARTICLEVIEW _groupId=13025&_EXT_ARTICLEVIEW_articleId=49731&_EXT_ARTICLEVIEW_version=1.0& _EXT_ARTICLEVIEW_i=4&_EXT_ARTICLEVIEW_curValue=1&_EXT_ARTICLEVIEW_redirect =%2Fweb%2Fguest%2Fcac-khu-vuc-kinh-te.

7. CPV Documents, 2000, 2017.

8. https://www.msn.com/vi-vn/money/topstories/gang-th%C3%A9p-th%C3%A1i-nguy%C3%AAn -%C4%91%E1%BB%A9ng-tr%C6%B0%E1%BB%9b c.c.-b%E1%BB%9D-v%E1%BB%81c-ph%C3%A1-s%E1%BA%A3n/ar-BBVKH55.

9. See Ari Kokko, Curt Nestor, and Le Hai Van on FDI in this volume.

10. http://baodauthau.vn/dau-tu/de-xuat-bai-bo-dung-nhieu-quy-hoach-76539.html.

11. http://vanban.chinhphu.vn/portal/page/portal/chinhphu/hethongvanban?class_id=1&mode =detail&document_id=192206.

12. http://vanban.chinhphu.vn/portal/page/portal/chinhphu/hethongvanban?class_id=2&mode=detail&document_id=194427.

13. BBC Vietnamese, "Kinh tế—Thủ tướng Dũng 'không sai' về Vinashin."

14. An Ninh Thủ Đô, "Tam quyền phân lập không phù hợp với thể chế chính trị ở nước ta."

15. Thúy Hiền, "Hiệu quả sản xuất kinh doanh của doanh nghiệp nhà nước còn thấp."

16. Hiếu Công, "Doanh nghiệp Nhà nước đang gánh số nợ 1,6 triệu tỷ đồng."

17. VnEconomy, "12 đại dự án ngành Công Thương: Đã giảm nợ 124 tỷ đồng."

18. VTC News, "'Củi khô, củi tươi' và bản lĩnh của người 'đốt lò.'"

References

An Ninh Thủ Đô. "Tam quyền phân lập không phù hợp với thể chế chính trị ở nước ta" (The separation of powers is not suitable for the political system in our country). October 9, 2013. https://anninhthudo.vn/chinh-tri-xa-hoi/tam-quyen-phan-lap-khong-phu-hop-voi-the-che-chinh-tri-o-nuoc-ta/515038.antd.

BBC Vietnamese. "Kinh tế—Thủ tướng Dũng 'không sai' về Vinashin" (Prime Minister Dũng not wrong about Vinashin). December 8, 2011. https://www-bbc-com.translate.goog/vietnamese/business/2011/12/111208_viet_pm_vinashin?_x_tr_sl=vi&_x_tr_tl=en&_x_tr_hl=en&_x_tr_pto=sc.

Communist Party of Vietnam. Documents of the Party, Party Program, Party Status (in Vietnamese). Hanoi: National Publishing House for Political Literature Su That, 1986, 1991, 2000, 2006, 2011, 2017, 2021. https://nhandan.com.vn/tin-tuc-su-kien/bao-cao-chinh-tri-cua-ban-chap-hanh-trung-uong-dang-khoa-xii-tai-dai-hoi-dai-bieu-toan-quoc-lan-thu-xiii-cua-dang-621155/.

Dang Phong, ed. *History of Vietnam's Economy*. vol. 2: *1954–1975* (in Vietnamese). Hanoi: Publishing House for Social Sciences, 2005.

Hiếu Công. "Doanh nghiệp Nhà nước đang gánh số nợ 1,6 triệu tỷ đồng" (State-owned enterprises are carrying a debt of 1.6 million billion dong). *Zing News*, May 28, 2018. https://news.zing.vn/doanh-nghiep-nha-nuoc-dang-ganh-so-no-1-6-trieu-ty-dong-post846322.html.

Le Dang Doanh. "Market Economy with Socialist Orientation in Vietnam and the Concept of the Social and Ecological Market Economy." In *The Social and Ecological Market Economy: A Model for Asian Development*, edited by Corinna Küsel, Ulrike Maenner, and Ricarda Meissner. Eschborn, Germany: GTZ, 2008.

———. "Reform of SOEs and State-Owned Economic Group: A Systemic Approach and a Roadmap?" Presentation at DSI-UNDP Workshop, Fortuna Hotel, Hanoi, October 28, 2011.

Nguyen Duc Thanh. *The Economy at a Crossroads*. Hanoi: Vietnam Centre for Economic and Policy Research, 2012.

Nguyen Van Canh. *Vietnam under Communism, 1975–1982*. Stanford, CA: Hoover Institution Press.

Ronnås, Per, and Orjan Sjöberg. *Economic Reforms and Development Policies in Vietnam*. Stockholm: SIDA/SSE/CIEM, 1990.

Thúy Hiền. "Hiệu quả sản xuất kinh doanh của doanh nghiệp nhà nước còn thấp" (The production and business efficiency of state-owned enterprises is still low). BNEWS, November 6, 2018. https://bnews.vn/hieu-qua-san-xuat-kinh-doanh-cua-doanh-nghiep-nha-nuoc-con-thap/101442.html.

Tran Van Tho et al. *Vietnam's Economy 1955–2000*. Hanoi: Publishing House of Statistics, 2000.

Van Arkadie, Brian, and Ray Mallon. *Vietnam: A Transition Tiger?* Canberra: Asia Pacific Press, 2004.

VnEconomy. "12 đại dự án ngành Công Thương: Đã giảm nợ 124 tỷ đồng" (Twelve big projects of industry and trade: Debt reduction of VND 124 billion). October 17, 2018. http://vneconomy.vn/12-dai-du-an-nganh-cong-thuong-da-giam-no-124-ty-dong-20181017183810565.htm.

VTC News. "'Củi khô, củi tươi' và bản lĩnh của người 'đốt lò'" ("Dried firewood, fresh firewood" and the bravery of the "burner"). June 30, 2022. https://vtc.vn/cui-kho-cui-tuoi-va-ban-linh-cua-nguoi-dot-lo-ar685003.html.

PART II

The Economy and the Environment

CHAPTER 6

Explaining Vietnam's Economic Growth Experience

Vu Thanh Tu Anh and Dwight H. Perkins

Vietnam today is seen by many as another Asian economic tiger that is moving rapidly from a poor rural society to a modern middle-income country with an economy dominated by manufacturing and urban services. The focus of the first part of this chapter is to explain briefly how this relatively rapid transformation was achieved and to explore some of the influences and policies that have held the economy back from realizing its full potential. The second and final part of the chapter will attempt to explain whether Vietnam will be able to sustain that relatively high economic growth rate for the next decade or two. Put differently, it will also present an argument by the authors of this chapter as to what changes Vietnam must make to sustain high gross domestic product (GDP) growth.

Vietnam's sustained economic growth did not begin until the late 1980s. Prior to that, war and preparation for war prevented sustainable economic development through 1975. After reunification, the end of fighting and bombing probably made it possible for parts of the economy to recover, but the end of large American wartime aid and expenditures in the south also led to the collapse of many businesses dependent on that aid and expenditure. A notable exception was the steady increase in paddy yields resulting from the introduction of high-yielding varieties from the International Rice Research Institute, which had begun in the early 1970s and continued to the end of the decade. Rice output therefore increased significantly, but rural development in the south more generally was hampered by the attempt in the late 1970s to impose a Soviet-style collective farming system, which was strongly resisted by farm households that had gained ownership of their land from wartime land to the tiller land reform. The negative impact of the collectivization effort on farm incomes led the government to introduce a contract system (in the north as well as the south) in 1981 that in effect returned management of crop production to the farm household. Continued state control of most agricultural marketing, however, meant there was no general boom in farm incomes of the kind that occurred in China in the early 1980s, when the collective system there was abolished and markets for farm products freed up. Food production, particularly in the north, remained barely sufficient to feed the population, and Vietnam continued to import grain.

The attempt to impose a centrally planned command system on the economy of the south, together with other measures taken by the government, led to a depressed urban economy. The ethnic Chinese community, which owned and managed most of the private businesses in the south, fled the country in large numbers, along with many others. Nationwide, it was only continued large subsidies from the Soviet Union that covered the cost of half of total Vietnamese imports that kept the economy functioning, albeit at a low level. (For an in-depth discussion of the economy during the pre-1986 reform period, see the chapter by Le Dang Doanh in this volume.)

In the mid-1980s Vietnam was poorer than most of the world's developing economies, with a per capita GDP comparable to or below that of Myanmar and Cambodia in the 1980s, or Chad (before oil) and Haiti. The official data suggest that Vietnam's economy grew at 5.1 percent per year in the 1980s, or around 3 percent per capita,[1] but if these figures are accurate, they must mainly represent recovery from the negative impact of the policies of the late 1970s, which continued into the 1980s. Exports in the mid-1980s were less than US$1 billion, and imports were nearly three times that, with the deficit financed mostly through subsidies from the Soviet Union.

This situation changed dramatically in the late 1980s. The political changes began in 1986, but most of the major economic policy changes began in 1989. The Soviet withdrawal from Eastern Europe that quickly led to the end of the Soviet trading bloc COMECON, of which Vietnam was a member, effectively reduced or eliminated the major market for Vietnamese manufactured exports. Soviet difficulties leading to the breakup of the Soviet Union also ended Soviet subsidies. These external events, combined with Vietnam's lackluster economic performance in the late 1980s, effectively forced dramatic policy changes on the government. The government responded in 1989 by freeing up most prices, including the exchange rate, and opening up to foreign trade with few restrictions. Shops that were mostly empty at the beginning of the year were overflowing with both domestic and foreign goods by the end of the year. The large deficit on the foreign trade current account was partly filled by offshore oil wells beginning to produce at that time. Equally important was the freeing up of rice prices (and the prior end of collectivization efforts in agriculture in the south) that changed Vietnam from being a large importer of rice into a large exporter. The liberalization of Vietnam's trade regime culminated with normalization of relations with the United States and the end of the American embargo in 1995 (other countries had ended it earlier).

Freeing up prices and liberalizing foreign trade, however, do not by themselves constitute a complete economic development strategy. The rest of the first part of this chapter is devoted to how that broader development strategy took shape and what impact it had on the country's economic performance. We will begin by describing the performance of the economy and some of its major components over the roughly three decades since the beginning of the reform era, and then turn to how the outcome of various policy choices helps explain that performance.

The reform era growth performance of Vietnam is presented in figure 6.1. The growth rate jumped to 5 percent per capita in 1989, fell back in 1990 and 1991, and then surged to over 6 percent in 1992–94, peaking in 1995 at over 7 percent. This initial spurt in growth following major economic reforms was common to several East Asian economies. For

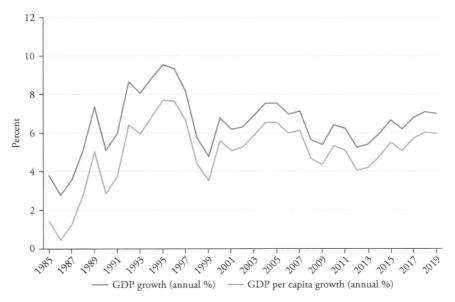

FIGURE 6.1 GDP and GDP per capita growth rates
Note: Vietnam's GDP in consultation with the United Nations was revised upward by
25.4 percent in 2019 for the years 2010–17 and after. This revision, however, has not changed
the GDP per capita growth rates. Given that the revision applies only to the most recent
decade's data, it is not possible to use these revised figures when calculating the sources of
growth in the past. As a result, all calculations here are based on the GDP data published
prior to the upward revision.
Source: Vietnam Investment Review, January 29, 2022, https://vir.com.vn/statistical-upgrade
-aids-revision-of-gdp-efforts.

China, as for Vietnam, much of the initial acceleration in growth came from simply dismantling the Soviet-type centrally planned command system, with all of its many distortions. In South Korea and Taiwan, a similar spurt occurred through the shift from an
inward-looking import substitution regime with an overvalued exchange rate to an export-
oriented regime with a sharply devalued exchange rate.

Vietnam's turn outward also explains some of the growth acceleration. In Eastern
Europe and the Soviet Union, however, the sudden dismantling of the centrally planned
command economy initially had a strong negative impact. Why Vietnam's performance
in the initial years of reform was similar to that of China and different from that of Eastern Europe and the Soviet Union is beyond the scope of this chapter. The explanation in
part, however, begins with the fact that the southern part of the country only briefly ex-
perimented with a Soviet-type system in both agriculture and commerce, making return
to a market system much easier.

After peaking in 1995–96, Vietnam's GDP and GDP per capita growth rates fell back,
with the per capita GDP growth rate fluctuating between 4 percent and 6 percent, averaging about 5 percent annually. Whether 5 percent per capita growth per year is considered
an impressive or mediocre GDP per capita growth rate depends on the countries with

Table 6.1
Per capita GDP levels compared

	Year	GDP per capita	Year	GDP per capita	Average growth rate
Korea	1963	1,050	2002	16,735	7.35%
				22,997	
China	1978	308	2014	6,108	8.65%
				12,759	
Vietnam	1989	420	2017	1,834	5.41%
				6,172	
Indonesia	1967	709	2017	4,131	3.52%
				11,188	
Thailand	1960	571	2017	6,126	4.25%
				16,278	
Malaysia	1960	1,353	2017	11,521	3.76%
				26,808	
Sub-Saharan Africa	1970	1,325	2017	1,648	0.47%
Latin America and Caribbean	1960	3,655	2017	9,356	1.66%

Source: World Bank, WDI online.

Note: The early year data are data in 2010 US dollars and the later year data are in both US dollars and purchasing power parity estimates in 2011 dollars.

which Vietnam is compared. Data for a few selected economies in Asia and for regions of Africa, Latin America, and the Caribbean are presented in table 6.1.

As the table indicates, Vietnam's growth rate lagged significantly behind that of China and South Korea during their reform periods but was higher than that of the best-performing Southeast Asian countries, and far ahead of the performance of sub-Saharan Africa, Latin America, and the Caribbean. It should be noted, however, that many of these countries started their periods of growth from a higher, in some cases much higher, per capita income than did Vietnam. Fast growth from a lower per capita income base, other things being equal, is generally easier.

The Nature of Growth in the 1990s

The challenges faced by the Vietnamese economy in the late 1980s, as noted above, were daunting. The collapse of the Soviet Union and COMECON was the most notable change. But the low quality of Vietnamese consumer manufactures compounded the problem of switching to markets in high-income market economies. The US-led embargo of trade with Vietnam also made it difficult to switch export markets to high-income market economies and blocked access to most bilateral and multilateral foreign aid. At the same time, partly due to the end of Soviet aid, the country's domestic investment rate had fallen and was far too low to sustain a high rate of GDP growth. Inflation, which had been

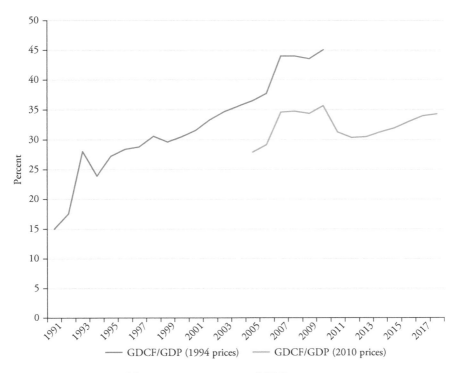

FIGURE 6.2 Gross capital formation as percentage of GDP
Source: National Statistical Office of Vietnam, *Statistical Yearbook*, various issues online and in print.

running at over 300 percent per year in 1986–88, had fallen, but was still averaging 70 percent per year in 1989–91.[2]

Estimates of the share of investment or gross domestic capital formation in GDP in the 1986–89 period vary by wide margins depending on whether one uses data in current or fixed prices, or with the data published in the early 1990s versus later reconstructed estimates (see figure 6.2). Given the high rate of inflation, estimation would have been difficult, but there is ample reason to believe that the true share of GDP measured in market prices or even contemporary prices was very low, perhaps below 10 percent per year. Given the high rate of inflation, households would have had little reason to save Vietnamese *dong*, whether in cash or in bank accounts. Nor could they buy land or real estate, traditional hedges against inflation, given that much of the real estate was owned by the state, and identifying who had user rights was still being sorted out into the early 1990s. The GDP growth rate for 1986–89 was 4.1 percent a year, and electricity use per capita rose by 20 percent, so the political changes in 1986 did produce some growth even before the major liberalization of 1989.

It was the major policy changes beginning in 1989 and 1990, however, that produced major growth and structural changes for the better. The balance of payments crisis disappeared, the investment rate climbed rapidly, and GDP growth soared to 8 percent a year by 1992. As pointed out above, the balance of payments crisis disappeared as rural reforms led to a boom in rice production that replaced the need for sizable imports of rice, returning the Mekong Delta to its more traditional role of being a rice exporter. At the same time, oil wells being drilled offshore began to produce and export. Hoa Binh, a major hydro project, increased the output of electricity further. State investment more than doubled, rising from 7.6 percent of GDP in 1991, and probably less in 1988, to 16.1 percent in 1993.[3] With the move to a market economy in 1989, foreign direct investment also rose from negligible levels before that to US$1,106 million of actually implemented capital by 1993 and US$2,352 million in 1995, or 7.4 percent and 13 percent of GDP, respectively.[4] The 1991–94 data are actually in 1989 fixed prices, but these were not much different from the 1994 prices. The earlier year prices are much higher than the 2010 prices, probably because the end of the embargos on Vietnam led to capital goods being available to Vietnam at much lower prices.

Where did the government find the new revenue to finance this state investment expansion? Vietnam did not begin publishing government budget figures until 2000, but one can roughly estimate where the new revenue was coming from. Oil revenues, customs duties, and state-owned enterprise revenues were, together, 68 percent of total government revenue in 2000. Oil revenue did not exist before 1989, but rose to perhaps 45 percent of the 2000 level by 1995. Customs duties on 1995 imports would have been more than three times the level of 1989–92, and state enterprise revenue would also have risen rapidly from the depths of 1989. Without knowing the total budget revenues of 1989, it is not possible to estimate what share of total revenue these three sources of revenue would have produced, but basically by 1995 the government had probably experienced more than a doubling of total revenue over the first half of the 1990s, while GDP was rising at roughly half that rate. It was this revenue boom that allowed the government to increase state investment at 19 percent a year (in real 1989 prices) between 1989 and 1995. Most of that rise occurred in fact in only two years, 1992 and 1993, when state annual investment rose by 57 percent per year, an extraordinarily high figure but one that did not put a major strain on the budget or cause an accelerated rise in prices. Retail prices in these two years rose at 17.5 and 5.2 percent per year, down from a rate of 67 percent a year in 1990 and 1991.

For political and equity reasons involving the desire to ensure that all regions of the country received comparable shares of this rising investment, the investment was not allocated efficiently, however. Efficient allocation would have required a much larger share of investment going to the fastest-growing areas—mainly the largest cities, and Ho Chi Minh City in particular. As the data in figure 6.3 indicate, that was far from the case, with the two major development centers (Hanoi and Ho Chi Minh City) in effect subsidizing expenditures in the rest of the country.

Ho Chi Minh City, the most dynamic economic area in the country, in fact, contributed by far the largest share of its revenue to other regions. As indicated in figure 6.4A, the share of revenue that the city was allowed to retain declined steadily over time, as contrasted to Hanoi, whose share actually rose slightly. It is therefore not surprising that the HCMC's revenue per capita was always higher, and at the same time its expenditure per capita has always been lower than Hanoi's, both by very wide margins (see figure 6.4B).

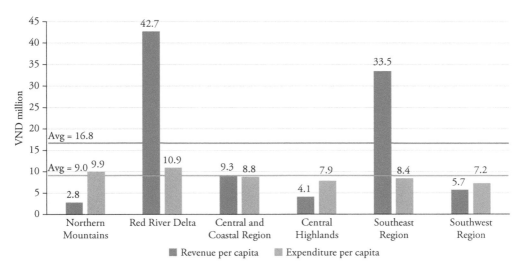

FIGURE 6.3 Revenue and expenditure per capita
Note: Data for 2020 are estimates approved by the National Assembly and published by the MOF.
Source: Authors' estimation from Ministry of Finance's Budget Transparency Data.

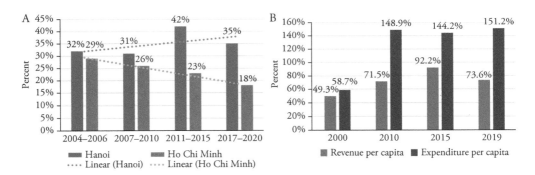

FIGURE 6.4 Budget comparison between Hanoi and Ho Chi Minh City
Note: Data for 2019 are estimates approved by the National Assembly and published by the Ministry of Finance.
Source: Authors' calculation based on Ministry of Finance's Budget Transparency Data.

More generally, this political bias in budget allocation can also be observed at the regional and national levels—going from north to south, the regional expenditure per capita tends to decline, and this pattern has persisted over time.

The investment story of the 1990s was, therefore, first and foremost a story of rapidly rising state investment in infrastructure and state enterprises. For the first half of the century, it was also a story of rapidly rising implemented investment by foreign enterprises, but this leveled off and then fell in the latter half of the 1990s. particularly during the Asian financial crisis of 1997–98. Domestic private investment was done mainly by households, farmers, shopkeepers, and the like, with the non-household private sector amounting to no more than 1 or 2 percent of total investment or GDP. GDP growth in the 1990s was thus a combination of rapidly rising state and foreign investment combined with efficiency improvements from abandoning the Soviet-style centrally planned command economy. The efficiency issue will be explored more formally later in this chapter. But the incremental capital output ratio's rise in the 1990s (figure 6.3) indicates the likelihood that the dominance of comparatively inefficient state investment in capital formation in that period partly offset the efficiency gains from the move to reliance mainly on market forces in the allocations of goods and services.

Changes in the Economic Growth Model after 2000

In 1999 the government passed an Enterprise Law that was primarily designed to give domestic private firms clear legal status. In 2005 another Enterprise Law was passed to bring all enterprises under a consistent framework that applied to them whatever their ownership. The policy debates that led to the passage of these laws are discussed in depth in chapter 5 of this volume. Here we are mainly interested in the laws' impact on private-sector growth. The 1999 law was seen at the time as an effort to give the domestic private sector many of the same rights available to both state enterprises and foreign enterprises. Accelerated growth in the domestic private sector was anticipated. The trade agreement with the United States in 2001 was expected to stimulate foreign direct investment, but was also seen as making it easier for the domestic private sector. And finally, negotiations to join the World Trade Organization were completed and Vietnam joined the WTO in January 2007. Many expected that that would further stimulate the domestic private sector as well as exports.

As the data in figure 6.5 indicate, however, a boom in private enterprise growth as defined by the government statistical authorities never really occurred. The share of the formal domestic private sector in Vietnamese official data rose slightly after 1999, but basically leveled off at less than 10 percent of GDP. The household sector, however, was also private. In the year 1995, 73 percent of this sector's output was from farming, but by 2017 the share of agriculture in household value added had fallen to 47 percent. Nonagricultural economic activities of households rose more than threefold, or over 7 percent a year from 2000 through 2017.[5] Agriculture, in contrast, as in most countries, grew much more slowly, at an annual rate of 3.4 percent after 1995. As the data in table 6.2 indicate, household nonagricultural activities, particularly after 2005, contributed somewhat more to GDP growth than the formal private sector, and in 2011–15 roughly as much as either the state or foreign investment sector. This pattern is not unusual in developing countries during their early stages of growth. Small firms often stay below the radar of the state regulatory and taxing authorities, and that presumably was what was happening in Vietnam.

The underlying reason for this relatively weak performance of the domestic private sector is that the sector faced formidable barriers that constrained its development. First and foremost, these barriers stemmed from the dualistic nature of Vietnam's socialist-

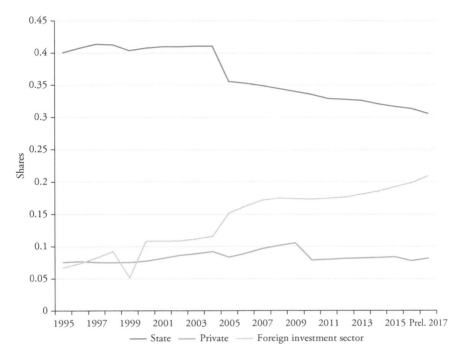

FIGURE 6.5 GDP shares by ownership
Note: This figure is distorted by (a) shares up to 2004 were in 1994 prices, while those after were in 2010 prices, so the more substantial change in shares from 2004 to 2005 results from relative price changes of the different sectors—specifically, agriculture prices relative to industrial prices rose roughly 20 percent from 1994 to 2010; the household share in GDP is particularly affected by this price change, and so was left out of the figure; (b) from 2010 on, ownership shares included a category "product taxes less subsidies on production," with no indication of how those taxes and subsidies affected the different ownership shares. The data for ownership were thus calculated as a percentage of GDP minus "product taxes less subsidies on production"; and (c) for 1999 and 2001, the breakdown included a category called "mixed," and this was added to the private share since that appeared to be what it was taken from.

oriented market economy. The party-state's overarching goal was and is to achieve high rates of economic growth in order to maintain its legitimacy, while keeping intact its absolute political power. This fundamental political economic dilemma explains why Vietnam adopted market-oriented reforms, allowed private ownership and the functioning of markets to a certain extent, and actively integrated into the world economy. But, at the same time, the Vietnamese party-state has tried very hard to maintain a large SOE sector despite its indisputable inefficiency, and has even found various ways to subsidize and shield this sector from international competition after Vietnam became a member of the WTO and joined the CPTPP.

It was and still is widely recognized that domestic private enterprises face many fundamental challenges: first, although private ownership is recognized on paper, enforcement of such rights is weak; second, private enterprises are not treated equally in terms of

Table 6.2
Contribution to growth by ownership sector (sector contribution to GDP increase by period, in %)

	1996–2000	2001–2005	2006–2009	2011–2015	2016–2018
State	42.5	40.3	28.4	26.3	19.9
Collective	5.6	4.1	3	3.4	3.1
Private	8.1	14.3	18.6	9.9	15.6
Household	22.8	18.6	24.7	35.7	27.4
(HH-agriculture)	15.9	11	11.8	10	5.8
(HH-nonagriculture)	6.9	7.6	12.9	25.7	19.9
Foreign investment	21.1	15	25.4	24.7	34.1

Note: These estimates were derived by the authors from the official data published by the Vietnamese statistical authorities. Because the official data are in 1994 prices for the earlier periods and in 2010 prices for the later years, and because there are some changes at various times in what is included in the ownership categories, these estimates are subject to errors created by the assumptions made in doing these calculations.

access to resources, especially land and credit; third, harassment of the private sector by government, at both central and local levels, has not decreased; and fourth, market-supporting institutions are either lacking or ineffective (for detailed discussion, see Pham Chi Lan,[6] Vu Quoc Tuan,[7] and Pham Duy Nghia et al.[8]).

Institutional weaknesses explain the limited significance of the private domestic enterprise sector in Vietnam. These weaknesses are also responsible for the clear differentiation within the private sector between cronies, who have close relationships with government officials (see chapter 7 in this volume), and regular small and medium-sized enterprises (SMEs) with little opportunity to gain access to important resources such as land and credit. It follows, as North[9] predicted, that the majority of large private enterprises concentrate in commercial or speculative activities, most in the real estate sector. SMEs, on the other hand, being crowded out by the SOE and FDI sectors, find it very difficult to make long-term investment to scale up and become large enterprises. SMEs, as noted above, are also subject to legal and illegal intervention by local officials. This explains why Vietnam has very few large-scale private domestic manufacturing enterprises. Thirty years of reform certainly helped many entrepreneurs accumulate wealth, but failed to create internationally recognized private (or public) manufacturing enterprises.

The rise of household nonagricultural activities did contribute to the declining share of the state's contribution to GDP, but of even greater importance was the dramatic rise in the GDP share of foreign direct investment, which passed 20 percent for the first time in 2017 and rose to 34 percent in 2018. Foreign direct investment is discussed systematically in chapter 8 of this volume. Here our concern is mainly with its impact on the rate of investment and the growth of GDP. The increase that began after 2004 was particularly dramatic, with actually implemented capital investment rising from US$2.7 billion in 2004 to US$11.5 billion in 2008, with production in the sector rising from 11.6 to 17.5 percent of GDP. As the data in table 6.2 indicate, foreign investment contributed roughly a quarter of the growth in GDP beginning in the 1990s and continuing up to the present. One of several reasons for the acceleration in foreign direct investment was the desire of some multinationals to diversify beyond China, and this tendency was strongly reinforced by the US-China trade "war" in 2019.

We have gone into the ownership issue at some length because it is central to understanding why Vietnamese GDP growth, while rapid by the standards of most developing countries, as noted above, has fallen below the rates achieved by the highest-growth East Asian economies. It is the performance of the state sector together with the small share of the formal private sector that is at the heart of what is holding Vietnam back from achieving the kinds of growth rates experienced by economies such as South Korea and Taiwan during their high-growth decades. The Vietnamese government apparently concluded that 6 to 7 percent economic growth was sufficient to allow them to pursue growth-slowing policies that served other goals.

To begin with, the productivity and the rate of return on assets of the state-owned sector have been consistently below that of both the foreign investment sector and the formal domestic private sector. There are a number of studies that make this point. Vu Thanh Tu-Anh, for example, points out that Enterprise Survey data indicate that the return on assets of the state-owned enterprise sector was only two-thirds that of the total enterprise sector in the early 2000s. He also estimated that ten of the eighteen State General Corporations, despite having monopoly privileges and numerous state privileges, had a return on assets that was below that of the return on assets of the economy as a whole.[10] In a systematic and sophisticated comparison of total factor productivity for state-owned, privately owned, and foreign-owned manufacturing enterprises for the years 2001–10, Tran Xuan Huong demonstrates that privately owned enterprises had higher productivity than the state-owned when controlling for the size of enterprises (more state-owned firms are large relative to the privately owned), and foreign-owned had higher productivity than domestic privately owned.[11]

We will return to productivity measures later in the chapter. The main point here is that Vietnam's state enterprises have not performed as well as their domestic privately and foreign-owned enterprises. Furthermore, the leaders of the country were fully aware that this was the case and that the impact was a slower rate of GDP growth than otherwise would have been the case. The Vietnamese leadership, however, was not single-mindedly focused on maximizing the growth rate of GDP. Early in the Đổi Mới reform period, they had accepted that the Soviet command system was not working well, and by the early 1990s had changed the main economic goal to one of creating a "socialist-oriented market economy." The fact that China around the same time formally established a similar goal of achieving a "socialist market economy" no doubt made it easier for Vietnam to define reform in a similar way. In China, however, the government and Party had taken a little over a decade of experimentation (1978–92) before it accepted the term as defining what the economic reforms were about. In Vietnam the term was adopted almost from the start of reform.

In neither Vietnam nor China has a socialist market economy been a euphemism for moving toward a fully capitalist system dominated by private enterprises. In Vietnam the goal from early on in the reform period was to have a vibrant state-owned enterprise sector. As much as possible, the Vietnamese government wanted key sectors of the economy to be dominated by enterprises that were owned and controlled by the state and not by foreigners or domestic private entrepreneurs. How the leadership of the country has attempted to achieve this goal can best be illustrated by the way it has approached the transformation of State General Corporations into giant, highly diversified State Economic Groups.[12]

The government and Party had been attempting to create a strong state-owned sector from at least 1994 on, but the first mention of the creation of giant State Economic Groups was at the Third Plenum of the Ninth Party Central Committee meeting in 2001. When Vietnam joined the WTO in 2005, the government and Party leaders feared that WTO membership would open up the economy, and large strategic industries in particular would be taken over or replaced by large foreign multinationals. WTO provisions in effect prohibited many of the measures used by the state to support state-owned enterprises, such as easy access to credit and a requirement that enterprises purchase key inputs from domestic sources. The formation of giant State Economic Groups could get around these provisions. As conglomerates they could own their own banks and their suppliers could be incorporated as members of the group, among other advantages.

One model that the Vietnamese leadership had in mind in pushing these large groups was South Korea's giant *chaebol*, a few of which (Samsung, LG, etc.) have become among the most successful multinational corporations in the world. But there are several critical differences between Vietnam's State Economic Groups and the Korean *chaebol*. Both received large support from the government in the first years of their existence and when they entered into new sectors of the economy, but that is where the similarity ends. The Korean firms were privately owned and were largely responsible for picking their own leadership. The subsidies they received, while large, came to an end after a short period, typically after five years. By that time the Korean *chaebol* were expected to be internationally competitive and major exporters. Vietnam's State Economic Groups, in contrast, are wholly owned by the state. The Party and government pick the top management and, so far, most depend almost entirely on the domestic market. Over the domestic market they often have a de facto monopoly because of various provisions in the law that may not violate WTO rules inhibiting entry by foreign or private firms.

Is China a model for Vietnam that is more consistent with Vietnam's current emphasis on state-owned enterprises? China has many state-owned corporations listed among the largest corporations in the world. But few of these state enterprises are major exporters. They depend in some cases on effective monopoly of their local markets and various legal provisions such as those in the banking and financial sectors that limit foreign entry. China's exports come overwhelmingly from the foreign and domestic private enterprises. China, of course, has a huge domestic market that can support large domestically oriented state-owned enterprises. Vietnam's domestic market is roughly 5 percent of China's.

Vietnam's Economy at the Beginning of the 2020s

Before one can look into Vietnam's likely economic growth future, one needs to have a comparative picture of how the current stage of its economy compares with countries that have gone through a similar development experience in the late twentieth and twenty-first centuries. As pointed out at the beginning of this chapter, Vietnam was one of the poorest countries among those in Asia that subsequently achieved sustained economic growth over several decades. The data in table 6.3 show where Vietnam stood as of 2017.

As the data in the table indicate, Vietnam is about where China was eleven years earlier. We cannot make a precise comparison with two of the other three countries because the World Bank does not publish PPP per capita estimates before 1990 for these countries, but one can get a rough picture of where Vietnam stood. In 2017 it was similar to Thailand in 1990 and similar to where Korea was in 1980 and Malaysia in 1970.[13] Vietnam in 2017, therefore, was a long way back from the per capita GDP when growth in most high-performing economies slowed markedly. This occurred at roughly PPPUS$16,000 in the East Asian economies of Japan, South Korea, and Taiwan, and in China at PPPUS$12,000 around 2013 (all in 2011 prices). For a larger sample of countries, the period when GDP growth decelerated markedly ranged from PPPUS$12,000 to 16,000.[14]

Vietnam is thus a long way, at least a decade and possibly longer, from when GDP growth is likely to decelerate, whatever policies are pursued. But Vietnam is not very far from when many of these other countries made the transition from labor-intensive manufactures dependent on low-cost labor to internationally competitive heavy and higher-technology industries. Vietnam has heavy industries, although little that could be called high-tech, but as pointed out above, these industries produce almost exclusively for the domestic market. The country's domestically produced exports have grown rapidly, but they are mainly made up of agricultural and fishery products (cashews, shrimp, etc.). There are a few domestic manufacturing firms that export, but the overwhelming share of

Table 6.3
GDP per capita (PPP 2011, international $)

	Year	(PPP per capita)
Rep. Korea	1990	11,632
Malaysia	1990	10,551
Thailand	1990	6,550
China	2006	6,411
Vietnam	2017	6,171

Source: World Bank, WDI online, March 7, 2019. The World Bank does not report Purchasing Power Parity GDP for these countries prior to 1990. The revised GDP figures would probably give Vietnam PPP GDP per capita of a little over $8,000 in 2017, but no official estimate of PPP GDP is available as this is being written.

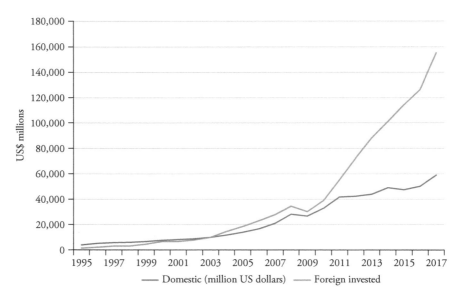

FIGURE 6.6 Exports from the domestic and foreign invested sectors
Source: Various issues of National Statistical Office of Vietnam, *Statistical Yearbook.*

manufactured exports comes from the foreign-invested sector, and that sector has grown much more rapidly than the domestic one (see figure 6.6).

The government does classify many of these manufactured exports as heavy industry, but this sector is largely made up of consumer electronic products, where the valued added in Vietnam mainly involves assembly of components and other low-tech contributions. A central issue going forward is whether Vietnam will be able to build heavy and high-technology sectors that are internationally competitive, or whether the foreign investment sector could do it for them. Singapore to some degree and Malaysia to a large degree have relied on foreign investment in this area, but these two countries have world-class infrastructure, speak English, and have other advantages that are particularly attractive to foreign investors. Before we attempt to tackle whether Vietnam can move up the technology ladder and create internationally competitive industries while doing so, we first need a more systematic framework for analyzing what is holding Vietnamese industry back.

The Underlying Sources of Barriers to Rapid Growth

The method we will use for speculating about future Vietnamese economic growth is the growth accounting framework that explains economic growth as being the product of increases in capital, the labor force, and the education of that labor force, or human capital, together with the productivity of these inputs, or total factor productivity. We first apply that approach to the country's economic performance from 1991 to 2019,[15] and then speculate about what is likely to happen to the factor inputs and productivity over the next decade or two. As this analysis will demonstrate, much of the answer to what happens to future economic growth will depend on the various elements that facilitate or hold back total factor productivity. The purpose of this forecast, therefore, is not to predict precisely what will happen to the Vietnamese economy but to identify the influences that will determine whether that economic performance will be rapid or slow.

Before turning to the growth accounting framework, it is helpful to first look at the simpler framework of the relationship over the past three decades between the rate of investment (gross capital formation as a percent of GDP) and the growth rate of GDP. The relevant data are in figure 6.2 earlier in the chapter and in figure 6.7. As the data in figure 6.2 indicate, the investment rate started the reform period at a very low level but rose quickly, passing 20 percent of GDP by 1995 and reaching close to 30 percent by 2006. The impact of this investment on GDP as measured by the capital-output ratio followed a similar pattern. Thanks to the gains from the early major market reforms, output rose rapidly, even when the investment rate was low, producing a capital output ratio of a little over 2 in 1989–92 before rising to over 3 by 1996 and then soaring up to around 5 by 1998 and staying at that high level through 2013. The initial jump to such a high capital output ratio for

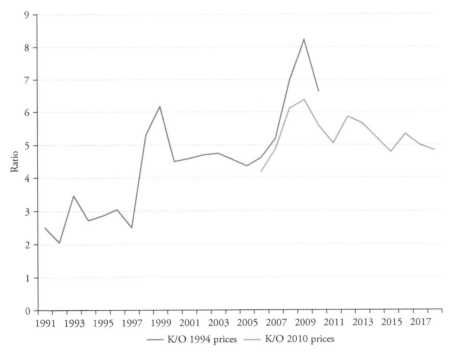

FIGURE 6.7 Incremental capital output ratio
Source: National Statistical Office (online and 1986–90, 1996, 1998, and later yearbooks).
The 1994 relative prices of capital goods were substantially higher than capital goods prices in 2010, probably at least in part because of the embargos in place prior to 1995. The 1991–95 ratios actually used 1989 prices for the capital formation estimates, but the 1989 and 1994 fixed prices appear to have been quite similar.

Table 6.4
Vietnam sources of growth, 1991–2018 (growth rates, in %)

GDP	1991–1995	1996–2000	2001–2005	2006–2010	2011–2015	2016–2019	2011–2019
GDP	8.18	6.95	7.51	7.01	5.91	6.78	6.3
K	2.18	9.59	10.11	10.04	4.06	6.24	5.03
.38K	0.8284	3.6442	3.8418	3.8152	1.5428	2.3712	1.9114
L	2.35	2.34	2.9	2.77	1.5	0.85	1.22
L×humK index	3.75	4.04	5.04	4.89	3.51	1.94	2.81
.62*L	1.457	1.4508	1.798	1.7174	0.9300	0.5270	0.7564
.62*(L×humK)	2.3256	2.5071	3.1266	3.0342	2.1762	1.2028	1.7422
TFP1	5.8946	1.855	1.9159	1.1696	3.4372	3.8818	3.6322
TFP2	5.026	0.7987	0.5416	0.1606	2.191	3.206	2.6464

Sources: A full explanation of the methodology used in deriving these estimates is reported in appendix A, which will be available on the websites of the authors. TFP2 is calculated using employed labor enhanced by human capital growth rates, while TFP1 uses the growth rate of employment unadjusted for human capital. The 1990–2010 data are calculated from data in 2010 prices, while the 2011–18 estimates are calculated from data in 2010 prices.

a country in the early stages of development could be thought of as partly artificial. The financial crisis that hit some of Vietnam's ASEAN neighbors hard in 1997–98 and beyond did to a limited degree also slow Vietnam's GDP growth rate, despite the fact that its investment rate was continuing to rise.[16]

The continuation of the high capital output ratio well beyond the end of the impact of the financial crisis on growth or for the years 2010–13, however, requires a different explanation. Vietnam's investment in these years was not producing as much GDP growth as one would expect for a country in the early stage of development and with such a high investment rate. Something else was going on, and to understand that we need to move to the growth accounting framework. Our estimates using this framework are in table 6.4. The sources of growth methodology are controversial, and the assumptions made in support of this use of an aggregate production function suggest caution in deriving precise conclusions from the results. But it is still the best methodology we have for quantitatively separating out the contributions to growth of investment, the growth of the labor force, the rising education of that labor force, and productivity growth or total factor productivity (TFP).

There are also data issues that can differ from one country to another. For Vietnam, for example, the conventional method for measuring the contribution of education to growth requires data that are not readily available. We have instead used the Barro-Lee index of education, and that index indicates a very rapid rise in the educational level of the Vietnamese population, hence a larger contribution of education or human capital to economic growth. There is little doubt that the rise in the education level of Vietnam's population during the period covered in our estimates was in fact unusually rapid. In 2009, 72.1 percent of the population over the age of five had completed at least primary education (grades 1–5), whereas twenty years earlier in 1989 that figure was only 29.9 percent. Graduates of upper-secondary school and university over that same period rose from

6.8 percent of the population over age five to 20.8 percent.[17] For a more in-depth look at Vietnam's education system, see chapter 12 of this volume. Overall, our results are broadly similar to those of Tran and Do, and Vu, although these studies only cover the story to 2010.[18]

The results for 1991–95 are consistent with the earlier discussion of growth in this period, when investment rates were low but the pace of reform and transition from a command to a market economy was rapid. Most of the growth came from an expansion of employment and of the human capital of those employed, together with a rise in total factor productivity. The investment rate was low, but the productivity gains from moving to a market economy were large. In the next five years (1996–2000) the pace of reform with the normalization of relations with the United States continued, but not as rapidly as the dramatic abandonment of central planning in favor of reliance on market forces in 1989–91. The rate of total factor productivity growth thus fell. Instead, in 1996–2000 the rate of capital formation rose substantially, and the growing capital stock accounted for 52 percent of GDP growth, in contrast to 10 percent in the previous five years. Growth in TFP and GDP in this period was probably also slowed to some degree by the financial crisis that affected several East Asian economies in 1997–98.

During the first decade of the twenty-first century, the capital stock and the investment rate continued to rise, and employment and human capital also grew rapidly. However, the worldwide recession of 2008–9 led to a brief fall in GDP growth, and TFP in the latter part of the decade fell even further, contributing little to GDP growth. In the second decade of the twenty-first century, the rate of investment and the growth rate of the capital stock and of employment slowed markedly. GDP growth also fell, but was sustained to a degree by a rise in TFP growth from the low figures of the previous decade.

In 2020 Vietnam successfully avoided much of the impact of the COVID-19 pandemic. Vietnam's GDP actually grew by 2.91 percent in 2020, far below earlier rates of growth because of disruptions in international trade and the impact of pandemic controls on the domestic economy. In 2021, however, the pandemic hit Vietnam hard, with major lockdowns, particularly in and around Ho Chi Minh City, and the growth rate, though still positive, fell to 2.58 percent.[19] The disruptive impact of COVID-19 in 2022 continued both within Vietnam and in markets worldwide. We have not included these pandemic years in our growth accounting calculations. Accurately estimating realized investment, the growth rate of the labor input, and the contribution of education, given all of the pandemic disruptions, would be difficult to impossible. The calculation would also have little relevance to our use of growth accounting to project alternative GDP growth rates going forward.

For the whole twenty-four-year pre-pandemic period (1996–2019), GDP growth averaged 6.8 percent a year, with TFP accounting for only 0.96 percent of that growth rate. Compared with Latin America and Africa, Vietnam's growth over this period was impressive. When compared with the rapid growth periods of South Korea, Taiwan, and China, however, the performance was less impressive. In those economies TFP growth for long periods was over 2 percent per year, making possible average GDP growth rates of 8 and 9 percent over much of their early catch-up growth.[20] It should be noted, however, that as China has reemphasized state-owned enterprises and relied increasingly on large state-led infrastructure investments to sustain growth, TFP there has fallen to 1 percent or less a year.

Forecasting Future Growth

A central issue for the future is whether Vietnam, post-pandemic, can continue to grow over the next one or two decades at a pace similar to or higher than the experience of the past three decades, or whether growth is likely to slow or even come to a halt. Forecasting long-term growth is fundamentally different from attempting to predict growth in the next one or two years. For short periods, all kinds of events, many of them unpredictable, come into play. Over the longer run these short-term effects tend to even out. A useful way of looking at the range of possible growth scenarios for Vietnam is to use the same growth accounting framework that was used to analyze Vietnam's past performance. What is likely to happen to the growth rate of the labor force, the education of that labor force, the rate of investment, and the likely productivity that alternative policies might produce?

In forecasting the future, we have put the economic growth of Vietnam during the COVID-19 pandemic of 2020–22 aside. Vietnam did better than most countries in limiting the number of COVID-19 cases and deaths. The impact on world trade and the measures to contain the virus, as previously pointed out, did lead to a significant fall in Vietnam's growth rate of GDP. In making our forecasts for the future, however, we are assuming that the decline in the GDP growth rate in 2020–22 will be followed by a rapid recovery to the country's long-term growth trend line, probably in 2023. In making this assumption, we are also assuming that world trade will recover to something like its pre-pandemic growth trend line.

The most straightforward component of the forecast is the projection of the labor force and the likely dependency ratio. A large share of the labor force through 2040 is already born. The current labor force is mainly those age fifteen to sixty-four, but over the next two decades many of those fifteen to nineteen will still be in school, and one also needs to forecast the likely death rate of those at later ages. For the age-specific death rate, demographers have done the work for us (see figure 6.8). The growth rate of the total population aged fifteen to sixty-four has already begun to slow, from 1.4 percent over the 1998–2007 decade to 0.4 percent over the 2007–17 decade. From 2018 through 2030, the fifteen to sixty-four population age group is forecast to grow at around 0.6 percent per year, falling to under 0.2 percent from 2030 through 2040. Because the share of the population aged fifteen to twenty-two that is still in school will continue to grow during this period, we expect that this age group's labor force growth will cease growing through 2030 and may be slightly if not significantly negative from 2030 through 2040. Labor's contribution to GDP growth will thus come mainly from the increasing quality of human capital resulting from continuing increases in the level of education. Using the Barro-Lee

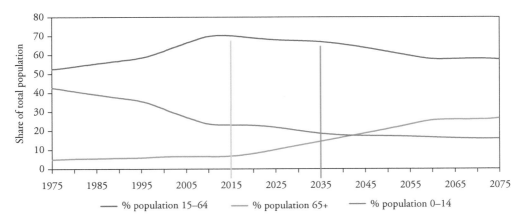

FIGURE 6.8 Declining share of working population
Source: World Bank and MPI, *Vietnam 2035.*

approach for estimating the average number of years of schooling of the population, we assume that Vietnam will increase that average at roughly the same pace as China, South Korea, and Taiwan in the twenty years after they reached a national average of 9.4 years of schooling (Vietnam's 2018 average). However, we assume that the rate of return on the additional years of schooling will be significantly higher than the rate assumed in the Penn world tables.

Estimation of the future rate of growth of the capital stock can be done in two different ways that produce essentially similar results. One way is to first estimate the share of gross capital formation (the rate of investment) in GDP. Given that Vietnam's dependency ratio is likely to remain much the same over the next two-plus decades, based on the life cycle theory of saving and investment, the gross capital formation rate is also likely to remain the same. In our analysis, however, we will also briefly discuss the implications of different rates of investment.

To get the growth of the capital stock, we must then also assume alternative rates of GDP growth and apply the investment rate to those GDP figures. As in our estimates of the historical data, we assume a depreciation rate of 9 percent and that the share of labor and capital income in national income will continue to be 0.62 for labor income and .38 for capital income. The alternative methodology is to simply assume alternative rates of growth of the capital stock. If we assume the rate of growth of the capital stock is 7 percent, we get results similar to those obtained in the first methodology by assuming that GDP is growing at 7 percent. It then becomes straightforward to estimate the impact of alternative rates of capital stock and GDP growth on the contribution of the growing capital stock to growth.

There are also two approaches that can be used to explore likely future rates of growth of GDP and total factor productivity (TFP). The approach we will use asks what level of TFP would be required to obtain 5, 7, or 9 percent growth in GDP. The alternative approach would have been to estimate what rates of growth would be produced by alternative

Table 6.5
TFP growth required for alternative GDP growth rates

	5% GDP growth rate	7% GDP growth rate	9% GDP growth rate
.62xLgrowth rate + HK Index			
2022–30	0.87	0.87	0.87
2031–40	0.81	0.81	0.81
.38×K growth rate			
2022–30	1.691	2.1166	2.5574
2031–40	1.8582	2.565	3.2908
TFP growth rate			
2022–30	2.44	4.01	5.57
2031–40	2.33	3.625	4.90
GDP growth rate	5	7	9

Source: See appendix A on Perkins's Harvard University website.

estimates of TFP. The estimates for 5, 7, and 9 percent growth are presented in table 6.5. We assume a rate of investment (Gross capital formation/GDP) of 32 percent throughout the two decades plus.

As the estimates in table 6.5 indicate, Vietnam should be able to maintain an annual GDP growth rate of 5 percent if it can continue to achieve a growth in productivity (TFP) a bit higher than what has been achieved since 2010. That is a slower rate of GDP growth than was attained in 2011–19. The main reason is that the contribution of labor and human capital to growth will be slower over the next twelve to twenty-two years than was the case in the recent past. If the investment rate were to be raised from 32 to 38 percent over the next twelve to twenty-two years, the contribution of the growth of capital stock would be raised by half a percentage point and TFP lowered by that amount over the next twelve years, but a 38 percent investment rate would not significantly raise the capital stock growth rate or lower the TFP growth rate for the 2031–40 decade over what would be achieved with a 32 percent investment rate. A similar result applies to the impact of raising the investment rate from 32 to 38 percent for the capital stock and TFP growth rates needed in order to achieve 7 or 9 percent growth. The higher investment rate leads to raising the contribution of the growth of the capital stock and lowering the TFP growth rate by half a percent from 2022 to 2030, but the increased investment rate leaves the capital stock and TFP results for 2031–40 much the same as the 32 percent investment rate.

To achieve a 7 percent rate of growth over the next nine to twenty-two years, therefore, Vietnam is likely to have to raise its total factor productivity growth higher than in any recent period in the past, although not higher than has sometimes been achieved elsewhere, notably in China during the first three decades of its post-1978 economic reform effort.[21] To reach 9 percent GDP growth, however, would require a rate of productivity growth far higher than any country has ever achieved on a sustained basis. Even if one assumed an accelerated increase in the education level of the population and an investment increase similar to the nearly 50 percent of GDP rate achieved in

China (2009–14), Vietnam would still have to attain an unprecedented level of productivity growth.[22]

To be clear, the estimates in table 6.5 are not forecasts of what the likely growth rate will be over the next nearly two decades. They are instead an estimate of what Vietnam will have to accomplish just to achieve a growth rate anywhere close to what it has achieved during the past two or three decades. Growth rates of 6 to 7 percent were achieved in Vietnam over the most recent decades, in part because of a rapid growth in export-oriented, labor-intensive industry and employment together with major improvements in education, mainly at the primary and secondary levels. Those rates of employment growth cannot be sustained over the next one or two decades. The steady replacement of Soviet-style inward-looking economic institutions with outward-looking, market-oriented ones also contributed to productivity. Dismantling inefficient command economy practices, however, is also largely in the past. Market-supporting institutional reforms going forward, such as in the financial sector (see chapter 9 of this volume), will be more complex and will take more time.

The TFP impact of the shift of millions of workers out of low-productivity agriculture into high-productivity urban employment, in contrast, is likely to continue for the next decade, but not much beyond that time. Employment in agriculture began declining at a rate of roughly 1 million a year in 2014, and if that rate continues for another eight to ten years, agricultural employment will be half of what it is today. Most working-age adults left in agriculture will be over the age of forty, when migration to the cities and urban employment is unlikely. In our calculations this shift in employment from low-productivity agriculture to higher-productivity urban jobs contributes roughly 0.6 percent a year to TFP in the 2020s. That source of productivity growth will largely disappear in 2031–40.

As indicated above, increases in the rate of investment or capital formation as a share of GDP will also increase the growth rate of the capital stock, but only for a decade when the rise is from 32 to 38 percent. If one followed the Chinese experience from 2000 to 2011 by raising the rate of gross capital formation as a share of GDP from 34 percent to 48 percent, one still gets similar results. For Vietnam, we raised the rate from 32 to 50 percent over 2019–40, and this did lead to a significantly more rapid growth of the capital stock of 3.4 to 3.8 percent, reducing the TFP growth required to achieve 7 and 5 percent GDP growth by a full percentage point for 2019–30. But the gain in the growth of the capital stock was only 0.5 percent for 2031–40, reducing the required TFP growth by only 0.16 percent. Furthermore, a rise of that magnitude in the investment rate would almost certainly lead to a substantial decrease in the rate of return to that investment, as in fact has happened in China.

The reason for going through these numerical exercises is to make one simple point. Vietnam is not going to sustain a rapid growth rate by simply raising the rate of investment in either physical or human capital. Higher productivity will be required simply to maintain the GDP growth rates of the past, and that higher productivity will have to be achieved with the help of supportive policies. The concluding section of this chapter will summarize from our earlier discussion what we believe those supportive policies need to be.

Finally, we note that the above calculations of future growth patterns suggest that some of the goals set at the Thirteenth Party Congress in 2021 will be difficult to achieve. The 2025 target of a per capita GDP of US$4,700–5,000[23] will be difficult to achieve given that the GDP growth rate for the first two years of that period averaged only 2.7 percent a year. The Congress's assumptions that GDP would have to grow at 6.5–7 percent a year to achieve the target, and that 45 percent of the growth would come from TFP growth, however, are similar to our calculations in table 6.2, where 51 percent of a 7 percent GDP growth would have to come from TFP. Vietnam came close to achieving 7 percent growth in 2016–19, and TFP accounted for 47 percent of that growth in our calculations. The TFP growth in 2016–19, it should be noted, was the highest rate of TFP growth rate achieved by Vietnam other than during the first years of the Đổi Mới reforms.

Policies to Achieve High Productivity Growth

If we assume that Vietnam will continue to support an outward-looking, export-oriented economy, the policies that will have the greatest impact on Vietnam's future rate of productivity growth begin with those related to the ownership of modern industry and services. The key question is whether the domestic private sector will be freed up to expand its share of GDP and whether Vietnam will continue to attract large amounts of foreign direct investment. Freeing up the domestic private sector will also require accompanying major reforms in the financial sector (see chapter 9 in this volume) and other market-supporting institutions. Continuing emphasis on protecting the central role of state-owned enterprises is not likely to be consistent with rapid growth.

Furthermore, this challenge of maintaining both a high rate of investment and a higher level of total factor productivity than in the recent past will have to be accomplished while moving from a manufacturing sector that is focused on labor-intensive, low-cost products to more sophisticated technology- and capital-intensive industries. As the data in figure 6.9 indicate, Vietnam's real wages, as in all rapidly growing countries before it, are rising rapidly.

To move to more complex and higher-technology industries in the coming two decades, Vietnam will have to increase its competitiveness in a wide range of areas (Figure 6.10). As the data in the World Economic Forum's competitiveness report indicate, Vietnam ranks poorly in many areas that are critical to moving up the technology ladder. The country ranks 93rd, for example, in the quality of its "education and skills" and 102nd in "innovation capacity."

Moving up from labor-intensive to more technologically sophisticated industries and services will, in addition, require major increases in both the quantity of education and quality improvements in tertiary education in particular. Quantitatively, there is little doubt that the education level of the country will continue to rise rapidly (see the discussion of education in chapter 11 of this volume). The issue is whether the quality of that

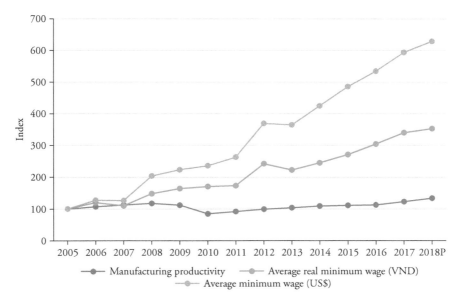

FIGURE 6.9 Growth rates of labor productivity and minimum wages
Source: Authors' calculation from data published by MOLISA and GSO.

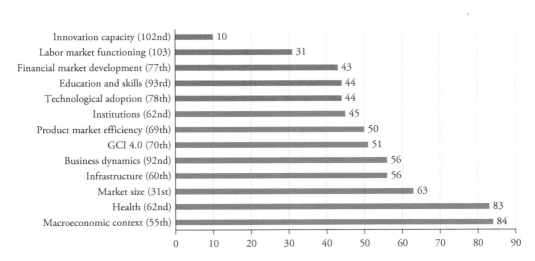

FIGURE 6.10 Vietnam's competitiveness 4.0
Source: World Economic Forum, *The Global Competitiveness Report, 2017–2018*.

education will experience equivalent improvement. Vietnam's universities today do not appear to be producing enough highly qualified engineers and scientists needed to expand the more sophisticated industries and the research organizations that support them. No Vietnamese universities are in the top few hundred in the most respected published assessments of international universities around the world. China's experience of investing heavily in education, along with structural reforms in education, and research over the past two decades give some idea of what will be required. Vietnam cannot hope to duplicate the quantity of effort China is putting in, but it will at least need to make a comparable qualitative effort per capita.

Continuing to attract foreign direct investment will also require major improvements in Vietnam's infrastructure if the country is to compete on something other than cheap labor with countries like Malaysia and China. The contribution to GDP growth of this investment in infrastructure will depend as much on the efficiency with which that infrastructure is constructed as it does on the quantity. The dilemma is whether demands for distributing infrastructure spending equitably, as in the past, will undermine efforts to remove infrastructure bottlenecks in regions where most of the GDP growth is occurring.

Notes

1. Derived from General Statistical Office, *Economy and Finance of Vietnam, 1986–1990*, 15.
2. The 1986–89 figures are from General Statistical Office, *Economy and Trade of Vietnam*, 160; 1990–91 data are available in a number of publications of the General Statistical Office of Vietnam.
3. These percentages were derived from General Statistical Office, *Nien Giam Thong Ke 1996*, 17 and 159. The data are in 1989 prices.
4. The official figure for foreign direct investment is somewhat lower, at 10 percent of GDP in 1995, but we have multiplied the dollar figure for implemented capital in Le Dang Doanh, "Foreign Direct Investment in Viet Nam," by the 1994 exchange rate and divided that into GDP in 1995 at 1994 prices.
5. The growth rate over this period cannot be calculated precisely because the Vietnamese statistical authorities removed some taxes and subsidies from the ownership sector production data in 2010, whereas before that date the data presumably included taxes and subsidies by sector.
6. Pham Chi Lan, "Development of Legal Environment."
7. Vu Quoc Tuan, "Enterprises Development."
8. Pham Duy Nghia et al., "Unplugging Institutional Bottlenecks."
9. North, *Institutions, Institutional Change and Economic Performance*.
10. Vu Thanh Tu-Anh, "Does WTO Accession Help Domestic Reform?"
11. Tran Xuan Huong, "The Evolution of Productivity," 87–88.
12. The discussion of the political economy of this transition is based on Vu Thanh Tu-Anh, "Does WTO Accession Help Domestic Reform?" The reader is referred to the original article for a more complete discussion of this transition.
13. These estimates assumed that Korea per capita GDP was growing at 6 or 7 percent in the 1980s and Malaysia's at roughly half that rate.
14. The East Asian growth slowdown estimates are from Perkins and Rawski, "Forecasting China's Economic Growth," and the broader sample is from Perkins, *East Asian Development*, 155. The original data in these sources was in 2000 prices but was converted to 2011 prices using the US GDP price deflator.
15. Reliable capital and human capital data for the 2020–21 pandemic years are not available for growth accounting calculations.
16. Vietnam did not experience a financial crisis at this time in large part because the country's businesses had not taken out large numbers of short-term dollar and other hard currency loans unhedged for changes in the foreign exchange rate, as had firms in Thailand, Malaysia, and Indonesia.
17. Vietnam's 2009 census.
18. Tran and Do, "The Role of TFP"; and Vu Minh Khuong, "Boosting Vietnam's Productivity."
19. General Statistical Office, January 16, 2022.

20. Perkins, *East Asian Development*, 58–62. The growth accounting methodology used to calculate the sources of growth in China, Taiwan, and the Republic of Korea was similar to the methodology used for Vietnam.

21. Perkins, *East Asian Development*, 62.

22. It should be noted that these estimates do not take into account the pandemic year slowdowns of 2020 through 2021 and 2022. Or to put it differently, these calculations in effect assume that the slowdown of the pandemic years will be made up with a brief period of accelerated growth after 2022 if the pandemic has ended by then or at least is no longer disrupting the economy.

23. Vietnam's Party Congress used the revised GDP figures of 2019 and after.

References

General Statistical Office. General Statistical Office. *Economy and Finance of Vietnam, 1986–1990*. Hanoi: Statistical Publishing House, 1991.

———. *Economy and Trade of Vietnam, 1986–1991*. Hanoi: Statistical Publishing House, 1992.

———. *Nien Giam Thong Ke 1996*. Hanoi: Statistical Publishing House, 1996.

Le Dang Doanh. "Foreign Direct Investment in Viet Nam: Results, Achievements, Challenges and Prospects." Presentation at the IMF Conference on FDI, August 2002.

National Statistical Office of Vietnam. *Statistical Yearbook*. Hanoi: Statistical Publishing House, various issues online and in print.

North, Douglas. *Institutions, Institutional Change and Economic Performance*. Cambridge: Cambridge University Press, 1990.

Perkins, Dwight H. *East Asian Development: Foundations and Strategies*. Cambridge, MA: Harvard University Press, 2013.

Perkins, Dwight H., and Thomas G. Rawski. "Forecasting China's Economic Growth to 2025." In *China's Great Economic Transformation*, edited by Loren Brandt and Thomas G. Rawski. Cambridge: Cambridge University Press, 2008.

Pham Chi Lan. "Development of Legal Environment for Businesses in Vietnam: The Memorable Paths." In *Renovation in Vietnam: Recollection and Contemplation*, edited by Dao Xuan Sam and Vu Quoc Tuan. Hanoi: Tri Thuc Publishing House. 2008.

Pham Duy Nghia, Nguyen Xuan Thanh, Huynh The Du, Do Thien Anh Tuan, Ben Wilkinson, Vu-Thanh Tu-Anh, Dwight Perkins, and David Dapice. "Unplugging Institutional Bottlenecks to Restore Growth." Policy discussion paper prepared for the 2013 Vietnam Executive Leadership Program (VELP), 2013.

Tran, T. D., and T. N. Do. "The Role of TFP in Vietnam Economy Growth." In *The 16th Productivity and Quality Forum*. Hanoi: Vietnam Productivity Center, 2012;

Tran Xuan Huong, "The Evolution of Productivity in Vietnam's Manufacturing Sector." Ph.D. dissertation, University of Wollongong, 2014.

Vu Minh Khuong. "Boosting Vietnam's Productivity as a Strategic Approach to Deepening Economic Reforms: Urgency, International Experience, and Policy Recommendations." Draft, December 17, 2014.

Vu Quoc Tuan, "Enterprises Development: Reflection on a Process." In *Renovation in Vietnam: Recollection and Contemplation*, edited by Dao Xuan Sam and Vu Quoc Tuan. Hanoi: Tri Thuc Publishing House, 2008.

Vu Thanh Tu-Anh. "Does WTO Accession Help Domestic Reform? The Political Economy of SOE Reform Backsliding in Vietnam." *World Trade Review* 16, no. 1 (January 2017): 85–109.

World Bank and Vietnam Ministry of Planning and Investment. *Vietnam 2035: Toward Prosperity, Creativity, Equity, and Democracy*. Washington, DC: World Bank, 2016.

World Economic Forum. *The Global Competitiveness Report 2017–2018*. Geneva: World Economic Forum, 2017.

CHAPTER 7

The Evolution of Large Domestic Businesses and Oligarchs in Vietnam

Nguyen Xuan Thanh

The economic transition of Vietnam from a centrally planned to a market economy and from one of the world's poorest nations to a middle-income country over the last thirty years has been driven by the rapid growth of a dynamic private sector. Vietnam today has almost 650,000 domestic private companies. According to the government and the Vietnam Chamber of Commerce (VCCI) classification, large companies account for only 1.2 percent of the total number of enterprises in Vietnam.[1] But in 2021, forty of the top 100 companies ranked by sales were domestic private firms.[2] With the growth of these large domestic private companies, there emerges a number of wealthy individuals who are now billionaires and multimillionaires in Vietnam.

Winters defines oligarchs as "actors who command and control massive concentrations of material resources that can be deployed to defend or enhance their personal wealth and exclusive social position."[3] Using this framework, Vietnamese billionaires and multimillionaires are classified as oligarchs because they have (1) active control of large private companies, (2) businesses in real estate and/or banking that give them rent-seeking opportunities, (3) support and protection from the political elites, and (4) various strategies and mechanisms to defend their wealth.

Searching for Vietnamese Oligarchs

In March 2013, for the first time, *Forbes* magazine named Vietnam's first billionaire, Pham Nhat Vuong, whose net worth was estimated at US$1.5 billion.[4] Since then, the number of Vietnamese billionaires whose wealth can be verified through their ownership of shares in Vietnam's stock exchanges has risen to nine. Table 7.1 lists these nine individuals. As all of them have accumulated wealth from real estate and banking and are shown in the later sections of the chapter as actively building political connections and

Table 7.1

Vietnamese billionaires based on ownership of shares traded on Vietnam's stock exchanges, December 2021 (> US$200 million)

Name	Company name	Industries	Companies under control Rank in Vietnam's top 500 firms[a]	Market capitalization (US$ million)	Ownership control[b] (%)	Market value of owned shares (US$ million)	Net worth estimated by Forbes (US$ million)
Pham Nhat Vuong	Vingroup	Real estate (retail, health care, education, automotive, technology)	5	15,886	63.7	10,115	7,300
Nguyen Thi Phuong Thao	Vietjet Air	Airlines	57	2,950	46.0	1,458	2,800
	HDB	Banking	50	2,698	3.8		
	Sovico	Real estate					
Bui Thanh Nhon	Novaland	Real estate	116	7,701	31.4	2,406	2,400
Tran Dinh Long	Hoa Phat Group	Steel	13	6,896	35.0	2,412	2,200
Tran Ba Duong	Thaco	Automotive	18	4,018[c]	71.0	2,853	1,600
	Dai Quang Minh	Real estate					
Ho Hung Anh	Masan Group	Consumer products	15	7,330	21.7	2,898	1,600
	Techcombank	Banking	28	7,860	16.6		
Nguyen Dang Quang	Masan Group	Consumer products	15	7,330	25.3	1,872	1,200
	Techcombank	Banking	28	7,860	0.3		
Do Anh Tuan	SSH	Real estate		1,686	65.0	1,644	
	KSF	Real estate		1,011	54.2		
Ngo Chi Dung	VPB	Banking	19	6,938	14.8	1,028	

Source: Author's estimates based on data from Hanoi and Ho Chi Minh City's stock exchanges and ownership disclosed by the Vietnam State Securities Commission. *Forbes's* data are taken from the 2021 List of World Billionaires, accessed at https://www.forbes.com/billionaires/#6026c68a25tc on February 1, 2022.

Notes:

[a] *Vietnam Report*, List of Top 500 Vietnamese Companies 2021, http://vnr500.com.vn. Companies are ranked based on annual volume of sales. *Vietnam Report* ranks the top 500 including state-owned, domestic, and FDI companies.

[b] Ownership control is based on combined ownership of shares by individual billionaires and their relatives, either directly or indirectly through investment vehicles.

[c] Thaco is not listed. The market capitalization of Thaco is based on the prices of Thaco's shares traded on the over-the-counter (OTC) market.

Table 7.2

Vietnamese multimillionaires based on ownership of shares traded on Vietnam's stock exchanges, December 2021 (> US$200 million)

Name	Companies under control					Market value of owned shares (US$ million)
	Company name	Industries	Rank in Vietnam's top 500 firms[a]	Market capitalization (US$ million)	Ownership control[b] (%)	
Nguyen Van Dat	PDR	Real estate	313	1,511	60.4	913
Ho Xuan Nang	Vicostone	Construction materials	212	795	79.5	632
Lo Bang Giang	VPB	Banking	19	6,938	7.5	522
Bui Hai Quan	VPB	Banking	19	6,938	6.7	464
Nguyen Hieu Liem	Novaland	Real estate	116	7,701	5.4	418
Nguyen Van Tuan	GEX	Manufacturing	66	1,485	22.6	335
Do Huu Ha	HHS	Manufacturing		157	48.5	340
	TCH	Manufacturing	265	727	36.3	
Bui Xuan Huy	Novaland	Real estate	116	7,701	3.7	287
Nguyen Duy Hung	SSI	Finance	276	2,019	9.6	234
	PAN	Agriculture	145	376	10.7	
Dang Thanh Tam	KBC	Real estate		1,152	14.8	219
	SGT	Tech		114	23.7	
	ITA	Real estate		684	3.1	
Nguyen Duc Tai	Mobile World	Trading, tech	9	2,112	9.6	203

Source: Author's estimates based on data from Hanoi and Ho Chi Minh City's stock exchanges and ownership disclosed by the Vietnam State Securities Commission.

Notes:

[a] *Vietnam Report*, List of Top 500 Vietnamese Companies 2021, http://vnr500.com.vn. Companies are ranked based on annual volume of sales. *Vietnam Report* ranks the top 500 including state-owned, domestic, and FDI companies.

[b] Ownership control is based on combined ownership of shares by individual millionaires and their relatives, either directly or indirectly through investment vehicles.

protection, they are considered oligarchs. Table 7.2 lists Vietnamese multimillionaires whose market value of listed shares under ownership exceeds US$200 million. Many of the multimillionaires listed in Table 7.2 can be considered oligarchs since they get most of their wealth from real estate or banking businesses and have been actively cultivating political support for wealth defense.

Table 7.3

Vietnamese oligarchs who control large unlisted private companies in real estate or banking

Name	Company name	Industries	Rank in Vietnam's top 500 firms
		Companies under control	
Duong Cong Minh	Him Lam Group	Real estate, finance	179
	Lien Viet Post Bank	Banking	64
	Sacombank*	Banking	29
Truong My Lan	Saigon Commercial Bank	Banking	22
	Van Thinh Phat	Real estate	
Thai Huong	TH Milk	Dairy products	
	Bac A Bank	Banking	129
Do Quang Hien	SHB*	Banking	37
	T&T	Finance, real estate, trading	126
Do Minh Phu	Doji Group	Jewelry	11
	Tien Phong Bank*	Banking	68
Nguyen Thi Nga	Seabank	Banking	106
	BRG	Real estate	
Vu Van Tien	An Binh Bank	Banking	158
	Geleximco	Real estate, trading, finance	154
Dang Van Thanh	Thanh Thanh Cong	Sugar, trading, finance, real estate	
Doan Nguyen Duc	Hoang Anh Gia Lai*	Real estate, rubber, sugar, hydropower	
Vu Quang Hoi	Bitexco	Real estate	

Source: Author's determination based on large unlisted companies drawn from Vietnam Report, List of Top 500 Vietnamese Companies 2021.

* These companies are listed. However, the oligarchs' main source of wealth comes from the unlisted companies.

Despite some rapid growth in recent years, Vietnam's stock market capitalization is still only 84 percent of GDP, and there are just 749 joint stock companies listed in the Ho Chi Minh City and Hanoi exchanges. In addition, there are 892 companies traded in the OTC market.[5] There are more oligarchs who control Vietnam's large unlisted companies. Table 7.3 lists the oligarchs who control the largest unlisted private companies in Vietnam. While the exact value of their wealth cannot be determined using market prices, the large sizes of the real estate companies or banks under their control very likely make them multimillionaires and oligarchs.

Table 7.4 lists four people under the category of former oligarchs. The first three former oligarchs were multimillionaires up until the mid-2010s but were put in jail as they failed in their wealth defense. The fourth on the list was arrested in 2022 for stock market manipulation. Given the lack of publicly available information, these lists are certainly not exhaustive, but they do include the most prominent oligarchs in Vietnam.

Table 7.4
Vietnamese former oligarchs

Name	Companies under control	
	Company name	Industries
Ha Van Tham	Ocean Group	Real estate, trading
	Ocean Bank	Banking
Nguyen Duc Kien	Asia Commercial Bank	Banking
Tram Be	Southern Bank	Banking
	Sacombank	Banking
	Binh Chanh Construction	Real estate, construction
Trinh Van Quyet	FLC Group	Real estate
	FLC Faros	Construction
	GAB	Manufacturing

The Rise of Vietnam's Private Sector and the Origin of Private Wealth

THE MULTI-SECTORAL ECONOMY

Unlike the Soviet Union and China, which largely collectivized their entire economies once the Communist Parties gained power, private economic activities still existed in Vietnam during the period of central planning. Before 1992, the private sector already played a very important role in agriculture and services; it was mainly in Vietnam's industrial sector where the government's role was disproportionately large. By the early 1990s, the agricultural sector was almost entirely private. Household farms accounted for 97.1 percent of agricultural value added in 1990. In the service sector, private firms (mostly in trade) accounted for 55.8 percent of value added in 1990. In the industrial sector, non-state enterprises accounted for 37.2 percent of value added in 1990. A significant proportion of Ho Chi Minh City's (HCMC) economic activities in trade and small-scale manufacturing continued to exist outside of the state plans and were subject to market forces during the 1980s.[6] However, almost all private businesses existed as household-based and/or informal units. In 1991, there were only 122 formal private enterprises in Vietnam. With the adoption of a new constitution in 1992 that formally defined the economy as "a multi-sectoral commodity economy functioning in accordance with market mechanisms under the management of the state and following a socialist orientation," the formal domestic private sector was recognized legally. Within a year, the number of private enterprises increased from 122 to 4,361.[7]

However, throughout the 1990s, setting up a private business was very difficult and time- and resource-consuming, with a complicated licensing regime. Each and every new private enterprise had to be approved and licenses signed by the chairman of the city or provincial People's Committee. During this process, promoters and founders of new private enterprises had to obtain many sublicenses from various government agencies, with authorities at various levels of government having excessive discretionary power.

Another big constraint facing the private sector in Vietnam during the 1990s was access to credit, as the banking system was dominated by state-owned banks that catered mostly to state-owned enterprises (SOEs) with directed lending. In 1992, state-owned banks accounted for 84 percent of the banking system's total assets, and 83.6 percent of domestic credit went to the government and SOEs. By 1999, the numbers were still 82 percent and 63 percent, respectively.[8]

However, even in this very difficult business environment, some private companies were established and grew big, making their owners the richest people in Vietnam today. Two main factors contributed to the origin of private wealth and the rise of oligarchs in Vietnam, namely businesses in Ho Chi Minh City taking advantage of the Đổi Mới (Renovation) policy and money from Vietnamese doing business in Eastern Europe.

ORIGIN OF PRIVATE WEALTH: HO CHI MINH CITY AND ĐỔI MỚI POLICY

Just like Russia and China, Vietnam had no oligarchs under socialism and central planning. As the communists took power in North Vietnam in 1954, local oligarchs had no choice but to either move south or emigrate abroad. A very few wealthy families that chose to remain in Hanoi had to quickly turn over their assets to the state. After 1975, when the country was unified, a similar process happened in the south, with much of private wealth destroyed. But throughout the second half of the 1970s, Hanoi was unable to fully install central planning in the south. As already mentioned, a significant proportion of HCMC's economic activity in trade and small-scale manufacturing continued to exist outside of the state plans and were subject to market forces. Vo Van Kiet, chairman of HCMC People's Committee, who later became the city's Party chief and Vietnam's prime minister, appreciated the importance of market forces and allowed prominent businesspeople in the city to trade in order to keep the city's economy alive. As a result, while there were no large private material resources, entrepreneurship still existed in the south during the 1980s.

When many market-oriented reforms as part of the Đổi Mới policy were implemented in the early 1990s, there was already a group of businesspeople in HCMC who stood ready to take advantage of price liberalization and lack of competition to seek profits from arbitrage trading. They would later become the first generation of Vietnamese oligarchs.

Truong My Lan, who built Van Thinh Phat Group, belongs to this generation. She first started in the restaurant and trading businesses, then moved into real estate and hotels. She gained prominence with the redevelopment of An Dong Market and new investment in the Windsor Plaza Hotel in the mid-1990s. During this time, she played up her business skills and Hong Kong financial backing through the connections of her husband, Eric Nap Kee Chu. Toward the late 1990s, she began to rely on various political connections to seek new business opportunities and defend her wealth.[9]

The story of Dang Van Thanh and his Thanh Cong Group is very similar. Dang Van Thanh started out as the owner of a small factory producing sugar syrup and rubbing

alcohol. Market reforms allowed him to supply his products to many state-owned enterprises that were previously prohibited from procuring supplies outside of the central planning system. From there, Thanh was able to develop his family-based production unit
into a sugar empire. At the same time, he also moved to create a credit cooperative that
eventually turned into one of the largest private banks in the country.[10] By the mid-1990s,
Dang Van Thanh and Truong My Lan had already become very wealthy and were in a
position to deploy their material resources.

Tram Be and Doan Nguyen Duc are two southern businessmen who both made their
first fortunes in forestry products and wood processing. Doan Nguyen Duc grew up on
Vietnam's south-central coast. He started out producing tables for schools in the Central
Highlands, then moved into wood processing, and eventually built Hoang Anh Gia Lai,
a diversified business group with businesses in real estate, rubber, and hydroelectricity
generation.[11] Tram Be grew up in the Mekong Delta in a very poor family, moved to Saigon
as a boy, working in the city's major traditional markets. His first business was in wood
processing and then construction, real estate, and finance.[12] Both Tram Be and Doan
Nguyen Duc needed the entire 1990s and early 2000s to truly become oligarchs.

ORIGIN OF PRIVATE WEALTH: EASTERN EUROPE

The second road through which Vietnamese oligarchs first built their wealth was Eastern
Europe. During the 1980s, Vietnam managed to send many of its brightest high school
graduates to the former Soviet Union and other Eastern European countries for university
education. The process was fairly merit-based through the implementation of a very competitive university entrance examination.[13] Many Vietnamese students who graduated in
Eastern Europe in the early 1990s decided to stay and go into private business in the post-
Soviet market liberalization. Young, smart, and supported by strong Vietnamese community networks, many of them built successful ventures in export-import, restaurants, and
food processing, often through loans in informal financial markets. Eventually, they
brought their money and their own business style back to Vietnam, which meant (1)
doing risky deals for large expected profits, (2) using high financial leverage, and (3) sparing
no financial expenses in securing political support.

Pham Nhat Vuong, Vietnam's first billionaire, is in this category. Vuong went to
study mineral extraction in Moscow in the late 1980s. After graduating in 1993, he moved
to Ukraine to start his restaurant and then a food-processing business. After becoming
Ukraine's processed-food king, he sold his instant noodle business to Nestlé. The sale
price was not disclosed, but Vuong's business was valued at US$150 million. The money
was then channeled back to Vietnam to help Vuong develop major real estate projects in
Hanoi, HCMC, the coastal city of Nha Trang, and Phu Quoc Island, eventually making
the company the largest real estate developer and Vuong the richest person in Vietnam.[14]

Similar to Pham Nhat Vuong, Ho Hung Anh and Nguyen Dang Quang cofounded
an instant noodle business in Russia. Unlike Vuong, Anh and Quang brought their original business back to Vietnam by establishing Masan Group, which started by producing
instant noodles and soy sauce. The money from Russia was also used by Anh to gain

majority ownership of Techcombank. Masan is now one of the largest domestic consumer product companies and Techcombank is one of the largest joint stock banks in Vietnam.[15]

Pham Thi Phuong Thao and her husband Nguyen Thanh Hung set up Sovico in 1992 as a trading company, with wealth originating in the former Soviet Union, where they did their undergraduate and graduate studies. Using business connections in Russia, Sovico's business was imports of heavy machinery and industrial materials in the early 1990s. From 1997, it moved into real estate and banking. In 2007, Thao founded Vietjet Air, the first truly private and budget airline in Vietnam. With Sovico as a holding company investing in banking, real estate, and airlines, Thao became the first female billionaire in Vietnam in 2017, when Vietjet was listed in the Ho Chi Minh City stock exchange.[16]

Nguyen Duc Kien can also be seen as having the Eastern European connection. Kien passed the university entrance exam to Vietnam's Military Technical Academy and was sent to Hungary for undergraduate education in communication in the early 1980s. Graduating in 1985, some years before the collapse of the Soviet Union, Kien came back immediately to Vietnam and started working at the Vietnam National Textile and Garment Group (Vinatext), which engaged heavily in garment trading between Vietnam and Russia in the late 1980s. By the early 2000s, he had managed to take control of Asia Commercial Bank (ACB), the largest joint stock commercial bank in the country at that time, and three other smaller banks.[17]

SOES, PRIVATIZATION, AND OLIGARCHS

The rise of many oligarchs in the world, in Russia in particular, was through privatization of SOEs. Braguinsky documented that of 296 Russian oligarchs, 132 were SOE managers, political elites, and their relatives.[18] During a period of mass privatization and lack of a strong legal framework, public officials and senior managers of SOEs used insider information, manipulation in asset valuation, and loan/share swaps to take control of privatized SOEs.

Vietnam's SOE equitization policy also gave some opportunities for the managers and their connected parties to accumulate wealth. However, the Party and the government of Vietnam chose the name equitization instead of privatization to suggest that the state would continue to hold major stakes in the equitized firms. As a result, the opportunities were limited for either SOE managers or outside investors to take control and/or engage in asset stripping.

In any case, equitization in Vietnam has proceeded very slowly. The Party still designates the state sector as having the leading role in the economy. The defining feature of the Vietnamese economy has been dualism, a strategy that sought to retain the dominance of the state sector while opening to foreign investment and permitting the emergence of a vibrant private sector.[19] Dualism was thought to be necessary to ensure political support for the transition to a market economy. Under this strategy, state economic groups were established. Diversifying into non-core businesses, setting up new subsidiaries, and securing contracts in noncompetitive ways were channels for the managers to accumulate private wealth. At the local level, HCMC and many other cities and provinces also saw the accumulation of private wealth by public-sector officials and managers through many newly established local SOEs and siphoning of public funds and assets into private firms.[20] While many public-sector officials and SOE managers became very wealthy, their wealth was still not large enough for them to turn into oligarchs. There is no manager or former manager of SOEs who appears in the top forty richest people in Vietnam's stock market. The richest former SOE managers and their families own shares of the equitized firms under their management that are worth only about US$50–120 million.[21] There are richer public-sector officials and SOE managers whose wealth is hidden and cannot be verified. And there are public-sector officials and managers or their relatives who built their own private businesses, but none of them became multimillion-dollar companies. Their main source of power remains their position as agents of the state to manage state-owned assets, sources that cease to exist upon job transfers or retirement.

The Growth of Large Private Firms and Oligarchs

PRIVATE SECTOR AND THE 1999 ENTERPRISE LAW

Overall, Vietnam had done very well over a decade since the launch of *Đổi Mới*. The economy grew rapidly up to 1997, averaging 8.3 percent per year during 1991–97. While avoiding serious damage from the Asian financial crisis and the slowdown in the world economy, Vietnam's GDP growth fell to 5.8 percent in 1998 and 4.8 percent in 1999. A positive response to the crisis was the promulgation of a new Enterprise Law in 1999. The law was drafted and passed as the government increasingly recognized that the economy needed a larger formal private sector in addition to foreign direct investment to create jobs and GDP growth. The main effect of the new law was the simplification of the procedures needed to start a new business and the abolition of sublicenses. An explosion of new private companies was recorded immediately after the implementation of the Enterprise Law (figure 7.1).

The successful implementation of the Enterprise Law and expanded global market access provided by new trade agreements were the driving forces for the growth of export-oriented domestic private companies. Figure 7.2 shows the growth of industrial output by SOEs, FDI companies, and domestic private companies from 1995 to 2013. The domestic private sector really took off around 2000 and surpassed the SOE sector by 2006 in terms of output value. A high concentration of labor-intensive garment companies is found in the southeast, in Ho Chi Minh City, Dong Nai, and Binh Duong. The region also attracts local private investments in plastics, rubber, and chemicals. Outdoor furniture products and animal feed businesses developed on the south-central coast. An export-oriented seafood-processing cluster emerged in the Mekong Delta. Lacking a dynamic market economy and constrained by the central planning mindset of local leaders, northern provinces lagged behind their southern counterparts in terms of private-sector development throughout the 1990s and early 2000s.[22] The 1999 Enterprise Law helped created a

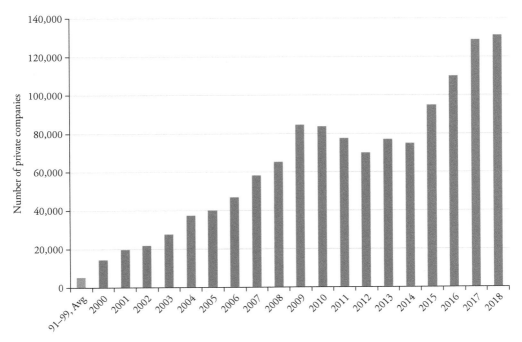

FIGURE 7.1 Number of newly registered private companies
Source: Agency of Business Registration, Ministry of Planning and Investment.

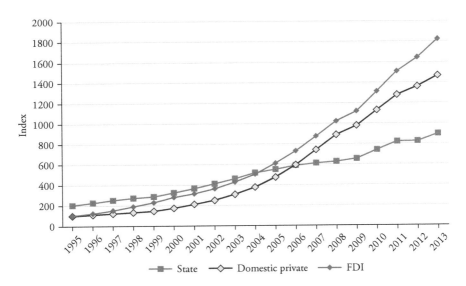

FIGURE 7.2 Growth of industrial output by form of ownership
Source: Author's calculation based on data published by Vietnam's General Statistics Office.

wave of new private companies in the north. The emergence of the formal private sector in the northern provinces surrounding Hanoi, with immediate positive impact on tax revenue and job creation, in turn helped change the attitude of public officials toward local private businesses there.

However, it is important to note from figure 7.2 that the FDI sector has grown much faster than the domestic private sector. On the one hand, FDI companies enjoy much more generous preferential treatment from the government in terms of tax incentives and access to land and infrastructure services. On the other hand, FDI companies can use external institutions to avoid many institutional obstacles facing the domestic private sector such as protection of property rights, access to credit, and access to technology.

Although the 1999 Enterprise Law did a great deal to reduce the licensing costs and entry barriers for domestic private businesses, it did not create a level playing field in the business environment of Vietnam. As a result, while many private firms were established, they were small in size and unable to become larger. In 2002, an average private company in Vietnam had seventy-four employees and US$1.5 million in capital. Also in that year, super-small companies, those that have no more than ten employees and US$130,000 in either revenue or capital, accounted for 53.1 percent of the total number of private companies. In 2011, an average private company in Vietnam had only thirty-four employees and US$2.2 million in capital. And the share of super-small companies went up to 65.6 percent in the ten-year period.[23] In this still difficult business environment, most of the private companies that managed to become larger were those that moved aggressively into real estate and banking.

OLIGARCHS AND THEIR REAL ESTATE
AND BANKING BUSINESSES

Earlier sections have shown that most of Vietnam's current biggest oligarchs made their first money based on their own entrepreneurial spirit and risk-taking behavior, either in the most economically dynamic parts of Vietnam or in Eastern Europe during the early 1990s. This experience sets Vietnam apart from China and Russia, where major roads to riches were being top SOE managers with insider access to strip assets or being relatives/subordinates of senior Party leaders. During the next phase of evolution, they moved into real estate and/or banking, exploiting loopholes in government land policy and financial regulations for rent-seeking and the accumulation of material resources.

As a real estate developer, Vuong's Vingroup possesses the unique capacity to secure land titles at prime locations and execute projects on time with quality workmanship. Unlike many of his peers, Vuong did not go into banking, but chose to focus on real estate. Up until 2006, Vingroup financed its projects using equity finance, borrowing from sources outside of the formal banking system, and advances from customers. The rapid expansion of Vietnam's banking system since 2006 allowed Vingroup to tap credit provided by commercial banks. During 2009–12, the state-owned Vietinbank became the biggest lender to Vingroup. Through loans and corporate bonds, the bank financed Vingroup's biggest residential and commercial real estate developments in both Hanoi and Ho Chi Minh City. BIDV is another large state-owned bank that helped finance Vingroup. From 2005 to 2018, Vingroup grew 642 times in total assets, 1,207 times in total debt, and 90 times in after-tax profits.[24]

Ho Chi Minh City Housing Development Bank (HDBank) was originally founded and owned by a number of local SOEs under the direction of the city government. Nguyen Thi Phuong Thao began buying shares of the bank in 2003 and became its largest shareholder. Pham Thi Phuong Thao also turned her Sovico into a holding company and started investing in real estate and banks during this time. In 2005, Sovico acquired the Furama Resort complex in Da Nang and set up Phu Long Real Estate to develop the Dragon City Project in Saigon South. Saigon Sovico Phu Quoc was set up in 2008 to develop resorts on Phu Quoc Island. In 2007, Vietjet Aviation JSC was established. Its three major shareholders were Sovico, HDBank, and T&C Investment JSC. In 2009, Sovico acquired all of the Vietjet shares from T&C. After this transaction, Sovico owned 70 percent and HDBank owned 30 percent of Vietjet charter capital. As air travel boomed in Vietnam, Vietjet expanded and became the largest domestic carrier. Thao became Vietnam's first female billionaire when the airline was listed in the Ho Chi Minh City stock exchange in 2017.[25]

Techcombank was originally controlled by Le Kien Thanh, the son of Le Duan, Vietnam's Party first secretary and then general secretary. Ho Hung Anh bought into the bank in the early 2000s and quickly increased his stake. Le Kien Thanh left in 2005. Another major shareholder, Nguyen Thi Nga, left in 2007, leaving Ho Hung Anh in total control of the bank. Under Anh, Techcombank grew extremely quickly and was known for its aggressive lending strategy during the asset bubble years of 2006–8. Corporate and individual borrowers consider it to be an "easy" bank to get financing for their speculative investments. Headquartered in the north, by 2012 the bank had surpassed its more well-known southern peers such as ACB and Sacombank in terms of total assets. From 2005 to 2018, Techcombank's assets and after-tax profits increased by thirty and forty-one times, respectively.[26]

As of late 2011, Asia Commercial Bank (ACB) was the largest joint stock bank in terms of both total assets and loans. ACB was also seen by the market and depositors as having the best financial health, with high profitability. Its average ROE during 2006–11 was 28.0 percent.[27] In its ownership structure, ACB had three major shareholder groups— Tran Mong Hung's family, Nguyen Duc Kien's family, and a group of foreign shareholders (including Standard Chartered Bank, Dragon Capital, and Connaught Investors).[28] However, Nguyen Duc Kien managed to dominate both the board and the management of the bank. Kien and his family founded and owned six companies: Asia Investment JSC (ACI), B&B Trading Investment JSC, ACB Hanoi Investment JSC (ACBI), Asia Hanoi Finance Investment (ACI-HN), Asian Group (AFG), and Thien Nam Export-Import Commercial JSC. By controlling the board and the management of ACB, Kien directed the bank to finance his companies to invest in securities (including shares in ACB itself) and gold accounts directly and indirectly through ACB Securities Company (ACBS) and commercial banks in which ACB was a major shareholder. Cross-ownership and connected financing were used by Kien to accumulate wealth (see figure 7.3).

Truong My Lan, Dang Van Thanh, and Tram Be in Ho Chi Minh City also set up similar cross-ownership structures among their real estate and banking businesses in an aggressive drive to grow their businesses.

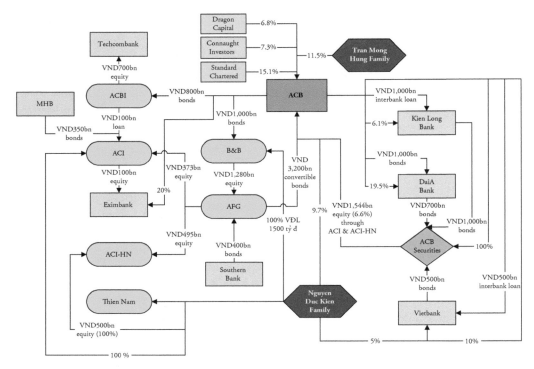

FIGURE 7.3 The structure of ownership, investment, and lending between ACB and affiliated institutions
Note: The data were as of December 31, 2011.
Source: Author's estimation based on the financial statements, annual reports, prospectuses, and management reports by ACB and affiliated institutions, 2010–11.

Truong My Lan acquired control of three Ho Chi Minh City-based banks—SCB, Tin Nghia, and Ficombank—by using loans from one bank to buy shares in the others. The three banks in turn financed real estate companies under her Van Thinh Phat Group (see figure 7.4).

Sacombank was founded in late 1991 as the State Bank of Vietnam gave out licenses to set up a dozen of Vietnam's first joint stock commercial banks. It was formed after the merger between Go Vap Economic Development Bank and three credit cooperatives—Tan Binh, Lu Gia, and Thanh Cong—the last of which was founded by Dang Van Thanh.[29] Under Thanh's leadership, Sacombank became one of the largest private banks between the mid-1990s and 2011. Parallel to the development of Sacombank was the expansion and interlocking ownership structures between nonfinancial companies under the control of Dang Van Thanh. The Thanh Cong Household Business Unit was transformed into Thanh Cong Co. Ltd. in 1999 and Thanh Cong Manufacture Trading JSC in the mid-2000s. In 2011, Thanh established Thanh Cong Group, with Thanh Cong Investment JSC as the core and the five original member companies in trading and sugar production—Bourbon Tay Ninh, Ninh Hoa Sugar, Thanh Cong Trading, Dang Huynh, and Thanh Ngoc. These businesses all received financing directly or indirectly from Sacombank (see figure 7.5).

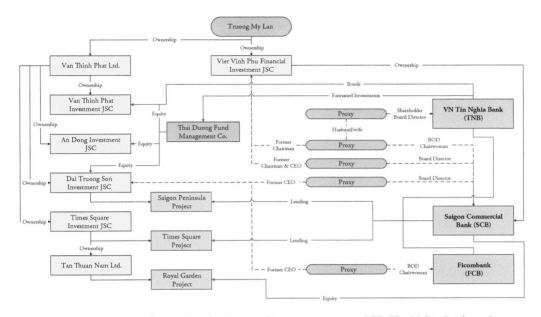

FIGURE 7.4 The structure of ownership, lending, and investment among SCB, Tin Nghia Bank, and Ficombank
Source: Author's estimation based on the financial statements, annual reports, prospectuses, and press releases by the banks and affiliated companies as of September 30, 2011.

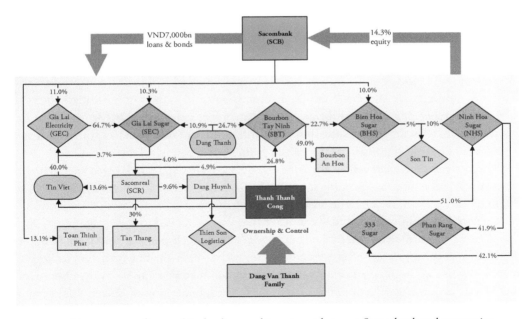

FIGURE 7.5 The structure of ownership, lending, and investment between Sacombank and companies affiliated with Dang Van Thanh's family
Source: Author's estimation based on financial statements, prospectuses, and annual reports of Sacombank and businesses affiliated with Dang Van Thanh's family, 2010–12.

Political Connections, Threat from the State, and New Mechanisms for Wealth Defense

To continue to build up their material resources and defend their wealth, almost all of the oligarchs had to develop strong political connections, which happened during the late 1990s and the entire 2000s. Their experience with building political connections has resulted in this being the key method to defend wealth. Many oligarchs strategically built relationships with one or a group of senior leaders from one political institution. They bet on the rise of this center of power for the continuation of protection and further growth of their wealth. Richer oligarchs were able to cultivate relationships with multiple political leaders or institutions. They deployed their material resources even to competing political factions, and thus ensured broad-based support for their businesses. It is not a coincidence that oligarchs in this group are those that made their wealth first in Eastern Europe. Their larger initial wealth allowed them to pursue the costly strategy of buying support from multiple state leaders.

Suffering from macroeconomic instability during 2008–11, Vietnam's economic growth slowed significantly. Losses in SOE and public investment projects and wrong economic decisions made by different political leaders were exposed. That set the stage for intense infighting and open competition among different political leaders and institutions in Vietnam's political system. The political infighting posed tremendous challenges to the oligarchs, making the wealth defense strategy based on a single relationship with one political leader or institution less effective, even disastrous. That was the cause of the fall of three oligarchs listed in table 7.4.

Kien's problem began when his ACB was investigated for irregular financial dealings with other banks. In 2012, Nguyen Duc Kien was arrested on charges of fraud and illegal trading of shares and gold. In June 2014, Kien was sentenced to a thirty-year prison term.

In October 2014, Ha Van Tham and several senior managers of PetroVietnam were arrested together during an investigation that first focused on deposits from PetroVietnam's subsidiaries to Oceanbank, but later expanded to widespread corruption at the state-owned business group. Tham received a life sentence in May 2018.

After the merger between Southernbank and Sacombank, Tram Be was seen as firmly in control of the new largest joint stock bank in Vietnam. But in 2015, he was forced to hand all of his shareholder rights at the merged bank to the State Bank of Vietnam. He was arrested in August 2017, and a year after that was sentenced to four years in prison.

During this turbulent time, the oligarchs who hedged their political risks by building relationships and support on a broader base continued to flourish. But even this strategy of wealth defense has become vulnerable as anti-corruption investigations intensify. Officials arrested are not just oligarchs or senior managers of SOEs, but senior officials in local governments and the central government, members of the Party Central Committee and Politburo.

Transferring funds to offshore accounts and oligarchs securing foreign citizenship have been reported. However, these actions are seen not as wealth defense, but as measures to maintain a minimum level of living standard in case their oligarchic empires are destroyed. Moving the oligarchs' companies abroad or listing them on foreign stock exchanges proved to be infeasible as Vietnamese companies have yet to be global or even regional players.

Two new wealth defense strategies have emerged recently. One strategy is to invite the participation of large international strategic investors and subject the business interests to the framework of international law (British or Singapore) instead of Vietnamese law. All businesses of the five Vietnamese billionaires are now listed and have large international investors and funds as major shareholders.

The other new strategy is for the oligarchs to replace the role of SOEs as instruments of the state to implement its industrial policy. Facing the spectacular collapse of Vinashin and then the massive losses incurred by other state-owned conglomerates, the Party and the government at the start of a new political term in 2016 could no longer deny the failure of their past industrialization strategy. While still not abandoning the leading role of the state sector officially, leaders in the Party and the government have been quiet about giving support and preferential treatment to SOEs. A new relationship is being formed between the state and the oligarchs, and this time it is official: the oligarchs are encouraged to go into new industries such as heavy industry, automotive, and technology as part of the government's new industrialization policy. VinFast producing cars and VinTech in AI and high-tech applications are two of the most frequently mentioned company names these days in Vietnam.

Conclusion

This chapter presents an analysis of the formation and evolution of oligarchs and the businesses under their control during the last thirty years of transition from central planning to a market economy in Vietnam. Based on the initial identification of a number of well-known oligarchs, there are two distinct sources of original wealth, namely the dynamism of the market economy already existing to some extent in Ho Chi Minh City before the economic reform and the Eastern European connection. Detailed case studies show that many oligarchs resort to the building of cross-ownership structures and political connections to ensure further wealth accumulation and wealth defense. Vietnam's economic growth slowdown after the global financial crisis and internal political fighting within the state system are posing tremendous challenges to the oligarchs, making many of their existing political relationships much less effective—even disastrous—in defending their wealth. In response, the oligarchs are now actively inviting the participation of large international investors and employing the protection of international legal systems. And most recently, a new cozy relationship is being forged between the government and the oligarchs as their businesses are encouraged to invest in new industries with the government's official support.

Notes

1. VCCI, *Vietnam Annual Business Report*, 2018, 66. According to the 2018 ranking, of the top 100 companies ranked by sales, thirty-four were private, forty-eight were either state-owned or equitized (i.e., partially privatized), and eighteen were FDI.
2. The list of top Vietnamese companies is compiled annually by *Vietnam Report*, http://vnr500.com.vn.
3. Winters, *Oligarchy*, 6.
4. Noer, "Vietnam's First Billionaire."
5. Vietnam State Securities Commission, "Number of Listed Companies in Vietnam as of December 2021," http://www.ssc.gov.vn.
6. Tran Du Lich et al., *Kinh Tế Việt Nam Giai Đoạn Chuyển Đổi*, 8.
7. Data provided by the former State Planning Commission of Vietnam.
8. Data from World Bank, *Vietnam Financial Sector Review*, World Bank Country Report, 1995, and IMF, *Vietnam Selected Issues*, IMF Staff Country Report No. 99/55, July 1999.
9. Nha Dau Tu, "Gia tộc giàu có Trương Mỹ Lan."
10. Dau Tu Viet Nam, "Doanh nhân tuổi Tý: Ông Đặng Văn Thành."
11. Doanh Nhan Duong Thoi, "Ông Đoàn Nguyên Đức và câu chuyện có học."
12. Nong Nghiep Viet Nam, "Con đường làm giàu của Đại gia Trầm Bê như thế nào?"
13. According to the Ministry of Education and Training, only 5 percent of high school graduates could pass the entrance exam at that time, and only those with the top scores could go to Eastern Europe.
14. Ismail, "Vietnam Billionaire Bets on Move from Gold to Land."
15. Minh Son, "Comrades: Vietnam's Two New Billionaires."
16. Vietnamnet, "Khối tài sản khủng từ thời sinh viên của nữ tỷ phú CEO Vietjet Air."
17. Vnexpress, "Chân dung Bầu Kiên."
18. Braguinsky, "Postcommunist Oligarchs in Russia," 307–49.
19. Dapice, "Vietnam's Economy."
20. Gainsborough, *Changing Political Economy in Vietnam*.
21. Cafef.vn, "Top 200 người giàu nhất trên thị trường chứng khoán."
22. Dapice et al., "History or Policy."
23. The data were taken from VCCI, *Vietnam Business Annual Report*, 2012.
24. Vingroup's financing sources and growth numbers are based on its audited financial statements from 2005 to 2018.
25. Ownership information and data are from audited financial statements and annual reports of HDBank (2007–18) and Vietjet Air (2017–18).
26. Techcombank's audited financial statements and annual reports (2005–18) and Techcombank's Prospectus for Bond Public Offering, December 2, 2010.
27. ACB's audited financial statements (2006–11).
28. ACB's Prospectus for Listing in Hanoi Stock Exchange, October 30, 2006.
29. BizLive, "Sacombank."

References

BizLive. "Sacombank: Từ hợp tác xã tín dụng tư nhân đến ngân hàng nửa quốc doanh" (Sacombank: From private credit cooperatives to a quasi-state-owned bank). November 8, 2015. https://nhipsongkinhdoanh.vn/chan-dung-doanh-nghiep-sacombank-tu-hop-tac-xa-tin-dung-tu-nhan-den-ngan-hang-nua-quoc-doanh-post1317876.html.

Braguinsky, Serguey. "Postcommunist Oligarchs in Russia: Quantitative Analysis." *Journal of Law and Economics* 52, no. 2 (2009): 307–49.

Cafef.vn. "Top 200 người giàu nhất trên thị trường chứng khoán" (Top 200 richest in the stock market). April 13, 2019. http://s.cafef.vn/top/ceo.chn.

Dapice, David. "Vietnam's Economy: Success Story or Weird Dualism? A SWOT Analysis." Paper prepared for the United Nations Development Programme and the Prime Minister's Research Commission of Vietnam, 2003.

Dapice, David, Nguyen Dinh Cung, Pham Anh Tuan, and Bui Van. "History or Policy: Why Don't Northern Provinces Grow Faster?" Paper prepared for the United Nations Development Programme, 2004.

Dau Tu Viet Nam. "Doanh nhân tuổi Tý: Ông Đặng Văn Thành, bước đường thăng trầm và duyên nghiệp nhà bang" (The year-of-the-rat businessman: Dang Van Thanh, a journey of ups and downs and the banking karma). January 25, 2020. https://dautuvietnam.com.vn/doanh-nhan/doanh-nhan-tuoi-ty-ong-dang-van-thanh-buoc-duong-thang-tram-va-duyen-nghiep-nha-bang-a4580.html.

Doanh Nhan Duong Thoi. "Ông Đoàn Nguyên Đức và câu chuyện có học" (Doan Nguyen Duc and the education story). March 20, 2017. https://doanhnhanduongthoi.com/ong-doan-nguyen-duc-va-cau-chuyen-co-hoc-92-3635.html.

Gainsborough, Martin. *Changing Political Economy in Vietnam: The Case of Ho Chi Minh City.* London: RoutledgeCurzon, 2003.

Ismail, Netty. "Vietnam Billionaire Bets on Move from Gold to Land." *The Independent*, October 29, 2012. https://www.independent.co.uk/news/world/asia/vietnam-billionare-bets-on-move-from-gold-to-land-8230185.html.

Minh Son. "Comrades: Vietnam's Two New Billionaires Have 'Intertwined' Interests." *Vnexpress*, March 6, 2019. https://e.vnexpress.net/news/business/companies/comrades-vietnam-s-two-new-billionaires-have-intertwined-interests-3890549.html.

Nha Dau Tu. "Gia tộc giàu có Trương Mỹ Lan: Bí ẩn từ hồ sơ Panama đến hồ sơ xin thôi quốc tịch Việt Nam" (The wealthy family of Truong My Lan: From the Panama Papers to the application to renounce Vietnamese citizenship). October 28, 2017. https://nhadautu.vn/gia-toc-giau-co-truong-my-lan-bi-an-tu-ho-so-panama-den-ho-so-xin-thoi-quoc-tich-viet-nam-d3979.html.

Noer, Michael. "Vietnam's First Billionaire and the Triumph of Capitalism." *Forbes*, March 25, 2013. http://www.forbes.com/sites/michaelnoer/2013/03/04/vietnams-first-billionaire-and-the-triumph-of-capitalism/.

Nong Nghiep Viet Nam. "Con đường làm giàu của Đại gia Trầm Bê như thế nào?" (What was the road to riches of oligarch Tram Be?). August 20, 2017. https://nongnghiep.vn/con-duong-lam-giau-cua-dai-gia-tram-be-nhu-the-nao-d200416.html.

Tran Du Lich, Luong Huu Dinh, Vo Thanh Thu, and Tran To Tu. *Kinh Tế Việt Nam Giai Đoạn Chuyển Đổi* (Vietnam's economy in transition). Ho Chi Minh City: Saigon Times Press, 1996.

Vietnamnet. "Khối tài sản khủng từ thời sinh viên của nữ tỷ phú CEO Vietjet Air" (The enormous wealth of the Vietjet Air CEO billionaire from her time as a college student). March 12, 2017. https://vietnamnet.vn/vn/kinh-doanh/doanh-nhan/forbes-xep-hang-nu-ty-phu-ceo-vietjet-air-dua-vao-dau-360866.html.

Vnexpress. "Chân dung Bầu Kiên" (A portrait of manager Kien). August 22, 2012. https://vnexpress.net/chan-dung-bau-kien-2722005.html.

Winters, Jeffrey. *Oligarchy.* New York: Cambridge University Press, 2011.

CHAPTER 8

FDI in Vietnam

Policies, Effects, and Linkages to the Local Economy

ARI KOKKO, CURT NESTOR, AND LE HAI VAN

Vietnam has emerged as one of the most attractive emerging market destinations for foreign direct investment (FDI) over the past decades. Foreign investors have contributed significantly to the country's economic development since the early stages of the economic reform and transition process that was launched in the late 1980s, and the importance of FDI has grown since 2007, when the country joined the World Trade Organization (WTO). FDI inflows jumped from US$4.1 billion in 2006 to more than US$8 billion in 2007 and averaged over US$18 billion per year in 2015–21.[1] Among developing economies, only the BRICs (Brazil, Russia, India, China) and Singapore, Mexico, and Turkey have managed to achieve notably higher FDI inflows during the past few years. Although FDI has mainly focused on labor-intensive manufacturing, Vietnam has also become a destination for high-tech enterprises. For example, the leading foreign investor in Vietnam is now South Korea's Samsung. The company's first investment in the country was made in 1996 (production of color television sets for the domestic market), but its presence has increased strongly since 2009, when it established a factory complex in the northern Bac Ninh Province and began to shift its export-oriented production of mobile telephones from China to Vietnam. Vietnam accounted for nearly half of Samsung's global production of mobile telephones in 2017, when the direct employment in its main production facilities outside Hanoi reached 107,000 people. At the same time, Samsung alone accounted for a staggering 26 percent of Vietnam's total exports. Vietnam's success in attracting firms like Samsung has led the country's leaders to be optimistic about future economic development, and it has been assumed that FDI will help Vietnam reach the objective of the Eleventh Party Congress in 2011 to become "a modern and industrialized nation." Apart from the direct effects of FDI on employment, household income, tax payments, and infrastructure, it has been expected that foreign investors will contribute to the development of local industrial capacity through various kinds of spillover effects. Empirical evidence from Vietnam as well as other countries suggests that some of the modern technologies used by foreign multinational enterprises (MNEs) can be diffused to local firms, raising their productivity and competitiveness.[2] The literature on spillovers has identified a potential for horizontal spillovers, where local firms learn from FDI in their own industry, but has tended to emphasize the importance of vertical spillovers, which occur as a result of linkages between local firms and foreign MNEs, for example, in the form of supplier or subcontracting relationships.[3]

However, the Samsung example has raised concerns about the development impact of FDI. While Samsung's direct contributions to the national economy in terms of employment, income, and export revenue were substantial already in 2014, the record with respect to vertical spillovers was disappointing. At that time, there were only four domestic first-tier suppliers in the company's Vietnamese value chain, mainly producing the cardboard boxes into which the mobile phones were packaged—the other sixty-three first-tier suppliers in Vietnam were all foreign-invested enterprises (FIEs), mostly Korean and Japanese firms that had already been part of Samsung's Chinese supply chain.[4] Given the relatively simple tasks assigned to the domestic suppliers, there was little scope for spillovers of advanced technology. The weak integration between FIEs and local firms— and the observation that Vietnam has not quite managed to become a "modern and industrialized nation" despite the large inflow of FDI—has contributed to an ongoing critical discussion about Vietnam's FDI policies. Foreign investors like Samsung have benefited from various FDI incentives, including tax holidays and reduced land rents. The formal arguments for providing such incentives typically emphasize the existence of spillovers, which means that free market solutions will generate too little FDI.[5] Yet, if there are only marginal spillovers, then the main result of FDI incentives may be to cement the competitive disadvantages of local investors who do not qualify for tax holidays and other benefits that are available mainly to FIEs.

The purpose of this chapter is to describe and discuss Vietnam's FDI policies and the effects of FDI from the early 1990s to the present. The analysis consists of two parts. The first of these summarizes data on FDI inflows and FDI policies during the period 1988–2021. This section also discusses the determinants of FDI inflows, where trade liberalization and global economic events like financial crises have moderated the impact of regulatory reform. The second section turns to a discussion of the productivity and spillover effects of FDI. The main question is how FDI has influenced local firms— what has been the impact of FDI on local competitiveness, growth, productivity, and technological competence? Here, the general pattern seems to resemble the Samsung case mentioned above. Vietnam has managed to attract large amounts of FDI, which has created millions of jobs, directly (in the MNEs) as well as indirectly (through various demand and multiplier effects), but the results in terms of FDI spillovers have been weak. One reason is the weakness of the domestic supporting industries (SI) sector. It is hard for FIEs to find local suppliers that can meet the required standards related to technology, quality, delivery times, and contract volumes. Section 3 provides a brief discussion of how the FDI policy framework for the period 2020–30 may look. The major challenge is the need to shift from simply attracting FDI to strengthening the linkages to the local economy and upgrading the position of local firms in global value chains (GVCs). At the time of writing (mid-2022), the "Strategy for Foreign Investment Cooperation 2021–2030" has just been approved, but its implementation is awaiting guiding regulation in several different policy areas. However, the relatively open debate on FDI policy during the past few years gives some useful insights into the plans and considerations of Vietnamese policy-makers. Our tentative assessment of the new policy framework is spelled out in the concluding remarks section at the end of this chapter. We agree that the shift in focus from aiming to attract FDI to optimizing the development impact of FDI is well founded, but there is a risk that the necessary reforms require larger changes than what Vietnamese leaders are prepared to carry out. To fully benefit from FDI inflows, more resources should be used to empower the private sector and raise the capacity and competence of local firms to make them more attractive as partners to foreign MNEs and better able to take advantage of the potential spillover benefits from FDI. A stronger focus on local firms would also improve the resilience of the domestic economy in case international developments result in fundamental restructuring of GVCs, international trade, and FDI linkages. However, it is not clear how eager the Communist Party of Vietnam is to support the emergence of a strong private sector, which would by its nature be fragmented, unpredictable, and relatively difficult to control.

FDI Inflows and FDI Policy

FDI INFLOWS 1988–2021

FDI has become an increasingly important part of the Vietnamese economy since 1988, when legislation allowing and encouraging inward investment was introduced. According to Vietnam's Foreign Investment Agency (FIA),[6] more than 34,500 FIEs were in operation in the country at the end of 2021. In total, these enterprises represented US$408 billion in registered approved investment capital, of which US$251 billion had been implemented.[7] Despite the ongoing COVID-19 pandemic during 2020–21, inflows in FDI continued at a remarkably high rate, with registered and implemented FDI reaching nearly the same levels as during 2019.

Figure 8.1 summarizes full year data on FDI inflows from 1988 to 2021 and provides some broad indicators of the role of FDI in the national economy during this period. Both registered and implemented FDI have fluctuated over time, with notable dips in connection with the Asian financial crisis and the global financial crisis when external events have reduced FDI flows across the world. The notable peak is 2008, when WTO membership boosted the attractiveness of the Vietnamese market and several megaprojects with values at above US$1 billion were registered. However, the underlying trend is one of substantial increases over time, and Vietnam is now a major emerging market destination for FDI.

Although FDI inflows (in particular, implemented FDI) were small in absolute amounts and did not exceed 10 percent of GDP during the first decade after 1988, FDI still left a notable mark on the local economy already at that time. Foreign-invested enterprises accounted for 30 percent of exports already in the early 1990s, and their share of total investment reached nearly one-third by the mid-1990s, before the outbreak of the Asian financial crisis. Since then, the ratio of FDI inflows to GDP has increased gradu-

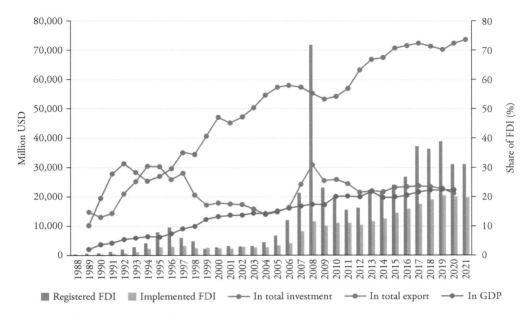

FIGURE 8.1 Overview of FDI in Vietnam, 1988–2021
Source: FIA Vietnam, "Báo cáo đầu tư nước ngoài vào Việt Nam"; Ministry of Planning and Investment internal database.

ally, reaching above 20 percent in the last few years. The share of FDI in total investment has fluctuated more and stabilized at a somewhat lower level than in the mid-1990s. The area where the role of FDI has expanded most remarkably is exports. In recent years, FIEs have accounted for around 70 percent of Vietnam's exports. As a result of FDI, Vietnam has entered GVCs in several industries, such as garments, footwear, furniture, and electronics.

Figures 8.2 and 8.3 illustrate the distribution of the stock of registered FDI capital across broad industry groups and investor source countries by the end of 2021. Figure 8.2 shows that the manufacturing and processing industry dominates, with more than one-half of total investment. Manufacturing investments have dominated FDI inflows, in particular during the last decade. Real estate and construction jointly account for about 18 percent of the FDI stock, the capital-intensive energy/utility sector holds 8 percent, and wholesale and retail trade and the hospitality sector account for 5 percent of the FDI stock (but a much larger share of the number of investment projects). The remaining thirteen industry categories in the Vietnamese statistics accounted for less than 10 percent of the aggregate FDI stock.

Figure 8.3 shows that the distribution of FDI across investor countries is relatively concentrated. Excluding tax havens, the top ten source countries cover 86 percent of the registered FDI capital stock. The dominance of Vietnam's East Asian neighbors is obvious, with South Korea, Japan, Singapore, Taiwan, and Hong Kong/China as the largest investors. FDI sourced from the EU, primarily the Netherlands, the UK, and France, accounts for 6.5 percent. The role of US investors (2.5 percent) is probably

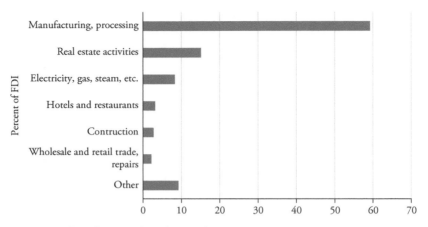

FIGURE 8.2 Cumulative FDI stock per industry
Source: FIA Vietnam, 2022.

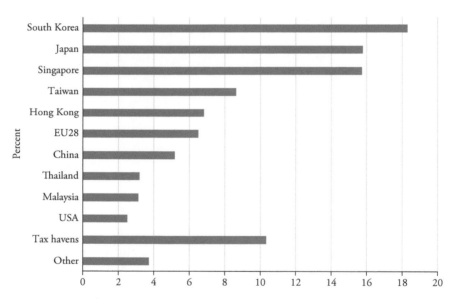

FIGURE 8.3 Cumulative FDI stock per investor country
Source: FIA Vietnam, 2022; calculation by authors.

underestimated since many American FDI projects are conducted by US affiliates in other Asian countries.

Even though FDI reached all sixty-three provinces in Vietnam, the geographical distribution of FDI is heavily skewed toward more developed provinces. By the end of 2021, more than three-quarters of FDI inflows were concentrated to Ho Chi Minh City and adjacent provinces in the south (44.0 percent), Hanoi with the hinterland in the north (27.1 percent), and to a smaller extent Da Nang with surrounding provinces in the central part of the country (4.7 percent).[8]

FDI POLICY: GRADUAL REFORM OVER TIME

Vietnam's economic reforms during the past thirty-plus years have not only affected domestic economic actors, but also changed the legal framework for foreign direct investors operating in or contemplating entering Vietnam. These changes explain much of the fluctuation in FDI flows outlined in figure 8.1. The policy reforms reflect to some extent an ideological shift in the Communist Party of Vietnam, but FDI policy has also responded to foreign investors' complaints and changes in the external environment, such as changes in the FDI regimes of competing host countries. The FDI policy framework during the past decades can be divided roughly into four phases. The first phase, in which the Vietnamese economy was gradually opened to foreign investors, lasted from the earliest reforms in 1988 to 1996, the year before the onset of the Asian financial crisis. The second phase, from 1997 to 2005, was characterized by efforts to overcome the negative impacts of the regional financial crisis and deepen Vietnam's integration with the world economy. The promulgation of the common investment law in 2006, which introduced the same legal framework for domestic and foreign investors, marked the beginning of the third phase. This phase was also strongly influenced by Vietnam's accession to the WTO in 2007. The fourth and current phase in Vietnam's international integration process is driven by major changes in foreign investment policies, reflecting the ambition to increase the development impact of FDI.

From 1988 to 1996 The Vietnamese government issued the first set of regulations governing FDI already in 1977, two years ahead of China's legislation on FDI.[9] However, the international political situation at the time, notably the US trade and investment embargo imposed on Vietnam, effectively blocked the inflow of foreign investment. Vietnam's first Foreign Investment Law (FIL) was instead approved in December 1987 and came into effect in 1988. The ambition was to attract foreign capital, modern resources, technology, and advanced management skills for economic development. FDI inflows were promoted in sectors where new ventures would create employment, produce import substitutes and export goods, contribute to the efficient exploitation of natural resources, build infrastructure, and increase the supply of foreign currency.

Little of this happened during the first years. After the long period of socialist planning and isolation from the global economy following Vietnam's invasion of Cambodia, the policy environment was complex and highly restrictive; unsurprisingly, the initial responses of foreign investors were cautious. Much of the capital invested in the first years was registered in joint ventures for offshore oil exploration projects. Other FDI projects were small joint venture operations with Vietnamese state-owned enterprises (SOEs), typically located in Ho Chi Minh City. Many of the early ventures failed—the investment permits of more than half of the FDI projects licensed in 1988–90 were withdrawn before the completion of the project, and there was often a long lag between the initiation of the FDI project and its implementation.[10]

New legislation introduced in 1990 supported the development of the nascent domestic private sector. The FIL was also amended in 1990 to allow private firms to participate in

joint ventures, but it took many years before any domestic private firms grew strong enough
to be attractive as joint venture partners. Amendments to the FIL were introduced in 1992,
and a new FDI law was eventually promulgated in 1996. The formal changes introduced
during this period aimed to make Vietnam more open to foreign investors by liberalizing
investment requirements and adding sectors where FDI was allowed. To reduce bureaucracy and red tape, licensing processes were gradually standardized and simplified, foreign
investors were permitted to establish wholly foreign-owned subsidiaries rather than joint
ventures, and policies were adjusted to promote export-oriented FDI.

Foreign investors were also strongly influenced by other dimensions of the legal
framework. A pilot project for setting up the first export-processing zone (EPZ) was carried out in Ho Chi Minh City in 1991. This provided both a legal and physical base for
foreign export-oriented companies. The management board of Tan Thuan EPZ (now the
Ho Chi Minh City Export Processing and Industrial Zones Authority) was established in
1992 to further facilitate foreign investment by simplifying administrative procedures.
This was the first provincial body authorized to issue licenses for foreign investment. New
regulations introduced in 1994 allowed management boards of industrial zones (IZs) in
selected provinces to license FDI projects with registered capital up to US$5 million—the
licensing of larger projects was still the prerogative of the central authorities.

By that time, trade liberalization had added significantly to the attractiveness of Vietnam as a location for export-oriented FDI. The US trade embargo on Vietnam that had
been in force since the unification of the country in 1975 was lifted in 1994, and diplomatic relations with the US were normalized in 1995. This made it possible for American
firms to consider Vietnam as a potential trade partner and investment location. Other
potential investors, for example, Japanese MNEs, also saw the end of US sanctions as a
cue to increase their engagement in Vietnam. In the same year, Vietnam joined the Association of Southeast Asian Nations (ASEAN) and its free trade area AFTA, which provided
a boost to FDI inflows from its Southeast Asian neighbors.

FDI inflows gradually increased in response to the more open policy framework.
Registered FDI grew from a few hundred million USD per year in 1988–89 to nearly
US$10 billion in 1996. However, given the complex business environment and high risk of
the Vietnamese market, implemented FDI remained much lower, reaching US$2.9 billion
in 1996. Although well below registered FDI, implemented FDI still accounted for nearly
one-third of total investment in the mid-1990s. The exports of FIEs grew from US$199
million to US$2.2 billion between 1989 and 1996, with a large change in export structure
from crude oil to an increasing share of manufactured goods.

From 1997 to 2005 The objectives of the second FIL issued in 1996 were to attract more FDI
to support the industrialization and modernization of the economy, to raise export capacity, and to reallocate resources to develop the underdeveloped and remote areas of the
country. The law and supporting decrees delegated licensing responsibility to provincial
authorities and opened new sectors for FDI. For example, new regulations in 1997 allowed provincial People's Committees to grant investment licenses for non-conditional
projects with total registered capital up to US$10 million in Hanoi and Ho Chi Minh

City, and up to US$5 million in neighboring provinces—a right that was further extended to all provinces in 1998.

The sectors and areas where FDI inflows were considered particularly important were identified in special lists of priority sectors and districts announced in 1998. Moreover, central and provincial authorities were authorized to encourage FDI in these priority sectors and locations through special preferential fiscal and financial incentives. This included, for example, more generous tax credits and simpler procedures for land leasing and site clearance.[11] In most cases, the incentives offered to foreign investors were more generous than those available for domestic private investors. The promulgation of numerous bilateral investment treaties (BITs) and double taxation treaties (DTTs) during the late 1990s added to the bias in favor of foreign investors. BITs were considered important for reducing the perceived risks among foreign investors contemplating entry into an emerging economy with complex regulations and government interventions. The investment guarantees provided by the BITs have allowed foreign investors to enjoy a level of political risk insurance that is still not available for domestic investors.

The most important formal incentive for inward FDI around the turn of the millennium was the bilateral trade agreement (BTA) with the United States. The removal of the embargo in 1994 had resulted in the establishment of some trade and FDI linkages, but the US remained a marginal destination for Vietnamese exports because of high US import tariffs. When the BTA went into effect in late 2001, tariffs on imports of Vietnamese goods were substantially reduced. Vietnamese exports to the US doubled in one year and grew fivefold in three years after the agreement came into effect.[12] Reforms focusing on the service sector were particularly important. Before the BTA, there had been substantial FDI inflows in services, but mainly concentrated in development of hotels, restaurants, and resorts. Now, FDI was gradually allowed also in business services like auditing, IT services, and banking and finance. However, the slow phasing-in of the commitment to liberalizing service FDI delayed much of the sector's FDI inflows to 2007–8. Moreover, the various reforms called for in the agreement were designed to be WTO-consistent— the BTA could be interpreted as a credible commitment pointing toward Vietnamese WTO membership.

Despite the more favorable legal environment and the strong increase in trade with the US, FDI did not grow much during the 1997–2005 period. FDI inflows contracted during three consecutive years (1997–99) because of the Asian crisis. The initial fall in registered FDI was dramatic, from the nearly US$10 billion recorded in 1996 to US$2.2 billion in 1999. During the years before the Asian crisis, FDI had been dominated by regional investors that were now weakened by their domestic financial troubles. As a response, the Vietnamese government emphasized the importance of facilitating already existing investors, and government missions were assigned to provinces to identify problem areas and discuss solutions. As a result, realized FDI did not fall as dramatically as registered FDI.

Revisions of the FIL in 2000 and 2003 also aimed to maintain FDI inflows. In addition to simplification of investment procedures, the revisions introduced rules for restructuring FIEs, including regulation for mergers and acquisitions (M&A) activities, incentives for expansion projects, and reductions of withholding taxes for foreign investors. This resulted in growing levels of registered FDI from around 2004.

Although FDI inflows remained lower during the post-crisis years, there were important changes in the structure of FDI. The export orientation of FDI started increasing already during the Asian crisis. In 1997, FIEs had accounted for about one-third of Vietnam's exports, and this share grew to nearly 60 percent by 2005, although the FDI share of total investment and GDP did not change much. Increasing exports of garments, textiles, furniture, and other consumer goods to the US market contributed to this development. US firms had increased their FDI in Vietnam, including FDI from their regional affiliates, in response to the BTA, temporarily overtaking the "traditional" Asian top performers in the rankings of foreign investors.[13]

From 2006 to 2020 The common Investment Law promulgated in 2005 (in effect in 2006) ended the distinction between domestic and foreign investment. Under the new legal framework, the provincial People's Committees were given full authorization to govern all FDI projects in their province. Similarly, the management boards of IZs and EPZs were granted control over all projects in their zones. Vietnam's accession to the WTO in 2007 and the opening of additional sectors for foreign competition (as promised in the US BTA from 2001) created new opportunities and investment motives for foreign investors. As a member of the WTO, Vietnam not only has access to the export markets of other member countries at relatively low most favored nation (MFN) tariffs, but membership also brings a more predictable business environment at home, to the benefit of foreign as well as domestic investors. FIEs participating in GVCs are among the main beneficiaries of the more open and transparent trade environment brought by the WTO.

The decentralization of FDI management to provinces and industrial zones was accompanied by a range of provincial-level policies to accelerate FDI inflows. One consequence was increasingly intensive competition between provinces in attracting investment in general and FDI in particular. In some cases, provincial-level FDI policies offered investment incentives that were significantly more generous than those provided by the national policy framework. A large number of provincial investment promotion centers were set up during this period. Almost all of Vietnam's giant FDI projects (i.e., projects with registered capital of more than US$1 billion) were also registered during this time. The peak, with eleven licenses for such megaprojects, came in 2008. Like other WTO members, Vietnam could no longer require FIEs to meet specific export targets, and with increasing domestic demand and purchasing power, foreign investors clearly preferred to locate in IZs rather than EPZs. This led to a boom in IZ development; already by 2012, Vietnam had established 283 IZs located in fifty-eight out of the country's sixty-three provinces/cities.[14]

Apart from WTO membership and changes in domestic FDI policies, there were important external events that influenced FDI during the 2006–15 period. The rapid increases in Chinese labor cost had started cutting into the competitiveness of the most labor-intensive manufacturing operations in China's coastal provinces at this time.[15] Vietnam was considered a feasible alternative location, given its high political stability, low labor cost, and proximity to China's coastal manufacturing hubs. Samsung's decision to establish production of mobile telephones in Vietnam is one illustration of this specific investment motive.

However, the boom in inward FDI during 2007 and 2008 was short-lived because of another external event—the global financial crisis that erupted in October 2008. The crisis resulted in a sharp drop in international trade and investment and a recession affecting most OECD countries during 2008 and 2009, and actually implemented FDI in Vietnam remained below the 2008 level until 2014.

The introduction of a new Law on Investment and a new Law on Enterprise in 2015 has contributed to the increase in FDI inflows since that time. The new laws confirmed the principle of free enterprise in Vietnam, removed most foreign ownership restrictions in Vietnamese companies, reduced bureaucracy in the foreign investment approval process, and brought corporate governance rules closer to international standards. The 49 percent foreign ownership cap in Vietnamese joint stock companies was abolished, which facilitated FDI in the form of M&As as well as foreign portfolio investment in the Vietnamese securities and stock markets.

In addition to the more favorable legal framework, the FDI boom in the last few years is also related to several important external drivers of FDI. For example, Vietnam has recently entered into several broad plurilateral trade agreements—including the Comprehensive and Progressive Agreement for Trans-Pacific Partnership (CPTPP), the free trade agreement with the European Union (EVFTA), and most recently the Regional Comprehensive Economic Partnership (RCEP)—which reduce trade barriers between the member countries and require institutional reforms for transparency and harmonization of regulations.[16] Moreover, continuing increases in Chinese labor costs and the trade conflict between the US and China since early 2018 contribute to a shift of labor-intensive, export-oriented manufacturing from China to Vietnam.

From 2020: The Next Generation of FDI Policy The next generation of FDI policy is currently under development following a broad consultancy process started in 2017. The new policy framework is intended to result in a shift of focus from the volume of FDI to the quality and development impact of FDI: key features are higher value added, better jobs, stronger linkages between FIEs and local firms, and stronger spillover benefits of FDI. The formal laws and regulations making up the new FDI policy framework were still under development at the time of writing (mid 2022), but we will return to a discussion of the objectives and possible features of the policy package in our concluding remarks at the end of this chapter.

Spillover Effects of FDI

TECHNOLOGY DIFFUSION AND SPILLOVERS

FDI has a very visible and important direct role in the Vietnamese economy, accounting for large shares of investment and formal employment and most of the country's manufacturing exports, as shown in the previous section. Demand and income multipliers linked to FDI contribute to large amounts of indirect employment. FIEs source inputs from local firms, which creates employment and income, and the earnings from FDI-related employment are largely spent on goods and services supplied by local firms, adding further to aggregate demand. However, it is widely debated how FDI has influenced the technology and productivity of local firms. Has FDI resulted in technology transfer and technology spillovers that have raised the capacity of local industry, or has it instead crowded out local firms and led to slower growth and development of domestic capability than what might have been possible with a less FDI-dependent industrialization strategy? These are obviously difficult questions, since nobody knows how the alternative development path would have looked. The discourse has therefore focused on identifying correlations between FDI and the growth rates of productivity or efficiency in local firms. This has also turned out to be a complex task.

One reason is that FDI influences local firms in several different ways. The productivity of local firms may be affected by FDI in their own industry (horizontal FDI) through demonstration effects, labor mobility, and competition for market shares, but FDI in other industries is also likely to matter. FDI in upstream sectors changes the cost and quality of necessary intermediate inputs, while FDI in downstream industries may change the demand for the goods produced by local firms. These vertical effects may take place purely through the market, or they may operate through the formal linkages between local firms and FIEs, when local companies source inputs directly from FIEs, or act as suppliers and subcontractors to them. In some instances, it is possible that learning and spillovers of foreign technologies take place between local firms, some of which are linked to FIEs, and not only through direct links between FIEs and local firms. Moreover, the diffusion of foreign technology is likely to depend on the technology gap between foreign and local firms and the absorptive capacity of local firms. Generally, there will be both winners and losers—the most likely beneficiaries are those local firms that have both the human resources to understand foreign technology and the financial resources to invest in the new technologies. These resources are not evenly spread between industries and geographic locations, which adds further complications. Moreover, even a strong positive correlation between foreign presence and local productivity growth does not prove causality: foreign firms may simply be attracted to those industries and locations that grow fast for other reasons.

Hence, it is not surprising that the results from studies on the impact of FDI on local industry vary widely and are sometimes contradictory. In addition to the complications discussed above, results diverge depending on the periods of analysis, data sets, and empirical methodologies.

EARLY STUDIES: INDUSTRY AND PROVINCIAL DATA

The first generation of studies on the impact of FDI dates to the late 1990s and early 2000s and used aggregated industry and province-level data to explore the impact of FDI. For example, Hemmer and Nguyen analyzed the role of FDI in poverty reduction during the 1990s and distinguished between a direct effect of FDI through employment creation and indirect effects that worked through the impact of FDI on provincial economic growth.[17] They could not find any significant employment effects, but did find a strong provincial growth effect that was assumed to promote poverty reduction. Pham studied the growth effects of FDI and found that foreign presence resulted in higher domestic savings and investment rates (hence faster output growth) during the period 1988–98.[18] The results also suggested that differences in FDI flows across regions tended to increase the gap between rich and poor provinces.

A few years later, Hoang and colleagues examined provincial growth during the period 1995–2006, and confirmed the positive direct impact of FDI, but noted that it was hard to find any clear signs of indirect effects or spillovers.[19] Anwar and Nguyen also looked at provincial growth in 1995–2006 and argued that only some Vietnamese regions had sufficient absorptive capacity (in terms of human capital and technology) to benefit from spillovers.[20] Vu, Gagnes, and Noy distinguished between different sectors in 1990–2004 and found that the growth effects of FDI were much higher in manufacturing than in food production or services.[21] In a second paper, Anwar and Nguyen analyzed a panel covering twenty-two manufacturing industries in 1995–2005 to distinguish between horizontal and vertical spillover effects. They found no signs of the former, presumably because negative competition effects neutralized any positive spillovers from demonstration effects and labor mobility. However, they did find strong signs of spillovers from backward linkages, that is, spillovers related to contacts with the FIEs purchasing inputs from local firms. In addition, their results highlighted the importance of absorptive capacity: "industries with a higher stock of human capital gain more benefits from vertical backward spillovers."[22] Overall, the findings from these early province- or sector-level studies showed strong growth effects of FDI that differed across regions and industries, weak evidence of horizontal spillovers, but some signs of spillover benefits from linkages to foreign investors in downstream sectors. Large technology gaps and weak absorptive capacity were the likely reasons for the relatively weak impact on local productivity.

Summarizing a review of the development effects of FDI, Schaumburg-Müller had already concluded that results had not lived up to expectations. Apart from the arguments mentioned above, he noted that most of the early FDI went into joint ventures with SOEs, while the underdeveloped private sector was largely neglected.[23] By the early 2000s, the new Enterprise Law and other policy reforms had strengthened the position of the private sector, but it was still not closely connected to FIEs through linkages and subcontracting relationships.

This notwithstanding, there were studies providing case-based evidence of spillovers and learning from foreign investors. For example, Le reported that foreign firms contributed significantly to human capital development through on-the-job training.[24] By the early 2000s, summary data indicated that 300,000 workers, 25,000 technicians, and 6,000 managers had been trained by FIEs in Vietnam. Some of these had transferred their skills to local industry, contributing to "observed improvements" in local firms in sectors like trade, tourism, machinery and equipment, and construction. The study also referred to case studies showing technology spillovers from foreign firms to their Vietnamese joint venture partners, and from the joint ventures to other Vietnamese firms.

FIRM-LEVEL DATA: FOCUS ON VERTICAL SPILLOVERS

From the early 2000s, researchers gained access to micro-data sets that make it possible to study the effects of FDI across different types of local firms. This has helped bridge the seemingly contradictory results from macro-level studies that find only limited spillovers and case studies where learning and technology transfer are more visible. Surveying the first round of Vietnamese micro-data analyses, Pham concluded that they added support to the hypothesis that there are positive FDI spillovers in Vietnamese industry.[25] Among other contributions, the survey highlighted Nguyen Dinh Chuc and colleagues, who added evidence of positive productivity effects from access to new, improved, or less costly intermediate inputs supplied by FIEs,[26] and Nguyen Ngoc Anh and colleagues, who confirmed the importance of vertical spillovers from supply chain linkages in manufacturing.[27]

Most of these early micro-data studies were carried out by Vietnamese research groups and were rarely published in leading journals. However, several qualified publications have appeared since 2010. One of the earliest was Le and Pomfret, who reported positive wage spillovers from horizontal as well as vertical FDI, particularly when both foreign and domestic firms were engaged in training activities.[28] One of the few later studies focusing on wage spillovers is Nguyen, Sun, and Beg, who found on balance a negative effect of FDI.[29] The likely reason is that FIEs generally pay higher wages and attract the most high-quality workers, leaving domestic firms with less-qualified workers who are likely to be paid less.

Using firm-level data for the manufacturing industry in 2000–2006, Le and Pomfret went on to examine the distinction between horizontal and vertical productivity spillovers and found evidence of spillovers from backward linkages from FIEs.[30] These spillovers were larger for local firms with higher labor quality, suggesting higher absorptive capacity. The estimated horizontal spillover effect was negative, presumably because the tougher competition from more productive FIEs outweighed any positive effects of demonstration and imitation. Export-oriented FIEs did not generate any negative competition effects of this type. The authors also recorded some differences between wholly owned FIEs and joint ventures: the positive vertical spillovers were larger and the negative horizontal spillovers were smaller for joint ventures. One reason could be that the technologies of wholly owned FIEs were more advanced, more difficult to absorb, and connected to stronger competition effects. The joint ventures' stronger networks with local industry could also explain their more positive impact. The main policy recommendation suggested by Le and Pomfret was to strengthen the linkages between FIEs and domestic firms.[31] An important prerequisite for this would be additional investment in relevant education and training, as well as incentives for domestic firms to engage in R&D and human capital upgrading to bolster their absorptive capacity.

Newman and colleagues added a dimension to the debate about vertical spillovers by distinguishing between those effects that operate through direct linkages with foreign firms and those that work through the market. Like most other studies, they found backward spillovers from FDI.[32] These effects were particularly strong for local firms with formal supply linkages to joint ventures rather than wholly owned FIEs. They also found negative forward spillovers affecting local firms purchasing inputs from upstream sectors with FDI. The proposed reason for this finding was that FIEs often gain a dominant market position and raise input prices for domestic downstream producers. However, these negative effects were significantly smaller for local firms with direct linkages to upstream FIEs, perhaps because these firms could simultaneously benefit from productivity-enhancing technology and knowledge transfers. The study did not find any evidence of horizontal spillovers, presumably because any positive effects of labor mobility, demonstration, and imitation were offset by negative competition effects.

Focusing on vertical spillovers through value chain participation, Ni and colleagues looked at how the origin of the foreign investors affected outcomes. Their assumption was that the degree of local sourcing could be affected by factors such as distance, preferential trade agreements, and institutional or technological differences between the investor and Vietnam. Their findings for 2000–2011 suggested that FDI from Asian firms generated positive backward spillovers to domestic firms but negative horizontal spillovers—FDI from non-Asian MNEs did not generate any significant spillovers at all. Furthermore, distinguishing between Asian investors, they found that Chinese and Taiwanese MNEs were the main sources of the significant spillover effects, while MNEs from Japan, Korea, and other Asian countries did not generate significant spillovers of any kind.[33] The proposed reasons were differences in the sourcing behavior of MNEs. Firms from South Korea and Japan preferred using suppliers from their own country or other foreign partners, because Vietnamese suppliers were often not able to meet their quality, cost, and delivery requirements. Chinese and Taiwanese investors, by contrast, operated with less sophisticated technologies and tended to choose local suppliers to minimize costs. Hence, the authors emphasized the importance of supply chain linkages and highlighted the crucial role of local technological competence: when the gap with respect to foreign technologies is too high, there is little local sourcing, and spillover benefits are limited.

The importance of local technological capability and absorptive capacity has recently been stressed also by Wrana and Nguyen, who examined the "strategic coupling" between MNEs and local industry. They argued that even if Vietnamese firms were to some extent integrated into global value chains operated by foreign MNEs, and even if there were transfers of technology from the MNEs to local firms, the impact on the technical efficiency of local industry was small.[34] Vietnamese suppliers gained access to new machinery and production technology, but their total factor productivity did not improve much as a result. Referring to the *Global Competitiveness Report 2016–2017*, they noted that the efficiency of technology transfer from MNEs to domestic firms in Vietnam ranked among the lowest in Asia, even behind regional neighbors like Indonesia and Cambodia.[35] The performance of local suppliers in Vietnam's Red River Delta was reported to be particularly disappointing, as the total factor productivity (TFP) growth rates among MNE suppliers were no higher than those of non-suppliers. The main reason was arguably a relatively large technology gap between local and foreign firms, coupled with the low absorptive capacity of local firms.

FIRM-LEVEL DATA: REGIONAL PATTERNS

The regional patterns of FDI spillovers have been explored in several recent studies. Revisiting their earlier 2010 study on regional growth using detailed firm-level data to estimate TFP in eight Vietnamese regions in 2000–2005, Anwar and Nguyen largely confirmed their initial finding that the impact of FDI varied systematically across regions. In the updated analysis, they argued that the positive effects in provinces with higher absorptive capacity were mainly generated through vertical backward spillovers, that is, through supplier relationships with foreign MNEs.[36] These backward spillovers were absent in regions with low absorptive capacity. Their conclusion was that regions with better technology, a larger stock of human capital, and a more developed financial system would gain more from FDI spillovers, both because foreign investors would be attracted by these qualities and because they would raise the absorptive capacity of local firms.

Tran, Pham, and Barnes looked deeper into the geographical pattern of FDI effects by estimating spatial spillover models on the firm-level data set used by Anwar and Nguyen. They found that productivity spillovers decayed quickly with increasing distance between foreign and local firms, so that intra-regional spillovers were much larger than inter-regional spillovers.[37] The intra-regional (i.e., provincial) effects of FDI included positive spillovers to local firms in supplier sectors (backward spillovers), but negative effects on firms in customer sectors (forward spillovers) and firms in the same sector (horizontal spillovers). FDI in neighboring provinces generated positive spillovers in all three dimensions, but these effects were much smaller in magnitude than the intra-provincial spillovers. Interestingly, they also recognized a social interaction effect among local firms. Contacts between local firms seemed to strengthen the positive backward spillovers and reduce the negative horizontal and forward spillovers. These benefits are probably linked to agglomeration effects and knowledge flows between local firms that strengthen their absorptive capability and competitiveness. Hence, one of the policy recommendations is to encourage clustering of local firms in relative proximity to downstream FIEs.

In another recent contribution, Huynh and colleagues explored an updated firm-level data set for 2011–15 and detected a slightly worrying pattern for regional spillovers. In qualitative terms, they found similar positive backward spillovers and negative forward and horizontal spillovers, as have many other studies. However, they also found that the negative effects tended to outweigh the positive spillovers during this period.[38] Their four policy conclusions were to (1) continue supporting backward FDI spillovers through participation in the value chains of FIEs, (2) raise the absorptive capacity and competence of local industry through investment in human capital and technology, (3) promote supporting industries through incentives for technology transfer and upgrading, and (4) provide a "truly fair business environment" for local firms. This new angle to the debate on the need to create a level playing field—this time, from the perspective of local private firms—provides an interesting flashback to an older discourse on FDI promotion and the need to establish a level playing field for foreign investors. Now, the level playing field argument is put forth not to maximize the inflow of FDI, but rather to promote the competence of local firms and the development effects of FDI. Wrana and Nguyen make a similar argument in their discussion of the disappointing spillover effects of FDI (especially in the Red River Delta). They claim that institutional entrepreneurship initiatives, for example, cooperative vocational training programs, have almost exclusively focused on the FIEs' specific skill demands and that they have barely reached local firms. Their main policy recommendation is therefore that "national and local authorities must increasingly consider the needs of private domestic firms" in industrial and development policy reforms.[39]

SUMMARY: SPILLOVER EFFECTS AND FDI LINKAGES

Summarizing the empirical evidence on the spillover effects, two observations stand out. First, the signs of horizontal spillovers are weak, but local firms seem to benefit from backward spillovers from FDI. These spillovers are particularly strong for local firms with formal linkages to FIEs—in other words, firms that have managed to enter the supply chains of FIEs record higher productivity. Forward spillovers are generally negative, except for firms with formal linkages to upstream FIEs. Second, the impacts of FDI vary across the provinces of Vietnam, with stronger positive effects in more developed provinces. One reason seems to be the higher education level and absorptive capacity in these locations, but it is also likely that agglomeration effects are important. Local firms that operate in clusters seem to be better at learning from FIEs and responding to negative horizontal spillovers. This finding highlights the importance of the match between FIEs and local firms. If FIEs operate in sectors that are not vertically linked to local industry, then it is likely that learning and spillovers will remain limited.

Both observations emphasize the vertical links between FIEs and local industry: the Vietnamese economy generates spillover benefits from FDI mainly when local firms qualify as suppliers to FIEs. However, in many locations and industries, this does not happen, primarily because the technological and industrial capabilities of local firms are too weak. Hence, FIEs rely to a large extent on imports or prefer to employ other foreign firms as suppliers. Apart from stronger technological capabilities and larger scale, the foreign-invested suppliers benefit from a more favorable regulatory and institutional environment than local firms. Many of the fiscal and financial incentives provided to foreign investors have not been available for domestic investors, the investment guarantees from BITs do not apply for domestic firms, and even the institutional initiatives that are available sometimes focus on the needs of FIEs rather than local industry.

The weakness of the Vietnamese supporting industry (SI) sector was painfully demonstrated in 2014 when Vietnam's domestic manufacturing industries inadvertently gained the reputation of "not being able to produce screws": after publishing an invitation to tender, Samsung's procurement division failed to find local suppliers capable of meeting the required standards and order volumes of screws and other less sophisticated inputs.[40] Government surveys confirmed the weak state of the sector. It was estimated that domestic enterprises were only capable of providing about 10 percent of the total demand for materials, parts, and components in manufacturing in 2016, and that only three hundred local Vietnamese enterprises were taking part in FIE-led supply chains in Vietnam.⁴¹ At that time, the Vietnamese SI sector consisted of around 3,300 enterprises, with 1,800 enterprises producing parts and components and 1,500 enterprises providing inputs to the garment and footwear sector. Most of the SI sector's leading firms were FIEs. The great majority of domestic firms were small and medium-sized enterprises (SMEs), with 70 percent employing fewer than a hundred workers and 91 percent employing fewer than five hundred workers.

The small size and low productivity of local firms are the main reasons for the weakness of the domestic SI sector.[42] GVC suppliers face strict quality standards, technological requirements, and delivery terms; order volumes are large, and price-cost margins small. Small firms rarely have the resources or technical capabilities to engage in the R&D, innovation, and specialization needed to meet the specific demands of large industrial customers. Small size also means that they are unable to compete on price with FIEs that benefit from scale economies. To strengthen the linkages with FIEs, Vietnam will need a more productive and competitive domestic private sector where firms have opportunities to grow over time. This calls for comprehensive reforms that go beyond traditional FDI policy, and include investments in education, skills, and technology; measures to improve the business environment for private firms, including SMEs; programs to match local suppliers with FIEs; and institutional reforms to create a level playing field for the domestic private sector.[43]

Next-Generation FDI Policy

Vietnamese authorities are acutely aware that the development effects of FDI have not been as positive as expected, that the value added in the operations of FIEs has been too low, and that the linkages and spillover effects of FDI have remained small. In addition to launching a Supporting Industry Development Program in 2017, the government therefore initiated a process to revise the broad policy framework for FDI. The main objective of this revision is to increase the focus on the quality and development impact of FDI. The final outcome—a twelve-page policy document entitled "Strategy for Foreign Investment Cooperation 2021–2030"—was approved in June 2022.[44] The guiding legislation necessary for implementation of the strategy had not been published at the time of writing (September 2022), but tracing the steps of the legislative process may give some insights into the challenges faced by Vietnamese policymakers aiming to strengthen the development effects of FDI inflows. The relatively open consultancy process during the early stages of the process, when the Ministry of Planning and Investment (MPI) and the World Bank affiliate International Finance Corporation (IFC) circulated their joint analysis and recommendations for next-generation FDI policy, reveals some of the objectives and core considerations of Vietnamese authorities as well as other stakeholders. Before turning to these, however, it is appropriate to note that the government's policy decisions are subject to several constraints.

CONSTRAINTS ON GOVERNMENT POLICY

Some decades ago, a developing country government might have tried to maximize linkages and spillover effects of FDI using a policy mix including local content, joint venture, and technology transfer requirements and other interventions directly affecting the production decisions of foreign investors. Today, governments have less discretionary power in the FDI policy area. It is risky to discriminate against foreign firms and difficult to impose strict performance requirements on them. WTO rules and various international investment agreements circumscribe trade measures such as trade barriers, export subsidies, and quantitative restrictions, but also instruments used to regulate the behavior of FIEs, such as local content and technology transfer requirements.[45] The policy space is further constrained by conditions attached to grants and credits in bilateral and multilateral development cooperation, as well as regional integration agreements.[46]

These policy restrictions are highly relevant for Vietnam. In addition to being a member of the WTO since 2007, by 2019 Vietnam had signed seventy-one double taxation agreements, sixty-one bilateral investment treaties, and twenty-six plurilateral or bilateral treaties with investment provisions.[47] The treaties with investment provisions include ASEAN and AFTA, the USBTA, the EVFTA, the CPTPP, and the RCEP, most of which contain promises to open the Vietnamese market to foreign investors and rules constraining Vietnam's ability to manipulate the behavior of FIEs. At the same time, agreements like the CPTPP, the EVFTA, and the RCEP provide opportunities to connect to new GVCs and strong motives for the government to introduce reforms that help local firms diversify and enter these GVCs with higher value-added activities.

Domestic considerations may also limit the policy space. Apart from purely political and ideological preferences, it is likely that specific interest groups may influence policy decisions. For example, the World Bank discusses the "commercialization" of state institutions and the granting of various privileges (related, for example, to taxation, public procurement, and access to land and finance) to SOEs, FIEs, and a limited number of well-connected domestic private firms.[48] While the international agreements discussed above aim to ensure that foreign firms are not discriminated against, they do not ban bad treatment of some domestic firms. In the past, this has meant that the relatively weak efforts to build critical market institutions and guarantee property rights and fair competition have limited the growth potential of private SMEs, leading to the emergence of new large enterprises.[49] In the current context, this is worrying because most of the enterprises in the Vietnamese economy, including the strategically important SI sector, are privately owned SMEs that have not had any large voice in the Vietnamese policymaking process in the past. There is a risk that future policies will also cater primarily to SOEs, FIEs, and the few privileged private firms that have the ear of Vietnam's political decision makers (see chapters by Nguyen Xuan Thanh and Le Dang Doanh in this volume).

RECOMMENDATIONS FOR "NEXT-GENERATION
FDI STRATEGY 2020–2030"

To promote an inclusive policymaking debate, MPI and IFC presented their joint recommendations for Vietnam's "Next-Generation FDI Strategy" in 2018. The broad recommendations for next-generation FDI policy focused on a set of priority sectors to be targeted for FDI promotion and a number of "breakthrough reforms" needed to attract the kind of FDI that Vietnam wants.[50]

The short-term priorities for proactive investment promotion involved SI sectors such as high-grade metals, plastics, high-tech components, industrial machinery and equipment, and services such as logistics and maintenance. Other short-term priority industries were automotive and transport equipment and environmental technologies. To exploit existing natural resources, high-value innovative agricultural products and niche tourism services were targeted. Pharmaceuticals and medical equipment, IT and knowledge process outsourcing, fintech, and education and health care services were among the sectors identified as medium-term priorities. To make up for the limited number of jobs provided by these new priority sectors, it was recognized that other types of FDI, including basic assembly and business processing operations, would be necessary for employment generation for a long time, especially in less-developed provinces.

Figure 8.4 shows eight "breakthrough reforms" that would be needed to realize the shift to next-generation FDI. While some of them focus on the way FDI policy is carried out, others address more fundamental reform needs in policy areas that are not directly under the control of the agencies directly responsible for FDI policy (such as FIA). Most of the proposed reforms dealing with the efficiency of investment promotion (reforms 3, 4, and 7 in figure 8.4) are relatively uncontroversial, and require primarily that FIA—the part of the MPI managing FDI policy—is granted sufficient resources in terms of financial and human capital to take on more demanding tasks. The establishment of a "next-generation FIA" (reform 2) is more difficult and requires changes in the relations between different government agencies—to lead in strategy implementation, the new FIA would need a broader mandate to initiate policy reforms involving not only FDI promotion but also export promotion, SME development, FDI linkages, special economic zones, innovation, and outward FDI. Considering the existing shortcomings related to horizontal policy coordination—for example, overlaps and insufficient cooperation between ministries[51]— such a mandate to lead and coordinate strategy implementation would be valuable, but probably also hard to achieve, precisely because of the weak coordination and cooperation between ministries.

The other four reform requirements address some of the fundamental weaknesses in the Vietnamese economy. These are not only reasons why linkages and spillovers from FDI have been weak, but also why Vietnam is not a more prosperous and developed economy. The shortage of skills (reform 1) is a problem for FIEs looking for Vietnamese suppliers, but it is also a challenge for the economy at large. The weaknesses in the Vietnamese business environment and investment climate (reform 5) have probably scared away some foreign investors and added to the operating costs of those MNEs that have

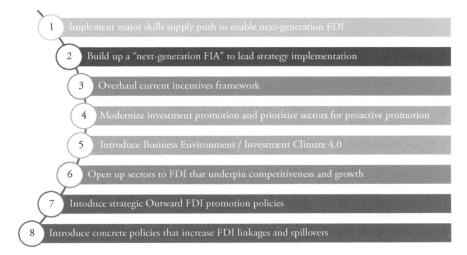

1 Implement major skills supply push to enable next-generation FDI

2 Build up a "next-generation FIA" to lead strategy implementation

3 Overhaul current incentives framework

4 Modernize investment promotion and prioritize sectors for proactive promotion

5 Introduce Business Environment / Investment Climate 4.0

6 Open up sectors to FDI that underpin competitiveness and growth

7 Introduce strategic Outward FDI promotion policies

8 Introduce concrete policies that increase FDI linkages and spillovers

FIGURE 8.4 Eight breakthrough reforms for next-generation FDI
Source: MPI/IFC, *Recommendations on Vietnam Next Generation FDI Strategy and Vision 2020–2030.*

nevertheless entered Vietnam, but they are even more costly for domestic SMEs trying to grow and prosper. Entry barriers and other rules that restrict FDI in sectors such as communications, logistics, education, health, and financial services (reform 6) limit the efficiency and competitiveness of FIEs as well as domestic firms. The need for policies that increase FDI linkages and spillovers (reform 8) is obvious, and various initiatives have already been launched, as in the form of the Supporting Industry Development Program and other schemes. Hence, more effective implementation of existing policies would perhaps be more important than entirely new policies.[52]

Overall, the "breakthrough reforms" included important policy improvements with a high payoff. Comprehensive investment in education and skill development, improvements in the business environment for private firms, reductions in regulatory entry barriers, and stronger efforts to implement economic reforms that have already been announced are low-risk investments. They are likely to strengthen the local economy and generate growth and development irrespective of how foreign investors respond to them in the short term. If FDI flows to Vietnam increase, the returns will be larger, not only because of the direct benefits of FDI, but also because stronger and more competitive local firms will be better able to collaborate with and learn from FIEs.

The major challenge is that the proposed "breakthrough reforms" would require comprehensive change in the Vietnamese policy environment. Commenting on the reform proposals, Kelhofer argued that it is necessary to change not only policy, but also the motivations and mindsets of both investors and policymakers to maximize value added and spillovers from FDI.[53] Table 8.1 illustrates the nature of this fundamental shift. It also reveals how broad and deep the reforms must be in order to reach the next-generation strategy targets. The gap between the existing motives of foreign investors (low

Table 8.1
Changes in investment motives and policies for next-generation FDI strategy

Existing situation	Next-generation FDI strategy targets
Investors' primary motives: • Low labor costs • Low-cost utilities • Risk-diversification alternative to China	Investors' primary motives: • High labor skills • Resource-efficient technologies • Superior location within ASEAN FTA
Nature of investment promotion: • Reactive, cross-sector, open-door • "When investors come"	Nature of investment promotion: • Proactive, targeted promotion • "To attract the investors Vietnam wants"
Main marketing tools: • Broad incentives to attract investors • Based on short-term cost advantages	Main marketing tools: • Holistic sector strategies to attract investors • Based on long-term competitive advantages
Incentives focus: • Fiscal incentives • Based on dollar value of FDI	Incentives focus: • Performance-based incentives • Based on local value-addition
Consequences: • Dual economy with little local content	Consequences: • High local value addition

Source: Adapted from Kelhofer, "Recommendations for a Next Generation FDI Strategy 2020–2030."

costs) and the envisioned status of Vietnam as an economy that has highly skilled labor and resource-efficient technologies to attract investors is particularly wide. Clearly, it will take years to create long-term competitive advantages that are based on abundant labor skills and technological assets. This should therefore be the time frame for the new policy framework. The gap also highlights the systemic nature of the necessary reform process. FDI policy on its own cannot create skilled labor and resource-efficient technologies— these will require more comprehensive reforms that cover education, innovation policy, and the business environment at large.

"THE STRATEGY FOR FOREIGN INVESTMENT COOPERATION 2021–2030"

Following the debate around the "Next Generation FDI Strategy," Vietnamese authorities have taken several steps to lay the groundwork for the necessary reforms. In August 2019, the Politburo issued a resolution calling for fundamental changes in FDI promotion policy to overcome the shortcomings of the institutional framework and to improve the international competitiveness of the domestic business and investment environment.[54] The resolution resulted in several initiatives, such as a government action program to improve the FDI environment issued in April 2020, the establishment of a special inter-ministerial working group in charge of proactive FDI promotion (June 2020), and a revision of the Law on Investment (June 2020, in effect from 2021). Further guidance on the implementation of the Law on Investment was issued in 2021, including a revised list of foreign-invested business activities subject to market access restrictions; a set of selective investment incentives for prioritized FDI projects; and a list of 157 projects, mainly in infrastructure, calling for over US$71 billion in FDI during the period 2021–25. Finally, in early June 2022, the government approved "The Strategy for Foreign Investment Cooperation 2021–2030."[55]

The twelve-page policy document outlines several quantitative objectives for FDI inflows, such as targeting investment from more developed economies in Asia (including China and India), Europe, and the United States; increasing the number of Fortune Global 500–listed MNEs investing in Vietnam; and improving the position of Vietnam in the World Bank's Business Environment ranking. Nine measures are proposed for increasing the efficacy of FDI, partly overlapping with the recommendations from MPI and IFC. Four of these measures address the effectiveness and efficiency of FDI promotion and the management of FDI, while the other five focus on the need for comprehensive reform to strengthen the economy's quality and competitiveness. The objectives include developing an ecosystem of science, technology, and innovation; strengthening the SI sector and its linkages to global value chains; and deepening Vietnam's integration with the international economy.

The actual implementation of the FDI strategy is pending the promulgation of guiding legislation in a wide range of policy areas. The success of next-generation FDI policy will to a large extent depend on how far this reform process will reach. In other words, the key reforms for improving the development effects of FDI in Vietnam might not be those focusing directly on potential foreign investors or incumbent FIEs, but rather those that aim to create an enabling environment for the domestic private sector.

Concluding Remarks

Vietnam's rapid development over the past thirty years is the result of a continuous reform process where an inward-oriented economic system characterized by central planning and control has gradually given way to a more market-oriented and internationalized economy. The development has been particularly fast in some dimensions. For example, the ratio of exports to GDP exceeds 100 percent—the only countries recording higher ratios are small economies like Luxembourg, Hong Kong, Singapore, Malta, and Ireland.[56] The inflow of FDI as a share of GDP (at over 6 percent) and the inward FDI stock as a share of GDP (around 50 percent) are also remarkably high for a country at Vietnam's income level. Reforms focusing on decentralization, deregulation, trade liberalization, and investment in IZs and other forms of infrastructure, together with an abundant supply of low-cost labor, have clearly been effective in enticing foreign MNEs to locate export-oriented activities in Vietnam.

However, not all dimensions of development have evolved equally quickly. The challenge highlighted in this chapter is the relatively weak integration between FIEs and domestic firms. The lack of strong linkages has meant that some of the potential benefits of FDI have been lost: the technology and productivity spillovers that could have helped domestic firms become more competitive and move into higher value-added activities have been limited. One reason for the "missing linkages" is the weakness of the Vietnamese private sector. Few domestic firms have been able to meet the tough conditions for joining foreign-controlled GVCs, and the lead MNEs have therefore often chosen to bring their foreign suppliers to Vietnam or import the needed materials and components.

The crucial question is why the domestic private sector has not been able to respond more strongly to the opportunities that emerged with the inflows of FDI. Some answers have been suggested above. Most of Vietnam's private firms are too small to invest efficiently in R&D, innovation, and specialization. It is hard to find highly skilled workers, and the competition from SOEs and FIEs is tough because both types of firms enjoy various privileges and incentives that are not available to private SMEs. In short, too few SMEs have managed to grow large enough to become attractive partners to FIEs. As discussed in the chapter by Le Dang Doanh in this volume, the Vietnamese private sector, with emphasis on SMEs, is still struggling to remain competitive in a setting with heavy government intervention and FIEs and SOEs that enjoy various policy-related privileges. A relevant question for future research is why the Vietnamese private sector has not managed to copy the Chinese private sector's success in generating "capitalism from below," as discussed by Nee and Opper.[57]

The main objective of Vietnam's "Next-Generation FDI Strategy" is to improve the development effects of FDI by strengthening the linkages between FIEs and the local economy. Some of the "breakthrough reforms" recommended by Vietnamese authorities and Vietnam's development partners address the key issues directly.[58] Investment in education and skill development, improvements in market institutions and the business environment, and lower regulatory entry barriers are necessary for promoting and empowering the domestic private sector. If these reforms are carried out, there are good chances that Vietnam will be better able to leverage FDI to reach the next stage of development.

Will this happen? At present, in 2022, forecasting the future is unusually difficult. There is substantial uncertainty connected to current global events, such as the rapid pace of technological change, sometimes summarized in the term Industry 4.0; the COVID-19 pandemic; and the drawn-out trade conflict between the US and China. Each of these could by itself lead to changes in global trade and investment patterns that would impact Vietnam and the perceived need to carry out radical reform. For example, Vietnam's relative success in maintaining export production during the pandemic could add to its attractiveness as an investment location and reduce pressure for other reforms. The most likely scenario is perhaps one where the impacts of different global events are contradictory, and where Vietnam takes some steps in the right direction but stops short of fundamental systemic reform. Such a gradual reform process would be historically consistent with Vietnam's experiences of economic transformation during the past thirty years. However, at the same time as gradualism might guarantee a high degree of political continuity, it would leave the private sector in a relatively weak position. If domestic private firms are unable to link up with and learn from the FIEs operating in Vietnam, it will also be difficult for them to develop the sustainable competitive advantages that Vietnam needs to become a modern and industrialized nation.[59]

Notes

1. Data provided by Foreign Investment Agency, Hanoi.
2. See Blomström and Kokko, "Multinational Corporations and Spillovers"; Nestor, "Technical Intensity of FDI."
3. Giroud, "MNEs Vertical Linkages"; Giroud, "Mind the Gap."
4. Tong, Kokko, and Seric, "Linking FDI and Local Firms."
5. Blomström and Kokko, "The Economics of Foreign Direct Investment Incentives"; Le, "The Impact of Investment Promotion."
6. FIA Vietnam, "Báo cáo đầu tư nước ngoài vào Việt Nam."
7. Data on registered FDI reflect foreign investors' capital commitments based on estimated project costs, as approved by Vietnamese authorities. Data on disbursements refer to the actual implementation of committed capital over time.
8. FIA Vietnam, "Báo cáo đầu tư nước ngoài vào Việt Nam."
9. Government Decree no. 115/CP, April 18, 1977.
10. Kokko, Kotoglou, and Krohwinkel-Karlsson, "The Implementation of FDI in Viet Nam."
11. Huynh et al., "Productivity Spillover from FDI."
12. Parker, Phan, and Nguyen, "US-Vietnam Bilateral Trade Agreement."
13. Parker, Phan, and Nguyen, "US-Vietnam Bilateral Trade Agreement."
14. Vo and Nguyen, "Experiences of Vietnam in FDI Promotion."
15. Yang, Chen, and Monarch, "Rising Wages."
16. World Bank, *2019 Investment Policy and Regulatory Review.*
17. Hemmer and Nguyen, "Contribution of Foreign Direct Investment to Poverty Reduction."
18. Pham, "Regional Economic Development"; Pham, "The Economic Impact of Foreign Direct Investment Flows."
19. Hoang, Wiboonchutikula, and Tubtimtong, "Does Foreign Direct Investment Promote Economic Growth?"
20. Anwar and Nguyen, "Foreign Direct Investment and Economic Growth."
21. Vu, Gagnes, and Noy, "Is Foreign Direct Investment Good for Growth?"
22. Anwar and Nguyen, "Absorptive Capacity, Foreign Direct Investment-Linked Spillovers and Economic Growth," 565.
23. Schaumburg-Müller, "Rise and Fall of Foreign Direct Investment."
24. Le, "Does FDI Have Impacts on the Labor Productivity of Vietnamese Domestic Firms?"
25. Pham, "Assessment of FDI Spillover Effects."
26. Nguyen et al., *FDI Horizontal and Vertical Effects.*
27. Nguyen et al., *Foreign Direct Investment in Vietnam.*
28. Le and Pomfret, "Foreign Direct Investment and Wage Spillovers."
29. Nguyen, Sun, and Beg, "How Does FDI Affect Domestic Firms' Wages?"
30. Le and Pomfret, "Technology Spillovers from Foreign Direct Investment."
31. Le and Pomfret, "Technology Spillovers from Foreign Direct Investment."
32. Newman et al., "Technology Transfers, Foreign Investment and Productivity Spillovers."
33. Ni et al., "The Origin of FDI and Domestic Firms' Productivity."
34. Wrana and Nguyen, "'Strategic Coupling' and Regional Development."
35. Schwab, *Global Competitiveness Report.*
36. Anwar and Nguyen, "Is Foreign Direct Investment Productive?"
37. Tran, Pham, and Barnes, "Spatial Spillover Effects from Foreign Direct Investment."

38. Huynh et al., "Productivity Spillover from FDI to Domestic Firms."

39. Wrana and Nguyen, "'Strategic Coupling' and Regional Development," 10.

40. VietNamNet, "Vietnam Can Produce PhDs."

41. MOIT, "Báo cáo về thực trạng."

42. World Bank, *Vietnam*.

43. World Bank, *Vietnam*; Hollweg, Smith, and Taglioni, *Vietnam at a Crossroads*.

44. Decision 667/QD-Ttg, June 2, 2022.

45. Thrasher and Gallagher, *21st Century Trade Agreements*.

46. Johnson, *Space for Local Content Policies and Strategies*; Tong, Kokko, and Seric, "Linking FDI and Local Firms."

47. World Bank, *2019 Investment Policy and Regulatory Review*.

48. World Bank, *Vietnam 2035*.

49. World Bank, *Vietnam*.

50. MPI/IFC, *Recommendations on Vietnam Next Generation FDI Strategy*.

51. Kelhofer, "Recommendations for a Next Generation FDI Strategy."

52. Kelhofer, "Recommendations for a Next Generation FDI Strategy."

53. Kelhofer, "Recommendations for a Next Generation FDI Strategy."

54. Politburo Resolution No. 50-NQ-TW.

55. Decision 667/QD-Ttg, June 2, 2022.

56. Vietnam's relatively low level of development is a partial explanation for the high export ratio: the numerator (exports) is measured in international prices, whereas the denominator (GDP) is largely based on lower domestic prices for goods and services (such as labor and domestically produced non-tradables). Vietnam's PPP-adjusted GDP is roughly three times larger than GDP at nominal prices and exchange rates.

57. Nee and Opper, *Capitalism from Below*.

58. MPI/IFC, *Recommendations on Vietnam Next Generation FDI Strategy*.

59. Ari Kokko's contribution to this chapter has been supported by Danida project grant 19-M05-CBS.

References

Anwar, Sajid, and Nguyen Lan Phi. "Absorptive Capacity, Foreign Direct Investment-Linked Spillovers and Economic Growth in Vietnam." *Asian Business & Management* 9, no. 4 (2010): 553–70.

———. "Foreign Direct Investment and Economic Growth in Vietnam." *Asia Pacific Business Review* 16, nos. 1–2 (2010): 183–202.

———. "Is Foreign Direct Investment Productive? A Case Study of the Regions of Vietnam." *Journal of Business Research* 67, no. 7 (2014): 1376–87.

Blomström, Magnus, and Ari Kokko. "The Economics of Foreign Direct Investment Incentives." In *Foreign Direct Investment in the Real and Financial Sector of Industrial Countries*, edited by Heinz Herrmann and Robert E. Lipsey. Hamburg: Springer Verlag, 2003.

———. "Multinational Corporations and Spillovers." *Journal of Economic Surveys* 12, no. 3 (1997): 247–77.

FIA Vietnam. "Báo cáo đầu tư nước ngoài vào Việt Nam" (Reports on inward FDI in Vietnam). Hanoi: Foreign Investment Agency, 2022. http://fia.mpi.gov.vn/Home.

Giroud, Axèle. "Mind the Gap: How Linkages Strengthen Understanding of Spillovers." *European Journal of Development Research* 24, no. 1 (2012): 20–25.

———. "MNEs Vertical Linkages: The Experience of Vietnam after Malaysia." *International Business Review* 16, no. 2 (2007): 159–76.

Hemmer, Hans-Rimbert, and Nguyen Thi Phuong Hoa. "Contribution of Foreign Direct Investment to Poverty Reduction: The Case of Vietnam in the 1990s." Entwicklungsökonomische Diskussionsbeiträge no. 30, Justus-Liebig-Universität Gießen, November 2002.

Hoang Thi Thu, Paitoon Wiboonchutikula, and Bangorn Tubtimtong. "Does Foreign Direct Investment Promote Economic Growth in Vietnam?" *ASEAN Economic Bulletin* 27, no. 3 (2010): 295–311.

Hollweg, Claire, Tanya Smith, and Daria Taglioni, eds. *Vietnam at a Crossroads: Engaging in the Next Generation of Global Value Chains*. Washington, DC: World Bank, 2017.

Huynh, T. N. Hien, Nguyen V. Phuong, Trieu D. X. Hoa, and Tran T. Khoa. "Productivity Spillover from FDI to Domestic Firms across Six Regions in Vietnam." *Emerging Markets Finance and Trade* 57, no. 1 (2019): 59–75. doi: 10.1080/1540496X.2018.1562892.

Johnson, Lise. *Space for Local Content Policies and Strategies: A Crucial Time to Revisit an Old Debate*. Bonn: Deutsche Gesellschaft für Internationale Zusammenarbeit, 2016.

Kelhofer, Kyle. "Recommendations for a Next Generation FDI Strategy 2020–2030." Paper presented at Vietnam Economic Forum, Hanoi, January 21, 2019. http://vietnameconomicforum.vn/upload/20624 /20190121/Kyle_Kelhofer_IFC_Country_Director___Eng.pdf.

Kokko, Ari, Katarina Kotoglou, and Anna Krohwinkel-Karlsson. "The Implementation of FDI in Viet Nam: An Analysis of the Characteristics of Failed Projects." *Transnational Corporations* 12, no. 3 (2003): 41–78.

Le, Hai Van. "The Impact of Investment Promotion on Attracting Foreign Direct Investment in Developing Countries." Ph.D. dissertation, Trinity College, Dublin, 2018.

Le, Quoc Hoi, and Richard Pomfret. "Foreign Direct Investment and Wage Spillovers in Vietnam: Evidence from Firm Level Data." *ASEAN Economic Bulletin* 27, no. 2 (2010): 159–72.

———. "Technology Spillovers from Foreign Direct Investment in Vietnam: Horizontal or Vertical Spillovers?" *Journal of the Asia Pacific Economy* 16, no. 2 (2011): 183–201.

Le, Thanh Thuy. "Does FDI Have Impacts on the Labor Productivity of Vietnamese Domestic Firms?" *International Economy* 11 (2008): 35–56.

MOIT. "Báo cáo về thực trạng và giải pháp thúc đẩy phát triển công nghiệp hỗ trợ Việt Nam" (Report on the current situation and solutions to promote development of supporting industries in Vietnam). Hanoi: Ministry of Industry and Trade, 2018.

MPI. *30 Years of FDI Mobilization in Vietnam: New Vision, New Opportunities in New Era*. Hanoi: Ministry of Planning and Investment, 2018.

MPI/IFC. *Recommendations on Vietnam Next Generation FDI Strategy and Vision 2020–2030*. Hanoi: Ministry of Planning and Investment and International Finance Corporation, 2018.

MPI/UNDP. *Industry 4.0 Readiness of Industry Enterprises in Vietnam*. Hanoi: Ministry of Planning and Investment and United Nations Industrial Development Organization, 2019.

Nee, Victor, and Sonja Opper. *Capitalism from Below: Markets and Institutional Change in China*. Cambridge, MA: Harvard University Press, 2012.

Nestor, Curt. "Technological Intensity of FDI in Vietnam: Implications for Future Economic Development and Emerging Clusters." In *Clusters and Economic Growth in Asia*, edited by Sören Eriksson. Cheltenham, UK: Edward Elgar, 2013.

Newman, Carol, John Rand, Theodore Talbot, and Finn Tarp. "Technology Transfers, Foreign Investment and Productivity Spillovers." *European Economic Review* 76 (May 2015): 168–87.

Nguyen, Dao Thi Hong, Sun Sizhong, and A. B. M. Rabiul Alam Beg. "How Does FDI Affect Domestic Firms' Wages? Theory and Evidence from Vietnam." *Applied Economics* 51, no. 49 (2019): 5311–27.

Nguyen, Dinh Chuc, Gary Simpson, David Saal, Nguyen Ngoc Anh, and Pham Quang Ngoc. *FDI Horizontal and Vertical Effects on Local Firm Technical Efficiency*. Hanoi: Development and Policies Research Center, 2008.

Nguyen, Ngoc Anh, Nguyen Thang, Le Dang Trung, Pham Quang Ngoc, Nguyen Dinh Chuc, and Nguyen Duc Nhat. *Foreign Direct Investment in Vietnam: Is There Any Evidence of Technological Spillover Effects*. Hanoi: Development and Policies Research Center, 2008.

Ni, Bin, Mariana Spatareanu, Vlad Manole, Tsunehiro Otsuki, and Hiroyuki Yamada. "The Origin of FDI and Domestic Firms' Productivity: Evidence from Vietnam." *Journal of Asian Economics* 52 (October 2017): 56–76.

Parker, Steve, Phan Vinh Quang, and Nguyen Ngoc Anh. "Has the U.S.-Vietnam Bilateral Trade Agreement Led to Higher FDI into Vietnam?" *International Journal of Applied Economics* 2, no. 2 (2005): 199–223.

Pham, Hoang Mai. "The Economic Impact of Foreign Direct Investment Flows on Vietnam: 1988–98." *Asian Studies Review* 27, no. 1 (2003): 81–98.

———. "Regional Economic Development and Foreign Direct Investment Flows in Vietnam, 1988–98." *Journal of the Asia Pacific Economy* 7, no. 2 (2002): 182–202.

Pham, Tien Hoang. "Assessment of FDI Spillover Effects for the Case of Vietnam: A Survey of Micro-Data Analyses." In *Deepening East Asian Economic Integration*, edited by Jenny Corbett and So Umezaki. Jakarta: ERIA, 2009.

Schaumburg-Müller, Henrik. "Rise and Fall of Foreign Direct Investment in Vietnam and Its Impact on Local Manufacturing Upgrading." *European Journal of Development Research* 15, no. 2 (2003): 44–66.

Schwab, Klaus, ed. *Global Competitiveness Report 2016–2017*. Geneva: World Economic Forum, 2016.

Thrasher, Rachel Denae, and Kevin P. Gallagher. *21st Century Trade Agreements: Implications for Long-Run Development Policy*. Boston: Boston University, 2008.

Tong, Yee-Siong, Ari Kokko, and Adnan Seric. "Linking FDI and Local Firms for Global Value Chain Upgrading: Policy Lessons from Samsung Mobile Phone Production in Viet Nam." Vienna: UNIDO, 2019.

Tran, Toan Thang, Pham Thi Song Hanh, and Bradley R. Barnes. "Spatial Spillover Effects from Foreign Direct Investment in Vietnam." *Journal of Development Studies* 52, no. 10 (2016): 1431–45.

VietNamNet. "Vietnam Can Produce PhDs but Cannot Produce Fasteners." *VietNamNet Bridge*, June 27, 2015. https://english.vietnamnet.vn/fms/education/134396/vietnam-can-produce-phds-but-cannot-produce-fasteners—na-deputy.html.

Vo, Tri Thanh, and Nguyen Anh Duong. "Experiences of Vietnam in FDI Promotion: Some Lessons for Myanmar." In *Economic Reforms in Myanmar: Pathways and Prospects*, edited by Hank Lim and Yasihori Yamada. Bangkok: IDE-JETRO, 2012.

Vu, Tam Bang, Byron Gangnes, and Ilan Noy. "Is Foreign Direct Investment Good for Growth? Evidence from Sectoral Analysis of China and Vietnam." *Journal of the Asia Pacific Economy* 13, no. 4 (2008): 542–62.

World Bank. *2019 Investment Policy and Regulatory Review: Vietnam*. Washington, DC: World Bank, 2020.

———. *Vietnam: Enhancing Enterprise Competitiveness and SME Linkages*. Hanoi: World Bank, 2017.

———. *Vietnam 2035—Towards Prosperity, Creativity, Equity, and Democracy*. Washington, DC: World Bank, 2016.

Wrana, Jöran, and Nguyen Thi Xuan Thu. "'Strategic Coupling' and Regional Development in a Transition Economy: What Can We Learn from Vietnam?" *Area Development and Policy* 4, no. 4 (2019): 454–65.

Yang, Dennis Tao, Vivian Weijia Chen, and Ryan Monarch. "Rising Wages: Has China Lost Its Global Labor Advantage?" *Pacific Economic Review* 15, no. 4 (2010): 482–504.

CHAPTER 9

The Political Economy of Financial and Capital Markets

JAY ROSENGARD AND HUYNH THE DU

The development of Vietnam's financial and capital markets is reminiscent of the 1993 American film *Groundhog Day*, a comedy in which the main character is caught in a time loop and constantly relives the same day. The difference is that for Vietnam's financial sector, the time loop is a decade.

Government policy has vacillated between regimes of financial repression, characterized by tight control and excessive regulation, to rapid liberalization and deregulation of financial and capital markets without accompanying improvements in the technical capacity and political independence of prudential oversight. This has resulted in one potentially cataclysmic crisis each decade since reunification in 1975, despite significant development of the financial sector in terms of size and depth, diversity and complexity, viability of state-owned commercial banks, degree of financial inclusion, and quality of prudential oversight.

Each crisis has compelled the government to reassert its control over the financial sector and mitigate the negative impacts of the crisis. However, rather than proceeding to address the underlying causes of the crisis, the government has instead disengaged from active and effective financial sector regulation and supervision. The government effectively has been a recurrent victim of its own success, eventually precipitating another crisis about ten years later, since successful short-term interventions have deprived the government of the requisite political mandate to undertake critical long-term fundamental reforms resisted by entrenched interests. The political economy of financial sector reform has thus revolved around the struggle to achieve balance among three sets of competing objectives: financial sector liberalization versus financial repression, technical competence versus political control, and policy ideology versus implementation pragmatism.

The second decade of the twenty-first century ended without any financial sector crisis or general macroeconomic turmoil. In fact, government-reported economic indicators looked good at the end of 2019, and the economic impact of the COVID-19 pandemic has been relatively moderate. Nonetheless, there are also several indicators of financial sector risks and vulnerabilities. Moreover, although we now have safe, effective, and widely available vaccines, the ultimate economic impact of the COVID-19 pandemic is still unknown. It is neither inevitable that Vietnam will face a fourth financial sector crisis in the next few years, nor is it certain that it can avoid one in light of growing risks from private sector conglomerates. At present, one can make a compelling argument for either scenario. Whether the "Groundhog Decade" syndrome has run its course or will be repeated once again remains an open question.

This chapter examines the political economy of financial and capital markets in Vietnam by first presenting an annotated chronology of financial sector development, and then providing a cross-cutting, multidimensional assessment of progress to date and future challenges.

Overview

CHRONOLOGY OF FINANCIAL SECTOR DEVELOPMENT

There are convincing arguments that financial sector development plays a vital role in facilitating economic growth and poverty reduction.[1] This applies to Vietnam as well. Financial and capital markets have played a significant role in the remarkable development of Vietnam over the past three decades.[2] They have fostered the accumulation of funds for savings and investment, intermediated between surplus capital and the productive utilization of this capital, facilitated efficient payment systems, and generated sophisticated risk management products. Although there is not a consensus on whether macroeconomic growth is a prerequisite for financial sector development or vice versa, clearly there are important synergies between the two, and it is unlikely Vietnam would have such a vibrant, rapidly growing economy without a financial sector that has evolved to offer a comprehensive portfolio of standard financial instruments via a wide variety of financial institutions.

However, despite these accomplishments, the financial sector has also repeatedly generated substantial risks and considerable fiscal costs to the economy.[3] Government policy has been like a pendulum swinging between regimes of financial repression with strict control and overregulation to swift liberalization and deregulation of financial and capital markets without better prudential oversight, technical capacity, or political independence.[4]

The result has been a significant crisis each decade since reunification in 1975. Every crisis has forced the government to reassert authority over the financial sector in order to reduce adverse effects of the crisis. However, instead of dealing with fundamental causes of the crisis, the government has withdrawn from active and effective financial sector regulation and supervision.[5] In other words, the government regularly has ended up being a victim of its own success, eventually leading to another crisis about a decade later, because successful short-term actions have left the government without the necessary political mandate to undertake critical long-term structural reforms strongly opposed by special interests. The political economy of Vietnam's financial sector reform thus is characterized by the difficult pursuit of an elusive balance among three sets of competing goals: financial sector liberalization versus financial repression, technical capability versus political dominance, and policy ideology versus implementation practicality.

The evolving policy framework for financial sector development in Vietnam, together with its many oscillations, is evident in the pronouncements of the political reports of the Communist Party of Vietnam (CPV) Congresses since 1976 (see appendix A).

These tumultuous ups and downs, with an overall positive trajectory of financial sector development in Vietnam, are punctuated by the four principal crises summarized below.

Late 1970s–Late 1980s: From an Unacknowledged Financial Sector to a Liberalized Financial Sector and Collapse of the Credit Cooperatives Until the mid-1980s, Vietnam's financial system was totally repressed. Since market mechanisms were forbidden, there were no acknowledged private financial institutions. The financial sector was not formally sanctioned during this period, although at the time it consisted of the central bank, the State Bank of Vietnam (SBV), and four policy banks (Agriculture Bank, Construction Bank, Foreign Trade Bank, and Industrial and Commercial Bank). The SBV was charged with the dual functions of money issuance and treasury operations, whereas the four policy banks were restricted to treasury functions.

This period was also characterized by a dual economy. The allocation of resources through the central planning mechanism did not work well, and the role of fiat money as a medium of exchange disappeared since the prices were set by the government. As a result, a barter economy emerged.[6] However, financing and exchange of a significant portion of goods was undertaken through market mechanisms.

At the beginning of this period, there was also no awareness of the role of money and the phenomenon of inflation in a market economy. Political leaders simply ordered SBV to print and put a large amount of money into circulation.[7] In 1985, there was a bold price, wage, and monetary reform under which the government pumped an enormous amount of money into circulation, causing hyperinflation: the aggregate inflation from 1986 to 1988 was approximately 10,000 percent.[8]

Failure of the 1985 reform, compounded by external difficulties, compelled the government to launch an even more fundamental reform, the Đổi Mới (Renovation) reform of 1986, with the objective of creating a "socialist-oriented market economy."[9] Shortage of capital for businesses was considered an underlying constraint for economic development, while at the same time there was a widespread belief that the people held a large amount of underutilized capital.[10] The government therefore deregulated and liberalized the financial sector in response to this quandary. All organizations could establish credit cooperatives to mobilize and use capital without any restrictions or prudential requirements. As stated in the Second Plenary of the Sixth Central Committee in 1987, permission was granted "to robustly implement the policy of mobilizing capital among people and economic organizations in many forms and many channels to ensure benefits for depositors." Unfortunately, liberalizing the financial sector did not solve the shortage of enterprise capital. Many Ponzi schemes[11] appeared instead, the monthly interest rate peaked at 24 percent, most of the over 7,000 credit cooperatives that were created went bankrupt, and many executives were arrested and sentenced.[12] Vietnam was thrown into a financial crisis.

Late 1980s–Late 1990s: Poor Prudential Oversight and Bank Collapses After the credit cooperative crisis, Vietnam started to establish a two-tier banking system: the central bank and commercial banks, including branches of foreign banks and private banks. Furthermore, the four policy banks (state-owned commercial banks, or SOCBs) became quasi-commercial. At the same time, some credit cooperatives were upgraded to become joint stock commercial banks (JSCBs) or private banks.[13] The government also issued prudential requirements based on Basel I.[14]

During this period, there were two ways for private businesses to acquire loans. First, they could develop close relationships with SOCBs and state-owned enterprises (SOEs), allowing them to take advantage of this perceived "quasi-public" status. Some private companies used trade credit through foreign trade with SOCBs to generate capital for real estate speculation.

Second, businesses (or business groups) could create their own banks to lend to themselves because of rudimentary and unclear ownership regulations, permitting these banks to become subsidiaries or "backyards of businesses," often to engage in non-core business activities. For example, the trading company Minh Phung established over a dozen subsidiaries to circumvent regulations and acquire a substantial amount of capital for real estate speculation. In addition, due to this cross-ownership between companies and banks, some JSCBs became instruments for companies to mobilize and inappropriately use capital. More problems appeared after the East Asian financial crisis (EAFC) of 1997–98. In the late 1990s, some JSCBs went bankrupt, and the government ordered SOCBs to take over these banks;[15] the government also put executives in prison and even sentenced some to death. Fortunately, the size of these banks was small in absolute terms as well as relative to the economy, and government intervention was quick, so unlike the experiences of many other countries, this phenomenon did not lead to systemic collapse. The effort to equitize state-owned enterprises was kicked off during this period as well. There were also preparations to establish a stock exchange.

Late 1990s–Late 2000s: Clamping Down, Loosening Up, and Another Crisis The consequence of the EAFC and bank collapses created tremendous stress on Vietnam's financial sector. Nonperforming loans (NPLs) in the early 2000s were approximately 30 percent of total loans outstanding and 15 percent of GDP.[16] From the early 2000s, the government pursued two contradictory policies: adoption of enhanced prudential requirements consistent with international practices, while at the same time permitting rural banks to be upgraded to become urban banks, allowing them to do business nationwide. As the market was booming after Vietnam joined the WTO in early 2007, businesspeople saw opportunities and found creative ways to own JSCBs. Optimism was high, the stock index peaked in March 2007, and the real estate market skyrocketed.

However, a new cycle of malfunctions began, and previous mistakes were repeated, especially issues related to asset bubbles, cross-ownership, and use of the state-dominated banking system to build up state-owned conglomerates.[17] Vietnam faced another financial crisis in the late 2000s.

From the Late 2000s: Building a More Prudentially Sound Financial Sector On the brink of a crisis, the Eleventh CPV Congress in January 2011 determined that its priority remained high and stable economic growth. However, the direction has completely changed since the conclusion of the Politburo of the CPV in March 2011. The government has prioritized stability over growth, with a series of strong measures. First, it arrested and prosecuted bank owners and executives. A number of powerful figures were sentenced to many years in prison. Second, it created the Vietnam Asset Management Company (VAMC) in 2013 to cleanse domestic bank balance sheets of NPLs. NPLs in banks have reportedly decreased, but there are doubts about NPL data quality.[18] Third, it took over seriously distressed banks through the zero-price method. In 2015, the SBV took over three banks. Fourth, it introduced prudential regulations based on Basel II, especially Circular 41/TT-NHNN in 2016.

Although conditions have improved, albeit at a high fiscal cost, financial sector risks are still significant. For example, there is still the temptation to prime the economy through credit growth. Another vulnerability is systemic risk entailed in the persistence of interlocking cross-ownership between companies and banks (see figure 9.1) and the rapid expansion of private conglomerates (see section "The Futile Search" below).

DIMENSIONS OF FINANCIAL SECTOR DEVELOPMENT

In the context of the above-summarized chronology of financial sector development in Vietnam, both progress achieved to date and future challenges can be assessed in five key dimensions:

- Size and depth of financial and capital markets
- Diversity and complexity of institutions and instruments
- Viability of state-owned commercial banks (SOCBs)
- Degree of financial inclusion
- Quality of prudential oversight

The remainder of this chapter thus will be organized first around these five metrics for assessing the strengths and weaknesses of financial sector development in Vietnam, followed by an analysis of the complex interactions between the government's financial sector development strategies and its efforts to identify a national engine of industrialization and modernization.

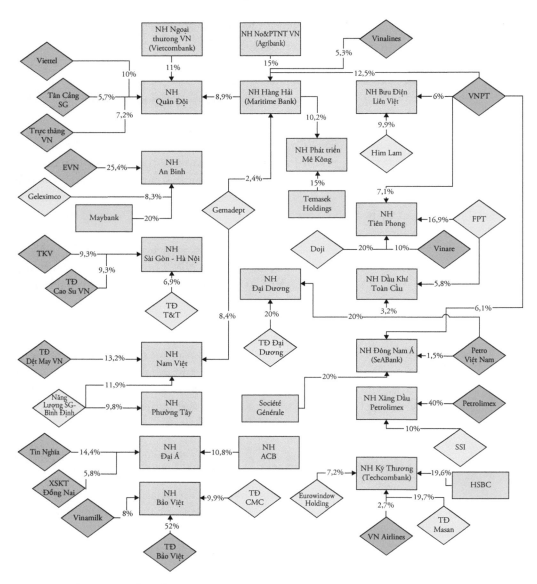

FIGURE 9.1 Cross-ownership of banks in Vietnam
Source: Nguyen, *Vietnamese Commercial Banks.*

Size and Depth of Financial and Capital Markets

There has been significant progress in the growth of the financial sector in Vietnam, and indirect financing through financial institutions has dominated (see figure 9.2). Financial depth has risen from essentially zero under a one-tier banking system to 227 percent of GDP at the end of 2019 under the current two-tier banking system and complementary capital markets, made up of credit to the economy (133 percent), market capitalization of

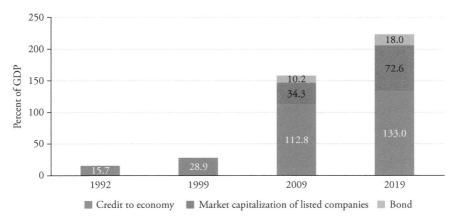

FIGURE 9.2 Vietnam's financial depth (percentage of GDP)
Source: Authors' rendering from the data of Ministry of Finance and State Bank of Vietnam.

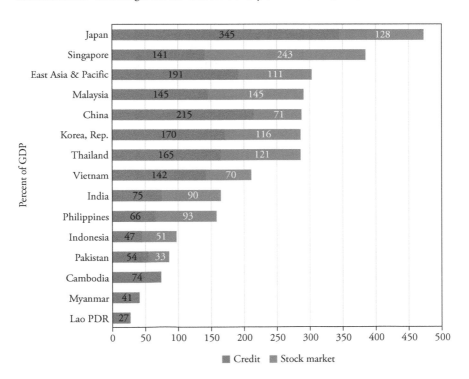

FIGURE 9.3 Financial depth (percentage of GDP) of selected countries in Asia
Source: World Bank, "World Development Indicators."

listed companies (73 percent), and bonds (18 percent). Current financial depth is relatively higher than other lower-middle-income countries in Southeast Asia (see figure 9.3)—for example, the Philippines (159 percent) and Indonesia (98 percent)—but considerably lower than upper-middle-income Southeast Asian countries such as Thailand (286 percent) and Malaysia (290 percent).

However, the financial sector has periodically grown too large when used as an instrument to stimulate unsustainable levels of growth, generating macroeconomic risks and vulnerabilities such as hyperinflation and a substantial increase in NPLs. This occurred after the 1985 price, wage, and monetary reforms, prompting the launch of the Đổi Mới comprehensive reform of 1986, and then again about twenty years later, contributing to another financial and banking crisis and a reining in of excessive credit expansion. These crises are good examples of the government's struggle to achieve a balance between policy extremes and then taking advantage of a disruptive disequilibrium to undertake necessary but unpopular policy reforms.

Diversity and Complexity of Institutions and Instruments

The financial sector's dynamic growth has been accompanied by a substantial diversification of institutions: Vietnam now has not just four policy banks channeling state financing, but also domestic private commercial banks; foreign banks; and finance, leasing, and insurance companies, as well as two stock exchanges (see figure 9.4).

Foreign banks (including branches and joint ventures) grew the most, quadrupling from sixteen in 1994 to sixty in 2018, but then dropped 50 percent to twenty-nine in 2020, while the number of JSCBs has declined from a peak of fifty-one in 1998 to twenty-eight in 2020 (see table 9.1). However, in terms of total assets, the share of foreign banks has remained modest, at around 10 percent, whereas the share of state-owned banks and policy banks has declined from 100 percent in 1990 to 43 percent as of June 2022, while

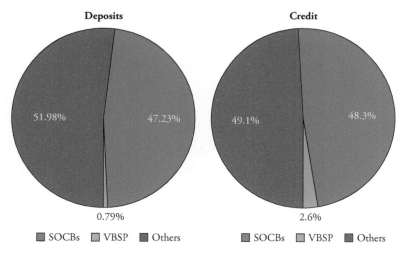

FIGURE 9.4 Share of deposits and credits by financial institution
Source: State Bank of Vietnam.

Table 9.1
Bank types over time

	1989	1990	1994	1998	2005	2009	2017	2018	2020
State-owned banks	4	4	4	4	4	5	7	7	7
Policy banks				2	2	2	2	2	1
Joint stock commercial banks			46	51	37	34	28	28	28
Foreign banks			16	27	36	46	60	60	29
Finance and leasing companies						21	26	26	26
Cooperative bank							1	1	1
People's Credit Funds/co-ops	>7,000	160				997	1,178	1,183	1,181

Source: Authors' compilation from annual reports of the State Bank of Vietnam and others.

Table 9.2
Composition of assets by bank type

	1994	1998	2005	2017	2018	2022 (06/22)
State-owned banks	89	82	60.4	45.7	45.7	41.4
Policy banks			14.5	5.0	2.6	1.7
Joint stock commercial banks		10	14.7	40.3	41.2	44.2
Foreign banks		8	9.2	9.5	10.3	9.8
Finance and leasing companies				1.4	1.5	1.6
Cooperative bank				0.3	1.3	0.3
People's Credit Funds			1.2	1.0		1.0
Whole system	**100**	**100**	**100**	**100**	**100**	**100**

Source: Authors' compilation from annual reports of the State Bank of Vietnam and others.

the share of JSCBs has grown from 10 percent in 1998 to 44 percent as of June 2022 (see table 9.2).

These institutions now offer a full portfolio of financial instruments, including loans for investments and working capital, consumer finance, leasing, factoring, derivatives, hybrid products, bonds, and equity investment opportunities. In terms of the sectoral composition of credit, as of May 2020, approximately 30 percent was for industry and construction; one-quarter for trade, transportation, and telecommunication; 9 percent for agriculture, forestry, and fisheries; and 37 percent for other activities (see figure 9.5).

It is more difficult to accurately evaluate credit quality in Vietnam. According to official data, NPLs account for only 2 percent of total loans outstanding at the end of 2018. This is equivalent to $6 billion, or 2.5 percent of GDP. However, alternative SBV calculations based on NPLs cleansed from bank balance sheets by VAMC indicate NPLs at about 9 percent of total loans outstanding.

Another challenge is Vietnam's continued overreliance on banks and debt for financial intermediation (see figure 9.2 and table 9.3), and the problem of cross-ownership

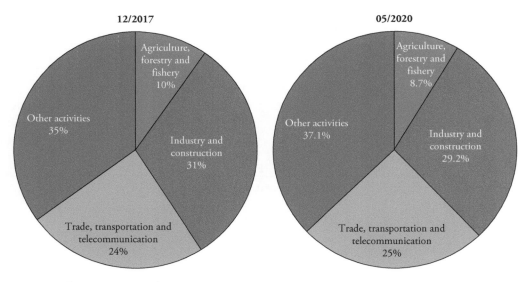

FIGURE 9.5 Loan composition by sector
Source: State Bank of Vietnam.

Table 9.3
Key financial indicators

No.	Item	1993	1999	2004	2009	2014	2019
1	Domestic credit to private sector (% of GDP)	16.5	28.2	58.7	103.3	100.3	137.9
2	Domestic credit to private sector by banks (% of GDP)	16.5	28.2	58.7	103.3	100.3	137.9
3	Inflation, consumer prices (annual %)		4.1	7.8	6.7	4.1	2.8
4	Official exchange rate (LCU per US$, period average)	10,641	13,943	15,746	17,065	21,148	23,050
5	Lending interest rate (%)	32.2	12.7	9.7	10.1	8.7	7.7
6	Consumer price index (2010 = 100)		48.9	55.3	91.6	143.6	163.5
7	Stocks traded, total value (% of GDP)				31.1	16.0	12.1
8	Market capitalization of listed domestic companies (% of GDP)				31.4	28.2	57.2

Source: World Bank, World Development Indicators.

between companies and domestic private commercial banks has reemerged. The risks created by cross-ownership have been exacerbated by the opaque and complex structure of these entanglements and the channeling of credit to non-core business activities.[19]

There is also an urgent need to enhance consumer protection, especially for both conventional consumer finance and in the rapidly growing field of fintech.[20] Currently it is difficult for consumers to calculate the true cost of credit and the risks of new credit instruments.

Viability of State-Owned Commercial Banks (SOCBs)

An integral component of the maturing of Vietnam's financial sector has been reform of the SOCBs. The SOCBs have been undergoing an incremental program of equitization, commercialization, and corporatization since the early 2000s. Incombank has made the most progress and is now over one-third equitized, whereas Vietcombank is approximately one-quarter equitized, BIDV is 20 percent equitized, and Agribank is still entirely state-owned (see figure 9.6).

The principal strategy has been to use equitization not only to raise money for the government, but also as a means to make the SOCBs more competitive with private banks by increasing transparency and depoliticizing personnel and lending decisions. For example, the bulk of equitization at both Incombank and Vietcombank has been via strategic investors: Tokyo-Mitsubishi UFJ Bank and the International Finance Corporation now own 28 percent of Incombank, and Mizuho Bank and Singapore's GIC Private Limited now own 15 percent of Vietcombank. Following this same strategy, BIDV has sold a 15 percent share to Korea's KEB Hana Bank.

However, the state remains the majority owner of all SOCBs, so these banks are still hampered by a contradictory dual mission of being commercially viable while serving as an effective agent of development. Moreover, voluntary SOCB ownership of domestic private commercial banks has created conflicts of interest (see figure 9.1). SOCBs have also been instructed to take over distressed domestic private commercial banks, thereby assuming the entire burden without compensation.

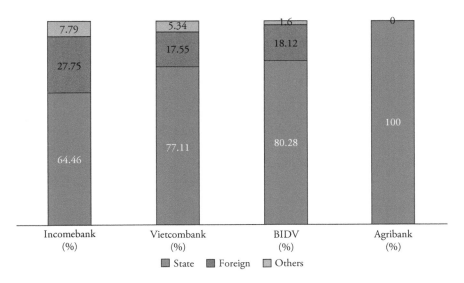

FIGURE 9.6 Ownership structure of SOCBs
Source: Authors' compilation from bank statements.

Degree of Financial Inclusion

Financial inclusion is important to ensure inclusive economic growth by providing equal access to formal financial services,[21] and thus, equal opportunity to benefit from Vietnam's macroeconomic progress. Financial inclusion has gradually expanded over the past few decades, but is still quite low when compared with figures for East Asia and the Pacific (excluding high-income countries). For example, the percentage of people fifteen years of age or older with an account in a financial institution rose by 50 percent from 2011 to 2017 (21.4 to 30.0 percent), but is still less than half of the regional total in 2017 (70.3 percent). The gap is even wider for Vietnam's most vulnerable population, namely those with a primary education or less, those in rural areas, and those whose income is in the lowest 40 percent (see table 9.4).

The fintech total and disaggregated numbers tell a similar story. For example, the percentage of people fifteen years of age or older who made or received digital payments in the past year rose from 18.1 to 22.7 percent from 2014 to 2017, but was just over a third of the regional total in 2017 (58.0 percent). The number and value of transactions via mobile devices show a similar trend. Through September 2018, mobile devices were used for 122 million transactions totaling Đ1,100 trillion; this is a 30 percent and 126 percent rise, respectively, when compared with September 2017, a large increase but from a very low base.

Nonetheless, fintech growth has accelerated recently, with digital payments the most fertile part of the fintech ecosystem. Digital payments are estimated to total about US$8.5 billion in 2019, dominated by digital commerce, and are projected to expand to US$13.7 billion by 2023, with 62 million users increasing to 70 million users over the same period (see table 9.5). Leading companies and brands in this domain include M_ Service's mobile payments app MoMo and ZION's Zalo Pay, integrated with its Zalo messaging platform. The second largest fintech segment is peer-to-peer (P2P) lending, for example, Growth Wealth, a P2P lending platform for small and medium-sized enterprises (SMEs).

Vietnam's financial inclusion is relatively low when compared with similar countries, primarily because its interventions have been state-dominated poverty alleviation policies rather than market-driven commercially sustainable initiatives. The main institution for the provision of microcredit has been the Vietnam Social Policy Bank (VSPB), but its operations have contracted significantly over the past few years. From 2002 to 2016, VSPB disbursed 31.9 million micro loans totaling Đ433 trillion, but by the end of 2016, total micro loans outstanding were only Đ38.7 trillion, accounting for just one-quarter of VSPB's loan portfolio and 0.7 percent of total loans outstanding in Vietnam (see table 9.2).

Consequently, financial institutions that provide microbanking services to low-income families and family businesses have seen these operations as a social or regulatory obligation rather than a new profit center. The services are thus highly subsidized, undercutting any incentives providers might have to develop appropriately priced new financial products and delivery systems for this market segment.

Table 9.4
Financial inclusion in Vietnam

Indicator	2011		2014		2017	
	Vietnam	Asia Pacific (excluding high income)	Vietnam	Asia Pacific (excluding high income)	Vietnam	Asia Pacific (excluding high income)
Financial institution account (% age 15+)	21.4	55.1	30.9	68.9	30.0	70.3
Financial institution account, primary education or less (% age 15+)	4.5	49.8	15.3	63.6	12.8	62.7
Financial institution account, rural (% age 15+)	16.5	50.2	26.1	66.9	24.6	68.7
Financial institution account, income, poorest 40% (% age 15+)	—	—	18.1	39.0	22.7	58.0
Made or received digital payments in the past year, primary education or less (% age 15+)	—	—	7.3	24.9	8.9	47.2
Made or received digital payments in the past year, income, poorest 40% (% age 15+)	—	—	11.4	23.5	12.6	43.0

Source: World Bank, *The Global Findex Database 2017.*

Table 9.5
Fintech in Vietnam

Market segment	Value		Users		Transaction value per user	
	2019 estimate	2023 projection	2019 estimate	2023 projection	2019 estimate	2023 projection
1. Digital payments	$8.5 billion	$13.7 billion	61.8 million	70.2 million	$137.5	$195.2
Digital commerce	$8.3 billion	$12.9 billion	51.1 million	55.9 million	$162.7	$232.0
Mobile POS payments	$218 million	$782 million	10.7 million	14.3 million	$20.5	$54.7
2. Alternative financing	$0.72 million	$1.29 million				
Crowd funding	$0.46 million	$0.71 million				
Crowd investing	$0.26 million	$0.58 million				

Source: Statista, September 2019, https://www.statista.com/outlook/295/127/fintech/vietnam.

Quality of Prudential Oversight

Accompanying these changes has been substantial improvement in prudential oversight. Regulation and supervision of credit institutions by SBV, of stock exchanges and security companies by the State Securities Commission (SSC), and of insurance companies by the Ministry of Finance (MOF) have been strengthened. Moreover, the government has created the National Financial Supervisory Commission (NFSC) to provide financial sector long-term policy formulation and macroeconomic oversight. A key objective of these prudential oversight institutions has been to gradually bring Vietnam into conformance with international standards and practices.

International standards of assurance were first comprehensively applied in Vietnam with promulgation of the State Bank and Credit Institutions Law in 1997 and implementation regulations on safety ratios and lending limits in 1999. Some Basel I standards were also included in the 1999 regulations, for example, the capital adequacy ratio (CAR). However, due to a technical misunderstanding, the mandated capital adequacy ratio (Tier I) was double the Basel I requirement, namely 8 percent rather than 4 percent. Consequently, even five years after this regulation was issued, none of Vietnam's banks met the specified CAR requirement.[22]

In 2005, SBV issued a number of new regulations to replace the 1999 regulations. In addition to correcting the CAR requirement, the 2005 regulations specified separation between the activities of commercial banking services (major credit and payment activities) and investment banking services (securities-related operations). In 2006, the prime minister issued a list of capital requirements for credit institutions; banks had to have a minimum charter capital of Đ3 trillion by the end of 2010. This requirement caused fraud in banks as it fueled interlocking cross-ownership (see figure 9.1). One of the most serious regulatory errors was to allow rural private banks, whose business activities had been limited to a single province, to be upgraded to nationwide urban private banks. This enabled many businesspeople to quickly own their own banks and expand their businesses out of their core activities into real estate speculation and the purchase of other companies. Nevertheless, the 2005 and 2006 regulations were another significant step in building the necessary foundations of banking safety in Vietnam.

In the late 2000s, the prudential oversight agencies in Vietnam again tried to apply international practices and standards to further enhance the quality of their regulatory and supervisory functions. However, the main problem—the interlocking cross-ownership between JSCBs and private companies, as well as the inappropriate relationships many companies have with SOCBs, SOEs, and government officials—has not changed. The situation has in fact gotten worse as the cross-ownership has become much more complex and sophisticated, commensurate with the growth of Vietnam's economy and financial sector.[23]

Consequently, as asset markets soared after Vietnam joined the World Trade Organization in 2007, especially stocks and real estate, many companies used capital from their core businesses and borrowed from financial institutions to speculate in these assets. Then Vietnam was hit with a "double whammy": macroeconomic mismanagement, particularly in mishandling large capital inflows, resulting in very high inflation (nearly 30 percent); and the global financial crisis. Asset bubbles burst: property markets crashed, and the stock index dropped from nearly 1,200 points in March 2007 to around 200 points in February 2009. A lot of companies and banks were hit hard by this downturn; many small banks become insolvent, and the government had to either take over some or order them to merge. Many bank officials and businesspeople were also arrested and sentenced. A large restructuring program was launched in 2011, and although conditions have improved, the root problems remain.

There is therefore still a long way to go before prudential supervision in Vietnam conforms with international best practices.[24] For example, although in 2016 the Politburo recognized the importance of applying Basel II capital adequacy requirements by issuing Resolutions 07-NQ/TW and 51/NQ-CP, together with Circular 41/2016/TT-NHNN, mandating that all commercial banks must fulfill Basel II capital adequacy requirements by the beginning of 2020, the deadline has passed with just over half of the commercial banks meeting this requirement.

Another major challenge confronting prudential regulators is oversight of rapidly growing shadow banking, particularly when linked to real estate development, as well as treatment of innovative fintech institutions and instruments. Collapse of the commitment to pay a 12 percent rate of return to investors in a Condotel project in November 2019, widely covered by the media, is an indicator of current regulatory challenges. Nonetheless, since the early 1990s, when simple prudential requirements were mandated for financial institutions in Vietnam, there have been significant technical improvements in the prudential oversight of the financial sector.[25]

The Futile Search for an Engine of Industrialization and Modernization

It is difficult to separate the trials and tribulations of financial sector development in Vietnam from the government's futile search for an engine of industrialization and economic modernization for the past three decades of reform. The prominent protagonists in this drama have been the SOEs, FDI, and domestic private sector conglomerates.

Enthusiasm about SOE potential reached its peak in the mid-2000s, when the government decided to upgrade large public corporations to become business groups or conglomerates. Some companies expanded rapidly into many sectors. However, failure followed shortly afterward and was a major cause of the crisis in the late 2000s. State-owned conglomerates appointed to develop key industries have had significant problems, and many executives, together with government officials, have been charged with corruption and mismanagement of the state assets. Vinashin is a typical case of such hope and failure. Since the government assigned it to develop the shipbuilding industry and gave it US$750 million, the first-ever government international bond issuance in 2005, it expanded into many types of businesses. It even owned a pineapple production plant. When on the brink of collapse in 2010, its assets totaled Đ104 trillion, equivalent to 5 percent of Vietnam's GDP at the time and an eightfold increase since 2004.

Considerable hope has also been placed in FDI as a driver of national industrialization and modernization. The government has therefore promoted many policies to attract FDI, hoping this would provide a catalyst to develop key industries. Expectations have been high that FDI firms would bring capital, technology, and management skills to help industrialize and modernize Vietnam's economy. In terms of the volume of capital attracted and the amount of export revenue generated, Vietnam has been extremely successful; exports now surpass GDP. However, with a few exceptions, Vietnam has had much less success in using FDI to build key industries such as garments and textiles, sugar, shoes and leather, automobiles, steel, and electronic equipment. Vietnam has not been able to climb to higher rungs of global value chains.[26] For example, hope for the high-tech industry was very high when Intel decided to invest in a billion-dollar assembly plant in 2006. However, results have not met these expectations. Likewise, Oasis in Vietnam has generated only a modest value-added margin for Vietnam's economy.[27] The FDI sector has essentially taken advantage of Vietnam's investment incentives without bearing the burdens entailed in developing Vietnam's economy.[28] It has been immunized from Vietnam's system in the form of economic enclaves and could leave when opportunities to earn significant profits dissipate, as in many other countries. The expectation that FDI firms would help industrialize and modernize Vietnam's economy has not been fulfilled, at least not yet.[29]

The government's new hope is that domestic private companies and Vietnamese billionaires will drive industrialization and modernization of Vietnam. Some private companies have indeed been successful and have played vital roles in key industries such as airlines, retail, and car assembly. Now there are also Vietnamese billionaires. Many senior national leaders have expressed their belief that private conglomerates will develop high value-added domestic industries. This hope has risen dramatically in recent years, as indicated by the following two examples.

The first case is Vingroup, the largest private company in Vietnam. Vingroup's assets in the third quarter of 2019 totaled Đ357 trillion, equivalent to 5.9 percent of Vietnam's 2019 GDP. Vingroup has expanded from its core real estate business into retail, health care, education, and agriculture. It is also planning to invest US$2 billion in automobile manufacturing (and sell the products in the US), as well as to produce electric cars. However, business results to date have been disappointing. In its 2019 third quarter financial report, Vingroup disclosed it earned profits just in real estate, while it incurred losses in all of its other business activities. Vingroup sold its retail and agriculture businesses in December 2019 to focus on manufacturing, even though the retail business was its second largest sales generator; its sales for the first three quarters of 2019 were half those of the real estate business and equivalent to the sale of all other businesses combined. Furthermore, Vingroup recently decided to cancel its plan to open an airline subsidiary after nearly a year of planning.

The second case is Truong Hai, Vietnam's largest car assembly company. Truong Hai has expanded aggressively into real estate, and in 2019 revealed an ambitious plan to invest in agricultural production. However, things do not seem to be going as planned; Truong Hai's chairman complained recently about difficulty obtaining bank loans for his agriculture business. Expansion and restructuring are natural in business. They are healthy and normal undertakings when pursued in a thoughtful and prudent manner. However, international experience, for example, the EAFC of 1997–98, has taught us that it is a substantial risk for both firms and entire economies when large companies recklessly divert significant resources, both internal and debt-generated, to activities far from their core business and often speculative in nature.[30] Moreover, one of the major contributors to past crises in other countries has been inappropriately close business–government interactions that have amplified and compounded systemic financial and economic vulnerabilities.[31]

But we can also look closer to home. Vietnam paid a steep price over a decade ago as SOEs expanded their businesses in this manner. Major conglomerates such as Vinashin and PetroVietnam got into problems of such magnitude that, as described earlier, they triggered a national economic crisis in Vietnam. This was not a one-off event. The nature of the previous three financial sector crises in Vietnam is quite similar. The cause of the crisis in the late 1980s was clear. The financial sector was rapidly and completely liberalized, then Ponzi schemes emerged as credit cooperatives mobilized capital by paying interest up to 24 percent per month. A decade later, large private companies established or bought banks to serve as their capital-generating facilities for real estate speculation, creating an asset bubble that burst after the EAFC hit. In the late 2000s, the culprit of the crisis was SOEs and private companies expanding into non-core business activities for which they lacked a competitive advantage.

The impact of these crises to date has not been cataclysmic because the size of the financial sector has been relatively modest when compared to the size of the national economy. Moreover, when state-owned conglomerates faced troubles, the management of those companies was limited in its authority to incur further risk because of regulatory restrictions and due to their status as civil servants. The situation could be much more serious if a crisis is triggered by private conglomerates, whose leaders have far greater authority to incur excessive risk. This reckless behavior can be compounded by acute moral hazard if the conglomerates believe they are "too big to fail" and that, ultimately, the government will bail them out in a crisis.[32] It would be good for Vietnam, and for the conglomerates themselves, if these bets pay off. But not only are these big gambles for the companies, but they also pose a large risk for both creditors and the national economy.[33]

Vietnam's "Groundhog Decade"

As mentioned in the introduction, the development of Vietnam's financial and capital markets reminds one of the American film *Groundhog Day*, in which the star is trapped in a time loop and repeatedly relives the same day. However, for Vietnam's financial sector, the time loop is about ten years. Nevertheless, the story certainly repeats itself.

Vietnam's story begins with government intervention to regulate the financial sector in order to mitigate a series of market failures. This is common, and indeed a necessity, around the world. As noted at the beginning of this chapter, financial services are essential to the robust and sustainable development of a nation's economy, and therefore are considered a quasi-public good. Although it is possible to exclude households and businesses from financial services, and these services can be rivals in consumption with services capacity limitations, because of the positive externalities of financial services, governments instead encourage access and utilization. This was the primary rationale for Vietnam's extensive deregulation and liberalization reforms in the mid-1980s, mid-1990s, and mid-2000s.

Of special concern to governments is the occurrence of incomplete markets such as savings for low-income households and credit for micro, small, and medium enterprises. These constitute the "unbanked majority" in many developing countries, even though financial institutions have demonstrated that these markets can be very profitable, for example, Indonesia's Bank Rakyat Indonesia (BRI), Bangladesh's Grameen Bank, and Mexico's Compartamos Banco. Despite the commercial successes, most banks perceive these markets as high risk and low return, so government policies are often promulgated to encourage greater financial inclusion. This is the main reason Vietnam created its two policy banks.

Information asymmetries also compel governments to intervene in the financial sector. For example, governments try to ensure bank soundness by effective prudential oversight (see section on "Degree of Financial Inclusion" above) so that people have confidence in bank savings products, and most countries, including Vietnam, offer deposit insurance to further increase customer confidence. On the credit side, the borrowers know best if they are willing and able to repay their loans, so to deal with cases of default, government-created legal systems like that in Vietnam provide for the seizure and liquidation of collateral.

Finally, in the event of macroeconomic disequilibrium, bank prudential norms are often adjusted, for example, to either increase or decrease money in circulation, depending on the nature of the crisis; Vietnam has periodically adjusted interest rates, as well as reserve and liquidity requirements, to help achieve monetary policy objectives.

The story continues with the nature of government interventions, which sometimes result in government failures and often make things worse. This is also part of Vietnam's recurring saga. When the government deregulates and liberalizes the financial sector to foster growth, competitiveness, and access, but without adequate prudential oversight, markets are unconstrained by public interest concerns and behave accordingly. Moral hazard pervades the financial sector, since financial institutions can take excessive risks without suffering full negative consequences. The sector is also subject to adverse selection, since those taking excessive risk have a competitive advantage over more cautious and compliant financial institutions. The negative impact is compounded by amplification of macroeconomic policies, for example, transforming inflation to hyperinflation. These cascading negative results occurred in Vietnam in the late 1980s and late 1990s; they repeated themselves again in the late 2000s. When the government then overreacts by excessive regulation, imbalance shifts in the opposite direction with equally destructive results. These government policies can reduce access to essential financial services, creating debilitating credit crunches; and diminish innovation, entrepreneurship, and competitiveness in the financial sector through financial repression. Vietnam experienced this in the early 1980s, early 1990s, and early 2000s.

The cycle is completed when the government once again deregulates and liberalizes the financial sector without addressing the conditions that enabled the crisis to emerge and flourish. Government disengagement without a more effective way to mitigate the perpetual underlying market failures that prompted previous government actions simply sets the stage for the next financial sector crisis. This is the principal systemic risk currently facing Vietnam. It has been about a decade since Vietnam's last financial sector crisis, and the dominant risks today are the same as those that preceded previous crises.

Unlike other export-oriented Asian countries with open economies, Vietnam's financial sector is less vulnerable to the negative effects of external slowdowns in economic growth or trade conflicts between other countries. About three-quarters of exports from Vietnam are generated by self-financed FDI entities, and trade finance by Vietnamese banks is relatively low risk—it is usually short-term and securitized by trade invoice payments.

Instead, the dominant risks are domestic, and quite familiar:

- Temptation to use the financial sector to stimulate the economy, with the past risks of overheating, inflation, speculation, and asset bubbles.
- Ownership and operational entanglements of companies and financial institutions that are exceedingly complex and extremely opaque, with the past risks of both financial and real sector systemic contagion and collapse.
- Contributing factors that are a toxic mixture of limited capacity and political interests, resulting in both technical weaknesses and principal–agent conflicts between public leaders and the constituents they are supposed to serve.

Only Vietnam's success in strengthening prudential oversight of its financial and capital markets and managing counterproductive political interests will prevent a fourth financial sector crisis, and thus a continuation of its recurring "Groundhog Decade."

The natures of the three financial crises are similar in that a small number of companies having interrelationships with financial institutions were able to mobilize substantial capital to speculate in financial assets or real estate, or engage in Ponzi schemes. The first financial crisis, the credit cooperatives crisis of the late 1980s, occurred when the government allowed business entities to mobilize capital without any prudential requirements. As a result, Ponzi schemes proliferated. The second financial crisis, in the late 1990s, took place when big private companies, and partnerships between private companies and SOEs owning banks or having close relationships with banks, used debt-generated capital to speculate in real estate, as well as some commodities such as fertilizers and agricultural products, through letters of credit. The third financial crisis, in the late 2000s, was triggered by state-owned conglomerates that failed to create key industries such as shipbuilding, steel, and chemicals, while at the same time expanding their business into other

non-core areas, together with private companies owning banks or having close relationships with banks that used loans to speculate in real estate and financial assets.

The second decade of the twenty-first century ended without any financial sector
crisis or general macroeconomic turmoil. In fact, government-reported economic indicators looked good at the end of 2019: GDP growth was at a relatively robust 7.0 percent;
inflation was just 2.8 percent, much lower than the 4.0 percent target; unemployment was
just 2.0 percent; the exchange rate was stable; the trade surplus was US$9.9 billion; and
foreign exchange reserves increased by US$20 billion, rising to US$80 billion, equivalent
to 16.5 weeks of imports. Financial sector indicators were also favorable: credit growth was
just 13.7 percent, the lowest in the last five years, and reported NPLs were only 1.9 percent.[34]
Moreover, although Vietnam's stock market index (VN-Index) quickly plummeted nearly
a third when the COVID-19 pandemic hit in early 2020, it bounced back. Even at the
peak of the second wave of the pandemic in Vietnam, the VN-Index in early September 2020 was down only about 6 percent from the end of 2019. To date, the pandemic's
overall economic impact has also been relatively moderate. Nonetheless, there are also
several indicators of financial sector risks and vulnerabilities:

- Just over a half of all commercial banks have met the mandated Basel II capital adequacy
  ratio requirement. This could also have the unintended perverse effect of triggering
  unhealthy cross-ownership of financial institutions to mobilize the requisite capital, as
  banks tried to do previously to meet the minimum charter capital requirement of
  Đ3 trillion.[35]

- Financial sector regulation has become even more challenging in Vietnam as financial
  institutions have expanded and diversified their businesses to encompass all types of
  financial services, and even nonfinancial activities, while at the same time each segment
  is overseen by a different government agency, creating coordination problems and
  opportunities for regulatory arbitrage. For example, the State Bank of Vietnam is in
  charge of the banking sector, whereas the Ministry of Finance is in charge of the
  securities and insurance markets.

- Although reported NPLs are low and there have been improvements, not only do some
  believe the actual number of NPLs is much higher, but even the official figures identify
  some very weak banks when disaggregated (see section on "Size and Depth of Financial
  and Capital Markets" above).

- Despite low inflation, interest rates for both deposits and lending are still quite high (see
  table 9.6). Compared to the Consumer Price Index in 2019 of 2.79 percent, the deposit
  rate of 8.76 percent is indeed high. Moreover, the 2 percent difference between the
  highest and the lowest rates is also very large. Since March 2020, the Central Bank has
  lowered key interest rates several times, but deposit lending rates have dropped only
  slightly. This means that there could be some structural problems among banks. Since
  banks face the risk of contagion, the whole system could be in danger if just one bank
  gets into trouble, especially if it is relatively large and was perceived as sound.

- Expansion of private conglomerates, especially since the direct financial sector exposure
  of banks to conglomerate business expansion and indirect bank vulnerability to a sharp
  downturn in the real sector are both unknown at present, even if several large conglomerates report a balance sheet consisting of about one-third equity (see table 9.5 and
  table 9.7).[36]

Table 9.6
Highest deposit interest rates of banks in 2020

	01/2020	08/2020
SCB	8.76	8.25
Eximbank	8.5	8.4
Viet Capital	8.2	7.4
SHB	7.9	7.2
VPBank	7.9	6.8
Maritime Bank	7.8	7.1
ACB	7.8	7.25
Sacombank	7.7	7.8
TP Bank	7.6	7.6
Dong A Bank	7.6	7.6
MB Bank	7.6	7.4
VIB	7.6	7.59
HDBank	7.5	7.3
Techcombank	7.4	5.9
Vietcombank	6.8	6.6
Vietinbank	6.8	6.5
BIDV	6.8	6.5
Agribank	6.8	6.8

Source: Bnews, "Lãi suất tiết kiệm ngân hàng rục rịch đi xuống" for 01/2020; and Topbank, "Lãi suất tiết kiệm tháng 8/2020: Cập nhật mới nhất từ các ngân hang" for 08/2020.

Table 9.7
Balance sheet indicators of selected conglomerates

Firm	Item	III/2019	2012	Annual growth (%)	Increase (2012–19)
VinGroup	Assets	357,159	55,818	26.1	6.4
	Equity	125,408	10,557	36.3	11.9
	Equity to assets	35.1%	18.9%		1.9
Trường Hải	Assets	74,835	12,718	28.8	5.9
	Equity	31,162	4,333	32.6	7.2
	Equity to assets	41.6%	34.1%		
FLC	Assets	29,111	2,123	45.4	13.7
	Equity	9,097	1,199	33.6	7.6
	Equity to assets	31.2%	56.5%		

Source: Company financial reports.

- There are indications of substantial shadow banking, entailing potentially serious systemic risks. Many real estate companies have mobilized capital by committing themselves to fixed high returns (such as 12 percent). However, when real estate prices stop increasing and liquidity is low, companies face difficulty in paying the promised returns. Recently, the owner of Cocobay, a large project in the central region, announced it would break its commitment to pay 12 percent returns. There are indications that other companies are facing the same situation, which raises the question of whether they too will default on their commitments to investors and thus trigger a systemic collapse.

- Although we now have safe, effective, and widely available vaccines, the ultimate economic impact of the COVID-19 pandemic is still unknown. To date, many big firms have incurred large losses, and conditions for most businesses have gotten much tougher; during the first seven months of 2020, nearly 63,500 firms, equivalent to 9 percent of active enterprises, have registered to either suspend or close their business.

It is neither inevitable that Vietnam will face a fourth financial sector crisis in the next few years, nor is it certain that it can avoid one in light of growing risks from private sector conglomerates. Signals are mixed. The key question is whether these conglomerates will become more internationally competitive or increasingly problematic. At present, one can make a compelling argument for either scenario. Whether the "Groundhog Decade" syndrome has run its course or will be repeated once again remains an open question.

Appendix A

FINANCIAL SECTOR DEVELOPMENT STRATEGY
PRONOUNCEMENTS IN THE POLITICAL REPORTS OF THE
COMMUNIST PARTY OF VIETNAM CONGRESSES SINCE 1976

- Fourth Congress (1976): Rapidly transform the finance and banking sector into the socialist model of a mono-banking system.
- Fifth Congress (1982): Use the mono-banking system to support economic plans.
- Sixth Congress (1986): Permit establishment of credit cooperatives and allow the banking sector to follow some market mechanisms.
- Seventh Congress (1991): Establish a two-tier banking system, including joint stock banks.
- Eighth Congress (1996): Establish a securities market.
- Ninth Congress (2001): Promulgate prudential requirements and develop the securities market.
- Tenth Congress (2006): Develop a sustainable and complete financial market, and open this market in accordance with international commitments.
- Eleventh Congress (2011): Restructure the financial system.
- Twelfth Congress (2016): Continue to restructure the financial system.

Notes

1. King and Levine, "Finance and Growth"; Klein and Olivei, "Capital Account Liberalization"; Zhuang et al., *Financial Sector Development*.
2. Anwar and Nguyen, "Financial Development and Economic Growth"; Tran and Vu, "Vietnam: The Dilemma"; Vuong, "The Vietnamese Financial Economy."
3. Leung, "Banking and Financial Sector Reforms."

4. Rosengard and Huynh, *Vietnam's Financial System Reform*; World Bank, *Finance and Private Sector*.

5. Stockport et al., "Prudential Supervision, Banking and Economic Progress."

6. Dang, *Vietnam's Economic History 1945–2000*; Dao and Vu, *Renovation in Vietnam*.

7. Dang, *Vietnam's Economic Reasoning*; Kovsted et al., *Financial Sector Reforms in Vietnam*.

8. Kovsted, Rand, and Tarp, *From Monobank to Commercial Banking*; Rosengard and Huynh, *Vietnam's Financial System Reform*.

9. Dang, *Vietnam's Economic Reasoning*; Dao and Vu, *Renovation in Vietnam*.

10. Nguyen, "Xử lý lạm phát và đổi mới."

11. A Ponzi scheme is a fraudulent investment scam that promises excessive rates of return with minimum risk. Ponzi schemes are similar to pyramid schemes in that they generate returns for early investors by acquiring new investors. The key difference is that Ponzi scheme participants believe their returns are actually generated by their investments, whereas pyramid scheme participants are aware that their earnings come from new investors. Regardless of investor perceptions, both Ponzi and pyramid schemes are destined to fail, since eventually promised returns to existing investors exceed resources provided by new investors—both schemes simply run out of money.

12. Kovsted et al., *Financial Sector Reforms in Vietnam*.

13. Vuong, *The Vietnamese Financial Economy*.

14. Kovsted, Rand, and Tarp, *From Monobank to Commercial Banking*; Rosengard and Huynh, *Vietnam's Financial System Reform*. Basel I, also known as the 1988 Basel Accord, is a set of minimum capital requirements for banks to reduce credit risk that was issued by the Basel (Switzerland) Committee on Banking Supervision.

15. Rosengard and Huynh, *Vietnam's Financial System Reform*.

16. Huynh, *Dealing with Non-Performing Loans in Vietnam*.

17. Nguyen, *Vietnamese Commercial Banks*.

18. Nguyen, *Vietnamese Commercial Banks*.

19. Nguyen, *Vietnamese Commercial Banks*.

20. Bain & Company, *The Future of Southeast Asia's Digital Financial Services*.

21. Jahan et al., "The Financial Inclusion Landscape."

22. Rosengard and Huynh, *Vietnam's Financial System Reform*.

23. Nguyen, *Vietnamese Commercial Banks*.

24. Stockport et al., "Prudential Supervision, Banking and Economic Progress."

25. Tran, "Về đích Thông tư 41."

26. Perkins, Thanh, and Anh, *Vietnam's Industrial Policy*; Nguyen, Luu, and Trinh, *The Evolution of Vietnamese Industry*; Vu et al., *A Retrospective on Past 30 Years*; Vu, "Does WTO Accession Help Domestic Reform?"

27. Huynh et al., *Intel Products Vietnam*.

28. FETP, *Khơi thông những nút thắt*.

29. These issues are examined in greater depth in the chapter by Vu Thanh Tu Anh and Dwight H. Perkins, as well as in the chapter by Ari Kokko, Curt Nestor, and Le Hai Van, both in this volume.

30. Chang, "Business Groups in East Asia"; Choe and Pattnaik, "The Transformation of Korean Business Groups"; Sung and Kim, "Chaebol Restructuring after the 1997 Crisis."

31. Goldstein, *The Asian Financial Crisis*; Haggard and MacIntyre, "The Political Economy of the Asian Economic Crisis"; Dooley, "Origins of the Crisis in Asia"; Hunter, Kaufman, and Krueger, *The Asian Financial Crisis*.

32. Mishkin, "Anatomy of a Financial Crisis."

33. The formation of these conglomerates and oligarchies is analyzed in detail in the chapter by Nguyen Xuan Thanh in this volume.

34. SBV, *Điều hành chính sách tiề*.

35. Nguyen, *Vietnamese Commercial Banks*.

36. Issues related to large domestic private conglomerates are addressed extensively in the chapter by Nguyen Xuan Thanh in this volume.

References

Anwar, S., and L. P. Nguyen. "Financial Development and Economic Growth in Vietnam." *Journal of Economics and Finance* 35, no. 3 (2011): 348–60. doi: 10.1007/s12197-009-9106-2.

Bain & Company. *The Future of Southeast Asia's Digital Financial Services.* 2019. https://www.bain.com /insights/fufilling-its-promise/.

Bnews. "Lãi suất tiết kiệm ngân hàng rục rịch đi xuống" (Bank savings interest rates are about to go down). July 1, 2020. https://bnews.vn/lai-suat-tiet-kiem-ngan-hang-ruc-rich-di-xuong/144465.html.

Chang, S. J. "Business Groups in East Asia: Post-Crisis Restructuring and New Growth." *Asia Pacific Journal of Management* 23, no. 4 (2006): 407–17. doi: 10.1007/s10490-006-9013-4.

Choe, S., and C. Pattnaik. "The Transformation of Korean Business Groups after the Asian Crisis." *Journal of Contemporary Asia* 37, no. 2 (2007): 232–55. doi: 10.1080/00472330701254062.

Dang, P. *Vietnam's Economic History 1945–2000.* 2002.

———. *Vietnam's Economic Reasoning.* Hanoi: Thong Tan Publishing House, 2008.

Dao, S., and T. Vu. *Renovation in Vietnam: Remember and Rethinking.* Hanoi: Tri Thuc Publishing House, 2008.

Dooley, M. P. "Origins of the Crisis in Asia." In *The Asian Financial Crisis: Origins, Implications, and Solutions*, edited by William C. Hunter, George G. Kaufman, and Thomas H. Krueger. Boston: Springer, 1999. doi: 10.1007/978-1-4615-5155-3_4.

FETP. *Khơi thông nhũng nút thắt thể chế để phục hồi tăng trưởng* (Unleash institutional bottlenecks to restore growth). Ho Chi Minh City: Fulbright Economic Training Program.

Goldstein, M. *The Asian Financial Crisis: Causes, Cures, and Systemic Implications.* Washington, DC: Peterson Institute, 1998.

Haggard, S., and A. MacIntyre. "The Political Economy of the Asian Economic Crisis." *Review of International Political Economy* 5, no. 3 (1998) 381–92. doi: 10.2307/4177277.

Hunter, W. C., G. G. Kaufman, and T. H. Krueger, eds. *The Asian Financial Crisis: Origins, Implications, and Solutions.* Boston: Springer, 1999. http://books.google.ca/books?id=P23tH6X5DTcC.

Huynh, D. *Dealing with Non-Performing Loans in Vietnam: Experience from China and Other Countries.* Ho Chi Minh City: FETP, 2004.

Huynh, T. Du, H. T. Dung, N. X. Thanh, and D. T. A. Tuan. *Intel Products Vietnam: 10-Year Investment Impact Study Report 2006–2016.* Ho Chi Minh City: Intel, 2017.

Jahan, S., J. De, F. Jamaludin, P. Sodsriwiboon, and C. Sullivan. "The Financial Inclusion Landscape in the Asia-Pacific Region." IMF Working Paper no. 2019/079. doi: 10.5089/9781498305440.001.

King, R. G., and R. Levine. "Finance and Growth: Schumpeter Might Be Right." *Quarterly Journal of Economics* 108, no. 3 (1993): 717–37. doi: 10.2307/2118406.

Klein, M. W., and G. P. Olivei. "Capital Account Liberalization, Financial Depth, and Economic Growth." *Journal of International Money and Finance* 27, no. 6 (2008): 861–75. doi: 10.1016/j.jimonfin.2008.05.002.

Kovsted, J., J. Rand, and F. Tarp. *From Monobank to Commercial Banking: Financial Sector Reforms in Vietnam.* Copenhagen: NIAS Press, 2005.

Kovsted, J., J. Rand, F. Tarp, D. T. Nguyen, V. H. Nguyen, and T. M. Thao. *Financial Sector Reforms in Vietnam: Selected Issues and Problems.* Hanoi: Central Institute for Economic Management, 2003.

Leung, S. "Banking and Financial Sector Reforms in Vietnam." *ASEAN Economic Bulletin* 26, no. 1 (2009): 44–57. doi: 10.2307/41317018.

Mishkin, F. S. "Anatomy of a Financial Crisis." *Journal of Evolutionary Economics* 2, no. 2 (1992): 115–30. doi: 10.1007/BF01193536.

Nguyen, H. "Xử lý lạm phát và đổi mới hệ thống ngân hàng. In *Đổi mới ở Việt Nam: Nhớ lại và suy ngẫm*, edited by S. Dao and T. Vu. Hanoi: Tri Thuc, 2007.

Nguyen, T. T. A., D. M. Luu, and D. C. Trinh. *The Evolution of Vietnamese Industry.* Washington, DC: Brookings Institution, 2014.

Nguyen, X. T. *Vietnamese Commercial Banks: From 2006–2010 Legal and Policy Changes to 2011–2015 Restructuring Incidents.* Ho Chi Minh City: FETP, 2016. https://www.fsppm.fuv.edu.vn/en/policy-papers/policy -research/vietnamese-commercial-banks-from-20062010-legal-and-policy-changes-to-20112015 -restructuring-incidents/.

Perkins, D. H., V. Thanh, and T. Anh. *Vietnam's Industrial Policy: Designing Policies for Sustainable Development*. Cambridge, MA: Ash Institute for Democratic Governance and Innovation, 2009.

Rosengard, J. K., and D. Huynh. *Vietnam's Financial System Reform: A Comparative Study with China*. Cambridge, MA: Ash Institute for Democratic Governance and Innovation, 2008.

SBV. *Điều hành chính sách tiền tệ chủ động, linh hoạt, góp phần kiểm soát lạm phát, ổn định kinh tế vĩ mô*. Hanoi: State Bank of Vietnam, 2020. http://sbv.gov.vn.

Stockport, G., C. Perryer, M. Kearns IV, and W. J. Ardrey IV. "Prudential Supervision, Banking and Economic Progress: Implementation of Risk Management Procedures in Joint Stock Banks in Vietnam." *SSRN Electronic Journal*, 2011. doi: 10.2139/ssrn.1463168.

Sung, T., and D. Kim. "How Chaebol Restructuring after the 1997 Crisis Has Affected Corporate Decision and Performance in Korea: Debt Financing, Ownership Structure, and investment." *China Economic Journal* 10, no. 2 (2017): 147–61. doi: 10.1080/17538963.2017.1319630.

Topbank. "Lãi suất tiết kiệm tháng 8/2020: Cập nhật mới nhất từ các ngân hang" (Savings interest rate in August 2020: Latest updates from banks). June 5, 2020. https://topbank.vn/tu-van/lai-suat-tiet-kiem.

Tran, G. "Về đích Thông tư 41: 'Tốt nghiệp' hay sự khởi đầu mới?" *Saigon Times*, January 5, 2020. https://www.thesaigontimes.vn/298897/ve-dich-thong-tu-41-tot-nghiep-hay-su-khoi-dau-moi-.html.

Tran, G., and T. T. A. Vu. "Vietnam: The Dilemma of Bringing Global Financial Standards to a Socialist Market Economy." In *The Political Economy of Bank Regulation in Developing Countries: Risk and Reputation*, edited by Emily Jones. Oxford: Oxford University Press, 2020.

Vu, T. T. A. "Does WTO Accession Help Domestic Reform? The Political Economy of SOE Reform Backsliding in Vietnam." *World Trade Review* 16, no. 1 (2017): 85–109. doi: 10.1017/S1474745616000409.

Vu, T. T. A., D. Dapice, N. X. Thanh, and D. T. A. Tuan. *A Retrospective on Past 30 Years of Development in Vietnam*. Ho Chi Minh City: FETP, 2015.

Vuong, Q. H. "The Vietnamese Financial Economy: Reforms and Development, 1986–2016." In *Routledge Handbook of Banking and Finance in Asia*, edited by U. Volz, P. Morgan, and N. Yoshino. New York: Routledge. 2019.

World Bank. *Finance and Private Sector Development*. Washington, DC: World Bank, 2014.

Zhuang, J., H. Gunatilake, Y. Niimi, M. E. Khan, Y. Jiang, R. Hasan, N. Khor, A. S. Lagman-Martin, P. Bracey, and B. Huang. *Financial Sector Development, Economic Growth, and Poverty Reduction: A Literature Review*. Manila: Asian Development Bank, 2009.

CHAPTER 10

Vietnam's Environmental Challenges and Opportunities

A Special Role for Agriculture

LE THI QUYNH TRAM AND MALCOLM F. MCPHERSON

This chapter examines Vietnam's environmental challenges and how changes in agriculture can help address them. Policymakers in Vietnam confront two opposing pressures. One is intensified environmental stress as farmers, herders, and fisherfolk transform natural resources to boost supplies of food and fiber, accommodate consumer preferences, and increase exports. The second is growing citizen demand for quality ecosystem services, cleaner water, fresher air, healthy habitats, and environmental amenities such as open spaces, multifunctional landscapes, and national parks.

Vietnam's rapid agricultural growth from the early 1980s was generated by increased inputs of land and labor, irrigation intensification, abundant surface and groundwater, high-yielding crops, improved livestock, and heavy applications of agrichemicals. The resultant gains in agricultural employment, output, income, exports, and rural welfare were critical to Vietnam's "renovation."

The environmental cost of these improvements has been enormous, magnified by government policy. The economic and social benefits generated by agriculture's expansion were so dramatic and so easily measured that they diverted official attention from the less obvious and largely unmeasured degradation of the nation's natural resources. Policymakers aggressively shifted resources from agriculture and rural development to promote urbanization and industrialization. In the process, they seriously underfunded the investments and largely ignored the implementation of policies that would have preserved the environment.

The most recent Socioeconomic Development Strategy, supported by decisions taken at the Thirteenth Party Congress, reaffirm the government's commitment to sustained growth and development, with Vietnam programmed to become a high-income country by 2045. Continued agricultural expansion will be essential to that goal. Since Vietnam's land frontier has closed and the agricultural labor force is declining, increased agricultural output can come only from improved productivity. The government will need to devise *and* implement policies that raise agricultural output per unit of land and labor without further impairing the sector's natural resources. Current agricultural and environmental policies will not suffice, especially given the intensifying effects of climate change, which Vietnam, as yet, has not begun to address effectively.

This chapter is arranged as follows. Section 2 reviews current trends in agriculture and the environment in Vietnam. Section 3 identifies how agriculture has been adversely affecting the environment and notes some tentative but positive responses. Section 4 examines changes in policy and economic and social behavior that would improve agriculture and the environment. Section 5 briefly summarizes the main points.[1]

Background

At the end of the war in 1975, Vietnam was in ruins.[2] Much of its infrastructure and productive capacity had been destroyed, agricultural output was low, and food insecurity was acute. Agent Orange and the unregulated clearing of hills and highlands had deforested large parts of the country. Cereal production in 1975 was 10.6 million metric tons (mmt), fell to 10.2 mmt in 1978, and rose to 12.1 mmt in 1980. Rice yields, which averaged 2.1 tons per hectare in 1975, were only 2 tons per hectare in 1980.[3] Arable land use barely changed, and rates of fertilizer application fell. Rising output came from increases in agricultural employment of roughly 3 million workers. During this period, crop, livestock, and wild fish production provided less than 90 percent of the minimum daily calorie requirement for Vietnam's population of around 50 million.[4] Almost half the population was malnourished, and more than 60 percent of children under five were stunted.[5]

Postwar recovery was impeded by the government's policies of collectivizing agriculture in the south and rusticating individuals and groups viewed as antagonistic to the Communist Party.[6] Vietnam's difficulties had deepened by the end of the 1970s.[7] The government sought alternatives. After noting the favorable reaction by Chinese farmers to the "household responsibility system," the government of Vietnam issued Directive 100.

Introduced in early 1981 and applying only to Haiphong Province, farmers were allowed to sell their "above quota" output at market prices.[8] The response was dramatic. The program spread, leading to higher productivity nationwide. Cereal yields, 1,980 kg per hectare from 1975 to 1980, averaged 2,490 kg over the next five years. Cereal production reached 16.6 mmt in 1985, an increase of 56 percent relative to its 1975 level. Livestock and fisheries (wild catch and aquaculture) increased as well, adding to the per capita food supply.[9] Social indicators reflected the improvements. Under-five mortality declined from 76.6 deaths per 1,000 live births in 1975 to 61.3 in 1985, and life expectancy at birth rose from sixty-one to sixty-nine years.

Though substantial, these gains were dwarfed by advances resulting from the 1986 reform program (*Đổi Mới*) and the 1988 Law on Land. The former was the foundation for Vietnam's "socialist-oriented market economy." The latter decollectivized agriculture by granting households land use rights that could be transferred, inherited, and leased. Subsequent amendments to the law (in 1993, 1998, 2003, and 2013) broadened those rights so that, de facto, land in Vietnam, particularly urban land, is (almost) private property.

These reforms were complemented by the 1987 Law on Foreign Investment, the 1991 Company Law, and, from the mid-1990s, a series of "enterprise laws" that stimulated the establishment of industrial parks and export processing zones. Enterprise formation and entrepreneurial activity accelerated, and in the process restructured Vietnam's economy and society.[10] Agriculture's relative contribution to national output fell, offset by increases in industry and services. Urban growth accelerated, per capita income rose markedly, and the rate of population growth declined.

Agriculture has been instrumental to these changes. Increased output of food and fiber boosted exports and strengthened linkages to processing, packing, marketing, and transport enterprises. Rising agricultural productivity freed up rural labor, particularly of young, better-educated workers. They were absorbed in thriving urban industries encouraged by government policies that eased regulations, extended markets, and promoted international trade. Being part of the world's fastest-growing region enabled Vietnam to attract large inflows of foreign capital. Finally, investor-friendly provisions in the Law on Land facilitated the conversion of agricultural land to support high rates of urban and industrial expansion.[11] The economy grew rapidly. Between 1990 and 2010, Vietnam's real GDP increased by 294 percent, equivalent to 7 percent per annum and 5.6 percent per capita.

Over the same period, value added in agriculture rose by 113 percent or 3.7 percent per annum with crop, livestock, and fish/aquaculture production increasing by 160, 253, and 426 percent, respectively. These gains resulted from higher labor productivity (+99 percent),[12] cereal yields (+68 percent), and additional arable land (+27 percent). Irrigation intensification contributed as well. Cereal output more than doubled, from 19.9 mmt in 1990 to 44.6 mmt in 2010, with total food production rising by 151 percent. When combined with an average reduction of about 40 kg in per capita rice consumption, a large rice surplus emerged. Since 1988, Vietnam has been a major world rice exporter.[13]

The consequences have been extraordinary. Food insecurity and malnutrition fell and poverty rates declined.[14] Health indicators improved significantly (particularly under-five mortality and childhood stunting) and life expectancy has approached levels common to high-income countries. Within less than a generation, Vietnam moved beyond the devastation of war to become a lower-middle-income, industrializing nation. It is now a major exporter of rubber, rice, cashews, coffee, fish and shrimp, and manufactured products, with a flourishing tourism sector.[15]

Since 2010, these growth rates have moderated, with several core indicators declining— the agricultural labor force (–8.4 percent), agriculture's share of GDP (–3.5 percentage points), and its employment share (–10.7 percent points). Nonetheless, the sector continues to make a major contribution to the economy and society[16] through increases in food output (+28.1 percent), and the production of crops (+28.6 percent), livestock (+32.5 percent), and fish/aquaculture (+52 percent). Finally, agricultural output per worker rose by 52 percent (or 4.3 percent per annum).

While impressive and widely praised, Vietnam's agricultural and broader economic successes have been environmentally devastating. Land degradation and habitat destruction have displaced and pauperized large numbers of natural resource–dependent households.[17] The environmental damage is evident as urban pollution,[18] contamination of marine ecosystems,[19] biodiversity loss,[20] coastal erosion,[21] river damage from sand mining,[22] cropland salinization,[23] primary forest destruction,[24] soil contamination,[25] water pollution,[26] land subsidence,[27] mangrove removal,[28] and excessive agrichemical use.[29] The unregulated dumping and discharge of toxic effluents has been widespread.[30]

Several indicators highlight the effects. CO_2 emissions have increased from 0.16 kg per dollar of output (in 2017 PPP terms) in 1990 to 0.36 in 2018 (the latest year reported).[31] Electricity production from hydro sources declined from 61.8 percent in 1990 to 31.6 percent in 2015, replaced by fossil fuels (coal, oil, and gas), which rose, correspondingly, from 15 to 63.3 percent.[32] Since 1990, PM 2.5 pollution exposure of the whole population has been above the WHO "guideline value." This pollution is carcinogenic.

Notwithstanding these adverse trends, Vietnamese living standards have risen markedly. In addition to declining poverty, increased life expectancy, and lower under-five mortality (noted already), living space per capita rose,[33] undernutrition fell,[34] access to clean water and modern sanitation expanded,[35] electricity spread nationwide,[36] transport services (boosted by motorcycle ownership) broadened,[37] and access to education, health care, and recreation facilities improved.

Three conclusions follow from these data. First, economic expansion raised income and some key elements of welfare while simultaneously degrading the environment. Second, Vietnamese living standards will continue to rise only if environmental management decidedly improves. Third, there is nothing "sustainable" about Vietnam's current "development" trajectory.

At present, the country's population is around 98 million, with projections showing it will peak at about 110 million by 2055.[38] Most of what Vietnamese do in their everyday lives transforms, and regularly exploits, the environment. They dam rivers; construct roads, bridges, buildings, and other infrastructure; drain wetlands; clear coastal mangroves; expand and intensify irrigation areas; industrialize livestock, horticulture, and aquaculture production; log forests and add to plantations; extend urban areas; discharge noxious gases into the atmosphere; generate contamination hotspots; deplete aquifers; and dump toxic substances into the environment (soil, rivers, lakes, and oceans). These actions permanently disrupt the immediate locations where they occur and often seriously degrade areas downstream, downwind, or downslope. With projected gains in incomes and material wealth associated with reaching high-income status in 2045, increased population, and rising rates of urbanization, environmental degradation will not cease. Climate change will exacerbate these effects. The government's current policies and growth orientation make environmental sustainability unachievable.[39]

Agriculture and the Environment

The dramatic expansion of agriculture from the early 1980s provided the foundation for Vietnam's "miracle economy."[40] It was critical to the government's development strategy of rapid industrialization, commercialization, and urbanization,[41] and affirmed for Vietnam's leaders that this orientation would enable the country to continue its progress.[42]

The downside of this approach has been widespread environmental deterioration. Overviews of agricultural pollution by the government and World Bank of the crops, livestock, and aquaculture sectors reveal a grim situation.[43] Using a common framework that links "drivers" of pollution to farm-level activities (waste management, feeding, agrichemical use), physical impacts (on air, land, water, and food), and socioeconomic and other effects (human health, ecosystem services, amenities), the studies show that agricultural activities have seriously polluted Vietnam's air, soil, and water.

Major problems include: "[p]ollution from livestock farms mainly comes from manure, feed, drugs and chemicals";[44] "[d]uring implementation and operation [of aquaculture activities], little attention is paid to monitoring of [environmental] compliance and enforcement";[45] and "[t]here have been few incentives for farmers to produce safe, clean or organic [crop] products."[46] They reflect a combination of poor management, weak oversight and regulation, and the lack of incentives to preserve natural resources.

These problems had not inhibited agriculture's expansion. Buoyant local and foreign demand for output allowed farmers to continue adding inputs to compensate for natural resource damage. However, recently access to quality water has become a major constraint, and agrichemical overuse is now locally toxic and creating reputational effects in foreign markets.[47]

The three studies concluded that environmental pollution is progressively undermining each sector's viability. Remedies suggested include upgrading waste management systems, enforcing existing environmental and phytosanitary regulations, limiting agrichemical use, employing water more productively, improving soil management practices, strengthening institutional oversight, and creating incentives that change producers' behavior.[48] Attention is also needed to overcome producers' "knowledge gaps," which promote the dangerous use of agrichemicals and "beggar-thy-neighbor" dumping of wastewater and toxic effluents. Each report urges improved coordination between the Ministries of Agriculture and Rural Development (MARD) and Natural Resources and Environment (MONRE) to rationalize their conflicting regulations and fragmented administration. The example in box 10.1 highlights how lack of policy coordination can undermine the environment.

Several constructive changes are occurring. Responding to local and foreign market pressures, private producers are improving product quality. Urban consumers have the purchasing power to switch from local products to imports, and export market standards are becoming increasingly stringent.[49] Nonetheless, sustained, large-scale reductions in agriculture's negative environmental effects will require stronger measures.[50]

The *Vietnam 2035* study, which was completed in 2016 by teams from the government and World Bank, has an upbeat assessment of Vietnam's prospects for "prosperity, creativity, equity and democracy." Readers are told:

> Energized by past success but by no means content, Vietnam now aspires to modernity, industrialization, and a higher quality of life. The aspirations reflect an emphasis on clean water and clear blue skies; a healthy, secure, learned, and equitable society; and an effective state accountable for improving material welfare.[51]

Box 10.1 Policies on Food, Irrigation, and Flood Mitigation

The cumulative impacts of agricultural "development" policies on the environment are illustrated by outcomes of government decisions on food security, irrigation expansion, and flood control.

The government's "rice first" policy was designed to deal with food deprivation in the 1970s and 1980s. To boost national rice production, farmers in the Upper Mekong Delta were encouraged to triple-crop rice. Despite repeated studies showing that the third crop loses money, farmers have remained locked in by communal irrigation schedules. Their small plots prevent them from shifting out of rice or leaving their land fallow.

Triple-cropping reduces soil fertility and intensifies pest and disease pressure. Farmers respond by increasing the application of agrichemicals. Since the Mekong Delta has no dedicated drainage, "used" water returns to the supply canals after flowing over farmers' fields. As water moves down the delta its chemical concentration increases, making it unsuitable for horticulture or aquaculture. Producers have adapted by expanding their use of groundwater. Extraction rates have been so pronounced that land is subsiding, exacerbating relative sea-level rise (RSL).

Flood control structures accelerate "flood season" flows downriver. This reduces dry-season flows, and when combined with RSL, increases saline intrusion throughout the lower delta. Again, producers compensate by using groundwater.

These interconnected effects—the result of long past and unremediated policy actions—reinforce the adverse spiral of declining water quality, diminishing freshwater supplies, and environmental pollution.

Four factors have contributed. The government maintains a national food security policy which inappropriately equates food security with rice supply (Ho and McPherson, "Food Security"). Irrigation has been extended without providing dedicated drainage. Flood control facilities prevent flood season flows from being stored upriver. The fourth factor is ineffective environmental regulation and management. MONRE is responsible for the Law on Environmental Protection but does not have the staff or capacities to effectively monitor farmer behavior. It also lacks the institutional stature to coordinate official entities—MARD, Ministry of Construction, state-owned enterprises (SOEs), and others—to implement the law and its regulations.

Considered separately within its context, each decision—enhancing food security, expanding irrigation, and mitigating floods—made sense. The problem has been the incapacity of the relevant government entities to respond to their adverse impacts *and* to act collectively to remedy their cascading damage.

Attaining these aspirations will be difficult. The study noted: "strong economic growth since the early 1990s and the ongoing economic and spatial transformations have brought with them severe stresses on the environment."[52] The stresses, many mentioned above, include land degradation and soil erosion, water/air pollution, water scarcity and salinization, deforestation, loss of biodiversity, and increasing rates of toxic greenhouse gas emissions. Contributing factors have been mangrove destruction, overfishing, the loss of primary forests, lack of urban wastewater treatment, effluent dumping, the sharp rise in PM 2.5 pollution in the major cities, and the contamination of coastal and marine ecosystems.[53]

There are "several underlying causes"—uncoordinated and inefficient public investment decisions,[54] public institutions that lack resources and do not enforce environment regulations, "market imperfections and pricing distortions [that] undercut private sector investment," "degradation of the resource base" by SOEs, and "poor coordination among key ministries with overlapping mandates." The study concluded that existing policies and practices will "place unsustainable pressures on land, water and energy resources."[55] These findings are consistent with the earlier discussion that attributed agricultural pollution to poor management, weak regulatory oversight by ineffective institutions, and distorted incentives.

To boost productivity without further impairing the environment, Vietnam will have to upgrade skills to improve management, strengthen institutions to enhance resource governance, and create incentives for producers and consumers to efficiently use *all* of the country's resources (physical, human, and natural).[56] We illustrate how these relate to agriculture by examining how to upgrade farmers' skills, enhance water governance, and appropriately value natural resources.

UPGRADING FARMERS' SKILLS

Vietnam's agricultural growth, as noted earlier, has been generated primarily through the use of additional inputs—land, labor, agrichemicals, and water. Most of these inputs are currently at, or beyond, their feasible limits. Land, labor, and water are supply constrained, and agrichemicals are being used excessively.[57]

The only degree of freedom is higher productivity. This will require farmers and all who support them to enhance their skills, knowledge, and techniques so that when combined with improved varieties of crops, fish, shrimp, tree crops, pastures, and livestock, output can continue to grow. Experience available both locally and abroad shows how this can be done, although Vietnam's situation is complicated by the rapid aging and increased feminization of the agricultural labor force.[58]

Progress requires several changes. First, the public sector will need to expand its support for adaptive agricultural research and development (R&D) that is both age and gender relevant.[59] At present, the few public resources provided for R&D in Vietnam typically highlight techniques and technologies suited to younger (mostly male) workers with significant levels of formal education and access to finance and mechanization. Second, all farming inputs need to be used socially efficiently. Incentives are needed to reduce the excessive use of agrichemicals and raise water productivity. Third, government's restrictions on land use in agriculture should be eased. Too much of Vietnam's limited supply of arable land is locked in low-value rice production because of the government's outdated "rice first" food security policy (mentioned above). Fourth, the public sector should aggressively invest in social overhead capital—roads, bridges, river ports, grain stores, outreach such as farmer field schools, and demonstration programs—that complement agricultural production.[60]

Policymakers will have difficulty making these adjustments. Their responses so far have failed to ensure that the productivity of *all* factors used directly *and* indirectly in agriculture will increase. Curiously, this point was a feature of the government's 2013 agricultural restructuring program (revised in 2017), which highlighted the need to "shift from quantitative development to qualitative development."[61] That shift would involve better-quality planning; encouraging private sector investment; enhancing the efficiency of public investments; reordering priorities in aquaculture, crops and livestock, forestry, science and technology, and irrigation; and promoting institutional reform (especially of SOEs and agricultural administration). Though the program was comprehensive, coherent, and compelling, almost a decade later it has been only partially implemented.[62]

ENHANCING WATER GOVERNANCE

Water governance relates to the efficient administration and management of all water resources—blue, green, and gray, surface and subsurface.[63] Water is not managed efficiently in Vietnam.[64] This is perplexing since much of the country's wealth and welfare derives from the social amenities, ecosystem services, and economic output generated by water use. Water productivity could be substantially increased by streamlining current water management, appropriately pricing (and costing) water in all its uses, maintaining water quality, and improving access to safe water by the poor.[65]

The tasks of managing water supply, quality, access, distribution, marketing, control, drainage, and pollution abatement in Vietnam are fragmented. Formal responsibility is assigned to multiple ministries, the prime minister's office, and a national council. Responsibilities often overlap, and there is no administrative mechanism for the relevant agencies to reconcile their differences so that the social allocation of water can be efficient.[66] Worse, due to their stovepiped organization, the staffs of the various agencies have no incentive to collaborate. At best, accountability is weak. These governance difficulties are accentuated by the replication of the national-level divisions at subnational levels. Long-standing problems go untended. For instance, water users in the Upper Mekong Delta have been largely indifferent to how their behavior—excessive agrichemical use, high rates of water extraction, and aggressive flood control measures—multiplies the difficulties of water users further down the delta.

Raising water productivity has several advantages. It increases the *effective* supply of water for ecosystem services (wetlands, aquifer recharge, mangrove preservation, and marine habitats), and it broadens access to water. The latter raises household welfare, improves equity, and creates an incentive for citizens to maintain water quality.

Water productivity will only increase if water users modify their behavior. Water fees were suspended in 2008 and have not been reinstated, so that farmers have no incentive to "save" water.[67] Direct evidence is Vietnam's exceedingly low water productivity relative to other Asian countries.[68] For that to change, the price paid for water needs to be raised to levels approaching its full social cost.[69]

So far, farmers have gained at society's expense. Water reallocated from farmers to other users in industry and urban areas would raise national output and income. Social welfare would increase as well, because the "freed up" water would sustain wetlands and coastal mangroves (helping to prevent coastal erosion), flush toxins from the soil, recharge aquifers, and increase dry season water flow thereby reducing crop losses from saline intrusion.[70]

Mismanagement of the nation's natural resources, of which declining water quality is one dimension, reflects a major governance failure. The most obvious failing is that the government does not fully and fairly enforce its existing environmental laws and regulations.[71] As noted earlier, households, towns and cities, industries, SOEs, and industrial parks regularly dump untreated effluents into the nation's rivers, lakes, and the ocean. Overuse of agrichemicals, also mentioned above, compounds the damage.

If water fees and charges were increased, the allocation, use, and quality of water would improve. Some observers argue that access to water is a "right" and a low price is needed to help the poor. The poor already have limited access to good-quality water and regularly bear high costs due to waterborne diseases and the consumption of polluted water. Higher water charges would help the poor by increasing water available for wetland preservation, supporting wild fish catch and aquatic production, and more regularly flushing the canals and pools from which they draw their household supplies.[72]

APPROPRIATELY VALUING NATURAL RESOURCES

Appropriate prices and costs should be extended beyond water to *all* natural resources. Since human, physical, and financial capital are typically valued through labor, capital, and monetary markets (even with some distortions), the missing element is a set of procedures for valuing Vietnam's natural resources and their associated ecosystems services.

The undervaluation of these resources and services systematically underrepresents their contribution to national income and welfare. It is a major reason, noted above, why the government focuses on GDP, which is measured and valued, at the expense of the environment, which is not. This bias can be remedied by modifying how projects and programs are formulated and broadening the national accounting system to include the contribution of natural wealth to growth and development.

Conventional cost-benefit methods used by official agencies in Vietnam are flawed. None of them includes estimates of the *permanent* loss of natural wealth required to generate the *transitory* flows of income each project or program is expected to yield. This deficiency explains the selection bias for activities that boost GDP. Adjusting the valuation procedures would not alter the social costs of these activities, since those costs are incurred whether or not they are measured.[73]

Changing project and program evaluation will be an important first step. This needs to be supplemented by other methods that measure the aggregate impact of natural resources on national income and wealth. Beginning in the 1990s, research by major international agencies and several national governments extended the conventional System of National Accounts (SNA) to create the System of Environmental-Economic Accounts (SEEA).[74] The goal has been to measure the full social contribution to national income and welfare of *all* productive resources.[75] These changes provide the means for more countries, including Vietnam, to promote "green" growth.[76]

Adopting this expanded system will take time,[77] although modest adjustments would produce immediate results. One is to introduce "payments for ecosystem services" for a much broader range of natural assets than currently. Vietnam has such a program.[78] Ecotourism charges, watershed services fees, and an "eco" adjustment to utility bills are now common. Another adjustment would be to begin "charging" for services provided by natural resources—through fees, taxes, or direct pricing—at levels that approximate their social value. Obvious candidates are irrigation and groundwater charges, user fees to upgrade water supply and drainage systems, timber stumpage fees, charges for livestock and aquaculture waste management, environmental levies on industrial parks, and license fees for discharging into the environment effluents such as untreated water and exhaust from electricity generation plants and vehicles.[79] A third change would be to tax carbon emissions, something that is being done by numerous countries and provincial governments.[80]

Vietnam already provides subsidies (primarily land use rights) to individuals who rehabilitate coastal mangroves. There are many advantages. Mangroves reduce coastal erosion, protect marine ecosystems, support household livelihoods, and expand the area available for shrimp and aquaculture production. A prominent example is Can Gio Biosphere Reserve. Devastated by war, this area is now a World Heritage Site and a popular ecotourism location close to Ho Chi Minh City.[81] It is part of the government's ongoing effort to conserve biodiversity. Beginning with Cuc Phuong National Park in 1962, Vietnam now has "30 national parks, 48 nature reserves, 11 species or habitat conservation areas, and 39 landscape protection areas, constituting 7.6 percent of the country's natural area."[82]

Vietnam's success in the scale and scope of its reforestation program is unique among developing countries. Due to war, rural collectivization, and poverty-induced overexploitation, the country's forest cover was less than 28 percent in the late 1980s. Several large-scale reforestation programs—initially 5 million hectares but subsequently expanded to 14 million hectares—began in the 1990s. The 1988 Law on Land and its amendments, reinforced by payments for forest ecosystem services, provide households with incentives to reforest degraded areas and prevent damage to existing forests. National forest cover in 2020 was 47.2 percent. Reforestation has multiple benefits—watershed protection, lumber to support Vietnam's thriving furniture exports, reduced soil erosion, slower siltation of dams and water storage facilities, and higher rates of aquifer recharge. It has also stimulated the expansion of tree and bush crops—tea, coffee, cashews, and rubber.[83]

A further initiative is counteracting the adverse effects of triple rice cropping—particularly on soil fertility—by reintroducing floating rice in the Upper Mekong Delta. Floating rice combined with fish production in the flood season is followed by vegetables or cassava and fallow in the dry season.[84]

In 2014, the government relaxed its restrictions on rice land. Farmers can now legally use some rice land for other productive purposes if that land can be replanted with rice should the government require.[85] This change enables farmers to grow more profitable crops and, in the process, reduce agrichemical pollution and the loss of soil fertility.

Vietnamese farmers have been adopting "organic" practices to meet urban consumer demand for higher-quality products.[86] This effort has been stimulated by the VietGAP program, which emphasizes "good agricultural practices."[87] Other beneficial methods that could be explored include precision agriculture, water supplementation through reverse osmosis, and the expanded use of drip irrigation.

Finally, as rising personal incomes increase the effective demand for amenities (open spaces, reduced congestion, cleaner habitats), some major municipalities, such as Da Nang, have expanded their recycling programs.[88] Growing amenity demand also accounts for climate-related activism, especially increasing citizen resistance to coal-fired power plants.[89]

Policy Implications

Policymakers in Vietnam seeking to modify the impact of agriculture on the environment need to reconcile divergent timescales. Agriculture produces output, income, employment, and exports, which are easy to measure and have immediate, tangible effects on national welfare. By contrast, the environment generates multiple, amorphous flows of "ecosystem services," which are difficult to measure because their effects are variable and slow to emerge. Citizens recognize quickly when employment or income declines, but it takes time to notice the cumulating adverse environmental consequences of diminishing wetlands, coastal erosion, depleted aquifers, denuded watersheds, contaminated landscapes, and polluted rivers, lakes, and the atmosphere.

With these consequences more than obvious in Vietnam, further delay in addressing them would only accentuate their damage and cost. The following actions are needed:

1. Vietnam should immediately begin valuing *all* its productive resources—natural, human, and physical—by adopting the SEEA. This will offset the widespread undervaluation of natural resources relative to human and produced capital. Full adoption will take time, but the effects can be accelerated by extending existing payments for ecosystems services, introducing broad-based carbon pricing by increasing the gasoline tax and electricity tariffs,[90] and including the full social costs of all resources used and affected by public investment activities.[91]

2. Because Vietnam's irrigation systems lack dedicated drainage, all environmental regulations relating to agricultural pollutants and effluent dumping in waterways, forested areas, and "open" landscapes should be strictly enforced.

3. Regulations and fees should be introduced to scale back groundwater extraction to match annual rates of aquifer recharge. The goal should be to price ground and surface water at levels approaching their social costs.[92] The very poor can be protected by "lifeline" fees referred to earlier.

4. Government support for irrigation expansion should end, especially in areas that can be returned to floating rice and alternative uses such as wetlands, biodiversity preserves, and marine habitats. Resources saved could be used to rehabilitate degraded natural resources and assist farmers in switching to higher-value crops (e.g., horticulture and floriculture) that are less intensive in their use of natural resources and toxic inputs.

5. Inducements and subsidies (such as land grants) should be expanded to accelerate coastal protection and the rehabilitation of degraded or denuded areas.

6. Long-term plans to selectively reengineer the Mekong and Red River Deltas to include dedicated drainage should be devised and sequentially implemented. Rationalizing the national system of water governance would accelerate that process.

7. Public expenditure on agriculture should be sharply increased. Specific areas include agricultural R&D, rural nonirrigation infrastructure, and programs that assist the aging, increasingly feminized agricultural work force adopt modern techniques and technology.

Finally, agricultural R&D should be directed to working with Vietnamese farmers to mitigate and adapt to the challenges posed by climate change.

None of these suggestions is new. The main problem is implementation. Vietnam has myriad laws, decrees, directives, strategies, and action plans related to both agriculture and the environment. Due to institutional fragmentation, dispersed authority, overlapping responsibilities, and corruption, most have been poorly implemented. None of this needs to happen. Vietnam is a "hard state" that is capable of achieving goals the government sets. Implementation failure reflects conscious policy choice.

The intensifying impacts of climate change may alter that. For decades, Vietnamese have known that their country is "particularly vulnerable" to climate change, a point highlighted in 1990 by the Intergovernmental Panel on Climate Change.[93] It has been forcefully reaffirmed by subsequent research showing that, in addition to the effects of sea level rise (specifically noted by the IPCC), the threats include higher temperatures, shifting rainfall patterns, intensified pest/disease damage, saline intrusion, increasingly violent storms, and climate refugees.[94]

This research also reveals that while the government has taken many relevant decisions and devised plans and strategies that would address these issues, its actions have been totally inadequate. That may change. In November 2021, the prime minister told COP26: "climate change response and the restoration of nature must become the highest priority in all development decisions."[95] *If* this sentiment gains traction, significant progress could be made. Vietnam already has a solid basis for action, with multiple mid-2000s initiatives and more taken recently.[96] They include the Law on Environmental Protection (2020), which tightens environmental standards and their monitoring; the socioeconomic development plan for 2021–25 (signed April 2020) that emphasizes climate change adaptation; the National Green Growth Strategy 2021–2030 (promulgated November 2021), which stresses the "smart circular economy" and raising "people's resilience in the face of climate change"; a national biodiversity strategy designed to expand protected areas; the commitment (announced at COP26) to reach net-zero greenhouse gas emissions by 2050; introducing a carbon trade exchange by 2025; and the formulation of an agricultural and rural development strategy for 2021–30 to target "ecological, sustainable agriculture."[97]

The implication is clear. In principle, Vietnam is well positioned to address critical agricultural, environmental, and climate-related challenges. *If* fully implemented, these initiatives would move Vietnam toward its *Vietnam 2035* aspirations (noted earlier) while confirming the prime minister's concluding remark to COP26: "our historic commitments and actions will help preserve a green planet, a sustainable habitat, and lasting happiness for generations to come."

Concluding Comments

Agriculture has made vital contributions to income, employment, exports, and rural welfare, but its activities have seriously damaged the environment. Vietnam will not prosper if the degradation continues. The land frontier has closed, the agricultural labor force is declining, surface and groundwater are scarce, and agrichemicals are being applied to excess. Future agricultural expansion will depend entirely on increasing output by using all productive inputs in ways that leave the environment unimpaired.

Success in this endeavor will require multiple constructive changes in the behavior of *all* agricultural producers and those who support them, especially the government. It will involve modifying the sector's product mix, upgrading farmers' skills and knowledge, increasing public support for agriculture and rural development, and creating an incentive structure that induces all stakeholders to protect the environment rather than exploit it.

The environmental problems created by agriculture are not due to lack of relevant knowledge. Producers—encouraged by higher net revenues derived from expanding local and foreign markets—regularly cut corners by misusing agrichemicals and contaminating the landscape, water bodies, and atmosphere. Regulators, insulated from accountability by Vietnam's stovepiped administrative structure, do not prevent this destructive behavior. Research demonstrates that although officials understand these matters, few of the necessary remedies have been acted upon. The environmental damage continues and, in the process, directly undermines efforts to counteract the effects of climate change. Recent statements by the highest government and Party officials suggest that appropriate measures will be taken. If they are, agriculture will indeed have a special role in preserving Vietnam's environment.

Notes

1. Unless explicitly referenced, all data in the chapter are from the World Bank, World Development Indicators Excel file, updated December 12, 2021, at https://databank.worldbank.org/reports.aspx?source=world-development-indicators. We accessed it in February 2022.

2. Vietnam's per capita GDP was $170, close to the bottom for low-income countries (LICs). World Bank, *World Development Report 1980*, 110.

3. Young et al., "Vietnam's Rice Economy."

4. Data are from "Health-Related indicators" in the Statistical Annexes of the World Bank's *World Development Report*, 1980 through 1984. Per capita daily calorie supply in 1977 was 1,801 (83 percent of requirements). It rose to 1,977 (90 percent) in 1980, and by 1985 was 2,280, equivalent to the World Health Organization's (WHO) recommended level. See World Bank, *World Development Report 1988*, table 29.

5. Data for this variable, respectively 61.3 percent and 61.5 percent, were first reported in the *World Development Report*, 1988 and 1993. Not all social indicators were weak. In 1975, Vietnam's literacy rate was 87 percent versus 38 percent for LICs. Corresponding data for 1978 for life expectancy at birth were 65.9 and 50 years. World Bank, *World Development Report 1980*, 110, and WDI online.

6. Raymond, "'No Responsibility and No Rice,'" 49–51.

7. Between 1977 and 1980, real GDP fell 8.5 percent. Le Dang Doanh, "Reform and Industrialization."

8. Raymond, "'No Responsibility and No Rice,'" 52–53.

9. From 1975 to 1985, total food supply increased by 69 percent, while population grew by 25 percent. Local food production displaced imports. Cereal imports, which were 1.86 mmt in 1974, declined to 0.46 mmt by 1985. World Bank, *World Development Report 1987*, 212.

10. GDF, "Vietnam's Industrialization Strategy."

11. Since all land in Vietnam is owned by the state, the government and its agents have had minimal difficulty "recalling" land from farmers and converting it to nonfarm uses. Land administration has been subject to rampant corruption and official abuse (McPherson, "Land Policy in Vietnam"). The Law on Land (2013) corrected some excesses, although it pushed the problem to the courts, widely viewed as unfair and corrupt (GAN Integrity, "Vietnam Corruption Report").

12. Vietnam's agricultural labor force peaked at 28+ million workers in 2001 and was above 27 million from 2000 to 2003. It was 25 million in 2010, 22 million in 2018, and 20 million in 2020. For the period 1990–2020, annual growth in labor productivity in agriculture (i.e., constant price value added per worker) was 4 percent.

13. From 2000 to 2020, rice exports averaged 5.38 million tons per annum, with a peak of 7.72 million tons in 2011 (www.indexmundi.com/agriculture/, using United States Department of Agriculture data).

14. Poverty reduction has been significant, although uneven across geographic areas and ethnic groups. World Bank, *Vietnam 2035*, xxiv–xxvi, chap. 6; OPHI, "Vietnam Country Briefing."

15. The trade data track this transformation. Exports (imports) of goods and services were 6.6 percent (16.6 percent) of GDP in 1986. In 1990, they were 36 percent (45.3 percent); 72 percent (80.2 percent) in 2010, and by 2020 were 105.6 percent (102.7 percent). Over that period, agriculture's share of exports dropped from 95 percent in 2000 to 11 percent in 2020, even as the sector's absolute contribution to exports grew robustly.

16. A point confirmed by the General Statistics Office in its end-2021 briefing on agriculture (GSO, "Socio-Economic Situation"). This source highlights some of the key, though transitory, difficulties created by COVID.

17. World Vision, *Mekong Delta Poverty Analysis*.

18. Jennings, "Industrial Growth Creates Nagging Air Pollution."

19. VNS, "Pollution Threat for VN Marine Life."

20. World Bank, *Vietnam 2035*, 252; Nash, "Vietnam's Empty Forests."

21. VNA/VNN, "Vietnam: Erosion Hits Thousands."

22. Timmins, "How the Scramble for Sand."

23. Smaygi et al., "Responding to Rising Sea Levels."

24. World Bank, *Vietnam 2035*, 250–52.

25. Ives, "In Mekong Delta."

26. Wilbers et al., "Spatial and Temporal Variability."

27. Gorelick, "Land in Mekong Delta Sinks."

28. World Bank, *Vietnam 2035*, 251.

29. World Bank, "Vietnam Development Report 2016."

30. VNN, "Industrial Zones Polluting Water with Chemicals."

31. Corresponding amounts of CO_2 were 0.27 and 2.7 metric tons per capita, an annual increase of 8.6 percent.

32. The contribution of renewables, other than hydro, to electricity generation in 2015 was 0.11 percent.

33. A GSO report, "20 Years of Renovation and Development," provides data from 1986 to 2005 (www .gso.gov.vn). Average living space per capita in 1993 was 8.3 square meters (sqm)—8.2 in urban areas and 8.4 in rural areas. By 2004, it had increased to 13.5 sqm (15.8 in urban areas and 12.8 in rural areas). Data for 2020 from the Ministry of Construction were 25.1 sqm in urban areas and 24 sqm in rural areas. NDO, "Vietnam Aims to Raise Housing Space."

34. The proportion of undernourished population declined from 0.2 in 2001 to 0.07 in 2019. The respective shares of stunted children fell from 0.43 to 0.23.

35. In 2000, access to improved water was 80.5 percent and 51.9 percent for sanitation. Corresponding data for 2020 were 96.8 and 89.2 percent.

36. Universal electricity coverage was achieved in 2012. Rural coverage had been 68.1 percent in 1990.

37. Half a million motorcycles were registered in 1995. By 2005, the number was 14 million and by 2016, 45 million. While sources vary, the total in 2020 was approaching 63 million (https://data.aseanstats.org). I am grateful to David Dapice for these data.

38. See World Population Review 2022 (www.worldpopulationreview.com/countries/vietnam-population).

39. That is, Vietnam will not meet, by 2030 or any foreseeable date, Sustainable Development Goal 15. This goal encourages countries to "protect, restore and promote sustainable use of terrestrial ecosystems, sustainably manage forests, combat desertification, and halt and reverse land degradation and halt biodiversity loss" (https://sustainabledevelopment.un.org/sdgs).

40. Vanham, "The Story of Viet Nam's Economic Miracle."

41. World Bank, *Vietnam 2035*, box 5.2, 249.

42. Pimhidzai et al., "Climbing the Ladder."

43. A broader environmental study, published at the same time, reached the same conclusion. Schirmbeck, "Vietnam's Environmental Policies."

44. Tung Xuan Dinh, "An Overview: Livestock," 35.

45. Nguyen Van Cong, "An Overview: Aquaculture," 24.

46. Nguyen Tin Hong, "An Overview: Crops," 45.

47. Tung Xuan Dinh, "An Overview: Livestock," 1.

48. These topics are reviewed in chapter 6 of each study.

49. Aquaculture producers are raising quality by explicitly adopting export standards. Nguyen Van Cong, "An Overview: Aquaculture," chap. 3.

50. Some perspective, however, is needed. Farmers do not gratuitously trash the environment since their livelihoods depend on natural resources. Furthermore, many farm-based activities have important environmental benefits. Rice fields, for example, help mitigate floods, nurture/restore aquatic ecosystems, provide wild foods, supplement household fish production, recharge aquifers, supply animal fodder, and, if managed appropriately, prevent erosion and improve soil productivity. Shivakoti and Bastakoti, "Multi-functionality of Paddy Fields."

51. World Bank, *Vietnam 2035*, 4.

52. World Bank, *Vietnam 2035*, 243.

53. World Bank, *Vietnam 2035*, 245–57.

54. As described in box 10.1.

55. World Bank, *Vietnam 2035*, 244–45.

56. A World Bank study covers much of the same material but muddles the message. Its subtitle, "Gaining More from Less," is biophysically impossible when applied to agriculture. No doubt the study sought to

emphasize the efficient use of resources. For that, *more* rather than fewer inputs will be required. Improving agriculture in Vietnam will not come from "gaining more from less." Rather, it will involve combining additional knowledge, information, skills, technology, and renewable energy with existing supplies of physical capital, land, and water in ways that raise output. It requires farmers to be better informed, equipped, and financed, more highly skilled, be served by improved logistics and deeper value chains, and enabled by constructive public policies. World Bank, "Vietnam Development Report 2016."

57. The impacts of these constraints are reflected in the lower growth rates of crop yields and crop, livestock, and aquaculture output evident in the relevant series reported in the World Development Indicators.

58. Le and McPherson, "Ageing and Feminization."

59. Older workers (particularly women) need special assistance. They have lower levels of formal education, and being poor, are less willing to risk adopting new techniques and innovative practices.

60. Ho and McPherson, "Complementary Investments."

61. "Approving the Project."

62. Weak implementation of agricultural policy in Vietnam is no surprise. When measured in terms of how the government acts, rather than what it states will be done, agricultural and rural development (ARD) have not been priorities. Over the last two decades, the share of ARD in the state budget has been around 6 percent, even as agriculture on average has employed 50 percent of the nation's labor force, generated 19 percent of its GDP, and, as noted earlier, made a major continuing contribution to exports. Besides the low level of public expenditure, agriculture has been taxed. The OECD's "producer support estimate" for 2018–20 relative to 2000–2002 shows that implicit and explicit taxation reduced gross farm receipts by 9.2 percent. OECD, *Agricultural Policy Monitoring and Evaluation*, chap. 4.30.

63. OECD, *OECD Principles on Water Governance*.

64. World Bank, *Vietnam 2035*, chap. 5.

65. This is part of Sustainable Development Goal 6, to which the government is committed.

66. Efficient allocation (roughly) equalizes the marginal social returns of water in each of its uses.

67. Farmers allocate a resource efficiently when its risk-adjusted marginal value product equals its price. When the price of water is zero, farmers use as much water as they believe each activity "needs."

68. World Bank, "Vietnam Development Report 2016."

69. This includes the costs (time, finance, effort, resources, cash) that farmers incur gaining access to, managing, and disposing of water, plus the amortization charges on canal construction and waterworks, the recurrent costs of maintaining and administering these facilities, and the forgone value of the water in its alternative uses such as ecosystem services, biodiversity maintenance, and household and industrial water supply. It also includes the costs associated with negative externalities such as the deleterious health effects of waterborne diseases, and pollution created by effluents and toxic substances.

70. Water saving in agriculture enhances the welfare of coastal residents. Increased river flow reduces their purchases of treated water and/or lowers the costs of traveling upriver to obtain freshwater.

71. "National Strategy for Environmental Protection"; "Law on Environmental Protection."

72. The poorest groups, particularly in urban areas, could be provided with water at a "lifeline" rate. This mechanism, common in electricity distribution, involves a low or zero charge for water consumption below a predetermined threshold (e.g., 100 liters per person per day), with higher charges for amounts beyond that limit.

73. Conventional cost-benefit analysis attributes the effect of "unmeasured" inputs to factors such as physical capital and human labor, which are measured. This overstates their contribution to the activity being evaluated, making their use appear more profitable/rewarding.

74. World Bank research has been critical to the valuation of natural capital and developing a broader measure of national wealth (Dixon and Hamilton, "Expanding the Measure of Wealth"). It led to the Wealth Accounting and the Valuation of Ecosystem Services (WAVES) initiative and stimulated United Nations and European Union support to improve natural resource valuation (World Bank, "Factoring Nature"; Australian Government, "Environmental Economic Accounting").

75. Shifting to SEEA reveals the rising social value (shadow price) of natural resources as their scarcity increases relative to human and produced capital (equipment, structures, information). With current technology and financial capacities, the stocks of natural resources and flows of ecosystems services are, for all practical purposes, fixed. That is not the case with human and other capital, which can be augmented

through investment (Johnson, "Population, Food, and Knowledge"). As these variable items accumulate, the relative supply of natural resources and ecosystem services declines. This raises their value.

76. These are "growth strategies [that] are focused on overall wealth rather than gross domestic product (GDP) as it is currently measured." World Bank, *Toward a Green, Clean, and Resilient World*, 1.

77. Through the Greater Mekong System Core Environment Program, the Asian Development Bank has been helping Vietnam value its "natural capital." Pham Quang Huy, "Exploring the Vietnamese Environmental Accounting."

78. Suhardiman et al., "Payments for Ecosystem Services"; World Bank, *Vietnam 2035*, box 5.6 and 268–69.

79. Because these fees lack a "market test," some observers reject them as arbitrary. International practice, however, provides practical, tested benchmarks. Yet, even if some arbitrariness remains, a positive charge induces more efficient use of resources, thereby reducing environmental degradation. When there is no charge, those features are missing.

80. Nurdianto and Resosudarmo, "Economy-Wide Impact of a Carbon Tax."

81. Green, "Preservation and Use of the Natural Resources."

82. World Bank, *Vietnam 2035*, 251.

83. Some benefits of reforestation have been undermined by illegal cutting of the country's remaining primary forest. World Bank, *Vietnam 2035*, 250–51.

84. Nguyen Van Kien, "Comparing the Costs and Benefits."

85. MARD, "Paddy Area Is Predicted to [Be] Cut."

86. Von Kote, "Vietnam's Farmers Struggle."

87. GAP also means "good aquaculture practices." Nguyen Van Cong, "An Overview: Aquaculture," 13 and chap. 6.

88. VNS, "Da Nang Cracks Down on Waste."

89. Mekong Eye, "Coal Power on the Rise"; Kotani, "Coal Backlash Creates Energy Dilemma."

90. ADB, *Pathways to Low-Carbon Development for Vietnam*.

91. None of the additional fees or charges (carbon taxes, access and user fees, waste management levies) will reduce national welfare, although there will be transitional distributional/equity effects, many of which will be positive. Vietnam is already incurring these costs as congestion, loss of amenities, soil erosion, pollution, contamination, and adverse health outcomes. Formally recognizing these effects through taxes and subsidies internalizes their costs.

92. Groundwater use would ease if surface water contamination were reduced (point 2).

93. IPCC, *Climate Change*, 135.

94. Matsuda, "The State of Environmental Problems"; IPONRE, *Viet Nam Assessment Report*; WB/ADB, *Climate Risk*; Van Hong Thi Ha and Nguyen Bang Nong, "Understanding Livelihood Vulnerability."

95. VGP, "Full Remarks by PM Pham Minh Chinh."

96. This information was reported on the official site for government news, www.en.baochinhphu.vn.

97. The Socio-Economic Development Strategy 2021–2030, approved during the Thirteenth Party Congress, encourages "strengthened resilience to climate related hazards . . . greener, smart and more efficient energy consumption and production . . . [and] conserved natural resources." Team Europe, "Socialist Republic of Vietnam."

References

ADB. *Pathways to Low-Carbon Development for Vietnam*. Mandaluyong City: Asian Development Bank, 2017.

"Approving the Project Agricultural Restructuring towards Raising Added Values and Sustainable Development." Prime Minister Decision No. 899/QD-TTg, June 10, 2013.

Australian Government. "Environmental Economic Accounting: A Common National Approach Strategy and Action Plan." Prepared by the Interjurisdictional Environmental-Economic Accounting Steering Committee for the Meeting of Environment Ministers, Canberra, 2018.

Dixon, John A., and Kirk Hamilton. "Expanding the Measure of Wealth." *Finance & Development* 33, no. 4 (1996): 15–18.

GAN Integrity. "Vietnam Corruption Report." GAN Integrity Business Anti-Corruption Portal, New York, 2019. www.GANintegrity.com/country-profiles/vietnam.

GDF. "Vietnam's Industrialization Strategy in the Age of Globalization." Graduate Institute for Policy Studies Development Forum, Tokyo, May 26, 2003.

Gorelick, Steve. "Land in Mekong Delta Sinks as Inhabitants Remove Ground Water." *Environmentalresearchweb*, September 4, 2014.

Green, Emily. "Preservation and Use of the Natural Resources in the Developing World: A Case Study of the Can Gio Biosphere Reserve, Ho Chi Minh City, Vietnam." *Occam's Razor* 1, no. 3 (2011).

GSO. "Socio-Economic Situation in the Fourth Quarter and 2021." Press Release, General Statistics Office of Vietnam, Hanoi, January 29, 2022. www.gso.gov.vn/data-and-statistics.

Ho Dang Hoa and Malcolm McPherson. "Complementary Investments to Improve the Efficiency of Rural Land Use." Policy Brief, Fulbright Economics Teaching Program and Ash Center for Democratic Governance and Innovation, Harvard Kennedy School, May 2010.

———. "Food Security and Land Policy in Vietnam." Policy Brief, Fulbright Economics Teaching Program and Ash Center for Democratic Governance and Innovation, Harvard Kennedy School, May 2010.

IPCC. *Climate Change: The IPCC 1990 and 1992 Assessments.* Geneva: IPCC, 1992. https://archive.ipcc.ch/ipccreports/far/wg_I/ipcc_far_wg_I_full_report.pdf.

IPONRE. *Viet Nam Assessment Report on Climate Change.* Hanoi: Institute of Strategy and Policy on Natural Resources and Environment, Government of Vietnam, 2009.

Ives, Mike. "In Mekong Delta, Rice Boom Has Steep Environmental Cost." *Yale Environment 360*, July 11, 2013.

Jennings, Ralph. "Industrial Growth Creates Nagging Air Pollution in Vietnam." *VOA News,* East Asia Pacific, November 5, 2019.

Johnson, D. Gale. "Population, Food, and Knowledge." *American Economic Review* 90, no. 1 (2000): 1–14.

Kotani, Hiroshi. "Coal Backlash Creates Energy Dilemma in Southeast Asia." *Nikkei Asian Review*, January 19, 2018.

"Law on Environmental Protection." National Assembly No. 55/2014/QH13, 2014.

Le Dang Doanh. "Reform and Industrialization." PowerPoint presentation, "Industrialization for Inclusive Development in Tanzania," Economic Society of Tanzania Annual Congress, Dar es Salaam, December 8, 2018.

Le Thi Quynh Tram and Malcolm McPherson. "The Ageing and Feminization of the Lower Mekong Basin Agricultural Labor Force." Policy Brief, Lower Mekong Public Policy Initiative, Fulbright Economics Teaching Program, Ho Chi Minh City, November 2015.

MARD. "Paddy Area Is Predicted to [Be] Cut by around 130,000 Hectares." Ministry of Agriculture and Rural Development, January 13, 2014. https://www.mard.gov.vn/en/Pages/paddy-area-is-predicted-to-cut-by-around-130000-hectares-1011.aspx.

Matsuda, Shinya. "The State of Environmental Problems in Vietnam." *Nihon Koshu Eisei Zasshi* 42, no. 6 (June 1995): 413–20.

McPherson, Malcolm. "Land Policy in Vietnam: Challenges and Prospects for Constructive Change." *Journal of Macromarketing* 32, no. 1 (March 2012): 137–46.

Mekong Eye. "Coal Power on the Rise: Mekong Region Digs In." *Mekong Eye*, February 15, 2016. https://earthjournalism.net/stories/coal-power-on-the-rise-mekong-region-digs-in.

Nash, Stephen. "Vietnam's Empty Forests." *New York Times Magazine*, April 1, 2019.

"National Strategy for Environmental Protection until 2020 and Vision toward 2030." Prime Minister Decision 1216/QD-TTg, September 5, 2012.

NDO. "Vietnam Aims to Raise Housing Space to 30 Square Meters Per Person by 2030." *Nhan Dan online*, October 15, 2021.

Nguyen Quang Thong. "Vietnam's Industrial Zones Create 'Massive Public Health Burden.'" *Thanhnien News*, January 11, 2015.

Nguyen Tin Hong. "An Overview of Agricultural Pollution in Vietnam: The Crops Sector." Washington, DC: World Bank Group, 2017. https://openknowledge.worldbank.org/handle/10986/29241.

Nguyen Van Cong. "An Overview of Agricultural Pollution in Vietnam: The Aquaculture Sector." Washington DC: World Bank Group, 2017. https://openknowledge.worldbank.org/handle/10986/29243.

Nguyen Van Kien. "Comparing the Costs and Benefits of Floating Rice-Based and Intensive Rice-Based Farming Systems in the Mekong Delta." *Asian Journal of Agriculture and Rural Development* 5, no. 9 (2015): 202–17.

Nurdianto, Ditya A., and Budy P. Resosudarmo. "Economy-Wide Impact of a Carbon Tax in ASEAN." *Journal of Southeast Asian Economies* 33, no. 1 (2016): 1–21.

OECD. *Agricultural Policy Monitoring and Evaluation 2021: Addressing the Challenges Facing Food Systems.* Paris: Organization for Economic Cooperation and Development, 2021. https://doi.org/10.1787/2d810e01-en.

———. *OECD Principles on Water Governance.* Directorate for Public Governance and Territorial Development, Organization for Economic Cooperation and Development Ministerial Council Meeting, Paris, June 2015.

OPHI. "Vietnam Country Briefing: Multidimensional Poverty Index Data Bank." Oxford Poverty and Human Development Initiative, University of Oxford, October 2021.

Pham Quang Huy. "Exploring the Vietnamese Environmental Accounting with an Introduction about the Green Accounting Information System." *Journal of Modern Accounting and Auditing* 10, no. 6 (June 2014): 675–82.

Pimhidzai, Obert, Linh Hoang Vu, Sergiy Zorya, Alwaleed Fareed Alatabani, Nga Thi Nguyen, and Sebastian Eckradit. "Climbing the Ladder: Poverty Reduction and Shared Prosperity in Vietnam, Update Report." Washington, DC: World Bank, 2018.

Raymond, Chad. "'No Responsibility and No Rice': The Rise and Fall of Agricultural Collectivization in Vietnam." *Agricultural History* 82, no. 1 (Winter 2008): 43–61.

Schirmbeck, Sonja. "Vietnam's Environmental Policies at a Crossroads." Hanoi: Friedrich-Ebert-Stiftung Vietnam Office, 2017.

Shivakoti, Ganesh P., and Ram C. Bastakoti. "Multi-Functionality of Paddy Fields over the Lower Mekong Basin." *MRC Technical Paper* no. 26. Mekong River Commission, Vientiane, 2010.

Smaygi, Alex, et al. "Responding to Rising Sea Levels in the Mekong Delta." *Nature Climate Change* 5 (2015): 167–74.

Suhardiman, Diana, Dennis Wichelns, Guillaume Lestrelin, and Chu Thai Hoanh. "Payments for Ecosystem Services in Vietnam: Market-Based Incentives or State Control of Resources?" *Ecosystem Services* 6 (2013): 64–71.

Team Europe. "Socialist Republic of Vietnam: Multi-Annual Indicative Program 2021–2027." 2021. https://ec.europa.eu>system>files, mip.2021-c2021-8997-vietnam-annex.en.pdf.

Timmins, Beth. "How the Scramble for Sand Is Destroying the Mekong." *BBC News*, December 19, 2019.

Tung Xuan Dinh. "An Overview of Agricultural Pollution in Vietnam: The Livestock Sector." Washington, DC: World Bank Group, 2017. https://openknowledge.worldbank.org/handle/10986/29244.

Van Hong Thi Ha and Nguyen Bang Nong. "Understanding Livelihood Vulnerability to Climate Change: Evidence from Quang Ninh Province, Vietnam." *GATR Journal of Business and Economics Review* 6, no. 2 (2021): 137–47.

Vanham, Peter. "The Story of Viet Nam's Economic Miracle." *World Economic Forum*, September 11, 2018. www.weforum.org/agenda/2018.

VGP. "Full Remarks by PM Pham Minh Chinh at COP26." Vietnam Government Portal, Government News, February 11, 2022. www.en.baochinhphu.vn.

VNA/VNN. "Vietnam: Erosion Hits Thousands All over Mekong Delta." Vietnam News Agency, Vietnam News Service, September 25, 2014.

VNN. "Industrial Zones Polluting Water with Chemicals." Vietnam News Network, February 23, 2016.

VNS. "Da Nang Cracks Down on Waste." Vietnam News Service, December 6, 2018.

———. "Mekong Delta Suffers as Factories Dump Waste into Local River System." Vietnam News Service, October 13, 2014.

———. "Pollution Threat for VN Marine Life." Vietnam News Service, August 22, 2016.

von Kote, Gilles. "Vietnam's Farmers Struggle to Meet Demand for 'Healthy Vegetables.'" *The Guardian*, May 5, 2014.

WB/ADB. *Climate Risk: Country Profile Vietnam*. Washington, DC: World Bank and Asian Development Bank, 2020.

Wilbers, Gert-Jan, Mathias Becker, La Thi Nga, Zita Sebesvari, and Fabrice G. Renaud. "Spatial and Temporal Variability of Surface Water Pollution in the Mekong Delta, Vietnam." *Science of the Total Environment* 485–86 (July 1, 2014): 653–65.

World Bank. "Factoring Nature into National Wealth Accounting." April 12, 2012. https://www.worldbank.org/en/news/feature/2012/04/12/factoring-nature-into-national-wealth-accounting.

———. *Toward a Green, Clean, and Resilient World for All*. Washington, DC: World Bank, 2012.

———. "Vietnam Development Report 2016: Transforming Vietnamese Agriculture: Gaining More from Less." Report no. AUS15856, East Asia and Pacific. Washington, DC, April 29, 2016.

———. *Vietnam 2035: Toward Prosperity, Creativity, Equity, and Democracy*. Washington, DC: World Bank, 2016.

———. *World Development Report*. Washington, DC: World Bank, various years.

World Vision. *Mekong Delta Poverty Analysis: Final Report*. World Vision Australia for Australian Government Agency for International Development, October 2004.

Young, Kenneth B., Eric J. Wailes, Gail L. Cramer, and Nguyen Tri Khiem. "Vietnam's Rice Economy: Developments and Prospects." Arkansas Agricultural Experiment Station, University of Arkansas, Division of Agriculture, Research Report no. 968, April 2002.

PART III

Human Welfare: Poverty, Family, Health, and Education

CHAPTER 11

Poverty Reduction and Inequality in Vietnam

DAVID DAPICE

It is now widely accepted that Vietnam was successful in reducing poverty from quite high rates to single-digit levels over the 1990–2020 period. These years were marked by strong growth in agriculture, mainly in family farms, huge gains in mostly FDI-sourced labor-intensive exports, with millions of direct and indirect jobs created, and rapid domestic business formation. After the 1999 Enterprise Law, the largest job gains came from domestic private firms that employed many more workers. The national reported Gini coefficient, which measures income inequality, has been fairly stable since 2000, but is of uncertain validity. Pockets of poverty remain, though even in those places poverty was declining—mainly in thinly populated remote highlands with high ethnic populations. So this is a striking success story. GDP growth averaged 6–7 percent a year from 1990 to 2019 and then slowed with the 2020–21 pandemic, but a good initial public health response suggests growth will resume after vaccinations are supplied. Rapid gains in poverty reduction continued through 2020 but likely faltered in 2021. This chapter aims to explain why poverty fell so much, how growth and other policies will or will not manage to continue diminishing poverty where it is still high, and the prospects for broadly based growth in the future.

It is common to use an official poverty income measure for poverty—it corresponds to the idea of a critical minimum income level. However, as a society grows richer, the old minimum poverty levels become less relevant. In 1990, having a bicycle helped one out of poverty. Now, a motorbike is more relevant. As Vietnam grows richer on average, a relative poverty measure (for example, any income less than a third or a half of the median income) is a better way to measure poverty in an increasingly middle-income society. In addition, public goods may be used to paint a richer picture of living conditions and security from shocks—called a multidimensional poverty measure.

The main sources of data on poverty come from household surveys and labor market surveys. The latter are a rich source of information on labor force structure, hours, wages, and returns to education, but consistent economy-wide wage data are only available in the last decade or so. And with 33 percent of the labor force in agriculture even now, wages do not always indicate incomes. The household surveys provide periodic data back into the 1990s, and the most recent survey is from 2020. Other surveys focusing on multidimensional poverty are more recent and will be mentioned in this chapter.

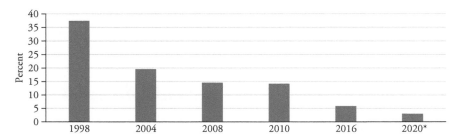

FIGURE 11.1 Poverty in Vietnam using an income-based poverty line
Note: A new higher real income level and methodology for the poverty line were applied after 2008, explaining the lack of progress in 2010. The income level from 2010 on was adjusted each year for inflation. In 2016, the poverty rate was reported by both that income measure and a newer and more demanding multidimensional poverty measure. After 2016, only the multidimensional number was reported. The 2020 income poverty rate is an estimate. (See box 11.1.)
Source: Statistical Yearbooks, various years.

Basic Data

A World Bank study from 2015 presents the basic income poverty data for Vietnam from 1993 to 2013.[1] In that period, even with some changes in methodology and measurement levels, it shows a decline of four-fifths or more in the rate of income poverty in Vietnam. There have been further declines since 2013, and by most definitions the income poverty rate is now in single digits—the General Statistical Office estimate for 2016 was 5.8 percent, based on the 2016 household survey and a price-adjusted income measure. Figure 11.1 updates the study to 2020. After 2016, the poverty rate was only reported using a multidimensional poverty measure. That measure showed a decline from 9.2 percent in 2016 to 4.8 percent in 2020.

In less academic terms, the number of registered motorbikes rose from 1.2 million in 1990 to 58 million in 2018,[2] or one motorbike for every 1.25 people from fifteen to eighty years of age. In a 2016 household survey, 92 percent of adults said they owned a motorbike—a rate that would suggest an even higher number than registrations, unless they were owned jointly. Given the cost of at least several hundred dollars for a motorbike, their ubiquity offers broad support for the notion that most people have indeed escaped grinding poverty.

Income Poverty and Multidimensional Poverty (MDP)—Further Details

A fuller description of multidimensional poverty is useful to describe ways that public services can reduce inequality and poverty. The MDP approach includes income but also incorporates variables about access to health care centers and health insurance, education, electricity, clean water, housing, public or private transfers, and certain durable goods.

Table 11.1
Income and multidimensional poverty in rural and urban areas

	2006 (Roelen et al.) (%)			2016 (GSO) (%)			2020 (GSO) (%)		
	Urban	Rural	Total	Urban	Rural	Total	Urban	Rural	Total
Income poverty rate	7.7	18.8	15.5	2.0	7.5	5.8	0.6*	4.5*	3.0*
Multidimensional poverty	12.0	43.4	36.7	3.5	11.8	9.2	1.1	7.1	4.8

* The 2020 income poverty data are estimated, assuming the proportional reduction from 2016 was the same as for MDP. The 2006 MDP data are for child poverty only.

Using an income cutoff for absolute poverty and a range above that for MDP, weights are developed for these variables, and households with less than half of a perfect weighted score (or one-third for severe poverty) are considered poor. In general, the poverty rate by this approach runs several percentage points above the rate measured only by income. In 2016, the national rate measured by MOLISA[3] income was 5.8 percent and the multidimensional rate was 9.2 percent (see table 11.1). However, the distribution and trend patterns remained similar. An estimate of 2020 income poverty by the income measure is that in total it fell to 3 percent, with rural areas about 4.5 percent. This assumes the relative fall in income and multidimensional poverty rates were similar. A virtue of the MDP approach is that it recognizes that public goods are important for the well-being of everyone, but especially lower-income families.

The movement of workers from low-income areas to high-income areas may not reduce multidimensional poverty quite as much as income poverty. Transfers sent back home can raise the income of the recipient household but may not move it closer to a good hospital or a high school—and these figure into multidimensional poverty. Indeed, if population growth is slow or even negative in a rural area, there may be less reason to extend improved services there.[4] However, the multidimensional poverty rate nationally in 2004 was estimated at 38.7 percent, and government programs combined with income growth brought this down to less than 5 percent by 2020, a decline of 87 percent, which about equals the proportional decline in income poverty.[5] It is also true that moving from rural to urban areas likely improves the multidimensional poverty rate for those who migrate, since urban services are better.

The Economic Basics

Why did poverty drop so much? The main immediate reasons were a near quintupling in income per capita and a *reported* fairly stable and equal income distribution. These two outcomes hinged on a high rate of investment in physical and human capital, an improving business environment, and greater integration into the world economy. There is also a

Box 11.1 Defining Poverty in Vietnam—A Rising Tide Lifts (Almost All) Boats

Definitions of poverty in the 1990s either just took the bottom fifth of the population (Vietnamese scholars) or (World Bank) assumed 70 percent of incomes were spent on food and then calculated how many households could not afford 2,100 calories per capita per day. The latter definition produced an estimated poverty rate over 50 percent in 1992–93. It was certainly higher in earlier years. After 2000, an expenditure-based approach was used. In 2002, spending of 160,000 *dong* (US$10.47) per capita per month was used for the "general poverty rate"; for the lower "food poverty rate," the levels were 146,000 (US$9.55) for urban and 112,000 (US$7.33) for rural spending. These were increased in line with inflation.

In 2010, the levels were adjusted upward and switched back to income. In 2010, the poverty income level was 400,000 (US$21.50) per capita per month for rural areas and 500,000 (US$26.86) for urban. These income levels were raised in line with inflation, so by 2016, the levels were 630,000 (US$28.72) for rural and 780,000 (US$35.56) for urban. Note that in 2016 the PPP GDP* per capita was nearly three times the market price GDP per capita, so in PPP terms the rural poverty income was US$83 per capita a month and US$103 a month for urban people. This is well over the "$2 a day" level often used in international estimates of poverty across countries.

In 2016, a "multidimensional poverty rate" was used. If a rural family had income below 700,000 *dong* (US$32) per capita a month *or* had 700,000–1,000,000 *dong and* at least three indicators measuring deprivation of access to basic social services, it was poor. For 2016 urban families, the per capita income levels were below 900,000 *dong* (US$41) or 900,000–1,300,000 *dong* (up to US$59) and a lack of access to services. All of these should be roughly tripled to get income in PPP terms. In 2016, the multidimensional poverty rate was 9.2 percent, while the older income-based poverty rate was 5.8 percent. If the 2016–20 national income poverty rate fell in the same proportion as the multidimensional rate, it would have been 3 percent in 2020.

---

* PPP refers to purchasing power parity, a way of adjusting market GDP to reflect a common international (usually US) set of prices for non-traded goods. PPP GDP in poorer countries is normally much higher than market-priced GDP. In Vietnam, it is about three times higher.

high degree of mobility within the country for most people, but not always for remote ethnic minority groups due to cultural issues.

Real GDP rose 7.4 times from 1990 to 2020, while population rose 44 percent, producing a jump in per capita output of about five times. Since people were living, if poorly, to start with, it stands to reason that an equally shared quintupling of incomes would bring most out of poverty. In 1990, as table 11.2 shows, there were 21.7 million working in agriculture and a real agricultural output of 42 trillion *dong* (1994 prices). By 2020, the

Table 11.2
Output per worker in agriculture and nonagricultural sectors (1994 constant prices)

	Agricultural GDP & workers GDP			Nonfarm GDP & workers GDP			Total GDP & workers GDP		
	GDP	Workers	Worker	GDP	Workers	Worker	GDP	Workers	Worker
1990	42	21.7	1.94	90	13.4	6.7	132	35.1	3.76
2020	119	17.7	6.72	862	35.9	24.0	982	53.6	18.30
Change:	*77*	*−4.0*	*4.78*	*772*	*22.5*	*17.3*	*850*	*18.5*	*14.54*

Notes: GDP is in trillion 1994 *dong*. Workers are in millions. GDP per worker is in million 1994 *dong*. All GDP data from the General Statistical Office, with calculations by author; the labor force is from the ADB, *Key Indicators*. Agriculture includes farming, fishing, and forestry. Constant price data after 2010 were converted to 1994 prices.

numbers working in agriculture fell to 17.7 million, but real agricultural output had risen to 119 trillion *dong*. So those remaining in agriculture enjoyed an average jump of 3.5 times their 1990 level—from 1.9 million to 6.72 million *dong* agricultural output per worker. This brought most rural people out of poverty, not even counting nonfarm jobs that they could access, at growing real wages, in the off-season. They also benefited if some family members sent money from urban jobs.

Those gains seem modest compared to the gains in nonagricultural sectors. Workers outside of agriculture rose from 13.4 million to almost 36 million laborers, while nonagricultural output rose nine times, from 90 trillion to 862 trillion *dong* in constant prices. In per worker terms, that is a jump from 6.7 million to 24 million *dong* per worker. Output per farm worker grew only 4.78 million *dong* compared to growth of 17.3 million *dong* per nonagricultural worker. This refers to average output, but the rapid rise in nonfarm workers suggests that marginal returns in nonfarm work were also much higher than in agriculture, which accounted for only 9 percent of GDP growth.

Agriculture accounted for 62 percent of all workers in 1990 and 33 percent in 2020. All labor force growth along with millions leaving farming after the early 1990s went into nonfarm jobs with much higher average productivity.[6] This, along with a 3.6-fold increase in output per nonfarm worker, accounted for much of the reduction in poverty. While the gain in output per worker was much less in agriculture, many poor rural families got out of poverty by boosting their real rural incomes 3.5 times. The drop in full-time farmers' share of jobs helped the progress in poverty, as did the growing availability of nonfarm jobs to supplement farmers' agricultural incomes.[7]

A Geographical Perspective

Another way to look at the poverty issue is to examine it from a geographical perspective. The Central and Northern Highlands aside, most low-income areas grew less rapidly in population than better-off areas. First, consider the relative income and population growth

Table 11.3

Relative incomes and population growth by select regions from household surveys

Region	Relative income in			Population growth from	
	1992–93	2003–4	2016	1992–2006	2006–20
All Vietnam	**1.00**	**1.00**	**1.00**	**21.2%**	**16.0%**
Rural	.91	.78	.80	11.4%	0.5%
Urban	1.76	1.64	1.43	71.6%	57.6%
Of which (fast-growing [in population] provinces/regions).					
Hanoi (including Ha Tay)	NA	1.34	1.57	35.1%	42.7%
Da Nang	NA	1.38	1.43	29.7%	48.1%
Southeast region*	NA	1.85	1.50	63.7%	32.6%
Central Highlands	NA	.80	.76	73.1%	22.2%
Rest of Vietnam	NA	.85	.81	13.7%	9.5%

Notes: * Ninh Thuan and Binh Thuan Provinces are kept in the south-central coast; classification varied over time. Likewise, Hanoi now contains Ha Tay Province, and Hanoi's population (with Ha Tay) has grown more rapidly than the remainder of the Red River Delta. These fast-growing areas accounted for 62 percent of population growth over 1992–2018 but had only a 23 percent share in 1992. Population and income data from statistical yearbooks.

**Box 11.2 Urban and Total Population Growth in Vietnam
from 2009 to 2019**

The change in national population from 2009 to 2019 as measured by the two national censuses was 10.36 million, while the growth in urban population was 7.71 million, a ratio of nearly three-quarters. However, many areas are officially rural but functionally urban, especially close to major cities. In addition, even with the census, some workers remain officially registered in rural areas but usually live and work in cities. One article suggested Ho Chi Minh City had a population of 13 rather than 9 million!* Taken together, it is likely that an even higher ratio of "actual" urbanization is going on. Research would be needed to determine the precise ratio, but earlier estimates by the GSO put the urban growth share at more than 90 percent.

* Quang Huy, "13 Million People in HCMC—How Many Have Houses?" *Zing News,* September 17, 2019. https://zingnews.vn/13-trieu-dan-o-tphcm-bao-nhieu-nguoi-co-nha-post990951.html.

---

of different regions relative to the national average: table 11.3 shows that the southeast, Da Nang, and greater Hanoi with their higher relative income, have attracted migrants from other parts of Vietnam—their population grew at two to three times the national average since 2006. In general, cities have accounted for most population growth lately (see box 11.2), and this has helped to reduce the disparity between rural and urban incomes.[8]

Only the Central Highlands and part of the Northern Highlands,[9] with their relatively open land and early in-migration, helped by national schemes to boost coffee and rubber production, have been below average in income but had above average population growth—and even they have recently had net negative migration. In general, and not surprisingly, people move to where they can earn more. Having workers move, and be allowed to move, to better opportunities accounts for much of the reduction in poverty, although the gains in agriculture were also very important, especially prior to 2006.

Regions with High Poverty Levels

The national income poverty rate in 1998 was 37.4 percent, and this fell to an estimated 4.3 percent with a higher real income poverty level by 2018. However, some regions remained with relatively high poverty levels. Table 11.4 provides data on regions with high poverty. Regions not enumerated all had single-digit poverty rates in both 2016 and 2020.

Poverty has been declining in every region by the income measure adopted by MOLISA and estimated by the General Statistics Office (GSO). Poverty, as measured by the more stringent multidimensional index, has practically disappeared in urban areas (at 1.1 percent) and has fallen to 7.1 percent in rural areas by 2020. It is still high in areas that are remote from major cities, high in isolated ethnic populations, and (for multidimensional poverty) need better public service provision. Attracting skilled teachers and medical personnel may be challenges in these areas, so higher budget allocations alone might not create rapid progress in service quality.

The data from the poorer regions show an 80 percent or better reduction in poverty in twenty years, even when the poverty income level has been moved upward. As of 2020, there is about 13 percent of the population living in provinces with relatively high, although declining, poverty. ("High" is an MDP rate of 10 percent or more.) These poorer provinces have a high proportion of ethnic minorities, which made up 73 percent of the

Table 11.4
Areas with high poverty rates

	Income-based poverty (%)				Multidimensional poverty (%)	
	1998	2008	2016	2020 (Est.)	2016	2020
All rural areas	44.9	18.7	7.5	4.5	11.8	7.1
Northern mt./midlands	64.5	31.6	13.8	8.6	23.0	14.4
Central coastal areas	42.5	18.4	8.0	4.5	11.6	6.5
Central Highlands	52.4	24.1	9.1	5.4	18.5	11.0

Source: 2009 and 2020 *Statistical Yearbook of Vietnam*, tables 308 (2009) and 365 (2020). Income poverty for 2020 is an estimate assuming the drop from 2016 is similar to the MDP change.

9 million poor people in the country, according to a 2020 World Bank study,[10] which also reported minorities had average consumption of less than half of the ethnic majority *Kinh*. However, incomes grew for this group at 5.7 percent a year from 2002 to 2014. It is true that this healthy rate was less than that enjoyed by the *Kinh* majority of 7.5 percent a year, but it indicates that even hard-to-reach groups were better off over this period, though more efforts will be needed to reduce ethnic inequality—which has been increasing. (All ethnic groups account for 14 percent of population, but many are well integrated. Isolated ethnic groups account for only 6–9 percent of total population.) There are thirteen provinces where ethnic minorities are more than half of the population, two in the Central Highlands and the rest in the northern mountains. These provinces had 10 million people in the 2019 census.

No attempt is made to present a documented critique of data quality in this chapter. It is natural to wonder if the data and reality are convergent or if problems in sampling or recording lead to biased results. In general, surveys tend to miss very high-income households and some transient workers. Because there seem to be cases when even population counts in urban areas seem to fall short in including transient workers, it could be that the poverty data are also skewed. However, most excluded workers are in relatively high wage areas and many are sending money back home. "Other" income sources account for 11–22 percent of total income from 2006 to 2016 in rural areas, and most of this is transfers. It is not likely that many of the uncounted workers would be in poverty, although these possible omissions could affect income inequality measures. For income poverty, it is likely that the trends are real, and the fraction reported as poor is not far off. For multidimensional poverty, any undercount of transient urban workers could result in more people with limited access to public services. However, official temporary residence cards are now easy to get, and access to public services is improving.

From these tables, we can see that the gains in nonfarm productivity and job mobility accounted for most gains in incomes. The agricultural productivity gains were important for those remaining in agriculture and moved most of those in farming who had been poor above the poverty line, if still well below average for nonfarm income levels. But, even in rural areas, the share of income from farming was falling as nonfarm sources had a predominant and growing share. As long as incomes were relatively equally distributed, the growth of real GDP per capita raised most people out of poverty, even as the poverty income line kept rising. The freedom of workers to move to better-paying jobs helped maintain this dynamic. In the last decade (2009–19), at least three-quarters of population growth has been in urban areas—indeed, Vietnam has reached a point where rural population actually starts to fall.[11] Given that average household incomes are nearly 80 percent higher in urban compared to rural areas (though only 40–50 percent more when cost of living differences are considered), the fact of migration and the gains from mobility are not surprising.[12]

Overall, even if a more comprehensive poverty measure is used, it appears that the downward trend and geographic patterns are similar to the income poverty measure, even if the estimated poverty levels are modestly higher. To put it another way, poverty is declining everywhere by any definition, but where it started higher it has not yet been lowered to levels of the more favored areas, even though workers are moving into those favored areas and earning more and arguably accessing better services. The questions for continued progress are, will the rapid uptake of labor in thriving areas persist, and can these areas continue to pay higher wages than other places? If not, can the other areas begin to play a larger role in keeping their own workers and reducing poverty with their own population and income growth?

Migrant Workers

Most labor force growth has been in cities due to migration. The area with the greatest population inflow (the southeast, including Ho Chi Minh City) has a reported multidimensional poverty rate of less than 1 percent. All urban areas in 2020 had a poverty rate of 1.1 percent compared to a national rate of 4.8 percent. However, while it is easy for a person to move to where there is work, it is not always easy to become a permanent resident. This can limit the government-funded education and health services for the worker or, especially, his or her children. Temporary workers also rarely get government jobs—they are largely private employees in manufacturing or services. There are local regulations determining how long one has to live in a city to become a permanent resident and get these services—in Hanoi, in addition to requiring three years of residence, there is even a requirement about the minimum living space while one is temporary. There are at least 5.6 million temporary residents who lack permanent status, according to a recent World Bank study.[13]

There are good reasons to reform the registration system, either by making it easier for migrants to become permanent residents—with no or shorter waiting periods in their new place of residence, and/or fewer differences between treatment of temporary and permanent residents. (This lessening of different treatment has been happening.) While some cities argue that this will result in inundation by poor rural folk, studies suggest that the fiscal impact of importing a worker is neutral or even positive. The tendency of the central government to take a high proportion of tax revenues from rich cities and provinces to use for subsidies to poor rural provinces may well upset that conclusion—the city looks at the net revenues, not gross revenues. Recalibration of interprovincial transfers makes sense anyway, since migrants often send a portion of their income back to their home province, and their incomes would be higher if their new residence worked better in terms of traffic and public services. It is interesting to note that in fast-growing Binh Duong Province (near Ho Chi Minh City), many "temporary" migrants are from ethnic minorities in remote provinces, and this may help to explain why ethnic poverty is falling. Overall, better treatment of migrant workers will further reduce poverty and speed growth. However, temporary registration is easy to get and access to public services for them is improving. As a result, mobility is high.

The movement of workers into urban areas, even if not always smooth, was much easier than in China where the *hukou* system made the migrant workers almost an underclass. Of course, Vietnam is smaller and has a common language for most workers, but it was a major political decision to allow millions of young workers to move without many restrictions or legal constraints. The high rate of labor-intensive FDI in the last five to ten years provided an economic reason to allow this and probably eased local concerns. In the last few years, the increase in FDI employment has equaled that of total labor force growth.

The pandemic has created difficult conditions for migrants, as their jobs are often lost, while travel restrictions prevent some from getting back to their home provinces. Emergency food distribution systems have gaps that often leave out the unofficial migrants. While these problems are likely temporary, there was real dislocation in some months of 2021, but the poverty data show a small decline for the year.

A Labor Market Perspective

Another lens to look at changes in income comes from looking at changes in jobs and wages. The Labor Force Surveys have been issued for over a decade and began to be issued quarterly in 2013 to 2018; an annual report was issued in 2020. They provide a rich regional and occupational breakdown of workers and their wages, as well as wages by type of employer. They do not always agree closely with the Living Standards Surveys. For example, monthly earnings of employees in urban areas are only about a third higher than rural monthly earnings, according to the Labor Force Surveys, while urban per capita incomes are 80 to 100 percent higher than rural per capita incomes in the Living Standards Surveys. (Incomes can include transfers that are not earnings, but the stability of work over the year may also be a factor explaining the differences.)

Vietnam used to be a nation primarily of household labor rather than employees. In 2002, 69 percent of all workers fell under "household labor," and these were mainly farmers, farm laborers, and service workers in family establishments. There were then 10.2 percent of all workers in the labor force working for the state and 15.6 percent working for collectives. Private paid workers—both domestic and foreign—were only about 5 percent. This is important because, if only a small fraction of the workforce works for wages, then changes in wages are not necessarily good indicators for gains in overall income or welfare. By 2019, 50 percent of the workforce was a paid worker or employer, and the groups equivalent to "household labor"—"own account worker" and "unpaid family worker"—had fallen to 50 percent. State workers fell to below 10 percent of total employed, so more than 40 percent of the total were private wage workers, including both domestic and foreign. Cooperative workers had all but disappeared.

This shift was substantial and rather rapid. While foreign employers did grow rapidly from a low base, they accounted for only 4.8 million or 8.8 percent of all employed in 2019. The biggest gains in absolute numbers came from the private domestic sector. This sector, which had 1.4 million private (domestic) workers in 2002, grew to 21 million in 2019. A part of this growth was caused by absorption of the collective sector, which numbered 6.1 million in 2002 but had collapsed by 2017. But most of the private growth was organic—a huge increase in the number of private enterprises and their workers.

Even if half of those employed are working for wages, it is likely that younger workers and new workers are proportionately overrepresented in the wage group. This is because most population growth has been in urban areas in the last decade, and paid workers and employers account for 62.7 percent of all urban workers, but only 37 percent of all rural workers. Most migration takes place among workers in their twenties and thirties, so those entering the labor force have been mostly urban and mostly wage workers.[14] Those leaving rural areas create a labor shortage, or fewer available workers, and that tended to drive up returns for those remaining, even if they did not work for wages themselves. A curious finding of the 2015 Migration Survey was that circular migration, common in much of Southeast Asia, was very low in Vietnam. Almost all migrants, at least in the survey, appear to be permanent rather than temporary migrants. In addition, women in 2015 were slightly more likely to migrate than men, so the impact of migration on labor returns would apply to both men and women to the extent there is a gendered division of labor.[15]

The wages of men and women are not equal, but overall female wages were 88–90 percent of male wages in 2017–19. The 2007 ratio was 87 percent for female to male wages, so there has been very modest progress toward equality in the last decade. The rapid expansion of labor-intensive export processing, often using mainly female workers, has no doubt helped to tilt the gender ratio in migration toward women and has contributed toward the slow progress in closing the male/female wage gap. FDI and state salaries are higher than private domestic salaries. Most job growth has been private, foreign, and especially domestic.

Wages have grown sharply in the last decade in real terms. Overall wages in 2007 were 1.4 million *dong* a month, and this rose to 6.7 million by the end of 2019 in current prices; correcting for the rise in consumer prices—if the 2007 CPI were set at 100, the 2019 index would be 235—the real wage in 2019 would be 2.8 million, a 100 percent real increase.

Curiously, real rural wages rose 100 percent, but real urban wages rose only 36 percent from 2007 to 2019, according to the Labor Force Surveys. Since the share of urban wage earners rose from 2007 to 2019, the total real wage increases of more than 100 percent *might* be right—*if*, as is likely, there were relatively more highly paid urban workers in 2019. The urban labor share with its higher wages increased from 26 percent to 32 percent from 2007 to 2019, but that is not enough to explain the discrepancy. It is very likely that urban wages, which were nearly twice rural wages in 2007, rose relatively more slowly than rural wages. As most population growth was in urban areas, the supply of workers rose sharply in those areas and did not grow much or at all in rural areas. This should have caused urban–rural wage differentials to shrink, as they did—urban wages were only 30 percent more than rural wages by 2019. All these published data are in nominal terms, and urban–rural inflation differences may accentuate the relative real rural gains.

Education and Wage Rates

One story told about Vietnam's growth is that it is driven by large numbers of workers in labor-intensive manufacturing. Of course, with only 9 percent of all workers employed by FDI firms in 2019, that looks to be an overly broad simplification. But more generally, if there were a huge expansion of jobs needing only rudimentary skills that are easily learned in a few weeks or months, then the returns to education may be rather low. Is this true?

In 2002, the labor force survey reported 80.3 percent of the workforce with no qualification and 3.2 percent with only short-term training. College and university workers were then just 4.2 percent of the total, and the rest (12.3 percent) were skilled or vocational workers with longer training. The group with no qualifications had fallen to 76 percent in 2020. The university and college category had risen from 4.2 percent to 14.9 percent. A new category, "midterm professional training," in 2019 was reported as 4.4 percent.[16]

The 10.7 percentage point increase in the share of university and college graduates from 2002 to 2020 is the most striking change, and the rise in "professional midterm" reflects an expansion of secondary schooling large enough that a separate category was initiated. Longer-term vocational training fell to 4.7 percent and short-term training disappeared—indeed, it appears to have been folded into "unskilled" by 2011. The decline in unqualified workers (if short-term vocational in 2002 is added to the unskilled) is notable—from 83–84 percent to 76 percent. The disappearance of the "skilled" group after 2002 makes comparisons difficult, but no strong increase in skilled and vocational workers is evident. Overall, as table 11.5 shows, there was significant upgrading in the share of academic educational levels of the workforce, but not in vocational or skilled workers.

The difference in wages for various levels of qualifications is only available for 2011–20. The data, as shown in table 11.6, support the view that real wages rose for all groups, but least in percentage terms for university graduates. The university workers continued to earn more than anyone else, but their real wages rose only 26 percent compared to an

Table 11.5
Changes in the training level of workers (% of total labor force)

2002 skill level (%)	2011 skill level (%)	2020 skill levels (%)
Unskilled, 80.3	Unskilled, 83.7	Unskilled, 76.0
Short training, 3.2	Vocational, 4.2	
Skilled, 8.5	Vocational > 3 months, 4.7	
Secondary vocational, 3.9	Secondary vocational, 3.7	Professional midterrm, 4.4
College or university, 4.2	College or university, 8.4	College or university, 14.9

Notes: The 2002 data are from the "Statistical Data of Labour-Employment in Vietnam 2002," Hanoi 2003, table 62. The 2019 data are from the online report of the 2019 Labor Force Survey, table 2.2, at https://www.gso.gov.vn/en/data-and-statistics/2021/05/report-on-labour-force-survey-2019/.

The 2011 data are from the online 2011 Labor Force Survey, table 18, at http://www.gso.gov.vn/default_en.aspx?tabid=515&idmid=5&ItemID=12541.

Table 11.6
Changes in real wages by level of training, 2011, 2020

Qualification	(Monthly wages in million *dong*)		
	2011 wages	2020 wages	Real % increase
No qualifications	2.59	4.65	+79%
Vocational training	3.70	5.32	+44%
Vocational school	3.10	NA	NA
Professional midterm	NA	4.83	NA
College	3.40	4.95	+46%
University	4.88	6.17	+26%
All workers	3.11	4.65	+49%

Notes: The 2020 data are from the Labor Force Survey as above, but from table 3.3. The 2011 data are from the 2011 Labor Force Survey, but from table 2.14. Data on consumer prices are from *Statistical Yearbooks* and online GSO sources. Wages are monthly and 2020 wages are deflated by the consumer price index with 2011 set as 100.

average real gain of 49 percent. Those with no qualifications saw a 79 percent rise in real wages over the same nine-year period. Other groups were in between the university and unqualified group gains. The job market responded by shifting in shares of workers toward those with more qualifications, but responding to supply changes in different types of labor through relative wage adjustments.

The slow real wage growth for university-educated workers also suggests that a lot of the labor demand growth was not in jobs that justified the rapid expansion of university education. Or it might be that the rapid growth in enrollments lowered the quality of graduates. The fact that workers with average or modest skills realized larger real wage gains than college or university graduates is surely one reason why income distribution has (reportedly) stayed relatively equal. On the other hand, a university-trained worker earns 33 percent more than an average worker and 51 percent more than an unqualified worker. So the existing differentials, though smaller than in 2011, are still large enough to attract more young workers to pay for a university education both from out-of-pocket costs and in reduced earnings while studying. Tripling the share of the college/university trained workforce, not just the new additions, in fifteen years is a notable achievement.

Still, the decline in "unskilled" workers is relatively slow. This may be due to a lack of available opportunities for vocational or higher academic education, even with their rapid expansion. Or it may reflect liquidity constraints. The cost of going to a Vietnamese public university is not high in terms of tuition—a few hundred dollars a year—but the cost of room, board, books, and so on can easily run US$200 a month in major cities, though somewhat less in lower-tier cities. Still, over four years, many students may have trouble financing more than US$10,000 in educational expenses. Private universities are often even more costly. The reportedly high unemployment or underemployment of many recent graduates may also depress willingness to invest in an education that may not pay off immediately.

The solution to this may lie partly in devising shorter and more targeted training opportunities that pay well, much as the 2011 wage survey showed vocationally trained workers earning 9 percent more than college-trained workers. Likewise, the 2020 wage survey showed vocationally trained workers of more than three months earning wages 7 percent higher than college-trained workers. This skill differential suggests that low- to mid-level traditional academic schooling may not be as productive as training focused on specific emerging job demands. The preference of many Vietnamese families to say their child has graduated from a college or university (and to pay for studying in a college) may explain the rapid growth of the higher academic segment even when other options pay well and cost less. It is remarkable that vocationally trained workers accounted for only 4.7 percent of the workforce in 2020. The independent survey of positions described as either "craft and related trades workers" or "plant and machine operators and assemblers" grew from 2010 to 2020—19.6 percent to 26.9 percent. This supports the need for more vocational training.

The educational growth has been shared among men and women. The share of college- and university-trained women (11.8 percent) in the female workforce in 2020 was slightly higher than for men (10.5 percent) in the workforce, but women also had a higher share in the "no technical qualification" group (80 percent) than the men (73.3 percent). The big difference was that many more men were vocationally qualified (8.3 percent) than women (0.7 percent). This may explain, in part, why vocational pay is so relatively high— that men predominate in the vocational job space and dominate relatively well-paid industrial jobs—though it would not explain the large gains made for workers with a vocational qualification.

Robustness of Gains in Reducing Poverty

If Vietnam can continue to combine brisk real GDP growth with a low population growth rate,[17] then the gains in poverty reduction would be secure and could continue, especially if the quality and extent of public services grew. When poverty rates get very low, poverty tends to be due to problems related to mental or physical health and misfortune, or to ethnic isolation, rather than broad economic opportunity. However, there are problems with this scenario that could slow progress and make income distribution less even.

1. Can growth continue at 6–7 percent a year? Most of ASEAN was growing slower even before the virus slowdown, and the "middle income trap" may be relevant for Vietnam. The trap refers to countries that have reached middle-income status but have trouble continuing necessary reforms as entrenched interests fight to maintain their position. GDP growth continues in such cases, often in the 3–5 percent a year range, but a slower rate of progress may create or highlight problems that faster growth covered up. In the case of Vietnam, the political economy is such that poor provinces get large subsidies from the central government, while thriving areas typically share a substantial portion of the revenues collected—Ho Chi Minh City pays 82 percent of its tax collections to the central government, getting to keep only 18 percent. The efficiency of many government transfers has also been questioned. Since most population growth is in the

southeast, Hanoi-Bac Ninh, and Danang, a transfer policy focused on investing more in areas with rapid population growth might be more helpful in reducing poverty than one focused on places where people are leaving. This assumes that decent education and health care will be provided everywhere, but that infrastructure would be built where it is needed after basic roads and electricity are in place. The very low population growth in most areas of low income suggests that the transfers are not keeping most local young people from leaving. Either Vietnam finds a way to make the transfers more productive in the poor areas or shifts some of that spending to the thriving urban areas where most population growth is. Without such an adjustment, urban growth will falter, and since cities provide about 80 percent of national growth,[18] it is likely that overall growth would also slow down. Unless the political allocation of fiscal resources can be more economically efficient, a slowdown in GDP growth is likely. This would slow gains in reducing poverty and improving livelihoods.

2. The huge gains in exports have employed millions of workers directly and probably as many indirectly, and helped real wage gains among those with modest education and training. Recent International Labor Organization reports on robotics suggest that over a decade or two, most jobs (75 percent or more) in sewing clothing, making shoes, and assembling electronics may be taken over by robots.[19] Even if this happens gradually, technical progress, supply chain regionalization, and rising trade barriers may make future job gains for entry-level workers difficult. With a high proportion—still more than three-quarters of all workers—classified as having no qualifications, these trends could knock out one of the pillars of past progress and slow any future gains. It is far from clear that capacity for retraining is adequate for the possible degree of displacement that the combination of technology, environmental damage, and trade barriers might throw up.[20] If young workers were displaced while the population ages, pensions could become difficult to maintain.

   A shorter-term concern is the fallout from the coronavirus and its impact both on family incomes and on FDI into Vietnam. While a continued shift of parts of the supply chain out of China will likely continue, there may well be less reliance on offshore or distant manufacturing in some sectors as well as slower economic growth in traditional export markets and consequently slower import demand growth from them. The ability of Vietnamese firms to add value to FDI exports by becoming core suppliers is currently weak and will have to improve as the increasing wage costs of low-skilled assembly labor drives factories to even lower-wage places. These are challenges and not insurmountable barriers. But Vietnam will have to raise its game if it wants to continue its rapid growth. Factory workers often stop working in factories after a decade or so, for a variety of reasons—the high pressure of the work, stress on eyes and muscles, or exposure to chemicals. Reskilling and finding jobs for these older workers, in addition to those older rural workers who may wish to leave farming, will be a challenge. Few training programs target these workers with limited or narrow skills, and entry-level jobs may be crowded if factory jobs shrink due to technology or shifting trade patterns.

3. Environmental challenges are growing, especially in the Mekong Delta. Heavy over-pumping of groundwater is lowering ground levels by 2–4 cm a year due to soil compression as water is removed—and this in many areas where the ground started at only 100 cm or less above mean sea level.[21] In addition, sea levels are rising due to ice melt and thermal expansion of the oceans. Tropical storms may also intensify, and removal of

mangrove barriers makes coastal areas more vulnerable. Upstream dams add to the challenges faced by reducing silt transport. Taken together, these shocks could cause significant problems in the Mekong Delta's agricultural economy, and instead of low or zero population growth, could drive many poorly skilled workers into the southeast region, where taxes (transfers to the center) are high and infrastructure is already stretched thin. Total Mekong Delta population is about equal to total population in the southeast, which is itself the economic engine of the country.

4. China is notorious for its air pollution, but is probably nearing "peak coal" and is trying to cut its use and reduce mortality from toxic chemicals and small particulate matter that lodges in the lungs. The Chinese Communist Party has responded to public concerns about dirty air. Vietnam's power plans and investments, to the contrary, expand coal use markedly, even though this will kill thousands of people a year. The new power development plan, PDP-8, made progress in some drafts in reducing reliance on new coal plants, but institutional inertia and existing plans still project a growing use of coal. If part of multidimensional poverty reduction comes from better health, a coal-heavy policy would move things backward. Air quality in major cities is already often below WHO standards, and burning millions of tons more a year of imported coal will make it worse. The availability of offshore gas or LNG and cheap renewable energy, along with the growth of low-cost electricity storage, makes this coal-heavy choice particularly strange given public protests against new coal plants.[22]

5. Finally, and less intuitively, the ability to sustain growth could depend on openness. There has been a move to closely control the online flow of information and discussion in Vietnam with the 2018 Internet Law. This law appears to follow China's example and reflects a fear of losing control more than an appreciation of the uses of such discussion in curbing corruption or highlighting problems that need attention. Since much future growth will come from well-trained individuals who know about artificial intelligence and information technology, Vietnam could drive out its best talent and end up slowing its growth in leading sectors. Since these sectors rely on highly mobile talent, the Party and government will have to decide where the greater risks lie—in losing control of online debates or losing growth through talent migration. Just as FDI employment growth has given the entire economy a lift, rapidly increasing IT skills could help the economy transition from low-skilled assembly to more productive jobs that help to sustain growth into upper-middle-income levels.

The Lack of Trend in Inequality

Inequality within a country is often observed increasing with the growth of globalization. Vietnam has opened up its economy in the last quarter century and had much higher levels of exports, imports, and FDI relative to its GDP. There is little data on wealth inequality, aside from the ownership of durable goods, so most discussions have focused on income inequality. The striking aspect of income distribution in Vietnam is that, according to survey data, it has not changed. See the graph (figure 11.2) for estimated values of the Gini coefficient from 1992 to 2018.[23] (A Gini coefficient of zero means perfect equality

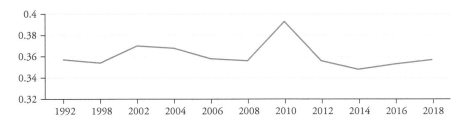

FIGURE 11.2 Gini coefficient in Vietnam from the Living Standards Surveys.
Source: World Bank database, https://data.worldbank.org/indicator/SI.POV.GINI
?locations=VN.

and 1.0 means perfect inequality. The Gini coefficient in China has been between 0.45 and 0.5 since 2000.)

Except for the excursion in 2010, there has been very little variation in this measure of inequality. While some European countries have Gini coefficients below 0.3, and South Korea has a stable Gini just below 0.33, the level of inequality shown here is lower than in most Asian economies. The question must be whether it is real or just statistical—due to inaccurate data.

The accuracy of income inequality data depends on the sampling and the accuracy of responses. There is every reason to believe that the middle of the income distribution is well covered. The governing system is well organized down to the block level, and most land ownership (or control) is also well known, although some high-level individuals may hold many apartments or houses and not declare them. Likewise, there may be some underreporting of transfers, which now exceed US$12 billion a year, or more than 5 percent of GDP. However, the main problem is whether very high-income or transient low-income households are adequately included in the sample (which was about 47,000 households in 2016), when the upper group might constitute only the top 1 percent and the larger, lower group is not necessarily in household lists. And if either group, but especially the rich, are included, does it fully and accurately respond to questions? There is no question that the General Statistics Office is professional and well trained. The people recording the information understand the survey and try to get the right answers. But if a high-ranking Party or government official gives an improbable answer, it may be awkward to press them.

An objective way to probe any possible shortfalls is to compare the survey data with other sources that are likely to be reliable. For example, there were 25 million households in Vietnam in 2016, and the Living Standards Survey of that year found 2.7 percent of the households surveyed owned a car, implying total cars owned at 675,000. Yet the number of registered passenger cars (excluding trucks, buses, or vans) in Vietnam in 2015 was 2 million, and more than 288,000 cars were sold in 2016.[24] So the survey coverage was less than one-third of registrations. This is a large discrepancy, which is unlikely to be explained by two-car families or government- or company-owned cars that may not fit into the category of family-owned vehicles. In any case, it does appear that the relatively wealthy families that own a car are not adequately sampled or did not respond. Owning a car is not secret or embarrassing to report.

If 6–8 percent of households in fact own a car and only a third that number are counted, it suggests that the inequality data are unreliable simply due to sampling problems. Only well-to-do people own cars, and many of them are apparently under-sampled unless they lied about having a car, which is unlikely. If the responses of high-income households that are surveyed are also flawed in terms of income received—there may be illegally received payments or a desire to avoid tax problems—then the reliability problems would be compounded. It is certainly counterintuitive that an economy that moved from collective agriculture and state-owned enterprises and nonfarm collectives in the late 1980s to its current configuration of largely private businesses outside of the relatively shrinking farm sector would *not* show some signs of changes in income distribution. *A tentative conclusion must be that the official data do not reflect reality and that we do not know the actual trends in inequality.*

Another interesting and counterintuitive fact comes from the ratio of food (and alcohol and tobacco) to total living spending. Remember that if a household in 1992 had a food to total spending ratio of 70 percent, they were considered poor. By 2001, the *average* spending on food had fallen to 56.7 percent and by 2016 to 51 percent. However, the top fifth of households were quite close to the overall average and showed little change in the food ratio (staying close to 45–46 percent in the decade to 2016) in spite of large reported real income gains. Using the consumer price index to correct for inflation, real incomes of the top fifth of households more than doubled from 2006 to 2016, yet the reported share of spending on food (and drink and tobacco) stayed close to 50 percent and did not drop. This is not plausible. Most people in the top fifth of households are already well fed, and while the quality of food (and its expense) can certainly increase with growing real incomes, it is very unusual to see the share of food spending remain this high as real income grows so strongly. This again suggests some combination of a failure to capture high-income households or getting responses that leave out pertinent spending.

It appears the basis for observing income inequality and arguably income has problems. It is not clear how to deal with this, because extracting "real" information is hard. Real income has surely grown strongly, but recorded consumer food spending patterns do not reflect this. However, purchases of durable goods do reflect rapidly growing ownership of motorbikes, cars, and smartphones in the last few decades. The preponderance of evidence is that real incomes grew a lot and broadly, but exactly which group got what portion of the gains is not at all clear.

If there are problems with estimating income distribution, there is a black hole regarding wealth. There are no data on wealth distribution, and while there has been furious building of apartments and a growth in the stock market (now worth US$150 billion, with realized and unrealized gains of about US$10 billion a year), it is very difficult to say what share of these assets is held by which part of the population, or how they relate to total wealth. Total wealth is probably about three to four times GDP, or roughly US$1,000 billion. There are reports by private market research groups reporting faster wealth growth in Vietnam than in China, and a total of two hundred ultra-wealthy individuals in 2017 with more than US$30 million in non–real estate assets, and 14,300 millionaires.[25] But the sources and reliability of such estimates are unknown, nor is it easy to fit into an overall picture of wealth holdings. It is safe to say that wealth is held much more unequally than income, and that income inequality is higher than official data show.

Even if the measurement of income inequality is shaky, other trends support the notion that inequality *might* not be strongly concentrating. The labor force survey shows wages of relatively unskilled workers have risen more than for the rapidly growing numbers of highly educated. Rural incomes and spending have grown in relative, but not absolute, terms faster than urban incomes. Numbers of urban workers have grown faster than rural workers, and urban incomes are much higher than rural incomes for most workers, though the relative differences are shrinking. The rise of labor-intensive exports has absorbed a lot of modestly educated labor and provided better wages than were available in agriculture, especially for women. Government programs to provide free education and health care, even in remote and poor areas, should also promote equality over time. These factors all tend to reduce the inequality of income and lower the poverty rate. To some degree, Vietnam is following the model of South Korea and Taiwan in moving low-productivity labor into labor-intensive exports and initially keeping inequality low.

Against these optimistic reasons to believe inequality has not grown much is the public finance system. Taxes in a socialist market economy are mainly levied on labor and at fairly high rates, but not on interest or capital gains. There is no effective annual real estate tax on urban property, which has rapidly risen in price. Many taxes are put on commodities, like sales or value-added taxes, and these do not tax unspent income, which is higher for the rich. Informal payments and fees ("red envelopes" for teachers or doctors and nurses) hit the poor and middle class more than the rich. On balance, the conclusion must be that some are doing much better than others and the official data miss a lot of what is going on.

In addition, there was a 2017 study from the ADB Institute,[26] though the analysis used data only from 2002 to 2010. They concluded that growth was only benefiting the upper fifth, but subsequent labor movements into the thriving areas weaken that argument. Their data caught the jump in the Gini in 2010, since reversed, at least officially. The flood of labor-intensive FDI in the last decade may well undercut their findings.

Tentative Conclusions

Poverty declined from well over half of the population in 1990 to low single digits by 2020. While continued growth will raise most incomes, as was the case in the past, it may not reduce residual poverty without better public services. The causes of poverty may move from low wages or a lack of work to family difficulties such as health issues—including damage from COVID to family finances and education—or the inability to move to places with better public services and insurance. This is especially true if unemployment becomes a systemic problem due to international shocks, as from the coronavirus. That is, there is both episodic poverty and long-running poverty. The latter is diminishing. The former may become more of a challenge.

The definition of poverty is best thought of as a moving target, and it is helpful to expand the concept of poverty beyond income, though still incorporating it, to include public services. The poverty income level itself has been, and should continue to be, moved up as average and median levels of income grow. Setting a poverty line relative to the average or median level of income is one way to recognize the importance of relative poverty, not just some minimum level that covers food and bare nonfood items.

Including clean air, water, and food in the definition of poverty would prompt the government to be more aggressive in dealing with those problems. If it is unhealthy to breathe, drink water, or eat, that is both a public health and a poverty issue.

The relatively high, though declining, levels of poverty in ethnic areas are not surprising, but suggest that additional effort may be fruitful in reducing isolation of these groups. This might be an area where NGOs can be helpful, as working at the village level is necessary, and local people tend to be trusted and effective in connecting their neighbors to opportunities.

The reasons for the rapid decline in poverty have been mainly economic. All workforce growth was in nonagricultural sectors, mainly urban, with higher earnings than rural areas provided. These new jobs were overwhelmingly private, both domestic and foreign. Changes in laws and regulations allowed these sectors to grow rapidly, though investing in health, education, and infrastructure were also supportive. The growth in agricultural output was helpful for those remaining in the agricultural sector. The movement of workers from rural to urban areas allowed incomes in rural areas to grow more quickly in relative terms than did urban incomes. This helped to maintain fairly equal income distribution.

It is likely that the upper-income households are not fully sampled and, if other countries are any guide, do not fully respond to income questions. This renders the income distribution data less reliable than wage or durable goods ownership data. However, income or expenditure for most households is likely to be reasonably well covered. The same cannot be said for wealth, which, aside from durable goods and housing quality, is ignored in household surveys, though data from banks, stocks, and company accounts allow some aggregate guesses. Real estate data are largely missing.

The future continuation of gains is uncertain, due to the political economy of taxes, transfers, and public investment as well as slow reform and a tendency to restrict openness.[27] Rising global protectionism, new technologies that displace labor, and difficulties in controlling pollution may restrict growth opportunities in Vietnam and drive talented people to other places. Supply chain risks may drive production closer to consuming nations. None of these problems are insurmountable, but failing to deal with them could put Vietnam into a position rather like Thailand's, with its slow growth, but at a lower level of income than Thailand now has. Avoiding this relative stagnation will be a major challenge for future government and Party leaders.

Notes

1. Demombynes and Linh Hoang Vu, "Demystifying Poverty Measurement in Vietnam"; another excellent study is Benjamin, Brandt, and McCaig, "Growth with Equity."

2. See "Vietnam Has 4th-Highest Number of Motorbikes."

3. MOLISA is a widely used abbreviation for the Ministry of Labor, Invalids, and Social Affairs.

4. A point seldom made in the aggregate data is the quality of electricity service in many rural areas. The amount and reliability of electricity is often less than required for many rural value-added activities, but EVN (the electric utility) has been improving its reliability in the last decade.

5. Roelen, "Monetary and Multidimensional Child Poverty," reports income and multidimensional poverty rates in Vietnam for 2004, 2006, and 2008. The 2016 and 2017 rates were in the 2017 *Statistical Yearbook*, 359. The 2018 multidimensional national poverty rate is reported in the GSO online review of 2018.

6. These findings are consistent with work by Brian McCaig and Nina Pavcnik, whose chapter in a 2017 IFRI study used data only through 2010. The trends in structural change have continued.

7. For example, in 1998, agricultural income (including agricultural self-employed earnings and livestock/fisheries) in rural areas accounted for 40 percent of total income. By 2016 this fraction had dropped to 27 percent (assorted living standards surveys.) Even workers identifying as agricultural get much of their income from other sources.

8. Benjamin, Brandt, and McCaig, "Growth with Equity," studied income inequality from 2002 to 2014 and found both gains within agriculture and, to a larger extent, the growth of wage labor markets sparked the reported widely shared growth.

9. The Northern Highlands have four high-poverty provinces with high population growth and others with lower, and the separate per capita incomes of each province could not be isolated, so they are not reported in table 11.3.

10. World Bank, "Vibrant Vietnam," 81. This study finds health and education outcomes for minorities are well below average.

11. A separate issue is whether some areas should be in the "urban" category due to their density and nonfarm activity but are still recorded as rural for population purposes. That issue is not considered here but would likely raise the share of population considered urban if an analysis were undertaken.

12. The 2017 Labor Force Survey reports urban *wages* only 36 percent above rural, or 10 percent in real terms. The 2016 Household Survey finds per capita urban *incomes* 88 percent higher than rural per capita incomes in nominal terms.

13. World Bank, "Vietnam's Household Registration System," ix.

14. The 2015 National Internal Migration Survey shows this clearly. On page 42, a graph shows that nearly three-quarters of migrants are in their twenties and thirties and an additional 13 percent are aged fifteen to nineteen. Only 15 percent are forty or older.

15. The 2015 Migration Survey (p. 37) reported a 16.8 percent migration rate for males and 17.7 percent for females. This was a reversal from the 2003 survey, which generally found slightly higher rates for men.

16. General Statistics Office, *Report on Labor Force Survey, 2020*, table 3.3.

17. Projections by the US Census Bureau international database show a growth of Vietnamese from ages sixteen to sixty-five of only 7 percent from 2018 to 2030. Virtually flat numbers of workers in the next decade are likely if more young people continue schooling. Population growth is projected to be 8.8 percent to 2030, or 0.7 percent a year, with a growing proportion of retired people. Extending working ages would tend to moderate these demographic trends.

18. From 2007 to 2019, 73 percent of all workforce growth was in urban areas, and urban per capita incomes in 2016 were 79 percent above rural incomes. In 2004, urban incomes were more than double rural incomes. If we take incomes as an index of productivity, about 82 percent of GDP growth was in urban areas.

19. Chung, Rynhart, and Huynh, "ASEAN in Transformation."

20. Working in a positive direction, many exporters are moving to Vietnam from China due to wage differences, the trade frictions with China, and its COVID-19 lockdowns. This has helped Vietnam, but it is unclear if the gains are durable.

21. See Phu et al., "Resource Governance, Agriculture, and Sustainable Livelihoods in the Lower Mekong Basin."

22. In addition, Vietnam's electricity use per unit of real PPP GDP is higher than China's. A lack of focused effort on conservation has resulted in much higher energy use per unit of GDP than anyone else in ASEAN as well.

23. The World Bank database provides the data in the graph, and it is lower than the income Gini index reported in the 2017 *Statistical Yearbook of Vietnam*, table 353, which shows a fairly stable index of about 0.43 from 2008 to 2016. It is likely the World Bank Gini is for expenditure inequality, which is typically less than income inequality. Adjustments for taxes, transfers, and savings (positive or negative) account for the differences. However, the 2020 *Statistical Yearbook* Gini index is 0.375, sharply lower than past estimates and in the range of the World Bank data.

24. The database of the International Organization of Motor Vehicle Manufacturers (OICA, http://www.oica.net/category/vehicles-in-use/) has data for passenger cars registered up to 2015. The figure for 2016 car sales is from *Vnexpress*, "Vietnam's Car Sales Hit Record in 2016 amid Tax Cuts," though the OICA data for 2016 suggest new (net?) registrations of 117,000.

25. Saigoneer, "Vietnam's Wealth Growth is the Fastest in the World: Report."

26. Sarma, Paul, and Wan, "Structural Transformation, Growth and Inequality," 681.

27. The Thirteenth National Party Congress resolution in early 2021 praised Đổi Mới and suggested carrying those policies forward combined with further rectification and anti-corruption efforts. This is a broad statement, and how it is applied will determine how successful the Party is in sustaining continued equitable and sustainable growth. See VietnamPlus, "13th Party Congress Adopts Resolution."

References

Asian Development Bank. *Key Indicators*. Mandaluyong, Philippines: Asian Development Bank, various years.

Benjamin, D., L. Brandt, and B. McCaig. "Growth with Equity: Income Inequality in Vietnam 2002–2014." *Journal of Economic Inequality* 15, no. 1 (March 2017): 25–46.

Chung, Jae-Hee, Gary Rynhart, and Phu Huynh. "ASEAN in Transformation: How Technology is Changing Jobs and Enterprises." International Labour Office, Working Paper no. 10, July 2016.

Demombynes, Gabriel, and Linh Hoang Vu. "Demystifying Poverty Measurement in Vietnam." Washington, DC: World Bank Group, 2015. https://openknowledge.worldbank.org/handle/10986/21691.

———. *Vietnam's Household Registration System*. Hanoi: Hong Duc, 2016. http://documents.worldbank.org/curated/en/15871468188364218/pdf/106381-PUB-P132640-ADD-ISBN-ON-BACK-COVER-PUBLIC.pdf.

General Statistics Office. *Report on Labor Force Survey 2019* (as well as other years). https://www.gso.gov.vn/en/data-and-statistics/2021/05/report-on-labour-force-survey-2019/.

———. "Statistical Yearbooks." https://www.gso.gov.vn/en/health-culture-sport-living-standards-social-order-safety-and-environment/publication/.

———. "The 2015 National Internal Migration Study." https://www.gso.gov.vn/en/data-and-statistics/2019/11/the-2015-national-internal-migration-survey-3/.

McCaig, Brian, and Nina Pavcnik. 2013. "Moving Out of Agriculture: Structural Change in Viet Nam." Working Paper 19616. Cambridge, MA: National Bureau of Economic Research, 2013.

Nguyen Quoc Anh, Tran Ngoc Thach, and Vo Anh Dung. "Data on Population, Family and Children." Hanoi, 2005.

Phu, Le Viet, Nguyen Van Giap, Le Thi Quynh Tram, Chu Thai Hoanh, and Malcolm McPherson. "Resource Governance, Agriculture, and Sustainable Livelihoods in the Lower Mekong Basin." Petaling Jaya, Malaysia: Strategic Information and Resource Development Centre, 2019. https://rgshirley.com/wp-content/uploads/2020/05/Resource-Governance_LMPPI.pdf.

Roelen, K. "Monetary and Multidimensional Child Poverty: A Contradiction in Terms?" The Hague: Institute of Social Studies, May 2017. https://onlinelibrary.wiley.com/doi/full/10.1111/dech.12306.

Roelen, K., F. Gassman, and C. de Neubourg. "Child Poverty in Vietnam: Providing Insights Using a Country Specific and Multidimensional Model." Maastricht: Maastricht Graduate School of Governance, 2009. https://collections.unu.edu/eserv/UNU:941/wp2008-008.pdf.

Saigoneer. "Vietnam's Wealth Growth is the Fastest in the World: Report." February 5, 2018. https://saigoneer.com/vietnam-news/12537-vietnam-s-wealth-growth-is-the-fastest-in-the-world-report.

Sarma, V., S. Paul, and G. Wan. "Structural Transformation, Growth and Inequality: Evidence from Vietnam." ADBI Working Paper no. 681, March 2017. https://www.adb.org/publications/structural-transformation-growth-and-inequality-evidence-viet-nam.

"Vietnam Has 4th-Highest Number of Motorbikes." Vietnam Colors (blog). July 25, 2019 https://www.vietnamcolors.net/2019/07/vietnam-has-4th-highest-number-of-motorbikes/.

Vietnamnet. "Vietnam Ranks Fourth among Countries with Largest Number of Motorcycles." July 24, 2019. https://vietnamnet.vn/en/society/vietnam-ranks-fourth-among-countries-with-largest-number-of-motorcycles-552924.html.

VietnamPlus. "13th Party Congress Adopts Resolution." February 1, 2021. https://en.vietnamplus.vn/13th-national-party-congress-adopts-resolution/195718.vnp#:~:text=13th%20National%20Party%20Congress%20adopts%20resolution%20The%2013th,closing%20session.%20VNA%20Monday%2C%20February%2001%2C%202021%2012%3A46.

Vnexpress. "Vietnam's Car Sales Hit Record in 2016 amid Tax Cuts." January 11, 2017. https://e.vnexpress.net/news/business/vietnam-s-car-sales-hit-record-in-2016-amid-tax-cuts-3527120.html.

World Bank. "Vibrant Vietnam: Forging the Foundation of a High-Income Economy." Washington, DC: World Bank Group, 2020. https://openknowledge.worldbank.org/handle/10986/33831.

———. "Vietnam's Household Registration System." Washington, DC: World Bank Group, 2016. https://openknowledge.worldbank.org/handle/10986/24594.

CHAPTER 12

Education, Skilling, and Opportunity
in a Market Leninist Order

JONATHAN D. LONDON

Future improvements in the welfare of Vietnam's citizens will depend significantly on the performance of the country's education system and, in particular, its effectiveness in promoting schooling, learning, and skilling as pathways to secure and gainful employment. In recent years Vietnam has been praised for having achieved strong education and learning outcomes at relatively low levels of income. However, beyond basic and lower-secondary education, the country's upper-secondary and postsecondary education subsectors reflect major weaknesses that, if left unattended, will retard the pace of gains in education, learning, and skilling in ways that will undermine the growth and sophistication of the country's economy and, ultimately, the well-being of Vietnam's citizens.

This chapter explores dimensions, sources, and limits of Vietnam's successes in education. It explains why improvements in the performance of upper-secondary education, higher education, and technical and vocational education and training (TVET) are especially urgent. It warns that the persistence of inequalities in Vietnam's education system and labor markets will significantly limit the prosperity of Vietnam and the welfare of its people, while also damaging social trust and further damaging the fragile legitimacy of Vietnam's nondemocratic political system. The chapter advances three claims. The first claim is that, despite its many strengths, the performance of Vietnam's education system—even in basic education—remains compromised by the institutionalization of governance practices that work against the Communist Party of Vietnam's (CPV) stated goal of promoting quality education for all. The second claim is that features of upper-secondary education, higher education, and TVET are limiting these subsectors' contributions to the promotion of quality education, skilling, and employment opportunities. The third claim is that, beyond contradicting the CPV's stated aims, the persistence and intensification of inequalities of access to quality education will do great harm by restricting the supply and demand for skilled workers, undercutting social trust and state legitimacy, and reducing prospective gains in welfare and national prosperity.

Education in Vietnam: Dimensions, Sources, and Limits of Success

In the first decades of the twenty-first century, Vietnam was viewed as a contemporary education outlier, having registered impressive gains in average years of schooling and high marks in international assessments of learning at comparatively low levels of income. Much of Vietnam's success in education stems from the CPV's political commitment to expanding access to basic education, to the determination of Vietnam's people in investing resources in their children's education, and to certain advantageous features of Vietnam's education system, education sector workforce and governance, and popular culture that allows it to deliver basic education at scale relatively better than all other lower-middle-income countries.

And yet Vietnam's education system exhibits numerous weaknesses. Among these, the most crucial stem from accountability gaps, educational inequalities, and the limited quality and accessibility of upper- and postsecondary education. Internationally, Vietnam is known as an education success story, a characterization that is misleading at best. Within Vietnam—and in stark contrast to the tone of international academic and policy literature, the overwhelming sentiment is that the education system is *underperforming* and can and must perform better. This is particularly true in upper- and postsecondary education. This chapter explains why this is the case and identifies key challenges the country faces moving forward.

AN INTERNATIONAL SUCCESS STORY?

For decades, Vietnam's performance on education has exceeded that of all other countries in its income group. In part, this is owing to specific features of Vietnam's social history, including the historical veneration of educational pursuits associated with Vietnam's conservative brand of classical Confucianism, the prominent role of education in Vietnamese anti-colonialism, and subsequent efforts to expand access to education in the north, the south, and on a nationwide basis since 1975. Since 1975, Vietnam's education system has seen periods of stabilization and gradual expansion before spiraling into crisis by the late 1980s and early 1990s in the context of an acute fiscal crisis of the state that attended the breakdown of central planning and hastened the movement to adopt a more market-based economy. At the time, Vietnam was among Asia's poorest countries, and its education system was in tatters. Viewed against this backdrop, Vietnam's achievements have been impressive in several respects.

Indicators of progress are reflected in summary statistics across a variety of dimensions. These include having achieved a 97.1 percent rate of youth literacy for the population of fifteen- to twenty-four-year-olds for both sexes by 2009;[1] explosive growth in enrollments, including near "universal" primary and lower-secondary enrollment; a doubling and tripling of net lower- and upper-secondary enrollment between 1992 and 2006 (a whopping, nearly three-year increase in average years of schooling between 1992 and 2014); and rapid growth in enrollments in postsecondary education driven by the increasing massification of higher education. Vietnam's results on 2012 and 2015 Program for International Student Assessment (PISA) attracted worldwide attention, as Vietnam's marks in language, math, and science far exceeded all other countries in its income groups and rivaled much wealthier OECD countries, including the US and the UK.

Other encouraging trends include the reduction in regional disparities in enrollments in basic education and the elimination of gaps in basic education between boys and girls. By 2010 educational inequalities between boys and girls in primary and secondary education had been overcome—with enrollment among boys somewhat trailing behind—while gaps in enrollment between rural and urban areas have fallen sharply. Significantly, enrollment in secondary and postsecondary education continues to lag for children and youth from lower-income households, and especially for ethnic minority groups, which, with the exception of ethnic Chinese, are vastly overrepresented among the poor. Within the ethnic *Kinh* majority population, girls lead boys in both enrollment and academic achievement. While levels of primary school completion and lower-secondary completion have increased, completion rates for upper-secondary education have grown at a relatively slower rate.

While the quantitative expansion of Vietnam's education system as measured by enrollments has been impressive, the significance of these gains is questionable. Vietnam's impressive gains in average years of schooling reflect thirty years of efforts to expand access to education after the calamitous late 1980s and early 1990s, when the breakdown of already anemic state socialist education occasioned a crisis in the education sector marked by 30 to 40 percent declines in enrollment and an exodus of teachers from their posts. By the mid-1990s the education system regained operational stability, and since then Vietnam has seen the rapid expansion of access to education for all, from primary school through to tertiary education. Notably, a rapid expansion in tertiary education occurred between 2000 and 2010, significantly driven by part-time, on-the-job training and certification programs, and tertiary enrollment subsequently declined. As will be discussed in detail later on, access to tertiary education is extremely unequal across different income groups, with social connections and cash playing a greater role than merit. Though it has expanded in recent years, TVET is often shunned in favor of paths to white-collar employment, a phenomenon common to many East Asian countries. Still, the quality and relevance of TVET remains uneven.[2]

Data on quantitative enrollment are of questionable meaning. First, while enrollment indicators have increased markedly, enrollment data, school completion rates, and measures of student performance across the last three decades are likely all inflated. As in many other bureaucratic authoritarian systems, the measurement of progress in Vietnam's education system reflects a political dynamic in which national, and especially local, officials are incentivized and rewarded for reporting good rather than accurate results. In Vietnam this practice is called "achievement syndrome" (*bệnh thành tích*), an affliction still widespread in 2020. Continued claims, for example, that Vietnam has achieved "universal secondary enrollment" are highly suspect and neglect that the "universalization" (*phổ cập giáo dục*) does not mean even close to 100 percent lower-secondary enrollment, let alone completion. Data on school dropouts are underreported and often only cover children who discontinue studies during the academic year. Progression to and completion of upper-secondary education remain limited among lower-income segments of the population. As Coxhead and Vuong show, from ages fifteen to eighteen, average school enrollments decline from over 90 percent to just over 50 percent, but with much sharper declines for lower-income and ethnic minority children. The persistence of large gaps in progression to upper-secondary education, they demonstrate, reflects slow and unevenly distributed increases in schooling attainment, which may undermine both the sustainability of economic growth and the distribution of its benefits, as the last year of schooling is the highest credential Vietnamese children will earn.[3]

Other qualifications concern quality. However impressive increased enrollments appear, Vietnam's school year at the primary and secondary levels remains among the shortest in the world in terms of classroom contact hours, and majorities of students in primary and secondary education do not study a full day. Despite very striking declines in enrollment disparities between boys and girls, and between rural and urban areas, the quality of education across and within provinces remains highly unequal, while access to quality education is often contingent on household income. Indeed, today in Vietnam, nominally public schools are divided into "high-quality schools" and even "high-quality classrooms," as opposed to normal schools and classrooms, with the availability of the former contingent on the payment of extra fees. In addition to being damaging from the perspectives of opportunity and growth, the institutionalization of these "pay to play" (i.e., pay extra or go home) principles is teaching children in Vietnam a harsh lesson about the role of money in shaping life chances.

The content of education at secondary and postsecondary levels remains a concern. While education in every country plays certain socialization functions, much of mass education in Vietnam is oriented toward political socialization functions, symbolized by the red scarf all Vietnamese children are compelled to don on a daily basis. With respect to the curriculum, much of it remains organized around the top-down transmission and rote memorization of selected material. Across Vietnam, impressive efforts are made to train "talented and gifted students" for international math competitions. One would hope these efforts are not at the expense of promoting better educational opportunities for all.

None of this negates Vietnam's substantial progress in boosting school enrollments; it simply invites a more nuanced view of the country's successes. Nuance is needed, for example, in assessing Vietnam's achievements in the areas of learning and skilling, even though Vietnam's performance does indeed appear to be outstanding given its income level. In the 2012 and 2015 PISA assessment of learning, Vietnam's marks approached or exceeded countries such as the UK and the US (see figure 12.1), raising questions about what Vietnam has done right to achieve such outcomes and what, if anything, the country's experiences might contribute to promote improvements in systems of education worldwide.[4] While no one doubts that Vietnam's performance is superior to other countries

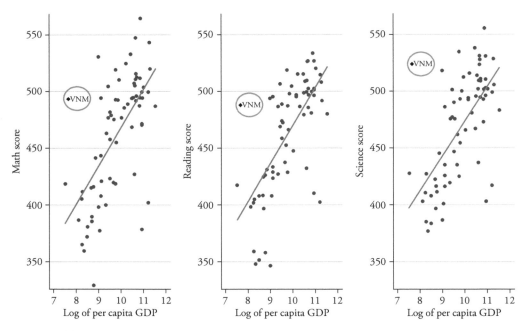

FIGURE 12.1 PISA test scores vs. country income level
Source: PISA database and World Bank's WDI database.

in its income group, there has been debate both outside and in Vietnam about the PISA results' meaning.

In a recent paper, Dang and associates find that Vietnam's strong results on PISA stand up even when controlling for the possibility that the sample of students is not representative.[5] Skeptics allege that the selection and preparation of students for the assessment was faulty. Education sector officials claimed this was not the case. While there are questions as to the validity of the PISA results, other assessments show that Vietnam performs better than all countries in its income group and many countries with much higher incomes.[6] Still, while domestic critics of Vietnam's education system recognize that their country does well compared to other countries with comparable incomes per capita, they emphasize that Vietnam's education system is nonetheless excessively geared to train certain (well-connected and well-resourced) students to test well and is much less successful in training all students how to learn. Notably, in 2019 UNESCO announced it could not verify Vietnam's 2018 PISA results.

EXTRAORDINARY LEVELS OF SUPPORT FOR EDUCATION WITH NOTABLE FINANCING GAPS IN KEY AREAS

While Vietnam faces many challenges in the education sector, the extraordinary support given to education in Vietnam would appear to bode well for the country's future. Three features of Vietnam's education that appear especially advantageous are high levels of po-

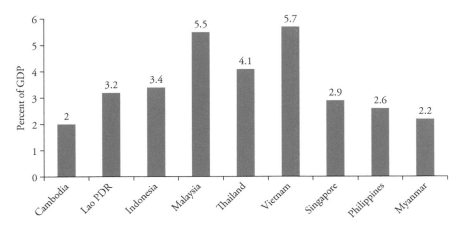

FIGURE 12.2 Public expenditure on education, Southeast Asia
Source: Created from *World Development Indicators 2018*, Government Expenditure on
Education, Total (% of GDP).

litical commitment to education, high levels of societal engagement in the education
sector as reflected both in financial contributions and civic engagement, and the professionalism of Vietnam's education sector workforce. Given these advantages and presum-
ing continued economic growth, the question is not whether there are sufficient resources
for education but rather what sorts of institutional arrangements and practices are required to enhance the education system's performance.

Political Commitment The CPV's commitment to education is striking and traces back to
the party's origins and beyond, to a core theme in Vietnam's anti-colonial struggle for
national independence. In the colonial period, formal education was restricted to a tiny
minority, and the right to education was a core principle in the struggle for national self-
determination. The importance of education was certainly clear among the first generation of anti-colonial leaders (e.g., Phan Chau Trinh), and was taken up by the CPV, both
as a political priority and as part of efforts to win popular support for its revolutionary
program. The CPV has maintained these political and ideological commitments over the
course of the nine decades of its existence.

In wartime and its aftermath, the promotion of education relied on mass mobilization efforts. In the context of economic growth, the CPV's commitment to education has
been reflected in its prioritization of education, both politically and in budgetary terms.
Over the last twenty years the CPV has maintained high levels of public support for education, approaching 5.7 percent of an expanding GDP in 2017, compared with 3.6 for Indonesia in 2015 and 2.6 for the Philippines in 2012 (see figure 12.2). Annually, education
spending accounts (by formal requirement) for 20 percent of the state budget, while private spending on education has continued to grow.[7]

The CPV has not merely spent more on education; it has redistributed resources for
education to poorer regions more than most other middle-income countries, permitting
rapid expansions in enrollment and average years of schooling nationwide. Still, as Vietnam

has grown wealthier and as the scale of public spending on education has increased, questions have arisen as to whether and to what extent the CPV and Vietnam's citizens are getting good value for the money. This prominent role of household finance only amplifies these concerns. Research by the current author and collaborators into subnational governance of Vietnam's education system seeks to establish how education priorities, expenditure, and management can be better aligned with the goals of promoting gains in learning in secondary education while also improving the ability of children to progress through the education system. Further, as will be explained below, major funding gaps remain at the postsecondary level.

Societal Commitment Beyond the CPV's political commitment to education, Vietnam reflects an extraordinary and multifaceted societal commitment to education, reflected not only in the traditional veneration of education and learning, but also, and no less importantly, in broad popular engagement along two key dimensions.[8] The first of these, perhaps somewhat surprisingly to those familiar with Vietnam, is financial participation—*up to half of the financial resources that flow into education on an annual basis comes through household payments* or, as CPV prefers, "household contributions." A second key dimension of participation, and perhaps again somewhat surprising, is seen in public opinion and the emergence of a public education sphere. As will be argued below, in combination with Vietnam's political commitment and with structures of communist accountability, the presence of an engaged fee-paying public may expand and deepen accountability.

Part of Vietnam's "societal buy-in" is thus literal. In the late 1980s, Vietnam experienced an acute fiscal crisis that effectively required the abandonment of central planning in favor of a market-based economy. The education system was hit hard, with many localities experiencing 30 and even 40 percent declines in enrollment over a two-year period, delays in staff pay lasting months, and shortages of books and teaching materials. To prevent the collapse of the public education system, Vietnam's government and people resorted to a system of formal and informal co-payments to finance education, an arrangement that persists until this day. While these arrangements should not be romanticized (for example, they have at times created space for opaque and corrupt practices), the fact that up to 40 percent of finance for *public* education is out of pocket has undoubtedly invited elevated levels of public engagement in the education system. Three additional points warrant emphasis. First, Vietnam's growing economy and political system promise returns to education (and/or to diplomas and titles) and this, together with the expectation of expanded economic opportunity, has incentivized household investments in education. Second, veneration of learning in Vietnamese culture has been widely noted, as has Vietnamese families' willingness to invest time and resources into their children's learning. Finally, as will be explored further later on, in certain aspects Vietnamese households are overspending.

An additional expression of societal commitment is at once striking and fascinating. Though Vietnam's political system limits expression and association, the country exhibits high levels of civic engagement in education. Though channels of expression and modalities of association may be limited to online activities, individual complaints and appeals mechanisms, and state-owned media, it is nonetheless clear that Vietnam exhibits dense civil society–like properties in the field of education. Somewhat paradoxically, controversies and scandals regarding perceived corruption or the questionable value of extensive informal payments have kept the citizenry engaged and the education sector workforce on its toes.

Viewed in positive terms, the lively debates on education policy in Vietnam reflect broad cognizance of the importance of a well-functioning education system and concern about the education system's perceived inefficiency and ineffectiveness, particularly in light of the considerable resources and energy the state and households commit to education and the country's continued lackluster performance with respect to productivity growth and industrial upgrading and the limited quality of postsecondary education. A further concern is whether more education spending buys better education and jobs, an issue to which we will return.

Professional Commitment and Layers of Accountability An additional advantageous feature of Vietnam's education system is the professionalism of its education workforce, which shows up on time, is driven by an ethos of commitment, and is subject to both performance and political accountability structures and mechanisms often missing in developing countries.[9] Part of this stems from circumstances of Vietnam's history. The expansion of education was—in both the north and the south—a central part of efforts at state building and nation building, and education in Vietnam under the Communist Party has a strongly political character. In the immediate postwar years, many teachers performed their duties virtually on a voluntary basis, while during the lean years of the early 1990s, many teachers remained at their jobs despite going months without pay.[10] To this day, education policy in Vietnam in conducted with patriotic zeal.

Surely, Vietnam's education sector workforce exhibits weaknesses, ranging from heavy reliance on outdated teaching methods to corruption (see below). Be that as it may, it is a workforce that has been trained through well-developed systems of teacher education, and one that reflects principles of discipline and seriousness of purpose that are often lacking in middle- and lower-income country contexts. In Vietnam, for example, absenteeism is all but unheard of, which may not be said of all other lower- and middle-income countries. Today, efforts to improve the teaching corps center on the adoption of new standards and new approaches to teaching (more about which below).

More recently, dozens of interviews carried out by the author with national policymakers and local officials and teachers suggest the ways in which Vietnam's political organization promotes consistent attention to education-sector goals from the level of policymaking to the daily management of the country's sixty-three provinces, more than 700 districts, and more than 11,600 communes and urban wards. With respect to political commitment, the research shows how the presence of Party cells and a perpetual political process promoting education-sector goals can be helpful for enhancing the coherence of local educational policy and practices at the school level. Related research has shown how, in the context of national debates about the merits and demerits of various teaching approaches, the country's education bureaucracy and workforce are increasingly if un-evenly willing to experiment with new approaches to teaching and learning,[11] including, for example, the adoption of student-centered approaches to learning and the selective use and modification of approaches used in other countries.[12]

A SUCCESSFUL UNDERACHIEVER?

Despite Vietnam's education system's many effective aspects and its famous PISA test re-sults notwithstanding, questions are raised about the system's underperformance with respect to learning, skilling, equity, and quality, and what to do about it are of the greatest interest to Vietnamese. Among Party leaders and policymakers, and even more resound-ingly among the general population, the resounding consensus is that Vietnam's educa-tion system is *underperforming* (if not performing badly) with respect to the promotion of learning. Recent literature on the political economy of education and learning has the observation that global gains in schooling as measured by enrollment rates and average years of schooling have been accompanied by highly disappointing gains in learning, reflected in the pithy observation that "schooling ain't learning."[13] Achievements notwith-standing, this axiom holds true in Vietnam.

Research on improving education systems has asked what features of countries' politics and public governance and what attributes of the education system (including accountabil-ity relations, finance, curriculum concerns, etc.) can help system performance.[14] While the foregoing discussion has touched on strengths of Vietnam's education system, it is also apparent that features of the politics and governance of education in Vietnam present major challenges. These include, as will be discussed presently, insufficiently accountable and counterproductive forms of decentralization.

Vietnam's Ministry of Education and Training (MOET) leads education policy, but the education and training system is decentralized in its functions. Foreigners unfamiliar with Vietnam may be surprised to know the country and its education system are gov-erned through a highly, and possibly overly decentralized, system within which Vietnam's sixty-three provinces are given unusually high levels of discretion with respect to the allo-cation of budgetary funds for education. An additional observation concerning decen-tralization is that, while in formal terms Vietnam's education policies require the collection of comprehensive data on education, including teacher, student, and school performance,[15] the reality is that the collection and (especially use) of information is extremely thin, ex-cepting all but a small minority of provinces. International agencies have expressed con-cerns about weaknesses in MOET's coordinating capabilities. Almost a decade ago the World Bank found Vietnam's education system lacking in the fields of strategic planning and oversight, calling for better coordination among key stakeholders in the education system and greater efficiency and equity in funding allocation.[16] By 2021 many of these weaknesses remained.

Take, for example, the manner in which education and training institutions are financed and managed at the local level. Two examples illustrate this point. The first concerns sub-national features of Vietnam's education system. Ongoing research explores variation in the way education policy is conducted across provinces.[17] The research suggests considerable variation in the manner in which local (especially provincial) bureaucracies set education-sector priorities along with wide variation and general weakness in education-sector information systems that are meant to promote efficiency in the allocation of resources and accountability in province, district, and school performance around the promotion of quality education for all.

Skilling Gaps While Vietnam's education system has performed admirably with respect to expanding enrollments, increasing average years of schooling, and eye-watering PISA results, its effectiveness in promoting the types of knowledge, learning, and skills that people need remains lacking. Weaknesses in Vietnam's education system are especially apparent in postsecondary education. What the World Bank observed in 2014 still holds today:

> Despite the impressive literacy and numeracy achievements among Vietnamese workers, many Vietnamese firms report a shortage of workers with adequate skills as a significant obstacle to their activity. A majority of employers surveyed [reported] hiring new workers is difficult either because of the inadequate skills of job applicants (a skills gap), or because of a scarcity of workers in some occupations (a skills shortage). Unlike many countries around the world today, Vietnam does not suffer from low labor demand; its employers are seeking workers, but they cannot find the workers that match their skill needs.[18]

As reported by Vu and Perkins in this volume, data from the World Economic Forum's competitiveness report indicate that "Vietnam ranks poorly in a wide variety of areas that are critical to moving up the technology ladder," including ninety-third in the quality of its "education and skills" and 102nd in "innovation capacity." In some respects, these shortcomings are due to technical aspects of education (e.g., content, pedagogy, etc.) that can, in principle, be adjusted through technical fixes, as will be discussed at greater length below. Others stem from the manner in which the education system is governed and the related and adverse effects of systemic incoherence around the promotion of skilled labor and, not least, the pervasive inequalities that drive and aggravate shortages of skilled graduates (see below).

In 2020 the Asian Development Bank (ADB) reported that labor productivity in Vietnam remained below that of other countries in the region and that productivity growth rates in some of the country's industrial sectors has actually declined.[19] In the same year, analysts estimated that only a tiny share (less than 5 percent) of the more than US$84 billion of electronics Samsung exports from Vietnam actually stayed in Vietnam. For decades, Vietnam's education system has been judged to be weak in promoting the kinds of soft and cognitive skills necessary for a globally competitive world economy, and severely lacking in promoting education on such basic themes as universal human rights. Overall, there is wide agreement that Vietnam can and should be more effective in promoting gains in learning and skilling, particularly given the extraordinary support given to education in Vietnam. This feature of Vietnam's education system recommends attention to secondary and postsecondary education, to which the discussion now turns.

Secondary and Postsecondary Education: Paths Forward

While Vietnam has been lauded for its successes in expanding access to primary and lower-secondary education, it is increasingly clear that the country's performance in upper-secondary, tertiary, and TVET is grossly inadequate to the country's needs, both with respect to access and equity and with respect to quality, relevance, and governance. The dimensions and implications of these deficiencies are increasingly apparent. Failure to improve the performance of these education subsectors at scale will limit the scope of gains in the productivity and sophistication of Vietnam's economy, constrain the growth of key industries, and slow the expansion of gainful employment in ways that will undermine both economic growth and well-being. Weak research and innovative capacity will limit the productivity and competitiveness of domestic firms and may reduce foreign investment in the long term. The indefensibly small scale of postsecondary graduates, the persistence of poor governance, uneven quality, anemic finance in higher education, and poor education–industry links in TVET are all major problems that must be addressed, as is the persistence of sharp inequalities of access to postsecondary education across the board. The discussion below clarifies problems in each subsector, detailing progress made and remaining performance gaps.

SECONDARY EDUCATION

The development of secondary education reflects both the great strides Vietnam has made in expanding access to schooling, and their limits. Principally, these are seen in the great successes in expanding access to lower-secondary education, but also the increasingly striking failure of the education system (and of policymakers) to grant sufficient numbers of Vietnamese access to full upper-secondary (i.e., high school) education. Twenty or perhaps as recently as ten years ago one could plausibly argue that Vietnam did not require large majorities of children to complete upper-secondary education. Today completion rates for upper-secondary education are lower than Vietnam requires. In 2019–2020, before the Covid pandemic, the participation rate in upper-secondary education in Vietnam was only 65 percent. Limited spaces and prohibitive costs restrict access, diminishing opportunities for learning and skilling, and restricting occupational trajectories in ways detrimental to the economy overall. Key challenges going forward include identifying ways and means to expand access to upper-secondary education and to better align the aims and content of secondary education with Vietnam's needs.

Some apparent gains in secondary education are misleading. Survey data that reflect over 70 percent net enrollment rates in upper-secondary education are dubious. Over the last two decades, annual growth rates in upper-secondary education have remained near 10 percent. In ongoing research, Coxhead notes a sharp decline in enrollments following the ninth grade, particularly pronounced among the lowest income/expenditure quintile of the population. He notes that in 2012, for example, 92 percent of twelve-year-olds were in school, compared to just 46 percent of eighteen-year-olds. Interestingly, Coxhead finds that estimated average returns to schooling are low in Vietnam, particularly in the private sector, and may have declined.[20] This trend would seem to be supported in the structural transformation of Vietnam's economy, which has included massive increases in low-skill, informal service and manufacturing jobs, the latter associated with processes of urbanization and Vietnam's inward FDI boom, developments that have increased demand for low-skilled labor.

In his contribution to this volume, David Dapice has illustrated that school leavers (i.e., those students who drop out of school) can earn higher incomes than those who complete secondary degrees and go on to higher education. This is consistent with an analysis of data for the 2000–2012 period by Coxhead and Shrestha, who found that across provinces, "a greater presence of foreign invested firms is associated with *significantly higher* rates of early exit [from] school, typically around the end of middle school," adding that these effects did not exist prior to Vietnam's FDI boom and associated economic policy reforms.[21] Whether this trend has continued will require further analysis.

All of this suggests that while modernization is associated with work in "modern" industries, the globalization of Vietnam's economy on the basis of low-skilled employment is not necessarily beneficial to the development of a skilled workforce. Indeed, the development of skilled jobs outside the state sector remains in short supply. For example, more than 50 percent of the labor force in the state sector have completed tertiary education, compared to less than 15 percent in foreign-invested firms and less than 5 percent in domestic private firms.[22] Such an outcome reflects, at the very least, an underdeveloped supply of skilled labor for the non-state economy and a private sector that exhibits low productivity across industry, agriculture, and services. Underlying this are unnecessary restrictions on the supply of skilled labor and sharp inequalities of access to postsecondary education. As Coxhead notes, divergent educational outcomes of different income groups become evident as children reach legal working age.[23] According to the World Bank, Vietnam should be expanding the numbers of students graduating upper-secondary school far beyond current levels; the country's rate of tertiary gross enrollment of 28 percent is among the lowest in East Asia.

HIGHER EDUCATION

Higher education remains a basic weakness in Vietnam's education system and its economy more broadly. Some two decades after the CPV supposedly prioritized education, the Party's political ability to promote significant improvements in the accessibility and quality of higher education is now in doubt. The World Bank argues that higher education in Vietnam can be usefully examined across key dimensions of performance, including equity and access, quality and relevance, research and technology transfer, governance, and resource mobilization and finance. In what follows I roughly follow this argument, while supplementing and critiquing the Bank's analysis where appropriate.

With respect to access and equity, Vietnam has seen a rapid increase and subsequent stagnation in growth of tertiary enrollment. By 2010 (and in 2020 still), roughly 2.3 million Vietnamese were attending universities, more than double that of 2000. Between 1999 and 2008, the number of universities in Vietnam more than doubled, from sixty-nine to 160. By 2018 it had reached 224. While tertiary enrollment has increased, Vietnam's 28 percent rate of gross tertiary enrollment for 2016 remained below the 33 percent average for Southeast Asia, and well below such countries as Malaysia (44 percent), China (48 percent), Singapore (83 percent), and Korea (93 percent). Tertiary enrollment figures can be misleading as up to 20 percent of those enrolled in tertiary education are in "short-cycled" versus fully fledged degree programs; within these, 60 percent of tertiary students were female.[24] Students from the lowest two income quintiles account for just 10 percent of enrollment, owing in part to lower-income students' much lower rate of upper-primary completion as well as to cost and other barriers lower-income upper-secondary graduates face.[25]

With respect to quality and relevance, numerous challenges persist, including poor linkages between higher education and industry, and the underdevelopment of research capacity. One way to address quality is through staffing. A decade ago, university staff tended to be undertrained, underpaid, and granted few opportunities to pursue research. Conditions have improved somewhat. Vietnam remains weak on research in both the physical and social sciences, and, with the possible exception of smaller international universities, still lacks a single university of international standard. The veritable great leap forward envisaged in 2006 by then–Minister of Education Nguyen Tien Nhan, which set a target of training 20,000 new PhDs by 2020, has significantly expanded the ranks of PhDs, but has not substantially affected the quality of Vietnamese universities. By 2017–18, Vietnam's universities had 74,991 teaching staff, of which 20,198 held PhDs. New plans to achieve 7 percent of teaching staff with completely foreign PhDs by 2025 imply an increase in staffing under this category of 6,825. Physical production targets are alive and well.[26]

In general, higher education in Vietnam remains weak with respect to research and technology transfer. The top university in Vietnam in 2020 stood in the 801st position globally, according to *Research Week*. Citation indicators place Vietnam lower than Indonesia, and much lower than countries such as Malaysia, Thailand, and Singapore, while Vietnam's rate of patents is less than a tenth that of Malaysia and less than 1 percent of world-leading China.[27] As the number of Vietnamese trained overseas increases, so too does the possibility of enhancing the quality of higher education in Vietnam. Be that as it may, working conditions in Vietnamese universities make it difficult for young scholars to remain active researchers.[28] As for non-state universities, their management remains subject to state oversight and intervention, with the hostile takeover of Hoa Sen University in Ho Chi Minh City and the delicate negotiations around the establishment and governance of Fulbright University as cases in point. The arrival of Fulbright together with the conglomerate Vin Group into higher education are noteworthy, in that both, along with several other universities, appear genuinely committed to supporting research.

Among the more promising developments are those seen in the gradual internationalization of Vietnamese universities, the continuous increase in Vietnamese students abroad, and the establishment and expansion of autonomous foreign universities, such as Fulbright

University Vietnam (FUV), which was formally established in 2016 with US State Department funds. With respect to the internationalization of Vietnamese universities, numerous
universities have developed collaborative relations with foreign universities. By 2017–18
more than 60,000 Vietnamese were studying overseas, including nearly 25,000 in the US.
While small in size, FUV offers truly innovative programs and aspires to offer American-
style liberal arts education of practical value to Vietnam. If there is a desire for proof, look
no further than FUV's inaugural conference on New Approaches to University Education
in Asia, sponsored by the university together with Coca-Cola.

The governance of postsecondary education, overseen by a combination of universities and various line ministries (rather than the Ministry of Education) and the prime
minister's office, adds excessive organizational complexity. Postsecondary education in
general has been shaped by pervasive and poorly regulated commercialization, resulting
in quality concerns.[29] While Vietnam's formal laws reflect a movement toward greater
autonomy, universities operate within a constrained decision space, particularly with respect to curriculum development and other areas, while academic freedom remains tightly
bound. The education bureaucracy continues to constrain local initiatives. In rural areas,
especially remote regions, recent efforts have been made to expand higher education, with
Thai Nguyen University being a recent example.

A final set of challenges concerns finance. One common indicator of political commitment to any policy priority is budgetary support. By this measure, the CPV's commitment to higher education is in itself in doubt. According to the World Bank, between
2004 and 2015, Vietnam's budgetary spending on tertiary education amounted to just
0.33 percent of GDP (well below that of Indonesia and Thailand and less than half the
rate of China), just 1.1 percent of total government spending, and just 6.1 percent of total
public spending on education and training.[30] Since 2015 there has been no major change
in these patterns. The consequences of this funding shortfall have been largely passed on
to students, adversely affecting enrollment expansion, especially among students from
lower- and middle-income households. By 2020, household payments remained the primary source (55 percent) of public universities' budgets, compared to 22 percent from the
state budget and 23 percent from other sources. Effective scholarship and loan schemes on
a large scale do not yet exist.

Thus far, the diversification of modalities of higher education provision and management has yielded limited gains. Discussion of whether public universities ought to be
privatized has faded.[31] By 2019, higher education in Vietnam still occurred largely within
the sphere of the state. Of 330 colleges and universities in 2007, roughly fifty were non-
state, accounting for roughly 12 percent of tertiary students. Vietnam's universities include
170 public universities, sixty private or people's founded universities, and five universities
with 100 percent foreign financing.[32] The scale of non-state universities is small by comparison. By 2020, government targets stipulate non-state providers of higher education
would account for 40 percent of enrollments. By 2017, however, roughly 1.5 million of 1.7
million enrolled in universities were in public universities. The recent policy to expand
higher education institutions' autonomy, encouraging them to self-finance, has met with
only limited uptake, including only twenty-three out of 171 public universities.

TECHNICAL AND VOCATIONAL EDUCATION AND TRAINING

Vietnam has seen rapid growth in the scale and scope of postsecondary technical and vocational education (TVET), but the contributions of this expansion to the development of a more productive and skilled workforce is the subject of debate, and Vietnam still has shortages of skilled workers and technicians. While the government has set ambitious plans for TVET, critics have found it to frequently lack specifics. The technical and vocational training that is in place tends to be beyond the reach of poorer segments of Vietnam's population. Among Vietnamese youth, as in other countries, there is a strong preference for white-collar work, even as white-collar jobs require upper-secondary or higher credentials.[33]

In the ADB's own words, "state-managed TVET and labor market support systems have remained weak, fragmented, and inadequately funded, most of them still performing poorly and lacking in ability to adapt to changing market demands." The dispersed organization of TVET education—even in the public sector—has made coordination difficult and frequently ineffective. Historically, vocational education in Vietnam has been administered through a variety of functional ministries, including education, health, construction, youth, women, and social affairs. The 2015 Law on Vocational Education put it under the authority of the Ministry of Labor, Invalids, and Social Affairs (MOLISA), even as a substantial share of the sector lies outside the authority and oversight of that ministry.

Nguyen and Nguyen (2019) provide an overview of efforts to improve the quality of TVET. They note that between 1999 and 2008 alone, the number of vocational schools (or colleges) nearly trebled, from eighty-four to 209, and ballooned to over 400 by 2017 before declining again more recently The growth of TVET has been characterized by a process of boom, bust, and stabilization. The period of rapid growth in TVET was characterized by pronounced unevenness in quality. Many training centers went belly-up, but since then the situation has stabilized. By 2015 Vietnam's government had identified 195 sets of national occupational skill standards, including 189 sets of test questions and practical skills tests for eighty-three occupations. By the same year, thirty-six centers for national occupational skills had been established, staffed by 1,785 assessors, of whom 120 had advanced certifications.[34]

Over the last decade, the government has sought to promote vocational training for the rural workforce. Government Decision 1956 of 2009 stipulated increased spending for this purpose, with specific efforts to provide rural workers with a greater set of transferable skills. Objectives included providing vocational training for around 1 million rural laborers annually, including 100,000 rural-based cadres and civil servants, improving the quality of training, generating jobs and employment, providing ideological training, and increasing the capacity of socioeconomic administrators in rural areas. The share of education spending going to vocational education is difficult to obtain, as much of the TVET and spending occurs *outside* the education sector. For the period 2010–14, TVET spending on average accounted for 1.2 percent of total public expenditures and the equivalent of

0.35 percent of GDP. This compares to around 1 percent of GDP in many European countries but accords with rates in Southeast Asian countries.[35] In the meantime, private (household) spending on TVET has increased more than fourfold since 2004, based on figures from the General Statistics Office and the Asian Development Bank.[36]

Spending on TVET, whether public or private, does not ensure quality or efficiency with respect to skills formation. As summarized by UNESCO-UNEVOC, perennial problems in the TVET sector include the quality of education; poor guidance, and inadequate information about TVET possibilities, which leads upper-secondary students to pursue higher education instead of TVET; the challenge of bringing in non-state providers able to deliver quality training at affordable costs; the low ratio of skilled workers working in the VET sector, which undermines scalability; the outdated technology used by TVET providers and domestic SMEs, which makes them unsuitable for employing TVET graduates; and diminishing the role of SMEs in TVET.[37] Efforts to promote financial autonomy for TVET institutions have encountered problems with the low management and financial capabilities that prevail among most TVET education providers. Ho and Tran provide an account of introducing foreign approaches to TVET in the Vietnam context. More recent efforts have aimed to enhance the quality of TVET, exemplified by joint Vietnamese-German efforts to establish "centers of excellence" in TVET capable of delivering high-quality training oriented to the demands of the Vietnamese markets and based on international standards in the fields.[38]

In the meantime, government support for the prioritization of TVET budgets for women are undermined by weak capacity and political will for gender-responsive budgeting at the local level and has yet to result in any sharp improvements. The efficacy of training and employment schemes directed at poor and ethnic minority labor has been compromised by the basic levels of training available. Overseas exports of unskilled minority and low-income labor for work has increased.

Prospects and Challenges

While Vietnam's education system has excelled in expanding the scale of basic education, teaching children to test, and transmitting dominant ideologies, there is wide agreement that it should and can be more effective in promoting gains in learning and in generating large-scale increases in skilled workers that experts within and outside the country agree the country needs. While the CPV has worked consistently and admirably to promote more equitable access to quality education in primary and lower-secondary education, progress in the fields of upper-secondary and postsecondary education has been slow, raising general concerns for Vietnam's future. With a desire to highlight some of the specific challenges Vietnam faces, but confronting space limitations, the discussion below addresses three sets of challenges, including inequality, corruption and education finance, and labor markets and opportunity structures.

EDUCATIONAL INEQUALITIES

In all countries, inequality is a fundamental feature of social life, even as features and magnitudes of inequality and their practical effects vary considerably across and within countries. In all countries, education systems, as major social institutions in their own right, both reflect and figure centrally in the determination of inequalities, variously contributing to the reproduction, intensification, and reduction of inequalities. The manner in which education systems shape inequalities is highly complex and context specific, reflecting not only political and socioeconomic circumstances in a given country or locality, but also general and specific features of education systems at various levels of governance. These features may include the goals and conduct of education policies, features of national and local education bureaucracies, as well as features of schools nationally, locally, and at different levels of the education system.

Unequal opportunities around education, skilling, and employment opportunities pose a threat to Vietnam's prosperity and the well-being of its citizens. Despite progress in basic education in particular, broad ranks of Vietnam's population are being effectively blocked from the educational opportunities that could and should be made available to them, effectively condemning them to precarious livelihoods in low-productivity, low-wage informal sectors, in which employment is uncertain and opportunities for upward mobility for individuals and households are limited. Urgent attention is needed to address the ways in which the education system is limiting opportunities for lower- and middle-income households, including expanding the number of students completing upper-secondary education. Studies show us that educational inequalities in Vietnam are on the rise, that the country has made slow progress on expanding full-day schooling (especially to poorer segments of the population), that enrollment in upper-secondary education has leveled off and lower-income students are dropping out, and that ethnic minorities lag far behind across a battery of indicators. Statistical analysis shows how education, skilling, and labor market opportunities can be dependent on the interaction of such variables as location, gender, ethnicity, socioeconomic status, and health/disability.[39] Yet the manner in which these variable dimensions of difference operate is not always amenable to statistical analysis. Such vital considerations as power relations and informal institutions fall into this category.

Educational inequalities are visible in the uneven quality of education. In the current context, efforts at improving education and skilling are being geared to the development islands of excellence within a broader sea of mediocrity. Alas, these "islands of excellence" are in limited supply and often available on a pay-as-you-go basis, effectively crowding out large shares of the population. The TVET sector, though expanding in scale, has thus far been able to achieve only incremental improvements in quality, despite encouraging movements toward closer ties with industry. Dropouts and school leavers face careers in the low-paid informal service sector, while graduates from universities and TVET centers enter a labor market with limited prospects, often owing to inadequacies of training, and often face the necessity of paying under the table for a job. At other moments, economic elites seem to legitimize inequality in self-serving ways. This is reflected in the frequently heard quip in Vietnam among defenders of inequality arguing that urban middle- and higher-income households that "have a demand" for better services should be permitted to buy them, which misses the point.

Vietnam's education system and its labor markets need to function in a more inclusive and less transactional manner. Until they do, shortcomings in secondary, vocational, and tertiary education will continue to retard gains in learning and skills formation, depress productivity growth, aggravate inequality, and unnecessarily slow improvements in living standards and national prosperity. The poor quality of higher education also drains national resources. As of 2017, Vietnamese households were estimated to have exported US$3 billion for the education of their children overseas.[40]

CORRUPTION AND EDUCATION FINANCE

Although it is unfair to tar the entire education sector workforce and system as corrupt, corruption stands out as a pervasive feature of Vietnam's education system and a systemic threat to its performance. Truong highlights the potentially distorting effects of corruption in the education sector and human capital formation. On the negative side, corruption, she finds, reduces positive effects of local public spending on educational achievement and worsens labor quality by diverting funds from their intended uses while discouraging investments of time and effort in accumulating knowledge and skills, adversely affecting the quality of labor. Seemingly mild forms of petty corruption such as under-the-table payments can be systematically ruinous, blocking the progression of children from lower-income households as if they were second-class citizens.[41]

In Vietnam, education ranks fifth among the twelve most perceived corrupt sectors.[42] Still, in the education system, as in labor markets as discussed below, there is a palpable sense that what matters most is not *what* you know or how well you *learn*, but rather who you know or how much you are willing to pay to for grades, a diploma, extra tutoring, opportunities to retake exams, the chance to sit in a "high-quality" classroom within a public school, and other institutionalized and pervasive informal costs attached to education in Vietnam. Advocacy groups note that corruption in the education sector is frequently associated with building and repair of schools, contracts for teaching equipment and printing textbooks, bribes of schools and teachers, schools' receipt of wage bonus allowances that never go to staff, teachers bribing school administrators to be assigned to classes they want, parents and students paying bribes to secure good grades, tip-offs on tests and test retakes, effectively coercing students to attend extra classes to the disadvantage of nonparticipating students, and collecting unofficial fees.[43] The widespread sale and purchase of diplomas (another frequent topic of scandal) adds a further disincentive to skills acquisition. Anecdotal evidence communicated to the author suggests securing a position in a Ph.D. program by means of cash payments can run in the range of US$10 to US$20,000. All of this suggests that to be effective, interventions intended to address inequalities (e.g., scholarships) need to address the manner in which markers of disadvantage intersect with formal and informal attributes of power relations (clientelism).

Vietnamese accounts of experiences in the education system around corruption, quality, and equity concerns show why education in Vietnam is a "lightning rod" issue, especially given Vietnam's high levels of public and household education spending, the tremendous energy and expense Vietnamese children and their families devote to learning, and the sense that the education sector is less effective in providing Vietnamese the skills they need.[44] A highly publicized corruption scandal in 2019 reaffirmed this sense. After being implicated in a large-scale high school cheating scandal involving children of officials, including his own (whose test results were conspicuously the best in his home province), Central Committee member and Hà Giang Province's Party Secretary Triệu Tài Vinh was removed from the position of provincial party secretary and "promoted" to the position of deputy chief of the Party's central economic committee.

A key contributor to corruption, but also the field that must ultimately contribute to its resolution, is to be found in the complex mix of formal and informal education payments and teachers' reliance on these payments. These arrangements pose challenges to all education stakeholders, yet represents a key policy and regulatory challenge that Vietnam must address. As Vietnam grows wealthier, there may be new opportunities to achieve long-sought-after breakthroughs in public sector salary reform or, at the very least, steps toward a more efficacious and transparent system. Across Vietnam there is a very significant, and often in urban areas a massive, difference between official salaries and what teachers can and do earn in the informal market. In order to bridge this credibility gap between what teachers earn publicly and what they earn in reality, the government has legitimized "household contributions" as part of its promotion of the "societalization" of education finance.[45] Moving forward, Vietnam's government, schools, and communities will need to achieve a more transparent set of regulations that can leverage public support and sympathy for teachers while also improving the accountability of schools and teachers.

LABOR MARKETS

Human capital theory suggests the development of skills is crucial to income gains and upward mobility in a given division of labor. Yet the assumption that increased spending on education will automatically lead to learning and skills formation is misbegotten. Vietnam is a case in point. While the CPV has consistently declared a commitment to developing Vietnam's human resources, its effectiveness in translating investments in education into a skilled workforce has been profoundly mixed. In secondary education, institutionalized features of the education system squeeze out low-income students, limiting opportunities for continuous learning. In higher education, inaccessibility, uneven quality, limited relevance, and underdeveloped research capacities are conspiring against further gains in human capital.

In the World Bank's Human Capital Index, Vietnam outperforms all middle-income countries, and its performance in education is the best in Southeast Asia. Yet the efficacy of its system of higher education is limited. Sung and Raddon's analysis shows how in Korea and Singapore, states shaped markets and used education and training as a vehicle for achieving long-term economic and social development goals, but also that recent times have seen the gradual erosion of these states' ability to do so, especially in the context of globalization, and even in the context of the sophistication of their economies and state regulatory functions.[46] China has performed better than Vietnam in equipping its population with skills through higher and technical education,[47] but the interest in and capacities for developing a comparably performing system in Vietnam appear limited.

Coxhead and Phan argue that Vietnam has developed a segmented labor market for skilled labor in which differential access to skills and credentials initially born of unequal access to education contributes to the expansion of inequalities. Additional inequalities are reflected in the uneven quality of education across regions and the ways in which the education system's operational features undermine equitable access to quality education.[48] Sarma and colleagues contend that improving skills acquisition for those at the lowest percentiles of the income distribution will be vital to reducing inequality.[49] While higher education and educational credentials in Vietnam are strongly associated with higher wages, the capital-skill complementary dynamic as described above has yet to materialize.

In neoclassical economics, the concept of capital-skill complementarity refers to a felicitous set of circumstances in which growth in skilled labor increases returns on capital investments, while the resulting increased capital stocks raise the productivity of labor, thereby, in principle, increasing incomes and (hence) returns to education and well-being. That this is the case reflects both the fantastical assumptions in neoclassical economics of a world without politics and power relations and actually existing features of Vietnam's education system, which prevents too many young people from getting the skills they need. As David Dapice has observed in his chapter in this volume, if more schooling does not produce needed work skills, investors will find Vietnam a high-cost location for upgrading but a low-cost destination for assembly work. Over the long term this will be counterproductive, as it will contribute to the reproduction of a labor force lacking sector-specific skills as well as such intangible skills as creativity, communication, and social-emotional skills that employers seek.[50]

Additional concerns regarding labor markets stem from emergent features of Vietnam's accumulation regime, which, as noted in other chapters, is heavily centered on speculative investments, especially in real estate development, and low-end manufacturing activities with few backward linkages to the domestic economy. While these points cannot be developed further for this chapter, the underlying points are that economic resources are being steered away from investments in industrial upgrading; meanwhile, opportunities to harness foreign investment for industrial upgrading are being squandered. The expansion of formal service-sector jobs such as in tourism, while carrying the substantial benefit of generating employment, will not contribute to the development of an advanced economy. As Malcolm McPherson has shown in this volume, limited skills are also hampering productivity gains in agriculture. Labor exports to neighboring and distant countries and limited years of employment within low value-added export processing zones offer limited short-term fixes with respect to employment and income, but unpromising strategies for the long term. As it stands, Vietnam's industrialization remains superficial, and this trend will continue without a political commitment to economic sophistication.

In a recent analysis, Coxhead and Vuong hypothesize a connection between increased participation in low-skill employment (e.g., in manufacturing and in service jobs in cities and in areas where manufacturing is centered) and slow and regionally uneven improvements in the rate of educational progression to upper-secondary school.[51] Whether growth in these kinds of employment is driven by slow growth in wage premiums (i.e., that higher wages can be achieved by secondary school leavers than those with upper-secondary and even undergraduate credentials) or the costliness of completing upper-secondary education (e.g., due to the need for extra classes, user fees, travel times, other costs) cannot be fully demonstrated. Paradoxically, the reduced rate of rise in the skill premium may be owing in part to the failure, thus far, of Vietnam's economic policies to generate and attract employment opportunities, owing, in part, to shortages of skilled labor. Employment in labor-intensive manufacturing draws most heavily from the lower middle-income (third to fifth deciles) of the population, not the upper half, according to the ILO.[52]

Ways Forward

Acknowledging the many strengths of Vietnam's performance on education and its impressive progress in improving living standards, the analysis presented in this chapter has suggested how and why the country is appropriately understood as *underperforming* with respect to learning, skilling, and the promotion of economic opportunity. It has emphasized the ways in which the acceleration of learning and skilling and the expansion of opportunities for gainful employment, economic security, upward mobility, and national prosperity have been restricted owing to institutionalized features of the country's education system and labor markets and the manner in which these are routed through prevailing power relations. Focusing on secondary, vocational, and higher education, this chapter explained how and why these rungs of Vietnam's education system have been and remain sites for both the development and underdevelopment of "human capital." Further, it has shown how and why institutionalized features of Vietnam's market-Leninist system mediate the manner in which learning and skilling are deployed, nurtured, and wasted in the country's globally linked market economy and the implications of this with respect to the welfare of its citizenry.

How Vietnam's education system performs with respect to preparing its citizens for life in local and global market orders has enormous implications for Vietnam's trajectory of social change in the near and long terms. At stake is not simply how many children go to school and how Vietnam fares on international tests. The development of the education system will determine the kinds of knowledge, skills, and intellectual curiosities and capabilities current and future generations will or will not acquire and will or will not be able to bring to bear on the development of their livelihoods, and will depend on the local and global economies within which their lives will play out. Vietnam's leaders have spoken routinely of their desire to boost productivity growth, speed the development of national innovative capacities, expand opportunities, and realize broad-based, sustained improvements in living standards for all Vietnamese. Achieving these goals will depend crucially on addressing challenges in the education system, only some of which have been highlighted in this chapter.

Efforts to improve the education system's performance need to be viewed in a broader context. As observers of Vietnam point out, in the short to medium term, addressing administrative, infrastructural, and logistical bottlenecks alone would accelerate Vietnam's growth going forward, and the country's comparative advantage will remain its low-cost and disciplined labor force for some time to come.[53] This suggests interventions in economic policy will be crucial in addressing bottlenecks in the education system. Granted, gains in productivity do not always depend on improvements in education systems (as a great deal of skilling takes place on the job or through automation). And increased skills or productivity will not necessarily lead to higher incomes for workers. Be that as it may, improvements in the performance of the education system in promoting learning and skilling will enhance the well-being of Vietnam's citizens and their quality of life.

Notes

1. UNESCO-UNEVOC, *TVET Country Profile: Viet Nam.*
2. Asian Development Bank, *Viet Nam: Technical and Vocational Education.*
3. Coxhead, Vuong, and Nguyen, "Getting to Grade 10 in Viet Nam."
4. Akmal, "Vietnam's Exceptional Learning Success."
5. Dang et al., "What Explains Vietnam's Exceptional Performance?"
6. See, for example, Espinoza Revollo et al., "Education and Learning."
7. World Bank data tables, 2018.
8. London, "Contemporary Vietnam's Education System."
9. McAleavy, Ha, and Fitzpatrick, *Promising Practice.*
10. London, "Contemporary Vietnam's Education System."
11. DeJaeghere et al., "Qualitative Video Study."
12. See, for example, Le, "Another Textbook Project?," 223–39.
13. Pritchett, *The Rebirth of Education.*
14. See, for example, Wales, Magee, and Nicolai, "How Does Political Context Shape Education Reforms?"; Levy et al., *The Politics and Governance of Basic Education*; Pritchett, "Learning about the Politics of Learning"; Hickey and Hossain, *The Politics of Education.*
15. Le Khanh Tuan, *Đánh giá Đội ngũ Giáo viên Bằng Phương Pháp Chỉ số.*
16. World Bank, *Vietnam Workforce Development.*
17. London and Nguyen, "Vietnam's Education System."
18. Bodewig et al., *Skilling Up Vietnam.*
19. Asian Development Bank, *Viet Nam: Technical and Vocational Education.*
20. Coxhead, "Must Try Harder?"
21. Coxhead and Shrestha, "Globalization and School–Work Choices."
22. Coxhead, "Must Try Harder?"
23. Coxhead and Shrestha, "Globalization and School–Work Choices."
24. UNESCO-UNEVOC, *TVET Country Profile: Viet Nam.*
25. World Bank, *Improving the Performance of Higher Education in Vietnam,* 3.
26. Quy Hien, "Sỏ có 7% giảng viên VN học tiến sĩ ở nước ngoài."
27. World Bank, *Improving the Performance of Higher Education in Vietnam,* 5.
28. It is estimated that, by 2007, more than 45,000 Vietnamese had university degrees from "Western" universities. Pham and London, "The Higher Education Reform Agenda."
29. London, "The Benefits and Limitations of 'Socialization.'"
30. World Bank, *Improving the Performance of Higher Education in Vietnam.*

31. For example, see Bùi Trọng Liễu, "Vì sao không nên cổ phần hóa đại học công?"
32. Vietnam.net, "Những con số "biết nói" về giáo dục đại học Việt Nam."
33. OECD, *Youth Well-Being Policy Review.*
34. UNESCO-UNEVOC, *TVET Country Profile: Viet Nam.*
35. Wright, *Financing TVET in the East Asia and Pacific Region.*
36. Asian Development Bank, *Viet Nam Secondary Education Sector Assessment, Strategy, and Road Map.*
37. UNESCO-UNEVOC, *TVET Country Profile: Viet Nam.*
38. Ho and Tran, "Appropriation of Foreign Approaches."
39. Dang et al., "What Explains Vietnam's Exceptional Performance?"; Coxhead and Phan, "Princelings and Paupers?"
40. Pham, "Bộ trưởng Giáo dục."
41. Truong Thi Hoa, "The Effects of Corruption on Human Capital."
42. Transparency International, "Corruption Perceptions Index 2016."
43. Towards Transparency, "Corruption in the Education Sector."
44. Viet V. Q., "Giáo dục Việt Nam."
45. London, "The Benefits and Limitations of 'Socialization.'"
46. Sung and Raddon, "Approaches to Skills in the Asian Developmental States," 565–83.
47. Che and Zhang, "Human Capital, Technology Adoption."
48. Coxhead and Phan, "Princelings and Paupers?"
49. Sarma, Paul, and Wan, "Structural Transformation, Growth, and Inequality."
50. Luong Hoai Nam, "Giáo dục và định mệnh quốc gia."
51. Coxhead, Vuong, and Nguyen, "Getting to Grade 10 in Viet Nam."
52. ILO, "Decent Work and the Sustainable Development Goals in Viet Nam."
53. Dapice et al., "Choosing Success."

References

Akmal, Maryam. "Vietnam's Exceptional Learning Success: Can We Do That Too?" *Rise Programme,* April 9, 2018. https://riseprogramme.org/blog/Vietnam_Exceptional_Learning_Success.htm.

Andrews, M. *The Limits of Institutional Reform in Development: Changing Rules for Realistic Solutions.* Cambridge: Cambridge University Press, 2013.

Ansell, B. W. *From the Ballot to the Blackboard: The Redistributive Political Economy of Education.* Cambridge: Cambridge University Press, 2010.

———. "Traders, Teachers, and Tyrants: Democracy, Globalization, and Public Investment in Education." *International Organization* 62, no. 2 (2008): 289–322.

Asian Development Bank. *Viet Nam Secondary Education Sector Assessment, Strategy, and Road Map.* Manila: Asian Development Bank, 2020.

———. *Viet Nam: Technical and Vocational Education and Training Sector Assessment.* Manila: Asian Development Bank, 2020.

Bodewig, C., R. Badiani-Magnusson, K. Macdonald, D. Newhouse, and J. Rutkowski. *Skilling Up Vietnam: Preparing the Workforce for a Modern Market Economy.* Washington, DC: World Bank Group, 2014.

Bùi Trọng Liễu. "Vì sao không nên cổ phần hóa đại học công?" March 9, 2008. http://www.diendan.org/viet-nam/co-phan-hoa-truong-111ai-hoc-cong.

Busemeyer, M. R., and C. Trampusch. "Review Article: Comparative Political Science and the Study of Education." *British Journal of Political Science* 41, no. 2 (2011): 413–43.

Che, Y., and L. Zhang. "Human Capital, Technology Adoption and Firm Performance: Impacts of China's Higher Education Expansion in the Late 1990s." *Economic Journal* 128, no. 614 (2018): 2282–2320.

Coxhead, Ian. "Must Try Harder? The Market for Skills and Economic Inequality in Indonesia and Vietnam." Presentation to the Institute for Developing Economies, Japan, 2017.

Coxhead, Ian, and D. Phan. "Princelings and Paupers? State Employment and the Distribution of Human Capital Investments among Households in Viet Nam." *Asian Development Review* 30, no. 2 (2013): 26–48.

Coxhead, Ian, and R. Shrestha. "Globalization and School–Work Choices in an Emerging Economy: Vietnam." *Asian Economic Papers* 16, no. 2 (2017): 28–45.

Coxhead, Ian, N. Vuong, and P. Nguyen. "Getting to Grade 10 in Viet Nam: Challenges from Deprivation, Discrimination, and a Booming Job Market." Discussion Paper no. 359. Jakarta: Economic Research Institute for ASIAN and East Asia, 2021.

Dang, H. A. H., and P. W. Glewwe. *Well Begun, but Aiming Higher: A Review of Vietnam's Education Trends in the Past 20 Years and Emerging Challenges.* Washington, DC: World Bank Group, 2017.

Dang, H. A. H., P. Glewwe, J. Lee, and K. Vu. "What Explains Vietnam's Exceptional Performance in Education Relative to Other Countries? Analysis of the 2012 and 2015 PISA Data." Bonn: Institute of Labor Economics, 2020.

Dapice, D., D. Perkins, X. T. Nguyen, T. T. A. Vu, T. D. Huynh, J. Pincus, and T. Saich. "Choosing Success: The Lessons of East and Southeast Asia and Vietnam's Future." In *A Policy Framework for Vietnam's Socioeconomic Development, 2011–2020,* edited by B. Wilkinson. Cambridge, MA: Harvard University Press, 2008.

DeJaeghere, Joan, Vu Dao, Phuong Luong Lan, and Phuong Nguyen. "Qualitative Video Study of Teaching and Learning Competencies in Vietnam: Some Initial Findings." *Rise Programme,* April 12, 2019. https://riseprogramme.org/blog/qualitative-video-study-teaching-learning-competencies-vietnam.

Doan, T., Q. Le, and T. Q. Tran. "Lost in Transition? Declining Returns to Education in Vietnam." *European Journal of Development Research* 30, no. 2 (2018): 195–216.

Doner, R. F., and B. Ross Schneider. "The Middle-Income Trap: More Politics than Economics." *World Politics* 68, no. 4 (2016): 608–44.

Espinoza Revollo, P., L. Benny, D. Le Thuc, and H. Nguyen Thi Thu. "Education and Learning: Preliminary Findings from the 2016 Young Lives Survey (Round 5): Viet Nam." Young Lives Factsheets, Young Lives, 2017.

Hickey, S., and N. Hossain, eds. *The Politics of Education in Developing Countries: From Schooling to Learning.* Oxford: Oxford University Press, 2019.

Ho, T. T. H., and L. T. Tran. "Appropriation of Foreign Approaches for Sustainable Development and Transformational Changes in Vietnamese Vocational Education." *Higher Education, Skills and Work-Based Learning* 8, no. 4 (2018): 527–43.

ILO. "Decent Work and the Sustainable Development Goals in Viet Nam." Hanoi: International Labour Organisation, 2019.

Kingdon, G. G., A. Little, M. Aslam, S. Rawal, T. Moe, H. Patrinos, T. Béteille, R. Banerji, B. Parton, and S. K. Sharma. *A Rigorous Review of the Political Economy of Education Systems in Developing Countries. Final Report.* London: Department for International Development, 2014.

Le, A. V., and P. H. Hoang. "Basic Education in Vietnam." In *International Handbook on Education in South East Asia,* edited by L. P. Symaco and M. Hayden, 1–23. Singapore: Springer, 2022.

Le, H. M. "Another Textbook Project? The Implementation of Escuela Nueva in Vietnam." *Educational Research for Policy and Practice* 17, no. 3 (2018): 223–39.

Le Khanh Tuan. *Đánh giá Đội ngũ Giáo viên Bằng Phương Pháp Chỉ số* (Teacher evaluation through statistical indicators methods). Hanoi. Education Press, 2018.

Levy, B., R. Cameron, U. Hoadley, and V. Naidoo, eds. *The Politics and Governance of Basic Education: A Tale of Two South African Provinces.* Oxford: Oxford University Press, 2018.

Levy, B., and M. Walton. "Institutions, Incentives and Service Provision: Bringing Politics Back In." ESID Working Paper no. 18. Manchester: Effective States and Inclusive Development Research Centre, University of Manchester, 2013.

London, Jonathan. "The Benefits and Limitations of 'Socialization': The Political Economy of Services in Viet Nam." Unpublished UNDP Policy Discussion Paper, 2013.

———. "Contemporary Vietnam's Education System: Historical Roots, Recent Trends." In *Education in Vietnam,* edited by Jonathan London. Singapore. ISEAS Press, 2011.

London, Jonathan, and Nguyen Hoang Phuong. "Vietnam's Education System: How Coherent is it for Learning." RISE Working Paper. https://riseprogramme.org/research 2022.

Luong Hoai Nam. "Giáo dục và định mệnh quốc gia" (Education and the fate of the nation). *Viet Nam Express*, August 28, 2014. https://vnexpress.net/giao-duc-va-dinh-menh-quoc-gia-3035920.html.

McAleavy, T., T. T. Ha, and R. Fitzpatrick. *Promising Practice: Government Schools in Vietnam*. Berkshire, UK: Education Development Trust, 2018.

Nguyen, D. T., and H. C. Nguyen. "Technical and Vocational Education and Training (TVET) in Vietnam." In *Vocational Education and Training in ASEAN Member States*. Singapore: Springer, 2019.

OECD Development Centre. *Youth Well-Being Policy Review of Viet Nam*. Paris: EU-OECD Youth Inclusion Project, 2017.

Pham T. M. T. "Bộ trưởng Giáo dục: Người Việt chi 3–4 tỷ USD cho du học mỗi năm." June 6, 2018. https://ndh.vn/thoi-su/bo-truong-giao-duc-nguoi-viet-chi-3-4-ty-usd-cho-du-hoc-moi-nam-1235985.html.

Pham, Thanh Nghi, and Jonathan London. "The Higher Education Reform Agenda: A Vision for 2020." In *Reforming Higher Education in Vietnam: Challenges and Priorities*, edited by Grant Harman, Martin Hayden, and Pham Thanh Nghi, 51–64. Dordrecht: Springer, 2010.

Pritchett, Lant. "Learning about the Politics of Learning." *Rise Programme*, March 21, 2019. https://www.riseprogramme.org/blog/learning-about-politics-of-learning.

———. *The Rebirth of Education: Schooling Ain't Learning*. Washington, DC: Center for Global Development, 2013.

———. "A Review Essay—*The Politics and Governance of Basic Education: A Tale of Two South African Provinces*." *Rise Programme*, June 28, 2019.

———. "Understanding the Politics of the Learning Crisis: Steps Ahead on a Long Road." In *The Politics of Education in Developing Countries: From Schooling to Learning*, edited by S. Hickey and N. Hossain. Oxford: Oxford University Press, 2019.

Quy Hien. "Sẽ có 7% giảng viên VN học tiến sĩ ở nước ngoài" (There will be 7% of Vietnamese lecturers studying for PhDs abroad). *Thanh Nien*, January 26, 2019. https://thanhnien.vn/se-co-7-giang-vien-vn-hoc-tien-si-o-nuoc-ngoai-post822905.html.

Sarma, V., S. Paul, and G. Wan. "Structural Transformation, Growth, and Inequality: Evidence from Viet Nam." ADBI Working Paper no. 681, March 2017. https://www.adb.org/publications/structural-transformation-growth-and-inequality-evidence-viet-nam.

Snilstveit, B., J. Stevenson, D. Phillips, M. Vojtkova, E. Gallagher, T. Schmidt, H. Jobse, M. Geelen, M. G. Pastorello, and J. Eyers. "Interventions for Improving Learning Outcomes and Access to Education in Low- and Middle-Income Countries: A Systematic Review." London: International Initiative for Impact Evaluation, 2015.

Sung, J., and A. Raddon. "Approaches to Skills in the Asian Developmental States." In *The Oxford Handbook of Skills and Training*, edited by C. Warhurst, K. Mayhew, D. Finegold, and J. Buchanan. Oxford: Oxford University Press, 2017.

Tikly, L. "Globalisation and Education in the Postcolonial World: Towards a Conceptual Framework." *Comparative Education* 37, no. 2 (2001): 151–71.

Tikly, L., and A. M. Barrett. "Education Quality and Social Justice in the Global South: Towards a Conceptual Framework." In *Education Quality and Social Justice in the Global South: Challenges for Policy, Practice and Research*, edited by L. Tikly and A. M. Barrett. London: Routledge, 2013.

Towards Transparency. "Corruption in the Education Sector." Hanoi: Towards Transparency Viet Nam, 2018. https://towardstransparency.vn/en/corruption-in-the-education-sector/.

Transparency International. "Corruption Perceptions Index 2016." Transparency International, 2017. http://transparency.org.tt/2017/01/26/corruption-perceptions-index-2016/.

Truong Thi Hoa, T. "The Effects of Corruption on the Human Capital Accumulation Process: Evidence from Vietnam." *Economics of Transition and Institutional Change* 28, no. 1 (2020): 69–88.

UNESCO-UNEVOC. *TVET Country Profile: Viet Nam*. Bonn, Germany: UNESCO-UNEVOC International Centre for Technical and Vocational Education and Training, 2018. https://unevoc.unesco.org/wtdb/worldtvetdatabase_vnm_en.pdf.

Viet, V. Q. "Giáo dục Việt Nam: nguyên nhân của sự xuống cấp và các cải cách cần thiết" (Education in Vietnam: The causes of its worsening performance and essential reforms). *Thời đại mới*, No. 13, March 2008. http://www.tapchithoidai.org/ThoiDai13/200813_VuQuangViet_1.htm.

Vietnam.net, "Những con số "biết nói" về giáo dục đại học Việt Nam" (The numbers that "talk" about Vietnamese higher education). August 11, 2017. https://vietnamnet.vn/vn/giao-duc/tuyen-sinh/nhung-con-so-biet-noi-ve-giao-duc-dai-hoc-viet-nam-389870.html.

Vegas, E., and A. Jaimovich. "The Importance of Early Childhood for Education and Development." In *Routledge Handbook of International Education and Development*, edited by S. McGrath and Q. Gu. Abingdon, UK: Routledge, 2015.

Wales, J., A. Magee, and S. Nicolai. "How Does Political Context Shape Education Reforms and Their Success?" ODI Dimension Paper no. 6. London: Overseas Development Institute, 2016.

World Bank. *Improving the Performance of Higher Education in Vietnam: Strategic Priorities and Policy Options*. Washington, DC: World Bank, 2020.

———. *Vietnam Workforce Development: SABER Country Report 2012*. Washington, DC: World Bank, 2012.

———. *World Development Report 2018: Learning to Realize Education's Promise*. Washington, DC: World Bank, 2018.

Wright, Robert Palmer. *Financing TVET in the East Asia and Pacific Region: Current Status, Challenges and Opportunities*, vol. 2. Washington, DC: World Bank Group, 2017. http://documents.worldbank.org/curated/en/494921508752195355/Financing-TVET-in-the-East-Asia-and-Pacific-Region-current-status-challenges-and-opportunitie.

CHAPTER 13

Family, Gender, and New Constellations

Crises and Changing Configurations in Late Đổi Mới Vietnam

HELLE RYDSTROM

This chapter explores the ways in which "the family" (*gia đình*) in late Đổi Mới Vietnam is undergoing transformations as a political institution, social organization, and lived experience. The notion of crisis, the chapter argues, provides an analytical vantage point to capture discrepancies between the ways in which the family is construed ideologically at the systemic level and how family life is experienced at the lifeworld level. Drawing on a combination of material, including ethnographic data, I focus on two examples, each of which indicates how an officially promoted family ideal is contested in a socioeconomically changing society. These two examples refer to, first, families that depart from a predominant heterosexual matrix and second, families that suffer from men's abuse of their female partner.

A family is assumed to be governed by a unique kind of affection due to love and morality rather than by contracts and regulations.[1] In the Vietnamese context, families are officially recognized as an ideological foundation and seen as the "cells" of society. A family is expected to consist of a heterosexual couple, preferably with two children, who are striving to live a "Happy and Harmonious Family Life" (*gia đình hạnh phúc hòa thuận*), and maybe even reaching the standard of a "Cultured Family" (*gia đình văn hóa*).[2] Families that do not live up to established family ideals tend to be seen as a hub for disruption and "social evils" (*tệ nạn xã hội*), an epithet that covers a variety of practices that are either prohibited or deemed to be immoral.[3]

This chapter draws on my various research projects on Vietnam, with generous funding offered by the research council (Sarec) of the Swedish International Development Corporation Agency (SIDA), the Swedish Research Council (VR), and the Riksbankens Jubileumsfond for the Advancement of the Humanities and Social Sciences. My gratitude goes to those who shared their experiences with me during various periods of fieldwork I have conducted in northern and even central Vietnam, but who cannot be mentioned for anonymity reasons. Thus, all names referred to are pseudonyms. Many thanks to Eva Hansson, Börje Ljunggren, and Dwight Perkins, as well as Le Dang Doan and Vu Thanh Tu Anh for inviting me to be part of the Harvard-Stockholm-Fulbright Vietnam book project. I appreciate the editorial assistance offered by Gretchen O'Connor.

The family, however, is transforming against the backdrop of Vietnam's rapidly developing economy.[4] Alternative family constellations have become more common, including divorce,[5] single female–headed households,[6] premarital cohabitation,[7] extramarital arrangements,[8] intercontinental relationships,[9] and same-sex partnerships.[10] Migration from rural to urban areas to search for employment is common,[11] and rural women especially migrate to distant countries to take up work, mainly in the domestic sphere,[12] to cover various family expenses such as health care and education, in an increasingly privatized economy.[13]

Changing Families

In accordance with official family ideals, the majority in Vietnam live in a heterosexual marriage; an organization that is defined by the General Statistics Office[14] as "a person who is recognized by the marriage laws or customs of the locality as married or self-identified as living with a person of the opposite sex as a married couple or in a union." Within the last ten years, the overall rate of unmarried persons has declined from 26.8 percent in 2009 to 22.5 percent in 2019.[15] The mean age at first marriage in Vietnam differs between men and women, in 2016 by 4.1 percent with 27.2 years for men and 23.0 for women, though with a higher mean age for both females and males in the urban areas.[16] Such figures not only imply that women are expected to get married, but even that the sex ratio balance is skewed.

Since 1999, the number of male births per 100 female births has grown steadily in Vietnam. In 1999, the sex ratio at birth was 107.0 male births to 100 female births, and in 2016, 112.2 male births to 100 female births.[17] As in other East Asian countries such as China and South Korea, sons are preferred over daughters in Vietnam. With the sex selective technologies, which became available in Vietnam by the late 1980s, the desire for having a son manifested demographically as an "erratic rise" in sex ratios at birth.[18] The preference for male progeny has paved the way for a phenomenon that has become known as "the missing girls."[19]

Lan, who is in her early forties, lives in the outskirts of Hanoi with her husband and their two children. She reflected upon having sons and daughters, saying, "I am happy with a daughter and a son because it is not good with two sons or two daughters," because this would in her mind impact negatively on the balance of a family. She also noted that "today you can have as many children as you want. It is not like it used to be when you only could have two children," thereby referring to couples who continue to have children until a male progeny is secured.[20]

In a survey from 2012, the United Nations Population Fund (UNFPA) found that 70.7 percent of male respondents in Vietnam prefer to have a son because of "lineage," while 51 percent refer to old-age support, and 49 percent to "ancestor worship." Loc, a young man from northern Vietnam, explained the meaning of male progeny by observing that "old people say that a father gives something special to his son. Only a son has the right to follow the tradition of his father. It is different with daughters. My fate would suffer if I only had girls. Families that continue to have girls suffer." Son preference is reflected in marriage figures by an overrepresentation of men, thus implying a shortage of female partners. In 2019, for example, 73.4 percent of men were ever married (a category that includes those who were married, widowed, separated, or divorced) and 81.5 percent of women.[21]

The General Statistics Office found that women in the lower age brackets marry to a larger extent than men.[22] However, the numbers decline after the age of thirty-nine, which implies that women are expected to get married earlier than men. Hence, in 2016, 88.8 percent of women aged thirty-five to thirty-nine were married, 2.3 percent widowed, 2.9 percent divorced, and 0.6 percent were separated. As for men in the same age group, 89.0 percent were married, 0.3 percent widowed, 2.3 percent divorced, and 0.5 percent were separated. These numbers not only indicate that women live longer than men, as fewer men are widowed than women, but also show an upward trend in the divorce rate, though it remains low.

In 2016, the divorce rate for men aged fifteen years and older was 1.2 percent and the separation rate 0.4 percent, while the rates for women in regard to the same two categories were 2.3 percent and 0.6 percent, respectively.[23] More women than men want to pursue with a divorce.[24] Changes in socioeconomic conditions, employment far from home, adultery, conflict, and violence are all factors that impact the divorce figures, according to research conducted by Nguyen Huu Minh.[25]

Single life is increasingly seen in Vietnam as an option for how to organize life. Younger people tend to delay marriage due to education and work plans in tandem with a growing feeling of independence from predominant norms, inspiration from global media, public debate on marriage, and experiences of violence in their childhood home.[26] The category "staying single and never getting married" applied in Vietnamese surveys can be taken as also including those who are cohabiting in a heterosexual relationship prior to marriage, as well as LGBTQ[27] persons who are living in a same-sex relationship, because official censuses do not account for such specified information.[28]

At an overall level, the single household rate (i.e., one-person households) increased from 7.2 percent in 2009 to 10.9 percent in 2019.[29] In 1998, 1.5 percent of men in the age bracket forty-five to forty-nine years were single and 3.5 percent of women. In 2009, these numbers had grown to 2.1 percent of men being single and 6.6 percent of women.[30] While the overall rate of unmarried persons among those aged fifteen years and older declined by 4.3 percent, the rates within the category "divorce or separation" increased from 1.4 percent in 2009 to 2.1 percent in 2019.

Younger generations, as noted by Nguyen Huu Minh, perceive marriage in a different light than older generations. Younger generations fancy the idea of staying single and never getting married. In 2006, 26 percent of young people aged twenty-two to twenty-five agreed with the idea of staying single, and the numbers had increased to 47.8 percent in 2009. More women than men agreed with the idea of remaining single and never getting married, as 55.4 percent of women considered singlehood as an option, compared to 50.4 percent of men. For both groups, these growing numbers signal changed attitudes to marriage, as also illuminated by findings that 8.7 percent of all households consisted of one person in 2016.[31] The prospect of staying single and never getting married especially appeals to urban youth in the age bracket twenty-two to twenty-five years, of whom 62.3 percent agreed that they would want to live a single life. As regards rural youth in the same age group, 50.4 percent agreed with the same proposition.[32]

Family arrangements are patrilocal, but a shift is currently taking place from an extended family organization to a nuclear one. In 2006, 64.8 percent of married couples aged eighteen to sixty lived together with the husband's family.[33] In 2019, 65.5 percent of the entire Vietnamese population lived in households composed of two to four persons, while the number of households consisting of five persons or more had declined from 28.9 percent in 2009 to 23.6 percent in 2019.[34]

As for extended families with several generations living together, the larger family is often divided into smaller generational units and separated household areas. While it is most common to live with the husband's parents and maybe even other members of his natal family, some couples decide to live with the wife's family. In any case, a man would usually be the head of the household, as 75.6 percent of those who are head of household are men and only 24.9 percent are women.[35]

According to my ethnographic data, sharing a household is appreciated as a way of providing intergenerational support and care; while ailing family members enjoy day-to-day support from younger kin, they look after the household's children. As Yen from northern Vietnam matter-of-factly stated, "My parents-in-law take care of family issues." She is in her early thirties and lives in the outskirts of Hanoi together with her husband and their three young children in a house that they share with Yen's parents-in-law. As both Yen and her husband have full-time factory jobs, Yen's mother-in-law takes care of the two youngest children, both of whom are under the age of three years.

Politics

Debates in Vietnamese society over the role of the family in postcolonial Vietnam resonate with both Confucian and Marxist ways of understanding the family and its function in society.[36] Studies on the Vietnamese family have examined kinship, hierarchies, gender, morality, reproduction, sexuality, and violence, as well as the family as a site for implementation of ideologies, policies, and economic priorities. As these studies elucidate, the family is understood as a critical political instrument in Vietnamese society.[37]

Vietnamese family politics echoes Friedrich Engels's writing on the family.[38] As society's "cellular form," the patriarchal and feudal family is imbued with norms and behaviors, according to Engels, which should be targeted and revoked. Social and economic inequalities could be eradicated, in the view of Engels (and Marx), through a revolution in the wake of which a socialist society would arise.[39] After the revolution in 1945, the family was thus identified by the Communist Party of Vietnam (Đảng Cộng sản Việt Nam) as a critical political and ideological tool. By the aid of the family, a new society should be developed by repealing a pre-revolutionary, feudal, patriarchal, and Confucian family type that worked as a vessel for "backward" (*lạc hậu*) norms and practices.[40]

Confucianism was the backbone of Vietnamese society from 1075 CE to 1919 CE.[41] Confucianism recognizes Heaven's Son, the emperor, as the ruler of a society in which harmony, order, and stability should prevail. To reach such goals, Three Bonds (*Tam Cương*) commanded a subject's loyalty to the emperor, children's piety toward their parents, and a wife's obedience to her husband.[42] In addition, Three Submissions (*Tam tòng*) clarified that a daughter obeys her father, a wife obeys her husband, and a widow obeys her son.[43] Even further instructions were provided for girls and women, such as the Four Virtues (*Tứ đức*), which described qualities desired in females, including industriousness (*công*), appearance (*dung*), speech (*ngôn*), and conduct/behavior (*hạnh*). Clearly, "a woman's place was by the hearth; her worth was largely measured by her skills at maintaining the warmth of that hearth, namely the well-being of her family."[44]

The Confucian family was critiqued by the Communist Party for being an oppressive institution.[45] Confucian vestiges were to be eradicated in postrevolutionary Vietnam to stimulate the building of a new "modern" (*hiện đại*) family guided by the principle of "equality of men and women" (*nam nữ bình đẳng*).[46] Capturing such tensions concerning the role of the family during Vietnam's societal transition process, in 1991, Rita Liljeström and Tuong Lai described in their edited volume *Sociological Studies of the Vietnamese Family* how a Confucian legacy in their view represented both a fine family tradition and an obstacle to the development of progressive and modern families in communist Vietnam.[47]

In postrevolutionary Vietnam, a family was understood to consist of a heterosexual, monogamous, and modern couple, with equal partners who had entered matrimony on a voluntary basis.[48] As a means of building such families, on December 28, 1959, the Law on Marriage and the Family was passed by the National Assembly to destroy "remnants of feudalism" and to build "happy, democratic and egalitarian families."[49] The new law had huge consequences for the rights of women and girls, as the law prohibited parental forced and early marriage, the use of property as a betrothal gift, mistreatment of women, concubinage, wife-beating (Art. 3), and endorsed the right to own property before and after marriage (Art. 15).[50]

Families

Over the years, official debates and campaigns have promoted family ideals, which have been aimed at mobilizing citizens to organize their lives in conjunction with principles such as affection, respect, and faithfulness.[51] Hence, in 1962, the "Cultured Family" (*Gia đình Văn hóa*) campaign was launched, and decades later, in the wake of the introduction of the Đổi Mới (Renovation) policy in 1986,[52] in July 1988 the Central Steering Committee adapted the goal to "build a harmonious, happy, [and] progressive family."[53]

Opening Vietnam's doors to the global market economy resulted in a major expansion of private-sector activity boosted by growing inflows of foreign investment. Agricultural and industrial production increased, multiple sectors were permitted, while enterprise and entrepreneurship thrived.[54] The reformation of the economy also meant far-reaching social changes, and general poverty reduction programs were implemented across the country. During this period, the image of the Cultured Family became an important leitmotif.

According to Le Thi, an official voice in Vietnam's public discourse, the family should function as an economic unit in transitional Vietnam, which was providing both for the family as such and for society at large.[55] Portraying the family as an economic engine, Le Thi implied the pertinence of building well-ordered families that did not suffer from any type of crisis, thereby distancing itself from "backward" tendencies.[56] Such sentiments are reiterated in the Marriage and Family Law of 2000, with its emphasis on the family as the foundation of a good society in which all citizens should contribute to the upholding of the "marriage and family regime" by:

> Building, perfecting, and protecting the progressive marriage and family regime, formulat[ing] legal standards for the conduct of family members; protect[ing] the legitimate rights and interests of family members; inherit[ing] and promot[ing] the fine ethical traditions of the Vietnamese families in order to build prosperous, equal, progressive, happy, and lasting families.[57]

The principle of equality between husband and wife is central to the law, as highlighted by the command that "husband and wife are equal to each other, hav[e] equal obligations and rights in all aspects of their family." Husband and wife, furthermore, are expected to be "faithful to, love, respect, care for, and help each other, so that they together can build a prosperous, equal, progressive, happy, and lasting family."[58]

The overall aim of the Vietnam Women's Union (Hội Phụ nữ Việt Nam), one of the mass organizations in Vietnam,[59] is to advance the conditions of women in Vietnam by representing their interests to the state, and state policies to its members.[60] While the central level of the union offers advice to the government in regard to law preparatory work, local unions organize a variety of activities such as small clubs where women can gather to discuss various topics including how to build and sustain a harmonious family.[61]

The role ascribed to women in achieving the goal of well-functioning, happy, and harmonious families, and by extension a thriving society, is salient for the union, according to which "building prosperous, equal, advanced, and happy families is the common goal of almost all the VWU's [Vietnam Women's Union's] programs and activities."[62] For the period 2017–22, for instance, the national Vietnam Women's Union runs an "emulation movement" to ensure that "women study actively, work creatively, and build happy families." For the same period, the union's Action Plan specifies as one of its "Main Tasks" (point 1.2) to "conduct communication, mobilization, and support for women to build prosperous, progressive, happy, and cultured families." This task is intended to "increase women's awareness of the positions and roles of the family, traditional values, and good family relationships."[63] To reach such goals, women's practice of *tình cảm* (sentiments/emotions/feelings) becomes a critical social capacity. *Tình cảm* is a quality appreciated in both men and women, though especially in women as a capacity thanks to which crises and conflicts may be avoided due to a woman's accommodating behavior.[64]

Crises

As a decisive moment that holds power to differentiate, a crisis appears as "conditions that make outcomes unpredictable."[65] A crisis can be seen as calling into question the structures of an order or system.[66] The boundaries of a crisis usually are assumed to be set by time, in the sense that a crisis is expected to have a beginning and an end. Identifying a difficult period with which one must deal, a crisis typically is seen as a phase imbued with challenges that, if overcome, may lead to renewal and improvement, as catharsis.[67]

A crisis, however, could also result in prolonged challenges and thus transmute from event into process.[68] In rupturing coherency and amplifying uncertainty for the future,[69] a crisis thus could evolve from a sudden "state of emergency"[70] into a "crisis of chronicity,"[71] an "interregnum," where the old is falling apart and progress is hampered.[72] Thus, rather than being a pivotal moment that eventually could result in a better future, a crisis could also transform into a new and painful normality.[73]

For my examination of the family, a crisis perspective can lay bare a chasm between a philosophy of history as portrayed by ideals, judgments, and assessments, on the one hand, and an empirical reality of lived experiences, which may contradict ideological narratives, on the other. Such discrepancies condition societal and/or individual crisis. At the lifeworld level, crisis experiences might lead to calls for recognition of new subjectivities and critique of political goals.[74] At the systemic level, challenges to dominant narratives can trigger a crisis of principles and ideological concerns.[75]

Families departing from official ideals might from a systemic viewpoint be denounced as struggling with a crisis in terms of being in an "unstable state of affairs during which a decisive change is impending."[76] Considered from within the family, at the lifeworld level, members of a family that diverges from official images might find themselves in a "situation that has reached a critical phase,"[77] thus affecting prospects for a "liveable life."[78]

Contingencies

With the implementation of the Đổi Mới policy, the Vietnamese government became increasingly concerned about societal challenges as those were thought to be induced by "social evils" (*tệ nạn xã hội*).[79] Social evils are assumed to be brought into the country by a global world that could corrupt Vietnam's "beautiful traditions and customs."[80] To handle this perceived threat, the Vietnamese government in 1995 launched a campaign to eliminate all social evils and "poisonous culture" (*văn hóa độc hại*). These referred to a wide range of social practices including homosexuality, sexually transmitted diseases, domestic violence, prostitution/sex work, drug use, and gambling.[81]

Newspapers, television, social media, and daily talk in contemporary Vietnam reverberate with the rhetoric of past campaigns against the backdrop of an increasingly globalized society.[82] While families, and especially women, have been under considerable pressure to adjust to the government's family campaign goals, these also speak to a concern in Vietnam about morality in a global world and how society, family, and young people are affected by such changes.[83] Growing up in a global community where values are seen as fluctuating, younger generations are thought to be particularly susceptible to values that might contest established traditions and lead to alternative lifestyles, including free partner choice, sexual encounters before marriage, cohabitation prior to marriage, single parenthood, and same-sex partnership.[84]

While the term "social evils" continues to circulate in public discourse in Vietnam,[85] the language has been moderated due to a recent shift in the focus of social policy. Various social problems have been addressed in a more direct way, and harm prevention strategies have been introduced to cope with various problems such as intimate partner violence.[86] The Department of Social Evils and Prevention, under the Ministry of Labor, Invalids, and Social Affairs (MOLISA), remains obliged to prevent and manage social evils, but rather than mainly condemning the existence of social challenges, the agency has applied an approach that is more problem solving.[87]

New Constellations

In the Law on Marriage and Family of 1986, homosexuality was circumvented and thus silenced.[88] The law from 2000, however, is explicit in defining homosexuality as an oppositional negative to the heterosexual regime that is the pillar of the law. The 2000 version of the Law on Marriage and Family repeatedly puts forward that the matrimonial union consists of a man and a woman in stipulating that "marriage is forbidden . . . between people of the same sex" (chap. 2, Art. 10.5). In this vein, the 2000 law prohibited cohabitation of same-sex couples without registration, that is, a marriage certificate.[89] Even though homosexuality as such was not banned by the law, in public debate same-sex sexuality tended to be stigmatized as immoral.[90]

This heteronormative matrix provides a framework for how the family is understood and from which it is difficult to escape, as highlighted by Cam from northern Vietnam. Cam, who is in his forties, remembered how he came out as gay to his parents, saying, "they accepted it, but from the beginning they were still very sad, of course, because every family in Vietnam wants their son to have a wife and to have kids later on. That is one of the most important things in Vietnamese culture: to have a son [so] their kids [can] follow the tradition and maintain the family line."[91]

Nonconforming family constellations are framed in Vietnamese society as if they were in a state of crisis that should be solved. Yet a path has opened for improved societal recognition of homosexuals in Vietnam, as Vietnamese nongovernmental organizations (NGOs) devoted to promoting the rights of LGBTQ people have gained some traction in Vietnamese society and obtained international support.[92] On August 5, 2012, the Vietnamese government thus allowed the first Pride Parade to be held in Hanoi,[93] while the Ministry of Justice and the Ministry of Health both have supported legal revisions to recognize LGBTQ people. The minister of justice even noted that it might be time to legalize same-sex marriage.[94]

At a workshop organized by the Ministry of Justice and the United Nations Development Programme (UNDP), "On Comparative Experiences in Protection of LGBT Rights in the Family and Marriage Relations," the chairman of the workshop signaled an understanding of the negative impact of a heterosexual family regime and how breaking with it can create crisis conditions in terms of discrimination against LGBTQ people in the family, and society more widely. In the words of the chairman, "The Marriage and Family Law needs some fundamental changes to reflect the principle of respecting and protecting at the highest level the human rights and citizen rights that Vietnam has committed to."[95]

As a first step in the process of a possible legalization of same-sex marriage and revision of the Marriage and Family Law, on September 24, 2013, the government issued Decree 110/2013/ND-CP, which removed the ban on same-sex marriage.[96] On June 19, 2014, the National Assembly followed up on the new decree by passing an amended Law on Marriage and Family, which, in line with the decree, removed the ban on same-sex marriage effective from January 2015. The National Assembly, however, has not legalized same-sex marriage.[97]

Since then, the Ministry of Justice and the Ministry of Health reportedly have been in a dialogue with the LGBTQ movement and have negotiated with the National Assembly for increased recognition of the rights of homosexual people, and more recently also of transgender people. One result of these struggles is illuminated by the ways in which the Civil Code was amended in 2015 with the Law on Gender Affirmation. The law is aimed at legalizing gender reassignment surgery and recognizing transgender people who have undergone a transition, but the law has not yet been passed by the National Assembly.[98]

Women's Union

The Women's Union has been hesitant to recognize homosexuality and same-sex marriage, and has tended to take new family constellations as if the institution of the family were in crisis. Thus, the realities of how misrecognition generates a state of crisis for the LGBTQ community by restricting people's potentialities have not been publicly acknowledged by the union. Not only has the central union been reluctant to accept same-sex marriage; it has even opposed legalization drafted to protect and recognize homosexuality.

Fighting for women's rights has not automatically included an engagement with LGBTQ rights. Rather, the conservative family ideals promoted by the union correspond with the official family discourse, including the social evils and poisonous culture campaigns, and thus a language embraced by the neo-Confucianism, which swept across Southeast Asia in the late 1990s and early 2000s.[99] Hence, the Vietnamese newspaper *Tuổi Trẻ* (Youth) observed that "the Vietnam Women's Union and several other agencies believe the state should not recognize same-sex marriage, since it is against the nation's customs and habits."[100] The international US-based news magazine *The Diplomat* similarly noted that "the most vigorous opposition [i.e., to legalizing same-sex marriage] has come from the Vietnamese Women's Union, which perceives same-sex marriage as a threat to traditional family ideals."[101] In other words, the union did not officially lend its systemic muscles to help curtail the crisis conditions under which those who depart from an influential heteronormative family matrix live.[102]

The Women's Union perpetuates the ideal of Cultured Family and projects, in doing so, an image of well-organized heterosexual families with women as central agents. For generations, the union has targeted women through campaigns to convey information about how to build a family.[103] Through billboards, educational pamphlets, and various activities, women have been instructed how to manage a household and take care of husband and children by nurturing them emotionally and supporting them practically.[104] The Cultured Family campaigns, in addition, have been promoted as a means to prevent and combat men's violence against their female partner because "'families of culture' . . . motivate and encourage behavioral change."[105]

Family Crises

According to nationwide findings, the ideal of "Happy and Harmonious Family Life" is repeatedly and brutally thwarted in Vietnamese families due to men's violence against their female partners. Figures show that 34 percent of ever-partnered women in Vietnam have reported a "lifetime experience of physical and/or sexual violence."[106] While such numbers accord with findings on gender-based violence on a world scale,[107] they are likely to be even higher in Vietnam, as intimate partner violence tends to be underreported in Vietnam as elsewhere in the world.[108]

International organizations have reported a global surge in gender-based violence during the coronavirus pandemic due to COVID-19–related lockdowns and stay-at-home orders, which by restricting movement have left women with their abusers. An already existing dire crisis of gender-based violence has been fueled and even exacerbated during COVID-19, creating what the UN has coined a "shadow pandemic." According to a UN Women report from 2021, based on worldwide data, 45 percent of all women have experienced partner violence or know of a woman who has been subjected to this kind of abuse during the COVID-19 outbreak.[109] A policy paper published by the UN Economic and Social Commission for Asia and the Pacific (ESCAP) in 2021 estimates a worldwide increase of 20 percent in men's violence against women in the domestic sphere during the pandemic.[110]

As a measure to prevent and combat the spread of the COVID-19 virus in Vietnam, under Directive no. 16/CT-TTg on the implementation of urgent measures, nationwide social distancing was mandated on March 31, 2020.[111] A study conducted in 2020 by the Institute for Social Development Studies (ISDS) and Hanoi School of Public Health found that out of 303 women aged eighteen to sixty living in Hanoi, 59 percent had experienced physical violence during the COVID-19 pandemic. Women interviewed for the report stressed that the frequency with which they had been subjected to physical or sexual male partner violence during the COVID-19 outbreak had increased compared to pre-pandemic levels.[112] A thirty-three-year-old woman interviewee voiced such disturbing tendencies, saying: "Previously, the frequency of his fights was five days a month, but then during the outbreak, it was almost every day."[113] The report concluded that "controlling behaviors, financial abuse, as well as psychological, physical, and sexual domestic violence occurred more frequently by at least 70 percent during the pandemic, compared to the pre-outbreak period."[114]

Domestic violence is intertwined with power balances in the family, Hanh from central Vietnam, who is in her late twenties, pointed out. She explained that gendered powers and relations have changed in Vietnam, noting that "'respecting men and degrading women' belongs to the past. It is different now. Men can't abuse women because that is domestic violence. Even if a man gets very angry, he is not allowed to abuse a woman. Today, women are much more respected than they were in the past."[115] While the law supports Hanh's understanding, intimate partner violence has been a serious problem in Vietnamese society prior to and during the COVID-19 outbreak, despite decades of campaigns launched and implemented nationwide to prevent and combat gender-based violence.[116]

Violence inflicts grave harm on bodies and minds and is defined by Vietnam's Law on Domestic Violence Prevention and Control (no. 02/2007/QH12) as "an intentional act by a family member which causes or potentially causes physical, spiritual [i.e., mental], and financial damage to other members of a family" (Art. 2).[117] Violence turns family life into a sphere of danger, harm, and unpredictability and, in doing so, leads to a new normal, an abusive ongoing crisis that truncates the horizon of a beaten woman and her potentialities for agency.[118]

Vietnam's Penal Code (no. 15/1999/QH10) and Law on Marriage and Family (2000) both stipulate that interpersonal violence is prohibited.[119] Article 21 (Para. 2) of the Marriage and Family Law of 2000 reads that "husband and wife are strictly forbidden to commit acts of ill-treating, persecuting, or hurting the honor, dignity, or prestige of each other." The Law on Marriage and Family, furthermore, states that the Women's Union should be in charge of violence prevention and should combat it by counseling and supporting victims of abuse through vocational training, credit, and saving programs. Such measures should be coordinated with relevant agencies, institutions, and organizations (Art. 34). Families, on the other hand, are requested by the law to solve violent disputes and crises immediately. If unable to settle a conflict, the matter should be brought to local authorities to be reconciled and solved (Art. 13).[120]

Reconciliation

In spite of efforts to end gender-based violence in the domestic sphere, there is a gap between the words of various laws stipulated to protect Vietnamese citizens against violence and the extent to which these laws have been implemented.[121] The strategies launched by local Women's Union units to prevent intimate partner violence differ locally but tend to include, first, prevention of violence through club meetings, and second, combating of violence through reconciliation. Chi, a leader of a northern local Women's Union unit, shed light on the ways in which club meetings organized by the union provide an important platform for raising women's awareness and knowledge about their legal rights:[122]

> In the clubs, women can share their experiences of violence. But sometimes the women feel too ashamed about the violence and therefore they do not like to share their experiences with others. Some women do not feel confident about disclosing their experiences and only use some general examples [to illustrate violence]. Usually, women do not report violence; only the extreme cases are reported to the authorities.

Local club meetings, according to my data, also focus on women's appropriate behavior, such as practicing *tình cảm* to stimulate family harmony. In this sense, women are encouraged to comply with a "hot" (*nóng*)—that is, angry—husband to avoid an "explosion" (*hăng lên*), which might be violent. Such advice inevitably places the onus for the violence on the victim rather than on the perpetrator.[123] When an abused woman reaches out to her local Women's Union for help, she would not uncommonly be advised to return to her violent husband. According to various studies, reconciliation is the most common strategy used by local unions to deal with a gender-specific violent crisis in a family.[124]

According to the *Keeping Silent Is Dying* report, 60 percent of abused female respondents in Vietnam are familiar with the Law on Domestic Violence Prevention and Control, while 87 percent of the same respondents have never sought any help from the authorities when physically abused by their male partner.[125] A leader of one of Vietnam's independent NGOs, Xuan, explained to me why a beaten woman is unlikely to ask for support and likely to stay with her violent partner to try to keep her family together. First, an abused woman might see the violence to which she is subjected as her "own fault" (*lỗi của em*). A beaten woman might blame herself for not behaving in ways that are thought to ensure a harmonious family life such as practicing *tình cảm* and thereby avoiding the violence. Second, an abused woman might be stigmatized by kin and neighbors because she is deemed incapable of maintaining her family. Hence, she may stay together with her husband despite his abuse, hoping to foster a harmonious and happy family life. And last, women might be "enduring suffering" (*chịu đau khổ*) rather than leaving their violent male partners due to a lack of professional guidance and support for women who want to pursue a divorce and escape gendered harm.[126]

A woman who is subjected to her male partner's abuse is confined to a family life, which is demarcated by a state of chronic crisis, as her family transmutes into a zone of exception where violence is inflicted upon her with impunity. When the ideal of harmonious family life translates from a rhetorical ideological goal into a squarely implemented reconciliation strategy, reconciliation can have hazardous consequences for women who live in a violent marriage.[127] While the notion of reconciliation may appear neutral and generate positive connotations by implying resolutions to a problem, in reality reconciliation comes to rationalize and gloss over continued gender-specific abuse experienced on the ground. Systemic harm and gender-specific violence at the lifeworld level can rebound in a reciprocal process, which provides the conditions for a vicious circle and mutual justification of harm.[128]

Such a circle reflects a damaging and dangerous crisis of violence. Even though the crisis appears chronic, many initiatives have been taken across Vietnam to draw attention to and break the vicious circle of gender-based violence and to help abused women to leave a violent male partner. These initiatives include, for instance, the social media #HearMeToo movement[129] and local Women's Union campaigns to actively fight men's violence against women, as seen in the central area of Vietnam. In addition, Vietnamese NGOs and the government have together launched various anti-violence campaigns such as "Say No to Violence" (*Nói Không với Bạo lực*), in tandem with the annual sixteen-day-long November UN Women–run global campaign "Say NO—UniTE to End Violence against Women."

Conclusions

The family is a site of political struggle in Vietnamese society. Officially, the family is rendered meaningful as a "cell" of society, a vehicle of economic development, and a vessel of gendered values. But the family also provides the social context for daily life practices and experiences, which, as I have shown, may not necessarily correlate with official ideological and idealized understandings of family life.

At the systemic level, challenges to official family ideals tend to be approached by the government and its various agencies as a crisis concern. Families that break with a heteronormative family ideal have been condemned in public discourse for not adhering to a heterosexual family norm even though the government increasingly has engaged in dialogue with the LGBTQ community. Regardless of anti-violence initiatives, families that are suffering from gender-based violence have been criticized by government agencies for not living up to the image of happy and harmonious family life, and an abused woman may be reproached for not managing her family appropriately.

Being held in the grip of a heteronormative family model or held captive in a violent marriage generates painful and damaging crisis conditions at the lifeworld level. Family members are confronted with hegemonic narratives about an ideal family life while, at the same time, they are experiencing the hampering of recognition and equal rights. Yet a crisis might for some eventually be turned into a stepping-stone on a path to empowerment and positive change, for example, when a woman terminates an abusive marriage or when a couple builds a same-sex family. Larger systemic recognition and respect for equal rights, however, demand structural systems of support for alternative family constellations such as same-sex marriage, on the one hand, and the prevention of men's violence against their female partners, on the other. The ways in which an overarching crisis like the coronavirus pandemic has fueled and exacerbated male partner violence must be taken into consideration when governmental strategies are developed to combat domestic violence.

Recent demographic figures indicate that perceptions of the family are being reconsidered in contemporary Vietnam in several ways; people are cohabiting before marriage, living together in same-sex relations, preferring a single life, or getting a divorce. While family configurations are becoming more heterogeneous, official family politics and discourse do not entirely reflect the realities of family life on the ground and the processes of transformation that the family is undergoing in rapidly changing late Đổi Mới Vietnam.

Notes

1. Collier, Rosaldo, and Yanagisako, "Is There a Family?"
2. Marriage and Family Law 2000, Art. 1; see also Le Thi, *The Role of the Family*; Nguyen Huu Minh, "Changes in Family Structure."
3. Nguyen-vo Thu-huong, *The Ironies of Freedom*.
4. Perkins, *East Asian Development Foundation*.
5. Nguyen Huu Minh, "Changes in Family Structure."
6. Phinney, *Single Mothers and the State's Embrace*.
7. Nguyen Huu Minh, "The Family in Contemporary Vietnam."
8. Horton and Rydstrom, "Heterosexual Masculinity in Contemporary Vietnam."
9. Braemer, *Love Matters*.
10. Newton, "A Queer Political Economy of 'Community.'"
11. Nguyen T. N. Minh, *Vietnam's Socialist Servants*.
12. Hoang Lan Anh, "Moral Dilemmas of Transnational Migration."
13. See Bales, Phuong, and Chen, this volume; London, this volume.
14. GSO, *Major Findings*, 13.
15. That is, those aged fifteen years and older.
16. GSO, *Major Findings*, 38.
17. GSO, *Major Findings*, 71.
18. Den Boer and Hudson, "Patrilineality, Son Preference."
19. Sen, "More than 100 Million Women."
20. On the two-child policy, see Bélanger and Khuat Thi Hai Oanh, "Second-Trimester Abortions"; Bélanger and Khuat Thu Hong, "Marriage and the Family"; Scornet, "State and the Family." On the desire for male progeny, see Rydstrom, *Embodying Morality*. The policy is under debate; see Báo Nhân Dân, "Health Ministry Proposes Relaxing Two-Child Policy"; Saigoneer, "Vietnam Wants You to Get Married."
21. CPHCSC, *The Viet Nam Population and Housing Census*, 49.
22. GSO, *Major Findings*.
23. GSO, *Major Findings*, 33–35.
24. Nguyen Huu Minh, "Changes in Socio-Demographic Characterstics," 375–77; Nguyen Huu Minh, "The Family in Contemporary Vietnam"; see also ISDS, "Social Determinants of Gender Inequality."
25. See the following by Nguyen Huu Minh: "Changes in Family Structure and Care Relations in Vietnam"; "Changes in Socio-Demographic Characteristics of the Vietnamese Family"; and "The Family in Contemporary Vietnam."

26. Nguyen Huu Minh, "Changes in Family Structure," 173–74.

27. LGBTQ stands for lesbian, gay, bisexual, transgender, and queer.

28. Nguyen Huu Minh, "Changes in Family Structure," 173–74.

29. CPHCSC, *The Viet Nam Population and Housing Census*.

30. Nguyen Huu Minh, "Changes in Socio-Demographic Characterstics," 375–76; see also ISDS, "Social Determinants of Gender Inequality."

31. GSO, *Keeping Silent Is Dying*, 22.

32. Nguyen Huu Minh, "Changes in Socio-Demographic Characterstics," 370–75.

33. Vietnam Family Survey 2006, quoted in Nguyen Huu Minh, "Changes in Family Structure," 175–76.

34. CPHCSC, *The Viet Nam Population and Housing Census*, 39.

35. ISDS, "Social Determinants of Gender Inequality," 27.

36. Tønnesson, *Vietnam 1946*.

37. Khuat Thu Hong, "Overview of Sociological Research"; Le Thi, "Gender, Growth and Scientific Study"; Hoang Ba Thinh, "Women and Family in Transition"; Mai Thi Tu and Le Thi Nam Tuyet, *Women in Vietnam*; Le Thi Nham Tuyet, *Vietnamese Women in the Eighties*; Tran Dinh Huou, "Traditional Families in Vietnam"; and Liljestrom and Tuong Lai, "Introduction," are examples of early studies of the family in Vietnam, which laid the groundwork for the next generation of research on Vietnamese families. Post-embargo research on family life has been carried out by scholars such as Bélanger and Khuat Thu Hong, "Marriage and the Family"; Barbieri and Bélanger, *Reconfiguring Families*; Le Thi, *The Role of the Family*; Drummond and Rydstrom, *Gender Practices*; Gammeltoft, *Women's Bodies, Women's Worries*; Nguyen T. N. Minh, *Vietnam's Socialist Servants*; Leshkowich, "Entrepreneurial Families"; Ngo Thi Ngan Binh, "The Confucian Four Feminine Virtues"; Nguyen Thi Thu Huong, "Rape Experiences"; Nguyen-vo Thu-huong, *The Ironies of Freedom*; Pettus, *Between Sacrifice and Desire*; Pham Van Bich, "The Changes of the Vietnamese Family"; Phinney, *Single Mothers and the State's Embrace*; Rydstrom, *Embodying Morality*; Rydstrom, "Encountering 'Hot Anger'"; Rydstrom, "Sexual Desires and 'Social Evils'"; Scornet, "State and the Family"; and Trinh Duy Luan, Rydstrom, and Burghoorn, *Rural Families in Transitional Vietnam*.

38. Engels, *The Origin of the Family*, 35.

39. See also Le Dang Doanh, this volume; Pham Duy Nghia, this volume.

40. Mai Thi Tu and Le Thi Nham Tuyet, *Women in Vietnam*.

41. Marr, *Vietnamese Tradition on Trial*.

42. Tran Dinh Huou, "Traditional Families in Vietnam."

43. Trinh Minh-ha, *Framer Framed*, 83.

44. Ngo Thi Ngan Binh, "Confucian Four Feminine Virtues," 50.

45. Le Thi, "Gender, Growth and Scientific Study"; Le Thi Nham Tuyet, *Vietnamese Women in the Eighties*, 23–33.

46. Barry, "Introduction."

47. Liljeström and Tuong Lai, "Introduction."

48. Hoang Ba Thinh, "Women and Family in Transition," 139–201; Tran Dinh Huou, "Traditional Families in Vietnam."

49. Mai Thi Tu and Le Thi Nham Tuyet, *Women in Vietnam*.

50. Moreover, abuse of daughters-in-law, adopted children, and stepchildren was explicitly prohibited (Art. 18), and divorce was introduced as an option for women.

51. Nguyen T. T. Huong and Rydstrom, "Feminism in Vietnam."

52. Ljunggren, *The Challenge of Reform*; Ljunggren, this volume.

53. Drummond, "The Modern Vietnamese Woman," 165.

54. Perkins, *East Asian Development Foundation*; see also Kokko, Nestor, and Le Hai Van, chapter 8 in this volume.

55. Le Thi, *The Role of the Family*.

56. Barry, "Introduction"; Hoang Ba Thinh, "Women and Family in Transition."

57. Marriage and Family Law 2000, Art. 1.

58. Marriage and Family Law 2000, Art. 19, 18.

59. See London, "Politics in Contemporary Vietnam."

60. Waibel and Gluck, "More than 13 Million."

61. Kwiatkowski, "Cultural Politics of a Global/Local Health Program"; Rydstrom, "A Zone of Exception."

62. Vietnam Women's Union, "Report on Ensuring and Promoting Women's Rights"; refers to the period 2007–12.

63. Vietnam Women's Union, "Action Plans."

64. Rydstrom, *Embodying Morality*; Rydstrom, "A Zone of Exception."

65. Habermas, *Legitimation Crisis*, 1. *Crisis,* a Latinized form of the Greek *krisis*, refers to "a turning point in a disease." See Bergman-Rosamond et al., "The Case for Interdisciplinary Crisis Studies."

66. Offe, "'Crisis of Crisis Management.'"

67. Roitman, *Anti-Crisis*; Walby, *Crisis.*

68. Offe, "'Crisis of Crisis Management.'"

69. Habermas, *Legitimation Crisis.*

70. Benjamin, *Illuminations.*

71. Vigh, "Crisis and Chronicity."

72. Gramsci, *Selections from the Prison Notebooks.*

73. See Rydstrom, "Machinery of Male Violence: Embodied Properties and Chronic Crisis amongst Partners in Vietnam"; Agamben, *Homo Sacer*; Arendt, *On Violence*; Mbembe, "Necropolitics"; Vigh, "Crisis and Chronicity."

74. Bergman-Rosamond et al., "The Case for Interdisciplinary Crisis Studies."

75. Endres and Six-Hohenbalken, "Introduction to Risks, Ruptures and Uncertainties."

76. Merriam-Webster online, https://www.merriam-webster.com/dictionary/crisis.

77. Merriam-Webster online, https://www.merriam-webster.com/dictionary/crisis.

78. Butler, *Frames of War.*

79. Rydstrom, "Sexual Desires and 'Social Evils'"; Vijeyaras, "The State, the Family."

80. Nguyen-vo Thu-huong, *The Ironies of Freedom*, 45.

81. Horton and Rydstrom, "Heterosexual Masculinity."

82. See, for example, *Giadinh Net.Vn* (Family net Vietnam).

83. Leshkowich, "Entrepreneurial Families."

84. Ngoc, "Words of a Generation."

85. Viet Nam News, "VN Gov't Steps Up Efforts."

86. Windle, "A Slow March from Social Evils."

87. MOLISA, http://pctnxh.molisa.gov.vn/default.aspx?page=define&key=site_introduction. The inclusion of "other social vices" in the amended Penal Code (Art. 5, 1) signals a change of policy. Vijeyarasa, "The State, the Family."

88. Khuat Thu Hong, "Overview of Sociological Research."

89. Australian Government, "Country Advice: Vietnam"; Tuoitrenews.vn, "Vietnam to Remove Fines."

90. Khuat Thu Hong, Le Bach Duong, and Nguyen Ngoc Huong, *Sexuality in Contemporary Vietnam*; Khuat Thu Hong and Nguyen The Van Anh, *Understanding and Reducing Stigma*; Tuoitrenews.vn, "A Legal Guide for Same-Sex Couples."

91. Horton and Rydstrom, "Reshaping Boundaries."

92. For instance, CSAGA, https://shelterasia.org/csaga-vietnam/; Australian Government, "Country Advice: Vietnam"; see also Hansson, this volume.

93. ABC News, "Vietnam Holds First Gay Pride Parade."

94. *Channels News Asia*, August 6, 2012; Mann, "Leading the Way"; Tuoitrenews.vn, "Vietnam to Remove Fines."

95. isee.org.vn, December 21, 2012.

96. Tuoitrenews.vn, "Vietnam to Remove Fines"; USAID and UNDP, "Being LGBT in Asia."

97. Horton and Rydstrom, "Reshaping Boundaries."

98. Nguyen Sen, "LGBT Rights."

99. See also Stivens, "Gendering Asia after Modernity."

100. Tuoitrenews.vn, "Vietnam to Remove Fines."

101. Mann, "Leading the Way."

102. Horton and Rydstrom, "Reshaping Boundaries"; Vietnam Women's Union, "Report on Ensuring and Promoting Women's Rights"; Vietnam Women's Union, "Program 2007–2012."

103. Barbieri and Bélanger, *Reconfiguring Families*; Hoang Lan Anh, "Moral Dilemmas of Transnational Migration."

104. Leshkowich, "Entrepreneurial Families."

105. Le Thi Nham Tuyet and Thi Phuong Tien, "Vietnam: Non-Violent Activities."

106. GSO, *Keeping Silent Is Dying*, 19–22; UN Women Vietnam, "Estimating the Costs of Domestic Violence," 13. For definitions of: (a) violence, see WHO, *World Report on Violence and Health*, 5; (b) gender-based violence, see the UN Declaration on the Elimination of Violence against Women (1993); and (c) intimate partner violence, see WHO, "Violence against Women."

107. UN News, "Ending Inequality Means Ending 'Global Pandemic'"; WHO, "Violence against Women."

108. UNFPA, "Gender-Based Violence"; see also Nguyen Thi Thu Huong, "Rape Experiences"; Viet Nam News, "VN Gov't Steps Up Efforts."

109. UN Women, "Measuring the Shadow Pandemic," 3, 5, 6.

110. UN ESCAP, "The Covid-19 Pandemic," 8; see also Usher et al., "Covid-19 and Family Violence."

111. ISDS and Hanoi School of Public Health, "Findings from a Research Study," 6; see also ILO Japan, "Covid-19, Situation"; Ministry of Health, *Thủ tướng chỉ thị*.

112. ISDS and Hanoi School of Public Health, "Findings from a Research Study," 6–7, 19–24.

113. ISDS and Hanoi School of Public Health, "Findings from a Research Study," 22.

114. ISDS and Hanoi School of Public Health, "Findings from a Research Study," 37.

115. That is, "showing respect for the superior and self-denial for the inferior" (*Biết kính trên nhường dưới*).

116. Kwiatkowski, "Cultural Politics of a Global/Local Health Program"; Rydstrom, "Encountering 'Hot Anger.'"

117. The civil rights of citizens entitle them to request the court or other relevant agencies to protect them (Art. 9) (Civil Code of 2005, no. 33-2005-QH11).

118. Rydstrom, "A Zone of Exception"; Rydstrom, "Machinery of Male Violence"; Rydstrom, "Disasters, Ruins, and Crises." See also Vigh, "Crisis and Chronicity."

119. In 1982, Vietnam ratified the Convention on the Elimination of All Forms of Discrimination against Women. In 2007, the Law on Domestic Violence Prevention and Control (Luật Phòng, chống bạo lực gia đình) was approved.

120. UN Women Vietnam, "Estimating the Costs of Domestic Violence."

121. WHO, "Violence against Women."

122. See also Pells, Wilson, and Nguyen Thi Thu Hang, "Negotiating Agency in Cases."

123. GSO, *Keeping Silent Is Dying*.

124. Kwiatkowski, "Cultural Politics of a Global/Local Health Program"; Rydstrom, "Machinery of Male Violence"; UNODC, "Research on Law Enforcement Practices."

125. Referring to 34 percent of all ever-married women in Vietnam ($n = 4,838$ interviewed women aged eighteen to sixty years) who had experienced physical and/or sexual violence. GSO, *Keeping Silent Is Dying*, 19–22.

126. Rydstrom, "Encountering 'Hot Anger'"; Rydstrom, "A Zone of Exception."

127. Kwiatkowski, "Cultural Politics of a Global/Local Health Program"; Rydstrom, "Machinery of Male Violence."

128. Bloch, *Prey into Hunter*.

129. UN Women Asia and the Pacific, "#HearMeToo."

References

ABC News. "Vietnam Holds First Gay Pride Parade." August 5, 2012. http://www.abc.net.au/news/2012-08-05/vietnam-holds-first-gay-pride-parade/4178626.

Agamben, Giorgio. *Homo Sacer: Sovereign Power and Bare Life*. Stanford, CA: Stanford University Press, 1998.

Arendt, Hannah. *On Violence*. Orlando, FL: Harcourt Brace. 1970.

Australian Government. "Country Advice: Vietnam." February 22, 2010. https://www.refworld.org/pdfid /50f7fb432.pdf.

Báo Nhân Dân. "Health Ministry Proposes Relaxing Two-Child Policy." October 10, 2017. https://en.nhandan .org.vn/society/item/5559702-health-ministry-proposes-relaxing-two-child-policy.html.

Barbieri, Magali, and Danièle Bélanger, eds. *Reconfiguring Families in Contemporary Vietnam*. Stanford, CA: Stanford University Press, 2009.

Barry, K. "Introduction." In *Vietnam's Women in Transition*, edited by Kathleen Barry. London: Macmillan, 1996.

Bélanger, Danièle, and Khuat Thu Hong. "Marriage and the Family in Urban North Vietnam, 1965–1993." *Journal of Population* 2, no. 1 (1996): 83–112.

Bélanger, Danièle, and Khuat Thi Hai Oanh. "Second-Trimester Abortions and Sex-Selection of Children in Hanoi, Viet Nam." *Population Studies* 63, no. 2 (2009): 163–71.

Benjamin, Walter. *Illuminations*. London: Pimlico Press, 1999. (Originally published 1968.)

Bergman-Rosamond, Annika, Thomas Gammeltoft-Hansen, Mo Hamza, Jeff Hearn, Vasna Ramasar, and Helle Rydstrom. "The Case for Interdisciplinary Crisis Studies." *Global Discourse: A Developmental Journal of Research in Politics and International Relations*, 2020. https://papers.ssrn.com/sol3/papers.cfm ?abstract_id=3907956.

Bloch, Maurice. *Prey into Hunter: The Politics of Religious Experience*. Cambridge: Cambridge University Press, 1992.

Braemer, Marie. *Love Matters: Dilemmas of Desire in Transcultural Relationships in Hanoi*. Ph.D. dissertation, Aarhus University, 2014.

Butler, Judith. *Frames of War*. London: Verso, 2010.

Collier, Jane, Michelle Z. Rosaldo, and Sylvia Yanagisako. "Is There a Family? New Anthropological Views." In *Rethinking the Family: Some Feminist Questions*, edited by Barrie Thorne and Marilyn Yalom. Boston: Northeastern University Press, 1992.

CPHCSC. *The Viet Nam Population and Housing Census of 00:00 Hours on 1 April 2019: Implementation, Organization and Preliminary Results*. Hanoi: Central Population and Housing Census Steering Committee, 2019.

Den Boer, Andrea, and Valerie Hudson. "Patrilineality, Son Preference, and Sex Selection in South Korea and Vietnam." *Population and Development Review* 43, no. 1 (2017): 119–47.

Drummond, Lisa. "The Modern Vietnamese Woman: Socialization and Women's Magazines." In *Gender Practices in Contemporary Vietnam*, edited by Lisa Drummond and Helle Rydstrom. Singapore: Singapore University Press, 2004.

Drummond, Lisa, and Helle Rydstrom, eds. *Gender Practices in Contemporary Vietnam*. Singapore: Singapore University Press, 2004.

Endres, Kirsten, and Maria Six-Hohenbalken. "Introduction to Risks, Ruptures and Uncertainties: Dealing with Crisis in Asia's Emerging Economies." *Cambridge Journal of Anthropology* 32, no. 2 (2014): 42–48.

Engels, Friedrich. *The Origin of the Family, Private Property and the State*. London: Penguin Classics, 2010. (Originally published 1884.)

Gammeltoft, Tine. *Women's Bodies, Women's Worries: Health and Family Planning in a Vietnamese Rural Commune*. Copenhagen: NIAS Press/Curzon, 1999.

Gramsci, Anthony. *Selections from the Prison Notebooks*. London: Lawrence and Wishart, 1971.

GSO. *Keeping Silent Is Dying: Results from the National Study on Domestic Violence against Women in Vietnam*. Hanoi: General Statistics Office, 2010.

———. *Major Findings: The 1/4/2016 Time-Point Population Change and Family Planning Survey*. Hanoi: Statistical Publishing House, 2017.

Guilmoto, Christophe Z. "Son Preference, Sex Selection, and Kinship in Vietnam." *Population and Development Review* 38, no. 1 (2012): 31–54.

Habermas, Jürgen. *Legitimation Crisis*. Cambridge: Cambridge University Press, 1992. (Originally published 1976.)

Hoang Ba Thinh. "Women and Family in Transition." In *Images of the Vietnamese Woman in the New Millennium*, edited by Le Thi Nham Tuyet. Hanoi: Gioi Publishers, 2002.

Hoang Lan Anh. "Moral Dilemmas of Transnational Migration: Vietnamese Women in Taiwan." *Gender and Society* 30, no. 6 (2016): 890–911.

Horton, Paul, and Helle Rydstrom. "Heterosexual Masculinity in Contemporary Vietnam: Privileges, Pleasures, and Protests." *Men & Masculinities* 14, no. 5 (2011): 542–64.

———. "Reshaping Boundaries: Family Politics and GLBTQ Resistance in Urban Vietnam." *Journal of GLBT Family Studies* 15, no. 3 (2019): 290–305.

ILO Japan. "Covid-19, Situation: Impacts and Responses. What Trade Unions and Employers Need to Know." Institute for Studies of Society, Economics, and Environment, December 21, 2012.

ISDS. "Social Determinants of Gender Inequality in Vietnam." Institute for Social Development Studies. Hanoi: Hong Duc Publishing House, 2015.

ISDS and Hanoi School of Public Health. "Findings from a Research Study on the Impact of COVID-19 on Domestic Violence against Women in Ha Noi, Viet Nam." Hanoi: Women's Publishing House, 2020.

Khuat Thu Hong. "Overview of Sociological Research of Family in Vietnam." In *Sociological Studies on the Vietnamese Family*, edited by Rita Liljestrom and Tuong Lai. Hanoi: Social Sciences Publishing House, 1991.

Khuat Thu Hong, Le Bach Duong, and Nguyen Ngoc Huong. *Sexuality in Contemporary Vietnam: Easy to Joke About but Hard to Talk About.* Hanoi: Knowledge Publishing House, 2009.

Khuat Thu Hong and Nguyen Thi Van Anh, eds. *Understanding and Reducing Stigma Related to Men Who Have Sex with Men and HIV.* Hanoi: Women's Publishing House, 2010.

Kwiatkowski, Lynn. 2011. "Cultural Politics of a Global/Local Health Program for Battered Women in Vietnam." In *Anthropology at the Front Lines of Gender Based Violence*, edited by Jennifer Wies and Hillary Haldane, Nashville, TN: Vanderbilt University Press, 2011.

Le Ngoc Lan, Nguyen Huu Minh, and Tran Quy Long. *Intra-Family Relationships of the Vietnamese Families.* Hanoi: Social Sciences Publishing House, 2011.

Le Thi. "Gender, Growth and Scientific Study on Women." *Vietnam Social Sciences* 4, no. 34 (1992): 3–11.

———. *The Role of the Family in the Formation of Vietnamese Personality.* Hanoi: Gioi Publishers, 1999.

Le Thi Nham Tuyet. *Vietnamese Women in the Eighties.* Edited by Vietnam Women's Union and Center for Women Studies. Hanoi: Foreign Languages Publishing House, 1989.

Le Thi Nham Tuyet and Thi Phuong Tien. "Vietnam: Non-Violent Activities to Prevent Violence." In *Women, Violence, and Non-Violent Actions*, edited by Aruna Gnanadason, Musimbi Kanyoro, and Lucia Ann McSpadden. Uppsala: Life and Peace Institute, 1996.

Leshkowich, Anne Marie. "Entrepreneurial Families." *Education about Asia* 13, no. 1 (2008): 11–16.

Liljeström, Rita, and Tuong Lai. "Introduction." In *Sociological Studies on the Vietnamese Family*, edited by Rita Liljeström and Tuong Lai. Hanoi: Social Sciences Publishing House, 1991.

Ljunggren, Börje, ed. *The Challenge of Reform in Indochina.* Cambridge, MA: Harvard University Press, 1993.

London, Jonathan D. "Politics in Contemporary Vietnam." In *Politics in Contemporary Vietnam: Party, State, and Authority Relations*, edited by Jonathan D. London. Basingstoke: Palgrave Macmillan, 2014.

Mai Thi Tu and Le Thi Nham Tuyet. *Women in Vietnam.* Hanoi: Foreign Languages Publishing House, 1978.

Mann, David. "Leading the Way: Vietnam's Push for Gay Rights." *The Diplomat*, April 18, 2014. http://thediplomat.com/2014/04/leading-the-way-vietnams-push-for-gay-rights/.

Marr, David. *Vietnamese Tradition on Trial 1920–45.* Berkeley: University of California Press, 1981.

Marriage and Family Law. December 29, 1986. National Assembly of Vietnam. http://www.refworld.org/docid/3ae6b54dc.html.

Mbembe, Achille. "Necropolitics." *Public Culture* 15, no. 1 (2003): 11–40.

Ministry of Health. *Thủ tướng chỉ thị: Cách ly toàn xã hội từ 0 giờ 1/4 trên phạm vi toàn quốc—Hoạt động của lãnh đạo bộ—Cổng thông tin Bộ Y tế (moh.gov.vn)* (Prime Minister's directive: Social isolation from 0:00 April 1 nationwide—Activities of ministry leaders—Ministry of Health Portal). March 31, 2020. https://moh.gov.vn/hoat-dong-cua-lanh-dao-bo/-/asset_publisher/TW6LTp1ZtwaN/content/thu-tuong-chi-thi-cach-ly-toan-xa-hoi-tu-0-gio-1-4-tren-pham-vi-toan-quoc.

Newton, Natalie. "A Queer Political Economy of 'Community': Gender, Space, and the Transnational Politics of Community for Vietnamese Lesbians (les) in Saigon." Ph.D. dissertation, University of California, Irvine, 2012.

Ngo Thi Ngan Binh. "The Confucian Four Feminine Virtues (*Tu Duc*)." In *Gender Practices in Contemporary Vietnam*, edited by Lisa Drummond and Helle Rydstrom. Singapore: Singapore University Press, 2004.

Ngoc A. B. "Words of a Generation." *Research Insight*, December 10, 2013. http://www.edelman.com/post /words-of-a-generation-vietnam/.

Nguyen Huu Minh. "Changes in Family Structure and Care Relations in Vietnam." In *Care Relations in Southeast Asia: The Family and Beyond*, edited by Patcharawalai Wongboonsin and Jo-Pei Tan. Leiden: Brill, 2019.

———. "Changes in Socio-Demographic Characteristics of the Vietnamese Family." In *Family and Social Change in Socialist and Post-Socialist Societies*, edited by Zsombor Rajkai. Leiden: Brill, 2015.

———. "The Family in Contemporary Vietnam." In *Routledge Handbook of Contemporary Vietnam*, edited by Jonathan D. London. London: Routledge, 2022.

Nguyen Sen. "LGBT Rights: Vietnam Recognizes Transgender People, but There Is a Flaw in Its Law." *This Week in Asia*, June 21, 2019. https://www.scmp.com/week-asia/society/article/3015423/lgbt-rights-vietnam -recognises-transgender-people-theres-flaw-its.

Nguyen T. N. Minh. *Vietnam's Socialist Servants: Domesticity, Class, Gender, and Identity*. London: Routledge, 2015.

Nguyen Thi Thu Huong. "Rape Experiences and the Limits of Women's Agency in Contemporary Post-Reform Vietnam." Ph.D. dissertation, University of Amsterdam, 2011.

Nguyen Thi Thu Huong and Helle Rydstrom. "Feminism in Vietnam: Women's Studies, Gender Research, and Intersections." In *Handbook of Vietnamese Studies*, edited by Jonathan D. London. London: Routledge, 2022.

Nguyen-vo Thu-huong. *The Ironies of Freedom: Sex, Culture, and Neoliberal Governance in Vietnam*. Seattle: University of Washington Press, 2008.

Offe, Claus. "'Crisis of Crisis Management': Elements of a Political Crisis Theory." *International Journal of Politics* 6, no. 3 (1976): 29–67.

Pells, Kirrily, Emma Wilson, and Nguyen Thi Thu Hang. "Negotiating Agency in Cases of Intimate Partner Violence in Vietnam." *Global Public Health* 11, nos. 1–2 (2016): 34–47.

Perkins, Dwight H. *East Asian Development Foundation and Strategies*. Cambridge, MA: Harvard University Press, 2013.

Pettus, Ashley. *Between Sacrifice and Desire: National Identity and the Governing of Femininity in Vietnam*. New York: Routledge, 2003.

Pham Van Bich. "The Changes of the Vietnamese Family in the Red River Delta." Ph.D. dissertation, Department of Sociology, Gothenburg University, Sweden, 1998.

Phinney, Harriet M. *Single Mothers and the State's Embrace: Reproductive Agency in Vietnam*. Seattle: University of Washington Press, 2022.

Roitman, Janet. *Anti-Crisis*. Durham, NC: Duke University Press, 2014.

Rydstrom, Helle. "Disasters, Ruins, and Crises: Masculinity and Ramifications of Storms in Vietnam." *Ethnos, Journal of Anthropology* 85, no. 2 (2020): 351–70.

———. *Embodying Morality: Growing Up in Rural Northern Vietnam*. Honolulu: University of Hawai'i Press, 2003.

———. "Encountering 'Hot Anger': Domestic Violence in Contemporary Vietnam." *Violence against Women* 9, no. 6 (2003): 676–97.

———. "Machinery of Male Violence: Embodied Properties and Chronic Crisis amongst Partners in Vietnam." *ASEAS, Austrian Journal of South-East Asian Studies* 12, no. 2 (2019): 167–85.

———. "Sexual Desires and 'Social Evils': Young Women in Rural Vietnam." *Journal of Gender, Place, and Culture* 13, no. 3 (2006): 283–303.

———. "A Zone of Exception: Gendered Violences of Family 'Happiness' in Vietnam." *Gender, Place and Culture* 24, no. 7 (2017): 1051–70.

Saigoneer. "Vietnam Wants You to Get Married before 30, Bear 2 Children." May 6, 2020. https://saigoneer .com/vietnam-news/18651-vietnam-wants-you-to-get-married-before-30,-bear-2-children.

Scornet, Catherine. "State and the Family: Reproductive Policies and Practices." In *Reconfiguring Families in Contemporary Vietnam*, edited by Magali Barbieri and Danièle Bélanger. Stanford, CA: Stanford University Press, 2009.

Sen, Amartya. "More than 100 Million Women Are Missing." *New York Review*, December 20, 1990.

Stivens, Maila. "Gendering Asia after Modernity." In *Gendered Inequalities in Asia: Configuring, Contesting, and Recognizing Women and Men*, edited by Helle Rydstrom. Copenhagen: NIAS Press, 2010.

Tønnesson, Stein. *Vietnam 1946*. Berkeley: University of California Press, 2010.

Tran Dinh Huou. "Traditional Families in Vietnam and Influence of Confucianism." In *Sociological Studies on the Vietnamese Family*, edited by Rita Liljestrom and Tuong Lai. Hanoi: Social Sciences Publishing House, 1991.

Trinh Duy Luan, Helle Rydstrom, and Wil Burghoorn, eds. *Rural Families in Transitional Vietnam*. Hanoi: Social Sciences Publishing House, 2008.

Trinh T. Minh-Ha. *Framer Framed*. New York: Routledge, 1992.

Tuoitrenews.vn. "A Legal Guide for Same-Sex Couples in Vietnam." April 17, 2013. http://tuoitrenews.vn /society/8841/a-legal-guide-for-samesex-couples-in-vietnam.

———. "Protest Gay Marriage Legalization in Vietnam." April 27, 2014. http://tuoitrenews.vn/lifestyle /18641/50-protest-gay-marriage-legalization-in-vietnam-study.

———. "Vietnam Removes Ban on Same-Sex Marriage." June 20, 2014. http://tuoitrenews.vn/society /20478/vietnam-removes-ban-on-same-sex-marriage.

———. "Vietnam to Remove Fines on Same-Sex Marriage." March 10, 2013. http://tuoitrenews.vn/society /13750/vietnam-to-remove-fines-on-samesex-marriage.

UN Economic and Social Commission for Asia and the Pacific. "The Covid-19 Pandemic and Violence against Women in Asia and the Pacific." November 23, 2020. https://www.unescap.org/resources/covid -19-pandemic-and-violence-against-women-asia-and-pacific.

UNFPA. "Gender-Based Violence." UN Population Fund, 2019. https://www.unfpa.org/gender-based-violence.

———. "Gender-Biased Sex Selection." UN Population Fund, 2018. https://www.unfpa.org/gender-biased -sex-selection.

———. "Study on Gender, Masculinity and Son Preference in Nepal and Vietnam." UN Population Fund, 2012. http://vietnam.unfpa.org/sites/default/files/pub-pdf/Masculinity_Report_Nepal_VietNam_ENG.pdf.

UN News. "Ending Inequality Means Ending 'Global Pandemic' of Violence against Women—UN Chief." November 19, 2018. https://news.un.org/en/story/2018/11/1026071.

UNODC. "Research on Law Enforcement Practices and Legal Support to Female Victims of Domestic Violence in Vietnam." Working Paper, UN Office on Drugs and Crime, 2011.

UN Women. "Ending Violence against Women." 2022. https://www.unwomen.org/en/what-we-do/ending -violence-against-women/facts-and-figures.

———. "Measuring the Shadow Pandemic: Violence against Women during Covid-19." 2021. https://data .unwomen.org/sites/default/files/documents/Publications/Measuring-shadow-pandemic.pdf.

UN Women Asia and the Pacific. "#HearMeToo: United for Advocacy and Concrete Interventions in Vietnam." December 3, 2018. http://asiapacific.unwomen.org/en/news-and-events/stories/2019/01/hearmetoo -united-for-advocacy-and-concrete-interventions-in-viet-nam.

UN Women Vietnam. "Estimating the Costs of Domestic Violence against Women in Vietnam." Hanoi: UN Women, 2012.

USAID and UNDP. "Being LGBT in Asia: Vietnam Country Report." Hanoi: USAID and UNDP, 2014.

Usher, Kim, Caroline B. Jones, Navjot Bhullar, Joanna Durkin, Naomi Gyamfi, Syadani R. Fatema, and Debra Jackson. "Covid-19 and Family Violence: Is This a Perfect Storm?" *International Journal of Mental Health Nursing* 30, no. 4 (2021): 1022–32.

Viet Nam News. "VN Gov't Steps Up Efforts to Prevent 'Social Evils.'" November 11, 2016.

Vietnam Women's Union. "Action Plans." 2022. http://vwu.vn/vwu-action-plans.

———. "Program 2007–2012." 2015. http://www.hoilhpn.org.vn/newsdetail.asp?CatId=78&NewsId =10103&lang=EN.

———. "Report on Ensuring and Promoting Women's Rights." Hanoi: Vietnam Women's Union, 2013.

Vigh, Henrik. "Crisis and Chronicity." *Ethnos, Journal of Anthropology* 73, no. 1 (2008): 5–24.

Vijeyarasa, Ramona. "The State, the Family, and Language of 'Social Evils.'" *Culture, Health, and Sexuality* 12, no. S1 (2010): S89–102.

Waibel, Gabi, and Sarah Gluck. "More than 13 Million: Mass Mobilization and Gender Politics in the Vietnam Women's Union." *Gender and Development* 21, no. 2 (2013): 343–61.

Walby, Sylvia. *Crisis*. Oxford: Polity Press, 2015.

WHO. "Violence against Women." March 9, 2021. http://www.who.int/news-room/fact-sheets/detail/violence-against-women.

———. *World Report on Violence and Health*. Geneva: World Health Organization, 2002.

Windle, James. "A Slow March from Social Evils to Harm Reduction." *Foreign Policy at Brookings*, 2016.

CHAPTER 14

Vietnam's Health System

Navigating Transitions in Protecting People's Health

Sarah Bales, Le Nhan Phuong, and Lincoln Chen

In the mid-1980s after the Resistance War against America, Vietnam's life expectancy was significantly higher than expected given its low GDP level.[1] Vietnam's successes, both then and now, have been attributed to the effectiveness of its public health measures and mobilization of the entire society's support to fight a common enemy. A big difference, however, is that in the earlier period resources were so limited that little could be allocated beyond the most basic services, so interventions had to focus on measures that could yield high health gains at low cost. Currently, however, providers of routine preventive and primary care services are competing with high-tech hospitals for the more abundant, but still inadequate, resources now available. When faced with an unexpected threat to national health, like COVID-19, the government is still able to mount a rapid and coordinated public health response. We argue, however, that it is less able to ensure the necessary balance in routine preventive and primary services that are needed by an aging population, and that will need to be provided in an equitable and sustainable way.

This chapter describes the evolution of the Vietnam health system since *Đổi Mới*, the opening of the economy to market-based reforms in 1986. These reforms have had mixed consequences for Vietnam's health care system. Although Đổi Mới raised living standards and improved health care, it has adversely affected health care financing. Into a publicly financed and publicly operated health system, Vietnam adopted policies to mobilize private, for-profit investments and encourage rapid revenue growth with insufficient consideration of appropriateness to medical need or the financial burden on households and the social health insurance fund. Each of these financial policies strained the structure, function, and performance of what has become a "mixed" public-private system. The net effect, so far, has been that demand and supply of routine health services and goods are increasingly determined by market forces, thus leading to complexities that include inequity, inefficiency, and insufficient quality.

Furthermore, while Vietnam's comparative success in controlling infection and death in the early phase of the COVID-19 pandemic[2] is reminiscent of its public health achievements in the pre–Đổi Mới era, the resurgence of COVID-19 due to the delta and omicron variants as the pandemic progresses is a reminder that Vietnam cannot rest on its laurels but must continue to find ways to involve the whole of society to overcome its health challenges.

Vietnam's Socioeconomic Situation and Health Outcomes

Vietnam has favorable socioeconomic conditions to achieve good health outcomes. The population is relatively large, at 97 million people, and growing slowly.[3] GDP per capita in 2020 was PPPUS$8,647, placing it in the group of lower-middle-income countries.[4] Although it seems implausible, trends in the Gini index indicate little increase in income inequality over time, with a 2018 estimate of 0.357.[5] Vietnam has received global recognition for its achievements in basic education,[6] particularly an increase in adult literacy from 88 percent in 1989 to 96 percent in 2019.[7] Between 2006 and 2020, Vietnam's income poverty rate fell dramatically, from 15.5 percent to 3.0 percent, and between 2016 and 2020 multidimensional poverty rates have declined from 9.2 percent to 4.8 percent.[8]

Vietnam has performed well on major health and demographic outcomes in comparison to other large middle-income ASEAN countries and to China. Life expectancy in Vietnam is higher at seventy-five years, while the infant mortality rate is relatively lower, putting Vietnam's performance above that of other lower-middle-income ASEAN countries, but still below that of Thailand and China.[9] Vietnam has reduced fertility to below replacement levels since 1999.[10] A disturbing aberration in this outstanding performance is the highly imbalanced sex ratio at birth, reaching 111.3 males to 100 females in 2020, placing Vietnam at the third worst in the world.[11] This is the result of strong patriarchal values and increased access to ultrasound technology and abortion of female fetuses as Vietnam's health system modernized.[12]

Vietnam's health service delivery system in relation to its population is not excessively large, although spending is robust. Physician density in Vietnam is in the mid-range, but the low nurse-midwife density means there are fewer than two nurses to support a single doctor, an imbalance with efficiency and quality of care implications.[13] Vietnam has 2.6 hospital beds per 1,000 population, which is lower than China, but higher than other ASEAN countries.[14] Vietnam's current health expenditure as a share of GDP is the highest among comparator countries in table 14.1 except for China.

Driving Force: Health Financing

Health financing modalities have been the driving force of many Vietnamese health reforms. Health financing encompasses the three functions of revenue collection, pooling, and purchasing, and also entails fund allocation decisions between these financing functions and service provision.[15] Although the ultimate objective of health financing is to protect and improve the health of the population, Vietnam's goal is aimed at equity, efficiency,

Table 14.1
Comparison between Vietnam and other countries

	Vietnam	Thailand	Philippines	Indonesia	China
Life expectancy at birth (years)	75	77	71	72	77
Infant mortality rate (per 1,000 live births)	17	7	21	20	6
Physicians (per 1,000 people)	0.8	1.0	0.8	0.6	2.2
Nurses and midwives (per 1,000 people)	1.5	2.8	4.9	2.4	2.7
Beds (per 1,000 people)	2.6	2.1	0.5	1.2	5.4
Current health expenditure/GDP (%)	5.2	3.8	4.1	2.9	5.4

Sources: Life expectancy at birth and infant mortality rate in 2020: World Bank, "World Development Indicators"; Human resources data: World Health Organization, "The Global Health Observatory." The indicator was recalculated to indicate health workers per 1,000 population. The most recent year varies by country—Vietnam (2016), Thailand (2020), Philippines (2020), Indonesia (2020), China (2019); Hospital bed data: OECD and WHO, *Health at a Glance*, 18; Health expenditure data 2019: WHO, "Global Health Expenditure Database."

and quality.[16] Equity aligns with the universal health coverage goals of financial protection and equitable access to effective services as well as prioritization of sustainable development goals. Efficiency focuses on providing the right services in the right place in the right way to achieve the greatest health benefit with the resources available. Quality focuses on technical effectiveness of health services and relations and communications to meet the health needs of the population.

Đổi Mới reforms transformed health financing in Vietnam, introducing another crucial objective of the health system—to mobilize additional financial resources to ensure the range of services that would meet the people's needs, while simultaneously attempting to sustain attention on the equity goals of financial access and protection for the poor.[17] This involved a substantial shift from the ideological position of state budget responsibility for funding all health services toward mobilization of resources from society (the population and private sector), even though the state continued to dominate health services provision.

Table 14.2 lists the key health financing policy streams that were initiated around the Đổi Mới period. In the early post–Đổi Mới years (the decade starting in the late 1980s), the financing policies aimed at mobilizing resources to provide adequate health goods and services, while reducing the financial burden on the state. Some of the earliest reforms included permitting doctors to open after-hours medical practices and sell pharmaceuticals to their patients for a fee, later expanding to promote establishment of private health facilities. User fees for curative care services were introduced in the public sector in 1989, allowing out-of-pocket payments to supplement the meager state supply-side subsidies. In 1992, contributory social health insurance (SHI) was introduced, with the aim of

Table 14.2
Evolution of market reform policies in the health sector

Year	Key health financing policies	Key health care system reforms
1987	Permit private after-hours practice and private sale of drugs (Circular 30)	
1989	Charge user fees in public facilities including exemption for disadvantaged groups (Decision 45)	Law on People's Health Protection: legal framework for the people's right to health care, four guiding principles, responsibility of state and non-state actors
1992	National health SHI system in the Ministry of Health (MOH) (Decision 958)	
1993	Further opening of private medical and pharmaceutical practice, including setting up private facilities (Ordinance 26)	
1994		Strengthening commune health network by ensuring staff salaries from central budget and mobilizing funds to build CHS in most communes. (Decision 58)
1996		National drug policy including quality assurance, access to essential drugs, and safe and rational use of drugs (Resolution 37)
1997	Social mobilization in the health and other sectors, paving the way for private investments in public hospitals (Resolution 90)	
2009		Law on Examination and Treatment: legal framework for quality assurance by mandating educational institution accreditation, health worker licensing, and continuing education

mobilizing financial contributions from society in a risk-pooling mechanism to improve the quality of curative care services, with enrollment initially focused on civil servants and other formal sector workers.[18] To further augment resources for priority public health programs, such as the Expanded Program on Immunization, the government mobilized funding through international organizations. The strategy to mobilize capital investments in the health sector, including private investments in public facilities, was initiated as early as 1997 to overcome state budget insufficiency to keep up with the growing needs of the health sector. Fund mobilization was primarily focused on curative care, except for external assistance, which focused on preventive health programs.

Summary statistics on health financing show that Vietnam's situation is similar to its ASEAN peers and China (see table 14.3). All these countries have launched SHI and strive to achieve universal health coverage through a combination of contributory and government-subsidized coverage. In 2020, Vietnam's health insurance coverage reached 90 percent, a level above Indonesia, but not quite as high as the other countries. About half of current

Table 14.3
Health financing in Vietnam and other countries

	Vietnam	Thailand	Philippines	Indonesia	China
Population covered by SHI (%)	88	100	98	85	97
Domestic general government health expenditure/current health expenditure (%)	48.6	76.1	31.9	48.4	56.7
Domestic private health expenditure/current health expenditure (%)	49.4	23.6	65.5	51.1	43.3
External expenditure/ current health expenditure (%)	2.0	0.2	2.6	0.5	0.0
Current health expenditure per capita in PPP Int$	376	671	372	368	841
Out of pocket health expenditure per capita in PPP Int$	170	75	197	127	303

Notes: Data on the population covered by health insurance is from the following. Vietnam (2018): Calculated using data from GSO, *Statistical Yearbook 2019,* 99 and 215; Thailand (2019): Sumriddetchkajorn, "Universal health coverage and primary care, Thailand," 415; Philippines (2018): PhilHealth, *2018 Stats and Charts,* 2; Indonesia (2018): Anindya, "Impact of Indonesia's national health insurance," 2; China (2015): Fang, "Enhancing financial protection under China's social health insurance," 2. Other health finance indicators refer to 2017: WHO, *Global Health Expenditure Database.*

health expenditures are contributed from private sources, 92 percent of which are out-of-pocket payments. Out-of-pocket payment per capita amounts to PPPUS$170 annually. For the ASEAN comparison countries during the same period, only Thailand (at 24 percent) had less than a quarter of total expenditures coming from private sources. In China, the private share of expenditures reached 43 percent, almost double that in Thailand. Reducing out-of-pocket spending to 15–20 percent of total health expenditure is associated with reduced incidence of catastrophic spending.[19]

Importantly, Vietnam's ideological commitment to health equity for curative care was sustained during this period of fund mobilization. The introduction of the curative care user fees in 1989 included a list of groups entitled to exemptions—including people with disabilities, orphans, elderly people with no family support, people with specific illnesses, ethnic minorities in remote areas, and children under age six. This was expanded in 1994 to include members of poor families. Although these exemptions were initially unfunded, gradually these entitlement groups were incorporated into SHI through government budget subsidies of the premiums (for the poor in 2002) or funding of fee exemption cards (for children under age six in 2005). In 2008, the Law on Health Insurance consolidated all these entitlements into premium subsidies, which guaranteed state budget funding for this purpose, with further expansion of groups entitled to subsidies to include the near poor or those newly escaped from poverty.

In the early post–Đổi Mới period, the government continued to earmark allocations of central budget funding for diseases that had been the focus of the pre–Đổi Mới period, such as malaria, common infections, and vaccine-preventable diseases.[20] In addition, the government mobilized external assistance focused on national health target program activities, gradually expanding their scope to cover other diseases that caused a high burden among vulnerable groups, such as HIV/AIDS, tuberculosis, schizophrenia, leprosy, and child malnutrition. Initially, the government continued to partially subsidize providers, mobilizing user fees to supplement the meager state budget for providing services, but not setting fees so high that services became unaffordable to the population.

The hospital autonomy policy began as an effort to allow hospital directors greater financial and organizational decision-making power, but the goal has continued to evolve. The initial policy encouraged revenue generation and allowed hospital directors to use operating surplus to top up salaries of staff and reinvest in the facility.[21] Over time, the government goal has evolved toward weaning public service delivery units off state supply-side subsidies, instead allowing them to charge full cost-recovery fees to cover their operating costs. This transition toward full financial autonomy has been most strongly implemented in state curative care facilities, although there is also pressure for public health and preventive medicine facilities to gain a higher share of their revenues through user fee collection.

Đổi Mới moved very strongly toward setting prices for medical services and goods through the market mechanism. Policies allow pharmaceutical and device suppliers to set their prices without restrictions such as reference pricing. Competitive tendering determines prices for procurement of drugs used in public hospitals and paid by health insurance.[22] Private providers, including private wards and services of public hospitals, set prices for their services with little regulatory oversight. Medical equipment procurement prices have not been tightly regulated. The main exception to market-set prices is the Ministry of Health's (MOH) administratively set fees charged in government hospitals using government-invested equipment and the prices paid by the SHI fund. When user fees were first introduced, they were expected to cover only part of the costs of delivery, since payroll and other overhead costs were paid by the state budget. As part of the autonomy policy, gradually, different cost components have been estimated and incorporated into the user fees. The costing approach relies on technical norms for inputs (such as hours of surgeon time or costs of medical gloves) and unit prices based on actual purchases by hospitals. Challenges have arisen because norms are somewhat arbitrary and some costs, such as depreciation, vary substantially across facilities, in part because of variation in the purchase price of equipment.

Mobilization of private financing to invest in medical equipment in public hospitals and encouragement of private investments have effectively transformed the Vietnamese health sector into a "mixed" profit-oriented sector, where providers are focused on revenue-maximizing objectives, rather than people's health protection. During the early years of *Đổi Mới*, state budget funds were inadequate to invest in much needed medical equipment.

To cope with this shortfall in state budget investment funds, the government encouraged private investors to provide capital, including through loans or profit-sharing arrangements. Few regulations existed to ensure rational equipment and infrastructure investments and avoid overcapacity. The shortage of equipment was so bad in the early years that even public facility staff were encouraged to invest their own capital into equipment in the facility where they worked, despite obvious conflicts of interest.[23] The consequence has been a focus on increasing volumes of high-tech, high-cost services, which have profit-generating potential, and corresponding neglect of primary health care, routine disease prevention, and health promotion.[24] Growth of private financing has led to reduced attention to SHI patients in public wards of public hospitals. Dual public-private practice by public hospital doctors moonlighting in the private sector, and dual public-private services within public hospitals lead to relative neglect or poorer service attitude of doctors serving insured patients in public wards.[25] This is because the fees per service in public wards are generally lower than in private wards or in the private practice outside the health facility. In fact, the for-profit and nonprofit distinction between private and public facilities is being blurred under hospital autonomy and social mobilization of investments.

A series of state budget laws have been passed, gradually devolving public finance to the provinces and eliminating earmarking. Before and in the early years of *Đổi Mới*, the MOH controlled medical facilities by controlling their budgets. The ministry was able to ensure priority disease control activities through target programs, where funds and program activities were tightly controlled from the central level. Under the state budget laws, the MOH lost an important control lever, and continues to struggle to ensure that the provinces will allocate their limited resources toward achieving national health priorities. In responding to COVID-19, the government reverted to central allocation of state budget targeted toward implementing a comprehensive set of measures, including border control preventing foreigners coming from infected countries, widespread molecular testing of exposed (not only symptomatic) cases, comprehensive contact tracing, enforced isolation or quarantine of infected people, and lockdown of high-infection zones. The provinces were given some discretion in how they use central COVID-19 control funds, depending on their local situation, but were held accountable for results.[26]

Financial protection mechanisms instituted since Đổi Mới have focused on increasing population covered by SHI, while neglecting other goals. The 2013 constitution enshrined citizens' right to universal health insurance coverage, and the prime minister's office monitors provincial health insurance coverage rates, leading to a high level of attention paid to this goal. However, little attention has been paid to ensuring that Vietnam Social Security (VSS) can maintain the SHI fund balance, as the package is continuously expanded, and tariffs have increased substantially to achieve full cost recovery, while premiums remain relatively unchanged and low, on average about US$53 per year.[27] Despite high SHI coverage, out-of-pocket spending remains high, because health facilities have incentives to overprescribe items that are not covered by health insurance. Financial protection indicators have been improving, with catastrophic spending (i.e., the proportion of population spending more than 10 percent of household consumption on out-of-pocket health care expenditure) falling from 15.9 percent of households in 2004 to 9.2 percent in 2012, although they are beginning to rise again, reaching 10.0 percent in 2018.[28] The poor continue to face financial and geographic access barriers when they require higher-level facilities to meet their health care needs. The private health insurance market is responding to demand from the better-off population who want financial protection when using private health services. Compared to 105.259 trillion VND in total SHI benefit payments,[29] private claim payments on net retained premiums amounted to only 4.769 trillion VND, or about 4.3 percent of total health insurance claims in 2019.[30] Private health insurance marketing materials indicate fewer restrictions on drug lists and services and long lists of preapproved facilities to receive cashless services compared to the SHI package. However, these insurance packages tend to exclude long lists of diseases and generally do not provide coverage beyond sixty or sixty-five years of age. This imposes some threats to SHI if private insurers can sell policies that don't supplement, but rather replace, SHI and skim younger, healthier patients.

Despite the strengths Vietnam has due to the creation of a single-purchaser SHI scheme in 1992 and achieving high population coverage, the institutional arrangements are fragmented across multiple government units, leaving VSS few tools and little authority to be an effective purchaser of health services for the population. Strategic purchasing consists of making effective decisions about what to purchase to meet population health needs, from whom to purchase these services or goods, and with what payment mechanism. Current institutional arrangements in Vietnam give the MOH authority to determine the health insurance benefits package and set policy on provider payments, including the payment rates. However, the MOH has little incentive to design these policies in a way that would achieve VSS goals of balancing the SHI fund. Without authority to implement strategic purchasing functions, VSS is left with few tools to control the appropriateness or quality of services provided by curative care facilities.

The fee-for-service mechanism introduced to pay for curative care services is strongly associated with overprovision of unnecessary health services, particularly when no hard global budget is imposed. Health facility managers are highly focused on ensuring revenues to pay adequate salaries to retain staff, and in many facilities, incentives induce individual practitioners to "mine" their patients to extract maximum revenues. High-tech investments are prioritized because they bring in more revenues. Lack of attention to cost-effectiveness or measures to ensure compliance with diagnostic and treatment guidelines results in clinical practice that varies widely across facilities, leading to substantial conflicts between the purchasers and providers when reviewing the reasonableness of insurance claims. Although policymakers are aware of these issues, and have even put in place a policy allowing alternative payment mechanisms since 2006, the complexities of coordinating policy among VSS, the MOH, and the Ministry of Finance have stymied policy development. Efforts to design a prospective case-based payment mechanism (specifically, diagnosis-related group payments) to incentivize providers to become more efficient have been ongoing for more than a decade, but so far have failed to come to fruition.

Health financing reforms have substantially transformed the health system, yet other policies and institutions needed to counterbalance the strong financial incentives in the health system have lagged, particularly those related to oversight and accountability. Although Vietnam has had medical associations since the 1950s, their role has been largely information sharing, rather than holding practitioners accountable to ethical and professional standards. Up to now, no domestic hospital accreditation body has been established, and hospital quality criteria focus more on structural indicators rather than ensuring compliance with treatment protocols or health outcomes of patients, such as mortality, readmission, or hospital-acquired complications. In recent years, health information systems have rapidly computerized, especially in the SHI claims review system, creating an invaluable information resource for promoting efficiency, equity, and quality of services. However, currently the statistical and analytical capacity to analyze these large databases lies outside the agencies that control the data.

Health System Reforms Post–"Đổi Mới"

Reaffirming its ideological commitment to health care equity, the government in 1989 issued a Law on People's Health Protection and a series of parallel health system policies (see table 14.2). Equity was prioritized in 1994–96 with policies to strengthen the CHSs, including covering commune health staff payroll through central budgets and a national essential drug policy to ensure use of affordable and effective drugs.

Since *Đổi Mới*, Vietnam's health system has experienced major expansion and deepening of its health infrastructure. Currently, Vietnam has a four-tier system (national, provincial, district, and commune), with the district and commune levels together constituting the grassroots health system. Between 1995 and 2018, the number of state curative care health facilities increased from 12,556 to 13,319, while the number of treatment beds in state health facilities (excluding commune health stations) went up from 172,642 in 1995 to 273,316 in 2018. Although in 1995 there were only 1,801 doctors working at the commune level, by 2018, 90.8 percent of the approximately 11,100 CHSs were staffed by doctors.[31] The preventive medicine and public health networks extend throughout the country. By 2020 all sixty-three provinces had created provincial centers for disease control by integrating the various facilities providing public health and preventive medicine services. Additionally, every district has a district health center, which may be a separate preventive medical facility or integrated with the district hospitals.

By 2018, there were 228 private hospitals with 21,122 beds located in forty-seven out of sixty-three provinces.[32] Although the health sector does not compile statistics on private, nonhospital health service providers, enterprise statistics from 2017 indicate that there are nearly 2,000 registered private enterprises (including private hospitals) and over 27,000 small and medium enterprises operating in the health and social assistance sectors, which does not include pharmacies, but does include some non-health enterprises such as private nursing homes and substance abuse rehabilitation facilities.[33] Vietnam also has 62,000 mostly private retail pharmacies.[34]

In the pre–Đổi Mới era, the health system focused on inexpensive basic public health interventions such as immunization, health education, and health promotion provided through the CHSs and vertical disease-specific programs.[35] Since *Đổi Mới*, public health programs funded by the state budget have expanded, adding activities to combat HIV/AIDS and noncommunicable diseases (NCDs), while integrating program delivery into the routine activities of grassroots health facilities and provincial centers for disease control. At the same time, the curative care sector has taken off, with some hospitals now capable of providing highly sophisticated surgeries like organ transplants and coronary bypass. In 2018, the MOH reported that health facilities provided 3.5 million CT and MRI scans, 24.3 million ultrasounds, and 3.5 million surgeries, while the GSO reported that about one in twelve people had an inpatient admission and one in three people had an outpatient contact.[36]

It is straightforward to understand how these financial mobilization efforts impacted on key parameters of Vietnam's health care system. Inequity has worsened as facilities are weaned off state budget subsidies and expected to cover costs through fee collection, putting pressure on them to overprovide services, while social insurance coverage only mitigates some of the costs of services. Private commercial financing targets the richer end of the market with expensive high-tech services, creating pressure for the social health insurance fund to compete with private insurers to provide better financial protection for this market. Foreign aid has traditionally focused on disease-targeted programs, which are struggling to replace those funds with domestic funding sources. Provincial budgets are under financial strain, preferring to invest in curative care, which generates revenues, rather than public health, which relies on state budget funding. The net impact of these financial policies has led to challenges of health equity, health system inefficiencies, and poor quality of care.

INEQUITY

Although improving on many national health indices, Vietnam's health system has been challenged by health inequities, defined as differences in health (health disparities or inequalities) that are unnecessary, avoidable, and considered unfair and unjust because they are rooted in social injustices that make some population groups more vulnerable than others.[37] The health inequities are manifested by disparities in health status that may be found across many attributes—age, sex, ethnicity, residence, and especially living standards.[38] Disparities are not static but dynamic, with some growing and others narrowing. Figure 14.1 shows large geographic disparities in childhood mortality indicators in 2019. The under-five mortality rate per 1,000 live births in rural areas (25.1) is more than double that in urban areas (12.3), and the rate in the Central Highlands (35.5) is 2.8 times higher than in the southeast (12.7), the region with the lowest rate. Similar differences in magnitude of risk are also seen with infant mortality rates.

Substantial inequity also exists in use of basic health services. About one in five mothers from poor households and ethnic minority mothers received no antenatal care, and one in three ethnic minority and one in four poor mothers did not have a skilled attendant at the

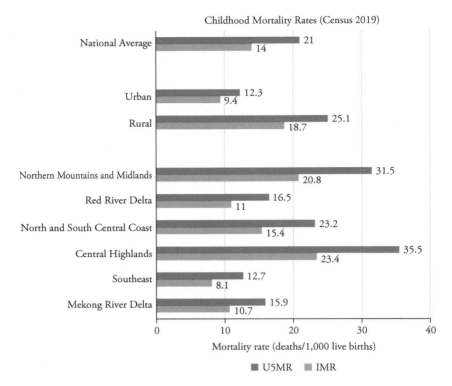

FIGURE 14.1 Disparities in childhood mortality rates
Note: IMR = Infant mortality rate; U5MR = Under 5 mortality rate.
Source: Central Census Steering Committee, *Results of the 2019 Population Census*, 1990–91.

birth of their child, yet for ethnic majority and nonpoor women use of these services was nearly universal. On the other hand, richer women are experiencing excess medical interventions—the cesarean section rate among the rich, at 46 percent, was three times higher than the rate among the poor.[39] Figure 14.2 shows that for outpatient care, better-off people have greater access, but for inpatient care, poorer quintiles have higher utilization. This likely reflects higher need for hospitalization among poorer people, who may delay care until they are very sick, but also the tendency of hospitals in more remote areas to admit patients who must travel long distances to seek care. People living in the mountainous regions of the North and Central Highlands and ethnic minorities also have a greater reliance on under-resourced commune health stations for both inpatient and outpatient care than other regions and the *Kinh* majority.[40]

Financial protection is another important equity concern in the health sector. Household out-of-pocket spending has continued to rise over time in Vietnam, still accounting for more than 40 percent of total health spending. Yet Vietnam has managed to reduce catastrophic spending and impoverishment rates associated with health spending.[41] This reflects in part the financial protection resulting from subsidized health insurance cover-

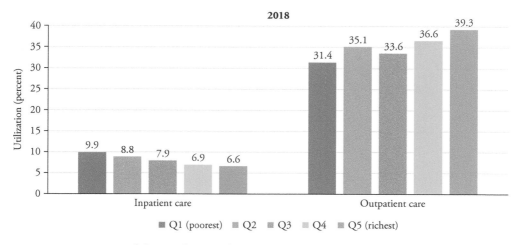

FIGURE 14.2 Proportion of the population seeking curative care services in the past 12 months by income quintile
Source: General Statistics Office. *Vietnam Household Living Standards Survey 2018*, 192–93.

age targeted to the poor and other vulnerable groups in the Health Insurance Law. However, low levels of out-of-pocket spending among the poor also reflect their lower utilization of health care services and greater reliance on grassroots health care providers.

INEFFICIENCIES

Inefficiencies and wasteful spending are an important challenge for Vietnam's health system, as they are for most countries in the world. With the level of resources Vietnam currently spends on health services, a higher level of health could be attained, and fewer people would face unmet needs. Although Vietnam's MOH has developed many national diagnosis and treatment guidelines, there is no mechanism in place to ensure that doctors or hospitals comply with them. Instead, financial incentives of the fee-for-service payment system, combined with the profit motives of social mobilization, the salary top-up system within the hospital autonomy policy, and the provider moral hazard (resulting from third-party payment for health services on behalf of patients) create strong incentives for hospitals and physicians to overprescribe services and inputs to care and extend length of stay to boost revenues. The health sector is looking toward provider payment reform to incentivize greater efficiency and cost savings in health service provision.

As in many other countries, corruption contributes to health system inefficiency. In Southeast Asian countries, the most common corrupt practices in the health sector include nepotism, mismanagement of resources, regulatory capture of the sector by pharmaceutical and medical providers, bribery, and informal payments.[42] Lack of trust in the integrity of quality regulation in the health sector due to possible regulatory capture leads consumers to choose and providers to provide more expensive options than necessary. Health- and pharmaceutical-related businesses also end up spending large amounts on marketing, including payments to induce providers to procure and prescribe their products, which leads to inflated prices for consumers and/or the insurance fund.[43] Low official salaries of health workers in public facilities create pressures for health care providers to boost facility revenues to top up salaries, which can lead to providing more services and inputs to care than may be needed by patients. In 2022, with a monthly base salary of 1.49 million VND[44] and the highest salary coefficient for a high-level doctor of 8.0,[45] the highest monthly salary would be 11.92 million VND. According to a website collecting information on market salaries, the average monthly remuneration of an acute care nurse is 15.6 million VND, a general medical practitioner is 34.9 million VND, and a surgeon is 51.6 million VND.[46] Lack of regulation of medical equipment procurement has also resulted in artificial inflation of prices so facilities can charge a higher depreciation cost in the service price. This means society spends a high amount on many unnecessary inputs to care to achieve a surplus to boost health worker income. Patients concerned about whether they are getting all the care they need may also be induced to make informal payments to providers. Public complaints about the necessity for bribery for access and use of public services is rampant in health care, but also in education and most public services, with adverse impacts on national development. The Vietnam Provincial Governance and Public Administration Performance Index (PAPI) provides evidence that corruption remains a problem in Vietnam's health sector. In 2019, 31 percent of respondents agreed with the statement that bribes and corruption are prevalent in public health care services, although this is a decline from the peak of 38 percent in 2016, and the proportion of people reporting that they have to pay a bribe to obtain better service at public district hospitals has declined to just 5 percent in 2019.[47] During the CO-VID-19 pandemic, the government took a strong stance against corrupt behaviors that undermined the fight against the pandemic, such as inflating procurement prices of COVID test kits, price gouging, and hoarding of personal protective equipment. The Minister of Health and the Hanoi People's Committee Chairman were expelled from the Communist Party and arrested for their involvement in corruption related to CO-VID-19. Similar strong measures may be needed to restore trust in the health sector regulatory agencies.

Health systems imbalance between overcrowded high-tech hospitals in major urban centers and under-resourced primary care CHSs stands out as a major weakness of the current system. In the post–Đổi Mới period, CHSs continued to provide primary health care focused on public health measures and infectious disease control. But population needs, preferences, and purchasing power were changing, and demand for diagnosis and treatment services was increasing, both for common conditions like child respiratory infections and for increasingly prevalent NCDs. Instead of investing in primary curative care services at the CHS, however, the state health sector focused investments on hospitals. At the grassroots level, district hospitals became the main provider of primary curative care and gradually developed an increasing level of specialization. A large share of state investment funds and mobilization of private capital was channeled to the development of highly specialized, high-tech services in large central and provincial hospitals. The hospital autonomy policy has also put great emphasis on revenue generation, including development of higher-priced private services within public hospitals. Patients began to associate higher-priced, high-tech services with quality, reducing their desire to seek care at the CHS and increasing their dependence on hospitals for even the most basic curative care services. This is striking when looking at trends in the source of outpatient care between 2008 and 2018. During this period, the public hospitals' share of total outpatient visits rose from 31 to 51 percent, while the share seeking outpatient care in the CHS and regional polyclinic fell from 26 to 19 percent, and in the private sector fell from 41.5 to 29.2 percent.[48]

Excessive emphasis on curative care rather than integrated curative, preventive, and promotive services has also been influenced by post–Đổi Mới arrangements for financing recurrent costs of health service delivery. There is great concern in the health sector that the policy of devolving financial responsibility to localities, particularly for preventive services and programs, in a context of inadequate provincial revenues, declining donor funding after Vietnam became a middle-income country, and many competing demands for state spending, will lead to underfunding of these services. At the same time, the expansion in CHS treatment services covered by health insurance is leading CHS staff to focus on increasing the volume of treatment services to boost incomes from this more stable funding source, rather than disease prevention and health promotion.

In contrast to neglected routine preventive medicine services, Vietnam's pandemic preparedness and response has been very strong. Vietnam has received extensive technical assistance on infectious disease control from various development partners over several decades. Vietnam has had opportunities over the past two decades to test its readiness, leadership, and coordination through global pandemics and pandemic threats, such as SARS and avian influenza. The government's historical tendency toward self-reliance has led to substantial investments in vaccine research and production, and laboratory testing capacity. Early on in the pandemic, Vietnam had enlisted the support of the private sector for development and production of COVID-19 test kits and COVID-19 vaccine development.[49] Vietnam's initial successes in keeping case counts and deaths at low levels were achieved through basic public health measures like mask wearing, testing, contact tracing, quarantine, social distancing, and international flight restrictions. However, Vietnam was slow to procure vaccines and was caught off guard when the highly infectious delta variant arrived in April 2021. Slow reactions to outbreaks in the south, likely due to economic pressures to maintain production and growth, led to a massive ballooning of cases in the fourth wave, from fewer than 20,000 cases from the beginning of the epidemic until the end of June 2021, to over 11.4 million cases by the end of August 2022.[50] Although the government accelerated COVID-19 vaccination in response to this outbreak, particularly in areas with high infection rates, the lack of supplies, large population, and low starting point (less than 1 percent fully vaccinated at the beginning of the fourth wave), meant the population had low immunity, with the tragic consequence that deaths rose from ninety-two to 32,000 between June and the end of December 2021, reaching 43,000 by the end of August 2022.[51] However, national prioritization to procure and administer vaccinations quickly reversed the situation; by the end of February 2022, Vietnam ranked eighth in the world for vaccines administered and tenth in the world for persons boosted per 100 population.[52] This high societal immunity allowed Vietnam's authorities to avoid further strict social and economic restrictions, accepting a massive increase in COVID-19 cases with low mortality rates and limited pressure on hospitals, and since May 2022 has lifted COVID-19 flight restrictions.

INSUFFICIENT QUALITY

There are legitimate concerns over quality of health services in Vietnam. The growing violence against medical staff and complaints about health facilities are symptoms of growing mistrust of doctors due to patient perceptions of over-servicing, medical errors, and lack of legal recourse.[53] Like China, the Vietnamese government is concerned over implications for political stability. The focus of quality improvement in the post–Đổi Mới period was on adopting high-tech specialized technologies in hospital settings, somewhat neglecting the fact that quality of health care is multidimensional. Professional technical competence is of fundamental importance, but socio-humanistic interactions of the care experience and patient satisfaction should not be neglected.

The grassroots health care network is presently ill-equipped to respond to the changing health care needs and population expectations. A national survey tested doctors on their ability to respond to vignette scenarios in six provinces.[54] Results indicated that CHS doctors had limited knowledge about managing clinical case presentations; district doctors had better knowledge but spent less time asking questions in patient examinations and ordered more tests. In addition, communes have weak infrastructure, which is often dilapidated and lacking in basic equipment, contributing to poor staff morale. Low salaries and limited opportunities for income generation at the CHS continue to hinder the ability to attract and retain highly qualified family doctors to work at the CHS. The linkages between primary and tertiary care are weak and fragmented. And CHSs still lack the capacities, including human, financial, and infrastructure resources, for prevention and control of NCDs. At the same time, the CHSs face increased competition from the private sector (including moonlighting by state health workers) and improving geographic access for the population to hospital care.[55]

To overcome these shortcomings, reforms are underway in medical education and workforce accreditation and certification.[56] The 2009 Law on Examination and Treatment (in table 14.2) was formulated to ensure accreditation of medical education, residency training, and certification of clinical practice.[57] The Ministry of Education has accredited seventeen public and twenty-four private medical schools by the end of January 2022.[58] Competency standards for nurses, midwives, and medical technicians have been strengthened, while those for other allied health professionals are in early development, for example, physical therapists. The legal framework was further strengthened in 2017 on practicum training for health professionals, with a new decree that proposes a national testing center for licensing of medical graduates, establishes accreditation standards for residency training, and certifies competencies, especially for post-residency specialists. The challenge now is to move beyond laws and regulations to implementation.

The MOH has put several policies in place aimed at improving competencies of the existing workforce. One mechanism is to organize rotations of professionals from higher-level facilities to lower-level facilities and practical training in specific skills for lower-level staff at higher-level facilities.[59] New requirements for continuing medical education have also been put in place, although enforcement has proven difficult, particularly with the lack of systematic continuing medical education resources and opportunities.

Health facilities are also adopting more quality assurance measures. The MOH has developed quality standards and annually assesses achievement of these standards. The MOH developed patient satisfaction surveys and requires hospitals to use them for internal quality improvement, and an external entity to implement them for government oversight. However, these efforts are still largely focused on inputs or conditions amenable to quality, with little attention paid to actual processes to achieve clinical quality and desired health outcomes. Feedback mechanisms to hospitals remain weak, and little quality information is disseminated to the general population to provide information to use in selecting where to seek health care.

Although Vietnam has many professional medical associations, they do not yet have a formal role in quality assurance, standards setting, or continuing medical education. The MOH and provincial health departments, with limited human and financial resources, and conflicting roles as both regulator and service providers, are facing substantial challenges in implementing the quality assurance function. A more balanced role will have to be found for a government-professional partnership. The role of professional societies along with government should be purposefully designed to ensure quality, defined as effectiveness of services acceptable to the population.

Emerging Challenges and Opportunities

The goal of all health care systems is to impact positively on health status, ensure patient satisfaction, and offer financial protection against catastrophic expenditures. Today, Vietnam is at a crossroads in health: How can it sustainably meet the health needs of its people? That Vietnam needed to raise resources to finance a more technologically advanced health care system for the whole country is beyond dispute. Nearly all mobilizing efforts have impacts, some positive and some negative, on health equity, health care efficiency, and quality of care. Vietnam has been pragmatic in moving forward into the unchartered territory of how a socialist state and economy can be transformed into a mixed public-private health care system.

Like China, Vietnam is undergoing an intensive and rapid demographic and epidemiologic transition. Driven by lower fertility and improved longevity, Vietnam's population is aging. In 2020, 12.3 percent of the population was age sixty years or older, but this group's population share is projected to more than double to 27.2 percent by 2050.[60] Aging will place enormous demands on family-based care in addition to public services.

Professional care skill requirements will broaden to include not only medicine and nursing but ancillary support services like social work, visiting assistance at home, physical and occupational therapy, and rehabilitation, which are currently underdeveloped.

Along with an aging population, the burden of disease has shifted rapidly from communicable disease and maternal, neonatal, and nutritional conditions to chronic diseases in adults and the elderly. In 1986, the major causes of illness were cardiovascular disease, respiratory infections, and maternal-neonatal conditions. Today, NCDs constitute the major disease burden, including cardiovascular diseases, cancers, musculoskeletal disorders, and diabetes.[61] To these diseases of aging and lifestyle are added new threats like motor vehicle accidents, HIV/AIDS, air pollution, and vulnerability to climate change. Many common risk factors for NCDs are widespread—smoking, alcohol, fatty and salty diet, and physical inactivity. There are also comparatively neglected and poorly recognized (and also stigmatized) health problems like mental illness, substance abuse, and health-related disabilities.

New prevention and treatment strategies will have to be developed and effectively implemented in Vietnam. A multisectoral approach, beyond medical services, will be mandatory since many risk factors must be managed outside of the health sector. A good example is Vietnam's success in capping the explosive growth of HIV/AIDS. With the support of the Global Fund to Fight AIDS, Tuberculosis, and Malaria and the US-provided President's Emergency Plan for AIDS Relief funds, Vietnam has been able to engage sectors beyond health to reduce transmission and ensure antiretroviral coverage of HIV-positive cases. Entirely fresh and energetic strategies will be required in information and education communications on smoking cessation; alcohol consumption; dietary advice; regulation of salt, sugar, fats, and other food additives in processed foods; and physical fitness activities in schools and communities. The Vietnam Health Program initiated in 2019 provides a useful framework but will require substantial resources and cross-sectoral accountability mechanisms to ensure effective implementation. Lessons may need to be learned from the communication strategies during the COVID-19 response, which succeeded in mobilizing the population to comply with public health measures, despite inconveniences and costs.

The recent merging of multiple preventive medicine units into the provincial centers for disease control, the merging of district hospitals and district preventive medicine centers, and greater cohesion between the commune and district levels should also facilitate coordination and integration of related activities within the health sector; however, there is a need for closer supervision to ensure provinces allocate adequate resources for these new entities to complement the SHI funds in implementation of a comprehensive package of preventive and curative care services to achieve national health goals.

The health system for treatment will have to be revamped, especially at primary and home levels. In an era of NCDs and aging-related disabilities, rehabilitation and home-based care will be crucial. Medical knowledge and practice among family members in households will determine the success of prevention and treatment. Many people lack the ability to take care of their own health or have not taken responsibility to do so. Entirely new primary home-based care systems will need to be designed and implemented.

This will call for changing roles for government and nongovernment entities. Government's role will shift increasingly to stewardship and governance. Increased attention will need to be paid to ensure safety, avoid fraud, and promote value for money in health care services. Government financing should focus on disease prevention since people will, on their own, seek curative treatment but not invest sufficiently in prevention and promotion. An authoritative body will be required to systematically track and monitor key quality and equity indicators, and ensure that action is taken when inequities occur. These governance efforts will require better use of administrative data and new information technology for real-time monitoring. Rather than delivering services, government will have to promote universal availability of equitable primary health care and incentivize appropriate, quality, and effective care.

Government policies and regulations on health financing are needed for both private and public sectors to ensure a level playing field for achieving affordable, quality, and effective services with financial protection from catastrophic expenditures. Vietnam should build upon its single-payer system and begin to realign incentives of provider payments for quality and effectiveness. The goal must be to set incentives to overcome fragmentation toward an integrated health system.

In Vietnam, public curative care services have developed rapidly, accounting for a growing share of outpatient care and dominating inpatient care with over nine in ten visits in public facilities. Private health insurance is developing to cover services at private facilities or other services not covered by SHI. Private medical schools are being developed to train medical staff for labor export, but also to fill gaps in capacity domestically. Little is known about private health services, health insurance, or medical training, indicating limited government regulation and oversight of these sectors. There is the tension that the public-private mix may emphasize profits rather than health protection, high revenue-generating potential of hospitals, and high tech versus the more important essential basic health services, which are underfunded and of poor quality.

Importantly, Vietnam should enhance and enforce quality control in both the public and private sectors to avoid fraud and to ensure safety. There is a need to change incentives away from volume of services toward patient outcomes, or at least a bundling of services under capitation and/or case-based payments to reduce strong incentives for excess investment in high-tech services to overprovide to patients for revenue maximization. Concern about incomes of doctors needs to be taken into consideration, because simply paying official salaries without these additional revenues from volume maximization may push doctors to the private sector, leading to a public sector brain drain.

Civil society can play a critical role. This may be under-recognized and underappreciated. In many countries, civil society groups operate as "consumer watchdogs," identifying and stopping malpractice, fraud, safety violations, or wasteful expenditures (and charges). Also, in many countries, professional associations play a most critical role in professional conduct and professional validation. For many health risks related to behavior, civil society organizations provide public education to enable the population to minimize risky behavior. Health literacy campaigns are important health promotion tools. The new social media can be used for patient education, to help to moderate patient expectations, and to guide patient health-seeking behavior.

Vietnam should grasp fresh opportunities to uphold its traditional global leadership role as an admired and tested model of health equity. Although Vietnam is keeping pace with neighboring countries, indeed doing better than many in terms of basic health indicators, many emerging challenges, such as the ongoing COVID-19 pandemic, demand innovation and strong governmental and civil society responses. Vietnam has thankfully improved on underlying social determinants of health (education, housing, poverty alleviation) and basic public health measures. Vietnam's health system has moved beyond a socialist system as in Cuba, but it did not abandon wholesale state-supported grassroots facilities like China.

All countries are grappling with dynamic public-private blends. Vietnam's health reforms are complex and present many tensions, paradoxes, and dilemmas. Continuing changes and challenges can be expected. Reexamination of health care prevention and treatment will be required to enhance access and improve quality. Health inequity can emerge as a growing problem as the economy diversifies, especially if the voice and role of civil society are not advancing adequately. Professional competency may improve with reform of education, accreditation, and certification. However, it can also worsen if misguided provider incentives are not corrected and if patient dissatisfaction is not tackled. The danger is that excessive focus on hospital-centric high-tech care will not address the core problem of universal affordable access with quality. Financial protection will be essential if Vietnam is to avoid catastrophic health expenditures. Private commercial investments in health care have already become entrenched. There is no going back. Strong government oversight, regulation, and evaluation will be necessary to continue to protect the health of the public.

Notes

1. World Bank, "World Development Indicators."
2. National Technology Center for COVID-19 Prevention and Control, *COVID-19 Data*.
3. World Bank, "World Development Indicators."
4. World Bank, "World Development Indicators."
5. World Bank, "World Development Indicators."
6. London, chapter 12 in this volume.
7. World Bank, "World Development Indicators."
8. Dapice, chapter 11 in this volume.
9. World Bank, "World Development Indicators."
10. World Bank, "World Development Indicators."
11. World Bank, "World Development Indicators."
12. Rydstrom, chapter 13 in this volume.
13. World Health Organization, "The Global Health Observatory."
14. OECD and WHO, *Health at a Glance*, 18.
15. Gottret and Schieber, *Health Financing Revisited*.
16. Politburo Resolution 46 (2005); Communist Party Resolution 20 (2017).

17. London, "Reasserting the State."

18. World Health Organization, *Social Health Insurance*, 1.

19. Xu et al., "Exploring the Thresholds," 16.

20. Ministry of Health Decision 1188/QD-BYT.

21. Government Decree 10, no. 10/2002/ND-CP.

22. Law on Pharmacy, no. 105/2016/QH13.

23. Government Decree no. 69/2008/ND-CP.

24. Vo and Lofgren, "Institutional Analysis of the Fiscal Autonomy."

25. Le et al., "Health Insurance and Patient Satisfaction."

26. Fforde, "Vietnam and COVID-19."

27. General Statistics Office, *Statistical Yearbook of Vietnam 2020*, 215.

28. World Bank, "World Development Indicators."

29. General Statistics Office, *Statistical Yearbook of Vietnam 2020*, 215.

30. Ministry of Finance, *The Annual Report of Vietnam Insurance Market 2020*, 42.

31. Ministry of Health, *Health Statistics Yearbook 1995*, 52; Ministry of Health, *Health Statistics Yearbook 2018*, 102.

32. Ministry of Health, *Health Statistics Yearbook 2018*, 58.

33. General Statistics Office, *Results of the 2017 Economic Census*, 79.

34. Ministry of Health, *Health Statistics Yearbook 2018*, 109.

35. World Bank, "Growing Healthy"; Ministry of Health, "55 Years of Vietnam's Revolutionary Health Sector Development"; Witter, "'*Doi Moi*' and Health."

36. Ministry of Health, *Health Statistics Yearbook 2018*, 120, 124; General Statistics Office, *Results of the Viet Nam Household Living Standards Survey 2018*, 191.

37. Partnership for Action in Health Equity, *Health Equity in Vietnam*; World Health Organization, "Health Inequities and Their Causes."

38. Hoang Van Minh and Nguyen Viet Hung, "Health and Social Determinants of Health."

39. General Statistics Office and UNICEF, *Viet Nam Multiple Indicator Cluster Survey 2014*, 157.

40. General Statistics Office, *Results of the Viet Nam Household Living Standards Survey 2018*, 199–212.

41. Teo et al., *The Future of Health Financing in Vietnam*, 19.

42. Zúñiga, "Anti-Corruption in the Health Sector."

43. Nguyen et al., "Corruption Practices in Drug Prescribing."

44. Decree 38/2019/ND-CP.

45. Integrated document 01/VBHN-BNV (2016), Decree on Salary for Civil Servants.

46. Salary Explorer, "Health and Medical Average Salaries in Vietnam."

47. CECODES et al., "The 2019 Viet Nam Governance and Public Administration Performance Index (PAPI)," 95.

48. General Statistics Office, *Results of the Viet Nam Household Living Standards Survey 2018*, 199.

49. Ministry of Health, "List of COVID-19 Diagnostic Biological Products"; Le, "Vietnam Targets Human Trials of Covid-19 Vaccine."

50. National Technology Center for COVID-19 Prevention and Control, *COVID-19 Data*.

51. National Technology Center for COVID-19 Prevention and Control, *COVID-19 Data*.

52. World Health Organization, "COVID-19 Dashboard."

53. Thanh Nam, "Khi ngành y còn đơn độc"; VNS, "Violence against Vietnam's Health Workers."

54. World Bank and Health Strategy and Policy Institute, *Quality and Equity in Basic Health Care*.

55. World Bank and Health Strategy and Policy Institute, *Quality and Equity in Basic Health Care*.

56. Fan et al., "Medical Education in Vietnam."

57. Vian et al., "Confronting Corruption in the Health Sector."

58. Ministry of Education and Training, "Danh sách các cơ sở giáo dục đại học được công nhận đạt tiêu chuẩn chất lượng giáo dục."

59. Takashima et al., "A Review of Vietnam's Healthcare Reform."

60. United Nations, "World Population Prospects 2019."

61. World Health Organization, *Noncommunicable Diseases (NCD) Country Profiles, Vietnam*.

References

Anindya, Kanya, John Tayu Lee, Barbara McPake, Siswanto Agus Wilopo, Christopher Millett, and Natalie Carvalho. "Impact of Indonesia's National Health Insurance Scheme on Inequality in Access to Maternal Health Services: A Propensity Score Matched Analysis." *Journal of Global Health* 10, no. 1 (2020): 1–12.

CECODES, VFF-CRT, RTA, and UNDP. "The 2019 Viet Nam Governance and Public Administration Performance Index (PAPI): Measuring Citizens' Experiences." Hanoi: Centre for Community Support and Development Studies, Centre for Research and Training of the Viet Nam Fatherland Front, Real-Time Analytics, and United Nations Development Programme, 2020.

Central Population and Housing Census Steering Committee. *Kết quả Tổng điều tra dân số và nhà ở Thời điểm 0 giờ ngày 01 tháng 4 năm 2019* (Results of the 2019 Population and Housing Census, April 1, 2019). Hanoi: Statistical Publishing House, 2019.

Fan, A. P., D. T. Tran, R. O. Kosik, G. A. Mandell, H. S. Hsu, and Y. S. Chen. "Medical Education in Vietnam." *Medical Teacher* 34, no. 2 (2012): 103–7. https://www.researchgate.net/publication/221790483_Medical_education_in_Vietnam.

Fang, Hai, Karen Eggleston, Kara Hanson, and Ming Wu. "Enhancing Financial Protection under China's Social Health Insurance to Achieve Universal Health Coverage." *BMJ* 365 (2019): l2378.

Fforde, Adam. "Vietnam and COVID-19: More Mark (Zuckerberg) than Marx." *Melbourne Asia Review*, October 29, 2020. DOI: 10.37839/MAR2652-550X4.13.

General Statistics Office. *Results of the 2017 Economic Census*. Hanoi: Statistical Publishing House, 2018. https://www.gso.gov.vn/du-lieu-va-so-lieu-thong-ke/2019/03/ket-qua-tong-dieu-tra-kinh-te-nam-2017/.

———. *Results of the Viet Nam Household Living Standards Survey 2018*. Hanoi: Statistical Publishing House, 2019. https://www.gso.gov.vn/default.aspx?tabid=512&idmid=5&ItemID=19615.

———. *Statistical Yearbook of Vietnam 2019*. Hanoi: Statistical Publishing House, 2020. https://www.gso.gov.vn/en/data-and-statistics/2020/09/statistical-yearbook-2019/.

———. *Statistical Yearbook of Vietnam 2020*. Hanoi: Statistical Publishing House, 2021. https://www.gso.gov.vn/du-lieu-va-so-lieu-thong-ke/2021/07/nien-giam-thong-ke-2021/.

General Statistics Office and UNICEF. *Viet Nam Multiple Indicator Cluster Survey 2014: Final Report*. Hanoi: Statistical Publishing House. 2015. https://www.gso.gov.vn/wp-content/uploads/2019/04/6.MICSVIETNAM2014310815.compressed.pdf.

Gottret, Pablo, and George Schieber. *Health Financing Revisited*. Washington, DC: World Bank, 2006.

Hoang, Van Minh, and Nguyen Viet Hung. "Health and Social Determinants of Health in Vietnam: Local Evidence and International Implications." *International Journal of Public Health* 62, no. S1 (2017): 1–2.

Le, Duc-Cuong, Tatsuhiko Kubo, Yoshihisa Fujino, Truong-Minh Pham, and Shinya Matsuda. "Health Care System in Vietnam: Current Situation and Challenges." *Asian Pacific Journal of Disease Management* 4, no. 2. (2010): 23–30.

Le, Nga. "Vietnam Targets Human Trials of Covid-19 Vaccine This Year." *Vnexpress*, July 23, 2020. https://e.vnexpress.net/news/news/vietnam-targets-human-trials-of-covid-19-vaccine-this-year-4134347.html.

Le, Nga, Wim Groot, Sonila M. Tomini, and Florian Tomini. "Health Insurance and Patient Satisfaction: Evidence from the Poorest Regions of Vietnam." *MERIT Working Papers* 2018-040. United Nations University–Maastricht, Economic and Social Research Institute on Innovation and Technology (MERIT), 2018.

London, Jonathan D. "Reasserting the State in Viet Nam Health Care and the Logics of Market-Leninism." *Policy and Society* 27, no. 2 (2008): 115–28.

Ministry of Education and Training. "Danh sách các cơ sở giáo dục đại học được công nhận đạt tiêu chuẩn chất lượng giáo dục" (List of universities accredited as meeting educational standards). January 31, 2022. https://moet.gov.vn/giaoducquocdan/khao-thi-va-kiem-dinh-chat-luong-giao-duc/Pages/Default.aspx?ItemID=7742.

Ministry of Finance. *The Annual Report of Vietnam Insurance Market 2020*. Hanoi: Finance Publishing House, 2021.

Ministry of Health. "55 Years of Vietnam's Revolutionary Health Sector Development (1945–2000)." Hanoi: Medical Publishing House, January 2001.

————. *Health Statistics Yearbook 1995.* Hanoi: Health Statistics and Informatic Division, n.d.

————. *Health Statistics Yearbook 2018.* Hanoi: Health Statistics and Informatic Division, 2020. https://moh.gov.vn/thong-ke-y-te.

————. "List of COVID-19 Diagnostic Biological Products at General Department of Preventive Medicine." 2020. http://vncdc.gov.vn/vi/phong-chong-dich-benh-viem-phoi-cap-ncov/13987/danh-sach-cac-sinh-pham-chan-doan-covid-19.

National Technology Center for COVID-19 Prevention and Control, National Cybersecurity Center, Ministry of Information and Communications. *COVID-19 Data.* 2022. https://covid19.ncsc.gov.vn/dulieu.

Nguyen, Tuan A., Rosemary Knight, Andrea Mant, Husna Razee, Geoffrey Brooks, Thu H. Dang, and Elizabeth E. Roughead. "Corruption Practices in Drug Prescribing in Vietnam: An Analysis Based on Qualitative Interviews." *BMC Health Services Research* 18, no. 1 (2018): 587.

OECD and WHO. *Health at a Glance: Asia/Pacific 2018: Measuring Progress towards Universal Health Coverage.* Paris: OECD Publishing, 2018. https://doi.org/10.1787/health_glance_ap-2018-en.

Partnership for Action in Health Equity. *Health Equity in Vietnam.* 2011. http://cphs.huph.edu.vn/uploads/tainguyen/sachvabaocao/HealthequityPerspective.pdf.

PhilHealth. "2018 Stats and Charts." 2019. https://www.philhealth.gov.ph/about_us/statsncharts/snc2018.pdf.

Salary Explorer. "Health and Medical Average Salaries in Vietnam." 2022. http://www.salaryexplorer.com/.

Sumriddetchkajorn, Kanitsorn, Kenji Shimazaki, Taichi Ono, Tesshu Kusaba, Kotaro Sato, and Naoyuki Kobayashi. "Universal Health Coverage and Primary Care, Thailand." *Bulletin of the World Health Organization* 97, no. 6 (2019): 415–22. https://www.who.int/bulletin/volumes/97/6/18-223693/en/.

Takashima, K., K. Wada, T. T. Tra, and D. R. Smith. "A Review of Vietnam's Healthcare Reform through the Direction of Healthcare Activities (DOHA)." *Environmental Health and Preventive Medicine* 22, no. 1 (2017): 74.

Teo, Hui Sin, Sarah Bales, Caryn Bredenkamp, and Jewelwayne Salcedo Cain. *The Future of Health Financing in Vietnam: Ensuring Sufficiency, Efficiency, and Sustainability.* Washington, DC: World Bank, 2019.

Thanh Nam. "Khi ngành y còn đơn độc trong 'cuộc chiến' chống bạo lực." *Nhan Dan*, April 23, 2018. https://www.nhandan.com.vn/chinhtri/item/36188702-khi-nganh-y-con-don-doc-trong-cuoc-chien-chong-bao-luc.html.

United Nations, Department of Economic and Social Affairs, Population Division. "World Population Prospects 2019." 2019. https://population.un.org/wpp/Download/Standard/Population/.

Vian, Taryn, Derick W. Brinkerhoff, Frank G. Feeley, Matthieu Salomon, and Nguyen Thi Kieu Vien. "Confronting Corruption in the Health Sector in Vietnam: Patterns and Prospects." *Public Administration and Development* 32, no. 1 (2012): 49–63.

VNS. "Violence against Vietnam's Health Workers Seen Growing." *VietnamNet Bridge*, November 3, 2015. https://english.vietnamnet.vn/fms/society/145300/violence-against-vietnam-s-health-workers-seen-growing.html.

Vo, Minh Thi Hai, and Karl Lofgren. "An Institutional Analysis of the Fiscal Autonomy of Public Hospitals in Vietnam." *Asia & the Pacific Policy Studies* 6, no. 1 (2019): 90–107.

Witter, Sophie. "'Doi Moi' and Health: The Effect of Economic Reforms on the Health System in Vietnam." *International Journal of Health Planning and Management* 11, no. 2 (1996): 159–72.

World Bank. "Growing Healthy: A Review of Vietnam's Health Sector." Washington, DC: World Bank Group, 2001.

————. "World Development Indicators." 2022. https://databank.worldbank.org/source/world-development-indicators.

World Bank and Health Strategy and Policy Institute. *Quality and Equity in Basic Health Care Services in Vietnam: Findings from the 2015 Vietnam District and Commune Health Facility Survey.* Washington, DC: World Bank, June 2016.

World Health Organization. "COVID-19 Dashboard." Geneva: World Health Organization, 2022. https://covid19.who.int./

————. "Global Health Expenditure Database (GHED)." Geneva: International Health Partnership, 2022. https://apps.who.int/nha/database.

———. "The Global Health Observatory." 2020. https://www.who.int/data/gho/data/indicators/indicator-details/GHO/.

———. "Health Inequities and Their Causes." February 22, 2018. https://www.who.int/news-room/facts-in-pictures/detail/health-inequities-and-their-causes.

———. *Noncommunicable Diseases (NCD) Country Profiles, Vietnam.* 2018. https://www.who.int/nmh/countries/vnm_en.pdf.

———. *Social Health Insurance: Report of a Regional Expert Group Meeting. New Delhi, India, 13–15 March 2001.* New Delhi: World Health Organization, June 2003. https://apps.who.int/iris/bitstream/handle/10665/206364/B3457.pdf?sequence=1&isAllowed=y.

Xu, Ke, Priyanka Saksena, Matthew Jowett, Chandika Indikadahena, Joe Kutzin, and David B. Evans. "Exploring the Thresholds of Health Expenditure for Protection against Financial Risk." *World Health Report*, 2010. http://digicollection.org/hss/documents/s18268en/s18268en.pdf.

Zúñiga, Nieves. "Anti-Corruption in the Health Sector in Southeast Asia." Transparency International, 2018. https://www.u4.no/publications/anti-corruption-in-the-health-sector-in-southeast-asia.pdf.

PART IV

The Changing International Economic and Political Context

CHAPTER 15

The Evolution of Vietnamese Foreign Policy in the "Doi Moi" Era

Alexander L. Vuving

In December 1986, the Sixth Congress of the ruling Communist Party of Vietnam (CPV) instituted profound changes in the country's domestic and foreign policy and elevated *"đổi mới"* (reform, literally: renovation) to the status of a grand cause (*sự nghiệp lớn*). Every subsequent congress of the CPV reaffirmed this grand cause, and the post-1986 period became known as the *doi moi* or reform era. The status and persistence of *doi moi* have given rise to a popular narrative that Vietnam is "in transition"—from state-command to market-driven economy and from totalitarianism to democracy. Similarly, the dominant view on Vietnamese foreign policy in the period portrays it as the unfolding or implementation of a new orientation characterized by international integration, diversification, and multilateralism that was introduced in the latter half of the 1980s. However, the linear progress suggested by these narratives is misleading at best. The interaction of international changes and domestic politics has shaped Vietnam's strategic trajectory in the *doi moi* era as a zigzag course with several directions.

Tracing the evolution of Vietnamese foreign policy since the 1980s, this chapter identifies four major turning points in the last four decades (see table 15.1 for a summary). As Vietnam's foreign policy lies in the interface between Vietnamese and world politics, its evolution reflects changes in both environments. The turning points of Vietnamese foreign policy were triggered by events in the international arena that fundamentally altered the environment of Vietnam's quests for resources, security, and identity. When Vietnam's ruling elites responded to these changes, they set in motion corresponding changes in Vietnamese domestic and foreign policy. The evolution of Vietnam's foreign policy thus roughly corresponded with the evolution of the Vietnamese state. This chapter will tease out the complex relationships between the international environment, the nature of the Vietnamese state, and Vietnamese foreign policy, and shed light on the worldviews and motives behind Vietnam's foreign policy.

The interaction between international and domestic politics is channeled through multiple "conveyor belts," the most consequential of which can be called "policy currents."[1] These are broad schools of thought regarding the fundamental structures and dynamics of the world, the desired place of the country in the world, and the relationships between

Table 15.1
Major turning points in Vietnamese foreign policy, 1980–2022

Year	International cause	Domestic effect	Foreign policy guidelines and national security strategy
1986	Deep crisis and large-scale reform in the Soviet bloc, with Gorbachev's *perestroika*, *glasnost*, and new thinking	Rise of modernizers	Resolution No. 13 of the Politburo, May 1988
1989	Collapse of Communist regimes in Eastern Europe	Dominance of anti-Westerners; rise of rent-seekers	Resolutions of the Third Plenum of the Seventh Central Committee, June 1992
2003	US unipolar power, vividly displayed by the US invasion of Iraq	Prevalence of rent-seekers	Resolution of the Eighth Plenum of the Ninth Central Committee, July 2003
2014	China's aggressive expansionism, graphically shown by the installation of a giant oil rig, the HYSY-981, within Vietnam's exclusive economic zone	Rise of moderates; fall of anti-Westerners	

the key components of the country. These policy currents evolve with the development of views on those questions, while their memberships are often fluid and not always mutually exclusive. Five major Vietnamese policy currents were distinguishable in the last four decades. Their different constellations characterize different phases in the evolution of the Vietnamese state and foreign policy. During the first three years after the launch of *doi moi*, until 1989, the general orientation of Vietnamese politics was that of a neo-Stalinist state in reform as a new policy current that placed the nation above any political party rose to prominence. This policy current aspired to modernize and industrialize the country and saw a historic opportunity to achieve these goals in the trends of globalization and a technological revolution that characterized the contemporary world. Between 1989 and 2003, however, the dominant policy current saw the antagonism between two social orders, socialism and capitalism, as the elemental source of world dynamics. Its central objective in the period was to fight Western influence and frustrate perceived Western strategy. As it placed the Communist Party above the nation, its ultimate goal was to preserve Communist Party rule. The general orientation of this period was that of a neo-Stalinist state in tactical retreat, which allowed modernization and international integration to advance to some extent in subordination to anti-Westernism. Between 2003 and 2014, the dominant policy current was a "child" from the "marriage" of anti-Westernism and modernization. Highly pragmatic, it was flexible about the relationship between the nation and the Communist Party. Like modernization, it emphasized international integration, but its preference within international integration differed from that of modernization. If it sometimes sought to modernize the country or to preserve Communist Party rule, it was because it saw opportunities to extract rent in these processes. The dominance of this policy current has transformed the neo-Stalinist state into a rent-seeking one that retained many Leninist practices and institutions due to their usefulness. Marxist-Leninist ideology served as a fig leaf to cover the embarrassing rent-seeking nature. Starting in 2014, the rent-seeking state has been on a correction course as rent-seeking was rivaled by moderation, the policy current of the middle of the road between modernization and regime survivalism, the previous incarnation of which was anti-Westernism. Events in Vietnam's relations with China and the United States in 2014 were the last push to morph anti-Westernism into regime survivalism, which accepted the Western-led international order while endeavoring to preserve Communist Party rule in Vietnam. Thus, by the latter half of the 2010s, all major Vietnamese policy currents shared the integrationist worldview, although each strove to anchor Vietnam to a different place in the world. For modernizers, the ideal place was an advantageous position to compete in the world market; for rent-seekers, it was a comfortable place to collect rents; for regime survivalists, it was a secure abode to maintain Communist Party rule.

Throughout the *doi moi* era, Vietnamese politics evolved from a neo-Stalinist state into a rent-seeking state, both employing the Leninist regime, but the trajectory was far from linear. The following four sections will each examine a phase in the evolution of Vietnamese politics since the mid-1980s. The concluding section will briefly address the key challenges and potentials for change lying ahead for Vietnamese foreign policy.

A Neo-Stalinist State in Reform, 1986–89

In the mid-1980s, a prolonged economic crisis and near-famines that started in the late 1970s, coupled with two concurrent wars of attrition—military conflicts with China along the northern border and a counterinsurgency war in Cambodia—and the diplomatic isolation resulting from the military intervention in Cambodia, forced Vietnam's ruling elite to adopt large-scale reform. After trying different directions of economic reform since 1979, the CPV announced a comprehensive reform program at its Sixth Congress in December 1986 and, in the spirit of "renovate or die" (*đổi mới hay là chết*), declared "renovation" as a grand cause of the Party. This partial but large break with the past was accelerated by the election of Truong Chinh, who had turned from a conservative to a reformer during 1983–86, as Party chief to replace the deceased Le Duan in July 1986.[2] Vietnam's severe economic crisis was part of a systemic governance and economic impasse that haunted the Communist countries. Responding to this predicament, newly elected Soviet leader Mikhail Gorbachev introduced a radical reform program, commonly known as *perestroika* (restructuring) and *glasnost* (openness, transparency), announced at the Twenty-Seventh Congress of the Communist Party of the Soviet Union in February 1986. As the Soviet Union was financing a large part of Vietnam's government budget through massive economic and military aid, the new Soviet policy exerted a strong pressure for reform in Vietnam. At the same time, "new thinking" (новое мышление, *novoe myshlenie*), the ideology undergirding the new Soviet policy, provided reform-minded Vietnamese with concepts and arguments to see and understand the world in a new light. Although elements of the new worldview had been present among Vietnamese policymakers since the early 1970s, the Gorbachevian new thinking was most instrumental in boosting the new worldview's coherence and legitimacy. The new worldview introduced the largest turning point in Communist Vietnam's foreign policy as it fundamentally broke with the old orthodoxy that had guided the state's behavior since the late 1940s. It did not replace the old orthodoxy, however, and the competition of the two *Weltanschauungs* would shape Vietnam's grand strategy throughout the *doi moi* era.

The old worldview through which Vietnamese leaders made sense of the world originated from the Stalinist and neo-Stalinist worldviews of the Soviet Union. Adopting the Stalinist worldview, Vietnam's Communist leaders divided the world into "two camps"—a socialist camp headed by the Soviet Union and a capitalist camp led by the United States—and explained international outcomes as the results of "four contradictions"—between the socialist and the capitalist systems, between the bourgeoisie and the proletariat, between oppressed peoples and colonialism, and among imperialist countries themselves. In the early 1970s, a third, neo-Stalinist, key tenet was added, which saw global progress as driven by "three revolutionary currents" represented by the socialist bloc, the communist and working-class movement in the capitalist countries, and the national liberation movement. While the Soviet variant stressed the leading role of the Soviet Union in the socialist system and the revolutionary currents, the Vietnamese variant emphasized Vietnam's role as the "spearhead" (*mũi nhọn*) of the world's national liberation movement, an element that was absent in the original Soviet variant. Similarly, when Vietnamese Communists embraced the Stalinist worldview in the 1940s, they assigned their country the role of an "outpost" (*tiền đồn*) of socialism against capitalism-imperialism in Southeast Asia.[3]

Although no less coherent, the new worldview was far less developed than the old worldview. Its elements were scattered in the writings and speeches of reform-minded intellectuals and politicians, most notably Nguyen Co Thach (foreign minister, 1980–91; vice premier, 1987–91), Vo Van Kiet (vice premier, 1982–91; prime minister, 1991–97), General Vo Nguyen Giap (vice premier, 1955–91), and Vo Chi Cong (president, 1987–92). The new worldview later found its more comprehensive and coherent statements in Kiet's memo to the Politburo, dated August 9, 1995, and Thach's book on world dynamics, published in 1998.[4]

If the old worldview was solidified by the binary structure of the Cold War and the role of the Vietnam War in this global conflict, the new worldview took shape in the waves of technological revolution and globalization that have swept the world since the 1970s. Inspired by the success of the newly industrialized countries in the Asia-Pacific, influenced by "new thinking" in the Soviet Union, and drawing from Vietnam's own experience, the new worldview rose to prominence in the second half of the 1980s and served as the intellectual backbone of efforts to "renovate foreign policy thinking" (*đổi mới tư duy đối ngoại*) during these pivotal years. It portrays the world as a single system and a single market where nations big and small are interdependent and, although big powers have the most say in world politics, smaller countries can achieve agency and prosperity by finding an

advantageous place in the international division of labor, riding on the tides of technological revolution (called "scientific-technical revolution" in the 1980s) and globalization
(called "internationalization" in the 1980s), and engaging in an "economic race" to development. Based on this image of the world, new thinkers advocated peaceful coexistence
with China, the United States, and ASEAN; the priority of economic development in national security strategy; integration into the global and regional economy; finding a niche
in the world's transition from the industrial age to the information age; and the primacy
of national interests over ideological solidarity in international relations.[5] This new world
outlook, couched in the old language of a struggle between socialist and imperialist forces,
underlay the foreign policy guidelines and national security strategy titled "Maintaining
the Peace, Developing the Economy," commonly referred to as Resolution 13, which was
adopted by the CPV Politburo in May 1988.[6]

In the spirit of the new worldview, Vietnam decided to withdraw its troops from Cambodia and Laos and cut its standing military forces by half, from about 1.2 to 0.6 million.
In December 1987, Vietnam passed its first Foreign Direct Investment Law, which was
touted as one of the most liberal in Southeast Asia at that time as it allowed fully foreign-
owned enterprises. In November 1988, CPV chief Nguyen Van Linh told visiting Philip-
pine Foreign Minister Raul Manglapus that Vietnam was "eager to join ASEAN," a
grouping that was still generally thought to be an extended hand of the United States and
the West.[7] In December 1988, Hanoi removed the characterization of China as a "hege-
monist aggressor" from Vietnam's Constitution. On the economic front, both the exigen-
cies of an economy in crisis and the reorientation of foreign policy plugged Vietnam into
its surrounding region and the Western-led world market. Vietnam's exports to the "capitalist world," using convertible currencies, surged to 44.6 percent in 1988 and, with 58.5 percent
of the total exports in 1989, surpassed the country's exports to the socialist countries for
the first time.[8]

However, Resolution 13 met with enormous internal opposition. Shortly before its passage, the April 1988 issue of the Party's central ideological forum *Tạp chí Cộng sản* (Communist Review) published a long article by Defense Minister Le Duc Anh in which he
argued that "imperialism led by US imperialists always directs its vehement attacks to the
socialist states in order to exterminate them" and warned of illusions about the anti-
Communist objectives and schemes of the imperialist-capitalist West. Anh's article was a
veiled counterattack on an earlier long article in the February issue of the same journal by
Phan Doan Nam, a close aid of Thach, which heavily criticized the two-camp worldview
and outlined the new thinking in foreign and security policy that would lend Resolution
13 its new direction.[9]

Resolution 13 itself was a compromise document that imparted the new worldview in
the language of the old. After its undisclosed adoption, the struggle between new and
old thinking continued, with the tide of battle tilting toward new thinking in 1988, then
returning to a delicate balance in the first half of 1989. The resurgence of old thinking in
Vietnam went hand in hand with the advance of radical changes and the resultant weak-
ening of Communist party rule in the socialist countries. In March 1989, about a month
after Hungary's Communist party approved the transition to a multiparty system, the Sixth

Plenum of the Sixth CPV Central Committee rejected pluralism and laid out the "basic principles of *doi moi*" which reaffirmed the Party's adherence to the socialist road and Marxism-Leninism as the Party's ideological foundation. The new worldview was dealt a severe blow at the Seventh Plenum of the Central Committee in August, which was convened to discuss "some pressing issues of ideological work in the current domestic and international situation," while it was overshadowed by Poland's appointment of the first non-Communist head of government in the Soviet bloc. In his remarks concluding the Plenum, General Secretary Nguyen Van Linh resurrected the two-camp worldview and, in an unmistakable attack on Thach and other proponents of the new worldview, claimed that the dismissal of the old worldview "has led certain persons to mistakenly believe that the nature of imperialism has changed." Contrary to the spirit of Resolution 13, Linh declared, "we do not nurture the illusion that the imperialist forces are willing to achieve peaceful coexistence with us." Marshaling a long list of evidence in support of the two-camp, four-contradiction doctrine, Linh argued that the fundamental conflicts between Communists and the United States remained vivid and highly relevant, and what had changed were their manifestations only. He stated:

> It is for this reason that the class struggle between socialism and capitalism to resolve the issue of who will defeat whom continues all over the world. It is for this reason that we need to further promote proletarian internationalism and socialist internationalism and join hands with other socialist forces, revolutionary forces, and progressive and peace-loving peoples worldwide in creating a combined strength to oppose the imperialist and reactionary forces. We must further sharpen the determination to protect the socialist Fatherland, effectively cope with all dark plots and acts detrimental to our country's security and territorial integrity, and frustrate the imperialists' and other reactionary forces' schemes aimed at causing our nation and other socialist countries to break away from the socialist path.[10]

These words are worth quoting in full because, as it turned out, they articulate the principal tenets of the conservatives' agenda for many years to come.

A Two-Headed Grand Strategy, 1989–2003

The successive collapses of Communist regimes in Eastern Europe in the second half of 1989 caused psychological shock waves across the socialist countries. In Vietnam, they prompted Linh and his fellow conservatives, who felt regime survival at stake, to seek an anti-Western alliance of the remaining socialist countries to preserve Communist Party rule. As their quest proved sterile in Eastern Europe, they turned to China, hoping that Beijing would assume leadership of the socialist world and form a strategic alliance with Vietnam despite fresh hostility between the two.[11]

Domestic struggle between old and new thinkers in the run-up to the Seventh CPV Congress in June 1991 as well as the policies toward Vietnam of China and the United

States cemented the anti-Westerners' prevalence over the modernizers. Eager efforts by anti-Westerners, notably General Secretary Linh and Defense Minister Anh, to reconcile with China led to a summit meeting at Chengdu in September 1990, the first between Chinese and Vietnamese leaders since China invaded Vietnam in 1979, and then to the renormalization of relations in November 1991.[12] Shortly after the Chengdu meeting, from which he was excluded at China's request, Foreign Minister Thach reached out to the United States, staying there for weeks, but returning empty-handed. The United States waited a week after the Chengdu summit to agree to talk about normalization with Vietnam; announced in April 1991, its vision for normalization was a multistage road map that would take several years to complete. It restored diplomatic relations with Vietnam in July 1995, a year after ASEAN approved Vietnam's accession to the group. The US approach was to stay one or more steps behind China and ASEAN in engagement with its former enemy.[13] Inside Vietnam, the position of the anti-Westerners was further strengthened after they managed to remove Tran Xuan Bach, the leading proponent of pluralism and a senior Politburo member, from the Central Committee at its Eighth Plenum in March 1990. At the Twelfth Plenum in May 1991, General Giap, another prominent reformer, fell victim to a fake plot fabricated by the military intelligence agency, which destroyed his chance to stay on the Central Committee.[14]

The new arrangement of leadership that was elected at the Seventh CPV Congress in June 1991 had an anti-Westerner, Do Muoi, as the new Party chief; another anti-Westerner, Le Duc Anh, as the new state president; and a modernizer, Vo Van Kiet, as the new prime minister, with Anh assuming, unprecedentedly, the authority to oversee defense, security, and foreign policy. The most vocal critics of pluralism at the March 1990 plenum, including Dao Duy Tung, Nguyen Duc Binh, Nong Duc Manh, and Nguyen Ha Phan, were the rising stars in the new Politburo and Secretariat. This first CPV congress after the Cold War laid the foundation for a neo-Stalinist state in tactical retreat. It ensured that conservatives both enjoyed an overwhelming majority in the Politburo and had veto over important issues, while economic reform and international opening were necessary in the post-Cold War environment. As a result, reform and opening were implemented half-heartedly in a piecemeal manner.

At its Third Plenum in June 1992, the first after the disintegration of the Soviet Union, the Seventh Central Committee discussed foreign policy guidelines and national security strategy in the new situation. It reaffirmed the new foreign policy approach set out in Resolution 13 and announced at the Seventh Congress, summarized by the keywords "diversification" (*đa dạng hoá*), meaning to include in the focus of foreign policy not just political and military aspects but also economic and technology cooperation, and "multidirectionalization" (*đa phương hoá*), meaning to include in the priority of foreign policy not just socialist and traditionally friendly states but also regional and major capitalist countries. It reiterated the slogan proclaimed at the Seventh Congress, "Vietnam wants to befriend all countries in the world." But like the Seventh Congress, it also emphasized "solidarity with socialist countries." It set the foreign policy priority first on relations with Communist states, second with countries in the Asia-Pacific region, and third with the advanced industrial countries in the West.[15] While identifying economic opening as a main foreign policy objective, it stressed that fighting "peaceful evolution," an imagined scheme thought to be orchestrated by the West to subvert the Communist regime, was the "top urgent" national security task. A classified directive attached to the national security strategy, drafted by the Le Duc Anh faction, instructed Party cadres on the geopolitical proximity between Vietnam and foreign countries. Neatly reflecting the two-camp perspective, it divided the world into four concentric circles. According to this directive, Vietnam's closest friends were the four remaining Communist states—China, Laos, Cuba, and North Korea—plus Cambodia, which was co-ruled by the originally Vietnam-installed Cambodian People's Party. The second innermost circle included the former socialist countries in Eastern Europe, where Hanoi hoped for a resurgence of Communist parties, and India, a major Asian power that was most friendly to Vietnam among the non-Communist states. Despite the new priority toward the neighboring and regional countries, the ASEAN states were placed in the third circle. The rest of the world constituted the fourth, outermost, circle, with the United States being kept at the largest distance.[16]

Vietnam's accession to ASEAN resulted from the interaction of four major forces. It was pushed vigorously by Vietnamese modernizers, most notably Prime Minister Kiet and Foreign Minister Nguyen Manh Cam, and supported by tailwinds within ASEAN, mainly from Indonesia and Malaysia; but it also faced strong headwinds in ASEAN, especially from Singapore, and was persistently braked by Vietnam's anti-Western leaders, most stubbornly CPV Executive Secretary Dao Duy Tung, who ranked fourth in the Party nomenclature. According to Cam, ASEAN membership was the key to Vietnam's break from international isolation, but for Tung, "ASEAN is the extension of SEATO [Southeast Asia Treaty Organization]" and ASEAN membership would increase the threat of "peaceful evolution."[17] Party chief Muoi and President Anh only changed their minds and approved Vietnam's joining of ASEAN after their respective visits to ASEAN countries in October 1993 and April 1994.[18]

The year 1995 was a big milestone on Vietnam's road to joining the world. It marks the country's accession to ASEAN, the establishment of diplomatic relations with the United States, and the signing of the EU-Vietnam Framework Cooperation Agreement. Partly inspired by this "bumper crop," Prime Minister Kiet proposed a new vision for Vietnam's domestic and foreign policy that, based on the single-market worldview, envisaged a democratic nation fully integrated into the outside world. However, this proposal, presented in his August 9, 1995 letter to the Politburo, met with fierce attacks from anti-Westerners and led to the forced resignation of its drafter, former Ambassador Nguyen Trung.[19] Characteristic of the political environment in which these modernizers lived, former Foreign Minister Thach's 1998 book, another manifesto of the new worldview and Vietnam's modernization, was confiscated by the authorities immediately after its publication.

Seeing the world through the two-camp perspective and fearing "peaceful evolution," anti-Westerners continued to obstruct relations with the West, especially the United States. A US-Vietnam Bilateral Trade Agreement (BTA) that would open the market of each to the other was strongly supported by both the Clinton administration and integrationists in the Vietnamese government but persistently delayed by anti-Westerners dominating the

CPV's top leadership. Its scheduled signing in September 1999 was postponed only a few days in advance due to efforts of Party chief Le Kha Phieu, former Party chief Muoi, former President Anh, and chief ideologue Nguyen Duc Binh. The revised version signed a year later, in the words of Prime Minister Phan Van Khai, "did not achieve any progress," but it cost Vietnam billions of US dollars in exports.[20]

As anti-Westerners were tenacious in blocking relations with the United States, they were equally obstinate in seeking a strategic alliance with China. The idea of an anti-US and anti-Western Sino-Vietnamese alliance that was initiated by Party chief Linh and Defense Minister Anh in the aftermath of the fall of Communist regimes in Eastern Europe was Linh's primary motive at the Chengdu summit in September 1990.[21] Although it met with Chinese reticence at that time, it was renewed at every inaugural visit of a new CPV chief to Beijing—Do Muoi in 1991, Le Kha Phieu in 1999, and Nong Duc Manh in 2001—until the anti-Westerners lost their dominance in the Politburo in the mid-2000s. Although it was consistently dismissed by China, Vietnam's cadres were informally instructed that China was the strategic ally and the United States the fundamental enemy.[22]

It was in this spirit that Phieu made large concessions to China in the Sino-Vietnamese border agreements that, when signed in 1999 and 2000, were the first to demarcate their boundaries on land and in the Tonkin Gulf since the inception of the two Communist states. These territorial losses and Phieu's obstruction of US-Vietnam relations were among the charges his opponents cited to oust him at the Ninth Party Congress in April 2001.[23] Replacing Phieu as Party chief, Nong Duc Manh characterized Vietnam and China as "comrades plus brothers" and, in the joint statement issued during his inaugural trip to Beijing in December 2001, two months after the US invasion of Afghanistan, he agreed with China to "strongly condemn hegemonism by political superpowers in international affairs." This was the first time Vietnam ever publicly vowed to join forces with China against another great power's "hegemonism"—but it was also the last.[24]

A Rent-Seeking State in Disguise, 2003–14

In July 2003, the Eighth Plenum of the Ninth CPV Central Committee passed a resolution titled "Strategy for Safeguarding the Fatherland in a New Situation" to replace the national security strategy of June 1992. While the 1992 strategy emphasized "fighting peaceful evolution," the new strategy states that its "top important task" is to "maintain peace and stability to successfully realize the cause of socialist-oriented industrialization and modernization." Two years earlier, at the Ninth Congress, the CPV had set out the goal that Vietnam should become an industrialized country by 2020. What makes the new strategy, commonly referred to as Resolution 8, a major turning point in Vietnamese foreign policy is its removal of ideology as a key criterion for determining friends and foes. The new principle distinguishes between "partners" (*đối tác*) and "opponents" (*đối tượng đấu tranh*), in which partners are defined as "anyone whose policy is to respect Vietnam's independence and sovereignty and to establish and broaden a friendly, cooperative, equitable, and mutually benefiting relationship with Vietnam," and opponents as "anyone whose dark schemes and actions are in opposition to our country's objectives in the cause of constructing and safeguarding the Fatherland."[25] By the 1992 strategy's definition, China is the strategic ally and the United States the strategic enemy. According to the 2003 strategy's principle, however, China can be both a partner and an opponent, and so can the United States, depending on their actual policy, intention, and action. In a nutshell, Resolution 8 rehabilitated Resolution 13.

The immediate consequence of Resolution 8 was Vietnam's reorientation of its relationship with the United States. Between August and December 2003, Hanoi dispatched four major ministers and a deputy prime minister to Washington. In November 2003, General Pham Van Tra became the first defense minister of Communist Vietnam to set foot in the Pentagon. During this visit, the two countries agreed that their defense ministers would visit the other country every three years and Vietnam would host a US warship every year, beginning later the same month. These rules would be faithfully kept until 2017, when Defense Minister Ngo Xuan Lich returned the 2015 visit of Secretary of Defense Ash Carter, and Vietnam received an increased number of visiting US warships. As the US ambassador to Hanoi at that time recalled, "until the second half of 2003, this progress [of US-Vietnam relations] moved at a slow pace," but in late 2003, "Vietnamese leaders informed us they would now welcome major steps that they had resisted for years." He also noted, "our access to top leaders became much easier, and we began a dialogue on strategic issues that Hanoi had previously considered off-limits."[26]

What caused the Vietnamese to adopt this sea change? The "new situation" to which the new strategy was a response was largely defined by US unipolar power, which was vividly demonstrated by the US invasion of Iraq in March 2003. For Vietnam's anti-Westerners, who dominated the ideological, defense, and security branches of the party-state, this pushed their hope for a resurgence of world socialism indefinitely further into the future. More urgently, they worried whether Vietnam or North Korea would be the next target of a US invasion.[27] However, viewing the world as a single system dominated by great powers, Vietnam's integrationists, who were more numerous in the diplomatic and economic branches of the party-state and often represented official Vietnam to Western diplomats, worried more about the imbalance of power favoring China as a result of US involvement in the Middle East.[28]

Resolution 8 provided a solution to both concerns. By removing ideology as the foreign policy compass, it allowed anti-Westerners to jump on the US bandwagon and integrationists to balance against China. Two conditions made Resolution 8 possible. First, US policy was to engage with Vietnam, not to subvert or isolate it. More importantly, the Bush administration, driven by geostrategic objectives, increasingly recognized Vietnam's strategic potential and wanted to strengthen relations with Vietnam as an important partner.[29] Second, the benefits of reform and opening had rendered the integrationists—those who see the world as a "single system" rather than "two camps"—the majority in the ruling elite, particularly the CPV Central Committee.[30]

Unlike the pioneer integrationists of the late 1980s, who were mostly modernizers, most of the integrationists of the early 2000s were rent-seekers. The "brackish water" of Leninist politics and a market economy that characterized the 1990s provided fertile ground for rent-seekers to thrive. They adopted the view of the world as a single market, but, while modernizers sought to enhance the country's competitiveness in the world market, rent-seekers strove to exact payment from society. To this end, rent-seekers supported international integration because it made available a large source of income, but they preferred authoritarian politics because it helped them to create barriers and exact payment. By the latter half of the 1990s, rent-seekers constituted a distinct bloc in Vietnamese politics that "uses money to manipulate politics, and once having access to Communist Party power, uses the political monopoly to reap hyper-profits."[31]

Resolution 8 removed a major obstacle on the road of Vietnam's integration into the world. Preparations for joining the World Trade Organization (WTO) were initiated by Prime Minister Kiet immediately following the "bumper crop" of 1995. But the process moved at a snail's pace for years because anti-Westerners wanted to wait until globalization would be led by socialist forces. As chief ideologue Nguyen Duc Binh, who held the most dogged veto in the Politburo against the BTA and the WTO, argued, "We are not against globalization but we will only join the proletarian-led globalization and should not participate in the current bourgeois-led globalization."[32] Anti-Westerners continued to torpedo the process until the Tenth CPV Congress in April 2006, and Vietnam missed its self-imposed deadline to join the WTO by 2005. At the Tenth Party Congress, anti-Westerners finally lost their plurality in the Politburo and rent-seekers became the largest bloc in the country's highest decision-making body.[33] Soon after the Tenth Congress, Vietnam was willing to make major concessions to the United States, which was the last to conclude an agreement to accept Vietnam's membership in the group. Vietnam officially acceded to the WTO at the start of 2007. Unlike most other countries, for which the WTO was little more than a global trade agreement, Vietnam saw its accession to the international organization as adoption into a new family. Debates among the ruling elite were not just about the impact of lower trade barriers but, more fundamentally, revolved around whether Vietnam was willing to change the way it organized its social, economic, and political life.

Membership in the WTO required substantial institutional adjustment. Vietnam's response was to relax the economy, restructure the administration, introduce some non-essential appearances of democracy, but tighten the Party's grip on political decision making.[34] These institutional adjustments and the prevalence of the rent-seekers in the ruling elite, including their dominance of the economy and their plurality in the Central Committee and the Politburo, effectively changed the nature of the party-state from a neo-Stalinist state to a rent-seeking state. They were like the last quantitative amount that led to a qualitative change: a neo-Stalinist state in tactical retreat morphed into a rent-seeking state in disguise. While the operational ethos of the neo-Stalinist state is to control all aspects of society to maintain power, that of the rent-seeking state is to create privileges, regulations, and other barriers to commercialize them. In the 2000s, Vietnam relaxed state control over many aspects of the economy and society, but, at the same time, the administration was further overstaffed, the number of new regulations that required licenses and permits skyrocketed—which the Vietnamese called the "plague of petty permits" (*nạn giấy phép con*)—and the state-owned enterprises became "dinosaurs in a juvenile economy," with privileged access to land, credit, and politics but without public accountability.[35]

As the operational ethos of the state changed, so did its foreign policy objectives and approach. The Eleventh CPV Congress in January 2011 endorsed "comprehensive integration" (*hội nhập toàn diện*) into the international community, and Resolution 22 of the Politburo in April 2013 reaffirmed this major policy with instructions on international integration in a full range from economic to political, security, technological, and educational areas. In November 2013, Vietnam replaced the 1992 Constitution with a new one to reflect the new thrust in international integration. In one instance, the new constitution revised the mission of the Vietnamese military to allow it to participate in the United Nations' peacekeeping operations, which it did starting in 2014.

After joining the WTO, Vietnam became a free trade agreement (FTA) enthusiast. By 2014, it signed six multilateral FTAs as an ASEAN member and two bilateral FTAs with Japan (VJEPA) and Chile (VCFTA). These were, however, low-level "traditional FTAs" that focused on lowering tariffs. In the latter half of the 2000s, Vietnam started negotiations toward "new-generation" FTAs that went far beyond tariffs to emphasize trade liberalization and market opening for both domestic and foreign entities. In 2008, at the invitation of the Bush administration, Vietnam joined the Trans-Pacific Partnership (TPP) negotiations, which envisaged a comprehensive and strategic economic agreement that affected not only trade liberalization but also labor rights, human rights, government procurement, and state-owned enterprises. Already from the beginning, Vietnam's decision to join the TPP was motivated not only by a vast foreign market for Vietnamese goods; it also hoped to act as a counterweight to China and an external push for domestic reforms.

On the strategic plane, the rent-seeking state did not lean on one side—the side of the Communist regimes fighting the West—as the neo-Stalinist state; instead, it endeavored to cast a wide web of partnerships with many actors around the world (see table 15.2 for a summary). In 2001, when China was still Vietnam's informal and one-way strategic ally, Russia became Vietnam's first strategic partner. The quest for strategic partners, propelled by integrationists and supported by their majority in the Central Committee and the Politburo after the Ninth Party Congress, became earnest as the United States prepared for its 2003 invasion of Iraq. General Secretary Manh's trip to China took place two weeks after the start of the Iraq War and was followed three weeks later by his visit to India, where he signed a Joint Statement on the Framework of Comprehensive Cooperation with this traditional partner. The first phase of Vietnam's quest for strategic partnerships was focused on the major powers resident in Asia—China, Russia, India, and Japan. In 2006, Vietnam was the first destination abroad of newly elected Japanese Prime Minister Shinzo Abe, during whose visit the two countries pledged to work toward a strategic partnership. The following year, India became Vietnam's second strategic partner. In 2008, when the search for a strategic ally had been abandoned, China and Vietnam became each other's first "comprehensive strategic cooperative partner." In fact, it was China that bestowed this mouthful epithet to Vietnam, as it did to Laos, Cambodia, Myanmar, Russia, and Thailand in the following years. As China was elevated to a higher

Table 15.2
Timeline and formal hierarchy of Vietnam's foreign relationships

Year	Special strategic relationship	Comprehensive strategic partnership	Strategic partnership	Comprehensive partnership
	Laos			
	Cambodia			
1991	*China*[i]			
2001			Russia	South Korea
2003				India[c]
2004				*South Africa*[d]
2006			*Japan*[a]	
2007			India	Chile
				Brazil
				Venezuela
2008		China*		
2009			Japan	New Zealand
			South Korea*	
			Spain	
2010			United Kingdom	Argentina
2011			Germany	Ukraine*
			Italy	European Union
2012		Russia		
2013			Thailand	United States
			Indonesia	Denmark
			Singapore	
			France	
2014		*Japan*[e]		
2015			Malaysia	
			Philippines	
2016		India		
2017			*Germany*[s]	Myanmar
				Canada
2018			Australia	Hungary
2019	Laos[g]		*United States*[p]	Brunei
			New Zealand[a]	Netherlands
2020			New Zealand	
2021		*South Korea*[a]		
2022		South Korea		

Source: Author's compilation.

Notes:

* The term "cooperative" or "cooperation" is added to the official designation of the partnership.

[a] *Agreed to work toward*

[c] Officially called "comprehensive cooperation," not "partnership"

[d] *A "partnership for cooperation and development," not a "comprehensive partnership"*

[e] *Upgraded to "extensive" but not "comprehensive"*

[g] Upgraded to a "great friendship" from a "traditional friendship"

[i] *One-sidedly regarded informal strategic ally by Vietnamese conservatives*

[p] *Planned but postponed due to Party chief Trong's health issues*

[s] *Suspended due to the Trinh Xuan Thanh kidnapping*

level, Japan became Vietnam's third strategic partner in 2009. The second phase of Vietnam's quest was focused on the major advanced industrial countries. Within three years, from 2009 to 2011, Vietnam established strategic partnerships with Japan, South Korea, Spain, the United Kingdom, Germany, and Italy. Its offer of a strategic partnership with France was rejected in 2007, and the Franco-Vietnamese strategic partnership was not declared until 2013. Vietnam's bid for a strategic partnership with Australia was also rebuffed in the late 2000s and again in 2014. However, as Canberra perceived a growing Chinese threat, it agreed to become Vietnam's strategic partner in 2018 and proposed, in May 2021, to elevate bilateral ties to "comprehensive strategic partnership" by 2023. In the third phase of its quest, Vietnam signed a series of strategic partnerships with major ASEAN members, starting with Thailand, Indonesia, and Singapore in 2013, followed by Malaysia and the Philippines in 2015.

The wide web of strategic partnerships cast by the rent-seeking state tilted markedly toward non-Western powers and showed a clear deference to China, which was Vietnam's first "comprehensive strategic cooperative partner." In 2012 and 2016, Vietnam's strategic partnerships with Russia and India, respectively, were upgraded to "comprehensive strategic partnerships," elevating these countries to the highest rank, just below the special relations with Laos and Cambodia in Vietnam's hierarchy of foreign relationships. The non-Western tilt and the deference to China resulted in large part from the anti-Western influence in the ideological, defense, and security branches of the party-state, most heavily in the Ministry of Defense. Different Vietnamese policy currents preferred different pathways in dealing with China. After the pursuit of solidarity with China on an ideological basis failed repeatedly to yield the desired outcomes, anti-Westerners, along with many of the moderates and some rent-seekers, placed their hope on deference as the main way to placate, and thus to make China peaceful and cooperative toward Vietnam. Most integrationists, however, believed a combination of leveraging the counterweight of other major powers, interlocking of mutual interests, and enmeshment of China in international institutions was more effective than deference.[36] In the first half of the 2010s, when the South China Sea dispute rose to top the agenda of Vietnam's foreign policy due to China's actions in the region, Vietnam's military leadership still believed that the biggest threat came from the United States. Speaking in September 2012, the head of the military's Education and Information Department, Major General Nguyen Thanh Tuan, stressed, "We should not be ambiguous and lose vigilance about China's scheme to take exclusive control of the East Sea [South China Sea]."[37] Writing in December 2012, however, both Defense Minister General Phung Quang Thanh and the military's chief political commissar, General Ngo Xuan Lich (who would succeed Thanh as defense minister in 2016), warned, "The hostile forces [Vietnam's code name for the United States] are pursuing the strategy of 'peaceful evolution' in earnest to sabotage our country's revolution [Thanh's version: "to change the political regime in our country"] and, when the opportunity arises, they will be ready to launch an invasion war using high-tech weapons [Thanh's version lacked "using high-tech weapons"]."[38]

This tilted approach has increasingly been put to the test since the late 2000s, when China became more "assertive"—that is, aggressive but not very aggressive—in the South

China Sea. Illustrative of Vietnam's deference to—and false hopes about—China, the ex-altation of their bilateral relations to "comprehensive strategic cooperative partnership" in 2008 was bracketed by anti-China public protests in 2007—the first since 1988, when China seized six reefs in the Spratly Islands and killed seventy Vietnamese sailors—and a new height of Chinese harassment of Vietnamese fishermen in the South China Sea in 2009. In the manner of "salami slicing," China ratcheted up its assertiveness in the South China Sea, first every two years, then every year. In 2005, China's Maritime Police killed nine Vietnamese fishermen in the Tonkin Gulf. In 2007, China pressured BP to abandon its oil and gas exploration contracts with Vietnam. In 2009, China detained and seized a rec-ord number of Vietnamese fishing boats. In one instance, a Chinese government vessel rammed and sank a Vietnamese boat. In 2011, Chinese vessels twice cut the cables of Viet-nam's hydrocarbon exploration ships within Vietnam's exclusive economic zone (EEZ). In 2012, China opened to bidding nine oil and gas blocks that lay entirely within Vietnam's EEZ after Vietnam passed its Maritime Law. In 2013, China started large-scale land rec-lamation at several of the reefs it occupied in the Spratly and Paracel Islands.[39] Combin-ing deference and soft balancing, Vietnam's response included quiet lobbying of major powers and the ASEAN members, occasional tolerance of anti-China public protests, and seeking talks to reach agreements with China; its buildup of maritime forces, encourage-ment of public discussion, and search for international allies remained insufficient.[40] Thus, when a bigger test came in 2014, Hanoi was caught by surprise.

A Rent-Seeking State on Correction Course, 2014–Present

On May 2, 2014, China parked a giant drilling platform that cost over US$1 billion, the *Hai Yang Shi You 981*, in waters southwest of the Paracel Islands. As the place lay on the Vietnamese side of the median line between the Vietnamese and Hainan Island coasts, well within what Vietnam considered its EEZ, Hanoi's red line was crossed. Staying seventy-five days in that area, the oil rig sparked the worst crisis in Sino-Vietnamese relations since 1988. During these two and a half months, news about the standoff topped the headlines of Vietnamese media, and the public was given nearly free rein in discussing the sensitive is-sue. For about a week from May 11, anti-China protests broke out across Vietnam in unpre-cedented large scale. The government initially lauded these protests as displays of "patrio-tism," but then subdued them after riots led to burning and looting of foreign factories and the killing of Chinese nationals.

The oil rig crisis proved to be a litmus test and a game changer. It helped the Vietnam-ese to clearly see China as the largest security threat and the United States as a friend in need. It destroyed the last remnants of Vietnam's trust in China and removed the last ob-stacles between Vietnam and the United States. During the incident, Washington was the most robust in speaking out against Beijing. After the incident, some members of the Viet-namese National Assembly called China an invader and an enemy, breaking a taboo that had been in place since the renormalization of Sino-Vietnamese relations in 1991. In early

October 2014, when Secretary of State John Kerry met with visiting Foreign Minister Pham Binh Minh, the United States announced its decision to partially lift a decades-old weapons embargo against Hanoi in order to help Vietnam improve its maritime security.[41]

The oil rig crisis caused Vietnam to move past the geopolitical equidistance between Beijing and Washington. This crossing was theoretically possible with Resolution 8, but Hanoi had been careful not to do so, both to reassure Beijing and to warn off domestic opposition. However, China's crossing of Vietnam's red line rendered this position untenable. Although Vietnam refrained from involving the United States during the crisis in order to fulfill one of China's conditions to withdraw the oil rig, Hanoi accelerated its rapprochement with Washington immediately after its removal.[42] In July 2015, General Secretary Nguyen Phu Trong paid a historic visit—the first ever by a CPV chief—to the White House. The invitation was delivered to him by Secretary of State Hillary Clinton in 2012, two years after she offered to raise US-Vietnamese relations to "strategic partnership." Washington wanted the visit to take place in 2013, but Hanoi was hesitant and instead sent President Truong Tan Sang to announce a US-Vietnam "comprehensive partnership."[43] Nguyen Phu Trong's trip was preceded by an advance trip by General Tran Dai Quang, the first official visit by a Vietnamese minister of public security to the United States, during which Quang affirmed that Hanoi would allow the US Peace Corps to operate in Vietnam. This marked a significant change in the Communist regime's attitude toward its ideological challenger. As late as 2009, a major document by the CPV Propaganda Department described the Peace Corps as an organization specializing in anti-Communist propaganda and subversion. For the first time ever, Communist Vietnam now trusted America more than it did Communist China.[44] The last major obstacle to a strategic partnership was removed in May 2016, when President Barack Obama completely ended the ban on lethal weapons sale to Vietnam on the eve of his visit to Vietnam, during which Vietnam also became the 142nd Peace Corps country.

Chinese aggression—and American friendship—have profoundly affected the worldviews of Vietnamese leaders and the relative strengths of Vietnam's policy currents. On the eve of Trong's visit to the United States, Vietnam's chief defense diplomat Nguyen Chi Vinh said in an interview that Vietnam and the United States had "agreed not to be each other's enemy, not to harm each other's strategic interests," and that he trusted the US commitment never to invade Vietnam again.[45] The military's chief political commissar Ngo Xuan Lich also removed the possibility of a US invasion of Vietnam in his April 2015 article that repeated most of the contents of the December 2012 article, although he continued to warn against "peaceful evolution" as a major threat to the regime.[46] With these new perceptions, the two-camp worldview died out in the Vietnamese leadership and the anti-Western policy current associated with it reached a final demise. Anti-Western and anti-American sentiments continued to exist, but as a general direction of policy, anti-Westernism morphed into regime survivalism, which accepted the Western-led international order while clinging to the primary objective of preserving the Communist regime. The net effect of the 2014 turning point was the fall of anti-Westernism as a policy current and the rise of moderates, who sat on the fence between regime survivalism and modernization.[47]

The rent-seeking state faced new conditions in the post-2014 environment. Because of the public's total distrust of China and the domestic pressure stemming from this, it had to partially decouple from China, and without a better option, it had to more closely couple with the West. The public's distrust of China forced the government to refuse Chinese finance in public projects. Vietnam paid lip service to China's Belt and Road Initiative as a way of deference to Beijing, but public scrutiny and the fear of "debt traps" prevented Vietnam from substantially participating in One Belt One Road.[48] Concerned about national security risks, Vietnam excluded China's Huawei from its 5G network, but, characteristic of its precarious position vis-à-vis China, it did so without a formal ban. Instead, Vietnam's largest mobile carriers—all were state-owned companies—simply signed contracts with Sweden's Ericsson, Finland's Nokia, and South Korea's Samsung, Huawei's rival suppliers of 5G equipment.[49] In June 2018, the Politburo had to withdraw the Special Zones Act just a few hours before its scheduled passage by the National Assembly, in response to intense public pressure, which would burst into protests across the country and flare up into riots in Binh Thuan Province following the postponement of the bill. A second attempt by the rent-seeking state to pass a slightly revised version of the bill in 2019 also buckled under heavy public pressure. The public perceived the proposed Special Economic Zones as gates wide open to China's peaceful invasion of Vietnam.[50]

The partial exit from the Chinese orbit was paralleled by a partial alignment with the West. By late 2015, the Politburo in Hanoi removed the last obstacles to the TPP negotiations by making major concessions on labor rights, government procurement, and state-owned enterprises, things that cut to the core of the regime. At its Fourteenth Plenum in January 2016, the Eleventh Central Committee endorsed the TPP agreement. Even without the United States, Vietnam joined the other TPP members and in November 2017 signed a slightly revised TPP, now called "Comprehensive and Progressive Agreement for Trans-Pacific Partnership" (CPTPP), which maintained high labor and environmental standards, among other items. After the US withdrawal from the TPP, Vietnam stepped up lobbying the European Union for an EU-Vietnam Free Trade Agreement (EVFTA). Like the TPP, the EVFTA also goes beyond the dismantling of tariffs and opening of markets; its noneconomic provisions are intended to enforce higher standards of human rights and environmental protection, promote Western values, and make Vietnam more attractive to Western investors. Signed in June 2019, the EVFTA was described by the EU as "the most ambitious free trade deal ever concluded with a developing country."[51] In April 2020, Vietnam joined the US-led informal grouping dubbed "Quad Plus," which included Washington's closest friends in the Indo-Pacific and discussed, among others, the restructuring of the supply chains out of China to prevent excessive dependency on this challenging market.[52]

China's 2014 oil rig move was paralleled by Beijing's massive artificial island building in the South China Sea, both marking a new phase in China's bid for dominance in the region. Upon completing the island building in mid-2017, China went on to harass and disrupt Vietnam's hydrocarbon drilling in the South China Sea, forcing Hanoi to scrap new projects within its own EEZ and pay an estimated US$1 billion in contract breakage fees.[53] At the other side of Vietnam's territory, China successfully pulled Cambodia and

Laos closer into its orbit. Hanoi now felt dangerously squeezed by Beijing's bid for regional hegemony. By 2018, the CPV Politburo green-lighted the preparation for a Vietnam-US strategic partnership. As the plan went, a second visit by Party chief Trong to the United States in late 2019 was to announce this upgrade, but his health issues and then the coronavirus pandemic pushed this landmark indefinitely into the future.[54] Despite the pandemic, the defense ministers of Japan and Vietnam visited each other in September and November 2021, during which they raised bilateral defense cooperation to a "new level," which included among other things an agreement that allowed Japan to provide defense equipment and technology to Vietnam. Asserting Vietnam's subregional leadership, Party chief Trong hosted a "summit meeting" with his neighboring counterparts, Cambodian People's Party chief Hun Sen and Lao People's Revolutionary Party chief Thongloun Sisulith, in September 2021, the first of its kind since the end of the Third Indochina War. In February 2019, Vietnam and Laos had formally elevated their "traditional friendship" to "great friendship." The non-Western tilt of Vietnam's web of partnerships has shifted into a non-China tilt as Vietnam deepened its strategic ties with all major powers other than China, strove to play a "core role" in ASEAN, and tightened its special relations with Laos and Cambodia.

The geopolitical shift away from China and toward the West put an additional but substantive pressure on the rent-seeking state to correct itself. As early as December 2011, shortly after becoming CPV chief, Trong launched a major anti-corruption campaign to combat the graft that had pervaded the rent-seeking state and thrown many state-owned conglomerates into technical default. The campaign effectively created a bipolar structure of Vietnamese politics that centered on Trong, who was often supported by President Sang, on one side, and Prime Minister Nguyen Tan Dung, who sat at the apex of the biggest rent-seeking network in the country, on the other. The tide of the battle between the two camps seesawed throughout the years until late 2015, on the eve of the Twelfth CPV Congress, when Trong decisively emerged victorious.[55] Trong's trip to the United States in the summer of that year certainly boosted his legitimacy, but had Dung defeated Trong, Dung would also have had to put the rent-seeking state on a correction course, albeit one of his own style.

In Lieu of a Conclusion

The four turning points examined in this chapter span a bridge between the last stage of the Soviet-US hegemonic contest and the first stage of the Sino-US superpower rivalry.[56] The latter is forming the largest geopolitical vortex in Vietnam's international environment. Navigating this vortex requires a new map and new skills that are different from the ones that proved useful in the last four decades. Vietnam is responding to the vagaries of international relations by "acting like bamboo," as Party chief Trong suggested at an important conference on Vietnamese foreign policy in December 2021.[57] But bamboo diplomacy, while providing flexibility and resilience, is no substitute for maps. Vietnam needs a new worldview to guide its action in the "new situation."

Table 15.3
The next turning point in Vietnamese foreign policy

Likelihood	International cause	Domestic effect	Foreign policy implications
High	New height of Chinese expansionism crosses Vietnam's red line	Rise of modernizers	Alignment and stronger ties with the US, Japan, India
High	Sharp deterioration of Cambodia-Vietnam relations and China supports Cambodia	Rise of modernizers	Alignment and stronger ties with the US and the West
Medium to high	Major crisis involving the US at home or elsewhere cripples US power in the western Pacific	Prevalence of moderates	Stronger ties with Russia, India, Japan; leadership of ASEAN
Medium to high	China is in a deep and severe crisis that cripples its external power	Rise of rent-seekers	Friends to all, including China
Medium to low	The US prevails over China in a local crisis or conflict	Rise of modernizers	Stronger ties with the US
Medium to low	China prevails over the US in a local crisis or conflict	Prevalence of moderates	Stronger ties with Russia, India, Japan
Low	China abandons Marxism-Leninism	Rise of modernizers	Stronger ties with the US, Japan, India
Low	Sharp deterioration of Lao-Vietnamese relations and China supports Laos	Rise of modernizers	Alignment and stronger ties with the US and the West

A characteristic of Vietnamese foreign policy after the Cold War is that it is often based on the views of a bygone era. Russia's full-scale invasion of Ukraine in 2022 helped Hanoi to validate its "bamboo" approach and "four no's" policy (no military alliances, no siding with one country against another, no foreign basing on Vietnamese soil, no use of force), but it also heralded a new Cold War between the United States and the West versus Russia and China. It immediately broke the web of partnerships upon which Hanoi's "bamboo" approach and "four no's" policy were predicated and squeezed Vietnam out of its usual balancing act. But Hanoi persisted with its old worldviews and a new one is unlikely to be adopted until the next turning point in Vietnamese foreign policy (see table 15.3 for a horizon scanning and its forecasts).

Notes

1. Some other "conveyor belts" include domestic institutions, public opinion, and party factions.
2. Huy Đức, *Bên thắng cuộc*, vol. 1, 285–390.
3. Palmujoki, *Vietnam and the World*; Porter, "The Transformation of Vietnam's World-View."
4. Võ Văn Kiệt, "Thư gửi Bộ Chính trị"; Nguyễn Cơ Thạch, *Thế giới*.
5. These views were ample on the pages of the Party's premier ideological forum, *Tạp chí Cộng sản* (Communist Review), during 1987–89, and the Foreign Ministry's newly established magazine, *Quan hệ Quốc tế* (International Relations), during 1990–91.

6. Resolution 13 was classified, but its main contents were presented in some interviews with and articles by its architect, Foreign Minister Thach, especially Nguyễn Cơ Thạch, "Những chuyển biến mới."

7. Thayer, "Vietnamese Foreign Policy."

8. Vũ Hồng Lâm, "Lịch sử quan hệ Việt-Trung."

9. Phan Doãn Nam, "Một vài suy nghĩ"; Lê Đức Anh, "Nâng cao cảnh giác."

10. Nguyễn Văn Linh, "Phát biểu."

11. Huy Đức, *Bên thắng cuộc*, vol. 2, 61–67; Trần Quang Cơ, *Hồi ức và Suy nghĩ*.

12. Trần Quang Cơ, *Hồi ức và Suy nghĩ*.

13. Vuving, "Grand Strategic Fit," 241.

14. Huy Đức, *Bên thắng cuộc*, vol. 2, 67–83, 135–41.

15. Đỗ Mười, "Thời cuộc hiện nay"; Hồng Hà, "Tình hình thế giới."

16. Thành Tín, *Mặt thật*, 334–35.

17. Huy Đức, *Bên thắng cuộc*, vol. 2, 273–74.

18. Nguyen Vu Tung, *Flying Blind*.

19. At the highest echelon of the party-state, Kiet's vision was openly supported by Foreign Minister Cam and Politburo member Vu Oanh but opposed in various ways by Party chief Muoi, President Anh, chief ideologues Dao Duy Tung and Nguyen Duc Binh, CPV Executive Secretary Nguyen Ha Phan, and the military's chief political commissar Le Kha Phieu, who in December 1997 would become Party chief. See Huy Đức, *Bên thắng cuộc*, vol. 2, 304–11; Nguyễn Chí Trung, "Thực chất từ Đại hội Đảng"; Nguyễn Trung, *Tôi làm "chính trị,"* 68–72.

20. Huy Đức, *Bên thắng cuộc*, vol. 2, 344–50.

21. Trần Quang Cơ, *Hồi ức và Suy nghĩ*.

22. Vuving, "Strategy and Evolution," 814–17. Conversations with Vietnamese officials, Hanoi, 2003.

23. Huy Đức, *Bên thắng cuộc*, vol. 2, 333–44, 354–59.

24. Vuving, "Strategy and Evolution," 817; "Vietnam-China Joint Statement."

25. Ban Tư tưởng-Văn hoá, *Tài liệu Học tập*; the quotes are on pp. 25, 44, 46, 47.

26. Burghardt, "Old Enemies Become Friends."

27. Ban Tư tưởng-Văn hoá, *Tài liệu Học tập*, 26–30, 37–41; Vuving, "Grand Strategic Fit," 240.

28. Burghardt, "US and Vietnam."

29. Burghardt, "US and Vietnam."

30. Vuving, "The 2016 Leadership Change," 427–29. Of the ruling troika elected at the Ninth VCP Congress, the top leader was anti-Western (General Secretary Manh), but the other two were integrationist (President Tran Duc Luong, a rent-seeker, and Prime Minister Phan Van Khai, a modernizer). Luong and Khai were reelected, but in their previous term, 1997–2001, the power of the ruling troika was overlaid by that of the anti-Western–dominated emeritus troika of Muoi, Anh, and Kiet.

31. Vuving, "Vietnam: A Tale of Four Players," 369.

32. Huy Đức, *Bên thắng cuộc*, vol. 2, 349.

33. Vuving, "The 2016 Leadership Change," 427–29.

34. Vuving, "Vietnam: Arriving in the World," 375–93.

35. Vuving, "Vietnam: A Tale of Four Players," 367–91; Vuving, "Vietnam in 2012."

36. Vuving, "Power Rivalry."

37. Nguyễn Thanh Tuấn, "Chủ quyền của Việt Nam."

38. Ngô Xuân Lịch, "Giá trị to lớn"; Phùng Quang Thanh, "Chiến thắng." The quote is from Lịch's version; Thanh's wording is slightly different.

39. Do Thanh Hai, *Vietnam and the South China Sea*.

40. Vuving, "Vietnam, the US, and Japan."

41. Vuving, "A Breakthrough in U.S.-Vietnam Relations."

42. Vuving, "Did China Blink in the South China Sea?"

43. Vuving, "A Tipping Point."

44. Vuving, "A Breakthrough in U.S.-Vietnam Relations"; Vuving, "Vietnam: A Tale of Four Players," 381.

45. Việt Anh, "Tướng Nguyễn Chí Vịnh."

46. Ngô Xuân Lịch, "Sức mạnh chính trị-tinh."

47. Vuving, "The 2016 Leadership Change," 426–32.
48. Vuving, "Vietnam in 2018," 386.
49. Nguyen Tung, "Viettel Moves Away."
50. Vuving, "Vietnam in 2018," 318, 386.
51. "EU-Vietnam."
52. Pompeo, "Remarks to the Press."
53. Hayton, "China's Pressure."
54. A Vietnamese attempt to upgrade the relationship to "extensive comprehensive partnership" during Trong's 2015 trip was aborted. Vuving, "Will Vietnam Be America's Next Strategic Partner?"
55. Vuving, "Vietnam in 2012," 325–47; Vuving, "The 2016 Leadership Change."
56. Space limits force me to abridge the conclusion and unsource many facts and assertions, for which I sincerely apologize.
57. Nguyễn Phú Trọng, "Xây dựng và phát triển."

References

Ban Tư tưởng-Văn hoá Trung ương (Central Department for Ideology and Culture). *Tài liệu Học tập Nghị quyết Hội nghị lần thứ Tám Ban Chấp hành Trung ương Đảng khoá IX* (Documents for the study of the resolution of the Eighth Plenum of the Ninth Party Central Committee). Hanoi: Nhà xuất bản Chính trị Quốc gia, 2003.

Burghardt, Raymond F. "Old Enemies Become Friends: U.S. and Vietnam." Brookings East Asia Commentary, November 1, 2006. https://www.brookings.edu/opinions/old-enemies-become-friends-u-s-and-vietnam/.

———. "US and Vietnam: Discreet Friendship under China's Shadow." *YaleGlobal Online*, November 22, 2005. https://archive-yaleglobal.yale.edu/content/us-vietnam-discreet-friendship-under-chinas-shadow.

Đỗ Mười. "Thời cuộc hiện nay và nhiệm vụ của chúng ta" (The present situation and our tasks). Report to the Third Plenum of the Seventh Central Committee. *Tạp chí Cộng sản* 8 (August 1992): 3–10.

Do Thanh Hai. *Vietnam and the South China Sea: Politics, Security and Legality.* New York: Routledge, 2017.

"EU-Vietnam: Council Adopts Decisions to Sign Trade and Investment Agreements." Press Release of the Council of the European Union, June 25, 2019. https://www.consilium.europa.eu/en/press/press-releases/2019/06/25/eu-vietnam-council-adopts-decisions-to-sign-trade-and-investment-agreements/.

Hayton, Bill. "China's Pressure Costs Vietnam $1 Billion in the South China Sea." *The Diplomat*, July 22, 2020. https://thediplomat.com/2020/07/chinas-pressure-costs-vietnam-1-billion-in-the-south-china-sea/.

Hồng Hà. "Tình hình thế giới và chính sách đối ngoại của ta" (World situation and our foreign policy). *Tạp chí Cộng sản* 12 (December 1992): 10–13.

Huy Đức. *Bên thắng cuộc* (The winning side), vol. 1: *Giải phóng* (Liberation). Los Angeles: OsinBook, 2012.

———. *Bên thắng cuộc* (The winning side), vol. 2: *Quyền bính* (Power). Los Angeles: OsinBook, 2012.

Lê Đức Anh. "Nâng cao cảnh giác, củng cố quốc phòng và an ninh của đất nước" (Heighten vigilance, strengthen national defense and security). *Tạp chí Cộng sản* 34, no. 4 (April 1988): 5–10.

Ngô Xuân Lịch. "Giá trị to lớn của nhân tố chính trị, tinh thần" (The great value of the political and spiritual factors). *Quân đội Nhân dân*, December 18, 2012. http://tapchiqptd.vn/vi/nhung-chu-truong-cong-tac-lon/chien-thang-ha-noi-dien-bien-phu-tren-khong-gia-tri-to-lon-cua-nhan-to-chinh-tri-tinh-than/1654.html.

———. "Sức mạnh chính trị-tinh thần của quân và dân ta trong cuộc kháng chiến chống Mỹ, cứu nước và vấn đề đặt ra đối với xây dựng Quân đội về chính trị hiện nay" (The political-spiritual strength of our military and people in the anti-US resistance to save the country and the issues in the present political building of the military). *Quốc phòng Toàn dân*, April 27, 2015. http://tapchiqptd.vn/vi/nhung-ngay-ky-niem-lon/suc-manh-chinh-tri-tinh-than-cua-quan-va-dan-ta-trong-cuoc-khang-chien-chong-my-cuu-nuoc-v/7406.html.

Nguyễn Chí Trung. "Thực chất từ Đại hội Đảng IX trở về trước (từ thập kỷ 90 thế kỷ 20) là vấn đề gì?" (What is the real problem prior to the 9th Party Congress?). Personal notes, July 21, 2002. https://www.danluan.org/tin-tuc/20090804/thuc-chat-tu-dai-hoi-dang-ix-tro-ve-truoc-tu-thap-ky-90-tk20-la-van-de-gi.

Nguyễn Cơ Thạch. "Những chuyển biến mới trên thế giới và tư duy mới của chúng ta" (New changes in the world and our new thinking). *Quan hệ Quốc tế* 3 (January 1990): 2–7.

———. *Thế giới trong 50 năm qua (1945–1995) và Thế giới trong 25 năm tới (1995–2020)* (The world in the last 50 years [1945–1995] and the world in the coming 25 years [1995–2020]). Hanoi: Nhà xuất bản Chính trị Quốc gia, 1998.

Nguyễn Phú Trọng. "Xây dựng và phát triển nền đối ngoại, ngoại giao Việt Nam hiện đại và mang đậm bản sắc dân tộc" (Building and developing a modern and national identity infused Vietnamese foreign policy and diplomacy). *Tạp chí Cộng sản*, December 14, 2021. https://www.tapchicongsan.org.vn/web/guest/media-story/-/asset_publisher/V8hhp4dK31Gf/content/xay-dung-va-phat-trien-nen-doi-ngoai-ngoai-giao-viet-nam-hien-dai-va-mang-dam-ban-sac-dan-toc.

Nguyễn Thanh Tuấn. "Chủ quyền của Việt Nam là bất khả xâm phạm" (Vietnam's sovereignty is inviolable). *Infonet*, September 29, 2012. https://infonet.vietnamnet.vn/bien-dao/chu-quyen-cua-viet-nam-la-bat-kha-xam-pham-134098.html.

Nguyễn Trung. *Tôi làm "chính trị": Những kỷ niệm và trăn trở* (I was doing "politics": Recollections and perplexing concerns). Self-published memoirs, version 2, July 19, 2018. http://www.viet-studies.net/NguyenTrung/Hoiky_NguyenTrung.pdf.

Nguyen Tung. "Viettel Moves Away from Huawei's 5G Technology." *Hanoi Times*, August 26, 2019. http://hanoitimes.vn/viettel-moves-away-from-huaweis-5g-technology-42438.html.

Nguyễn Văn Linh. "Phát biểu của đồng chí Tổng bí thư Nguyễn Văn Linh bế mạc Hội nghị 7 của Ban Chấp hành Trung ương Đảng" (Remarks by Comrade General Secretary Nguyen Van Linh concluding the Seventh Plenum of the Party Central Committee). *Tạp chí Cộng sản* 35, no. 9 (September 1989): 6–8.

Nguyen Vu Tung. *Flying Blind: Vietnam's Decision to Join ASEAN*. Singapore: ISEAS-Yusof Ishak Institute, 2021.

Palmujoki, Eero. *Vietnam and the World: Marxist-Leninist Doctrine and the Changes in International Relations, 1975–1993*. London: Macmillan, 1997.

Phan Doãn Nam. "Một vài suy nghĩ về đổi mới tư duy đối ngoại" (Some thoughts on renovation of foreign policy thinking). *Tạp chí Cộng sản* 34, no. 2 (February 1988): 50–54, 79.

Phùng Quang Thanh. "Chiến thắng 'Hà Nội—Điện Biên Phủ trên không' và những bài học cần phát huy trong sự nghiệp bảo vệ Tổ quốc hiện nay" (The victorious battle of "Hanoi—Dien Bien Phu in the air" and the lessons that should be brought into full play in the present cause of safeguarding the Fatherland). *Quốc phòng Toàn dân*, December 17, 2012. http://tapchiqptd.vn/vi/nhung-chu-truong-cong-tac-lon/chien-thang-ha-noi-dien-bien-phu-tren-khong-va-nhung-bai-hoc-can-phat-huy-trong-su-nghiep-/1642.html.

Pompeo, Michael R. "Remarks to the Press." Washington, DC, April 29, 2020. https://www.state.gov/secretary-michael-r-pompeo-at-a-press-availability-4/.

Porter, Gareth. "The Transformation of Vietnam's World-View: From Two Camps to Interdependence." *Contemporary Southeast Asia* 12, no. 1 (June 1990): 1–19.

Thành Tín. *Mặt Thật: Hồi ký Chính trị* (True face: Political memoirs). Irvine, CA: Saigon Press, 1992.

Thayer, Carlyle A. "Vietnamese Foreign Policy: Multilateralism and the Threat of Peaceful Evolution." In *Vietnamese Foreign Policy in Transition*, edited by Carlyle A. Thayer and Ramses Amer. Singapore: Institute of Southeast Asian Studies, 1999.

Trần Quang Cơ. *Hồi ức và Suy nghĩ* (Reminiscence and reflection). Unpublished manuscript, 2003.

Việt Anh. "Tướng Nguyễn Chí Vịnh: 'Việt-Mỹ cam kết không xâm hại lợi ích chiến lược'" (General Nguyen Chi Vinh: Vietnam and the United States are committed not to harm each other's strategic interests). *VnExpress*, July 2, 2015. https://vnexpress.net/tuong-nguyen-chi-vinh-viet-my-cam-ket-khong-xam-hai-loi-ich-chien-luoc-3241672.html.

"Vietnam-China Joint Statement." Vietnam News Agency, December 4, 2001. http://vietnamembassy-usa.org/relations/vietnam-china-joint-statement.

Võ Văn Kiệt. "Thư gửi Bộ Chính trị" (Letter to the Politburo). August 9, 1995. Reprinted in *Diễn đàn* 48 (January 1996): 16–19.

Vũ Hồng Lâm. "Lịch sử quan hệ Việt-Trung nhìn từ góc độ đại chiến lược" (History of Sino-Vietnamese relations from the grand strategic perspective). *Thời Đại Mới* 2 (July 2004). http://www.tapchithoidai.org/200402_VHLam.htm.

Vuving, Alexander L. "A Breakthrough in U.S.-Vietnam Relations." *The Diplomat*, April 10, 2015. http://thediplomat.com/2015/04/abreakthroughinusvietnamrelations/.

——. "Did China Blink in the South China Sea?" *National Interest*, July 27, 2014. https://nationalinterest.org/feature/did-china-blink-the-south-china-sea-10956.

——. "Grand Strategic Fit and Power Shift: Explaining Turning Points in China-Vietnam Relations." In *Living with China: Regional States and China through Crises and Turning Points*, edited by Shiping Tang, Mingjiang Li, and Amitav Acharya. New York: Palgrave Macmillan, 2009.

——. "Power Rivalry, Party Crisis, and Patriotism: New Dynamics in the Vietnam-China-U.S. Triangle." In *New Dynamics in U.S.-China Relations: Contending for the Asia Pacific*, edited by Mingjiang Li and Kalyan M. Kemburi. London: Routledge, 2014.

——. "Strategy and Evolution of Vietnam's China Policy: A Changing Mixture of Pathways." *Asian Survey* 46, no. 6 (November 2006): 805–24.

——. "A Tipping Point in the U.S.-China-Vietnam Triangle." *The Diplomat*, July 6, 2015. http://thediplomat.com/2015/07/a-tipping-point-in-the-u-s-china-vietnam-triangle/.

——. "The 2016 Leadership Change in Vietnam and Its Long-Term Implications." In *Southeast Asian Affairs 2017*, edited by Daljit Singh and Malcolm Cook. Singapore: Institute of Southeast Asian Studies, 2017.

——. "Vietnam: Arriving in the World—and at a Crossroads." In *Southeast Asian Affairs 2008*, edited by Daljit Singh and Tin Maung Maung Than. Singapore: Institute of Southeast Asian Studies, 2008.

——. "Vietnam: A Tale of Four Players." In *Southeast Asian Affairs 2010*, edited by Daljit Singh. Singapore: Institute of Southeast Asian Studies, 2010.

——. "Vietnam in 2012: A Rent-Seeking State on the Verge of a Crisis." In *Southeast Asian Affairs 2013*, edited by Daljit Singh. Singapore: Institute of Southeast Asian Studies, 2013.

——. "Vietnam in 2018: A Rent-Seeking State on Correction Course." In *Southeast Asian Affairs 2019*, edited by Daljit Singh and Malcolm Cook. Singapore: Institute of Southeast Asian Studies, 2019.

——. "Vietnam, the US, and Japan in the South China Sea." *The Diplomat*, November 26, 2014. https://thediplomat.com/2014/11/vietnam-the-us-and-japan-in-the-south-china-sea/.

——. "Will Vietnam Be America's Next Strategic Partner?" *The Diplomat*, August 21, 2021. https://thediplomat.com/2021/08/will-vietnam-be-americas-next-strategic-partner/.

CHAPTER 16

The Dynamics of Vietnamese-Chinese Relations

BILL HAYTON

The People's Republic of China is the Socialist Republic of Vietnam's largest neighbor, biggest trading partner, and oldest diplomatic supporter, yet the relationship between the two party-states is the most fraught of all Hanoi's external ties. The Communist Party of Vietnam (CPV) regards the Communist Party of China (CPC) as both an ideological friend and a risk to its nationalist legitimacy. For the Vietnamese state, China is both a vital economic benefactor and an existential security threat. As a state, China is too close, too large, and too assertive, but as a Leninist regime, China's ruling party is an ally against political pluralism. This contradiction between the CPV's ideological cooperation with the CPC and its simultaneous search for domestic legitimacy is the most important dilemma in the party-state's contemporary foreign relations.

This chapter will argue that, from the outset, the overwhelming priority of Vietnam's successive Communist leaderships has been regime survival; the maintenance of the Party's domestic power—or more specifically, the power and worldview of the dominant fraction within it.[1] Their second objective has been to assert the strategic autonomy of the Vietnamese state. The record since 1945 suggests the Party leadership will always prioritize its own leading role because it believes the Party represents the interests of the Vietnamese nation as a whole. From this I argue that current and future Party leaderships will require considerable ingenuity to overcome the increasingly contradictory imperatives of protecting strong political and economic ties with Beijing while also maintaining independence, resisting hostile moves, and containing growing anti-China feelings among the population.

Early Days, 1900–54

Party-to-party ties predated state-to-state ties by several decades. Right from the beginning of anti-colonial agitation in the 1910s, Vietnamese nationalists depended upon connections with southern China. Political and military ties between nationalists on both sides of the border grew much closer once the Guomindang (GMD) government was established in Guangdong in 1925.[2] Between 1925 and 1927, around two hundred Vietnamese were trained by Soviet, German, and Chinese instructors at the GMD's political-military Whampoa Academy. Important personal ties were also forged there between revolutionary leaders including Ho Chi Minh and Zhou Enlai. Many Vietnamese served with GMD and Chinese Communist forces right into the 1940s.[3] Once the Second World War was over, many of these veterans returned home, bringing to Vietnam experience of tactics and understandings of political organization. They translated Chinese military manuals into Vietnamese and established Chinese-style training schools. As a result, when Viet Minh nationalists formally declared independence from France as the Democratic Republic of Vietnam (DRV) in September 1945, they already had an embryonic army.[4]

Once open conflict broke out with the returned French colonial administration in December 1946, these forces became the DRV's protectors. As the fighting with the French and the French-backed "State of Vietnam" deepened, the Vietnamese received greater support from their political allies across the border. These links became even stronger after the Communist victory in China in 1949. From May 1950, the new Chinese government provided significant aid to the Viet Minh forces, starting with over a thousand tons of arms and ammunition in the first year and an eighty-strong group of military advisers. Most of the Viet Minh's military academy staff were relocated to southern China, and 30,000 Vietnamese were sent there for training. There is now evidence that "the Chinese played the determining role in choosing to take the French on at Dien Bien Phu," the battle that enabled the DRV to evolve from a rhetorical vision into a political reality.[5]

In short, the emergence of an independent and Party-led Vietnam was the result of its leaders' early and deep connections with the nationalist and communist movements across the border in China. Chinese connections enabled the Viet Minh to transition from agitators to state managers by 1954. There can be little doubt that, during this period, the Chinese side provided and the Vietnamese side received. How was this framed in the minds of those involved? It seems that the rhetoric of revolutionary solidarity between "big brother" China and "little brother" Vietnam masked the traditional condescension of the former imperial center toward its periphery.[6] This may have irritated some on the Vietnamese side, but even after the DRV took power in Hanoi in October 1954, the leadership continued to request ever-greater support from Beijing.

Partition, 1954–64

The result of the victory at Dien Bien Phu was France's agreement to withdraw its troops from Indochina. The Geneva Conference then mandated temporary partition pending elections on a future government. It has long been claimed that the leadership of the People's Republic of China pressured the DRV into accepting the partition against its wishes. However, recent discoveries in the Vietnamese archives suggest that partition was actually an outcome the DRV leadership had been prepared to accept from the out-set. Its military forces were exhausted, it faced a challenging domestic political situation, and it needed to avoid further interventions by France and the United States.[7]

This decision enabled the Communist leadership to secure a political victory and pre-pare for the next phase of political struggle.[8] Land reform had been a key objective of the Indochina Communist Party from its formation in 1929. However, it was only in Janu-ary 1950 that the Party, now known as the Vietnam Workers Party (VWP), became suffi-ciently strong to initiate a campaign.[9] It did so under the guidance of Luo Guibo, the head of the Chinese Political Advisory Group, whose advice had been specifically requested by the Vietnamese communists. The campaign stepped up further in 1953, following Luo's proposal for a mass movement to remove local elites. It was a Chinese-style plan, but it was not imposed on the VWP leadership against its will. They foresaw plenty of political ben-efits in the elimination of potentially oppositional forces from rural areas.[10]

For four years, the VWP leadership of the DRV imposed a violent campaign against those it defined as landlords. It may have been inspired by Chinese advice, but it was also a policy chosen by the Vietnamese leadership in the interests of reinforcing their own power base. Between 5,000 and 15,000 were executed and many tens of thousands more beaten and imprisoned.[11] By 1956, however, resistance to the campaign had grown suffi-ciently strong to worry those at the top of the VWP. In Nghe An and Ha Tinh Provinces, abuses by party cadres even provoked uprisings by villagers. In October of that year the government publicly apologized.

There is nothing to suggest that Chinese advice changed in late 1956, yet the VWP leadership called an abrupt end to land reform nonetheless. Faced with a direct threat to its domestic power base, and splits within its own ranks, the party changed course, defy-ing the disapproval of its bigger brother across the border. This created space for political criticism of the leadership, particularly in the pages of two publications: *Nhan Van* and *Giai Pham*. The arguments over policy were later portrayed as a battle to resist Chinese influence, but internally this episode was a fight between a dogmatic radical majority of the VWP and a "revisionist" minority. In 1957–58 the majority then proceeded to crush the political views of the minority.[12]

With their position now assured, the VWP hard-liners persuaded the Party's Central Committee in January 1959 to agree to intensify the war in southern Vietnam. This strained the VWP's relations with the Soviet Union (USSR), which was attempting to maintain an atmosphere of "peaceful coexistence" with the West. In 1962–63, the dominant group in the VWP chose to orient itself toward a sponsor, China, that would support the position it had already chosen. First Secretary Le Duan and his supporters, notably Le Duc Tho, then neutralized their opponents with a campaign against "modern revisionism" in 1963. This was, ostensibly, intended to root out those who favored the Soviet Union over China, but in reality, it eliminated those who prioritized the building of the economy in the north over the decision to return to revolutionary war in the south.[13]

China's role in Vietnamese policymaking had not been to dictate policy. Instead, it provided succor and advice for the more radical elements within the VWP. Chinese sup-port enabled the group around Le Duan and Le Duc Tho to pursue more extreme land reform policies, restart the armed revolution in the south, and adopt economic autarky. By the end of 1964, Le Duan's war in the south was well underway. This alarmed the Soviets, who decreased their aid to Hanoi, but pleased the Chinese, who increased theirs. In the context of its own split with Moscow, Beijing was able to deploy its support of Hanoi's war to promote itself as the authentic representative of Third World liberation movements, in contrast to the prevarication displayed by the Soviets. China had not ordered the Vietnamese escalation, but its backing had made a decision by Vietnamese hard-liners possible.

War, 1965–75

The ousting of the Soviet leader Nikita Khrushchev in October 1964 and his replacement by Leonid Brezhnev changed the USSR's policy toward Vietnam. Brezhnev's views on the global anti-imperialist struggle were much closer to those of the VWP leadership than Khrushchev's had been. Soviet Premier Alexei Kosygin visited Hanoi in early 1965, and substantial military supplies began to arrive in February. In effect, the Vietnamese hard-liners had caused a change in Soviet foreign policy. The Vietnamese leadership eased up on its "anti-revisionism" campaign and returned to a more balanced position between Beijing and Moscow. By then, however, the arrival of US ground forces in the Republic of Vietnam had destroyed Le Duan's expectations of a quick victory in the south.[14]

During meetings in May 1965 and March 1966, China's Premier Zhou Enlai urged visiting Vietnamese leaders to beware of Moscow's fickle nature and remember the great sacrifices made by their Chinese brethren.[15] Nonetheless, the increase in Soviet aid obliged Beijing to increase its own support for the DRV's military campaign.[16] The cumulative effect of Sino-Soviet competition increased the Vietnamese leadership's freedom of maneuver. They could worry less about offending one or the other capital since both were eager to support their struggle. Beijing was pushing for a Maoist guerrilla war, while Moscow advocated a conventional war strategy combined with negotiations. Keeping both sponsors happy required deft diplomacy, but the VWP leadership managed to maintain control over policy throughout. The competition between the two made Hanoi's autonomy possible.[17]

However, the increasing radicalization within China following the launch of the Cultural Revolution in May 1966 began to worry Hanoi. Thousands of Chinese advisers had already been deployed to the DRV. Chinese sources assert that between June 1965 and March 1968, a total of 320,000 soldiers served in the DRV, with the peak troop level reaching 170,000 in 1967.[18] By then, the Vietnamese leadership was fearful that this foreign army could attempt to impose Maoist policies in the areas where they were based. There were reports that some Chinese experts were demanding that the Vietnamese they worked with adopt anti-Soviet views. Their condescending manner was contrasted unfavorably with the "humble, very friendly, and respectful" attitude of their Soviet counterparts.[19] At this point, Vietnamese resentment of Beijing's "big brother" attitude began to affect state policy. Vietnamese intellectuals in the DRV were given political space to write about Vietnam's "history of resistance to Chinese aggression."[20] These concerns also spread to Laos, where in September 1968, under Vietnamese pressure, the communist Pathet Lao movement asked the head of the Chinese advisory team to leave the country.[21]

By 1969, Chinese actions in the DRV came to be seen as a threat to VWP rule. Le Duan may have been a hard-liner when it came to advocating war in the south, but he was not willing to see his state become subordinate to whoever emerged from the Cultural Revolution chaos inside China. Now blessed with the enthusiastic support of the Communist Party of the Soviet Union, the VWP was in a position to assert its national sovereignty as a means of protecting itself against Maoist madness. The year 1968 was the high point of Chinese aid to the DRV. It then fell until conditions changed again in 1971.[22] The USSR filled in the gap and the VWP leadership leaned further toward Moscow. Disputes between Hanoi and Beijing became more fractious, but power had moved in Hanoi's favor since any public criticism of China by the leading Third World liberation movement would have damaged Beijing's image in the eyes of the socialist world.

There were, however, clear limits to Hanoi's ability to influence the behavior of either of its main sponsors. Both Beijing and Moscow had moved in favor of a negotiated end to the war. Relations became worse after the visit of US President Richard Nixon to China in February 1972. Assured of Washington's intentions to work with China in a joint struggle against the Soviet Union, Beijing became less concerned about the American threat in Vietnam.[23] No longer able to play off its sponsors against one another, the DRV was obliged to reach a peace deal with the United States. In hindsight, however, it is clear that the DRV had no intention of abiding by the document it signed in Paris in January 1973; it merely paused for a few weeks until conditions became more propitious.

The Chinese leadership was now more concerned with the DRV's increasing tilt toward the Soviet Union, and this led it to oppose the rapid reunification of Vietnam. It preferred to see its neighbor divided and bogged down in war rather than united and allied with the Soviets.[24] Having increased its military aid to the DRV in 1972 and 1973, Beijing then cut it by half.[25] In 1974, the same calculations led the PRC to occupy the western half of the Paracel Islands (in the South China Sea) after evicting the forces of the RVN. The response from Hanoi was to increase its tilt toward Moscow, step up its military campaign for reunification, and occupy the RVN's positions in the Spratly Islands farther south. By April 1975, despite the objections of "bigger brother" in Beijing, Le Duan and his supporters had achieved their war aims and united the country under their leadership.

Rupture and Repair, 1975–91

As a result, the VWP leadership's priorities changed. Since 1945 its reason for conquering territory—whether as a rebel force against the French or as a Hanoi-based state against the RVN—had been to create a space for the implementation of communist policies. However, from early 1975, once it seemed assured of victory, the Party's priorities evolved into protecting sovereignty over territory as an end in its own right. It was, to borrow James Scott's phrase, "seeing like a state."[26] Internally, the Le Duan–led regime had constructed an effective security apparatus that could both snuff out dissent in the north and impose socialist control over the newly conquered south. Externally it had chased away the United States and, by the end of 1975, Vietnam was bordered entirely by communist states: China, Laos, and Cambodia. It should have been the best of times for East Asian communism. Instead, the next decade and a half was spent mired in wars of attrition.

What may have begun as a political dispute within the communist family was rapidly polluted by nationalism. Questions over the ownership of offshore islands, the exact line of national boundaries, and the loyalty of minority populations, which had been regarded as minor issues during the war years, rapidly became emotive rallying points. China's seizure of the strategic Paracel Islands in 1974 became a patriotic cause celebre in the RVN, prompting the DRV to reassess its previous nonchalance toward the issue. At around the same time, small-scale clashes occurred along undemarcated sections of the China-Vietnam land border. Hanoi said there were ninety incidents in 1974; Beijing later claimed there had been 121. At the same time DRV state media began talking about "the threat from the north" in an attempt to mobilize a new form of patriotic feeling among the people.

Le Duan's visit to Beijing in September 1975 did not go well: he reportedly resented his counterparts' "bigger brother" attitude. At the end of 1975, Beijing decided to reduce its economic and military aid to almost nothing. The Vietnamese felt they deserved more; the Chinese felt they had already given far beyond their means.[27] Shortly afterward, the DRV leadership requested closer military relations with Moscow, including the transfer of more advanced weapons. These began to arrive the following year, and, not coincidentally, the number of military confrontations along the border with China also increased. In late 1976 the renamed Communist Party of Vietnam (CPV) expelled from its Central Committee several senior figures who had served in various capacities in China, a move that Beijing could reasonably interpret as hostile. There were also reports of assaults against Chinese experts working on aid projects. Anti-Chinese feeling was also growing in the general population. This was exacerbated by Hanoi's policy of encouraging ethnic Chinese in the newly unified country to repudiate their Chinese citizenship and pledge loyalty to Vietnam, amid concerns that Beijing was attempting to recruit them as a "fifth column" (see Le Dang Doanh's chapter in this volume). From 1976, what was supposed to be a voluntary process became increasingly coercive. Chinese-language schools were closed, Chinese-owned businesses were nationalized, and thousands of ethnic Chinese were forcibly relocated away from border areas to "New Economic Zones." Under the difficult conditions of postwar trauma and enforced collectivization, the Chinese minority became an easy scapegoat.[28]

Within months of the victorious DRV changing its name to the Socialist Republic of Vietnam (SRV) in July 1976, the country was plunged into an economic and social crisis caused by the ongoing impact of the war, the leadership's neo-Stalinist policies, and large reductions in Chinese aid. Demands that the United States should pay war reparations came to nothing (see Miller's chapter in this volume). GDP per capita was less than one dollar per day, the state rice reserves were exhausted, only 63 percent of the government budget was funded, 3 million workers were unemployed, and law breaking was rampant.[29] Meanwhile, China increased its aid and military support to the Khmer Rouge regime in Phnom Penh. Hanoi began to fear strategic encirclement, particularly as the number of clashes on the border with Cambodia reached more than a thousand during 1977. Faced with an existential threat to the state's economy and therefore to the party's own position as its political leader, the Le Duan leadership took drastic action. The only likely source of economic aid was now the Soviet bloc. In a recent study based on a detailed work in the Vietnamese archives, Kosal Path argues that the CPV leadership decided in January 1978 that the only way to unlock this aid, while simultaneously tackling its border problems, was to deliberately trigger a crisis with China.

Relations between the Communist Parties of Vietnam and Cambodia had been hostile as far back as 1971. In May 1975, immediately after their revolutionary victories in their respective countries, they had clashed over disputed islands in the Gulf of Thailand. Cambodian forces attacked Vietnamese villages in early 1977, and by the end of September they had killed around a thousand Vietnamese civilians. The Chinese Party leadership attempted to mediate but without success. Relations between Hanoi and Beijing worsened in November 1977 when Le Duan, after a visit to Moscow, held talks with his Chinese counterpart Hua Guofeng and asked him for additional economic aid. Hua's refusal prompted Le Duan to criticize China's "reactionary" position at the subsequent ceremonial banquet. China's continuing friendly relations with Cambodia, even as the cross-border raids continued, only hardened attitudes. In February 1978, the VWP's Central Committee endorsed the Politburo's decision to invade Cambodia and, at the same meeting, also voted to abolish (the largely ethnic Chinese–owned) capitalist trade in the former RVN.[30]

According to Path, the Vietnamese Politburo's decision to invade Cambodia was therefore "a strategic one motivated by their belief that it would ensure full military and political support from Vietnam's great power ally, the Soviet Union, increase the flow of material and technology from the Soviet-led Council for Mutual Economic Assistance, and raise Vietnam's international standing in the Soviet-led socialist camp."[31] In other words, the Vietnamese leadership chose to invade Cambodia not just to eliminate the border security problem but also to deliberately place Vietnam on the front line of the confrontation within the communist world. This, it was assumed, would oblige the Soviet bloc to provide sufficient aid to the country for it to escape a potentially fatal economic crisis. The alternatives were a rapprochement with China, which would not have generated extra aid and could have obliged Vietnam to accept Cambodia's demands on the border, or a turn toward Western providers of aid, which would have required a rapid reversal of economic policy and a change of political worldview, jeopardizing CPV rule. Given the choice between starting a new war and losing power, Le Duan and his colleagues chose war.

The Party leadership spent 1978 preparing for confrontation. Central planning rules were relaxed to give local districts greater autonomy and so build up their resilience; military units were readied for action; state media talked up the "threat from the north"; and the ongoing border clashes were publicized domestically and internationally. In June, Vietnam joined the Soviet-led Council for Mutual Economic Assistance (COMECON), in November it signed the Soviet-Vietnamese Treaty of Friendship and Cooperation with the USSR, and in December—despite many public and private warnings from Beijing[32]—it invaded Cambodia. It took less than two weeks to evict the Khmer Rouge from Phnom Penh.

The Vietnamese leadership had assumed their alliance with the Soviet Union would deter Chinese retaliation. They were wrong. In fact, the Chinese leadership was determined to punish Vietnam because of that alliance. Its response came on February 17, 1979, the day that Vietnam's prime minister and army chief signed a friendship treaty with the newly installed Cambodian government. Tens of thousands of Chinese troops flooded across Vietnam's northern border. Deng Xiaoping had cleared plans for the invasion with US President Jimmy Carter during his visit to the White House three weeks earlier.[33] The Carter administration, eager to build relations with Beijing in order to outflank the Soviet bloc, assisted the Chinese by providing information about Vietnamese military positions and the weak state of Soviet forces stationed along the border with China.[34] Just as Hanoi hoped that its conflict with China would solidify its relations with the Soviet bloc, so Beijing expected that its conflict with Vietnam would grant it entry to a Western-led anti-Soviet community. Throughout the 1980s, China found itself part of an "unholy alliance" with the United States and members of ASEAN in support of a Cambodian opposition, which included the Khmer Rouge.

By the time the USSR strengthened its land units along the country's far eastern borders and deployed its ships to Southeast Asian waters, the Chinese leadership had declared its military aims achieved and announced the end of fighting. The Vietnamese provinces of Lao Cai, Lang Son, Cao Bang, and Mong Cai had been laid waste and over half a million people made homeless.[35] This was not the end of the northern border problem, however. The two sides continued to wage a war of attrition there for the next decade. Making the situation worse, Vietnam was now also bogged down in a counterinsurgency quagmire in Cambodia.

Ideologically, this period became the high point of Vietnamese "neo-Stalinism" (see also Vuving's chapter in this volume). In the words of Gareth Porter, "From the early 1980s to mid-1986, the Vietnamese Party had portrayed big power relations as a 'bitter struggle between two systems' in which the United States and its allies were stepping up the arms race and threatening world peace, and the People's Republic of China was aligned with the United States and the West against the world revolution."[36] In this, the Party leadership became even more belligerent than the Soviets. When Le Duan visited Moscow in May 1982, it became apparent that differences over China were becoming significant.[37] When the Soviet leader, Leonid Brezhnev, attempted to improve relations with China that year, he was told that one of the three obstacles was Vietnam's occupation of Cambodia.[38] Vietnam, however, was determined to destroy what it saw as China's proxy in Cambodia.

The Vietnamese offensive in 1984–85 destroyed the last of the major Khmer Rouge strongholds within Cambodia and, on August 16, 1985, Vietnam announced that its forces would totally withdraw from Cambodia by 1990. Stalemate, however, continued. It was only after the reorientation of Soviet foreign policy, beginning with Mikhail Gorbachev's Vladivostok speech in July 1986, that the Vietnamese leadership was forced to adjust its own outlook. At this point, changes in superpower relations, the perceived failure of Vietnam's existing economic policies, the cost of maintaining a vast standing army, and the death of Le Duan combined to create an opening for new thinking.

One school of thought was championed by Foreign Minister Nguyen Co Thach (father of Vietnam's current Deputy Prime Minister Phạm Binh Minh).[39] Thach argued, in effect, that the Soviet bloc was not going to win the economic war with capitalism and that, as a matter of survival, Vietnam needed to open relations with Western countries. In May 1987, the CPV's theoretical journal published, in the words of Gareth Porter, "its first critical evaluation of changes in the international situation," written by Thach's assistant, Phan Doan Nam. This was followed by a second article in February 1988.[40] In March 1988, Chinese forces occupied six features in the Spratly Islands, triggering a clash at Johnson Reef South in which sixty-four Vietnamese marines were killed. The need for relations with other powers was made even more obvious. A few months later, in May 1988, the Politburo approved Resolution 13, its first major document on foreign policy in four years. It acknowledged, in effect, that future economic development would require international cooperation. It called for a revised position on Cambodia and a new "diversifying and multidirectional" foreign policy.[41] Hanoi's last troops withdrew from Cambodia in September 1989 (by which time the conflict had killed at least 55,000 Vietnamese soldiers).[42]

Once again, the Vietnamese leadership faced a major strategic decision. It could, theoretically, have attempted to maintain its rule through mass coercion. Instead it chose to seek popular legitimacy by delivering a better standard of living to the people. However, the collapse of the socialist regimes in Central Europe in late 1989 alerted them to the likelihood that Soviet aid, estimated at US$3 billion that year, was unlikely to be maintained.[43] More alarming was the political threat to the Party's legitimacy. General Secretary Nguyen Van Linh warned against American-backed efforts at regime change.[44] A speech by Linh delivered to the Sixth Central Committee meeting of the Sixth Congress, in May 1989, was entitled "Why We Do Not Accept Pluralism."[45] Linh was the foremost proponent of economic renovation—*Đổi Mới*—but he was not prepared to allow liberalization to creep into the political sphere.

The Politburo's fears became more acute in February 1990 when the Soviet Communist Party formally renounced its constitutional leading role. The following month, by contrast, the Communist Party of China publicly reaffirmed its own leading role. Coming after the June 1989 crackdown in Tiananmen Square, it demonstrated to the Vietnamese that the CPC was serious about defending Leninism. In its own public statements, the Vietnamese Politburo was already following the Chinese path, asserting that Vietnam's unique history and state of evolution required a leading role for the Communist Party.[46] At this moment, the CPV's concern for domestic power outweighed its concern for strategic autonomy. In March, the Central Committee voted to expel one member of the Politburo, Tran Xuan Bach, who had urged the Party to adopt greater pluralism.[47]

In 1978 the Vietnamese Party leadership had switched loyalties from Beijing to Moscow in order to preserve their regime. A decade later the same instinct demanded a reverse switch. Tran Quang Co, one of the officials involved, recounted in his memoirs that the crisis obliged the Vietnamese leadership to seek a new protector.[48] Beijing's post-1989 international isolation created an opening for a rapprochement, and, in April 1990, Linh reached out via intermediaries in Laos. The timing was fortuitous. In July, the United States announced it was no longer willing to support a Cambodian coalition that included the Khmer Rouge and intended to contact Hanoi to discuss a settlement to the fighting. China would be left internationally exposed.[49]

The CPV leadership had a choice to make: open to the US, as Foreign Minister Thach desired, or to China as General Secretary Linh preferred. The guardians of Leninism won the argument. On September 2, 1990, Linh, Prime Minister Do Muoi, and Party éminence grise Pham Van Dong absented themselves from their own Independence Day celebrations and flew to Chengdu to meet Chinese leaders for the first time since the mid-1970s. The price of economic and political stability at home was to accept all of China's demands in Cambodia. Years of stalemate were ended by a hard-headed assessment of what was best for the CPV. That led to the Paris Peace Accords of October 1991 and the formal resumption of relations between Vietnam and China the following month.[50]

However, Vietnam's leadership was clearly unwilling to put all its faith in China. The CPV's Seventh Congress in June 1991 called for the country to "diversify and multilateralize economic relations with all countries and economic organizations . . . regardless of different sociopolitical systems." It was a rejection of the Party's former worldview of "two camps" locked in a death struggle, but it was less a turn to the West and more an attempt to shore up Leninism by opening the doors to international investment and trade while maintaining strong relations with a fellow communist regime in Beijing. The Congress saw the exit of Foreign Minister Thach, dismissed from the Politburo as part of the price for restoring relations with the CPC. Control of China policy passed to Defense Minister Le Duc Anh.[51] Once again, the China factor had become a resource for Party hard-liners to deploy in their struggle against those whom they perceived to be undermining communist rule in Vietnam.

As David Elliott's book *Changing Worlds* makes clear, the changes in Vietnam's "collective ideas" on politics and international orientation were not caused by a single external shock (the collapse of the USSR), but rather "a shock following an extended crisis which had weakened resistance to change."[52] Despite all its talk of national sovereignty, the CPV has never stood alone. One of the leadership's aims in normalizing relations with China had been to obtain some kind of alliance or security guarantee. Beijing declined the request.[53] Nonetheless, ever since it stopped being close to the USSR, the CPV's basic foreign policy orientation has been to keep close to (*thân*) China.

1992–2001, Coping with National Interests

Although the 1990s was a period of economic opening, Vietnam's basic security orientation remained stable. As the number of communist party-states dwindled, the CPV's reliance on the CPC increased. In June 1992, a key meeting of the Central Committee ordained a hierarchy of countries—with communist friends like China, Cuba, and North Korea at the top and the United States at the bottom. At the same time, the CPV also defined the country's top foreign policy priorities as regional cooperation and better relations with the world's economic powers. The intention was to combine Leninism with international integration ("market-Leninism," as London terms it elsewhere in this volume).

Over the following decade, the Vietnamese and Chinese leaderships worked to renew their relationship. There were at least eighteen meetings between senior leaders from both sides between 1991 and 2001. The most important benefit was a dramatic rise in cross-border trade: it increased almost a hundredfold, from just over US$30 million in 1991 to US$2.8 billion in 2001. The political relationship was, however, very different from the one that existed before 1975. The Chinese leadership shocked their Vietnamese counterparts by characterizing it as "comrades but not allies."[54] The two Communist Parties shared a political outlook on how to manage their own societies, but they had important differences over what they regarded as their national interests. In the past, territorial disagreements had been put aside in the cause of revolutionary internationalism. With that political struggle now over, questions of sovereignty became more difficult. In the aftermath of Tiananmen Square, the source of political legitimacy for the CPC had shifted from revolutionary history to nationalism.

In 1992 China promulgated a new Maritime Territorial Law formalizing its claim to the Paracel and Spratly Islands. The claims dated back to the 1900s and 1940s, respectively, but, unlike in previous decades, China now possessed the ability to assert them. There were confrontations over oil exploration off Vietnam's southeastern coast in 1994. Toward the end of that year, Chinese forces also occupied Mischief Reef, close to the Philippines.[55] The CPV became increasingly alarmed about threats to Vietnam's national interests. At the same time as it was pursuing closer party-to-party relations with Beijing, Hanoi also began to seek new partners through which it could increase its diplomatic leverage and strategic autonomy.

Vietnam acceded to ASEAN's Treaty of Amity and Cooperation in 1992 and became a founding member of the ASEAN Regional Forum in 1994.[56] China's moves had also provoked concerns in other Southeast Asian capitals, and in July 1995 the six existing members of ASEAN welcomed Vietnam into the group. Hanoi then began lobbying for the admission of Myanmar, Laos, and Cambodia in order to increase ASEAN's diplomatic weight and its own influence within ASEAN.[57]

That year, Vietnam also established official relations with the United States and signed a framework cooperation agreement with the European Union. In 1989 Hanoi had had relations with only twenty-three noncommunist states. By 1996 the number was 161.[58] At the same time, as a result of this international integration, Vietnam's economic situation was improving significantly. Growth averaged 8 percent between 1991 and 1996, and the economy doubled in size, relieving some of the political pressure on the Party leadership at home.[59] Yet there were concerns that growth would slow without further reforms.

In August 1995, Prime Minister Vo Van Kiet wrote a twenty-two-page memo to the Politburo urging the CPV to withdraw from the details of government and allow others to play a role in policymaking.[60] This call to separate Party and state was anathema to other leading members of the Politburo and initiated an epic battle for control over the future direction of the Party that continued into and beyond the Eighth Congress in June 1996. The battle was reflected in the Congress listing the "four dangers" facing the country as "lagging behind economically," but also "deviation from socialist orientation; red tape and corruption; and 'peaceful evolution'" (code for moves toward political pluralism).

As this power struggle was unfolding, Beijing made a move that caused a significant readjustment in Hanoi's foreign policy. On March 7, 1997, China deployed an oil-drilling platform, the *Kantan III*, into the Gulf of Tonkin. In response, the Vietnamese mobilized fellow members of ASEAN. When that failed to deter the Chinese, Hanoi invited the head of the US Pacific Command, Admiral Joseph Prueher, to visit. A week after those discussions, the Chinese withdrew the oil rig. A new phase in Vietnam's international relations had begun. Just three months later, China invited CPV General Secretary Do Muoi to Beijing. In his meeting with President Jiang Zemin, the two leaders agreed to settle their countries' border on land by 2000 and in the Tonkin Gulf before the end of 2000.[61] It appeared that by making a very public opening to the US, Hanoi had induced a significant shift in Beijing's attitude.

In December 1997, the rival strands of opinion within the CPV managed to find sufficient common ground to select a new Party leader: Le Kha Phieu, a political commissar from the military. He immediately initiated an enthusiastic turn toward China. During 1998, there were 148 formal exchanges between the two party-states, with fifty-two at vice-ministerial level or above. In 1999, the number of high-level visits jumped to eighty. It amounted to a determined move to shore up the Leninist position within the Party.[62]

However, the CPC leadership was not interested in forming an explicit ideological alliance with the CPV. Rather than describing the two states as brothers, comrades, or allies, the March 1999 agreement between the two Party general secretaries, Jiang Zemin and Le Kha Phieu, set out "16 Character Guidelines" for relations between the two countries: "long-term, stable, future-oriented, good-neighborly, and all-round cooperative bilateral relations." The CPC had prioritized China's national interest over a mutual ideological one. The CPV leadership was obliged to accept. Phieu then agreed to the necessary compromises on the northern border for agreement to be reached by the end of the year.[63] The final settlement was presented as fair, with Vietnam awarded 113 km² of the disputed territory and China 114 km².[64] However, no maps were published, and it seems that the disputed territory was ground that China had occupied after the 1979 border war. The net result was that, compared to the pre-1979 border, China gained territory.[65] Behind closed doors in Hanoi, Phieu and his supporters were strongly criticized for having sold out Vietnam's national interest in order to win support for their conservative approach to politics.

However, Phieu did not abandon his efforts. In early 2000, Phieu summarized the importance of China for a visiting Chinese delegation: "If China succeeds in its reform, then we'll succeed. If China fails, we'll fail."[66] According to Alexander Vuving, "It was at Phieu's initiative that China and Vietnam agreed to hold regular consultations on ideology." In June 2000, sixteen senior Vietnamese officials, including Politburo member and chief theoretician Nguyen Duc Binh, attended a two-day seminar in China on how to reform a socialist economy without losing Party control. At the event, Binh reportedly urged the Chinese to intensify solidarity among communist countries. Phieu also renewed the Vietnamese request for a two-way ideological alliance.[67] At this time, the CPV's concerns for domestic power outweighed their worries about strategic autonomy.

In what appeared to be an attempt to demonstrate his commitment to a closer Vietnam-China relationship, Phieu unilaterally made concessions in the negotiations over the maritime boundary in the Gulf of Tonkin. He also signed up to a Joint Statement for Comprehensive Cooperation in the New Century, which set out a framework for future bilateral relations, described by Zachary Abuza as "very pro-China and explicitly anti American." And that, more or less, finished Phieu's political career. The final straw came when he sat next to China's political heir apparent, Hu Jintao, at the CPV's Ninth Party Congress in April 2001.[68] By then, Phieu's failures were many and obvious. In the words of Carl Thayer, "Phieu was criticized for ineffective leadership, failure to revive Vietnam's stagnant economy, inability to root out widespread corruption in the party, and 'anti-democratic' behavior, . . . nepotism [and] of pursuing a 'pro-China' policy."[69] In the end, his attempts to use China to shore up his own ideological position, a tactic that had worked for previous general secretaries, became a liability, not a strength. He was accused of selling out the country for a cause that was now out of step with the needs of the times.

2001–13, Cooperation and Struggle

Phieu's failure to be reelected at the Ninth Party Congress in April 2001 was an obvious indicator that the "turn to China" of the previous four years was over. For the new General Secretary, Nong Duc Manh, Vietnam's priority was to catch up with more developed countries.[70] The Congress set a target of 7 percent economic growth each year for the next two decades.[71] There was consensus that this would require greater integration into the world economy. The Congress also reaffirmed Vietnam's commitment to a diversified foreign policy. Among the broader CPV elite, the perception was growing that a more powerful China would increasingly assert its own national interests at the expense of those of Vietnam. Before and during the Congress the state-owned media had published several stories about Chinese violations of Vietnamese sovereignty in the South China Sea and Vietnam's determination to protect its position. The Congress voted to upgrade bases on the disputed islands. There had been no mass protests against China. Instead, there had been a change of mood within the CPV elite: prioritizing Vietnam's strategic autonomy over ideological solidarity with China.

A month before the gathering, the Vietnamese leadership agreed to a new strategic partnership with Russia. In October, however, Russia announced that it could no longer afford to maintain the military forces that had been based at Cam Ranh Bay in central Vietnam since 1979.[72] They withdrew in May 2002; Vietnam was suddenly alone.[73] Hanoi's first response was to work with the other members of ASEAN to try and constrain China's behavior in the South China Sea. However, negotiations for a "code of conduct" between ASEAN and China were disappointing. The two sides could only agree on a political "Declaration" in November 2002, rather than the binding treaty the Vietnamese had hoped for.

In December 2001, China joined the World Trade Organization (WTO), giving its economy another huge boost. In November 2002, China and ASEAN signed a framework agreement laying out a road map toward a China-ASEAN Free Trade Area by 2010. Vietnam sought to diversify its economic relations by ratifying a long-delayed bilateral trade agreement with the United States in November 2001. However, with the US now embarked upon its "War on Terror," one part of the CPV leadership became concerned that China would fill the strategic void in Southeast Asia. Another part feared that the US's success in forcing regime change in Baghdad could be replicated against Hanoi. The result was another rethink of Vietnam's strategic options. According to Alexander Vuving, "In the aftermath of the U.S. invasions of Afghanistan and Iraq, writers in the CPV theoretical journal recognized for the first time the reality of a unipolar world." Those who believed the United States was fundamentally hostile to the Party, as well as those who wanted stronger ties with the US, were able to agree to a new approach. Resolution 8 at the Central Committee meeting in July 2003 removed the ideological element of Vietnam's foreign policy and elevated pragmatism into a principle.[74] Its conclusion was that "Hanoi no longer regarded any country as merely a partner (to cooperate with) or purely an adversary (to struggle against)." The resolution made clear there was no simplistic distinction between cooperation and struggle, and that elements of both could exist in Vietnam's relationship with any one country.[75]

With this ideological justification agreed, Vietnam was finally ready to open the door to greater military cooperation with the United States. The Vietnamese defense minister visited Washington in November 2003, and a week later the USS *Vandegrift* became the first American warship to visit Vietnam since 1975. According to the American ambassador, Raymond Burghardt, "Vietnam's leadership authoritatively conveyed its concerns about America's inattention to Asia during Deputy Prime Minister Vu Khoan's visit to the United States in early December 2003."[76] In further discussions that month, Vietnam's Vice Foreign Minister Le Van Bang (who had previously been in charge of Northeast Asian relations) told American diplomats in Hanoi about what he regarded as a "change of strategy" agreed by the CPC's Sixteenth Party Congress, in which China would be less inward-oriented. Bang told them China was "into everything" in a manner that he described as "aggressive" rather than merely "active." By contrast, he criticized American engagement with Southeast Asia as weak.[77] In 2003, therefore, the CPV leadership decided to enroll the US in its efforts to defend the state's strategic autonomy and the Party's popular legitimacy while avoiding any entanglements that might undermine its domestic power.

Vietnamese anxieties heightened in September 2004 when China and the Philippines agreed to joint oil and gas exploration in the South China Sea. The Vietnamese protested loudly and were allowed to join the Joint Maritime Seismic Undertaking (JMSU) in March 2005. However, this initiative failed to change the terms of the countries' disputes. China instead turned to more coercive measures. Where once Beijing had tried to use financial carrots to get its way in the South China Sea, from 2007 it increasingly turned to sticks to try and force international energy companies to abandon developments off Vietnam, the Philippines, and other Southeast Asian countries.[78]

Despite these developments, Vietnam continued to engage with China to resolve other outstanding issues. Two agreements, one on maritime delimitation and the other on fisheries cooperation, were ratified on June 30, 2004, ending their dispute in the Tonkin Gulf.[79] The agreements granted a larger share of the waters to China than might have resulted if the case had gone to international arbitration. The Vietnamese deferred to China, albeit in a relatively minor way, in the interest of reaching an agreement.[80] That was followed the following month by an agreement between the Vietnam Petroleum Corporation (PetroVietnam) and the China National Offshore Oil Corporation (CNOOC) to conduct joint exploration for oil and gas in the Gulf. It is notable that these negotiations continued despite the shooting deaths of eight Vietnamese fishermen in January 2005.[81] The leadership's response to that incident was not to inflame confrontation but to neutralize it through closer cooperation. Despite all the other difficulties in the relationship, the Tonkin Gulf has remained stable; reported incidents of clashes between fishing crews have largely disappeared.

In 2006 the two leaderships agreed to establish a China-Vietnam Steering Committee for Bilateral Cooperation at the deputy prime ministerial level.[82] Although it held its first meeting that November, progress was initially slow and participants were limited to the Party's structures in the military's General Political Department. Nonetheless, it has continued to meet annually. In October 2006, the two prime ministers agreed to complete the demarcation of their land border by the end of 2008,[83] a deadline that was later met. In June 2008, a summit of Party leaders in Beijing agreed to raise the two countries' bilateral relations to that of "comprehensive strategic cooperative partnership."[84] In 2009, they agreed to install a hotline for direct communication between senior leaders, and in November 2010 Vietnam and China held their first Strategic Defense and Security Dialogue. It is notable that Vietnam has matched its formal dialogues with China and the US, creating "defense dialogues" with both in 2004–5 and then "strategic dialogues" with both in 2010.[85]

The intensification of these bilateral arrangements paralleled an intensification in the two countries' disputes. In 2007, the Chinese authorities began pressuring international energy companies to abandon oil and gas developments off the Vietnamese coast. Several of them did so over the following years. In 2011, Chinese vessels obstructed energy companies' hydrocarbon surveys in the same waters. Vietnam's response was to both broaden its international engagements and also increase the capacity of its navy. In 2009 it began sponsoring international conferences on the South China Sea, and in 2010 hosted a tumultuous meeting of the ASEAN Regional Forum in Hanoi, at which the US secretary of state, quietly supported by most ASEAN members, made strong criticisms of China's behavior. Between 2010 and 2014, Vietnam's defense spending rose by 60 percent, with most investment going into maritime capabilities.[86]

But throughout the decade, even as Vietnamese concerns over China's growing influence and assertiveness grew, Hanoi continued to push new forms of dialogue with Beijing.

Although the CPV leadership had abandoned the idea of creating some kind of Leninist alliance, they continued to encourage party-to-party and state-to-state relations as a way of engaging their Chinese counterparts. Each year, officials took part in dozens of meetings, with discussions ranging from practical issues to larger questions of ideology. It is this author's contention that these efforts are more than just a means of managing a potentially hostile relationship. They are a mechanism for political learning and a manifestation of an ideological affinity between the two Communist Parties. By dividing issues into particular areas of responsibility, the two leaderships have created a method of crisis management. Difficult subjects can be "quarantined" (or "neutralized," in Brantly Womack's terminology[87]) in particular venues without necessarily disrupting the overall relationship.

Different types of contact are used for different purposes. The party leaderships set the overall agenda with occasional set-piece meetings between general secretaries. An annual ideology workshop between the two parties, involving members of their Politburos, has taken place every year since 2005. In 2006, then–National Assembly Chairman Nguyen Phu Trong told journalists after one such event, "China and Vietnam have many things in common, so we can share our views and learn from each other. The visit provided me a chance to learn how China has turned theory into reality, and it has a lot of experience in this area."[88] Carl Thayer has suggested that "party-to-party ties have been used to identify common ground between former antagonists."[89] However, it seems likely that these events play a more fundamental role in renewing and protecting Leninist ideas within both countries.

In summary, the 2000s were a period in which the enormous growth of China's economy generated and facilitated an ambition to become a regional power. Although from 2003, China's leaders talked about their country's "peaceful rise," Vietnamese observers became increasingly concerned about Beijing's real intentions. Perhaps even without being aware of it, the Chinese state, its agencies, corporations, and the many other actors within the People's Republic asserted their interests in and around Vietnam in ways that disconcerted the Vietnamese elite's desire for strategic autonomy. Vietnamese analysts were concerned about China's rising influence in Laos and Cambodia,[90] its apparent lack of concern for Vietnam's interests in the Mekong River catchment, its predatory behavior in the South China Sea, and its business activities within Vietnam itself. Making matters worse, in 2005 China became Vietnam's top trading partner, with the balance firmly in China's favor.

Modern economic and strategic concerns mingled with historical memories of Chinese domination to produce a rising tide of anti-China sentiment. This first expressed itself on the streets of Vietnam in December 2007, with spontaneous protests against China's actions in the South China Sea. There were further protests in 2009 against a decision to allow a Chinese company to exploit bauxite reserves in Vietnam's Central Highlands. The response of the Communist Party leadership was to suppress such criticism in order to maintain smooth relations with China. There was no suggestion that Hanoi would ever break Party and state ties with Beijing. Instead, it did the opposite, tightening relations but, at the same time, seeking friends and supporters in other capitals.

2014–Present, Coping with Xi

At the beginning of May 2014, a highly organized flotilla of vessels from China's oil industry, coast guard, navy, fishing industry, and other authorities escorted the country's
first deep-water oil rig (*HS981*) into an area of the sea near the Paracel Islands claimed by
both China and Vietnam. This prompted an immediate response from the Vietnamese
coast guard, which attempted to block the rig's progress. In a highly unusual move, the
Vietnamese authorities chose to publicize what was going on, prompting street protests
against the Chinese embassy in Hanoi and consulate in Ho Chi Minh City. Here, the
CPV copied a technique previously used by the CPC to signal both its displeasure and its
resolve in international disputes.[91] There were also protests against Chinese firms in some
industrial zones and attacks on Chinese contractors at the Ha Tinh steel works, in which
at least four Chinese workers were killed. (In these cases, however, it is likely that the
protests were prompted by workplace grievances unrelated to geopolitical disputes.) All
this took place during a meeting of the CPV Central Committee in Hanoi. However, in
a sign of the deep splits within the Party over how to respond, the meeting resolved to do
nothing more than closely monitor the maritime situation and seek its peaceful resolution. At sea, the standoff continued, with Vietnam facilitating international media coverage of its coast guard's resistance actions and mobilizing diplomatic support. On May 10
it persuaded ASEAN to issue a formal statement, "urging all parties . . . to exercise self-
restraint." This was the first time that ASEAN had ever taken a position on the Paracel
Islands—a purely bilateral dispute between Vietnam and China.

Reports suggest that Hanoi made many attempts to open communication with Beijing
but failed. Instead, it made a turn to the US. On May 20, Vietnam announced it would join
the US-sponsored Proliferation Security Initiative, which it had previously joined China in
opposing.[92] This had been a long-standing US request, so the timing suggested Vietnam's
acceptance was a deliberate opening to Washington. At the same time, however, Vietnam
turned down an invitation for Foreign Minister Pham Binh Minh to visit Washington.
That would have been a step too far, involving the US too obviously in a dispute with China
and thereby exacerbating it. At the Shangri-La Dialogue at the end of May, Phung Quang
Thanh, minister of national defense and third-highest ranking member of the Politburo,
tried to play down the significance of the crisis, describing China as "the friendly neighboring country" and calling for the peaceful resolution of the standoff.

On June 18, China's State Councilor Yang Jiechi visited Hanoi under the rubric of
the long-scheduled annual meeting of the Joint Steering Committee for Bilateral Cooperation. His public comments chastised Vietnam for its behavior during the standoff, but
it is believed that discussions behind closed doors with Foreign Minister Pham Binh
Minh and CPV General Secretary Nguyen Phu Trong marked the beginning of the two
sides' de-escalation.[93] In early July, the CPV Politburo was reported to have voted overwhelmingly to hold a meeting of the Central Committee to endorse international legal
action against China. A petition circulated among some prominent intellectuals calling
for Vietnam to "escape China's orbit."[94] On July 15, however, China brought the crisis to

a swift end by announcing the withdrawal of the oil rig a month earlier than planned. An excuse had been provided by the imminent arrival of Super-Typhoon Rammasun.

In late July 2014, Politburo member Pham Quang Nghi made an intriguing visit to the United States at the invitation of the State Department.[95] The Hanoi leadership appeared to be using the visit as a warning signal to Beijing that it had the option to pursue closer relations with Washington if it so chose. This was emphasized on August 14, when General Martin Dempsey became the first chairman of the US Joint Chiefs of Staff ever to visit Hanoi. However, by not sending its foreign minister to Washington and deciding against taking legal action against China, it appears that the Vietnamese leadership chose to deliberately de-escalate the situation. Beijing appears to have recognized the message and reconsidered the confrontation it had initiated. On August 27 it received Le Hong Anh, Politburo member, head of the Secretariat of the CPV Central Committee, and a former minister of public security.

This signaled an end to the crisis, which was confirmed two months later, on October 16–18, when Vietnam dispatched its most significant military delegation ever to visit Beijing. It proposed that "both militaries should remain calm, patient, show restraint, and strictly control activities at sea to avoid misunderstandings." On October 16 the Chinese and Vietnamese prime ministers met on the sidelines of the Asia-Europe Summit Meeting in Milan. At the end of the month (October 27) Hanoi hosted the seventh meeting of the two countries' Steering Committee for Bilateral Cooperation, with State Councilor Yang Jiechi and Foreign Minister Pham Binh Minh resuming their discussions.[96] Relations appeared to have returned to normal, at least in public.

It was significant that, immediately after the state-to-state meetings in October 2014, the two Communist Parties held their tenth "theory seminar" in the Vietnamese highland resort town of Dalat to share "experiences in building a socialist country under rule of law."[97] Politburo members responsible for ideology and propaganda led each side's delegation: Liu Qibao on the Chinese side and Dinh The Huynh on the Vietnamese. This suggests that a significant motivation for the seminar was to find ways to manage public opinion over the South China Sea disputes.

Even during the oil rig standoff, their most heated confrontation since normalization in 1991, the two leaderships limited the degree of escalation and made sure that some areas of the relationship, particularly trade, remained unaffected. The two sides opened and concluded their conflict resolution discussions through the state-to-state bilateral Joint Steering Committee. In between there were substantive party-to-party and military-to-military talks. Then, after the second meeting of the Steering Committee, the two parties had high-level talks on how to reconcile public opinion with the new reality.[98] Such party-to-party contacts help the CPV reassure the CPC that its actions to assert strategic autonomy will be kept within limits. As such they play an important role in Vietnam's diplomatic balancing, albeit one that is largely hidden from outside view.

Such discussions are not for show. They are part of a considered process of "ideological sharing" through which Vietnam's Communist Party learns from its Chinese counterpart. The CPV's post-2016 anti-corruption campaign, for example, shared some similarities with the anti-corruption campaign launched by President Xi Jinping in 2012. In January 2017, General Secretary Nguyen Phu Trong discussed the Chinese campaign with its mastermind, Wang Qishan, during his four-day visit to Beijing.[99] In May 2019, a Vietnamese delegation visited the CPC's Commission for Discipline and Inspection.[100]

Despite the ongoing difficulties in aspects of their bilateral relations, leaders from Vietnam continue to pay substantive visits to their Chinese counterparts. The CPV's Ho Chi Minh National Academy of Politics "maintains regular cooperation relationships with the three Chinese Communist Party schools," according to its own website, and high-ranking officials continue to be sent to Chinese institutions for training.[101] In a May 2018 interview with the Chinese news agency, the vice president of the Academy acknowledged that Vietnam is learning from the practical experience of China, particularly Xi Jinping's ideology regarding "the creative application and development of Marxism in the new context."[102]

Despite this ongoing closeness between the two parties, Vietnamese public opinion continues to move against China. The 2014 Pew Global Attitudes Survey suggested that just 16 percent of Vietnamese had a favorable image of China, with 78 percent having an unfavorable one. Only 21 percent thought China's growing economy was good for Vietnam, with 71 percent seeing it as bad. A 2020 survey conducted by the Institute of Southeast Asian Studies in Singapore found that 80 percent of those surveyed in Vietnam (described as working in academia, business and finance, the public sector, civil society, and the media) were "worried about [China's] growing regional economic influence." This was the second-highest proportion of the ten countries surveyed.[103] This figure rose to 90 percent in the 2021 survey, but fell to 73 percent in 2022.[104] A separate 2020 survey, sponsored by the Singapore-based Rajaratnam School of International Studies (RSIS), found 65 percent of Vietnamese respondents thought China was deliberately engaging in "debt-trap diplomacy" in order to buy influence or seek dominance.[105] Anti-China sentiment is easily aroused, as demonstrated by protests in August 2018 against a law on special economic zones that critics alleged would have allowed Chinese investors to take ninety-nine-year leases on Vietnamese land. The COVID pandemic demonstrated that suspicion of China continues. The 2022 survey of elite opinion referred to above found that just 4 percent of respondents trusted Chinese vaccines, compared to 80 percent for Western vaccines.[106]

This apparent polarization in attitudes toward China poses a serious problem for the CPV. While some in the Party, particularly those who came of age during the years of hostility in the 1980s, share a dislike of China, the leadership continues to see its Chinese counterpart as a model to emulate. The CPC has successfully energized its economy while remaining unchallenged in power, and that is exactly how the CPV would like its own future to unfold. However, as popular opinion becomes increasingly anti-China, overtly recognizing the CPV's debt to its Chinese counterpart becomes increasingly difficult. The aspects of the Chinese model Vietnam most wants to learn from include the "dark arts" of managing public opinion, organizing politicized anti-corruption campaigns, and maintaining robust Party control over the bureaucracy and private enterprises. These are vital to sustaining the Party's rule but are not the kind of issues that are ever openly discussed. We can only gain hints from the vague news releases provided by Party institutions. Only occasionally does this side of the relationship emerge. In August 2021, just before the visit of US Vice President Kamala Harris to Hanoi, the Chinese ambassador to Vietnam demanded an urgent meeting with Prime Minister Pham Minh Chinh. According to the Chinese embassy's version of events, Chinh stressed "the importance of the communication between Vietnam and China, noting the two countries will deepen inter-Party, foreign affairs, national defense, and public security cooperation, and guard against 'peaceful evolution' of hostile forces and their attempts to sow discord between the two countries."[107]

Conclusion

In general, Vietnamese-Chinese relations since normalization have progressed far better than most observers expected. A great many issues that could have prompted disputes such as land border demarcation, the Gulf of Tonkin boundary, and the growing trade deficit have either been resolved or managed. At the same time, one dispute—over the territorial and maritime boundary claims in the South China Sea—has come to overshadow all these areas of successful coexistence. To quote one of the Vietnamese Foreign Ministry's leading South China Sea analysts, "Vietnamese strategists are convinced that China's ultimate goal is absolute control of the South China Sea." However, even on this issue, "There are no signs of Vietnam hastily beefing up its defense at all costs, or falling into the embrace of other powers as a backstop to China's rise."[108]

Keeping close to China is the current default position of the CPV leadership. Over the past thirty years, the broadening of Vietnam's foreign relations and, in particular, its gradual engagement with the United States only occurred because, in successive crises, the "pro-Chinese" position has become untenable, and a majority within the CPV decided that failing to change course would threaten the Party's legitimacy and ability to rule. The current Chinese leadership is unlikely to ever form an alliance with Vietnam. If China were to grant Vietnam some special status on the basis of ideology, it would, in effect, be denying itself special regional status based on hierarchy as the preeminent power in East and Southeast Asia. Instead, China tries to shape Vietnam's external behavior by trying to set limits on its interactions with other states, in particular the United States.

China plays a doubly useful role for the CPV. China is a model from which to learn, but also an "other": a nationalist rallying point that helps to generate a sense of community among the Vietnamese population. In the words of Jürgen Haacke, the CPV benefits from "a continued sense of resentment vis-à-vis China that feeds on the rejection of Chinese superiority and the feeling of historically having been given a raw deal by the northern neighbour."[109] Trying to maintain a balance in this love/hate relationship is one of the most serious challenges facing the CPV. However, it has plenty of experience in managing such ideological contradictions and is more than likely to be able to keep doing so in the future.

Notes

1. See Vu, *Vietnam's Communist Revolution*, for more on the Vietnamese leadership's worldview.
2. Marr, *Vietnam 1945*, chap. 4.

3. Marr, *Vietnam 1945*, 257–58.

4. Goscha, "Building Force," 540–41.

5. Goscha, "Building Force," 556–59.

6. Marr, *Vietnam 1945*, 255–56, 261.

7. Asselin, "The Democratic Republic of Vietnam," 155–95.

8. Reilly, "The Sovereign States of Vietnam," 115.

9. Hy, *Revolution in the Village*, 158.

10. Vo, "Nguyễn Thị Năm and the Land Reform," 1–62.

11. Edwin Moïse suggests at least 5,000 (Moïse, "Land Reform," 78); Alec Holcombe argues for at least 15,000 (Holcombe, *Mass Mobilization*, 165).

12. Schütte, "Hundred Flowers in Vietnam"; Boudarel, *Cent Fleurs écloses*; Boudarel, "Intellectual Dissidence in the 1950s."

13. Grossheim, "'Revisionism' in the Democratic Republic of Vietnam," 451–77; Nguyen Lien-Hang, *Hanoi's War*, 42.

14. Nguyen Lien-Hang, *Hanoi's War*, 75.

15. Path, "The Politics of China's Aid."

16. Christensen, *Worse than a Monolith*, 146–80.

17. Nguyen Lien-Hang, *Hanoi's War*, 80.

18. Zhai, *China and the Vietnam Wars*, 135; Zhang, "The Vietnam War," 759.

19. Path, "The Politics of China's Aid," 693–95; Path, "The Sino-Vietnamese Dispute."

20. Path, "Hà Nôi's Responses."

21. Khoo, *Collateral Damage*, 139.

22. Zhai, *China and the Vietnam Wars*, 136.

23. Path, "The Economic Factor," 521–22.

24. Ross, *The Indochina Tangle*, 24–26.

25. Zhai, *China and the Vietnam Wars*, 136.

26. Scott, *Seeing Like a State*.

27. Path, *Vietnam's Strategic Thinking*, 24–25.

28. Path, "The Sino-Vietnamese Dispute," 199–205.

29. Path, *Vietnam's Strategic Thinking*, 36, 69.

30. Khoo, *Collateral Damage*, 120–25.

31. Path, *Vietnam's Strategic Thinking*, 4; Horn, "Vietnam and Sino-Soviet Relations," 729.

32. Ross, *The Indochina Tangle*, 224; Khoo, *Collateral Damage*, 127.

33. Mann, *About Face*, 98–100.

34. Chanda, *Brother Enemy*, 360; Zhang, "Deng Xiaoping and China's Decision," 25.

35. Path, *Vietnam's Strategic Thinking*, 83.

36. Porter, "The Transformation of Vietnam's World-View," 10.

37. Horn, "Vietnam and Sino-Soviet Relations," 731.

38. Womack, *China and Vietnam*, 201.

39. Path, "The Origins and Evolution," 171–85.

40. Porter, "The Transformation of Vietnam's World-View," 1–19; Dosch and Vuving, *The Impact of China*, 18.

41. Thayer, "Vietnam's Foreign Policy," 183–99.

42. Reaves, "Vietnam Reveals Cambodia Death Toll."

43. Duiker, "Vietnam: A Revolution in Transition," 367.

44. Vuving, "Grand Strategic Fit and Power Shift," 232.

45. Joiner, "The Vietnam Communist Party Strives."

46. Joiner, "The Vietnam Communist Party Strives."

47. Erlanger, "Vietnamese Communists Purge an In-House Critic."

48. Do, "Vietnam: Riding the Chinese Tide," 208.

49. Womack, *China and Vietnam*, 208.

50. Womack, *China and Vietnam*, 208.

51. Wurfel, "Between China and ASEAN," 150–51.

52. Elliott, *Changing Worlds*, 323.

53. Wurfel, "Between China and ASEAN," 151.

54. Do, "Vietnam: Riding the Chinese Tide," 209.

55. Hayton, *The South China Sea*, 127–28.

56. Thayer, "The Structure of Vietnam-China Relations."

57. Dosch, "Vietnam's ASEAN Membership Revisited," 244.

58. Goodman, "Vietnam and ASEAN," 594.

59. Riedel, "The Vietnamese Economy in the 1990s," 60.

60. Abuza, "Leadership Transition in Vietnam," 1108.

61. Vuving, "Grand Strategic Fit and Power Shift," 236.

62. Elliott, *Changing Worlds*, 185.

63. Amer, *The Sino-Vietnamese Approach*, 28.

64. Amer, "Sino-Vietnamese Border Disputes," 295.

65. Vuving, "Grand Strategic Fit and Power Shift," 233–34.

66. Chanda, "Friend or Foe?"

67. Vuving, "Strategy and Evolution," 805–24.

68. Abuza, "The Lessons of Le Kha Phieu," 140; Thayer, "The Tyranny of Geography," 348–69.

69. Thayer, "Vietnam in 2001."

70. Abuza, "The Lessons of Le Kha Phieu," 143.

71. Thayer, "Vietnam in 2001," 84.

72. Thayer, "Vietnam in 2001," 87.

73. BBC News, "Russia Closes Vietnam Naval Base."

74. Vuving, "Grand Strategic Fit and Power Shift," 239.

75. Do, "Vietnam: Riding the Chinese Tide," 212.

76. Burghardt, "US-Vietnam: Discreet Friendship."

77. US Department of State, diplomatic telegram, December 29, 2003, https://www.wikileaks.org/plusd /cables/03HANOI3351_a.html.

78. Hayton, *The South China Sea*, 135–44.

79. Nguyen, "Maritime Delimitation and Fishery Cooperation," 25.

80. BBC Vietnamese Service, "Nhìn lại Hiệp định Vịnh Bắc Bộ sau 10 năm."

81. Nguyen Hong Thao and Amer, "Managing Vietnam's Boundary Disputes," 313.

82. Thayer, "Vietnam and Rising China," 392–409.

83. Thayer, "Vietnam: The Tenth Party Congress and After," 391.

84. Le Hong Hiep, "Vietnam's Hedging Strategy," 348; Nguyen Thi Phuong Hoa and Nguyen Xuan Cuong, "Looking Back on Vietnam-China Relations," 8.

85. Hayton, *Vietnam and the United States*, 12.

86. Abuza, "Analyzing Southeast Asia's Military Expenditures."

87. Womack, *China and Vietnam*, 89–90.

88. Elliott, *Changing Worlds*, 302.

89. Thayer, "Vietnam and Rising China," 395.

90. Dosch, "Vietnam's ASEAN Membership Revisited," 250; Dosch and Vuving, *The Impact of China*, 16.

91. Weiss, *Powerful Patriots*.

92. United States Department of State, "Vietnam Supports the Proliferation Security Initiative."

93. Vuving, "Did China Blink in the South China Sea?"

94. Newsmax World, "Vietnam Communists Call for Democracy."

95. Embassy of the Socialist Republic of Vietnam, "Hanoi Party Committee Secretary Pham Quang Nghi Concludes U.S. Visit."

96. People's Republic of China, Ministry of Foreign Affairs, "China and Viet Nam Hold the Seventh Meeting."

97. Xinhua, "Chinese, Vietnamese Parties Hold 10th Theory Seminar."

98. Xinhua, "Chinese, Vietnamese Parties Hold 10th Theory Seminar."

99. Xinhua, "Senior Chinese Leaders Meet Vietnamese Party Chief."

100. Trọng Đức, "Đoàn cán bộ Ngành Kiểm."

101. Ho Chi Minh Academy, "Học viện Chính trị khu vực III."
102. Tao Jun and Bui Long, "Interview: What Vietnam Is Learning."
103. Tang Siew Mun et al., *The State of Southeast Asia*, 15.
104. Seah et al., *The State of Southeast Asia*, 21.
105. Rana, Chia Wai-Mun, and Ji Xianbai, *China's Belt and Road Initiative.*
106. Seah et al., *The State of Southeast Asia*, 14.
107. Global Times, "Vietnamese PM Urges Awareness."
108. Do, "Vietnam: Riding the Chinese Tide," 206.
109. Haacke, "The Significance of Beijing's Bilateral Relations," 125.

References

Abuza, Zachary. "Analyzing Southeast Asia's Military Expenditures." *CogitAsia*, May 7, 2015. Washington, DC: Center for Strategic and International Studies. http://cogitasia.com/analyzing-southeast-asias-military -expenditures/.
———. "Leadership Transition in Vietnam since the Eighth Party Congress: The Unfinished Congress." *Asian Survey* 38, no. 12 (December 1998): 1105–21.
———. "The Lessons of Le Kha Phieu: Changing Rules in Vietnamese Politics." *Contemporary Southeast Asia* 24, no. 1 (April 2002): 121–45.
Amer, Ramses. *The Sino-Vietnamese Approach to Managing Boundary Disputes.* Durham, UK: International Boundaries Research Unit Department of Geography, University of Durham, 2002.
———. "Sino-Vietnamese Border Disputes." In *Beijing's Power and China's Borders: Twenty Neighbors in Asia*, edited by Bruce Elleman, Stephen Kotkin, and Clive Schofield. Abingdon, UK: Routledge, 2013.
Asselin, Pierre. "The Democratic Republic of Vietnam and the 1954 Geneva Conference: A Revisionist Critique." *Cold War History* 11, no. 2 (2011): 155–95.
BBC News. "Russia Closes Vietnam Naval Base." May 2, 2002. http://news.bbc.co.uk/1/hi/world/europe /1964253.stm.
BBC Vietnamese Service. "Nhìn lại Hiệp định Vịnh Bắc Bộ sau 10 năm." January 22, 2011. http://www.bbc .co.uk/vietnamese/vietnam/2011/01/110122_bacbo_agreement_10years_on.shtml.
Boudarel, Georges. *Cent Fleurs écloses dans la nuit du Vietnam: Communisme et Dissidence 1954–1956.* Paris: Editions Jacques Bertoin, 1991.
———. "Intellectual Dissidence in the 1950s: The Nhan Van-Giai Pham Affair." *Vietnam Forum* 13 (1990): 154–74.
Burghardt, Raymond. "US-Vietnam: Discreet Friendship under China's Shadow." *YaleGlobal Online*, November 22, 2005. https://yaleglobal.yale.edu/content/us-vietnam-discreet-friendship-under-chinas-shadow.
Chanda, Nayan. *Brother Enemy—The War after the War: History of Indo-China after the Fall of Saigon.* New York: Harcourt Brace Jovanovich, 1986.
———. "Friend or Foe?" *Far Eastern Economic Review*, June 15, 2000.
Christensen, Thomas. *Worse than a Monolith: Alliance Politics and Problems of Coercive Diplomacy in Asia.* Princeton, NJ: Princeton University Press, 2011.
Do Thanh Hai. "Vietnam: Riding the Chinese Tide." *Pacific Review* 31, no. 2 (2018): 205–20.
Dosch, Jörn. "Vietnam's ASEAN Membership Revisited: Golden Opportunity or Golden Cage?" *Contemporary Southeast Asia* 28, no. 2 (August 2006): 234–58.
Dosch, Jörn, and Alexander L. Vuving. *The Impact of China on Governance Structures in Vietnam.* Bonn: Deutsches Institut für Entwicklungspolitik, 2008.
Duiker, William. "Vietnam: A Revolution in Transition." In *Southeast Asian Affairs 1989*, edited by Chee Yuen Ng. Singapore: ISEAS-Yusof Ishak Institute, 1989.
Elliott, David. *Changing Worlds: Vietnam's Transition from Cold War to Globalization.* Oxford: Oxford University Press, 2012.

Embassy of the Socialist Republic of Vietnam, "Hanoi Party Committee Secretary Pham Quang Nghi Concludes U.S. Visit." July 29, 2014. http://vietnamembassy-usa.org/news/2014/07/hanoi-party-committee-secretary-pham-quang-nghi-concludes-us-visit.

Erlanger, Steven. "Vietnamese Communists Purge an In-House Critic." *New York Times*, April 1, 1990.

Global Times. "Vietnamese PM Urges Awareness of 'Peaceful Evolution' at Meeting with Chinese Envoy ahead of Harris' Visit." August 25, 2021. https://www.globaltimes.cn/page/202108/1232394.shtml.

Goodman, Allan. "Vietnam and ASEAN: Who Would Have Thought It Possible?" *Asian Survey* 36, no. 6 (June 1996): 592–600.

Goscha, Christopher. "Building Force: Asian Origins of Twentieth-Century Military Science in Vietnam (1905–54)." *Journal of Southeast Asian Studies* 34, no. 3 (October 2003): 535–60.

Grossheim, Martin. "'Revisionism' in the Democratic Republic of Vietnam: New Evidence from the East German Archives." *Cold War History* 5, no. 4 (November 2005): 451–77.

Haacke, Jürgen. "The Significance of Beijing's Bilateral Relations: Looking 'below' the Regional Level in China-ASEAN Ties." In *China and Southeast Asia: Global Changes and Regional Challenges*, edited by H. K. Leong and S. C. Ku. Singapore: Institute of Southeast Asian Studies, 2005.

Hayton, Bill. "The Modern Origins of China's Claims in the South China Sea." *Modern China* 45, no. 2 (2019): 127–70.

———. *The South China Sea: The Struggle for Power in Asia*. New Haven, CT: Yale University Press, 2014.

———. *Vietnam and the United States: An Emerging Security Partnership*. Sydney: United States Studies Centre at the University of Sydney, 2015.

Ho Chi Minh Academy. "Học viện Chính trị khu vực III: Hiệu quả từ các phong trào thi đua" (Regional Political Academy III—Effect from emulation movements). July 7, 2020. https://hcma.vn/vanban/Pages/ke-hoach.aspx?ItemId=30474&CateID=0.

Holcombe, Alec. *Mass Mobilization in the Democratic Republic of Vietnam, 1945–1960*. Honolulu: University of Hawai'i Press, 2020.

Horn, Robert. "Vietnam and Sino-Soviet Relations: What Price Rapprochement." *Asian Survey* 27, no. 7 (July 1987): 729–47.

Huong Le Thu. "Bumper Harvest in 2013 for Vietnamese Diplomacy." *ISEAS Perspective* 4. (2014). https://www.iseas.edu.sg/images/pdf/ISEAS_Perspective_2014_04.pdf.

Hy V. Luong. *Revolution in the Village: Tradition and Transformation in North Vietnam, 1925–1988*. Honolulu: University of Hawai'i Press, 1992.

Joiner, Charles. "The Vietnam Communist Party Strives to Remain the 'Only Force.'" *Asian Survey* 30, no. 11 (November 1990): 1053–65.

Khoo, Nicholas. *Collateral Damage: Sino-Soviet Rivalry and the Termination of the Sino-Vietnamese Alliance*. New York: Columbia University Press, 2011.

Le Hong Hiep. "Vietnam's Hedging Strategy against China since Normalization." *Contemporary Southeast Asia* 35, no. 3 (December 2013): 333–68.

Mann, James. *About Face*. New York: Knopf, 1999.

Marr, David. *Vietnam 1945: The Quest for Power*. Berkeley: University of California Press, 1997.

Moïse, Edwin. "Land Reform and Land Reform Errors in North Vietnam." *Pacific Affairs* 49, no. 1 (Spring 1976): 70–92.

Newsmax World. "Vietnam Communists Call for Democracy, Shift Away from China." August 6, 2014. https://www.newsmax.com/world/asia/vietnam-communists-democracy-china/2014/08/06/id/587173/.

Nguyen Hong Thao. "Maritime Delimitation and Fishery Cooperation in the Tonkin Gulf." *Ocean Development & International Law* 36 (2005): 25–44.

Nguyen Hong Thao and Ramses Amer. "Managing Vietnam's Boundary Disputes." *Ocean Development and International Law* 38 no. 3 (2007): 305–25.

Nguyen Lien-Hang. *Hanoi's War: An International History of the War for Peace in Vietnam*. Chapel Hill: University of North Carolina Press, 2012.

Nguyen Thi Phuong Hoa and Nguyen Xuan Cuong. "Looking Back on Vietnam-China Relations since the Establishment of Strategic Cooperative Partnership." *Russian Journal of Vietnamese Studies* 4, no. 1 (2020): 8–17.

Path, Kosal. "The Economic Factor in the Sino-Vietnamese Split, 1972–75: An Analysis of Vietnamese Archival Sources." *Cold War History* 11, no. 4 (2011): 519–55.

———. "Hà Nôi's Responses to Beijing's Renewed Enthusiasm to Aid North Vietnam, 1970–1972." *Journal of Vietnamese Studies* 6, no. 3 (2011): 101–39.

———. "The Origins and Evolution of Vietnam's Doi Moi Foreign Policy of 1986." *TRaNS: Trans-Regional and -National Studies of Southeast Asia* 8, no. 2 (2020): 171–85. doi: 10.1017/trn.2020.3.

———. "The Politics of China's Aid to North Vietnam during the Anti-American Resistance, 1965–1969." *Diplomacy & Statecraft* 27, no. 4 (2016): 682–700.

———. "The Sino-Vietnamese Dispute over Territorial Claims, 1974–1978: Vietnamese Nationalism and Its Consequences." *International Journal of Asian Studies* 8, no. 2 (2011): 189–220.

———. *Vietnam's Strategic Thinking during the Third Indochina War.* Madison: University of Wisconsin Press, 2020.

People's Republic of China, Ministry of Foreign Affairs. "China and Viet Nam Hold the Seventh Meeting of the Steering Committee for Bilateral Cooperation." October 27, 2014. http://www.fmprc.gov.cn/mfa_eng/zxxx_662805/t1205122.shtml.

Porter, Gareth. "The Transformation of Vietnam's World-View: From Two Camps to Interdependence." *Contemporary Southeast Asia* 12, no. 1 (June 1990): 1–19.

Rana, Pradumna, Chia Wai-Mun, and Ji Xianbai. *China's Belt and Road Initiative: A Perception Survey of Asian Opinion Leaders.* Singapore: S. Rajaratnam School of International Studies, 2019.

Reaves, Joseph. "Vietnam Reveals Cambodia Death Toll." *Chicago Tribune,* 1 July 1988.

Reilly, Brett. "The Sovereign States of Vietnam, 1945–55." *Journal of Vietnamese Studies* 11, nos. 3–4 (2016): 103–39.

Riedel, James. "The Vietnamese Economy in the 1990s." *Asian Pacific Economic Literature* 11, no. 2 (November 1997): 58–65.

Ross, Robert. *The Indochina Tangle: China's Vietnam Policy 1975–1979.* New York: Columbia University Press, 1988.

Schütte, Heinz. "Hundred Flowers in Vietnam 1955–1957." Berlin: Department of Southeast Asian Studies, Humboldt-University, 2003.

Scott, James. *Seeing Like a State: How Certain Schemes to Improve the Human Condition Have Failed.* New Haven, CT: Yale University Press, 1999.

Seah, Sharon, Joanne Lin, Sithanonxay Suvannaphakdy, Melinda Martinus, Pham Thi Phuong Thao, Farah Nadine Seth, and Hoang Thi Ha. *The State of Southeast Asia: 2022 Survey Report.* Singapore: ISEAS-Yusof Ishak Institute, 2022.

Tang Siew Mun, Hoang Thi Ha, Anuthida Saelaow, Qian Glenn Ong, and Pham Thi Phuong Thao. *The State of Southeast Asia: 2020 Survey Report.* Singapore: ISEAS-Yusof Ishak Institute, 2020.

Tao Jun and Bui Long. "Interview: What Vietnam Is Learning from China's Socialist Model." *Xinhua,* May 8, 2018. http://www.xinhuanet.com/english/2018-05/08/c_137163346.htm.

Thayer, Carlyle. "The Structure of Vietnam-China Relations, 1991–2008." Paper for the Third International Conference on Vietnamese Studies, Hanoi, December 4–7, 2008.

———. "The Tyranny of Geography: Vietnamese Strategies to Constrain China in the South China Sea." *Contemporary Southeast Asia* 33, no. 3 (2011): 348–69.

———. "Vietnam and Rising China: The Structural Dynamics of Mature Asymmetry." In *Southeast Asian Affairs 2010,* edited by Daljit Singh. Singapore: ISEAS-Yusof Ishak Institute, 2010.

———. "Vietnam in 2001: The Ninth Party Congress and After." *Asian Survey* 42, no. 1 (January/February 2002): 81–89.

———. "Vietnam: The Tenth Party Congress and After." In *Southeast Asian Affairs 2007,* edited by Daljit Singh and Malcolm Cook. Singapore: ISEAS-Yusof Ishak Institute, 2007.

———. "Vietnam's Foreign Policy in an Era of Rising Sino-US Competition and Increasing Domestic Political Influence." *Asian Security* 13, no. 3 (2017): 183–99.

Trọng Đức. "Đoàn cán bộ Ngành Kiểm tra và Thanh tra đi nghiên cứu, học tập về công tác phòng, chống tham nhũng tại Trung Quốc" (A delegation from the Inspection Commission went to study and learn about the prevention of corruption in China). Ủy Ban Kiểm Tra Trung Ương (Central Inspection Commission of the Communist Party of Vietnam), May 28, 2019. http://ubkttw.vn/tin-tuc-thoi-su/-/asset

_publisher/bHGXXiPdpxRC/content/-oan-can-bo-nganh-kiem-tra-va-thanh-tra-i-nghien-cuu-hoc-tap
-ve-cong-tac-phong-chong-tham-nhung-tai-trung-quoc.

United States Department of State. "Vietnam Supports the Proliferation Security Initiative." Media Note, Office of the Spokesperson, May 22, 2014. https://web.archive.org/web/20140523212926/http://www.state.gov/r/pa/prs/ps/2014/05/226449.htm.

Vo, Alex-Thai. "Nguyễn Thị Năm and the Land Reform in North Vietnam, 1953." *Journal of Vietnamese Studies* 10, no. 1 (2015): 1–62.

Vu, Tuong. *Vietnam's Communist Revolution: The Power and Limits of Ideology.* Cambridge: Cambridge University Press, 2016.

Vuving, Alexander. "Did China Blink in the South China Sea?" *The Diplomat,* July 27, 2014. http://nationalinterest.org/feature/did-china-blink-the-south-china-sea-10956.

———. "Grand Strategic Fit and Power Shift: Explaining Turning Points in China-Vietnam Relations." In *Living with China: Regional States and China through Crises and Turning Points,* edited by Shiping Tang, Mingjiang Li, and Amitav Acharya. London: Palgrave Macmillan, 2009.

———. "Strategy and Evolution of Vietnam's China Policy: A Changing Mixture of Pathways." *Asian Survey* 46, no. 6 (November/December 2006): 805–24.

Weiss, Jessica Chen. *Powerful Patriots: Nationalist Protest in China's Foreign Relations.* Oxford: Oxford University Press, 2014.

Womack, Brantley. *China and Vietnam: The Politics of Asymmetry.* Cambridge: Cambridge University Press, 2006.

Wurfel, David. "Between China and ASEAN: The Dialectics of Recent Vietnamese Foreign Policy." In *Vietnamese Foreign Policy in Transition,* edited by Carlyle Thayer and Ramses Amer. Singapore: Institute of Southeast Asian Studies, 1999.

Xinhua. "Chinese, Vietnamese Parties Hold 10th Theory Seminar." November 4, 2014. http://news.xinhuanet.com/english/china/2014-11/04/c_127178393.htm.

———. "Senior Chinese Leaders Meet Vietnamese Party Chief on Stronger Ties." January 14, 2017. http://www.xinhuanet.com//english/2017-01/13/c_135980903.htm.

Zhai, Qiang. *China and the Vietnam Wars, 1950–1975.* Chapel Hill: University of North Carolina Press, 2000.

Zhang, Xiaoming. "Deng Xiaoping and China's Decision to Go to War with Vietnam." *Journal of Cold War Studies* 12, no. 3 (Summer 2010): 3–29.

———. "The Vietnam War, 1964–1969: A Chinese Perspective." *Journal of Military History* 60, no. 4 (October 1996): 731–62.

CHAPTER 17

Past Imperfect

Peacemaking, Legitimacy, and Reconciliation in US-Vietnam Relations, 1975–2020

EDWARD MILLER

In July 2020, the Stimson Center in Washington, D.C., hosted a webinar entitled "The U.S.-Vietnam Relationship and War Legacies: 25 Years into Normalization." Although the virtual gathering took place amid the global COVID pandemic, the mood was celebratory. Participants included officials of both the United States and the Socialist Republic of Vietnam (SRV) governments, along with scientific experts and international aid specialists. The webinar marked twenty-five years since the establishment of normal diplomatic relations between the US and SRV—an event that participants recalled as a major step toward reconciliation between the two countries in the aftermath of the Vietnam War. Much of the webinar focused on the two governments' ongoing efforts to resolve what everyone referred to as "war legacies." Those efforts included recovery of the bodies of both American and Vietnamese soldiers who were still listed as missing in action (MIA) from the war, as well as remediation of unexploded ordnance (UXO) and American-sprayed herbicides such as Agent Orange. US Ambassador Daniel Krittenbrink marveled at the comity between Washington and Hanoi, noting that "we use almost identical language to describe one another and our partnership and our interests."[1]

What explains the far-reaching transformation in United States-Vietnam relations since the end of the Vietnam War in 1975? Since the early 2000s, bilateral connections in diplomacy, trade, capital investment, education, and cultural exchange have thrived. Yet the current era of good feelings stands in stark contrast to the situation in earlier decades. For years after the end of the war, US-Vietnam relations were mired in suspicion and hostility, amid recriminations over MIAs, refugees, and reconstruction aid. This wariness lingered even after the establishment of normal diplomatic ties in 1995.

During the 1980s and 1990s, many observers interpreted the postwar tensions in US-Vietnam relations as the product of miscalculations and misperceptions. According to this view, officials in Washington and Hanoi were genuinely interested in postwar reconciliation, but each failed to grasp the constraints and motives that shaped the other's thinking. From this perspective, the history of US-Vietnam relations between 1975 and the 1990s reads as a tragic series of missed opportunities.[2] Another interpretation places the blame for the initial failure of reconciliation efforts more squarely on the United States. For these scholars, US leaders were unwilling to accept defeat in Vietnam after 1975, and they therefore resolved to continue to wage war against Hanoi "by other means."[3] More recently, some authors have focused on the gradual improvement in relations after the 1995 normalization. In these accounts, US-Vietnam reconciliation is depicted as the result of good-faith efforts by diplomats, officials, and other elites from both countries.[4]

This chapter examines the post-1975 history of US-Vietnam relations as a contentious and still incomplete peacemaking process. I draw on the work of Charles Kupchan, who examines whether and how enemy states move from war to peace. According to Kupchan, the path to peace begins with trust-building measures and reciprocal displays of restraint on low-stakes issues. These initial efforts at mutual accommodation, if successful, can pave the way for closer social and economic integration. Once the bonds of interdependence are sufficiently strong, the two parties can move to the final phase: the crafting of new narratives and identities in which old antagonisms are replaced by feelings of comradery and solidarity. In this model, peacemaking culminates in memory making, as the former rivals align their previously disparate narratives of the violent past.[5]

Even before the Vietnam War ended in 1975, US and Vietnamese leaders professed their interest in reconciliation. But neither side was willing to make peace at any price. In both the United States and Vietnam, memories of the Vietnam War were intertwined with concerns about the legitimacy and moral standing of the state and its leaders. In the aftermath of the war, US elites began to champion international human rights as a way to rehabilitate America's moral reputation, which had been badly tarnished by the war. Meanwhile, senior leaders of the ruling Communist Party of Vietnam (CPV) found themselves mired in their own legitimacy crisis, due to failed agricultural collectivization, hyperinflation, famine, and the onset of a new war with Cambodia and China. Such circumstances did not lend themselves to the kind of trust-building measures that are prerequisites for reconciliation. Although both US and SRV leaders were prepared to talk about rapprochement—and even held meetings during 1977 and 1978 on the possible normalization of diplomatic relations—neither government was prepared to accommodate the other for fear of undermining its own legitimacy claims.

The first meaningful moves to break the standoff were made by Vietnamese leaders in the late 1980s, following Hanoi's adoption of the Đổi Mới (Renovation) reforms and "new thinking" in foreign policy. But even after Vietnam signaled its new approach to Washington, progress toward reconciliation remained slow. Although the two governments finally normalized diplomatic ties in 1995, the old suspicions lingered. It was only during the early 2000s, and especially after 2010, that the two countries began to forge more substantive economic, social, and cultural connections. These new ties, in turn, enabled US and SRV representatives to craft new narratives of reconciliation. Yet these elite-led attempts to define US-Vietnam reconciliation around a discrete set of "war legacies" often glossed over some of the more contentious questions lurking in the history and memory of the war. In the early 2020s, US-Vietnam reconciliation remains incomplete, the remarkable recent progress notwithstanding.

Near Miss or Near Impossibility?

On May 7, 1975, just one week after North Vietnamese Army forces marched into the South Vietnamese capital of Saigon and ended the Vietnam War, the Democratic Republic of Vietnam (DRV) sent a message to the US government. Prime Minister Phạm Văn Đồng wrote that Hanoi looked forward to enjoying "good relations with the U.S." and to the early normalization of bilateral ties.[6] The administration of US President Gerald Ford did not immediately reply. However, Washington froze approximately US$70 million in US-based assets belonging to the now-defunct South Vietnamese government. It also imposed a near-total economic embargo on Vietnam, as well as on Cambodia and Laos. Several weeks later, the US State Department angrily denounced Đồng for describing the US wartime intervention in Vietnam as a "criminal war." DRV officials quickly fired back, stating that they would not allow searching for American MIAs until Washington fulfilled its obligation "to heal the wounds of war caused by the criminal U.S. war of aggression."[7]

The antipathy between the US and Vietnam governments in the spring of 1975 was not surprising, given the bloody history of the previous twenty-five years. What *was* surprising is that the two governments moved quickly after the war's end to explore the possibility of establishing formal diplomatic ties. In 1977, shortly after Jimmy Carter's election to the US presidency, American and Vietnamese diplomats began high-level talks on normalization. These talks continued for more than a year—only to be suspended in late 1978. What lay behind this early attempt at normalization? And did it mark a lost chance for an early breakthrough on reconciliation?

As dedicated Marxist-Leninists, CPV leaders had long viewed the world as being divided into two antagonist camps: the socialist (or "democratic") countries and the imperialist (or "anti-democratic") countries. During the Vietnam War, CPV General Secretary Lê Duẩn elaborated a distinctive version of this two-camp worldview that positioned the DRV's struggle against the United States as "the driving force of world revolution." As Tuong Vu has demonstrated, Lê Duẩn and his CPV comrades remained committed to this Vietnamese brand of "vanguard internationalism" throughout the Vietnam War. In their minds, the validity of the two-camp model was only reinforced by the withdrawal of US combat forces from Indochina in 1973 and by the defeat of South Vietnam in 1975.[8]

This does not mean, however, that CPV leaders were unable or unwilling to revise their approach to foreign policy. Although the 1986 launch of the *Đổi Mới* reforms is now correctly viewed as a major turning point in the history of Vietnamese diplomacy, recent research shows that some elements of Vietnam's "new thinking" about foreign relations first emerged more than a decade earlier, in the mid-1970s.[9] Even before the Vietnam War had ended, CPV and SRV leaders were already grappling with complex new international political realities. They also imagined how a postwar rapprochement with the United States might unfold.

The last years of the Vietnam War took place during a period of superpower détente. By 1972, US President Richard Nixon was engaged in high-profile "triangle diplomacy," in which he pursued rapprochement with both the Soviet Union and the People's Republic of China simultaneously. Nixon pursued this strategy in part because he hoped to persuade both communist powers to pressure Hanoi to end the Vietnam War on terms favorable to Washington. On that point, Nixon's efforts proved unsuccessful. But the mere willingness of both communist powers to welcome Nixon's overtures provoked grave concern among CPV leaders, whose war effort relied on massive amounts of Soviet and Chinese aid. By the time of the signing of the 1973 Paris Peace Accords, Hanoi's relations with both Moscow and Beijing were under considerable strain.[10]

In light of these developments, CPV leaders began to revise their thinking about foreign affairs. They continued to view international politics as a long-term contest between the socialist and imperialist camps, and they remained staunchly committed to "the eventual and complete triumph of socialism."[11] However, in CPV official reports and discourse, the traditional two-camp model was transformed into a three-tier structure. In addition to socialist and capitalist countries, CPV analysts now referred to "nationalist" countries that were not aligned with either of the two main camps. CPV leaders continued to treat China, the Soviet Union, and other socialist nations as Vietnam's most important foreign partners, and they fully expected that Hanoi's postwar relationships with those nations would cover the full spectrum of political, economic, cultural, and ideological ties. However, they also expected to forge new connections with the nationalist and capitalist countries. CPV officials such as Nguyễn Cơ Thạch—a senior diplomat who would later become a key architect of the Đổi Mới reforms—argued as early as 1973 that Vietnam needed trade and technology exchanges with the United States and other capitalist nations to meet its postwar development goals. These ties were necessary, Thạch argued, because "the world is now a [single] market"—a perception reinforced by the increased trade between communist-bloc states and capitalist nations.[12]

These changes in CPV approaches to international affairs help explain a key assumption of Hanoi's postwar foreign policy planning: the expectation that China, the Soviet Union, and the United States would all supply substantial amounts of postwar reconstruction and development aid to Vietnam. In the fall of 1975, Lê Duẩn led a high-level Vietnamese delegation on a two-month tour of China, the Soviet Union, and Eastern European communist states. CPV leaders treated the tour partly as a victory lap, but also as an opportunity to secure continued large flows of communist-bloc aid to Vietnam. Although the actual amounts of aid pledged to Vietnam were lower than anticipated, the Vietnamese still expected more aid would be forthcoming from socialist nations.[13]

Hanoi also had high hopes for postwar aid from the United States. Party officials believed that US leaders would be eager to gain access to the markets and resources of a reunified Vietnam—a notion reinforced by the interest of US oil companies in developing recently discovered petroleum deposits in the South China Sea.[14] In addition, CPV leaders were convinced that Washington faced considerable moral pressure to supply Vietnam with reconstruction aid. This conviction derived in part from Hanoi's recognition that the Vietnam War had been enormously controversial and unpopular in many parts of US society. CPV leaders reasoned that the American public would naturally support Vietnam's efforts to recover from US-inflicted wartime damage.

Hanoi's expectations about postwar American aid were also conditioned by prior US promises. In the 1973 Paris Agreements, Washington declared its desire for "an era of reconciliation" with the DRV and for contributing "to healing of wounds of war and to postwar reconstruction."[15] While no actual US aid commitments were included in the Accords, US President Richard Nixon assured Hanoi that such aid would be forthcoming. In February 1973, Nixon sent a secret letter to Prime Minister Đồng in which he pledged more than US$4 billion in reconstruction aid and other assistance to the DRV.[16] Even though Washington subsequently accused Hanoi of violating the Paris Agreements, CPV officials still believed that US officials could be compelled to honor Nixon's promises. A 1973 secret report to the Politburo cited global oil shortages and the resulting economic turmoil in the United States as an opportunity "to demand that the Americans pay compensation for their war of destruction in Vietnam." CPV officials wanted this compensation to be paid as war reparations, to show American responsibility for Vietnamese suffering.[17]

As it turned out, Hanoi had badly overestimated its ability to wring postwar aid from Washington. Following the fall of Saigon, most Americans seemed to want to forget about the war.[18] Moreover, US policymakers did not place high priority on finding economic opportunities for American businesses in postwar Vietnam. Most important of all, American officials had no intention of paying war reparations to Vietnam. This was especially true of Nixon, who viewed his secret 1973 aid pledge not as a compensatory measure, but as a realpolitik move. "We should help North Vietnam because the US is in a position to draw them inward and have influence on them in the future," Nixon told his cabinet in February 1973. "If we have no leverage, we have no influence."[19]

Gerald Ford, who succeeded Nixon as president following the latter's resignation in 1974, took a similar approach with Hanoi. Like Nixon, Ford dismissed DRV demands for reparations and denied that Washington had waged an immoral war in Vietnam. His administration also blocked Hanoi's attempts to join the United Nations—a move widely viewed as petty and vindictive. Nevertheless, Ford did not rule out the possibility of normalizing relations with Hanoi. Many of the administration's initial policy steps after the fall of Saigon—such as the imposition of the US economic embargo—were intended as temporary measures that could be dropped once a normalization agreement was in place. As early as June 1975, US officials told Hanoi that they bore "no hostility" toward the DRV and were prepared to hear proposals for postwar ties.[20] Yet Washington also signaled that it expected Hanoi's help with locating the approximately 2,000 US military personnel still listed as MIA in Vietnam. The Ford administration thus articulated the core principles of US policy toward Vietnam for the next two decades: US leaders were willing to pursue normalization, but would not accept any moral responsibility for the war or wartime suffering. Vietnam, meanwhile, would have to provide a "full accounting" of American MIAs.[21]

Ford's hard-line stance on relations with Vietnam seemed to offer an opening for Jimmy Carter, the Democrat who won the 1976 presidential election. In keeping with his call for a more moral foreign policy, Carter promised to seek normal relations with Vietnam "without preconditions." But he also echoed Ford's call for a "full accounting" of MIAs and rejected war reparations as a nonstarter. When asked in 1977 if the US had a moral obligation to help Vietnam repair the destruction inflicted by US forces during the war, Carter replied:

> Well, the destruction was mutual. You know we went to Vietnam without desire to capture territory or to impose American will on anybody. We went there to defend the freedom of the South Vietnamese. And I do not feel that we ought to apologize or castigate ourselves or assume the status of culpability.[22]

The idea of normalizing US relations with Hanoi was clearly appealing to Carter. But like American presidents before and after him, he had no appetite for reckoning with the history or morality of past US actions in Vietnam.

In March 1977, Carter dispatched a delegation to Hanoi under the leadership of Leonard Woodcock, the head of the United Auto Workers union. Although Woodcock's mission had no official standing, Carter instructed him to find out if SRV leaders would drop their demand for reparations. When Woodcock arrived in Hanoi, his hosts reiterated that the US was legally obligated to deliver the aid promised by Nixon, and that no cooperation on American MIAs would be forthcoming until that aid arrived. But then the Vietnamese appeared to soften their stance, stating that normalization, aid, and the MIAs could be treated as separate (albeit interrelated) issues. SRV officials also offered to establish an office to facilitate cooperation on searches for US soldiers' remains. Carter declared the mission a "superb success" and accepted Hanoi's offer to begin direct talks on normalization.[23]

But Carter was mistaken: the Vietnamese position had not changed. When US and SRV diplomats met in Paris, the incompatibility between their positions quickly became obvious. The US team was led by Richard Holbrooke, a State Department official who had served in Vietnam during the war. On the first day of meetings, Holbrooke got straight to the point. "May we go out this afternoon and announce normalization?" he asked Phan Hiên, his Vietnamese counterpart. Holbrooke offered assurances that normalization would clear the way for a few million dollars in private humanitarian aid for Vietnam, as well as additional indirect aid. To Holbrooke's astonishment, Phan Hiên stated that normalization was impossible unless Washington was willing to deliver the billions promised by Nixon. Later that day, Phan Hiên outlined Hanoi's position to the international press corps and also revealed the existence of Nixon's 1973 letter, which had not previously been made public.[24]

CPV leaders evidently believed that the news of Nixon's letter would provoke an upwelling of American public support for their demands. But the move had exactly the opposite effect. After hearing the news of the Nixon letter, the US House of Representatives voted to prohibit the administration from even raising the possibility of US aid with Vietnamese officials. In addition to opposing direct aid to Hanoi, Congress subsequently blocked the delivery of indirect US assistance via the World Bank and other international institutions.

After this inauspicious beginning, the US-SRV talks on normalization continued intermittently for more than a year. But the meetings were soon overshadowed by a growing military crisis in Southeast Asia. Starting in the spring of 1977, the Khmer Rouge government of Cambodia carried out a series of cross-border military raids that killed thousands of Vietnamese civilians in the Mekong Delta. The Khmer Rouge were backed by China, whose leader Deng Xiaoping accused the Vietnamese of siding against Beijing in its long-running rivalry with the Soviet Union. By mid-1978, Deng had suspended all aid and trade with Vietnam, prompting Hanoi to join the Soviet-led Council for Mutual Economic Assistance (COMECON).

With a new Indochina War looming, Vietnam finally signaled to the US in July 1978 that it would drop its demands for aid as a precondition to normalization. But the Carter administration was now split over how to proceed. While Secretary of State Cyrus Vance remained supportive of normalization with Hanoi, National Security Adviser Zbigniew Brzezinski pushed Carter to take a more confrontational line with the Soviet Union. Brzezinski hoped to complete the formal normalization of the US relationship with China by the end of the year—a goal that might be disrupted by a simultaneous American rapprochement with Hanoi. In September 1978, Carter decided to defer a decision on normalization with Vietnam until after the upcoming US congressional elections. For the Vietnamese, that was too long to wait. On November 3, the SRV and the Soviet Union signed a treaty of friendship and cooperation. Four days later, US diplomats informed their SRV counterparts that Washington was suspending the normalization talks.[25]

Because Vietnam and the United States appeared to come so close to normalization during 1977–78, journalists and historians have long viewed the aborted talks as a missed opportunity for reconciliation. But depicting these events as a lost chance for peace overlooks an important question: What *kind* of peace between Washington and Hanoi was possible in the late 1970s? Normalization of diplomatic ties does not lead inevitably or automatically to reconciliation. Even if the two governments had exchanged ambassadors in 1977, it is hard to see how normal relations could have prevented the Third Indochina War, or the disputes over Cambodia, refugees, and MIAs that defined US-Vietnam interactions throughout the 1980s. Moreover, Carter's desire "to face the future without reference to the past" remained anathema to CPV leaders, who viewed their legitimacy as inextricably tied to their military victory over the United States and to their self-perception as the vanguard of the global socialist camp. While it is evident that both Washington and Hanoi had a serious interest in normalization during the late 1970s, it is equally clear that they remained far apart on what "reconciliation" might entail. The war was over, but the basis for a durable peace had yet to emerge.

The Long Road to Normalization, 1979–95

On Christmas Day 1978, units of the People's Army of Vietnam (PAVN) invaded Cambodia in retaliation for the raids carried out by Khmer Rouge troops over the previous year. PAVN forces quickly seized Phnom Penh, forcing Pol Pot's government to flee. In response, China stepped up aid to the Khmer Rouge and launched its own punitive incursion into Vietnam's northernmost provinces in February 1979. The PAVN fought well against Chinese forces, who withdrew after less than a month of heavy combat. But the Vietnamese fared less well in Cambodia, where they soon found themselves bogged down in jungle warfare operations. Although Vietnam's decision to oust Pol Pot's genocidal regime seems justified in hindsight, Hanoi's occupation provoked fears that it was seeking to dominate its neighbors. The Vietnamese invasion was denounced by the United States, which joined China and the countries of the Association of Southeast Asian Nations (ASEAN) in demanding a PAVN withdrawal.[26]

For the government and people of Vietnam, the impact of the Third Indochina War was made more severe by an intensifying internal economic crisis. Shortly after its 1975 triumph over South Vietnam, Hanoi unveiled its first postwar five-year plan, which called for the country to move "rapidly, vigorously, and steadily to socialism." By late 1977, however, it was clear that the plan was in trouble. Economic growth and productivity fell, the transportation system was on the verge of collapse, food shortages were widespread, and the country's unemployment rate and trade deficit both soared. As tensions with Cambodia and China rose, Lê Duẩn and other senior CPV leaders doubled down on a fast-track collectivization strategy that included large-scale mass mobilization of the population. But these measures were strongly resisted by southern farmers, many of whom opted to reduce their output or to abandon agriculture entirely to avoid having to sell their produce to the SRV state at below-market rates. By 1979, food production had declined by up to 75 percent in some southern provinces, causing shortages across the country. Meanwhile, a botched currency exchange scheme, coupled with a campaign to seize the wealth of the country's "commercial capitalists"—the majority of whom were ethnic Chinese—fueled a sharp increase in inflation.[27]

War and escalating economic turmoil in Vietnam combined to create a third crisis in the late 1970s: a massive increase in the flow of refugees out of Indochina. Since the fall of Saigon, tens of thousands of Vietnamese had fled the country by land and sea. By early 1978, the plight of the so-called "boat people"—migrants making dangerous attempts to cross the South China Sea, often in overloaded and unseaworthy vessels—was attracting global media attention and sympathy. In the United States, prominent anti-communists lobbied the Carter administration to exempt Indochinese refugees from immigration quotas. Then, in the fall of 1978, the rate of seaborne departures from Vietnam exploded. The new wave included large numbers of *Hoa* (Vietnamese of Chinese descent), who had been targeted in the CPV's anti-capitalist crackdown. The number of refugee arrivals in other Southeast Asian countries soared from fewer than 3,000 in August 1978 to nearly 57,000 in June 1979. As conditions in refugee camps deteriorated, Thailand, Malaysia, and other ASEAN countries began "pushing" arriving ships back out to sea.[28]

For CPV leaders, the events of 1978–79 were more than just an unfortunate confluence of crises. They also posed a profound challenge to the legitimacy of the CPV and its right to rule. Just four years earlier, Party leaders had confidently predicted the advent of a new era of socialist development and material prosperity. However, the intensifying economic turmoil and the onset of a new war seemed to give the lie to these promises. Like its ally-turned-enemy, the Communist Party of China, the CPV would experience the late 1970s and early 1980s as a seemingly unending series of "legitimacy crises." For millions of Vietnamese, these years would be remembered as the "subsidy" (*bảo cấp*) period—a time of shortages, hardship, and unfulfilled promises.[29]

US leaders were also impacted by the events of 1978–79 in Southeast Asia, albeit in very different ways. In the eyes of Carter administration officials, the Third Indochina War was part of a new global Cold War offensive led by the Soviet Union. As a result, the war contributed to the unraveling of détente and to the "strategic reorientation" of Carter's foreign policy around Cold War objectives.[30] At the same time, the war in Indochina also intersected with another major theme of Carter's presidency: human rights. During his presidential campaign in 1976, Carter frequently declared his intent to make human rights one of the organizing principles of his foreign policy. Yet human rights had been notably absent from the earlier normalization negotiations with Vietnam.[31] It was only during 1978–79 that human rights and humanitarianism became central to US official thinking about Vietnam.

Carter's rise to the presidency took place amid the "human rights revolution" of the 1970s. Activists, lawyers, and legislators articulated a new notion of human rights as a category of international legal protection, rather than a set of principles enforced by sovereign states. This "revolution" was a global phenomenon, but it had had distinctive expressions in the United States. According to Barbara Keys, US politicians embraced human rights in the mid-1970s primarily to redeem America's tarnished moral reputation in the aftermath of the Vietnam War. By focusing attention on human rights violations (and violators) outside the United States, politicians and activists could avoid uncomfortable discussions of earlier American-perpetrated rights abuses in Vietnam and elsewhere.[32]

When the Indochinese boat people first gained global media attention in 1977, Carter resisted calls to allow more refugees into the United States. But as the exodus expanded, the issue became impossible to avoid, and Carter adopted a different approach—one that aimed to enhance US global legitimacy at Vietnam's expense. In July 1979, Carter dispatched Vice President Walter Mondale to an international conference in Geneva organized by the United Nations High Commission for Refugees (UNHCR). At the conference, the US consented to accept more refugees for resettlement and to expedite processing, and also agreed to cooperate with Vietnam to facilitate legal emigration. But Mondale also used his speech at the event to castigate Hanoi for "failing to ensure the human rights of its people." Although Mondale did not mention the well-documented cases of US-perpetrated rights violations in Vietnam during the war, this omission seemed to go unnoticed by conference participants, who gave Mondale a standing ovation.[33]

If Carter only belatedly connected US-Vietnam reconciliation to human rights, the same cannot be said of his successor, Ronald Reagan. Reagan expressed no ambivalence about the morality of the US intervention in the Vietnam War, famously describing it as a "noble cause." As a presidential candidate in both 1976 and 1980, he insisted that he would oppose normalization with Vietnam unless and until Hanoi provided a "full accounting" of American MIAs. While no such requirement appeared in the 1973 Paris Agreement—the text obligated both sides merely to "help each other" in recovering the remains of lost soldiers—conservative US politicians and MIA advocacy groups discerned that demanding the return of dead Americans would resonate with the public. As president, Reagan reframed "full accounting" as a humanitarian issue and made it a central focus of negotiations with Hanoi. He also allowed the National League of Families of American Prisoners and Missing in Southeast Asia—the leading element of the "MIA lobby"—to shape US policy agendas and even to join official delegations to Vietnam. In the process, he lent credence to the claims that some American prisoners might still be alive and languishing in Indochinese prison camps. By the mid-1980s, the mythology of US military personnel who had been "left behind" in Indochina in 1975 had gained wide acceptance in US society.[34]

While the MIA issue took on outsized importance under Reagan, his administration did not neglect other humanitarian and human rights issues in its dealings with Vietnam. In addition to continuing Carter's efforts to resettle "boat people" in the United States, the administration worked to facilitate legal Vietnamese emigration under the UN-established Orderly Departure Program. These efforts produced one of the most unexpected and re- markable consequences of the Vietnam War in the United States: the emergence of large and thriving Vietnamese American communities in California, Texas, and other states. Besides sponsoring the emigration of family members, Vietnamese Americans also lob- bied on behalf of particular groups of Vietnamese, such as the former South Vietnamese government supporters who had been imprisoned in SRV reeducation camps after the war. Meanwhile, other activists took up the cause of Vietnamese Amerasians (the children born in South Vietnam during the war to American fathers and Vietnamese mothers). In contrast to the slow and halting progress on MIAs, Washington and Hanoi concluded multiple agreements on migration during the 1980s.[35]

In addition to its demands about MIAs and refugees, the Reagan administration vowed not to normalize ties with Hanoi while PAVN troops remained in Cambodia. However, the leading role in the crafting of a peace settlement for the Cambodian war would be played not by US diplomats but by representatives of ASEAN. Although the ASEAN countries had joined the US and China in supporting the Khmer Rouge and other anti-Vietnamese resistance forces in Cambodia in 1979, they took the lead in devis- ing a formula for peace: a Vietnamese withdrawal followed by internationally supervised Cambodian elections. ASEAN diplomats eventually persuaded all the warring parties to endorse this formula—including Hanoi, which in 1985 announced plans for a unilateral phased withdrawal by the end of the decade. Following ASEAN-hosted meetings in Jakarta with all belligerents, the last Vietnamese units left Cambodia in 1989, clearing the way for an international peace agreement in Paris in 1991 and UN-backed elections in Cambodia in 1993. Cambodia's embrace of democracy would turn out to be fleeting, but as an exercise in regional peace-building, ASEAN's patient diplomacy was strikingly successful.[36]

Vietnam's efforts to wind down the Third Indochina War were connected to an even more consequential change in CPV policy and strategy: the adoption of the Đổi Mới re- forms. Since 1978, the balance of political power in Hanoi had tilted in favor of what one scholar describes as the "military first" faction of the CPV. Led by Lê Duẩn, Lê Đức Thọ, and Phạm Hùng, this group of leaders favored continued mass mobilization of the Viet- namese population and alignment with the Soviet bloc, with the goal of winning military victory over China. But by 1985, following another failed currency reform and a fresh bout of hyperinflation, the Party's legitimacy appeared more tenuous than ever. This provided an opening for reform-minded officials such as Võ Văn Kiệt and Nguyễn Cơ Thạch, who stepped up their calls for "new thinking" in both foreign and domestic policy. These efforts, coupled with the death of longtime CPV General Secretary Lê Duẩn in mid-1986, paved the way for far-reaching policy changes regarding private enterprise, price liberalization, foreign investment, agricultural production, and banking. Subsequent measures restored land use rights to individual Vietnamese households and provided farmers with greater control over their own labor.[37]

Vietnam's reform path during the Đổi Mới era was a slow arc rather than a sharp turn. Although the CPV's commitment to reform as a means of rebuilding its legitimacy was clear, so too was its determination to maintain its monopoly on power. The result was what one scholar aptly describes as "market-Leninism": support for Vietnam's integration into global trade and capital markets, coupled with efforts to maintain the CPV's monopoly on political power.[38] As we will see, the party's embrace of markets and the subsequent improvement of Vietnam's economic fortunes did not mean that the party's legitimacy crisis had ended. However, the Đổi Mới reforms did help the CPV to survive the shock waves produced by the collapse of communism in Europe during 1989–91. The reforms also steered Vietnam toward a globalized model of development and away from the two-camp schema that had defined the CPV's worldview since its founding.[39]

By the time that George H. W. Bush took office as US president in 1989, the CPV had significantly altered its approaches to both foreign affairs and domestic policy. In addition to making peace in Cambodia and seeking accommodation with ASEAN, Hanoi was also pursuing rapprochement with China, culminating in the 1991 restoration of full diplomatic ties. Meanwhile, Vietnam's internal economic reforms were beginning to pay off, as evidenced by improved growth and agricultural output, including a dramatic return to the country's traditional status as a leading exporter of rice.[40] SRV officials closed the last of the reeducation camps and expanded cooperation with the US and other countries on emigration. In 1991, Hanoi announced a policy of "becoming friends" with all countries of the world—a move that seemed to mark the formal abandonment of the two-camp worldview. The SRV also signaled new willingness to engage with Washington on MIAs, "for the sake of peace and stability in Southeast Asia."[41] All these Vietnamese moves, in tandem with sharply reduced Soviet aid to Vietnam, suggested that the time might be ripe for a new push for normalization with Washington.

But Washington was not yet ready. Although US humanitarian organizations, business leaders, Vietnam veterans, and some members of Congress advocated the lifting of the US embargo as a prelude to normalization, these efforts were opposed by the National League of Families and other "full accounting" advocates. Like his Republican predecessors, President Bush initially aligned himself with the League and its allies. Yet Bush viewed the lack of normal relations with Vietnam as a lingering effect of the "Vietnam syndrome"—a term that hawkish pundits used to complain about Washington's purported reluctance to use military force. In Bush's eyes, normalization with Vietnam might banish painful memories of American defeat.[42]

In 1991, shortly after the American-led victory over Iraq in the Gulf War, State Department officials outlined a new "road map" to US-Vietnam normalization. While the plan required stepped-up collaboration from Vietnam on MIAs, it also envisioned an end to the US embargo and an easing of aid restrictions *prior* to full normalization—an approach akin to what CPV leaders had demanded in 1977. The road map drew withering criticism from the National League and the MIA lobby, which denounced it as a surrender of Washington's "leverage" with Hanoi. These arguments were temporarily boosted in the summer of 1991 by the publication of sensational photographs that purported to depict American servicemen alive in Indochina. Although the photographs were soon shown to be fakes, they prompted the creation of a new Senate select committee that would spend more than a year investigating alleged "live sightings" and government cover-ups.[43]

The Bush road map was eventually implemented, but only during Bill Clinton's first term in the White House. Although candidate Clinton duly promised a "full accounting" of MIAs, his actions as president moved the US decisively toward normalization. In July 1993, Washington ended the long-standing ban on indirect US aid to Vietnam via international lending institutions. Six months later, Clinton lifted the US economic embargo—after the Senate narrowly endorsed the move. Key support was provided by Senators John Kerry, Bob Kerrey, Chuck Robb, and John McCain. As veterans who had served in Vietnam during the war, their testimony and that of other congressional veterans provided "political cover" to Clinton, who had faced criticism for avoiding military service during the war via draft deferments.

On July 11, 1995, Clinton announced that the United States and Vietnam had agreed to normalize their official relations. Although that date is now celebrated in the US and Vietnam as a moment at which both countries put their past enmities aside, Clinton's actual remarks on the occasion suggested otherwise. After reassuring Americans that the efforts to resolve MIA cases would continue, Clinton invoked a Reagan-esque version of Vietnam War history that affirmed the moral righteousness of the American war effort:

> Whatever we may think about the political decisions of the Vietnam era, the brave Americans who fought and died there had noble motives. They fought for the freedom and the independence of the Vietnamese people. Today the Vietnamese are independent, and we believe [normalization] will help to extend the reach of freedom in Vietnam.[44]

Normalization was an important achievement, but it did not yet herald the dawn of a new era of US-Vietnam reconciliation. The concessions made by both governments in the early 1990s were significant mainly as confidence-building measures and as displays of what Kupchan calls "reciprocal restraint." It was only in the years after 1995 that the two countries would move into the next phase of peace building: the creation of jointly authored narratives about the Vietnam War and its historical meaning for both countries.

New Connections, New Narratives, and "War Legacies," 1995–2022

In June of 1997, former US Defense Secretary Robert McNamara visited Hanoi. It was his second trip to the capital he ordered bombed during the Vietnam War. Two years earlier, SRV officials had warmly welcomed McNamara, noting the recent memoir in which he described his wartime decisions on Vietnam as "terribly wrong." But on this return trip, McNamara's hosts regarded him more warily. Over several days, McNamara and other retired US officials conversed with some of their Vietnamese counterparts, all of whom had served in the DRV military or Foreign Ministry during the war. McNamara hoped the discussions would shed light on wartime mistakes made by leaders in *both* governments, and perhaps reveal missed chances for a negotiated peace. But his Vietnamese hosts did not accommodate him. "The opportunities were missed by the US, not the Vietnamese side," a former deputy foreign minister admonished McNamara.[45]

McNamara's motives in Hanoi in 1997 were not hard to discern. "He was willing to accept blame," one journalist noted, "but he also sought to spread the guilt around, to extend the circle of error to the North Vietnamese."[46] In both his memoir and his visits to Vietnam, McNamara was seeking a kind of plea bargain. He would admit a measure of culpability for the war and the destruction it wrought, but he also wanted to depict his wartime mistakes as resulting from a broader problem of distorted worldviews and faulty assumptions.

McNamara did not get the plea deal he wanted in Hanoi in 1997. But his trip hardly marked the end of conversations between Americans and Vietnamese over the meaning and memory of the war. Beginning in the early 2000s, the United States and Vietnam entered a period of steadily warming relations. Amid a boom in bilateral trade and the flourishing of new cultural, educational, and business connections, the two governments began to collaborate in a steadily growing range of policy areas. Along the way, Americans and Vietnamese elites embarked on the first sustained efforts to craft shared narratives about reconciliation and what officials on both sides began calling the "legacies" of the war.

The evolution of the US-Vietnam relationship after 1995 took place amid extraordinary changes in economic and social life within Vietnam. In the early 1990s, Vietnam entered a period of high economic growth that exceeded all but the most optimistic predictions. Although not all the effects of this growth were positive—especially when factors such as pollution and environmental degradation are considered—the overall scope and scale of the transformation were astonishing, especially as measured by rising productivity, falling poverty, and improved educational outcomes.[47] Meanwhile, the skylines and built environments of Hanoi, Ho Chi Minh City, and other Vietnamese urban areas were transformed by a seemingly endless wave of construction and infrastructure projects.

As Vietnam's new era of growth unfolded, some observers concluded that the CPV had finally escaped from its long-running legitimacy crisis.[48] But not everyone was convinced. From early in the Đổi Mới period, a few CPV insiders argued that the time had come for an end to one-party rule.[49] Meanwhile, signs of dissatisfaction with the party-state were evident in other quarters. During 2008–9, a broad coalition of elites and groups of ordinary Vietnamese joined a movement to oppose government plans for expanded bauxite mining in Vietnam's Central Highlands. Using petitions, websites, and other media, movement participants attacked the plan on environmental protection grounds. They also challenged the state's plan to contract the mining work to Chinese-owned companies—a line of criticism that reflected intensifying animosity toward China in many sectors of Vietnamese society. Beneath these complaints, however, lay another concern: the widespread belief that CPV leaders were mortgaging Vietnam's national interest to line their own pockets.[50]

At first, the lingering doubts about the CPV's legitimacy did not seem to augur well for US-Vietnam reconciliation. In the years immediately after normalization, American and Vietnamese political leaders frequently professed a desire to look for common ground—only to then revert to a strategy of staking out the moral high ground. This dynamic was evident in 2000, when Bill Clinton became the first US president to visit Vietnam since the war. When CPV General Secretary Lê Khả Phiêu lectured Clinton about the "true nature of the resistance war" that Vietnam had waged against US imperialism prior to 1975, the president indignantly responded that the Americans who fought the war "were not imperialists or colonialists, but good people who believed they were fighting communism." Although some CPV leaders criticized Phiêu's comments as inappropriate and out of touch, others shared his concerns that rapprochement with Washington might undermine the Party at home.[51] In 2003, when human rights advocates in the US Congress proposed a measure that aimed to compel the release of Vietnamese political prisoners, Hanoi responded by suspending bilateral discussions on human rights for three years.

Some authors suggest that American-Vietnamese relations during the 1990s and afterward are explained mainly by the efforts of US-based corporations to secure access to Vietnam's consumer markets and labor resources.[52] In reality, however, the growth of US business interests and American investment in Vietnam was a slow and uneven process. After Clinton lifted the US embargo in 1994, the total volume of bilateral US-Vietnam trade the following year only amounted to US$250 million. Trade between the former adversaries actually declined in the late 1990s and did not break the US$1 billion mark until 2000. Meanwhile, American foreign direct investment in Vietnam lagged behind the amounts from Taiwan, Hong Kong, and South Korea. With the implementation of a 2001 US-Vietnam Bilateral Trade Agreement, two-way trade finally entered a period of rapid year-on-year expansion. This trend accelerated after Vietnam's 2007 accession to the World Trade Organization. By 2019, the total value of US-Vietnam trade had topped US$75 billion. Yet more than 80 percent of this trade was accounted for by soaring Vietnamese exports to the United States.[53]

In hindsight, the role of American corporations in US-Vietnam economic relations seems less important than that played by another set of actors: Vietnamese Americans. Because anti-communism was a central component of the political cultures of Vietnamese

American communities established in the United States after 1975, some members of those communities remained strongly opposed to building political and economic ties to the SRV. However, many other Vietnamese Americans took a different view. As Ivan Small shows, monetary gifts and remittances sent or carried to Vietnam by Vietnamese Americans after 1975 had far-reaching impacts on both givers and receivers.[54] Moreover, as Vietnamese American professionals came to Vietnam for travel, study, and work, many of them became involved in the country's burgeoning private business sector. In the 2010s, foreign tourists noted the presence of Starbucks coffee shops in Hanoi and Ho Chi Minh City and concluded that US corporations had taken over the Vietnamese retail coffee market. They were unaware that the presence of Starbucks in Vietnam was tiny compared to the market shares of Vietnamese rival chains—or that one of the most successful of those chains, Highlands Coffee, had been founded in 1998 by a Vietnamese American who grew up in Seattle.[55]

The growing visibility of Vietnamese Americans in Vietnam coincided with an unexpected development in Vietnamese public opinion: growing admiration for the United States among ordinary Vietnamese. This sentiment was evident in the large and enthusiastic crowds that Clinton drew during his 2000 trip. People turned out even though SRV media provided almost no advance notice of the visit.[56] By the 2010s, opinion poll data suggested that Vietnam was among the most pro-American countries in Asia, with three-quarters of Vietnamese expressing positive feelings toward the United States.[57] Many Vietnamese idealized the United States as a land of economic opportunity for immigrants—a view reinforced by their perception of Vietnamese Americans, who were typically viewed as successful and prosperous (if perhaps a little haughty). Vietnamese also admired the American educational system. During the 1990s and early 2000s, hundreds of Vietnamese received Fulbright fellowships to study in the United States; others were sponsored by the Vietnam Educational Foundation, a US agency seeded by South Vietnamese government assets frozen in 1975. By 2018, Vietnam ranked sixth as a source country for international students in the United States, with more than 31,000 Vietnamese students enrolled in American secondary schools and universities.[58]

For CPV leaders, the growing popularity of the United States in Vietnam presented a dilemma. Some argued that closer US ties could provide a counterweight to Chinese power; they also suggested that a formal partnership with Washington could enhance the party's legitimacy, given the Vietnamese public's overwhelmingly positive views of America (and its increasingly negative perceptions of China). But other CPV leaders were more cautious, warning that Washington still hoped eventually to end one-party rule in Vietnam by promoting the country's "peaceful evolution" into a liberal democracy. During the premiership of Nguyễn Tấn Dũng (2006–16), those who favored accommodation with Washington appeared to gain the upper hand. In 2013, Vietnam agreed to upgrade the bilateral relationship into a "comprehensive partnership." This decision seemed to pay off the following year, when China triggered a major crisis in the South China Sea by dispatching an oil exploration rig into waters claimed by Vietnam. The administration of Barack Obama responded by criticizing China and lifting a long-standing ban on maritime weapons sales to Vietnam. In 2015, US-Vietnam ties received another boost when

General Secretary Nguyễn Phú Trọng met Obama in Washington—the first-ever US visit by a sitting CPV chief. Although Trọng was a hard-liner and a skeptic about US intentions for Vietnam, he was gratified when Obama agreed that each government should respect the other's political system—a statement that CPV leaders interpreted as a US promise not to undermine the Party's legitimacy.[59]

For Obama and other US officials, the success of the Trọng visit turned on the general secretary's acceptance of a US-backed plan to liberalize labor laws in Vietnam. This was an essential step to securing Vietnam's participation in the Trans-Pacific Partnership (TPP), a multilateral trade deal that aimed to create a free trade zone among a dozen Pacific Ocean countries. Administration officials hoped that Vietnam's inclusion in the TPP might persuade other developing countries to join. But the entire initiative was thrown into doubt in November 2016, following the unexpected victory of Donald J. Trump in the US presidential election. Shortly after taking office, Trump pulled out of the TPP, claiming it would undermine US manufacturing. Yet Vietnam and the other ten participating nations proceeded to recast and ratify the pact without the United States. For CPV leaders, the main impact of the US withdrawal was not in the area of foreign trade—Vietnamese exports to the US continued to boom throughout Trump's presidency—but in Vietnam's domestic realm. Following the US pull-out, Trọng cracked down on the reformers and activists who hoped to use the TPP provisions to push for improved labor conditions and human rights in Vietnam.[60]

In the wake of Trump's withdrawal from the TPP and Trọng's consolidation of CPV authority, some observers wondered if the rapprochement between Washington and Hanoi might be ending. But officials in both governments remained strongly committed to the relationship. During Trump's tenure in office, the two sides expanded cooperation in trade, investment, and security. This cooperation was sustained in part by both sides' ongoing concerns about China and its aggressive stance in the South China Sea. In 2018, the USS *Carl Vinson* became the first US aircraft carrier to visit Vietnam since the end of the Vietnam War—a move widely viewed as a message to Beijing. But the continued warm relations were not driven solely by geopolitical considerations. The two governments also collaborated in other areas, including some that addressed "war legacies" and various other topics previously deemed off limits.

One high-profile collaboration involved Fulbright University Vietnam (FUV), billed as the country's "first nonprofit, independent university." Endorsed by both Trọng and Obama, FUV was a revamped and greatly expanded version of the Fulbright Economics Teaching Program (FETP), a US-funded school set up in Ho Chi Minh City in 1994 to provide training in market economics to mid-career Vietnamese civil servants. While FETP had operated mostly without fanfare for more than twenty years, the same would not be true of FUV. Official Vietnamese news reports of Obama's announcement noted that the university had been licensed by the SRV Ministry of Education and Training and that it would be "supervised" by CPV officials. Yet they also highlighted the university's dedication to "American values," including "academic freedom, autonomy, meritocracy, and transparency."[61] This narrative did not meet with universal approval; critics in Vietnam and the United States denounced the selection of former US senator and Vietnam veteran

Bob Kerrey to head the university's board of trustees, due to reports of his involvement in a 1969 massacre in the Mekong Delta.[62] But this critique failed to garner widespread attention or support in either country. Kerrey quietly stepped down, and the support of both governments for the university was undiminished.

In the area of "war legacies," the new spirit of cooperation extended into one of the most contentious issues in Vietnam War history: Agent Orange. Since the 1980s, the use of chemical herbicides by US forces—and the harmful effects of those chemicals on US soldiers—had loomed large in American memories of the war. Lawsuits eventually forced the US government to provide compensation and treatment to American veteran victims of Agent Orange. But this only made Washington more determined to avoid incurring similar obligations to the far more numerous Vietnamese victims of US herbicides (many of whom were born after the war, but who suffered the epigenetic effects from their parents' exposure to dioxin). Beyond the financial cost, such obligations might require the United States to revisit difficult questions about the morality of its wartime policies and practices in Vietnam—questions that every US president since 1975 had dismissed as invalid. As a result, US officials in Vietnam had long refused even to discuss the topic of Agent Orange. Of all the "war legacies" on which Washington and Hanoi might seek to cooperate, Agent Orange initially seemed one of the least promising.[63]

In 2006, a joint statement by US President George W. Bush and SRV President Nguyễn Minh Triết contained a brief reference to Agent Orange. This provided an opening for the Hanoi office of the Ford Foundation, which had previously collaborated with Vietnamese government scientists on Agent Orange issues, and for sympathetic members of the US Congress, who passed the first of a series of appropriations to support Agent Orange remediation at "hotspots" in Vietnam, along with aid for Vietnamese victims. By 2018, the US government had spent more than US$230 million on these efforts. In the coauthored words of Charles Bailey, an American public policy specialist, and Le Ke Son, a Vietnamese toxicologist, the United States and Vietnam had shifted "from enemies to partners."[64]

In crafting a common narrative about the US participation in Agent Orange remediation and victim assistance, US and SRV officials invoked the language of moral rectification. US Senator Patrick Leahy, who took a strong personal interest in the issue and led the efforts to pass the legislation, declared that the new measures showed that "instead of turning our backs on the problem, we had a moral obligation to do something about it." Yet Leahy and most other US officials were often deliberately vague about the actual moral infraction that the US had committed. The most revealing remark may be Son and Bailey's pithy summary of the US understanding of its obligation: "Let's fix this; it's a humanitarian concern that we can do something about."[65]

By framing Agent Orange as a humanitarian problem, the writers of these joint American-Vietnamese narratives subtly blurred the moral meaning of this and other "war legacies." Even as US officials acknowledged a moral obligation to cooperate with their Vietnamese counterparts to alleviate the contemporary effects of these "legacies," they avoided discussing some of the more intractable moral questions about the Vietnam War and the role of the United States in that conflict. Meanwhile, the CPV could plausibly portray the new US engagement on Agent Orange and other issues as an affirmation of its own official narrative of Vietnam War history—and, by extension, as an endorsement of the Party's legitimacy. Viewed as part of the decades-long peace process between the United States and Vietnam, the emergence of "war legacies" as a new arena of bilateral collaboration was an important and welcome development. But that hardly meant that the long-standing concerns about morality, legitimacy, and the historical meaning of the war had been laid to rest.

Conclusion

Since the US and DRV governments first declared their shared desire to enter an "era of reconciliation" in the Paris Accords of 1973, relations between the United States and Vietnam have never been as warm as they appear to be in 2022. While the 1995 normalization agreement between the two nations was a significant event, it was less of a turning point than an incremental step on the road to peace. With hindsight, it is evident that the seeds of reconciliation were planted during the 1980s, when CPV leaders embraced the "new thinking" of the Đổi Mới era and abandoned the two-camp view of international politics. The party's turn toward market-Leninism and a globalized development model paved the way for subsequent agreements with Washington on diplomatic ties, trade, security, and cultural exchange. Cooperation was also facilitated by Vietnamese Americans, who invested extensive economic and cultural capital in Vietnam, and by the rising popularity of the United States in the eyes of ordinary Vietnamese citizens. The combined effect of these trends was increased feelings of mutual trust between the two governments, leading eventually to the joint production of new narratives about reconciliation, progress, and "war legacies." There was nothing inevitable about this process. As demonstrated by the chronic tensions that still plague Washington's ties to other Cold War adversaries such as China, Russia, Cuba, and North Korea, the rise of US-Vietnam reconciliation was anything but foreordained. In an era in which rivalry and conflict within and across international borders seem to be rising ever higher, Americans and Vietnamese will do well to value the peace they have built together and to consider how they might make it even stronger.

Notes

1. Stimson Center, "The U.S.-Vietnam Relationship and War Legacies."
2. Chanda, *Brother Enemy*, 263–96; Becker, *When the War Was Over*, 385–405; Hurst, *The Carter Administration and Vietnam*.
3. Martini, *Invisible Enemies*; Franklin, *M.I.A.*
4. Osius, *Nothing Is Impossible*.
5. Kupchan, *How Enemies Become Friends*.

6. Ménétrey-Monchau, "The Changing Post-War US Strategy in Indochina," 68.

7. "Hanoi Premier Calls on the U.S. To Establish Normal Relations," *New York Times*, June 4, 1975, 3; "Hanoi Bars a Search for G.I.'s Unless U.S. Gives Postwar Aid," *New York Times*, June 12, 1975, 4.

8. Vu, *Vietnam's Communist Revolution*, 178–209; quotation on p. 201.

9. Path, *Vietnam's Strategic Thinking*, introduction and chap. 6.

10. Nguyen, *Hanoi's War*, chaps. 7 and 8.

11. Quoted in Vu, *Vietnam's Communist Revolution*, 215.

12. Path, *Vietnam's Strategic Thinking*, 26–27, 181–83; Vu, *Vietnam's Communist Revolution*, 207–8.

13. Path, *Vietnam's Strategic Thinking*, 24–25.

14. Vu, *Vietnam's Communist Revolution*, 216.

15. Agreement on Ending the War and Restoring the Peace, chap. 8.

16. Nixon, "US Promise of Postwar Reconstruction."

17. Path, *Vietnam's Strategic Thinking*, 181–83.

18. Ménétrey-Monchau, "The Changing Post-War US Strategy in Indochina," 66.

19. Diary Entry: February 16, 1973, H. R. Haldeman Diaries Collection, Richard Nixon Presidential Library and Museum, Yorba Linda, CA.

20. White House message no. 51044, Scowcroft to Oveson, June 11, 1975, in *Foreign Relations of the United States, 1969–1976*, vol. E-12: *Documents on East and Southeast Asia, 1973–1976*, Document no. 76.

21. Ménétrey-Monchau, "The Changing Post-War US Strategy in Indochina," 70.

22. "The President's News Conference of March 24, 1977," in *Public Papers of the Presidents of the United States: Jimmy Carter*, 501.

23. Becker, *When the War Was Over*, 386–89; Hurst, *The Carter Administration and Vietnam*, 32–35.

24. Becker, *When the War Was Over*, 390–91.

25. Ménétrey-Monchau, *American-Vietnamese Relations in the Wake of War*, chaps. 4 and 5.

26. On the Third Indochina War, see Chanda, *Brother Enemy*; Westad and Quinn-Judge, *The Third Indochina War*; Khoo, *Collateral Damage*; Zhang Xiaoming, *Deng Xiaoping's Long War*; Path, *Vietnam's Strategic Thinking*.

27. Ngo Vinh Long, "The Socialization of South Vietnam"; Path, *Vietnam's Strategic Thinking*, 30–37; St. John, *Revolution, Reform, and Regionalism in Southeast Asia*, 21–28, 45–48; see also the chapter by Le Dang Doanh in this volume.

28. Loescher and Scanlan, *Calculated Kindness*, chap. 7, esp. pp. 136 and 140. See also Lipman, *In Camps*, chap. 2.

29. The CPV's post-1975 legitimacy crisis is a primary theme of Huy Đức, *Bên Thắng Cuộc*. On the CPC's legitimacy crises, see Chen Jian, "Tiananmen and the Berlin Wall."

30. Sargent, *A Superpower Transformed*, 261–96.

31. Hurst, *The Carter Administration and Vietnam*, 125.

32. Keys, *Reclaiming American Virtue*. See also Moyn, *The Last Utopia*; Iriye, Goedde, and Hitchcock, *The Human Rights Revolution*.

33. Loescher and Scanlan, *Calculated Kindness*, 137–45; for Mondale's speech, see http://www2.mnhs.org/library/findaids/00697/pdf/UNSpeech19790721.pdf.

34. Franklin, *M.I.A.*, 137–40.

35. Demmer, *After Saigon's Fall*, chaps. 3–4; Valverde, "From Dust to Gold."

36. Acharya, *Constructing a Security Community in Southeast Asia*.

37. St. John, *Revolution, Reform and Regionalism*, 70–80; Vu, *Vietnam's Communist Revolution*, 252–64; Path, *Vietnam's Strategic Thinking*, chap. 6. See also the chapter by Le Dang Doanh in this volume.

38. London, "Viet Nam and the Making of Market-Leninism."

39. Path, *Vietnam's Strategic Thinking*, 180; Elliott, *Changing Worlds*, chaps. 2–3.

40. Dollar and Ljunggren, "Vietnam."

41. Vu, *Vietnam's Communist Revolution*, 252; Elliott, *Changing Worlds*, 121–22.

42. Martini, *Invisible Enemies*, 162–63.

43. Martini, *Invisible Enemies*, 162–63.

44. "Remarks Announcing the Normalization of Diplomatic Relations with Vietnam," July 11, 1995, in *Public Papers of the President of the United States: William J. Clinton*, 1074.

45. Shipler, "Robert McNamara and the Ghosts of Vietnam."
46. Shipler, "Robert McNamara and the Ghosts of Vietnam."
47. For in-depth analysis of these changes, see the chapters in this volume by Vu and Perkins; Kokko, Nestor, and Le; Le and McPherson; Dapice; and London.
48. London, "Viet Nam and the Making of Market-Leninism," 396.
49. Thayer, "Political Legitimacy in Vietnam."
50. Morris-Jung, "The Vietnamese Bauxite Controversy."
51. Huy Đức, *Bên Thắng Cuộc*, vol. 2, 376–77; Clinton, *My Life*, 930.
52. Martini, *Invisible Enemies*, 195–97.
53. US Census Bureau, "Trade in Goods with Vietnam."
54. Small, *Currencies of Imagination*.
55. Saini, "Why Starbucks Is Failing in Vietnam"; "Seattle Entrepreneur Establishes the Coffee Brand in Vietnam."
56. Lamb, *Vietnam, Now*, 262–67; Huy Đức, *Bên Thắng Cuộc*, vol. 2, 374–75.
57. Devlin, "40 Years After Fall of Saigon, Vietnamese See U.S. as Key Ally."
58. Ashwill, "Vietnam Student Enrolment in the US Holds Steady."
59. Vuving, "Will Vietnam Be America's Next Strategic Partner?"
60. Denyer and Nakamura, "Ripple Effect"; see also Eva Hansson's chapter in this volume.
61. Vuong Duc Anh, "Obama to Open First American-Style Private University in Vietnam Next Week."
62. Taft, "How a U.S.-Backed University in Vietnam Unleashed Old Demons." The author served on the Fulbright University board of trustees from 2017 to 2019.
63. Fox, "Agent Orange."
64. Le Ke Son and Bailey, *From Enemies to Partners*, 10.
65. Le Ke Son and Bailey, *From Enemies to Partners*, 14.

References

Acharya, Amitav. *Constructing a Security Community in Southeast Asia: ASEAN and the Problem of Regional Order*. London: Routledge, 2001.

Agreement on Ending the War and Restoring Peace in Viet-Nam. *United Nations Treaty Series*. no. 935, 1974. Document 13295.

Ashwill, Mark. "Vietnam Student Enrolment in the US Holds Steady." *University World News*, February 8, 2020. https://www.universityworldnews.com/post.php?story=20200205124654543.

Becker, Elizabeth. *When the War Was Over: The Voices of Cambodia's Revolution and Its People*. New York: Simon & Schuster, 1986.

Chanda, Nyan. *Brother Enemy: The War After the War*. New York: Collier Books, 1986.

Chen Jian. "Tiananmen and the Berlin Wall: China's Path toward 1989 and Beyond." In *The Fall of the Berlin Wall: The Revolutionary Legacy of 1989*, edited by Jeffrey Engel. New York: Oxford University Press, 2009.

Clinton, Bill. *My Life*. New York: Vintage Books, 2005.

Demmer, Amanda C. *After Saigon's Fall: Refugees and US-Vietnamese Relations, 1975–2000*. Cambridge: Cambridge University Press, 2021.

Denyer, Simon, and David Nakamura. "Ripple Effect: How a Trump Decision on Trade Became a Setback for Democracy in Vietnam." *Washington Post*, October 11, 2018. https://www.washingtonpost.com/graphics/2018/world/how-a-trump-decision-on-trade-became-a-setback-for-democracy-in-vietnam/.

Devlin, Kat. "40 Years After Fall of Saigon, Vietnamese See U.S. as Key Ally." Pew Research Center, April 30, 2015. https://www.pewresearch.org/fact-tank/2015/04/30/vietnamese-see-u-s-as-key-ally/.

Dollar, David, and Börje Ljunggren. "Vietnam." In *Going Global: Transition from Plan to Market in the World Economy*, edited by Padma Desai. Cambridge, MA: MIT Press, 1997.

Elliott, David. *Changing Worlds: Vietnam's Transition from Cold War to Globalization.* New York: Oxford University Press, 2012.

Fox, Diane Niblack. "Agent Orange: Coming to Terms with a Transnational Legacy." In *Four Decades On: Vietnam, the United States, and the Legacies of the Second Indochina War*, edited by Scott Laderman and Edwin Martini. Durham, NC: Duke University Press, 2013.

Franklin, H. Bruce. *M.I.A., Or, Mythmaking in America.* New Brunswick, NJ: Rutgers University Press, 1993.

Hurst, Stephen. *The Carter Administration and Vietnam.* London: Macmillan, 1996.

Huy Đức. *Bên Thắng Cuộc* (The winning side). Los Angeles: OsinBook, 2012.

Iriye, Akira, Petra Goedde, and William I. Hitchcock. *The Human Rights Revolution.* New York: Oxford University Press, 2012.

Keys, Barbara J. *Reclaiming American Virtue: The Human Rights Revolution of the 1970s.* Cambridge, MA: Harvard University Press, 2014.

Khoo, Nicholas. *Collateral Damage: Sino-Soviet Rivalry and the Termination of the Sino-Vietnamese Alliance.* New York: Columbia University Press, 2011.

Kupchan, Charles A. *How Enemies Become Friends: The Sources of Stable Peace.* Princeton, NJ: Princeton University Press, 2010.

Lamb, David. *Vietnam, Now: A Reporter Returns.* New York: Public Affairs, 2002.

Le Ke Son and Charles R. Bailey. *From Enemies to Partners: Vietnam, the U.S. and Agent Orange.* Chicago: G. Anton, 2017.

Lipman, Jana K. *In Camps: Vietnamese Refugees, Asylum Seekers, and Repatriates.* Oakland: University of California Press, 2020.

Loescher, Gil, and John A. Scanlan. *Calculated Kindness: Refugees and America's Half-Open Door, 1945 to the Present.* New York: Free Press, 1986.

London, Jonathan. "Viet Nam and the Making of Market-Leninism." *Pacific Review* 22, no. 3 (2009): 375–99.

Martini, Edwin. *Invisible Enemies: The American War on Vietnam, 1975–2000.* Amherst: University of Massachusetts Press, 2007.

Ménétrey-Monchau, Cécile. *American-Vietnamese Relations in the Wake of War: Diplomacy After the Capture of Saigon, 1975–1979.* Jefferson, NC: McFarland and Co., 2006.

———. "The Changing Post-War US Strategy in Indochina." In *The Third Indochina War: Conflict between China, Vietnam and Cambodia, 1972–1979*, edited by Odd Arne Westad and Sophie Quinn-Judge. London: Routledge, 2006.

Morris-Jung, Jason. "The Vietnamese Bauxite Controversy: Towards a More Oppositional Politics." *Journal of Vietnamese Studies* 10, no. 1 (2015): 63–109.

Moyn, Samuel. *The Last Utopia: Human Rights and History.* Cambridge, MA: Harvard University Press, 2010.

Ngo Vinh Long. "The Socialization of South Vietnam." In *The Third Indochina War: Conflict between China, Vietnam and Cambodia, 1972–1979*, edited by Odd Arne Westad and Sophie Quinn-Judge. London: Routledge, 2006.

Nguyen, Lien-Hang T. *Hanoi's War: An International History of the War for Peace in Vietnam.* Chapel Hill: University of North Carolina Press, 2012.

Nixon, Richard. "US Promise of Postwar Reconstruction: Letter to DRV Prime Minister Pham Van Dong, February 1, 1973." In *Vietnam and America: The Most Comprehensive Documented History of the Vietnam War*, 2nd ed., edited by Marvin Gettleman, Jane Franklin, Marilyn B. Young, and H. Bruce Franklin. New York: Grove Press, 1995.

Osius, Ted. *Nothing Is Impossible: America's Reconciliation with Vietnam.* New Brunswick, NJ: Rutgers University Press, 2022.

Path, Kosal. *Vietnam's Strategic Thinking during the Third Indochina War.* Madison: University of Wisconsin Press, 2020.

Public Papers of the President of the United States: William J. Clinton. Washington, DC: US Government Printing Office, 1998.

Public Papers of the Presidents of the United States: Jimmy Carter, 1977, Book 1. Washington, DC: US Government Printing Office, 1977.

Saini, Leon. "Why Starbucks Is Failing in Vietnam." *Better Marketing*, January 9, 2020. https://medium
.com/better-marketing/why-starbucks-is-failing-in-vietnam-e77a87c3eccb.

Sargent, Daniel. *A Superpower Transformed: The Remaking of American Foreign Relations in the 1970s.* New York:
Oxford University Press, 2014.

"Seattle Entrepreneur Establishes the Coffee Brand in Vietnam." Meetjohnsong (blog), May 20, 2012.
https://meetjohnsong.com/2012/05/20/a-seattle-entrepreneur-establishes-the-coffee-brand-in-vietnam/.

Shipler, David K. "Robert McNamara and the Ghosts of Vietnam." *New York Times Magazine*, August 10,
1997.

Small, Ivan. *Currencies of Imagination: Channeling Money and Chasing Mobility in Vietnam.* Ithaca, NY:
Cornell University Press, 2018.

Stimson Center. "The U.S.-Vietnam Relationship and War Legacies: 25 Years into Normalization." July 15, 2020.
https://www.stimson.org/event/the-u-s-vietnam-relationship-and-war-legacies-25-years-into-normalization/.

St. John, Ronald Bruce. *Revolution, Reform, and Regionalism in Southeast Asia: Cambodia, Laos, and Vietnam.*
Oxford: Routledge, 2006.

Taft, Isabelle. "How a U.S.-Backed University in Vietnam Unleashed Old Demons." *Politico*, February 4, 2018.
https://www.politico.com/magazine/story/2018/02/04/how-a-us-backed-university-in-vietnam-unleashed
-old-demons-216528/.

Thayer, Carlyle. "Political Legitimacy in Vietnam: Challenge and Response." *Politics & Policy* 38 (2010):
423–44.

US Census Bureau. "Trade in Goods with Vietnam." https://www.census.gov/foreign-trade/balance/c5520
.html.

Valverde, Kieu-Linh Caroline. "From Dust to Gold: The Vietnamese Amerasian Experience." In *Racially
Mixed People in America.* Edited by Maria P. P. Root. Newbury Park, CA: Sage, 1992.

Vu, Tuong. *Vietnam's Communist Revolution: The Power and Limits of Ideology.* New York: Cambridge University Press, 2017.

Vuong Duc Anh. "Obama to Open First American-Style Private University in Vietnam Next Week." *Vnexpress,* May 17, 2016. https://e.vnexpress.net/news/news/obama-to-open-first-american-style-private-university
-in-ho-chi-minh-city-next-week-3404377.html.

Vuving, Alexander L. "Will Vietnam be America's Next Strategic Partner?" *The Diplomat*, August 21, 2021.
https://thediplomat.com/2021/08/will-vietnam-be-americas-next-strategic-partner/.

Westad, Odd Arne, and Sophie Quinn-Judge, eds. *The Third Indochina War: Conflict between China, Vietnam
and Cambodia, 1972–1979.* London: Routledge, 2006.

Zhang Xiaoming. *Deng Xiaoping's Long War: The Military Conflict between China and Vietnam, 1979–1991.*
Chapel Hill: University of North Carolina Press, 2015.

Index

Page numbers for figures and tables are in italics.

Leninist-Stalinist party-state in USSR, 46
Le Quy Don, 47, 52, 53, 54
Le Thi, 305
Le Thi Cong Nhan, 81
Le Trong Hung, 30
Le Van Bang, 383
LGBTQ people, 302, 308–9, 312. *See also*
    homosexuality
Li, Eric X., 50
Liu Qibao, 387
loans to private businesses: financial instruments
    for, 211; before late 1990s, 206; micro loans by
    VSPB, 214; nonperforming, 206, 207, 210, 211,
    222; peer-to-peer lending, 214; sectoral composi-
    tion of, 211, *212. See also* capital markets; credit,
    access to; financial sector
Luo Longji, 46, 47

malnutrition, 229, 230, 327
mandarinates, precolonial, 45, 50, 51–53, 54
manufacturing sector: barriers to large-scale devel-
    opment of, 142; centered on low-end activities,
    293; demand for materials and components and,
    191; foreign direct investments in, 146, *146,* 179,
    180, 182, 184–85; heavy and higher-tech produc-
    tion in, 145–46; labor-intensive segment of, 294;
    small-scale outside of state plans, 162, 163;
    spillovers from FDI and, 187, 188; technology-
    and capital-intensive industries and, 154. *See also*
    industrial sector
market economy with socialist orientation, 113, 122,
    124, 127, 128; agriculture and, 229; deployment of
    learning and skilling in, 294; dualism as strategy
    in, 165; financial sector and, 205; with goal of
    domination by SOEs, 143–44; legal recognition
    of domestic private sector in, 162; party-state's
    absolute political power in, 140–41; taxation in,
    269. *See also* Đổi Mới (Renovation)
market-Leninism, 1–2, 19, 294, 406, 413
Marriage and Family Law of 2000, 305, 307, 308
Marxism: family issues and, 303; Vietnamese-
    Chinese cooperation and, 388
Marxism-Leninism, 3, 19, 23, 37, 59, 89, 349, 352.
    See also Leninism
mass organizations, 26, 34, 58, 61, 62, 91–92; in Party's
    countering of protests, 88; repression of 2005–7
    and, 83–84
master plans, 123–24. *See also* PAR master plans
McCain, John, 407
McNamara, Robert, 408
media: repressed in early 2000s, 83–84; subjugated
    role of, 35–36. *See also* press; social media

Mekong Delta agricultural sector, 9, 138, 233,
    238
meritocracy, 4, 46, 49, 50, 52, 53
MIAs (persons missing in action), 396, 398,
    400–401, 402, 404–5, 406–7
migration: to distant countries for work, 301; to
    urban areas, 259–60, 261, 301
military: Communist Party's control over, 28–29;
    fearing invasion by US in 2012, 360. *See also*
    armed forces
millionaires, 269; multimillionaires, 158, 160, *160*
minimum wage strike, 78, 84
modernization: foreign policy and, 348–49, 362; vs.
    rent-seeking, 357. *See also* industrialization and
    modernization
Mondale, Walter, 404
monetary policy, 220. *See also* inflation
monetary reforms of 1985, 205, 210
motorbike ownership, 251, 252, 268
multiparty democracy: condemned as ideological
    degeneration, 89, 90; imprisonment of a party's
    founder, 81; Petition 72 and, 84

National Assembly, 29–30, 62, 64, 65, 93–94, 127
nationalism, 19–20, 23, 38, 370–71, 375, 380, 389,
    399
national liberation movement, 350
National Party Congress, 59
natural resources, 236–38, 239
neo-Confucianism, 309
neo-Stalinist state, 348, 349–52, 375, 377; changed
    to rent-seeking state, 357, 358
NGOs, 34, 64, 127; domestic violence and, 311, 312;
    LGBTQ rights and, 308
Ngo Xuan Lich, 356, 360, 362
Nguyen Chi Vinh, 362
Nguyen Co Thach, 350, 351, 352, 353, 354, 378, 379,
    399, 406
Nguyen Dinh Loc, 84
Nguyen Du, 54
Nguyen Duc Binh, 353, 355, 357, 381–82
Nguyen Ha Phan, 353
Nguyen Manh Cam, 354
Nguyen Minh Triet, 412
Nguyen Phu Trong, 3, 23, 26, 27–28, 30, 31; on
    "acting like a bamboo," 13, 364–65; anti-corruption
    campaigns and, 364, 387–88; Chu Hao's expulsion
    from the Party and, 37; elected to National
    Assembly, 93; geopolitical shift away from China
    and, 364; need for reform and, 49; oil rig crisis of
    2014 and, 386; response to corruption scandals,
    77, 127–28; right of workers to organize and, 98;

Harvard East Asian Monographs
(most recent titles)